The Letters and Diaries
of
John Henry Newman

The Letters and Diaries

of

John Henry Newman

Edited at the Birmingham Oratory
with notes and an introduction

by

Gerard Tracey

Volume VI
The Via Media and Froude's *Remains*
January 1837 to December 1838

CLARENDON PRESS · OXFORD

1984

Oxford University Press, Walton Street, Oxford OX2 6DP
London Glasgow New York Toronto
Delhi Bombay Calcutta Madras Karachi
Kuala Lumpur Singapore Hong Kong Tokyo
Nairobi Dar es Salaam Cape Town
Melbourne Auckland
and associated companies in
Beirut Berlin Ibadan Mexico City Nicosia

Oxford is a trade mark of Oxford University Press

Published in the United States
by Oxford University Press, New York

British Library Cataloguing in Publication Data
Newman, John Henry
The letters and diaries of John Henry Newman.
Vol. 6: The Via Media and Froude's Remains,
January 1937 to December 1938
1. Newman, John Henry 2. Catholic Church
—Clergy—Correspondence
I. Title II. Tracey, Gerard
262'.135'0924 BX4705.N5
ISBN 0-19-920141-2

Library of Congress Cataloging in Publication Data
(Revised for volume 6)
Newman, John Henry, Cardinal, 1801–1890.
Letters and diaries.
Some volumes have imprint: Oxford, Clarendon Press.
1. Newman, John Henry, 1801–1890. 2. Catholic
Church—England—Clergy—Correspondence. 3. Cardinals—
England—Correspondence. I. Dessain, Charles
Stephen, ed.
BX4705.N5A4 1961 282'.092'4 61–65738
ISBN 0-19-920141-2

Set and printed in Great Britain by
New Western Printing Ltd, Bristol

Preface

WITHOUT the gradual building up at the Birmingham Oratory of a very full collection of Cardinal Newman's correspondence (an account of which will be found in the Introduction to Volume XI), the present work could not have been undertaken. Its aim is to provide an exhaustive edition of Newman's letters; with explanatory notes, which are often summaries of or quotations from the other side of the correspondence. Some of these letters *to* Newman, when they appear to have particular importance, or to be necessary for following a controversy, are inserted in the text. Every one of the letters written *by* Newman is included there, in chronological sequence. Should there eventually be any of his letters, whose existence is known to the editor, but of which he has failed to obtain a copy, this will be noted in its place. On the other hand, no attempt has been made to include a list of letters written by Newman and now lost, nor the brief précis he occasionally made of his reply, on the back of a correspondent's letter, although these are utilised for the annotation.

In order that the text of each letter may be as accurate as possible, the original autograph, when it still exists, or at least a photographic copy of it, has been used by the editor as his source. (The very few cases in which he has been content with an authenticated copy will be noted as they occur.) Always the text of the autograph is reproduced or, when the autograph has disappeared, that of the copy that appears most reliable. When only Newman's draft exists, that is printed. The source used in each case is to be found in the list of letters by correspondents.

Such alterations as are made in transcribing the letters aim, without sacrifice of accuracy, at enabling them to be read with ease. Newman writes simply and has none of those idiosyncrasies which sometimes need to be reproduced for the sake of the evidence of one kind or another which they provide.

The following are the only alterations made in transcription:

ADDRESS AND DATE are always printed on the same line, and at the head of the letter, even when Newman puts them at the end. When he omits or gives an incomplete date, the omission is supplied in square brackets, and justified in a note unless the reason for it is obvious. The addresses, to which letters were sent, are included in the list of letters by correspondents. The information derived from postmarks is matter for annotation.

THE CONCLUSION of the letter is made to run on, irrespective of Newman's separate lines, and all postscripts are placed at the end.

NEWMAN'S CORRECTIONS AND ADDITIONS are inserted in their intended

v

place. His interlinear explanations are printed in the text in angle brackets ⟨⟩, after the word or phrase they explain. His erasures are given in footnotes when they appear to be of sufficient interest to warrant it. Square brackets are reserved for editorial additions. All Newman's brackets are printed as rounded ones (the kind most usual with him).

NEWMAN'S PARAGRAPHS AND PUNCTUATION are preserved, except that single quotation marks are printed throughout, and double ones for quotations within them. (Newman generally used the latter in both cases.) Further, a parenthesis or quotation that he began with the proper mark but failed to complete, or completed but did not begin, is supplied. All other punctuation marks supplied by the editor are enclosed in square brackets. Newman's dashes, which frequently do duty either for a full stop, a semicolon or a comma (especially when he is tired or writing hurriedly), are represented by a '—' with a space before and after. His spelling and use of capitals are left unchanged, but 'raised' letters are lowered in every case.

NEWMAN'S ABBREVIATIONS are retained in the case of proper names, and in the address and conclusion of each letter, since these are sometimes useful indications of his attitude at the time. In all other cases, abbreviations are printed out in full, where Newman employs them.

When he uses the initials of proper names, the full name is normally inserted in square brackets after the initials, at the first occurrence in each letter, and more often if it seems advisable in order to avoid confusion. No addition of the full name is made in the case of Newman's correspondent, whether his initials occur at the beginning of the letter or in the course of it. When Newman uses only a Christian name, the surname is sometimes added in square brackets for the reader's convenience.

When transcription is made from a PRINTED SOURCE, typographical alterations clearly due to editor or printer are disregarded.

Sometimes Newman made HOLOGRAPH copies of his letters or of portions of them, when they were returned to him long after they had been written. In order that the reader may be able to see how much he copied and what changes he introduced, the copied passages are placed in quarter brackets ⌐ ¬, and all additions of any importance included in the text in double square brackets, or, where this is impracticable, in the annotation.

Newman's letters are printed in CHRONOLOGICAL ORDER, with the name of his correspondent at the head (except that those of each day are arranged alphabetically), and, when more than one is written to the same person on the same day, numbered, I, II. In the headings the name of the correspondent is given in its most convenient form, sometimes with Christian names in full, sometimes only with initials.

THE LIST OF LETTERS BY CORRESPONDENTS, at the end of each volume, shows whether the source used was an autograph, draft, printed source or copy, and in the last case, whether a holograph made by Newman later; and gives the present location of the source, as well as of any additional holograph copies or drafts. References to standard works have generally been omitted as being too numerous and already well known; the most relevant of them are referred to in the notes.

THE LETTERS WRITTEN TO NEWMAN, when inserted in the text, are printed in type smaller than that used for Newman's own letters, and headed by the name of the correspondent. These letters are not always arranged in chronological order, but may be placed either just before or just after the letter of Newman to which they are related. A list of them is given at the end of each volume in which they occur. These and the quotations from letters in the annotations are always, unless otherwise stated, printed from autographs at the Birmingham Oratory, and are transcribed in the same way as Newman's letters.

NEWMAN'S DIARIES COVER THE YEARS 1824 to 1879 (with a gap from July 1826 to March 1828). They are printed in a series of mottled copy books, 12 × 18 centimetres, printed for a year each, and entitled *The Private Diary: arranged, printed, and ruled, for receiving on account of every day's employment . . .'* with the exception of the four periods July 1847–May 1850, January 1854–January 1861, January 1861–March 1871, March 1871–October 1879, each of which is contained in a somewhat thicker copy book.

These diaries are printed complete for each day in which Newman has made an entry. It has been thought best to include Newman's record of persons to whom he wrote or from whom he received letters. At the end of each diary book are various notes, lists of addresses, of people to be prayed for, accounts, etc. These, also, are omitted, except for occasional dated notes of events, which, are inserted in their proper place. Of the rest of the notes, some are theological and will be reserved for a volume of Newman's theological papers, and others will perhaps have room found for them in any fuller edition of *Autobiographical Writings*.

Newman compiled with his own hands, on quarto sheets sewn together, a book of *Chronological Notes*, drawn largely from the diaries. Any new matter in these *Notes* is printed in italics with the appropriate diary entry, if any. (It should be noted that the diary entries themselves were sometimes written up considerably later than the events they record.)

Each volume is preceded by a brief summary of the period of Newman's life that it covers. Summary, diaries and annotation give a roughly biographical form to the whole, and will, it is hoped, enable the ordinary reader to treat it as a continuous narrative.

THE BIOGRAPHIES OF PERSONS are collected in the index of proper names at the end of each volume, in order to simplify the annotation of the letters. Occasionally, when a person is mentioned only once or twice, and a note is required in any case, biographical details have been given in the notes, and a reference in the index. (The editor will be grateful for information as to persons not identified.)

These notices have been compiled from such various sources—books of reference, letters at the Oratory, information supplied by the families or religious communities of the persons concerned, and by librarians and archivists—that the giving of authorities would be a very complicated and lengthy process. Like others faced with the same problem, the editor has decided usually to omit them. References are given, however, to *The Dictionary of National Biography*, or *The Dictionary of American Biography*, and failing them, to Boase's *Modern English Biography* or Gillow's *Bibliographical Dictionary of the English Catholics*. When the volumes of letters have been issued, a final index volume will be compiled for the whole work.

Letters found too late for inclusion at their right dates continue to come in. These will be placed at the end of the last volume of Anglican letters.

Contents

Abbreviations in Volume VI

THE abbreviations used for Newman's works are those listed in Joseph Rickaby, S.J., *Index to the Works of John Henry Cardinal Newman*, London 1914, with a few additions.

References to works included by Newman in his uniform edition are always, unless otherwise stated, to that edition, which was begun in 1868 with *Parochial and Plain Sermons*, and concluded in 1881 with *Select Treatises of St Athanasius*. From 1886, until the stock was destroyed in the 1939–45 war, all the volumes were published by Longmans, Green and Co. They are distinguished from other, usually posthumous, publications by having their date of inclusion in the uniform edition in brackets after the title, in the list of abbreviations below. The unbracketed date is, in every case, the date of the edition (or impression) used for giving references. (Once volumes were included in the uniform edition the pagination usually remained unchanged, but there are exceptions and minor alterations.)

Add.	*Addresses to Cardinal Newman with his Replies etc. 1879–82*, ed. W. P. Neville, 1905.
Apo.	*Apologia pro Vita Sua* (1873) 1905.
Ari.	*The Arians of the Fourth Century* (1871) 1908.
Ath. I, II	*Select Treatises of St Athanasius*, two volumes (1881) 1920.
A.W.	*John Henry Newman: Autobiographical Writings*, ed. Henry Tristram, 1956.
Call.	*Callista, a Tale of the Third Century* (1876) 1923.
Campaign	*My Campaign in Ireland, Part I* (printed for private circulation only), 1896.
D.A.	*Discussions and Arguments on Various Subjects* (1872) 1911.
Dev.	*An Essay on the Development of Christian Doctrine* (1878) 1908.
Diff. I, II	*Certain Difficulties felt by Anglicans in Catholic Teaching*, two volumes (1879, 1876), 1908.
Ess. I, II	*Essays Critical and Historical*, two volumes (1871) 1919.
G.A.	*An Essay in aid of a Grammar of Assent* (1870) 1913.
H.S. I, II, III	*Historical Sketches*, three volumes (1872) 1908, 1912, 1909.
Idea	*The Idea of a University defined and illustrated* (1873) 1902.
Jfc.	*Lectures on the Doctrine of Justification* (1874) 1908.
K.C.	*Correspondence of John Henry Newman with John Keble and Others, 1839–45*, ed. at the Birmingham Oratory, 1917.
L.G.	*Loss and Gain: the Story of a Convert* (1874) 1911.
M.D.	*Meditations and Devotions of the late Cardinal Newman*, 1893.
Mir.	*Two Essays on Biblical and on Ecclesiastical Miracles* (1870) 1907.
Mix.	*Discourses addressed to Mixed Congregations* (1871) 1909.
Moz. I, II	*Letters and Correspondence of John Henry Newman*, ed. Anne Mozley, two volumes, 1891.

O.S.	*Sermons preached on Various Occasions* (1870) 1927.
P.S. I–VIII	*Parochial and Plain Sermons* (1868) 1907–10.
Prepos.	*Present Position of Catholics* (n.d. 1872) 1913.
S.D.	*Sermons bearing on Subjects of the Day* (1869) 1902.
S.E.	*Stray Essays on Controversial Points* (private) 1890.
S.N.	*Sermon Notes of John Henry Cardinal Newman, 1849–1878*, ed. Fathers of the Birmingham Oratory, 1913.
T.T.	*Tracts Theological and Ecclesiastical* (1874) 1908.
U.S.	*Fifteen Sermons preached before the University of Oxford* (1872) 1909.
V.M. I, II	*The Via Media* (1877) 1908, 1911.
V.V.	*Verses on Various Occasions* (1874) 1910.

*   *   *

Boase	Frederick Boase, *Modern English Biography*, six volumes, Truro 1892–1921.
DNB	*Dictionary of National Biography*, to 1900, London, reprinted in 1937–8 in twenty-two volumes, the last being a Supplement, *DNB*, Suppl.
Liddon's *Pusey* I–IV	H. P. Liddon, *Life of Edward Bouverie Pusey*, four volumes, London 1893–7.
Brit. Crit.	*The British Critic, Quarterly Theological Review, and Ecclesiastical Record.*
Brit. Mag.	*The British Magazine, and Monthly Register of Religious and Ecclesiastical Information.*
D.R.	*The Dublin Review.*
Remains I–IV	*The Remains of the late Reverend Richard Hurrell Froude, M.A.*, two volumes, London 1838. Part the Second, two volumes, London 1839

NEWMAN'S ABBREVIATIONS IN THE DIARIES

A	Aunt
A F	[James] Anthony Froude
A M	Arthur *or* Anne Mozley
B N C	Brasenose College
C	Charles [Newman]; in context, Copeland, or Christie
C C C	Corpus Christi College
Ch Ch	Christ Church
F	Frank [Newman]; in context, Froude
G and R	Gilbert and Rivington
H	Harriett
H W	Henry Wilberforce
J	Jemima
J M	James [Bowling] Mozley
K	Keble
M (R) G	Maria (Rosina) Giberne
R	Rogers
R W	Robert Wilberforce; in context, Robert Williams
S W	Samuel Wilberforce
T	Tom [Mozley]
T M	Tom Mozley
W	Williams

W F   William Froude
W W   William Wilberforce

Abbreviations of fasting and of Breviary Hours are explained at their respective first appearances, 30 January and 11 February 1837.

Introductory Note

1 January 1837–31 December 1838

NEWMAN WAS ENGAGED in a wide variety of publishing ventures during these two years, but two works were to attract significantly different receptions—his *Lectures on the Prophetical Office*, and Froude's *Remains*.

In the *Lectures on the Prophetical Office of the Church*, Newman expounded the position of the Church of England as a 'Via Media', appealing to Scripture and the teaching of antiquity, as opposed to that of the now corrupt Roman Church, which appealed to its own infallibility, and that of Protestantism, which appealed to private judgement. He used the Caroline Divines as a main source: 'I say nothing, I believe, without the highest authority among our writers.' The work had originated in a controversial correspondence of 1834–5 with the Abbé Jager, and had been developed in a series of lectures, which were delivered in Adam de Brome's Chapel in May to July 1836. Newman revised his material later in 1836, and, on 11 March 1837, noted in his diary that his 'book on Prophetical Office came down'. He was satisfied with the effect it produced, writing to his sister Jemima on 25 April: 'It only shows how deep the absurd notion was in men's minds that I was a Papist; and now they are agreeably surprised . . . We have all fallen back from the Reformation in a wonderful way.' Newman even thought that 'perhaps under the cover of this surprise and the relentings attending it, I may be able to discharge some darts against common Protestantism without molestation.'

Early in 1837 Newman found himself in controversy in the columns of the Evangelical *Christian Observer*. The editor had criticised Pusey's *Tracts* on Baptism as based upon 'the darkest ages of Popery, when men had debased Christianity from a spiritual system, a "reasonable service," to a system of forms', and suggested that the 'learned Professor ought to lecture at Maynooth, or the Vatican'. He had concluded with a challenge to any of the Tractarians to explain that they did honestly believe all of the Articles and the Homilies. Newman took up the challenge, and his first letter was published in the February and March issues. Newman was worried at first that the editor would not insert his letter, and, although it was published, his text was crowded out by a much more extensive editorial commentary. A second letter appeared in April and May, but Newman decided against continuing the correspondence further after friends advised him that his language was too fierce, and likely to repel moderate Evangelicals. Newman wrote on 12 April: 'My present notion is to publish what will be almost a book on Justification—and perhaps in the Preface allude to the Christian Observer.'

Döllinger pronounced Newman's *Lectures on Justification* to be 'the greatest masterpiece in theology that England has produced in a hundred years'. Having just been involved in the *Christian Observer* controversy, Newman's natural target was the doctrine of justification by faith alone. Newman endeavoured to show that the traditional Protestant doctrine imprisoned men within themselves, examining their own feelings, and his final lecture is a masterly indictment of religious subjectivism. Again seeking to establish a 'Via Media', Newman also criticised what he conceived to be the deficient Roman formula of 'inherent righteousness'. Newman offered a more comprehensive definition: '. . . we are justified by grace, given through Sacraments, impetrated by faith, manifested in works.' Newman delivered the lectures in April and May 1837, and worked them up for publication in the following months. Several letters testify to the great pains which he took with the work, and he admitted: 'It has taken me much more time than any other book'.

The earlier of the *Tracts of the Times* had been flimsy productions, with little financial return. Pusey's *Tracts* 67, 68, and 69 on Baptism had initiated a new approach, and the later *Tracts* began to resemble small treatises. The response improved, and Newman reported with surprise on 29 January 1837: 'The Tracts have suddenly begun to sell apace.' Rivington, the publisher, undertook reprints of the earlier *Tracts*, and doubled the number of all future editions.

The idea of starting a specifically Tractarian journal or magazine was mooted in the early years of the Oxford Movement. Newman himself favoured a coalition with an already established publication, and he found a likely candidate in the *British Critic*. Founded in 1793 as a conservative monthly by William Jones of Nayland, the journal had been taken over, and turned into a quarterly in 1825, by a group of High Churchmen led by Joshua Watson, and they had since attempted to keep it alive, with increasing difficulty. Newman met Watson early in 1836 and, on his advice, came to an arrangement with the publisher to supply about a third of the articles for each issue. The scheme worked well for a while, but Newman soon became frustrated by the policy of the editor J. S. Boone. Great offence was caused in Oxford circles by a review of R. D. Hampden's introduction to the second edition of his Bampton Lectures, which appeared in the July 1837 issue. Newman was particularly disgruntled because Boone, in any case, had asked him to review the work. An article on the liberal Edward Stanley's installation sermon in the October issue proved the final straw. Newman declared his intention of withdrawing from the journal because of the matter, and Boone duly resigned. The search for a new editor began, and Newman, pointing out that the journal was now widely considered to be party organ, pressed for a man who would establish Catholic principles. Manning was a name acceptable to all sides, but he declined the offer for personal reasons. Eventually the historian S. R. Maitland accepted the editorship, but he had to resign after one issue because the critique of the Ecclesiastical Commission which Pusey had undertaken for the April number would have been an embarrassment to him in his post as Archbishop's Librarian at Lambeth. On 28 January Newman wrote to inform Manning: 'I am Editor of the British Critic, to my disgust, to come into play in July'.

Hurrell Froude had died on 28 February 1836, and a month later Newman received a collection of his papers from the Froude family. The Sermons, Becket Papers, Essay on Rationalism, and miscellaneous articles were put at Newman and Keble's disposal to publish as they thought fit. The editors spent a good while considering the best way to deal with the material, and they circulated it among friends to obtain their opinion. Newman wrote to Frederic Rogers on 1 June 1837: 'Keble, Pusey, Williams, Copeland, Wood and you are for the publication of F's papers.' Though personally enthusiastic about Froude's work, Newman wavered, writing the following day: 'I confess I have some fears about dear F's papers—but all parties but me are for the immediate publication'. However, Newman resolved his doubts, and his letter of 30 June to Keble gives a clear explanation of what he believed to be the best reasons for publication.

However, all was not settled, for two further items were to come up for consideration which were to have an important bearing on the reputation of the volumes. Newman reported to Rogers on 5 July that Isaac Williams had come up with the suggestion of including a selection of Froude's correspondence, an idea which Newman applauded. He explained to Keble a few days later that the correspondence would show that Froude had given 'the first hints of principles etc. which I and others have pursued and of which he ought to have the credit.' When Rogers wrote to Newman agreeing about the interest of the letters, he pointed out the possibility of giving the impression that the Tractarians were 'plotters'. On 25 August Newman received Froude's Private Journal of 1826–7, which Archdeacon Froude had sent for possible inclusion, and of which Newman had not previously known. In the Journal Froude had recorded details of his fasting, faults, and temptations. Newman's letter of 27 August to Keble shrewdly anticipates likely criticism of the Journal, particularly concerning Froude's omission of the name of Christ. However, the editors felt that they would be able to deal with such difficulties in the preface and notes. They also hoped to be able to offset the effect of Froude's strong anti-Protestantism by pointing to his severe strictures on the Church of Rome. Newman expected that different parts of the *Remains* would appeal to different readers, 'the sermons for parsons, the first volume for young people.' The arrangement of the volumes was finally decided during Newman's stay at Hursley in October, and the publication of the first two volumes was due in February 1838. Newman wrote to J. W. Bowden on 17 January about his fear of possible reactions, but concluded: '. . . on the whole I trust it will present, as far as it goes, a picture of a mind, and that being gained as a scope, the details must be left to take their chance.'

The response to the *Remains* fulfilled the worst of Newman's fears. People did not bother to look further than the first volume, which contained the Journal and the letters, with their revelation of the schemes of the Oxford men, and Froude's vitriolic denunciation of the Reformers. Evangelicals and Low Churchmen declared war, moderate Anglicans were disgusted, and the loyalty of the more cautious and conservative of the adherents of the Movement was strained. The only positive response came from a few of the younger, more extreme Tractarians, such as Frederick Oakeley and W. G. Ward, whose allegiance was to a large extent decided by the work. The *Edinburgh Review* and other journals were caustic in their criticism. Lord Morpeth raised the matter in the House of Commons, and Gladstone came to the defence of Newman and Keble. Godfrey Faussett, Lady Margaret Professor of Divinity, protested against what he termed the 'Revival of Popery' in the pulpit of St Mary's. It was widely rumoured that the *Remains* were the cause of the testimonial for a memorial to Cranmer, Latimer, and Ridley, which was started later in the year. The testimonial was certainly seen as a test for Newman and Pusey, and suspicions increased when they did not subscribe.

The Bishop of Oxford was due to deliver a triennial Visitation Charge in August 1838, and the word had spread that he was going to speak in favour of the *Tracts*. When the Charge was delivered it came as a severe disappointment to Newman. The Bishop stated that he found much to approve of in the *Tracts*, and insisted that 'in these days of lax and spurious liberality, anything which tends to recall forgotten truths, is *valuable*.' But the Bishop went on to add words of caution, though explaining: 'I have more to fear of the Disciples than of the Teachers.' Newman had a very high view of episcopal authority and, for him, 'a Bishop's lightest word ex Cathedra is heavy'. He explained the dilemma to Henry Wilberforce on 19 August: 'He has said that there are expressions in them [the *Tracts*] which may be of disservice to certain minds—and by not saying what, has thrown a vague suspicion over them all.' After discussing the matter in long letters to Keble, Newman decided that he ought to try and discover which *Tracts* the Bishop had been worried by and offer to withdraw them, otherwise he would have to consider discontinuing the series. The Bishop wrote to explain that he had certainly not intended to give the impression that Newman had formed. When the Bishop published the Charge he added a clarifying footnote to the relevant passage, and Newman felt able to continue with the *Tracts* without inconsistency, though he had certainly felt the incident to be a setback.

Another disappointment was the fate of a project undertaken by Newman's two young lay friends S. F. Wood and Robert Williams. Rogers wrote on 26 January 1838: 'Has Wood told you that he and R W talk of publishing a translation of the Breviary (or greater part of it) in monthly (?) numbers by subscription.' The project progressed through the year, and Newman himself contributed translations of hymns. On 3 November George Prevost sent Newman a rather peremptory note to inform him of how distressed he and some others (Thomas Keble in particular) were to hear of the translation. He suggested that Newman request the translators to suspend their work, he and his friends offering to defray any expense involved. Newman corresponded about the matter with Keble, who was himself doubtful about the wisdom of proceeding with the work at that time. Newman gave a good deal of consideration to possible ways of editing the translation to make it acceptable to moderate men. However, the translators, deciding to save Newman trouble and anxiety, gave their work up. Newman's letter of 21 November to Keble shows that this, and connected matters, had come as something of a blow to him.

There were other publications occupying Newman's attention at this time. The first two volumes of the Library of the Fathers appeared in 1838, and Newman gave R. W. Church a great deal of assistance with his translation of St Cyril's Catechetical Lectures. Newman himself brought out two editions of Latin Breviary hymns, and contributed prefaces to several of the older Anglican devotional works which were republished in Oxford around this time. In the summer of 1838 he delivered his 'Lectures on the Scripture Proof of the Doctrines of the Church', which were published as *Tract* 85.

Newman's diaries reveal the development of some stricter religious habits. On 11 February 1838 he began to make abbreviated notes of his recitation of the Breviary hours. Earlier in the same month he had likewise begun to note his regular fasting.

Longer letters of particular interest include that of 12 September 1837 to Lord Lifford about Evangelicalism; those of 25 March and 9 May 1837 to Henry Wilberforce about prayer; the letter of 4 June 1837 to his sister Jemima about Confirmation; and that of 23 March 1838 to S. F. Wood about the Church.

Newman's volumes of copied extracts from letters to himself, so much of which have been published in Volumes I–V, cease at the end of 1836, and Newman kept fewer autograph letters to himself from this time.

Summary of Events covered by this Volume

1837

11–12 January	Newman writes to the *Christian Observer* in defence of Pusey's *Tracts* on Baptism.
January	Rivington proposes double editions of the *Tracts* in future.
6 February	Newman begins his weekly soirées.
February	Second edition of *Lyra Apostolica*.
11 March	*Lectures on the Prophetical Office* published.
9 April	Newman begins weekly early Eucharist at St Mary's.
13 April	Newman begins Lectures on Justification at St Mary's.
8–9 June	Newman visiting at Bisley, Thomas Keble's parish;
10–12 June	at Badgeworth, J. F. Christie's parish;
13 June–1 July	at Cholderton, Thomas Mozley's parish.
3–12 October	Staying at Hursley with John Keble to discuss the forthcoming publication of Froude's *Remains*.

1838

January	Newman agrees to take the editorship of the *British Critic*. S. F. Wood and Robert Williams begin to translate the Roman Breviary.
24 February	The first two volumes of Froude's *Remains* published.
March	Third edition of *Lyra Apostolica*.
30 March	Newman's *Lectures on Justification* published.
30 April–3 May	Newman in London for the meeting of the S.P.C.K., staying with Frederic Rogers and Mr Bowden senior.
Midsummer	Newman takes a house for young writers in St Aldate's.
20 May	Godfrey Faussett preaches against the Tractarians in St Mary's.
25 June	Newman's *Letter to Faussett* published.
10–21 July	Newman in London, staying with J. W. Bowden at Roehampton.
14 August	The Bishop of Oxford alludes to the *Tracts* in his Charge.
1–15 October	Newman staying at Derby with the John Mozleys.
22–26 October	Newman visiting John Keble at Hursley.
October	Proposals for a Martyrs' Memorial in Oxford begin, allegedly intended to test Newman and others.
November	Translation of the Roman Breviary suspended.
30 November	Volume IV of *Parochial Sermons* published.

The Letters and Diaries
of
John Henry Newman

SUNDAY I JANUARY 1837 Circumcision did duty morning and afternoon preached Number 438[1] Palmer assisting at Sacrament dined at Pusey's, with Berkeley.

MONDAY 2 JANUARY T and H went from Cholderton to Town Eden went Williams went walked with Pusey read prayers at Littlemore every day this week but today. (*I believe there were daily prayers there from the time Chapel was opened*) visiting Mrs Birmingham 3 times wrote to Archdeacon Froude sent parcel to H

TO MRS THOMAS MOZLEY

⌐January 2. 1837

My book [[Prophetical Office]][2] is gone to Press—and makes me very anxious. I have taken immense pains with it, writing great portions of it from four to six times over.⌐

TO SAMUEL WILBERFORCE

[2 January 1837]

My dear Wilberforce

I was truly sorry to hear from Rogers that you were wondering you had not heard from me. I understood you to send me the Paper of the Winton Chapter[3] merely to look at and be returned at leisure; I did not suppose you wanted my opinion.

If I must give it, I can hardly speak very favorously [sic]. It seems to speak somewhat flippantly of Church Services which are the highest object of Chapters, but it is all written in a declamatory style, more fitted the platform of a Society than a grave body of Prebendaries. Any protest of course is better than none—for people do not weigh words—but I wonder the Chapter did not concoct something better.[4]

I felt much obliged by your information about Mrs W. and the little child.—I hope she is well by this time—One can never have very lasting sorrow, when one is sure that what is taken from us is *sure* of glory; which is a peculiar compensation for the loss of children.

Will you ask Robert two questions—1. If Mr Jebb will consent to send his Article (the history of the non-appearance of which I do not understand

---

[1] *S.D.*, 8, 'The Church and the World'.

[2] *Lectures of the Prophetical Office of the Church, viewed relatively to Romanism and Popular Protestantism*, London 1837. Later republished as *V.M.* I.

[3] The Address of the Dean and Chapter of Winchester to the Ecclesiastical Commissioners of 9 Dec 1836.

[4] The Address alluded to 'the intimate connexion which subsists between cathedral institutions and the maintenance of a sound theology. We do not make light of our daily services of prayer and praise . . . Neither would we depreciate the value of our Sunday services . . . But we beg leave to state it as our entire conviction, that the utility of cathedral institutions is not to be measured by considerations of this nature alone; and that their vast importance is to be traced, not only in the outward magnificence of the venerable fabrics . . . in the sacred and imposing effect of their choir service . . . but, in addition to these, in the aid which they give to the theological learning of the country . . .', *Brit Mag.*, 11, 1837 (March), 315-7.

to this hour, having heard nothing about it) to the British *Magazine*.[1]—2. If he can tell me, for I forget, *what* his authority was for the report of the immorality of Collier and Hickes[2]

Yrs most sincerely John H Newman

TO HUGH JAMES ROSE

Oriel College. January 3. 1837

My dear Rose,

I have delayed answering your letter till Pusey returned, to take his opinion about your inquiry about King's College and our University.[3] He says, and I agree with him, that the University would do nothing at all—that with the exception of one or two men our heads have not the first principles of government in their minds or the first elements of it in their character—and that it will be best first to try them with the Archbishop's plan of a theological examination which I suppose they are already upon.—β is Froude's initial in the Lyra. I was very sorry it had to stop, but the reason was simply this—The only ones I could *rely* on as forthcoming, were my own—and they were *all* written when I was abroad with the exception of two and a half. It went on then *till* the supply was exhausted. I should have run out sooner unless I had stimulated Keble to send some contributions.[4]

I have been wishing, ever since I left off, that is, the last 2 or 3 months, to send more 'Churches of the Fathers'—but my time and thoughts have almost been absorbed with books, questions and compositions on the subject of Romanism—I am publishing a sort of Via Media as far as it goes, and of course it makes me very anxious to be accurate. I do not think I deviate from our great writers in any point, certainly any point in which they agree

---

[1] John Jebb, Rector of East Farleigh and a friend of the Wilberforces, had proposed an article on Church Reform and the State which Newman had hoped would appear in *Brit. Crit.*, but it was not published.

[2] The non-jurors Jeremy Collier and George Hickes. The allusion is puzzling, especially considering that Collier was a leading critic of the immorality of the theatre of his day. However, Thomas Arnold, in his article on 'The Oxford Malignants and Dr. Hampden', had referred to Hickes as 'a man [who] like one or two of the Oxford conspirators, much vaunted by his party for the pretended holiness of his life . . . found his religion perfectly compatible with falsehood and malignity'.

[3] Rose wrote from King's College, London, 26 Dec. 1836: 'Do you think it at all possible that the Universities would give *us* an helping hand, by allowing residence or courses of study here to count for *some* terms (of course a *much* less number) passed with them. A very large proportion of our Students goes to Cambridge or Oxford. There are nearly 100 at Cambridge now and I believe 50 or 60 at Oxford. A little help now would be most precious. Our medical men are well disposed and came to me to express their wish that no one might be *allowed* to go for a degree to this new university unless he had passed an examination as to religious matters. I asked them whether, if we could gain something of time from the Universities, they would not prefer it—and I evidently saw they would grasp at it. In a few days, I hope that our Council will issue a quiet but decided declaration that with all respect to the King's Charter, they will not be driven from the principles on which they were founded.'

[4] The last two parts of 'Lyra Apostolica' had appeared in *Brit. Mag.* for September 1836, Rose hoped that the instalments might be continued. The last two parts of the 'Church of the Fathers' appeared in April and May, 1837.

—Doubtless, I shall make some mistakes after all—but not for want of pains—most of it has been re-written, not retranscribed, several times—good part from four to six times. This will account for my apparent idleness.

You deserve some rest by this time—No one can doubt the British Magazine has been of extreme service to the Church since it appeared. It is too valuable a work to let drop.

As to the [Ecclesiastical] Commission,[1] I have little opinion upon it. Chapters have been so mismanaged, and there is so little hope of improvement that I am disposed to take things as they come—except that I should feel some satisfaction in so infamous a commission (in which the laity exceed the Clergy) being upset. Νέμεσις would be gratified, and I do not think, to say the least, any harm could be done

Ever Yrs very truly John H Newman

Pray accept for yourself and Mrs Rose the kindest wishes which this season inspires.

TO HENRY WILBERFORCE

[[Jan 7. 1837]] [3 January 1837]

James Mozley looked over the Register list in the Library a month ago and found no books out in your name. I went on receipt of your last, and found Tertullian and Miller, not in their places. Kaye's Tertullian is out of print—and cannot be replaced at present. What the price of the new edition will be, I cannot divine.

You did not ask me to pay bills—you only wrote Bills to be paid—what could I make out of this? Giles etc are *not* paid

I wish I could tell you about the Books, but I really cannot—I should guess Tertullian with binding about 17s, Miller with the binding 15/ I have today paid 3/ for you for a fly

WEDNESDAY 4 JANUARY 1837   Stevens, Mr Hall, and Copleston to breakfast   married young Hedges to Miss Norman.   Copleston went to town

THURSDAY 5 JANUARY   letters from H. Thornton and Bridges

[1] Rose wrote, 'I am very doubtful as to the question as to Chapters. I believe that for the last 2 or 3 years my views have been dreadfully gloomy—and I must confess that now, I can see no hope whatever, humanly speaking of any successful struggle for the Cathedrals. Some slight modifications may be obtained—but any larger alteration of the measure I think is not to be looked for except by a complete upset of the Commission. And how that can be effected I do not see—The clergy evidently have little or no feeling as to the matter. The strong addresses of *all* the Archdeaconries in this Diocese to the Bishop calling him one of the chief Defenders of the Church at this crisis, show that *they* are not offended at the changes of which he is one of the movers—and if 6 or 700 clergy hereabouts are in this condition, I suppose it is the same elsewhere. The only movements are about other things, *Convocation* etc.—Nor again do I know what party would upset the Commission.'

TO MRS JOHN MOZLEY

⌐January the fifth 1837⌐

My dear Jemima

Stevens is kind enough to be the bearer of this—I forget whether you know him, but if he falls in your way, I think you will like him much.

If you find any misprints in the Lyra, please make a list and let them be printed and stuck in. I find one p 132 *en*compassed for compassed.

I had something to say to you, but forget what. Dicks has charged £10 for the Inventory etc!

I have been anxiously expecting ever since Aunt went to Derby, some news of her safe arrival. My love to her.

⌐My book [[Prophetical Office]] is all but finished—but very little has passed through the press. It is no *advance* on any thing I have said—but a systematizing, consolidating, supplying premises etc. I say nothing, I believe, without the highest authority among our writers, yet it is so strong that every thing I have as yet said is milk and water to it—and this makes me anxious. It is all the difference between drifting snow and a hard snow ball. It seems to me like hitting the Peculiars [[Evangelicals]] etc. a most uncommon blow in the face. Pusey however compared it to a blow that takes the breath out of one. He says they will be so out of breath as not to be able to answer—and that before they recover, one or other of us must give them another. While I laugh, I am still anxious, and have no great excitement, I assure you⌐

Ever Yrs affly John H Newman

FRIDAY 6 JANUARY 1837 Epiphany service in Chancel—read Number 328 administered Sacrament to Berkeley's sick person   Charles came and dined and slept here

TO MRS MARTIN JOSEPH ROUTH

[6 January 1837]

Dear Madam

I take the liberty of inclosing the accompanying note for your inspection, both because I do not like to make the request it contains to the President direct, lest it should be unpleasant to him, and also because I indulge the hope of having the benefit of your kind influence with him in furtherance of it.

But whatever decision yourself, or he come to about it, I hope you will excuse its boldness in consideration of the great value of the object which has led to my making it.

Yours &c J H N

TO MARTIN JOSEPH ROUTH

Oriel College Jan 6. 1837

Dear Mr President,

I wish to make a request, which any how I fear you will consider presumptuous, and perhaps will judge best to negative.

I have a book in the press in illustration of the Via Media between the extremes of Romanism and popular Protestantism as preserved in the English Church;—and I am encouraged by your kindness to me on several occasions to ask the great favor of being allowed to dedicate it to the President of Magdalen.

I cannot venture to hope that there is nothing in my volume of private and questionable opinion—but I have tried, as far as may be, to follow the line of doctrine marked out by our great divines, of whom perhaps I have chiefly followed Bramhall, then Laud, Hammond, Field, Stillingfleet, Beveridge and others of the same school.

Should you wish to see me, I will gladly wait on you at any time you appoint, and am,

Yours most respectfully John H Newman[1]

SATURDAY 7 JANUARY 1837   letter from F.   Charles went, I walking with him as far as Hedington hill   called on Routh who consented to have my Lectures dedicated to him.   Cornish returned

TO FREDERIC ROGERS

Oriel: January 7, 1837.

I want your impression of several things. Routh has been kind enough to accept my offer of dedication, and in a really pleasant way.[2] He said he had allowed very few dedications to him, and mentioned particularly the case of one person who wished to dedicate, and he advised him to address some one who could be a better patron, which the man did; but, said he, 'I will not say so to Mr Newman, as I am sure he is not looking to get on in life.' Perhaps I think it is so 'pretty' because it is flattering. However, what say

[1] Routh replied the same evening:
'My dear Sir,
    I shall be happy to see you at any time, that is agreeable, for the pleasure of conversing with you. With Mrs Routh's best Compliments,
                                        I remain Sincerely yours M. J. Routh.'
[2] Routh later wrote, '. . . a perusal of many of the acknowledged writings of Dr. Pusey and Mr. Newman enables me to express my admiration of the ardent piety, holy views, and scrupulous adherence to the ancient summaries of Catholic belief displayed in them. I likewise state my persuasion that these, in conjunction with other estimable works, have contributed to correct many erroneous notions too long prevalent amongst us, and subverting the unity and authority of the National Church.' J. R. Bloxam, *The Magdalen College Register*, Oxford 1881, IV, 35.

you to a dedication of this sort? *Study it, and fix your first impression, so as not to report it before you read on to see my reason for it:*—

'To Martin F. [sic] Routh, D.D., President of Magdalen College, who has been reserved to report to a degenerate age the theology of our Fathers, this volume is (most) respectfully inscribed, with grateful sense of his services towards the Faith, and with the prayer, that what he has witnessed to others may be his own comfort and support, in the day of account.'[1]

Is 'grateful sense' arrogant in me? But what I want you to do is, first, to correct it, next, to weigh this reason. I felt very unwilling to say anything in the Dedication which might (if it be not a bold thing to say) do Routh harm. I mean, I did not wish to flatter, particularly considering he has never been called upon for *active* services; so I have put at the end something serious and practical. But I want your *impression* of it.

What do you say to this title? 'Lectures on the Middle Way between Romanism and Popular Protestantism.'[2]

Then, what say you to this motto? Is there a chance of its being taken as arrogant and self-regarding?—'They that shall be of thee shall build the old waste places: thou shalt raise up the foundations of many generations; and thou shalt be called, The repairer of the breach, The restorer of paths to dwell in.' You see it is addressed by Isaiah to the *Church*,—i.e. the *Anglican*, by me.[3]

I am very anxious about this book. I cannot conceal from myself that it is neither more nor less than hitting Protestantism a hard blow in the face. I do not say whether the argument is good or not. I need not have the better of it, and yet may hit a blow. Pusey has seen one lecture, and he said, without my speaking, that it would put people out of breath, so that they would not be able to retort; and that before they recover their wind, we must fetch them a second blow. It is curious Froude compared my letter to Arnold[4] to a blow in the stomach; and the Bishop of Winton, the tracts, to shaking the fist in the face.[5] I speak seriously when I say I think I shall be considered an infidel. I have not room to say why.

[1] The final version of the dedication was, 'To/Martin Joseph Routh, D.D./President of Magdalen College/who has been reserved/to report to a forgetful generation/what was the theology of their fathers,/this volume/is inscribed,/with a respectful sense/of his eminent services to the Church,/and with the earnest prayer/that what he witnesses to others/may be his own support and protection/in the day of account.'

[2] Rogers shared Newman's apprehension about the phrase 'grateful sense', but approved of the rest of the dedication. He wrote concerning the suggested title, 'Could a direction post to the meaning be introduced into that part of the Title which does not tell? I rather like your title but not much. There is a kind of prosiness about it to me.—"Popular" is a rather amusing advance from "ultra".' The title used for publication was *Lectures on the Prophetical Office of the Church, viewed relatively to Romanism and Popular Protestantism.*

[3] *Isaiah*, 58:12. Newman did use this text for the motto.

[4] See letter of 16 Nov. 1833 to Anthony Grant and that from T. Arnold to Grant of 11 Nov., Volume IV, 105–8. Froude wrote on 20 Nov., 'Who would have thought of Arnold standing with his elbows a-kimbo and letting you knock his wind out?', p. 122. See also *Apo.*, pp. 33–4.

[5] This has not been traced. For C. R. Sumner's earlier, and quite favourable, attitude to the *Tracts*, see Volume IV, 97.

To my astonishment Rivington has just sent me word that the Tract [75] on the Breviary is coming to a second edition. I wish you would call or send him a [illegible word] letter to this effect, that Mr N will send Messrs. G. and R. a corrected copy of the Tract on the Breviary, and to bid him print off as he proposes, the 2nd part of Christian Liberty [*Tract* 30], sending a proof to Bowden.

Rivington had told me the Tracts were selling well, but 750 copies of the Roman Breviary since July last is portentous. I am getting into controversy with the Christian Observer *in its own pages*. I fervently hope I may be able to tease them usque ad necem, insaniam, or something else equally bad.[1]—

The flame is kindling at Cambridge,—tiny but true, I hope. The Bishop of Exeter, at the Consecration of some Churches, has been expanding the end of his Charge into Sermons in the most marvellous way, and is exciting quite a sensation. They say he quite throws off the political ground. Rose unasked has made the amende.[2] I have had more requests to read my Littlemore Consecration Sermon than any ever, I think.

What an egotistical letter this is!—as all mine are.

P.s.—Boone I see in the British Critic (end of article on Jebb)[3] goes on making us confessors and martyrs.[4]

---

[1] The *Christian Observer* of December 1836 attacked Pusey's *Tracts* 67, 68, and 69, on Baptism, as based upon 'the authority of the darkest ages of Popery, when men had debased Christianity from a spiritual system, a "reasonable service," to a system of forms, and ceremonial rites, and *opera operata* influences . . . The learned Professor ought to lecture at Maynooth, or the Vatican, and not in the chair of Oxford . . .' The editor, S. C. Wilks, concluded with a challenge concerning Pusey, '. . . what does he do with the Articles and Homilies? We have often asked this question in private, but could never get an answer. Will any approver of the Oxford Tracts answer it in print?' Newman wrote two letters in reply, the first of which was published in two parts in the February and March numbers of the *Christian Observer*. Both letters were published as *Tract* 82, and republished in *V.M.* II. For the details of the development of the controversy, see letters of 16 Jan., 16 March, and 12 April to J. W. Bowden.

[2] This may refer to the very favourable notice of *Lyra Apostolica* in *Brit. Mag.*, 11, 1837 (Jan.), 63–4.

[3] *Brit. Crit.*, 21, 1837 (Jan.), 207–8: 'But, in order that we may have something to dread, and hate, and execrate, a scape-goat has been prepared, on which the mountainous sins of Popery may be safely laid. And this devoted victim is no other than a school of studious and contemplative men; whose only crime it is, that they are intensely zealous (and, as some may think, rather unseasonably and indiscreetly zealous,) for primitive theology and discipline. In short, the balmy rebuke, which threatens no damage to the cranium, is to be reserved for the *Malignants of Maynooth*: while the hottest vials of our wrath must all be outpoured upon the *Malignants of Oxford*!'

[4] The autographs of most of Newman's Anglican letters to Rogers seem to have disappeared soon after Rogers's death. Quite a few were printed in *Moz*., which has been the main source for these volumes. However, an album of W. J. Copeland's has recently been discovered at Pusey House, which contains extracts which he made from the correspondence when he was planning a history of the Oxford Movement. Copies of letters not included in *Moz*. have been inserted in their chronological place (any missed in the previous volumes will be included in a supplement to Volume X). There are copies of some letters which were printed in *Moz*., but which contain phrases or passages which Anne Mozley omitted (as in the present letter). These have been incorporated when their position in the text is clear, otherwise they have been placed in footnotes. See the List of Letters by Correspondents for dates.

SUNDAY 8 JANUARY 1837 1st Epiphany letter from Grant [of] New College Cornish at St Mary's in morning I at Littlemore administering Sacrament I at St Mary's in afternoon preaching Number 231[1] Berkeley dined with me

MONDAY 9 JANUARY letter from J went to Tuckwell Copleston returned had prevalent influenza very unwell kept in doors the *whole* week (*from last year my rule had been to use the breviary daily, with such exceptions as would occur*)

TUESDAY 10 JANUARY letter from Pusey somewhat better [word illegible] this week wrote out Catena 3.[2] Wrote to Pusey and sent answer to Bishop's Questions

TO E. B. PUSEY

Oriel College. Jan. 10, 1837

My dear Pusey

Excuse this scrap of paper; I can find no more. It seems to me that Sewell is your man—then Oakeley.[3] Copeland would *do*—Williams would not— Every one has his place—for a popular preacher W. would not do. Oakeley is the safest card, for Sewell might be seduced into metaphysics. For myself I most heartily wish I may not be thought of—nor is it likely. Some years ago the Bishop of London mentioned it to me—but so much has happened in the interval that he may fairly be absolved, if he passes me over. It would break into my engagements here most sadly—Indeed I do not like to contemplate the chance of it. I could not refuse, I suppose—but certainly my path is clear before me at present without following up new openings.

I hoped by your return to have had the letter to the Christian Observer ready—but was yesterday seized with a violent influenza, and fear this week will be lost. They have periodical meetings at Islington—and we before now have been the subject of discussion.[4] Mr Hill goes up to report progress. Mr Wilson is a regular don—a conceited self sufficient man, with 18 (?) clergymen dependent on him, and looked up to as a Bishop. Nothing inspires me with greater hope for our cause, or rather brings home to me the fact that we are on the whole right and they on the whole wrong than the circumstance that they have less humility than I think we have.

[1] *P.S.*, VII, 18, 'Stedfastness in the Old Paths'.
[2] *Tract* 78, 'Catena Patrum. No. 3. Testimony of the Writers in the Later English Church to the duty of maintaining *quod semper, quod ubique, quod ab omnibus traditum est.*' Usually ascribed to Manning and C. Marriott although this entry suggests that Newman may have had some responsibility for the tract.
[3] Pusey had been consulted about a suitable person for the Whitehall Preachership. He had thought of Newman '(facile princeps)', then Oakeley, Copeland, I. Williams, Sewell, and H. Bull. Frederick Oakeley was appointed.
[4] Writing from Fairford on 9 Jan., Pusey quoted from a letter he had received from W. Dodsworth: 'I hear there was a most violent and abusive attack on us, at a meeting of clergy at Islington yesterday (Jan. 5.) and a great alarm expressed at the spread of High Church principles, which they did not scruple to denounce as *heretical*! This looks well for the cause, but is sad for them. I should think from the tone which I hear was assumed, we may expect open war'.
Daniel Wilson the younger, a leading figure among London Evangelicals, held regular clerical meetings at his vicarage in Islington. John Hill, of St Edmund Hall, took great pains at this meeting to assure those present that Tractarian views could in no legitimate sense be called Oxford views. See P. Toon, *Evangelical Theology 1833–56: a Response to Tractarianism*, London 1979, p. 31.

Grant has written to me to say he has failed in getting a Chrysostom and therefore wishes some other Father. So the 2nd Cor. I suppose is open. We ought to be civil to Mr Wood Warter.[1]

I think I agree most entirely with you about Dissenting Baptism.[2] What you say about confirmation, the Eucharist etc. would be most satisfactory, were it a point of mere speculation—or to account for what we otherwise knew. But in a practical question one wishes to go by what is safest. Then follows the balance of reading prayers, implying the absence of reparation or not using the rite at all. Could not a Bishop help one out of the difficulty? I mean in a case partially provided for by the Liturgy, he might authorize the omission of certain prayers—or of all the prayers. Or why should any talk be made about it in particular cases? As people do not know the fact that the Baptism was Dissenting, need they know the fact of the supplement? My head is not clear enough just now to follow this out.

Ever yours most affly John H Newman

I mentioned to the Archdeacon about the petition, but he said the Bishop was against it.

P.S. You have not given me the means of writing a more definite direction.

WEDNESDAY 11 JANUARY 1837   parcel with proofs of Lectures   sent up proofs to G. and R.

THURSDAY 12 JANUARY   letters from Pusey, Rogers, and M R G.   Ottley called   snow   wrote letter to Christian Observer   wrote to Pusey and Rogers

FRIDAY 13 JANUARY   letter from Bowden   wrote to Bowden, M R G. [,] Bridges and S W

TO JOHN WILLIAM BOWDEN

⌜Oriel College. Jan. 13. 1837⌝

My dear Bowden,

I was very glad to see your handwriting dated from the Stamps. It showed me you were again at your business, and the first painful period of your

[1] John Wood Warter had written to Pusey offering to translate for the Library of the Fathers, but he did not complete anything. See letter of 25 Jan. to Pusey about Grant.

[2] Pusey wrote, 'We ought to make up our minds, as soon as we can, on the validity of dissenting Baptism. For we shall have to commit ourselves . . . Qu. whether confirmation being at the hands of the Bishop, do not render valid, what before may have been invalid, as opposed to, or in separation from him? and then, whether the one sacrament do not virtually contain the other, when circumstances prevent the other being received? As Baptism is to infants the participation of the Body and Blood of their Lord, so the Eucharist may *fully* engraft the Adult into the Body of Christ, whatever may have been deficient before? I should have no difficulty about baptizing conditionally or otherwise in itself, looking upon the act (in your view) as a dutiful attempt to supply whatever may have been before deficient; but I have a decided repugnance, at present, to using the prayers, which imply the absence of regeneration, for one who has for half a life, been admitted to the Communion.'

This probably refers to Mrs Pusey, whose worries about her own baptism were increasing at this time. See note to diary entry of 14 April 1838 about her conditional baptism.

bereavement over. I have suffered the same too recently not to know how severe it must be to you; but it is still more so to your Father, and he is so much more thrown on himself. And very severe to your Aunt also.[1]

⌐The article on Bishop Jebb is not Mr Jebb's—the article is gone, I know not to this minute where—except that Boone, who did not write me word till it was too late to inquire (I suspect on purpose) has not had it.

I have been laid up with influenza since Monday and am sick of confinement—my cough not yet gone. We had a heavy snow here yesterday—and now a boisterous wind.

My new book is to be dedicated to Routh.

I spoke to Sewell about your article[2]—but he tells me he knows of no books, and does not recollect where he got the facts from I heard him mention.

My letter to the [[Christian]] Observer will go directly Pusey returns, whom I wish to see it, since it concerns him. I declare I doubt whether they will put it in. It will make them so angry.

Rose has made the amende so far as I am concerned, so I am very glad I mentioned his coolness to nobody.⌐

Thank you for your account of the Bill.[3] Will you say I will pay the money directly I get out to their name at Hammersley's. Did I know their Bankers I would send it to them.

⌐I suppose I shall be in Town after Easter, and then, (once more) about my teeth. I need not say that if you would and could then take me in I should rejoice—but my difficulty is having to go to Town to the Dentist daily.

I agree with you about S.W's article.[4]

There has been a mighty grand Conciliabulum at Islington, I believe they are periodical—at which we have been voted heretical, and open war denounced.[5] Earthen jars should not swing with iron ones, or the crockery will suffer. The Fathers are a match for many Daniel Wilsons.⌐

Ever yrs affectionately John H. Newman.

[1] Bowden's mother had died on 27 Dec. 1836.
[2] 'Church-Building', *Brit. Crit.*, 21, 1837 (April), 303–38.
[3] For items of Church plate and engraving for Littlemore Church. Bowden had negotiated with the firm in London about the matter.
[4] [[Samuel Wilberforce]] 'Sacred Poetry', *Brit. Crit.*, 21, 1837 (Jan.), 167–85. Bowden wrote, 'S.W. might have made more of the *principles* of the Lyra—anti-ultra-protestantism etc.'
[5] See the previous letter to Pusey. F. Rogers wrote at about this time: 'The Islington affair has, I suspect considerably spread your fame.—You and your friends are stage coach talk in this neighbourhood among the Peculiars [Evangelicals].'

TO MISS M. R. GIBERNE

⌜Oriel College. Jan. 13. 1837⌝

My dear Miss Giberne,

⌜I fear I shall not send you a bright letter, having had this epidemic Influenza upon me.⌝ Henry W. [Wilberforce] has not yet sent or mentioned your paper, which I shall be pleased to see. You ask what you had better write—why, I would try my hand at several subjects, and see which I got on best with. As to the History of England, the only difficulty is that people as yet are not ripe for seeing things in their true light; and perhaps we none of us have searched into facts enough to see how our principles act upon them. This would make tales or dialogues safer. However follow your fancy.

⌜I hear from London that your friends at Islington have lately voted us heretics, and we are to be proceeded against accordingly. *How* is not yet decided—Mr Goode is writing against Pusey. The Christian Observer too has attacked him and I am to take up the cudgels in its pages—and, if they will but stand up, I will do my utmost, they may rely on it, to use them in true yeoman fashion.[1] It amuses me beyond measure to see how angry these people are made by their very incapacity. They put me in mind of a naughty child put atop of the bookcase, very frightened, but very furious. You see when one knows one has all the Fathers round one, let be that little mishaps and mistakes may befall, yet on the whole one feels secure and comfortable.⌝

I fear H. W. in his way has been filling you with monstrous sayings on all subjects, and putting them off as ours.

⌜My new book is going through the Press and has cost me an immense deal of trouble.⌝ It is on the Pastoral Office of the Church, as opposed to Romanism and Popular Protestantism. I treat of Romanism's neglect of the Fathers; of Infallibility; of Private Judgment; of the Indefectibility of the Church; of Fundamentals of Faith, and of Scripture as its foundation. I suppose I shall not get beyond this—but I have other Lectures written. Not an inviting list you will say—yet I hope the discussion will interest more.

We are getting on very well with our subscriptions for the Catholic Fathers—and have more than enough Translators. It will give us an immense deal of trouble.

⌜Catholic principles are spreading here so surprisingly, as to make one anxious. In Exeter the Bishop of Exeter has been expanding the end of his Charge,[2] which was stronger than any thing we ever have said, into a series

---

[1] [[N.B. The point of controversy was Pusey's Tract on Baptism. J H N. Augst 29/62]]

[2] *Charge delivered to the Clergy of the Diocese of Exeter . . . at his Triennial Visitation in the months of August, September, and October, 1836*, London 1836. Most of the Charge was concerned with parliamentary measures affecting the Church, but in the conclusion (pp. 42–8) Phillpotts turned to the question of the ministry. He insisted on, '. . . the obligation of instructing the people in the real nature of Christ's Church, and the duties resulting from it both to the Ministers and to the people.' He exhorted ministers to a faithful and regular use of all the services laid down in the Prayer Book. 'Be not . . . afraid nor ashamed thus to assert the true authority of your ministerial office.'

of Sermons, which he has preached at different consecrations of Churches, to the creation of no small sensation among the Westleyans. He is said quite to have given up the political ground.

As to the Apocrypha, the word *inspiration* is most vague. In some of our Collects we speak of ourselves as inspired. The Old and New Testaments only have *plenary* inspiration.⌝ I wonder whether you could get some book of Martyrs (not Fox) I fear they are all in Latin. It would not be bad to ask at Brown and Keating's—Paternoster Row or at Bookham's Bond Street— and you might *select those* which were veritable etc.—abridging, or adding from other sources, or putting in remarks etc.

⌜As to fasting, this week I confess to being emaciated, but the Influenza is the cause. I have certainly been under the united effect of Influenza and Ipacacuanha, a precious partnership. But not otherwise⌝

Yours most sincerely John H Newman

SATURDAY 14 JANUARY 1837   letters from W F [William Froude] and Mr Merewether Eden returned   Pusey returned, and called.   wrote to W F

SUNDAY 15 JANUARY   2 Epiphany   Pusey read prayers in morning and preached Provost read prayers in evening   took a short walk first time

TO JOHN WILLIAM BOWDEN

⌜Oriel College. January 16/37⌝

My dear Bowden,

⌜I am putting a little trouble on you. It is about the Christian Observer.[1]

You know first they have challenged an answer from me [[us]]—then I wrote to know if they would put one in from me. In their reply you know, they express indignation that it should be thought doubtful. I have written my defence. Now Pusey says it is so 'playful and malicious' they will not put it in. The question is, with what face they can refuse? What *face* can they put upon it? e.g., 'Mr. Newman has sent up a rambling letter partly in praise of the tracts, partly against ourselves, which, though of considerable length, is not yet finished etc., etc., Under these circumstances we decline etc., etc.,' I do not know whether they *can* get out of the scrape, but I wish to provide for the chance as follows.

You know Hatchard enough to do as much as this; to call on him with my M.S. (forthwith) if possible, and to beg him to give it to Mr. Wilkes, and to *ask Mr. W. 'whether it will be inserted in the next number'* (not hinting the chance of rejection) '*If not*, Mr. Newman wants it back.' And that you will call for that answer and M.S. on a day to be fixed   Thus I shall be secure from an impertinent misrepresentation of its contents in a notice to

[1] See note to letter of 7 Jan. to Rogers about the origin of the controversy.

correspondents. If you see any great absurdity in this manoeuvre do not execute it.[1]

Do you observe you are a Lyræ⌐2

Ever yrs affly John H. Newman.

TUESDAY 17 JANUARY 1837   wrote to Rogers and Mr Whitworth
WEDNESDAY 18 JANUARY   letter from Acland   sent parcel to G and R inclosing note to Boone   parcel from G and R   wrote to Acland
THURSDAY 19 JANUARY wrote to J

TO MRS JOHN MOZLEY

Oriel College. ⌐Jan. 19. 1837⌐

My dear Jemima,

It is very kind in you and John to be thinking of doing what you mention about Aunt N [Newman].—of course I wish to do my part. You say £40 more per annum is requisite. Well—I will do of this whatever you and Frank do not do. Wait and see what F. will do before you say what you will do yourself.—Or I will arrange it in any other way you like. I should like my Trust money, when it comes into my hands, to be received (i.e. the interest of it) *with yours* by you and John. Then you can pay it over to Aunt in part of what I have to send her. Else the money will have a double journey.

Frank has written me an angry letter lately which has surprised me. It seems he has been all the while fidgetting about my giving a book to his wife.

[1] [[N.B. Mr Wilkes [S. C. Wilks] acted far more cleverly than to misrepresent my letter, without inserting it, as I feared. What he did was, to insert it, but to append a running comment of his own, which occupied nearly the whole page of letter press, leaving me a streamlet of text along the top of the page. The consequence was, that, whether readers studied his comment or not, they could not properly read and understand my Defence. The letter was afterwards reprinted as one of the Tracts in Volume 4 [*Tract* 82], under the title of 'A Letter to a Magazine' May 15. 1862.]]
Newman's first letter, dated 11 Jan., was published as 'Letter from the Rev. J. H. Newman upon the Oxford Tracts, with Remarks upon it', in two parts. The first part appeared in *The Christian Observer*, 422, 1837 (Feb.), 114–26. The editor published Newman's text in large print, generally occupying the top quarter of the page, and filled the rest of the page with his own notes in small print.
Wilkes explained in his prefatory note that the letter had arrived too late to be inserted in the correspondence section and would normally have been left for the next issue, but: 'We have, however, seen enough of the spirit of controversy to know that any delay would, by some staunch party-men, be attributed to other causes than the true one, the least violent of which would be, that we did not choose to let Mr. Newman speak until we had enjoyed a month to concoct an answer . . . we cannot, in duty, send our Reverend Correspondent's strictures to press without some notes—though being necessarily thrown off in rapid haste, they are intended only as *pro re nata* remarks . . .' Wilks went on to challenge the title Oxford Tracts, saying that they had no connection with the University as a whole, and only represented the views of a minority.
See letter of 16 March to Bowden about the continuation of the matter.
[2] [[i.e. in the Lyra Apostolica. The allusion is to our star-gazing atop of Trinity Chapel Tower with Ogle, when Bowden and I were undergraduates. Ogle or Bowden used to be great about 'Alpha Lyrae'.]] Alpha was the code letter for Bowden's poems in the *Lyra Apostolica*.

Why not say so then? I am sure it has given me trouble enough. He speaks as if I were treating *her* as I would not *him*, i.e. more kindly. Why I have done every thing *through* him, and through delicacy would not even write to her. When the book was received, *she* wrote to me, and I *then* answered it—which has excited F's displeasure. I am told that there has been a letter in the Morning Chronicle from Bristol from a person who says he has heard Frank say I wrote the article on Dr Wiseman. I do not care who knows it—people are very much out if they think I do—but how did F. know? it is like him to go chattering about, and very decent to have one brother speaking against another in mixed society. If he does it on religious grounds, then I have nothing to say of course; only I should find fault with his taste.

Charles made his appearance here unexpectedly on the Epiphany—he was walking to Town, without clothes. He slept here one night and pursued his journey. He declared he did it for exercise and health, but I thought it foolish this time of year. I fear he must have been laid up of the Influenza in London. I have had the Influenza, and for a week was laid on the shelf. I hope to hear a good account of you all at Derby by James. All the Littlemore people have had it—It has come to them as to me quite suddenly. I had not heard it was about and would not believe I had a cough; it came so entirely without preparation or exciting cause. Mrs Birmingham who has been ailing for 6 weeks died last night. Mrs Hedges is dead also, not comfortably. And Mrs (I do not know her name) at Mr Waddle's house, of the Influenza.

⌐Tell Miss Mozley that I fear I must decline the place in her poetical collection—I can never write except in a season of idleness—When I have been doing nothing awhile, poems spring up as weeds in fallow fields.

I have been reading Emma. Every thing Miss A [Austen] writes is clever, but I desiderate something. There is a want of *body* to the story. The action is frittered away in over-little things. There are some beautiful things in it. Emma herself is the most interesting to me of all her heroines. I feel kind to her whenever I think of her. But Miss A. has no romance, none at all. What vile creatures her parsons are! she has not a dream of the high Catholic $\tilde{\eta}\theta os$. That other woman, Fairfax, is a dolt—but I like Emma.⌐

I have nearly finished Southey's Westley,[1] which is a very superficial concern indeed—interesting of course. He does not treat it *historically*, in its connexion with the age, and he cannot treat it theologically, if he would. ⌐I do not like Westley—putting aside his exceeding self confidence, he seems to me to have a black self will, a bitterness of religious passion, which is very unamiable. Whit[e]field seems far better⌐

My best love to Aunt—thank her for her note—and apologize to her on your own score for having seduced me into filling up this third side to you instead of to her

Ever Yrs affectionately John H Newman

[1] Robert Southey, *Life of Wesley*, two volumes, London 1820.

P.S. The Tract on the Breviary has run through 750 copies in 6 months in the dead time of the year!

P.S. Thanks for your kind thoughts of me.

FRIDAY 20 JANUARY 1837   letter from Grant   went to T [Tuckwell]   administered Sacrament to Thomas Cox   wrote to Grant

SUNDAY 22 JANUARY   Septuagesima   letters from Christie, R Williams and Bramston did duty morning and afternoon   preached Number 439   wrote to Acland, Harrison and Bramston

MONDAY 23 JANUARY   Harrison's brother, Newman and Lowe to breakfast.   Keble came to Pusey   dined with Pusey

TUESDAY 24 JANUARY   letters from Boone, H, and Harrison   went to Tuckwell Keble's Lecture   wrote to Harrison, Acland, and Mr Merewether

WEDNESDAY 25 JANUARY   St Paul's   letter from Grant   Service in Chancel   read Number 330[1]   wrote to Grant

TO E. B. PUSEY

St Paul's Convern. [25 January 1837][2]

My dear Pusey

I have a letter from Grant this morning in answer to mine, begging off translating the *first* of Corinthians on account of its length and keeping to the *second*. He will let us have the *Second* in 6 months. Will it begin a volume? We must either make H. Cornish work, or Wood at the Galatians and Oxenham at the Philippians, or Grant's expedition will be thrown away.

Ever Yrs affly J H N

P.S. Send me the list of Fridays[3] and I will take it to King tomorrow morning. Williams will take Friday week Febr 3 and one late in the Term. I will take Febr 10. tho' I should *prefer* a later one.

THURSDAY 26 JANUARY 1837   letter from Harrison   Whately in Oxford with the Provost who was too ill to dine

FRIDAY 27 JANUARY   Whately went   went to T [Tuckwell]   first meeting of Theological.   Keble read—papers of subjects for Term printed   *meeting of Theological as usual, tho' I have not noted it.   (from this date on there are notices of fasting.)*

SATURDAY 28 JANUARY   Keble went to Hursley

SUNDAY 29 JANUARY   Sexagesima   letter from Miss Giberne   did duty morning and afternoon at St Mary's   Sacrament for Berkeley at St Aldate's   preached Number 440   buried Mrs Hillier   wrote to Christie, H W. [,] Miss Giberne

[1] *P.S.* VIII, 15, 'Sudden Conversions'.

[2] Newman wrote on the letter long afterwards, 'January 25. 1840(?)'. Grant had offered to translate St John Chrysostom's Homilies on I and II Corinthians for the Library of the Fathers. He wrote on 23 Jan. to explain that parochial duties restricted his time for the work and in the event he did not complete anything.

[3] Papers to be read at the Theological Society.

TO J. F. CHRISTIE

Oriel. Jan. 29. 1837

My dear Christie,

Things are nearly as flat here, as with you—constant employment is one's own resource—for the external world is flat and dry. The Influenza is the only relief. I had it for a week—all Littlemore had it—The Provost is abed —and so he was when Whately δέκατος αὐτὸς¹ came last week to his house —It seems certainly one of the most general pestilences, a very mild one but still such, any where. At Clapham they have offered up the 'prayer in general sickness—' Thornton tells me that his brother in Law in Kent sent to the butcher's—no meat was to be got—it was all bought up for broth—and the butcher was in bed. He sent to the poulterer's—the p's wife put her head out of the window, and said her husband and all her children were ill abed, and she had no fowls to sell—While he was meditating on this state of things, the Doctor of the Parish sent to him to say he was starving for want of victuals, and begged to know if he could send him any thing. At last they got some fowls from a farmer's. In London I hear shops have been shut up for days. It has been pretty mild here. At Abingdon this day week, they said not half the Churches round would be served. My sister writes me word, when they got back to Cholderton, they found every one had it.

You must not fancy about Mozley—at the same time be sure of this, that every one when he marries is a lost man—a clean good for nothing—I should not be surprised to be told that Mozley would not write another letter all his life.

The Tract on the Breviary,—which I published, not supposing it would answer, but because dear Froude wished it,—which was a dear one, and published at a dead time of year,—has in 6 months run out the whole edition. This is the most promising event that has happened since the Tracts began. Rivington says they have suddenly begun to sell, and is in haste getting reprints of some of them. He proposes to double all editions in future; viz to make them 1500.

There has been a meeting at Islington of Peculiars. They spouted one after another for two hours against the Oxford Tracts—that is called a 'Discussion'—Then they had 'Conversation' for another hour, which con-sisted of another man's getting up and saying he wished to explain a point, which he proceeded to do to the extent of the full hour. At this meeting a Mr Goode announced his intention of writing against Pusey, and was re-ceived with applause. Those peculiars are angry and frightened out of their skins. They cannot argue, and they won't be convinced.

If you will, in spite of my remonstrances, take old Sermons of mine, you must expect every inconvenience in them. So far from being distressed, I rejoice at your mishap.

¹ 'with nine others'.

When do you mean to come up to finish your Ridley?[1] *resolve* on a certain time. You must not keep putting it off.

Maurice is standing for the Political Economy Professorship and is taken up by all respectable people.[2] His opponents are Mr Twiss and Merivale. Thornton, Jeffreys, Rogers, Acland, Williams, Wood, Bowden etc are coming up. You must make your appearance. The time is not known yet. Out it will be before Easter.

We are getting on capitally with our Translations—but we Editors certainly have a most laborious work before us—

It is quite impossible that your living should exceed what a fellowship will carry. My book will not be out for a month yet.

W. Palmer of Magdalen seems a very nice fellow—but it is my misfortune now to have no middle man here between myself and others. I am cut off from the University, and live in my rooms.

I. Williams is wonderfully well, but he has had the Influenza lately. Cornish of Exeter is helping him regularly at Littlemore.

I am sorry to see your paper bordered with black

Ever Yrs affectionately John H Newman

TO MISS M. R. GIBERNE

⌐Oriel College. January 29. 1837⌐

My dear Miss Giberne,

My only excuse is, that I should have written last night, had there been a post; and then I should have had the satisfaction of my letter crossing yours on the road. I really am very much annoyed, but if you knew more of my correspondence, you would find me very irregular; sometimes very punctual, sometimes remiss, according as my engagements happen to be. I have been attempting to write to you every day since your most acceptable parcel arrived—and something has always prevented it. I did not like to take up my pen and scrawl a few lines. However under the circumstances, it was inexcusable. I have no doubt you have said 'I am sure Mr N. cannot have got the parcel—he is so punctual in acknowledging etc etc' See what a scrape I am in.

I hope I need not say, I am sure I need not, how very acceptable the portrait of my dear Mother was—I value it most highly—and it is a very great mark of your kindness, your sending it.

As to the Christ Church alto relievo, it is inimitable—I recognized it at once. It is just like the original, and beautifully done. I have not decided

---

[1] Christie wrote an article on 'Bishop Ridley's Remains', *Brit. Crit.*, 31, 1842 (April). T. Mozley, who was then editor, disliked the tone of the article and later commented 'Christie . . . did admire and like Ridley and . . . made him not only a saint but an authority.' T. Mozley, *Reminiscences chiefly of Oriel College and the Oxford Movement*, London 1882, II, 230.
[2] See letter of 12 Feb. to Keble.

where abouts to put it in my small room—so at present I have placed it upon my mantle piece as a temporary resting place—that every one may see it —and I have been commenting on it to all comers.

I found your four sovereigns—and thank you much for so liberal a contribution—but that is not the plan of the Library of Fathers. At Rivingtons, if you send there, you may get Prospectuses, and you will see the mode of subscribing. Persons may subscribe for a particular Father, or for a year, or for good. The price, I believe, is not to exceed 9/ (I am not sure) per volume—and there will be about 25—so your £4. will buy about a third of the whole. Any thing else you like me to do with it, I will gladly.

⌐I suppose I told you all in my last, whatever news there was—about the Tract on the Breviary having run out 750 copies in 6 months in the dull part of the year. So I will go on to your MS,¬ for which I thank you. It is done with spirit, as any thing would be, which you would set about; but I think the subject is not equal to what you should attempt. I mean, I do not wish you to write stories for children, but, as you proposed, for grown people. You spoke of history—the difficulty there is the want of definite views and accurate details—still I think you must not write mere tales for children. ⌐What say you to biography? I think I mentioned the Acta Sanctorum.¬ Why should you not make a Catholic Fox? ⌐did I mention the notion of illustrating the Calendar? It seems to me that a most delightful work might be written on the black letter days. Or again what say you to a plan I have had in my mind for some years, to form an *English* Calendar, arranging all our worthies on their death days. Or it would be a great thing if we had lives of saintly women, there being little biography of the sort.¬ Did H. Wilberforce suggest nothing?

I see you say in your letter of this morning that the money is to go to the Tract Fund—if so, thank you

I am really quite ashamed of my remissness

Yours very sincerely John H Newman

TO HENRY WILBERFORCE

Oriel College. ⌐Jan 29. 1837¬

My dear Henry,

⌐I hope I shall not annoy you by what I am going to say. It is better for both of us that you give over the Translation of St Austin. It will be a continual burden upon you, a vexation and anxiety to me. Be advised—it is best. What makes me write this, is hearing you are just going for a month from home.¬ Many men would find that a season of leisure for such an occupation. I cannot expect it in you. Be advised—give it up at once—I shall consider it given up and look out for some one else—except I receive before Ash Wednesday the translation of the first book complete.

Miss Giberne has been sending me something of hers to look at—but I wish something for grown people—something like the Acta Sanctorum etc —I wish you would think of some subjects to send her. Harrison has lost his sister.

With kindest remembrances to Mrs W.

Yrs ever affly John H Newman

P.S. ⌜The Tracts have suddenly begun to sell apace. We are to have double Editions in future.⌝

MONDAY 30 JANUARY 1837 King Charles f.b.[1] till one—then dined c.m: did duty in Chancel—read Number [376]

TUESDAY 31 JANUARY letters from Acland and J C F [Fourdrinier] inclosing Trust Receipt and £21.6.6. went to T [Tuckwell] wrote to J C F and Harrison

WEDNESDAY 1 FEBRUARY letters from Woodgate and Boone went to Littlemore f— no d. wrote to R Williams and Woodgate

THURSDAY 2 FEBRUARY Purification letter from R W. [,] J. and Harrison did duty in Chancel—read Number 276 W Pusey and his wife at Service. reading of Statutes. account day—Provost still too ill to dine Gaudy dinner

FRIDAY 3 FEBRUARY went to T f.d. Williams took tea with me—theological— Williams read third on Disciplina Arcani

SATURDAY 4 FEBRUARY Woodgate made his appearance walked with Williams and Philipps to Littlemore dined in rooms

SUNDAY 5 FEBRUARY Quinquagesima did duty morning and afternoon S S.[2] Marriott helping me. preached Number 441 (Woodgate preached University Pulpit)[3] dined with Pusey to meet Mr Bevan—Woodgate also to dinner.

MONDAY 6 FEBRUARY visited Mrs Beesley for first time Woodgate walked with me to Littlemore, where I read prayers Woodgate dined with me. had men to tea for first time—(Anderdon and Newman) (*This was the beginning of my weekly soirées, which went on till the affair of Number 90.*)[4]

TUESDAY 7 FEBRUARY Shrove Tuesday letters from C and Pope went to T (vid April 4) [letter] from J through J. M. who returned yesterday evening administered S Sacrament to Mrs Beesley dined with Williams

WEDNESDAY 8 FEBRUARY Ash Wednesday f br. till l. began Breviary letter from Acland visited Mrs Beesley Service in Chancel Churched Mrs Standen James M to tea wrote to H and J.

[1] A possible interpretation of the details about fasting which begin at this time is: f.b.= fasting breakfast; c. m.=collation meal, or, cold meal; f. d.=fast day, or, fasting dinner; no d. but l.=no dinner but lunch. Later there are other variants such as ½ f. b.; and ½ f. d.

[2] Sacrament Service.

[3] 'The Study of Morals vindicated and recommended', which was published in Oxford later in the year.

[4] James Mozley wrote to his sister on 21 Feb., 'Newman gives a tea-party now every Monday evening, in term. He has just started the thing. Last night went off very well—about eight or nine men. Conversation flowing continuously, and every one at his ease. Newman can manage a thing of this kind better than Pusey . . . We talked on a variety of subjects.' *Moz.* II, 224. Another undergraduate reported that Newman 'talks to me of every sort of subject except what is called Tractarianism, and that he has never mentioned.' ibid., 225n.

TO MRS JOHN MOZLEY

Oriel College. Ash Wednesday. Febr 8/37

My dear Jemima,

I have so many things to write about, that I shall forget half and ought to have written days ago. But first pray make excuses to Aunt for my not writing to her—it quite annoys me—but I cannot help it this time.— Rivington, I suppose, has by this time ordered the 2nd Edition of the Lyra —I do not know what (number) edition, but *I* should not be for a large one —I fancy the first has been *taken off* by our friends, in large quantities, for Presents etc. That the volume will ultimately sell, I doubt not—but I am not sanguine about its immediate success. Parker wants, if it is not too late, his *name* to be in the Title page—John must settle this with Rivington—it is nothing to me—except that caeteris paribus I should prefer it. P. also recommends (if not too late) the page should be made *exactly* to correspond with that of the Christian Year—e.g. Edn. 13th—also that the *paper* should be the same. (1) Of false prints I know none but 'new-encompassed' p 132 which should be 'new-compassed—' However I do not like *it*—put, *new-ventured* in the new Edition not that I like this, but it is rather better—(2) At p 9 last line for ('Truth's shafts' read '*Heaven's shafts*,' which is rather less harsh. It is bad, for 'heaven's peace' is just before—but I cannot think of any thing else.)[1] Yes, put the two last lines thus.—

'And learn to kneel before the Omniscient Ray,
Nor shrink, while Truth's avenging shafts descend.'

(3) Again, put the two first poems of 'Saints departed' under a separate head as BEREAVEMENT. This will alter the roman numbers *in the Table of Contents*. (4) In p 45. for 'Thy Church's' it should be '*My Mother's*'—I cannot think how it is not.

Now to another subject—Carr the Butcher has at last brought in his account—as follows—you must please verify it. His son *believes* he received *two* £10.s on Account which would reduce it to £36 etc. but does not know!—

Also Plowman has sent me in a little bill. I cannot find it. It is about 12s/6. Thank you for the money; especially for your advance on the next dividend. I have now all paid me but Frank and H's to make up their shares —which is about £14 or £15 together.—

I had a letter from Charles yesterday, which pained and frightened me much in one respect—He will always go forward in a daring way. He has been receiving the Sacrament, confessing at the same time something so shocking that I will leave his own words presently to tell his feelings. I do not pretend of course to analyze the state of his mind—but I am sure he should be not so daring.—I will write out the whole passage—the former

---

[1] Newman crossed out these two sentences.

part of which contains a curious witness which has somewhat comforted me about myself, tho' painfully as to Frank. Some time or other I will send you F's letter and mine. It so happened that Charles was with me the very morning I received F's letter. At first I put it in my pocket in disgust and said nothing—but at last I showed it Charles. I now think that F. perhaps is irritated at finding Charles justify me—at least I think so for want of knowing what to think.—On second thoughts I cannot quote you what Charles says of his present state of unbelief—he says he does not know whether he believes or not—but then adds something of such a nature as I am sure should have kept him from the Sacrament—In fact he seems to take religion as a *medicine*, which would be beneficial though he were an atheist. I say all this, dear J., because we ought all to think of him much in prayer, —of course Satan wishes to keep him.

'I certainly' he says 'have formed a very decided opinion by the writings I read, chiefly yours, at Cholderdon in respect to the difference of opinion between you and Frank, and he seems to me fundamentally wrong in setting himself up as a judge of the English Church, since it has such high and just claims on all consistent Christians. Indeed the impression I have received of the tone of his feelings is, that, to be consistent, *he* ought to be an unbeliever. I am afraid I have for the present lost all credit with him for speaking my mind. In a previous letter last $\frac{1}{2}$ year written after I saw you for $\frac{1}{2}$ an hour in Burlington Arcade, I had accused him of want of due candour in his representations to me, when I was with him shortly before (last June) at Bristol, of your doctrine. He now says that, if I thus accuse him of [lack of] good faith, he must decline all correspondence with me. But this is hasty in him, in fact it is written in a postscript—for I always allowed him to be honest. But from what I read at Cholderdon last Christmas and from what I have seen lately of your friends, I have now got a still stronger idea of his want of fairness and candour, be the cause of this defect what it may. For he told me what certainly surprised me that "you were striving with all your might to create a sect, and to put yourself at the head of it." These words he repeated more than once. From which I concluded that you were introducing some crotchets and novelties of your own. But I now find you are simply following the doctrine of the prayer book. Respecting his misunderstanding your letter to his wife, I told him, as you wished me, that you had shown me the correspondence, and that it plainly seemed to me that his letter to you was entirely founded on mistake. First that he must allow on consideration that he had reasoned on an incorrect proposition in assuming that it was inconsistent in any man in any circumstances to set his face against his brother and yet acknowledge him as such, and next that he was obviously mistaken in the fact that you had put his wife on a footing of nearer relationship than himself, and that the letters you had shown me from you and to you bore evidence that you had not done so. It would be desirable that F. should see he is quite mistaken in this little matter, as it might give him room to suspect that he may be so in more weighty ones; but he is so impatient and so wanting in steadiness of mind, that I suppose I shall not be able to get him candidly to confess he has misapprehended, besides perhaps I have quite lost credit with him by so decidedly taking your part which I should have done to some extent a year or two ago even, had I had better information of the real state of the case.'—It strikes me curious how F's party *impute motives*—they who of all men make such a clamour about personalities— What a very uncharitable thing it is, his saying I want to make a sect. *I* say nothing of *him*. I judge him in no way. I only say that God tells me to avoid persons who make divisions—and he makes a division. My conscience acquits me both of imputing any thing to him (I cannot if I would—such cases are far too puzzling for me in a flippant way to account for) and of having any wish to propagating peculiar opinions of any kind.

Ever yrs affly John H Newman

P.S. An *extempore* Prayer meeting in St Werburgh's?[1] The Bishop should be applied to—I willingly will agree to your plan about Aunt's expences.— Charles was tripped up and robbed near Uxbridge, but saved watch and money. He lost his hat. I heard from R and S. Wilberforce the morning of your letter. Not a word of any marriage. J. Marriott has had a pleurisy.

THURSDAY 9 FEBRUARY 1837   visited Mrs Beesley   walked to Littlemore with J M and Williams   Acland came and called   dined in rooms   Mrs Beesley died

TO C. P. GOLIGHTLY

Oriel—Feb 9/37

My dear Golightly

I am glad to say that the Tract Fund is in that comfortable state, that I am able to do, what I had always hoped to do, repay those who so kindly advanced money towards its formation. In consequence I have paid into your name the £50, which you gave three years since, and beg to acknowledge with many thanks the loan of it.

It is not often that money once given comes back to the donor, but here is a case w[h]ere it literally is on hand—and must, if kept, be applied to some new object

Ever Yrs most sincerely John H Newman

---

[1] The local parish church of the Mozley family in Derby. It was under Evangelical influence at this time. See T. Mozley, *Reminiscences, chiefly of Oriel College and the Oxford Movement*, London 1882, I, 194.

TO C. P. GOLIGHTLY

[February 1837]

My dear Golightly,

I am much obliged to you for the extract. Copeland, I am told, comes back next Wednesday.

By the bye I am told you have said that I have spoken in criticism, to say the least, of Pusey's Sermon, or Tract, or something or other.[1] Pray tell your informant it is an utter mistake from beginning to end. I am not aware of any thing which Pusey has written that I do not agree with.

Yours ever John H Newman

FRIDAY 10 FEBRUARY 1837 d.c m. at 1 letters from Rogers, C. Anderson, and Barter attended Archdeacon's meeting of Clergy about petition to Parliament about chapters Theological—I read 2nd on Ignatius[2]

TO AN UNKNOWN CORRESPONDENT[3]

Febr 10/37

Sir,

I wish I could return a more satisfactory answer to your letter than this is likely to prove, partly from the confined limits of a sheet of paper—

I do not exactly hold what you suppose viz 'that a person in order to become a true member of Christ's Visible Church, must, of necessity, be rightly and with faith baptized by a Clergyman who has been episcopally ordained.'—Lay baptism *under certain restrictions* has ever been admitted in the Church. About a century ago there was a controversy on the subject, the

---

[1] 'he [Golightly] was now gossiping all over Oxford about some of his old allies—not Pusey himself—in a way which . . . did not help him or others to understand them. Pusey, not having been himself attacked, with characteristic directness wrote to Golightly what the latter called 'a severe scolding,' and 'warned him against the dangerous occupation of talking over or against people.' Golightly was much ruffled; Pusey, he held, had not been justified in thus writing, either by seniority, or station, or by the terms of their acquaintance . . . Golightly from this time ranged himself in conscious, and . . . increasingly bitter opposition to the Oxford leaders.' Liddon's *Pusey* II, 12. See Letter of 18 Feb. to Henry Wilberforce.

[2] There are two papers of Newman's on St Ignatius preserved in the Archives of the Birmingham Oratory. The first, entitled 'Ignatius a witness for Catholic doctrine', would seem to have been that which Newman read to the Theological Society on 11 Nov. 1836. The second, just headed 'Ignatius', would have been that read on this occasion. Newman noted on them 'these are all used or superseded', and a good deal of the material seems to have been incorporated in his article 'Jacobson's *Apostolical Fathers*—Ignatius', *Brit. Crit.*, XXV, 1839 (Jan.), 49–76. (Later reprinted as 'The Theology of St Ignatius' in *Ess.* I, 222–62.)

[3] Signing himself 'K. X. T.', the correspondent wrote on 4 Feb. from Oxford and appealed to Newman as 'one of the great supporters of the discipline of our Church'. He asked if Newman was one of those who believed that baptism could only be validly administered by an episcopally ordained minister. He wondered, 'how it is that if a Dissenter should wish to become a Churchman, or rather desire to belong to the Church of England, he has not therefore to be baptized again . . .'.

most important work in which (as far as I know) was Laurence's[1]—with whom Waterland agreed, having first sided with Bingham, who took the opposite opinion. Laurence's view is that the early church allowed lay baptism, *when* done under the Bishop's sanction, not otherwise; this he proves by instances. I suppose it may be expressed *doctrinally* thus: that, whereas all Christians are in one sense priests, this particular gift attaches to them all that they may propagate Christianity, or make other Christians. Their own baptism gives them a power of baptising; but, as all gifts may be quenched, so is this gift when a layman attempts to exercise it without Episcopal authority. This account of the fact is a *theory*; and is a right theory, if supported by Catholic Antiquity, but a mere opinion, if not. Whether it is or not I know not (having only seen the first volume of Laurence's work—I believe there are two) but the *rule itself* that lay Baptisms without Episcopal sanction were not taken as valid, is, I believe, certain from Antiquity, however we account for it.

But with respect to Dissenters Baptisms, in the present condition of the church I would but say, *they are not certainly valid*—but I would not dare to pronounce the contrary (where the words and matters are preserved), because, so lax has been Episcopal jurisdiction, that it is impossible to say whether or not permission has been given. There was an attempt made at the beginning of last century to get the English Church to acknowledge Lay Baptism.[2] First it was tried in Convocation and the Lower House stopped it—then in the College of Bishops and Sharp Archbishop of York did the same. Still it is plain so near an escape gave great countenance to the irregularity. Again some Dissenters are bitterly hostile to the Church, others well-meaning men who wish to cooperate with it.—Hence the question of baptising Dissenters on joining the Church, is one of expediency (in the high sense of the word) in the particular case; viz whether on the one hand it is not *safer* to baptize them—or on the other, whether the certainty of its distressing and unsettling a number of persons, the anxiety it would create—even in many who were baptised in the Church, but not registered, or baptised at sea etc etc. the curious questions which would next rise about sprinkling, affusion, and immersion, would not be a reason against it in the case of persons who had been confirmed and habitually communicated; (vid. Euseb. Hist. vii.9) I would lay down two things, first that when there has

---

[1] Roger Laurence was one of several non-jurors who pressed the invalidity of presbyterian baptisms. In 1708 he published the first part of his *Lay Baptism Invalid*, which was answered by Joseph Bingham in his *Scholastical History of Lay Baptism* of 1712. Bingham tried to show that, although laymen were not allowed to baptise in ordinary cases, they had always been allowed to do so in extraordinary circumstances, without any need for rebaptism.

[2] The commitment of many High Churchmen to the invalidity of lay baptism meant that n 1712, 'the bishops thought it desirable to publish a collective declaration, first against the irregularity of baptism by lay persons, and then showing that "primitive and Anglican usage disallowed the reiteration of baptism." Three or four, however, of the bishops, headed by Sharp, declined to sign, not from any difference in view, but for fear it might encourage irregularities, and the Lower House of Convocation thereupon refused to consider the question.' C. J. Abbey, *The English Church and its Bishops 1700–1800*, London 1887, I, 40–1.

been an *intention* to obey God, He will mercifully accept it (2 chron. xxx. 18) e.g. should the water in sprinkling (no one observing it) not have touched the face *only* the clothes—and so in other cases—Next that the *authors* of irregularities are answerable. We did not begin to leave off immersion or to allow of Dissenting Baptism; the authors are nothing to us however, except by way of warning.—In the above you will observe I give no decision on the subject. I cannot—it depends on the individual case.

I conceive the English Church refuses to recognize the American only as acting under compulsion of the *State*.[1] We are in many ways in captivity

I am, Sir etc

SATURDAY 11 FEBRUARY 1837 (went to T?)   no M. L. or P of B[2]   Cornish obliged to go from illness in his family   Sir W Heathcote called   walked to Littlemore

SUNDAY 12 FEBRUARY   1st Lent   Marriott had news of his brother G's death   did duty morning and afternoon   preached afternoon Number 442   dined with C and W. [Copeland and Isaac Williams]

TO JOHN KEBLE

Oriel College. 1st Sunday in Lent
⌐[[February 12]] 1837⌐.

My dear Keble

I went to Banting yesterday about the plans—but I am very doubtful whether he will be able to produce them. I fancy they are lent; I said I wanted them directly. If they come in time, Sir W.H [Heathcote] shall have them.

⌐Maurice has published a rambling theory of Baptism, which shows him to be so unsettled in his views, that Wood has written down to me to ask whether I can consistently vote for him.⌐[3] I do not know, but at all events it

---

[1] The correspondent also found it 'unaccountable why the Church of England should refuse to recognize the Church of America, (though sound in faith and not differing from us in any essential points) and not even permit her Bishops to preach in our Church . . .'.

[2] 'Matins, Lauds, or Prime of Breviary'. In some later diary entries Newman used small letters for the Breviary hours, using 'th' (third) for 'terce'. The usual names of the hours are: matins, lauds, prime, terce, sext, none(s), vespers, compline. Later, M P and E P—Morning Prayer and Evening Prayer from the Book of Common Prayer—were added.

[3] Acland wrote on 7 Feb., 'I am most anxious about Maurice's letters to the Quakers . . . He has I am sure very much misunderstood Pusey, who I think, one point says just what M. makes him out not to say.—I am afraid he has been sadly misled by Eclecticism: and at the same time I think he has put forward some most important truth.' Acland felt that Maurice's theory was 'below his belief'.

Wood wrote on the following day, in alarm about Maurice, 'whether, considering all the late rows about Hampden etc, one ought to give them even the remote countenance which voting for him would, he being considered here as the man put forward by the "*Catholic party*." He went on to say, 'from a conversation with him I collected to be his notion (1) as to baptism; he denies it not only to be a change of *nature* but, any gift or deposit given once for all; and says that it relates to the *person* only, that it is the inchoation of *personal union* with the Head of the Church, and the time when the H. S. is assigned as the Guardian and Teacher of the child. (2) as to *sin* after baptism; this he merely considers a neglect pro tanto

is not a matter that should bring people up, I think. ⌜If you choose to send for 'Letters to a Quaker No 1 and 2, published at Darton's', you can judge for yourself.⌝ At any rate you ought to know.

⌜Gilbert and Rivington have sent me the amount of Tracts taken out [[by friends]] in my name. They come up to the serious sum of £70 odd⌝ of which yours are £16. 13. If you think they will *sell*, by all means keep them at Winton; else it is only diminishing the in coming sum I expect from Rivington. ⌜Please convey a message⌝ to this effect ⌜to S. Wilberforce, whose bill is £7. 8.⌝—If either of you have any sum to forward from the *sale* of course it will be acceptable.

Tell Wilson I am ashamed of not writing, but I have nothing to say—so he must be kind enough to accept my love instead

Ever Yrs affly J H N.

MONDAY 13 FEBRUARY 1837   Acland went   walked to Littlemore   had in evening Woolcombe, Ryder, Newman, Barker, and Shortlands.
TUESDAY 14 FEBRUARY letter from H   dined with Mr H Parker   wrote to M R G.

TO MISS M. R. GIBERNE

Oriel College. February 14. 1837

My dear Miss Giberne

I hope you have got rid of your Influenza long before this. Thinking I should but incommode you by writing was one reason why I did not answer your last at once—and I have been repaid for my delay—for a day or two since H Wilberforce sent your story of Little Mary, which is really quite beautiful. Much as I wish the Acta Sanctorum made available for Apostolical purposes, yet I willingly relinquish it for such stories as the one in question. I am sure such will do a great deal of good, and the more you write the better. I cannot tell you how much I have been pleased with it.

Your drawing of the Alto relief has been transferred to my inner room. Every time I look at it, there is something more and more taking in it. There is something so striking in their all being in the attitude of praying—and when I go in again, I am tempted to say 'What? you are all at it still?' if that were a reverent and proper speech. It seems an impressive emblem of the perpetual intercession of the Saints perfected waiting for Christ's coming. If there is any change I should have preferred, it would have been in the motto. Some text e.g., from Zech. xiv about our Saviour standing on Mount Olivet—or from Acts I or from Phil iii fin—etc etc. would have been better.

to claim and act upon this union; which may be remedied any moment, and the distance between the One and the other removed.'
For his strictures on Pusey see F. D. Maurice, *The Kingdom of Christ . . . in Letters to a Member of the Society of Friends*, London 1838, I, 91ff.

At present it fastens the mind too much upon these miserable agents of reform who ought to be forgotten on account of the intenser interest of the subject represented. So my dear Henry W. was at fault here—

Yours very sincerely John H Newman

P.S. I have not forgotten the sermons on Antichrist—though I did forget to mention them. You shall have them—but I could not lend them just at this minute—I am just now in want of them.[1]

WEDNESDAY 15 FEBRUARY 1837 sent parcel to C no d. buried Mrs Beesley or yesterday?

THURSDAY 16 FEBRUARY Maurice withdrew from the Political Economy Cornish returned dined in rooms wrote to Wood about the Political Economy

FRIDAY 17 FEBRUARY no d. Woodgate started for Political Economy Professorship walked with Pusey and his wife W and C to tea Theological—Williams read

SATURDAY 18 FEBRUARY no d. but l. letters from Rogers, H W and Anon: (no M. or L. of B) walked to Littlemore Marriott returned

TO HENRY WILBERFORCE

Oriel College. ⌜February 18/37⌝

My dear Henry

Let me congratulate you and Mrs W. as I do most sincerely on the happy event of which you give me notice.[2] I earnestly trust and pray that you have now committed to you an additional heir of heaven, who will be yours to all eternity. I am much pressed for time on Saturday evening; so you must excuse a hasty letter.

I have wanted to write ever since I got your packet. Two days after its appearance ⌜Pusey found so good a translation of the Confessions that he decided on adopting it, and printing from it. Therefore take the letters ⟨Epistles⟩ and your time.⌝ The truth is, my dear H., when men are free and easy about enims and veros, it proves they are not good scholars; and many as your qualifications are in a number of ways, I do not think that you have that particular precision and tenacity of thought which leads to scholarship.

⌜Woodgate is standing for the Political Economy Professorship. His College have taken it up warmly⌝—all the white corded parsons are to be evoked—and *we* are to have a sort of gathering. ⌜I have not time to write the whole history, which is amusing.⌝ March 2 is the day.

[1] 'Advent Sermons on Antichrist', which Newman originally preached in November and December 1835 and published in 1838 as *Tract* 83. He later republished them as 'The Patristical Idea of Antichrist', *D.A.*, pp. 44–108.
[2] Wilberforce's wife had just given birth to a daughter, Florence, who died in 1841.

⌜Golightly⌝ (DO NOT TELL) ⌜has sent Pusey a lecturing letter—and when Pusey, who argues with people too much, (out of kindness) replied somewhat *convincingly*, Golius replied that Pusey was too hard for flesh and blood. I wish the said G. were not so insufferably conceited.⌝

Your news about Miss Giberne shows there is no trusting women (not *her*) if it may be said. Keep the following secret. Knowing my sister Jemima and Miss Mozley were pursuing a similar plan, I wrote to sound Jemima on the possibility of all working together—She thought it best not [,] for reasons I need not say—but it was a profound secret. At present the Mozleys are at Brighton—and their literary labours suspended. How to get out of the scrape with Miss G. I know not. Perhaps I had better preserve a dignified silence, till fairly asked categorically

Ever Yrs affly John H Newman

My book will be out by the first of March—all going well.

SUNDAY 19 FEBRUARY 1837 2nd Lent M. of B. letter from C did duty morning and afternoon preached Number 443 buried Mrs L. Line dined in rooms. wrote to Wood

MONDAY 20 FEBRUARY went to Littlemore J M to dinner to tea with me Ryder, Hatsell, Newman, J. M. [,] Marriott, Church, and Daman

TUESDAY 21 FEBRUARY letter from J dined with W

TO MRS JOHN MOZLEY

Oriel College. Febr 21. 1837

My dear Jemima,

Thank you for your kind congratulations—thank Aunt also—It is to me quite portentous to think the age I am getting.

As to the Lyra, I wish John to decide entirely about the size—it is a thing he will understand better. Thank you for the measures. I agree with him. The only question is about any *new divisions* of stanzas, if there are to be any. But any how he is as good a judge as I can be—My principles would be these, not to divide *rhymes*—and not to divide where the sense would *seem so complete* as not to need turning over the page. The Greek in Keble's Lighting of Lamps is not placed quite as it should be in the first Edition— is it? I mean there is an awkward break in p 74. Part of p 75 should come into it. I do *not* want to see the proofs.

As to Charles, if I were not in a great hurry, I would quote his words. I wrote to him about them, and from his answer, it is plain *he* did not see what they conveyed. Nor did I mean to convey to you that he knowingly approached the Sacrament in an unbelieving frame; I meant more what one means by profaneness. His answer is so far satisfactory that he has let me into his feelings much more—and I rejoice to find a great many good ones. There is a mixture of others of a less pleasing description—but every thing cannot be done at once. I have written back to him to say that under the circumstances, though I should not have advised him to approach the Lord's table without more preparations, I will not venture to dissuade him from what he has begun—but speaking earnestly of the seriousness of it. I do *not* think he feels this enough. He says what is almost this in so many words—that he did not act religiously before because he was not elected, but that now he trusts he is—confesses he does not repent, nor does he see the need ⟨(*Do not tell at this even to Harriet or Aunt*)⟩—at the same time trusts that God will make him repent, if necessary, if he waits upon Him. This is just a sample of his state of mind, calling of course for our earnest prayers. I think he trusts himself too much; but, as I say, one can but be thankful he has already got as far as he has.

My dear J. how could Anne Mozley let out to M. Giberne that she knew M. G. was writing something. You have got me into great trouble—but you can *do* nothing, or it will be made worse. It seems such a breach of confidence in me

Ever yrs affly John H Newman

WEDNESDAY 22 FEBRUARY 1837   letters from Bowden and M R G   f.d.

THURSDAY 23 FEBRUARY   letter from Rivington, offering a 2nd Edition of 3rd Volume Sermons   f.d i.e. 1.   went to Littlemore   wrote to Anderson

TO C. H. J. ANDERSON

Oriel College, St Matthias' Eve [23 February] 1837

My dear Anderson,

Your letter was inexpressibly welcome—I thank you very much for it and for its kindness. It will always give me great pleasure, whenever it happens to me to fall in with you and Mrs Anderson, to whom I beg to be remembered most kindly.

I have myself in the course of the last year suffered the same bereavement, which you mention as having befallen yourself. Till the day before my dear Mother died, I did not know her danger—and had ever anticipated for her a long life—but it is all well.[1]

I wish the Tracts were printed in another form—We began them, not knowing they were to go on—taking the type at random—and now we find

---

[1] Anderson wrote on 7 Feb. to thank Newman for sending him a copy of *P.S.* III, which he and his wife had read with great profit. His mother had died recently and he had found Sermon 25, 'The Intermediate State', particularly consoling in the circumstances.

it very difficult or rather impossible to change it. For the volume never goes out of print all at once—but first one Tract, then another. I am glad to say the sale is good and increasing. It would be a great point to extend it into the North. Should you be able to do any thing in the way of a Depot, it would be so much gain—but I am not sanguine much would be done in any one place. The sale is here and there over England. What I think we should aim at is a library on all subjects for the middle classes and the Clergy—what the Christian Knowledge Society might provide. I am getting one or two ladies to write stories for children or young people. I have got another's hymns—and some of our men here have published lately the life of Ambrose Bonwick[1], and Vincentius's Commonitorium[2] in a convenient form. Parker too has lately published Jeremy Taylor's Golden Grove.[3] When once there was a respectable set of books on various subjects, a Depot would answer. But if you choose to take the trouble at present, you shall have it in your power to return any Tracts you order, should they not sell.[4]

I saw Lord H. Vane the other day. He passed through Oxford and called on me—A very pleasing man he is certainly—I wish he was in the way to get views on important subjects.

The Lyra, I am glad to say, has already come to a Second Edition

Believe me, My dear Anderson, Yours most sincerely John H Newman

TO JOHN KEBLE

⌐Oriel College Febr. 23.⌐ St Matthias' Eve. 1837

My dear Keble

Oakeley called on me today to say they had just heard from ⌐Woodgate⌐—and that he ⌐will not stand.⌐ I cannot say I altogether wonder at it—though I wish he would have sent his resolve two posts sooner.

Williams having written to you, I write to tell you this news. ⌐Oakeley and Harrison are still unwilling to give up the field, and talk of trying poor Rogers again—but I do not expect any thing will come of it.⌐

As to dear H F.'s [Froude] papers, I am almost of opinion that no notes

[1] *The Life of Mr Ambrose Bonwicke. To which are added, Thoughts on Christian Education, by William Beveridge . . .*, Oxford 1834. Ambrose Bonwicke was a young eighteenth century non-juror of St John's College, Cambridge, who died at the age of twenty two, in 1714, partly as a result of the ascetical discipline of his deeply religious life.

[2] *Vincentius of Lirins Commonitory*, Oxford 1836. The Latin text was published in Oxford in the same year.

[3] Jeremy Taylor, *The Golden Grove. A Choice Manual, containing what is to be believed, practised, and desired or prayed for . . . to which is added, a Guide for the Penitent . . .*, Oxford 1836.

[4] Anderson asked Newman's advice about means of circulating the *Tracts* in his area. He had considered setting up a depository. Many of the local clergy were Evangelicals and had scant regard for Church authority. He continued: 'What would I give to see the Village Churches open on all days, or even on Fasts and Festivals. But hoping to go (on the strength of your Sermons and the Tracts) to hear the Commination Service on Ash Wednesday I know of no place but the Minster at Lincoln to go to.'

should be put but simply explanatory—If so, I would leave out those I have put in the paper you first saw

Ever Yrs affectionately John H Newman

FRIDAY 24 FEBRUARY 1837   St Matthias   letters from M R G (inclosing MS) and Manning   Service in Chancel   read Number 286   dined in rooms   wrote to Manning and to E. W. [of] Colchester (anon)

FROM H. E. MANNING

Lavington, Petworth Feb 22, 1837.

My dear Newman,

You must think me a very faithless brother for not sending you the references I promised. A friend of mine has run away with the British M. (for December) and I have no other but—I daresay Newman you have no need of my help, and, I believe, if you should, the printed list is enough. But if not tell me, and as I am bent on extracting a speedy reply from you, I will do your bidding when it comes. I write to know two other things, and first whether the Election for the Pol: Econ: chair is of importance enough for us bumpkins to trudge up to Oxford. If so I will come. I hear Woodgate will stand. What are your wishes about it?

I am reading Justin through, and with very great pleasure. I should very much like to hear what you think of his expressions about the Millenium; and the Man of Sin. Does not Jerome say that every Ecclesiastical writer up to his day understood the ὁ ἄνθρωπος τῆς ἁμαρτίας[1] to be a person? I remember talking to you about Antichrist, when I was last in Oxford.

Chevallier's translation of the Apologies will I suppose make it needless for you to republish them. You intend also to put out the later Fathers first, as being less likely to scare our Protestant contemporaries. Is it not worth considering that the Ante Nicene Fathers sometimes use an undefined language about the Trinity, I mean a language, which had not been as yet fixed by Catholic agreement—and therefore the Nicene and Post Nicene should come out first—but I cannot doubt all this has been thought over by you 1000 times. By this arrangement Justin would not be wanted for a long time—and I should like to take first Chrysostom's Homilies on St. John, which I do not see taken as yet. Pray tell me whether this meets your approval. I have been writing, and waiting for your book, but as yet in vain.

Do you know Milner's End of Controversy?[2] Wiseman I think has evidently used it in his Lectures. It is very much what Dr. Parr said of Milner's writings bitter, and boisterous; but he puts true Catholic principles very unanswerably.

I want to know something on Thorndyke, and Montague—Bishop of Norwich. Will you tell me what to think about them. I see Milner quotes and lauds them, and somebody else—I think Forbes. They seem to be very good Catholics: and to go further than any I know in opposing Protestant lies, and prejudices against Catholicism.

And now, as I doubt not you think me a very troublesome fellow, I will let you go, only adding that, I have been very much pleased with the Lyra, and amused to boot with W's [S. Wilberforce] Review in the B. Critic.

Believe me, My dear Newman, Yours very sincerely, H. E. Manning.

Do you know of two men, or 1 man wanting a Curacy—We have one of £120 a year with a house in a large parish, and another with £100 and no house.

[1] 'the man of sin'.
[2] John Milner, *The End of Religious Controversy, in a friendly Correspondence between a Religious Society of Protestants and a Roman Catholic Divine*, London 1818.

TO H. E. MANNING

Oriel College. St Matthias'. [24 February] 1837

My dear Manning,

Woodgate will not stand. Perhaps it is not very surprising, but I suppose he would have been pretty sure if he had. It is, I fear, pretty clear that Merivale or the other man will have it. Many men are very much annoyed at this here—and I am glad to say the effort has not been *from us*—I say this, to show the growth here of such principles as we think true.

Justin is taken by this time—I believe we do not intend to publish *Chrysostom* upon St John, but *Augustine*. Heurtley of C C C has taken it.—Are you disposed for Optatus? I suppose not.—Let me hear again from you when you have any view—

My book, I expect, will be out next Wednesday. It is an anxious thing. I have to deal with *facts* so much more than in writing Sermons—and facts which touch people to the quick. With all my care I may have made some floors—and I am aware that I deserve no mercy from your Protestants—and if they read me, shall find none. Then again the Via Media is ever between the cross fires of Papists and Protestants.

Some one here is writing against Keble's Sermon[1]—Pusey is in the thick of a hailstorm. Really it is astonishing hitherto how well I have escaped —my turn will come. The amusing thing is that the unfortunate Peculiars are attacked on so many sides at once that they are quite out of breath with having to run about to defend their walls—Tradition, Baptism, Apostolical Succession, Faith and works, etc etc. No sooner do they recover their breath after one blow, but they receive another in their stomach.

I have made good use of your references in the forth-coming Catena.[2]— The Tracts have lately taken to selling so well, that Rivington has recommended in future printing double editions.

As far as I have an opinion, I consider Antichrist to be a person, yet future.

I know very little of Thorndike—what I do know of him, I like much. Bull speaks most highly of him.

The Lyra has already come to a Second Edition

Ever Yrs very sincerely John H Newman

---

[1] Keble's Visitation Sermon *Primitive Tradition recognised in Holy Scripture*, London 1836. The Sermon was attacked by the evangelical William Wilson in *A Brief Examination of Professor Keble's Visitation Sermon . . .*, Oxford 1837, which spoke of Keble's position as 'indirect opposition to the acknowledged principles of Protestantism'. Thomas Butt of Christ Church criticised the sermon in *Observations on Primitive Tradition, and its Connexion with Evangelical Truth*, London 1837.
[2] *Tract* 78. See note to diary for 10 Jan.

TO AN UNKNOWN CORRESPONDENT[1]

[24 February 1837]

Sir,

Whatever interpretations are assignable to this or that clause of the 17th Article, I suppose it carries on the face of it to all divines an Anti-calvinistic character, as Laurence and Copleston have shown.[2] I mean, there are certain expressions in it which are known to be the historical badges of the Anti-calvinist school.

The chief of these is that of 'election *in Christ*;' The Calvinists maintain an election of *individuals* to eternal life; the Lutherans an election of a *body*, Christ mystical, of which individuals do but (as I may say) *happen* to be members. The Calvinist considers the electing love of God directly to contemplate the individual—the Lutheran the body. The Calvinist considers the individual to persevere, the Lutheran the body, or again the Calvinists the individual, *quâ individual*, the Lutheran the individual *qua Christian*, so that if he ceases [to] be Christian, he ceases to be elected   Calvin says 'Praedestinationem vocamus aeternum Dei decretum, quo apud se constitutum habuit, quid de *uno quoque homine* fieri vellet—So the Lambeth Articles of 1595, drawn by certain Calvinists on the *admission* that our Articles were not clearly Calvinistic, say, 'God from eternity hath predestined *certain men* unto life; *certain men* He hath reprobated etc . . . There is predetermined a *certain number* of the predestinate, which can neither be augmented nor diminished.' In like manner in the Conclusions at Dort it is declared, 'that God, by an absolute decree, hath elected to salvation a *very small number* of men etc, . . . and secluded from saving grace all the rest of mankind, and appointed them by the same decree to eternal damnation, without any regard to their infidelity or impenitency.' This is the genuine Predestinarean doctrine, very different surely from that of our Article—

This contrast, while it historically designates, also explains the article in question. In it the whole course of election is declared as a matter of *doctrine*; that is, as all doctrine must be, without reference to failures or exceptions. The will and purpose of God is declared, the innate power and tendency of

[1] Using the initials 'E. W.', and writing from Dedham, near Colchester. He had been reading Newman's sermons, and wrote, 'I should very much like to hear your mode of explaining the seventeenth article of our Church, which *appears to me* to disagree with your interpretation of those passages of the New Testament which relate to election. I think as you do that by election and predestination in the New Testament we are to understand election to the blessings of Baptism, such as Regeneration, Adoption, Justification etc., and not necessarily an election to Eternal Life, as the Article seems to imply. The Article evidently teaches that all the Elect are saved, now, I do not think this is quite the doctrine of St. Paul.' he explained that he was a deacon and that this difficulty about the 39 Articles was giving rise to doubts about continuing to priest's orders.

[2] Richard Laurence's Bampton Lectures of 1804, *An Attempt to Illustrate those Articles of the Church of England, which the Calvinists improperly consider as Calvinistical*, Oxford 1804. Edward Copleston, *An Enquiry into the Doctrines of Necessity and Predestination . . . and an Appendix on the Seventeenth Article of the Church of England*, London 1821.

35

His provisions, and the actual history of the dispensation when looked on, as it were, at a distance. Looked at externally, what is it but the disengagement of an elect people out of a fallen race of free grace and a carrying them forward to eternal life? Is not this the very description we should give of it, were we called to do so? just as we say that God brought the children of Israel out of Egypt and settled them in Canaan. The words 'those' 'them' 'they' etc in the Article do not imply, and I suppose it is historically certain they were not meant to imply 'each individual of them' but the whole as a body. A Calvinist would have said 'he' and 'him'   I read the Article therefore as follows—'Predestination to life is the everlasting purpose of God, whereby etc. He hath decreed etc. to deliver from curse and damnation a body chosen out of mankind into His Son, etc etc—Wherefore that chosen company is called according to His purpose by His Spirit etc. it through grace obeys the calling: it is justified etc.'

As to the Millenium, as Christ was at once a sufferer and a conqueror, the son and Lord of David, yet it appeared not how beforehand, so it may be true that when He comes there may be little faith on the earth yet a millenium of peace and purity immediately precede the final judgment. Now put forward nay be substantially reconcilable, and at once right and to be wrong[1]—nor must we hesitate to declare what is told us, because we do not see how it stands with what is not told or partially told us. The whole dispensation is one of Mystery; and unfulfilled prophecy not in the least remarkable degree.

SATURDAY 25 FEBRUARY 1837   a cold   not M L or P of B.   dined in rooms
SUNDAY 26 FEBRUARY 3rd Lent   did duty morning and afternoon   preached Number 444   dined in rooms   took tea at Marriott's where Mr Hall   wrote to Bowden   sent back B's article in parcel to G and R

TO J. W. BOWDEN

[[Oriel College. Febr 26. 1837]]

My dear Bowden,

⌐You are very kind in your good wishes from year to year, and though I have been remiss in words, it is not as if I did not think of you.[2] I hope to hear a good account of your health the next time you write as Johnson gave me but a poor one. As I fear we shall not see you on Thursday (Woodgate not standing nor any one else on our side) I have sent back your M.S. to Rivingtons, Waterloo Place—whence you may take it or tell them to give it Boone, who is acquainted with it by name already.

I like it very much, and hope it will do good—it brings together a number

---

[1] Some words of the draft here and below are not properly decipherable.
[2] [[N.B Our Birth days were on the same day of the same month; February 21, his in 1798, mine in 1801.]]

of interesting facts and considerations. Do you see the Quarterly is to have one on Architecture in the forthcoming number—it is as if you and they were running a race—the case was the same with the Papacy.[1] I had nothing to remark on your Article in the way of criticism.⌐ You observe you had not filled up some dates—but you can do that in proof.

At present I suppose my beginning weekly Communion will be an hindrance to my coming to Town after Easter.⌐ You must let me know your further plans, as time goes on—when you go to the North etc. This is a shabby letter. By a stupid mistake, I have taken but half a sheet.

Ever yrs affly John H. Newman.

MONDAY 27 FEBRUARY 1837 letter from C bad cold not M or P of B. kept in doors and took medicine wrote to T. Keble—Heberden, Mr Willis, Barter, and H W

TO HENRY WILBERFORCE

Oriel College ⌐February 27. 1837⌐

My dear Henry

⌐There is no gathering [.] Woodgate will not stand, though pretty sure. We now see that no man of good principles can be found to understand the study of Political Economy. Is this a slur upon Good Principles or Political Economy?

It is said today the report about Hampdens being sent to Salisbury is true. If so, the Clergy must begin peti[ti]oning—I suppose it will be too late to petition the King, or too soon—so the Archbishop or the Chapter of Salisbury must be the party to be addressed⌐ You had better let friends know, to be in readiness. The movement should proceed from the country not from us

ever yr affly John H Newman

TUESDAY 28 FEBRUARY 1837 letter from James the W's brother in law †[2]

WEDNESDAY 1 MARCH letter from R. Williams c.m. baptized Martin's child wrote to R Williams and James

THURSDAY 2 MARCH letter from Manning election for Political Economy Professorship—Merivale gained it went to Littlemore—walked home with Woolcombe of Ch Ch wrote to Manning and Keble

[1] [[subject?]] J. S. Morritt's 'Hamilton . . . on Architecture' appeared in *Quarterly Review*, 58, 1837 (Feb.), and Bowden's 'Gothic Architecture' appeared in *Brit. Crit.*, 21, 1837 (April). Bowden's article 'Rise of the Papal Power' appeared in *Brit. Crit.*, 20, 1836 (July), and H. H. Milman's 'The Popes of the Sixteenth and Seventeenth Centuries' had appeared in *Quarterly Review*, 55, 1836 (Feb.).
[2] The anniversary of Hurrell Froude's death.

TO JOHN KEBLE

⌐Oriel College. March 2. 1837⌐

My dear Keble,

⌐The Act for the extinction of Sodor and Mann had a flaw in it⌐—and has to pass through Parliament again. It begins with the Commons tonight— Under these circumstances a last chance is afforded us. The bill stands *by itself*—so cannot plead being part of a whole—*though* it be thrown out, every thing else stands. ⌐We are very desirous you should send us a petition for this place—thinking you excel in that line, more than we do.⌐ But no time ought to be lost—⌐If S. Wilberforce is at home, will you send him a line, or a petition⌐—and perhaps you can do something in your own parts, or can write to someone. ⌐Do send us a strong petition—I will sign it with half a dozen even.⌐ I am no hand at that sort of thing myself; or would not ask you.[1]

No news here—⌐before I close, I shall hear who has got the Political Economy Professorship[2]—They say the Dean of Litchfield is to have the vacant see[3]—One report was that the Bishop of Oxford was to go there. If so, the Conge d'Elire will fall foul of Pusey—Only fancy our being under Hampden.—They say the Bishop of Salisbury[4] has died rich⌐—it is very likely considering he had no family and was a bad man of business—but I shall be sorry for the appearance, if it is so.—⌐The Duke has written to Hampden to resign the [[St Mary's]] Hall as being non resident⌐—in consequence he *sleeps there* every night. This was asserted at a Head of a House's table, so I suppose it is true; Also that he is to go back to live in the Hall— and that poor Mr Cox, after giving up his house in Beaumont Street, is to be cast on the world[5]—which occasions his friends (qu?) to say he is an ill used man. I hope [[Isaac]] Williams is as well as he looks. He is growing

---

[1] One provision of the Established Church Act of 1836 had been that the see of Sodor and Man should be suppressed and united with that of Carlisle. Robert Williams had written to Newman on 10 Jan. to inform him that there was a move afoot to oppose the suppression 'on account of some blunders in the Act'. He continued to keep Newman informed about the matter and asked for a petition about it from Oxford. Keble sent a draft petition on March 4. A Bill was passed in 1838 which repealed the suppression.

[2] Keble replied, 'I hear Merivale is the Pol. Oecon. which is I suppose . . . the right thing on the principle of *non sancta* NON SANCTIS.'

[3] Of Salisbury. Edward Denison was appointed. The Dean of Lichfield was H. E. J. Howard.

[4] Thomas Burgess. He had been known as an energetic Bishop when at St David's, but was nearly seventy when translated to Salisbury, his health was failing, and there were complaints about episcopal business. He left £70,000 and his wife and immediate executor had died before him. See T. Mozley, *Reminiscences chiefly of Oriel College and the Oxford Movement*, London 1882, I, 420–1.

[5] W. Hayward Cox was Vice-Principal of St Mary Hall. A rumour had reached the Duke of Wellington, as Chancellor, that Hampden, the Principal of the Hall, was not acting in conformity with the Statutes because he did not technically live in the Hall. The impression had been given that Hampden had turned the post into a sinecure, however, he held on to it. See H. Hampden, *Some Memorials of Renn Dickson Hampden*, London 1871, pp. 91–2.

fat.⌉ I write with a very cold hand—Excuse the scribble—Love to Wilson and believe me

Ever Yrs affly John H Newman

FRIDAY 3 MARCH 1837   f d   letters from Williams and Wood—and proofs of Tracts. cold bad—stayed in—did not go to Theological—Carey read   wrote to Wood and Mr Beaven

SATURDAY 4 MARCH   wrote to J

SUNDAY 5 MARCH 4th Lent   did duty morning and afternoon   preached Number 445   Marriott assisted me in Sacrament   dined with Williams in his rooms

MONDAY 6 MARCH   sent two proofs   had to tea Marriott, J M. [,] Ryder [,] Hatsell, Newman, Anderdon, Rogers (Exeter) A. Harrison and Bridges

TUESDAY 7 MARCH   letters from C and Manning   dined at Carey's   wrote to M R G

TO MISS M. R. GIBERNE

⌐Oriel College. March 7. 1837⌐

My dear Miss Giberne,

I received 'in due course' your packets and feel much obliged by them. If I am to decide, I should make the Aunt and Cousins peculiars—but perhaps you have already made up your mind; and no doubt in the best way, however it is. Do not go to the Acta Sanctorum—you are very well employed. ⌐The Christian Observer is in several ways doing good service. First he is obliged to puff us in a many ways—talks of Pusey's liberality and meekness —compares him and Keble to Fenelon.[1] All this must do great good. The peculiars cannot be more angry at our doctrines than they are—but they are apt besides to accuse us of underhand views. To say we are self indulgent College fellows—or dry and unspiritual—or selfrighteous—or ambitious and desirous of forming a party—or political and desirous of bringing in Sir R. Peel. When then the Christian Observer talks of Keble's amiableness and my truthfulness, why it is all so much gain.⌐[2] It obliges the said peculiars to

[1] 'We do not mean to apply personally to the Oxford Tract writers any one word that is offensive: their devoutness, though somewhat mystical, is intense; and, as an example of their love of good works, we need only notice Professor Pusey's munificent donation of 5000l. to the Bishop of London's church-building fund, under the anonymous title of 'One who seeks Treasure in Heaven.' *The Christian Observer*, 423, 1837 (March), 197.
'Let a Pusey, a Keble, or a Newman, or let a Fenelon, a Bellarmine, or a Borromeo, refine as they may in their own devout minds, and preach and practise as they may in holy and mortified lives, the rude multitude will transmute every thing to gross materiality and soul-deluding superstition: the wafer will be a sacred charm; holy water will sanctify evil deeds; fasts and alms will atone for sin ... Not all the Fenelons or Puseys that ever lived can prevent such results, when once the preaching of sacramental efficacy is set up against the preaching of justification by faith.' ibid., 166.
[2] 'Mr. Newman is, we are sure, a truth-loving man, and we therefore the more confidently appeal to him, that the public may understand what are the real points of discussion.' ibid., 153. The editor explained that the journal had refrained from attacking Keble's Visitation Sermon on Tradition as they did not want to 'wound even private friendships.' op. cit., 422, 1837 (Feb.), 121.

take a different ground, and meanwhile like the sheep in Cowper's Needless Alarm, to 'think again, yet know not what to think.' ⌜Then again they *allow* we can subscribe the Articles—this for them is much. Besides they talk of our influence and our zeal and our talents and so on, and all this is good as a puff. And then, if they let me reply to them, all this will be so much gain. They[1] cannot think worse of me than they do; they may be somewhat mollified—or at least some one here or there. To be sure, the said Observer does tell some abominable untruths—but no good is unmixed with evil⌝

The Clock strikes ten and I am obliged to conclude. I thought it better to send this hurried scrawl, than to keep you waiting

Yours very sincerely John H Newman

WEDNESDAY 8 MARCH 1837   buried Martin's Child   News of Denison being Bishop of Salisbury.   Examination began for Johnson Scholarship—Examiners Edwards, Walker and I.   9 or 10 theological candidates   preached sermon ⟨Number 327⟩[2] at Littlemore at John Smith's funeral who has been killed in the quarry   not n. v. or c.

THURSDAY 9 MARCH   Examination continued.   dined with W.   not v. or c.

FRIDAY 10 MARCH   not m or l.   letters from T Keble and Mr Goldsmidt   elected Mr Faber[3] Johnson Scholar (theological) Mr Donkin Mathematical Scholar (Utterton and Monro stood.) At Theological—Harrison read.

SATURDAY 11 MARCH   letter from R. Williams   My book on Prophetical Office came down   dined in hall

TO MRS E. B. PUSEY

Oriel March 11. 1837

My dear Mrs Pusey

I did not propose to send any parcel tonight, not being ready. Your account of Edward is disappointing indeed—I hoped he was quite to escape the influenza—and this too, so fine a day. Thank you about the proof—directly any copy comes from London, I will gladly take advantage of your offer—though I fear you had trouble enough with the Christian Observer. I hope you are yourself better than yesterday. I mean one of the accompanying books for William—but not knowing where he is, will not put his name in it. If he is in London, he shall receive it through Rivington

Yours very sincerely John H Newman

SUNDAY 12 MARCH 1837   fifth Lent   letters from Mr Willis and Mr Beaven   did duty morning and afternoon   preached Number 446

MONDAY 13 MARCH   Collections began   went to Littlemore—read prayers   Anderdon and Newman to tea—

[1] [[viz Evangelicals]]
[2] *P.S.* VII, 1, 'The Lapse of Time'.
[3] Frederick William Faber and William Fishburn Donkin, both of University College.

TUESDAY 14 MARCH   letter from Bowden   dined in hall   wrote to H W   and to
E Churton by Philipps

TO EDWARD CHURTON

Oriel College. March 14. 1837

Dear Churton,

Copeland has promised me from time immemorial the turnings of one of
his letters to you, to enable me to thank you for your kindness in several ways
—in the *matter* of your pamphlet, and your sending it to me.[1] And at last I
give him up as hopeless. The bearer of this has more interest in delivering it,
than Copeland in remembering me—so I suspect I shall at last reach as far
as you. He is standing for a school at York, of which you are Trustee or
Governor, and being a relative of mine I am interested in him. He is young,
but steady, has taken a very fair degree, and has a mature mind.[2]

I wish much you would turn your thoughts to writing an account of
Grotianism in our Church. Some of your remarks in your pamphlet lead me
to say so. We should be indebted to you for much light on a portion of our
history well worth studying. The question of Hales' and Chillingworth's faith
would come in. How came Taylor to be so liberal in his Liberty of Prophesying? and how far is Hammond tinctured as regards the Sacraments with
Grotianism?—After this would follow the history of the Cambridge Latitudinarians, and then the Lockites. However, I feel I am talking quite at
random to any one who knows the subject so much better than myself as
you do.

Believe me, My dear Churton, Yours very truly
John H Newman

TO HENRY WILBERFORCE

Oriel ⌈March 14/37⌉

My dear Henry

I must say what I have to say as quick as I can. A friend and relative of
mine, at present an inmate of Pusey's, by name Phillips, is standing for a
school at York—one of the Trustees of which is a person who (J Mozley
says) is a friend of yours—nomine Gray. If so, please to send him a line,
recommending Philipps to his notice as a respectable youth, who passed a
good examination (he was in the 3rd class) of studious habits and mature
character. The sooner you write the better.

[1] His Visitation Sermon, *The Church of England a Witness and Keeper of the Catholic
Tradition*, Durham 1836. See pp. 12–14, where he briefly discusses the adverse influence of
Arminian theologians, who were 'ill versed in the early history of the Church', upon English
divines concerning the role of tradition.
[2] John Bartholomew Phillips.

For myself, I am much vexed he stands, instead of availing himself of the advantage of being with Pusey—but that is his look out.

I hope Mrs W. is well and the little child—Wood is coming down here for Easter Week. My book is out—i.e. it has been in Oxford some days. ⌈The Commission is knock up—at least the Bishops and Lord Harrowby have withdrawn—⌉[1]

Excuse a shabby letter and believe me

Very affly Yrs John H Newman

P.S. ⌈Apostolicity is growing so fast in Oxford that I trust it is not too fast.⌉ Do not say all that I am going to say *from me*. ⌈At Magdalen two men have taken to wear the stole—Oakeley is growing prodigiously, and is Whitehall Preacher. Sewell's article in the Quarterly is reckoned in London the greatest triumph our principles have had.[2] At Exeter right opinions are strong. At Magdalen, Trinity, University and Oriel nucleuses are forming. Marriott goes the whole hog—Browell is much stronger—Christ Church alone is immobile⌉—Archdeacon Hodson's son (I know not at all what *kind* of a fellow he is) has taken up Apostolical views.

WEDNESDAY 15 MARCH 1837   f.d.   letters from Wood [,] Williams [,] Rogers [,] Archdeacon Froude and Mr Russell,   wrote to J. [,] Archdeacon F. [,] R Williams, Rogers and Mr Russell

TO JOHN FULLER RUSSELL

Oriel College, March 15. 1837.

Sir,

In answer to your letter received this morning I beg to inform you that I shall have great pleasure in subscribing to the work you propose editing

---

[1] Bowden wrote on 13 March, 'There is, I believe no doubt that all the Prelates resigned their seats at the Commission Board on Friday last . . . though the papers, with the exception of John Bull, do not seem to know any thing about it yet—If the Archbishop etc are now *really* disposed to be firm, they will soon be made to feel the mischief they have done by what they have already sanctioned—What a set ministers are!—They clearly intended by their bill only to amuse the dissenters—had they really meant it to operate they *must* have consulted the Abp about it before bringing it in—Come what may, the crushing of the odious Commission is a thing to be thankful for.' Rogers wrote about this time, 'there is a report about that all the Church Commissioners from the Archbishop—to Lord Harrowby have sent in their resignations—I am afraid it is too good to be true.'

Relations between the Bishops and the Government had recently deteriorated because of the proposed Church Rates Bill. The Bill proposed to abolish Church Rates and would have met the expenses which they had previously covered out of the incomes of Chapters. Bishop Blomfield wrote to the Bishop of Gloucester on 15 March that the Bishop Commissioners and three others had sent a letter to Lord Melbourne to explain that they 'decline concurring in any further recommendations while this measure is pending . . .'. The Bill was dropped after a while. See A. Blomfield, *A Memoir of C. J. Blomfield*, London 1863, I, 212–7.

[2] 'The Cathedral Establishments', *Quarterly Review*, 58, 1837 (Feb.), 196–254.

on the judgment of the later Anglican Church concerning the Rule of Faith.[1] So elaborate an undertaking is clearly, as you observe, in a different line from our brief extracts in the Catenas—but even if it interfered with them, at this crisis there cannot be too many efforts made in the way of exhibiting the genuine principles of our Church.

Wishing you all success in your publication,

I am, Sir, Your faithful Servant, John H. Newman.

THURSDAY 16 MARCH 1837   letters from Battanshaw and Bliss   Grant called   dined in Common Room with Eden and Daman.   all fellows gone but Eden, Daman[,] Litton and I   wrote to Bowden[,] R Williams and Rogers

TO J. W. BOWDEN

⌐Oriel College, March 16. 1837.⌐

My dear Bowden,

I owe you several letters at once, yet have so little to say, that I hardly know whether to write or not. I have sent to have the two mistakes corrected,[2] and hope they did not arrive too late—anyhow they shall be put as errata— Are you sure you did not put both readings 'high altar' etc., one above the other? I cannot conceive the printer's imagination would have been so lively as to originate. The only other hypothesis, is, Rogers's sisters who were kind enough to transcribe many of them, made the hallucination.

⌐You know I suppose, the third volume of Tracts has been some time since out of print. This in a month or two! There is no doubt Mr Wilkes's froth and fury arise from witnessing the spread of Apostolical opinions. I am constantly having letters of inquiry etc., from strangers. The Cathedral Article in the Quarterly,[3] I am told, is considered the greatest triumph of Apostolicism—When the Quarterly turns Apostolical, Burnham Wood may well begin marching, and all other equally strange movements take place. The amusing thing is that the poor [[Christian]] Observer is obliged to puff our munificence, meekness etc., to compare us to Fenelon etc.[4] He will do more good in this way than harm by his railing; for no one but thinks as bad of our views already as he can, who is peculiarly disposed.

[1] The work which Russell was bringing out, backed by subscription, was entitled *The Judgement of the Anglican Church (posterior to the Reformation) on the Sufficiency of Holy Scripture, and the Authority of the Holy Catholic Church in Matters of Faith . . .*, London 1838. See letter of 3 Jan. 1838 to Russell.
[2] In *Lyra Apostolica*.
[3] William Sewell's 'The Cathedral Establishments', *Quarterly Review*, 58, 1837 (Feb.), 196–254.
[4] The second part of Newman's letter was published in *The Christian Observer*, 423, 1837 (March), 141–98. However, the letter only occupied three and a half pages of print and from p. 145 was filled with the editor's animadversions. For the allusions to Fenelon see the first two notes to letter of 7 March to M. R. Giberne.

I suppose I shall not come to Town till I do not know when. Johnson told you the reason just at present. Wood [,] Williams, and Mathison are coming down here for Easter week⌉ When do *you* mean to look at Mr Slatters'? ⌈We are getting up addresses to the Archbishop of congratulation for his spirit of intercession to Parliament in behalf of the Isle of Mann (!) etc., etc., but I suppose not much will come of them. In Devonshire they are addressing the King on the ground of his Coronation Oath—I cannot say I wish the Ministers out—Even as to preferments, they will do pretty much the same as the Conservatives. Denison was just the man,[1] except as being too young, to be promoted by Sir R. Peel and I find the Conservatives in London praise generally the ecclesiastical appointments of this Ministry.[2] Even if Sir R. Peel extravagated into better men at any time, what would be his most ambitious ascent? To Rose, I suppose, who with his ten thousand excellences, yet has not the firmness for these times. What a good appointment Oakeley's is to the Whitehall Preachership. You will have very elegant and interesting, and very bold and Apostolical sermons from him

I was much rejoiced to hear your account of the Bishop of Hereford.[3] Somehow every thing is looking up at the present moment. Though we are in very low estate, our fluxion is positive.⌉

Ever yrs affly John H Newman.

FRIDAY 17 MARCH 1837   letters from Mr Goldsmidt and Woodgate   f.d.   wrote to Woodgate   no c.

TO H. A. WOODGATE

Oriel College. March 17/37

My dear W

As far as I have a view, I should say that the Communion on Good Friday is against both the $\mathring{\eta}\theta o\varsigma$ and the practice of the Primitive Church; but I suppose it is our custom, and there is an end of it. There being a Communion Service for the day, I do not say proves it, but looks that way. Hammond in his last illness is recorded by Fell to have received it on Good Friday, (as far as my memory goes).[4]—If you have been in the habit of

---

[1] [[E. Denison of Merton, just then made Bishop of Salisbury.]] He was aged thirty-six.
[2] [[N.B. It was said at this time that Lord Melbourne (the Premier) declared that 'the Bishops died to spite him'; he was so hard up for Liberal candidates for promotion. It was just after the Hampden matter too. When the see of Salisbury was vacant, it was said at the time ⟨1837⟩ that Mr (Sotheron) Estcourt (Conservative) went to Sir C. Wood (Whig and in the Ministry,) both Oriel men, and said 'Why not make E. Denison (a third Oriel man, and their contemporary) the new Bishop?' and that Lord Melbourne seized and acted on the suggestion. May 15. 1862.]]
[3] [[Grey? Lord Grey's brother.]] Edward Grey. Bowden had been greatly impressed by a sermon of his.
[4] See *The Works of Henry Hammond*, London 1674, I, 49.

44

celebrating it on the day, I would continue it, were I you. We always have it at St Mary's.

I think I should have done as you did about the Political Economy Professorship, had I been in your place—but I think you should have answered by return of post. Oakeley has published his remarks—and very valuable they are[1]—and Sewell his Inaugural Lecture, which is very valuable too.[2] I was much pleased to hear your sermon gave such general 'satisfaction' —and would certainly advise your recasting and repreaching for your next that one you preach some years since, as you thrown out [sic]. As to the Margaret Professorship, I do not suppose I should ever stand in your way —that is, I like my own ease and liberty too much to care to have any such office—but Greswell, I suppose, would be before us both—And again, I am not certain the University would have you. I think they look on you more as a moral philosopher than a Divine—the former is your *line*. Accordingly you were thought of and desired for the Political Economy Chair. Your Bampton Lectures would raise their notions—but still you will not show learning enough for these times.[3]

I congratulate you much on your success at Tunbridge Wells in the good cause. It is certainly most remarkable, how it seems to be prospering.

Denison's appointment, except that he is young, is a most respectable one for the present Ministers. I do not think Sir R. P. [Peel] would make a better ever—or hardly ever. Denison is just the style of man Sir R. P. would take. He seems to me the kind of man we must expect for the next 10 or 20 years—very respectable men of no principles in a strict sense of the word. Were it not that a Church spirit is rising such men would do us harm as our governors—but I think, that is I trust, we shall be too strong for them.

I am not quite sure whether I shall be here or not on the 4th   Excuse haste—the Clock has struck

Ever Yrs John H Newman

P.S. I have no time to read this over.

SATURDAY 18 MARCH 1837   letters from R Williams and H   no p.   sent parcel to Bliss   Harrison went   dined in Common Room with Eden and Litton and A.F. [Froude] with me.   no c.

SUNDAY 19 MARCH   Palm Sunday   did duty morning and afternoon—preached Number 449   Johnson, Ward (of Oriel) and Church dined with me in Common Room—Daman and Eden

MONDAY 20 MARCH   Passion Week   service through week at 11   Baptized Furley's

[1] F. Oakeley, *Remarks upon Aristotelian and Platonic Ethics, as a Branch of the Studies pursued in the University of Oxford*, Oxford 1837. Oakeley's Advertisement mentioned the interest and satisfaction which had been occasioned by Woodgate's sermon on 5 Feb. on *The Study of Morals Vindicated and Recommended*.
[2] Sewell's Inaugural Lecture of 25 May 1836 as Professor of Moral Philosophy.
[3] Woodgate had been appointed Bampton Lecturer for 1838.

son. dined in Common Room Ward with Daman—and Litton wrote to T. Keble

TUESDAY 21 MARCH letter from Christie f.d. (i.e.) l. snow

WEDNESDAY 22 MARCH letters from H W[,] C Marriott and W F. thick snow —lying, then thawing called on Mrs Parker dined in Common Room with Eden and Litton

THURSDAY 23 MARCH letters from R Williams (inclosing note from Mrs Thornton) proof from Br. M. [British Magazine][1] and letter from French Clergyman f.d. fresh thick snow sent back proof—wrote to R Williams, Archdeacon Wix and sent papers for [illegible]

FRIDAY 24 MARCH Good Friday m at 3 a m l at 8 p at 4 p m Br A[2] letters from Rogers and Mr Whitworth snow hard on ground wind east with frosty fog did duty morning and afternoon preached Number 352 Pusey assisted me in Sacrament f d

SATURDAY 25 MARCH duty at 11—f.d. Rogers came and dined in Common Room f. over by 6 P.M. then Wood and R Williams Mathison late at night.

TO HENRY WILBERFORCE

Oriel College. ⌜March 25.1837 Easter Eve⌝ and Annunciation

My dear Henry

You will see I write this *for you*—there are some things which are evidently not intended for your correspondent, and at any rate in so delicate a subject I would rather have your judgment in confirmation of my own, before any thing I said was reported[3]

It has long been on my mind that the sort of questions you send me would come upon us—and serious they are. Little as I see of persons, I feel sure that the thoughts of some, if not many, will take that direction—and how to advise?

I will say what I can in the order of your questions—'As to the length etc of prayers.'—⌜If we are to give hours to prayer during the day, I hold this to be quite impossible without forms⌝—even allowing, which I do not wish to deny, the abstract lawfulness and the occasional propriety of dispensing with them, and fully maintaining the piety and duty of spontaneous ejaculations etc. ⌜Then comes the question, *where* are the forms?⌝—I do not know of them, i.e. accessible, and without our own arrangement etc—⌜I hope we shall soon have Bishop Cosin's reprinted—and very suitable and excellent they are.[4] I could not recommend any thing better. The Breviary Devotions take up from 3 to 4 hours a day[5]—a time which may be easily

[1] For the last two installments of 'Letters on the Church of the Fathers', which appeared in the April and May issues.
[2] Unexplained; perhaps meaning 'Breviary all'?
[3] Wilberforce wrote on 25 March sending on questions from a lady enquirer, however, the part of the letter containing the questions was not kept by Newman. Wilberforce wrote that she had been enquiring since she had read Newman's sermons.
[4] See first note to letter of 3 May to M. R. Giberne.
[5] This would imply slow recital.

redeemed from the world. I like them uncommonly. They are very unexciting, grave, and simple. They are for the whole year, varying day by day more or less.⌐ This again I like much; ⌐it keeps up attention and rouses the imagination towards the course of the Christian year, without exciting it. Cosin's are only for the week, (or *day* rather, I think.) It is a great loss women do not know Latin and Greek *so far*. Latin devotions are majestic and austere— Greek are much more pathetic and animated—they are better fitted for praise and earnest expostulation. The great advantage of a dead language is that it keeps one sober.⌐ I should like, if I could, to find some make-up for those who are ἰδιῶται.[1]

⌐The Psalms should be the basis of all devotion—the more one knows of them, the more surprising they are—of course, being inspired. In the Breviary the 119th and superadded Collect is the rudiment of the whole Service—it is gone through every day [[⟨?⟩]]—and, considering its exceeding pathos, applicableness, and variety, I am very loth to give up such a usage, were I to determine. Another peculiarity of the Breviary is that the bulk and stress of the Service is in the morning—viz when our time is more our own and our mind most fresh. To leave the body of our prayers for night, is like putting off religion to a deathbed. By the bye here is a curious contrast between peculiarism[2] and the Catholic way. Evening Services are *peculiar*; they are made exciting, in order to answer. To return:—morning services *secure* the day's devotion. Further the Breviary Services simplify as the day proceeds—Compline is all but invariable through the year—here is something beautiful in this—Another characteristic of the Breviary Services is the shortness of the prayers they contain.⌐ Dear Froude used to say that 'long prayers' were peculiar and came in at the Reformation. ⌐Verses and Responses, Sentences, and Collects are much easier to attend to. This is one great excellence of the Psalms—as being not *continual addresses* to Almighty God, (which require a great effort and stretch of mind) but meditations on His attributes etc. mutual exhortations, interspersed with some more like prayers. Dear H.F. used to say the Eucharistic Prayer was the only long one in the Primitive Services. Another excellence of the Breviary Services is their precise *method*—I am sure, in order to attend,⌐ (I speak all this however from my *own* impression) ⌐we ought to know *where we are*⌐—This is a fault of an interminable career of prayers—and again much more of extempore. ⌐I speak under correction, but it does seem a good thing to have a definite *number* of prayers and psalms. This led the Romanists to their rosaries, beads etc.—I feel the *principle* to be important, though it may be abused into formalism.⌐—Nothing strikes me further on this part of the subject. —As to that I began just now, about the *rudiments* and development of the Breviary service, I would say this—of the devotions, the 119th Psalm is the basis—to this is to be added the matin Psalms, 12 a day which vary through

[1] 'private persons'.
[2] [[i.e. Evangelicalism]]

47

the week. On these are raised certain Psalms, Songs, and Hymns, as additions and embellishments. The Te Deum at Matins,—the Lauds (as a whole) *to* Matins—the Benedictus at Lauds etc. And then again in like manner, each separate Psalm and Song has its ornaments, first the Gloria, then the Antiphons—and lastly the whole of each Service is summed up by one solemn direct concise prayer, the Oratio or Collect—Now according as the Service is more or less festive or the reverse these ornaments increase or diminish— From Thursday to Saturday night in Passion Week, the day Services are little more that [than] 119th Psalm and the Collect—and this by slow steps —The highest feast has the Antiphons doubled—When we enter Lent, the Alleluia ceases, and the Te Deum. When we come to Passion Sunday (a fortnight before Easter) the Gloria begins to fail—on the Thursday in Passion Week it ceases—so do the Hymns the Antiphons etc etc.—

Now the question is, what is all this to the purpose?—Why, it is so far as this. Tastes and feelings so differ, that I never would *prescribe* for another —but if asked what *I* should wish Services formed upon, I should unhesitating say the model of the Breviary—The great difficulty is that, nothing set forth by authority, individuals have to form them for themselves.

I have not spoken of the Lessons—there we excel the Latins—we read more Scripture, but I like their *mode* of reading, i.e. not long passages of chapters—but short and broken portions with responses—attention is thus kept up, and the most beautiful and pathetic associations admitted—The termination too 'Tu autem Domine miserere nobis' with the answer 'Deo Gratias', is much more religious than 'Here endeth etc'—and the blessing at each beginning is in the same character.—

When we come to the question *what* Lessons are to be taken, this difficulty arises. One should like to take the 4 Church Lessons for the day, dividing them duly through the seven services, but they are not always such, particularly at the beginning of the year, that all people, women certainly, can read by themselves. Whether our Reformers were right or not in *all* they have put down to read in public, (that they were right in a great deal, I am sure) still there is a vast difference between reading in Church in God's presence and reading in private: In Church, at least it is a fitting penance, far lighter indeed than that shame which it may perchance be our lot to feel at the judgment. Again one cannot say, take sometimes, sometimes not, without bringing in the principle of Eclecticism—and if one says take the New Testament only, this is scarcely religious.—I hardly know what to advise.

As hints, however, on the whole subject,—I say as follows—Let the devotions of each day consist of a certain number of Psalms, with Hymns, Collects and Sentences—and let a certain portion of Scripture be read each day. I am finishing this in a great hurry, and shall send you another letter— if you will let me know whether this is to the purpose. It is well to recognize the 7 Penitential Psalms, e.g. for Friday—the Graduales—and the Messianic, and the Funeral; also the Litanies, e.g. of Jeremy Taylor in the Golden

Grove[1] (which is just published separately by Parker) and Bishop Andrew's intercessions,[2] if there are none more suitable or convenient.—But I am now writing at random.

As to St Austin, some people make marenests in the way of *doctrine*, Sam has somewhat the failing of making marenests of *facts*. Do not let him seduce you. I suppose the *fact* is, if I can recollect, that, *while* you were delaying to send any MS. I happened to write to Wood and ask him if he knew of any translator *in case* you took the Letters instead of the Confessions.

⌈Rogers, Wood, R Williams and Matthison are keeping holy day here⌉ and [J.B.] Mozley who is here desires all kind thoughts to you and Mrs W

Ever Yrs affly John H Newman

SUNDAY 26 MARCH 1837   Easter Day   Wood, R. Williams, J M and Rogers to breakfast in my rooms   did duty morning and afternoon   preached Number 450[3]   no one to assist me at Sacrament   dined with the rest at Pusey's.

MONDAY 27 MARCH   Easter Monday   letters from J and Mr Willis [of] Bath   Service in forenoon   Copeland preached University Sermon.   walked up all of us to Littlemore   Copeland, I. Williams, Berkeley, Rogers, Sheppard, Wood, and two others dined with me. (Matthison, J. M. and P. Claughton asked)   wrote to H W

TUESDAY 28 MARCH   letter from Belfield and from Mr Withy mentioning death of Henry *Audit and admission of 4 Probationers* Williams preached ⟨University Sermon⟩ and went   duty in mid day   dined, as did Matthison, Wood, R. Williams and Rogers with Copeland   wrote to Mr Withy

WEDNESDAY 29 MARCH   buried Godfrey's child?   not n. v. and c.   Acland breakfasted with us   Eden went?   Wilson came   dined with Provost, as did Matthison, Wood and Williams   wrote to J. [,] Dr Wordsworth and Hook

TO MRS JOHN MOZLEY

Oriel ⌈March 29/37⌉

My dear Jemima,

I heard from Mr Withy yesterday, what is in the Papers today, the death of Henry Withy at Tunbridge Wells. Woodgate had taken Mr W. into his house. I believe the Influenza is what was ultimately fatal to him—but he was in weak health a long while. I was very much concerned to hear it.

About my dividend, I want to give no *trouble* to John—else, I should be very glad to avail myself of his proposal for receiving it through Williams and Deacons—⌈I believe I am right in saying as follows—I have to give Aunt per annum £50 + £$\frac{40}{3}$ = £63.6.8. If then John is good enough to receive my dividends, I shall have to send besides (£63.6.8.—£35) £28.6.8.⌉

---

[1] Jeremy Taylor, *The Golden Grove. A Choice Manual, containing what is to be believed, practised, and desired or prayed for . . .*, Oxford 1836, pp. 103–21.

[2] *The Private Devotions of Lancelot Andrewes, Bishop of Winchester . . .*, London 1830, pp. 282–92.

[3] *P.S.* V, 7, 'The Mystery of Godliness'.

I am sorry the Lyra is so long about—Parker has been obliged to send all his copies to London—and has none here, tho' they are wanted.

⌜My new book[1] is selling very well.⌝

I hope I shall do good in the Christian Observer—but I shall be as brief as possible. When Pusey's doctrine is understood, it will be seen to be as little strange as it is Apostolic.

Love to Aunt and John

Ever Yrs affly John H Newman

Rogers, Wood, R. Williams, and Wilson (coming today) are keeping festival here.

TO CHRISTOPHER WORDSWORTH

Oriel College March 29. 1837

Dear Sir,

I beg to acknowledge the acceptable favor you have done me by sending me your Remarks on the Ecclesiastical Commission.[2] I had already ordered it, before it was published, and shall now read it with double pleasure

I am, Dear Sir, Your faithful Servt John H Newman

THURSDAY 30 MARCH 1837   letters from Mr Goldsmid and Mr Ostrehan   not v and c   Matthison, Acland and R. Williams went   Cornish went   dined with Pusey, as did Wood, Wilson, Rogers, Ryder, Copeland, Berkeley, etc.

FRIDAY 31 MARCH   letter from I. Williams   not v. and c.   walked with Pusey and Wood towards Bagley   A.F. [,] Daman, T. Ryder and J.M. dined with me—together with R, Wilson and Wood in my rooms wrote to Battanshaw, Belfield, Mr Goldsmid and Mr Ostrehan   and by Wilson to Keble

TO JOHN KEBLE

⌜Oriel. March 31 1837⌝

My dear Keble,

⌜[[Robert]] Williams has, I suppose, sent you from the Bishop of Sodor and Man a milk and water petition, which I suspect *here* will get no signatures at all. Without conciliating the many it will dishearten the few,⌝ who will not like so to address the Commons.

Parker is about to advertise the new edition of the Christian Year—and wishes to know if the Lyra may be advertised with it.

When you have done with F's MSS, please let me have them, as ⌜William F [[Froude]] is, I think, desirous they should soon be published.⌝ W. F.

[1] [[Prophetical Office]]
[2] *The Ecclesiastical Commission and the Universities; a Letter to a Friend*, London 1837.

50

comes here to take his degree next Term: I will try to make your and his visits to Oxford coincide.

I was congratulating myself on the coincidence of my own view about the Record of Faith with yours in your Sermon, and Wilson tells me we differ, which yet I hardly think. ⌐I am pleased at your liking the book [[Prophetical Office]]—yet if it conciliates some, it will frighten others, I fear.[1] A least I am not sanguine. I am glad to hear it is selling.⌐

I have said nothing more about your Sermons, since you lent me them. simply and solely because I feared I was teasing you. ⌐If I were to say what I really feel,⌐ (which I suppose I must, since you hint I feel differently,) ⌐I would say plainly that no greater benefit could in my opinion be granted to the Church than the publication of Sermons from you—and that on account of their *matter*, *not* only the authority of your name.⌐ You have *challenged* me to say this.[2]

⌐I am so glad you think of St Irenaeus,—but there is no hurry as to the *publication*⌐[3]

Ever Yrs very affly John H Newman

SATURDAY 1 APRIL 1837 Wilson and Wood went not c Mr Hope and Mr Bruce (*Lord Elgin*?)[4] to breakfast with R walked to Littlemore dined in Common Room Copeland and J. M. dining with me—Hatsell with Rogers. Copleston and Eden returned

SUNDAY 2 APRIL 1st Easter letters from M G and Boone, and letter of attorney from Messrs Williams. m. ns.[5] 1 and 2. did duty morning and afternoon preached Number 451[6] Browell assisting me in Sacrament Mr Scott of Ball. [Balliol] took Littlemore dined with P [Pusey] (Mrs P unwell) (Sir G Grey and Colquhoun *were* to have come) and Rogers and J. M.

MONDAY 3 APRIL letter from H W no th. s. n. or c. Rogers went walked to Littlemore with J.M. and P. part of the way—caught in heavy sleet and hail. Shortland and Boodle dined with me in Common Room Berkeley with Copleston.

TUESDAY 4 APRIL went to T [Tuckwell] for last time. (vid Febr 7) Mr Hall and J.M. to dinner sent letter to Christian Observer and power of attorney to Messrs Williams

WEDNESDAY 5 APRIL no s. n. c. went to Littlemore, reading prayers there. dined at Vice Chancellor's [A. T. Gilbert] to meet the new Proctors[7] wrote to Rogers

THURSDAY 6 APRIL baptized Standen's son Woodgate in Oxford who walked with me to Littlemore, where I read Colquhoun called dined with Berkeley. no v or c

[1] Keble had written to Pusey on 28 March about *Prophetical Office*: 'as far as I can judge from a cursory perusal it will go further than any thing yet to set him right with timid well meaning people. I wish I had seen the Lecture on the Rule of Faith before I wrote that Sermon of mine.'
[2] Pusey had written to Keble on 20 March, urging him on behalf of the Tractarians to publish a volume of his sermons. He explained, 'it is not fair to let Newman bear the whole brunt alone, as if his Theology were something peculiar, or as they call it, the Newmania.'
[3] Keble translated St Irenaeus against the Heresies for the Library of the Fathers. However, it was only published posthumously, in 1872.
[4] James Bruce, he succeeded as 8th Earl of Elgin in 1841, and was later created Baron Elgin. He was an old friend of J. R. Hope.
[5] 'nocturns'; the Breviary hour of Matins was divided into three nocturns.
[6] *P.S.* IV, 2, 'Obedience without Love, as instanced in the Character of Balaam'.
[7] W. J. Butler of Magdalen and W. Meech of New College.

FRIDAY 7 APRIL   letter from Rivington.   Pusey went to town   walked to Littlemore —read there   heavy fall of sleet and snow   no s. n. v. or c   dined in Common Room   Daman's brother there   wrote to Wood

SATURDAY 8 APRIL   letters from J[,] H W and Archdeacon F.   from H thro A.M. [Arthur Mozley]   breakfasted with Mr Hall at Merton   College term began   [letter] from James through W. Newman   walked to Littlemore with 2 Ms[Mozley]   dined with Palmer to meet Mr Todd

SUNDAY 9 APRIL   2nd Easter   Early Communion (first time)[1]   read Number 453 Berkeley assisted me   19 persons altogether   did duty morning and afternoon Woodgate was to have preached, but I preached Number   Woodgate and J.M. to dinner in my rooms—Marriott in evening

MONDAY 10 APRIL   Mr Todd breakfasted with me   snow and sleet every day, and lying *since the 3rd snow, sleet, hail continually—lying.* did not walk   dined at Provost's to meet Jelf   In evening in my rooms Bridges,   Ms, Newman, Ryder, Hatsell, Anderdon   no n v c

TUESDAY 11 APRIL   letter from Mr Darley   (a cold)   no m. l. p n v c   did not walk Woodgate chosen Bampton Lecturer   Pusey returned   dined at Trinity—thence to Pusey's where was Jelf.

WEDNESDAY 12 APRIL   letters from Rogers, Wilson, Pope, and Bowden   dined in hall   wrote to Wood, Bowden, and Manning   no v or c

TO J. W. BOWDEN

⌐Oriel. April 12. 1837
(The anniversary of my Election here).

My dear Bowden,

   Fearing my letter might cross one from you, I have delayed writing. I am very sorry to hear about Johnson; and hope he will soon get right again.

   ⌐As to the Christian Observer it seems as if Leslie's remark was right— viz., that one could not fight with scavengers without using the dirt from the kennel as well as they.[2] I say this because Rogers and perhaps Wood are dissatisfied with my letters to the Editor[3]—yet really I only see the choice

   [1] From this day Newman kept a record at the back of his diary of the numbers at early eucharist, the amount of the collection, and the charities to which he gave the money. In 1837 the numbers varied with the season from six to thirty-six, and the collection from 6s. 6d. to £12. 3s. After small sums 'to the Clerk for Bread and Wine', £107. 17s. was divided between 'Small Livings' (the diocesan branch of 'Small livings augmentation association') and 'Curates Fund' ('Society for promoting the employment of additional curates in populous places', cf. *Brit. Mag.*, 11, 1837, 694); and nearly £17 was 'carried on' to 1838, for which year see at 23 Dec. 1838. *Early* eucharist was usually only three times a month (four times when there were five Sundays).
   The Additional Curates Society had recently been formed after policy disagreements in the Church Pastoral Aid Society. Joshua Watson was a directing influence, and the Committee later included Bowden, Wood, Gladstone, Acland and R. Williams.
   [2] 'I grudge not the office of a scavenger, and the Herculean labour of cleansing so foul a stable; a sink and complication of the vilest heresies that have ever been broached in the Christian church . . .' in the preface to his attack on the Quakers, 'Satan disrobed from his Disguise of Light', *The Theological Works of the Rev. Charles Leslie*, Oxford 1832, IV, 364.
   [3] Rogers wrote on 11 April, 'As to the Christian Observer I should be for a treatise on Justification as you say and putting off S. O. [C. O. ?]—Wood I talked to, and he is I think against it. But R. W. [Williams] says that by Peculiars Wilkes is considered as having floored you: which is a reason for having your say out at any rate.—I confess I did not like at all your letter that you gave me to read, it is very amusing of course and a great ἐπιδειξις δυνάμεως, but I should think it would disgust many fair kind of Peculiars—I should think (reverenter

of not writing, and of lashing them. But this is nihil ad rem. As to my breaking off the correspondence, I do not see *how* I could continue it *after* they spoke about pounds, shillings and pence.[1] So I wrote to tell the Editor so.⌐ By the bye, perhaps you are not on those terms with Hatchard; but, were it possible, I should like to make out whether they intend *now* to publish in May the remainder of my letter. The Editor says it is gone to type, in his notice. On it would turn what I had best do—still since I can do nothing at once, I might as well sit patiently till May comes.

⌐My present notion is to publish what will be almost a book on Justification—and perhaps in the Preface to allude to the Christian Observer.[2] Or if the Editor does *not* publish the rest of my letter, *which I wish*, then *I* would publish *it* with such alterations as are necessary. By the bye, do you think you could do this? which I think would be best of all? get back the M.S.—or hinder the publication of the rest of my letter? for then it would appear fresh in my own book. However, I know this may be a delicate thing but I throw it out.⌐

dictum sit) they would consider it arrogant—pariticularly if they do not appreciate Mr W's folly.—It is not worthwhile criticizing, I suppose, but certainly I am *very glad indeed* it is not to appear.—Certainly I should have been glad if you had let Wilkes roar on without taking any notice of him—but now it seems to me you are so much in for it that you *must* put out your views unless you choose to submit to an appearance (in the eyes of many) of having nothing to say.'

Wood had written to Newman on 8 April to express his relief at the proposal to withdraw from the controversy. He went on to say, 'As to the question whether you should treat it separately or wait for the 'Sacerdotal office', as you seem to be gathering suggestions, I offer the following, the first of which will accord with your idea (to Rogers) of being œconomical at present, the 'Prophetical office' being thought *'judicious'*. Is not the 'peculiar' view of justification in some sense their stronghold, inasmuch as it is only false as being partial and distorted, and has there not been a *great school* on that side ever since the Reformation? It seems to me (and I'm sure it was the case with myself) that men must be induced to drop their notions on this point by being made good Catholics, and not vice versa. The last is like pulling at a horses tail instead of his bridle. If this be true it follows that the subject should be treated as *late* as possible.' He added that the Evangelicals ought to be happy to 'submit to *your* view, as it includes theirs, and does not, like Bulls, cast it out. But I would suggest; (1) how many are there who hold it as a mere *formula*, an empty form, and only possessing virtue under that *form*. So that unless you say 'Abracadbra' [sic] purely and simply, nothing more or less, (be your additions as beautiful as may be) they will be as deaf as if you said nothing at all. (2) Is not your view so closely connected with the Sacramental question that it will appear to much greater advantage conjointly with it? Besides, to disjoin them will spoil our notion of exhibiting the Via Media of the Anglican Church with regard to the relation of the two, *our* "justification" not superseding the Sacraments as Luther's was said to do, nor implying, as the Romish notion of "habitual and inherent justice" was said to do, the Romish notion of the Sacraments.'

[1] Newman's second letter was published in *The Christian Observer*, 424, 1837 (April), 243–63. The editor wrote: 'We have received from the Rev. J. H. Newman a manuscript of fifty-two pages, dated (we suppose commenced) March 3, but received March 13, with a message dated March 11, saying "Mr N. is anxious that it should appear in *the next* (the present) *Number in an entire state*; should this not be the case, Mr N. would feel himself at liberty to publish it . . . Mr Newman also says, "I have a claim in courtesy, nay, in justice, that you should put in the whole of this reply without a word of your own.' The editor protested against Newman's 'claim', and added, 'it is doubly hard to pay for printing and circulating thousands of copies'. Newman was allowed about three pages worth of text, the rest taken up by the editor's introduction and comments. The rest was published in May, see letter of 25 April to Bowden.

[2] [[N.B. As my Lectures on the Prophetical Office of the Church, rose out of my correspondence with the Abbé Jager, so those on Justification rose out of my controversy with the Christian Observer.]]

I am very much pleased indeed with your article in the B.C.[1] It is most interesting and instructive.

ᴦAs to the meeting in London, I have Lectures[2] going on of an evening now, which will hinder my going, I suppose—but some of us will make our appearance.

The Translation of the Confessions of St Austin are intended to appear in August—the Cyril Hieros: or a volume of Chrysostom in October—and thenceforward it will proceed, we trust, quarterly.ᴸ I am very dry of matter.

Ever yrs affly John H Newman

P.S. I think, *since* I have written to the Christian Observer withdrawing from the correspondence, you might well write to Hatchard for my M.S. which would discover *whether* it was to be published or not.

TO H. E. MANNING

Oriel College. April 12. 1837

My dear Manning

Anderdon's return reminds me I ought long before this to have acknowledged your last very kind letter, for which I sincerely thank you. It was quite unnecessary, though, as far as it expressed your friendly feelings to Pusey and myself, such expressions it is always a privilege to receive—and, considering how much one has to go through, which perhaps persons, like yourself, partly escape from your country life, not lightly to be prized. We have had a good deal of anxiety and trouble about the Translations—persons failing us etc.—if that caused me to write at all hastily to you, I am very sorry for it—though writing is so very untrue a representation of oneself, that I sometimes doubt whether one ever should be sorry or pleased at any thing one has written, as if the animus was every thing[.] I now understand you have taken Justin for good—as to Chrysostom, I do not think it would be wise for you or for us to settle between us any thing about it prospectively, while you have another in hand.[3] There is difficulty enough in arranging what is present, without anticipating the future.

We trust St Austin's Confessions will appear the first of August—Pusey has found a Translation he likes so much, that Henry Wilberforce having made the offer of taking the Letters instead, the coincidence decided us on publishing what was ready to our hands—which we shall ever do when we can.

I suppose a volume of Chrysostom will come out October 1—if we can

---

[1] 'Church-building: Gothic Architecture', *Brit. Crit.*, 21, 1837 (April), 303–38.
[2] [[on Justification]] Newman delivered the first Lecture the following day.
[3] See letter of 24 Feb. to Manning and that of 22 Feb. from Manning placed before it. In the event Manning did not contribute anything to the Library of the Fathers.

get our various translators to bear—else Cyril of Jerusalem—and then we hope to continue quarterly.

On looking at your letter, I see you ask about Justin's Apologies. This was our difficulty in publishing it, and occasioned my not answering your letter in October—we did not know what to do as regards Mr Chevallier.[1] Nor have we got over the difficulty. We had rather not be in it—but I suppose it must take its chance. An edition of the *whole* of a Father's works is no interference with a work selecting a particular Tract. As to Reeves's Translation.[2] If you have it, it would be best to use it—i.e. in whole or as a basis, according to your judgment. Sometimes we have found these Translations so diffuse, as to be useless.

I do not know that I have any thing else to say, except, what I trust there is no need of saying, that

I am, My dear Manning, Most sincerely Yrs John H Newman

TO E. B. PUSEY

[April 1837]

My dear P

Manning clings to Justin. I told Mr Beaven, if he had not begun, not to do so, till he heard from me—Since he has not written, I conclude that he has *not* begun. Whatever you tell me to write to him, I will. Manning owns he began without having received my answer. I sent my answer through Wood, and so I suppose the mistake arose.

Manning tells me the Record says Chrysostom was the first who used John iii. 5 of Baptism. I do not find it in Dionysius. The passage in Basil is as follows—

['Faith and baptism are two ways of gaining salvation, naturally united and inseparable. For faith is brought to completion through baptism, and baptism is given a foundation through faith'] liber de Spiritu Sancto 12 ⟨11 fin⟩[3]

I have thought what Harrison might most beneficially do—and no one so well as he—Extract catholicism from Frith, Phillpott and the other Martyrs[4]—Since we shall be attacked from this quarter, it will be something to make them a house divided against itself. Do think of this

Ever Yrs affly J H N

[1] Temple Chevallier, *A Translation of the Epistles of Clement of Rome, Polycarp, and Ignatius; and of the Apologies of Justin Martyr and Tertullian*, Cambridge 1833.
[2] William Reeves, *The Apologies of Justin Martyr, Tertullian, and Minutius Felix . . . translated from their originals: with notes*, London 1716.
[3] St Basil, *Opera Omnia*, ed. J. Garnier O.S.B., Paris 1730, III, 23–4. Newman quoted the passage in Greek.
[4] John Frith (*c.* 1503–33) and John Philpot (1516–55), Protestant Martyrs.

TO HENRY WILBERFORCE

Oriel College April 12. 1837
(anniversary of my getting in to Oriel)

My dear Henry

First as to your question about your Translation; I am sorry I should have discouraged you by any thing I said some months since. I could not say any thing *myself* one way or other about your Translation, as it fell to Pusey not to me—and I had not read a word of it. I gave you his message as accurately as I could at the time—though now I forget what it was. I do remember being somewhat surprised at the way you took his criticisms. Also I remember thinking it an advantage when he told me he had found a Translation which he thought so good that, without entering into the question whether yours were better or not, would set you at liberty for that other work (St Austin's Letters) which you had already made us an offer of taking instead, and which, as far as we know, is *not* translated. We (naturally) think it so much in advance when we find a Translation ready made to our hands, which will do. After all, Pusey felt so much for your kindness in the trouble you had taken on the first book, that he determined not to use the already published Translation so far—but to correct yours. What was inconsiderate in all this?[1]—I have said above that I thought this discovery an *advantage*—for I saw clearly enough, your Translation (owing to your other occupations) never would be finished in time—and it was a great anxiety to me to find week go after week and nothing come from you. As far as I recollect, at the time I begged you to give it up or send me some by Ash Wednesday, happening to write to Wood, I asked him to look about for us in case you ultimately relinquished it. *What* was inconsiderate in all this?—I am sick of explanations. Perhaps this will only get me into fresh difficulties. Why, My dear H W, cannot you take it for granted that words are not a suitable index of one's intentions?— I would say more, if I had any idea what is was [sic] I am considered to have been deficient in. We hope to bring out the Confessions on August 1.

James Mozley has done your errants [sic], I trust, long before this.

The last news I have heard is, what must not be told on *my* authority, that Mr Sanderson Robins, being engaged in preventing a lady turning

[1] A misunderstanding had occurred about Wilberforce's relinquishing the translation of the Confessions to Pusey. In his letter of 1 April he explained that he was satisfied with the arrangement and was 'delighted' that Pusey was going to make use of those pieces of translation which he had completed. On 16 May he wrote, 'I assure you that I never for a moment thought that either Pusey or you had acted with any inconsideration towards me . . . I felt that you had both of you good cause to complain of my dilatoriness . . .'
The difficulty seems to have grown out of a discussion between Samuel Wilberforce and Wood. Rogers wrote on 27 April that Wood, '. . . did say to S. W. that it was idle of H. to have thrown up the Confessions—and will never again say a word about one Wilberforce to another—but that he was led astray by your having written to him to ask him to suggest some translator for the Confessions—H. W. having taken the letters.' Wood wrote on 8 May that he had only passed a jocular remark and had certainly not implicated Newman in any way. See letter of 14 April to Keble.

Papist, after trying and failing with UltraProtestantism, took to our Tracts, and thereby not only reclaimed her but converted himself. I think it exaggerated.

The remaining questions[1] are scarcely precise enough to admit of answering—but any thing I can say I will if wanted. I am quite ashamed of a great deal I have said overleaf—but things barren and littleworth in themselves often *suggest* what is valuable to others—so I have not refrained

Let me conclude by earnestly begging any one who thinks good gained to her from what I have written (and I thank you much for what you have said, not that I am worthy of it) to do what I cannot doubt such a person would do, pray for me.[2] I should hold *that* as a sort of interest, which I have a fair right to expect my writings to bear. Indeed I need it much. I do not think I gain any comfort from such things as you have kindly told me, except this hope. Such things do not seem to comfort or cheer me; I feel so conscious I am like the pane of glass (to use the common simile) which transmits heat yet is cold. I dare say I *am* doing good—but I have no consciousness that I retain any portion of it myself—or that I am more of an instrument of God than Solomon, or Jehu might be. But if I think I am getting persons to pray for me in my life and in death, yea after death I gain something I can take hold of. Also when I hear such things as you have said, one is insensibly drawn in affection towards the unknown friend—and that of course is also a great comfort

Ever Yrs affly John H Newman

THURSDAY 13 APRIL 1837 no l. p. c. dined early service and lectures *twice a week for the season* began in Adam de Brome's Chapel in the evening—read Number 447 [*Jfc.*][3]

FRIDAY 14 APRIL letters from C. and Garbett. no p dined in hall wrote to C and Garbett

TO JOHN KEBLE

Oriel College ⌜April 14. 1837⌝

My dear Keble,

The accompanying letters would have been despatched to you long since, (and I hope the delay will prove of no consequence) but Copeland gave me

[1] From the person who had been enquiring about prayer. See letter of 25 March to Wilberforce.
[2] Wilberforce had heard of another lady who had turned from evangelicalism after reading Newman's sermons: 'the last thing I heard of her was that she said speaking of you "One only regrets that he can never know the sort of gratitude felt towards him by many of whom he knows nothing—but perhaps one day he will know it." '
[3] This was the first of the Lectures on Justification, which were delivered between this date and 1 June, usually on Mondays and Thursdays. The relation between the Lectures delivered and those published is uncertain. One more Lecture was delivered than published.

hopes that the Morrells were making up a parcel to you—As however I hear nothing of it, I delay no longer.

By ill luck your little note, which I have kept safe to reply to and made marks upon about some things I wished to say to you has vanished from my table at the very moment I want it.

I suppose, if we do not hear from you to the contrary, we may put your name as the intended Translator of Irenaeus in the forthcoming list. It does not of course absolutely bind you.

⌐The Christian Observer has revived the report of your giving the £5000.[1] Pusey says, *if* you think it worth while to notice it, keep this in view —*that every denial tends negatively to fix it on the right person*. Such gross indelicacy (though they mean it as praise) in them arises, as he says, from their thinking it no use doing good unless it is talked about. He says that, having given up the notion of heavenly rewards as selfrighteous, they take to earthly.

That dedication to Routh was quite on my mind for a while, and made me very anxious. I felt the chance of what you think, before hand and earnestly deprecated it. Those I showed it to entirely approved of it. Pusey thought it just what it should be. I should have sent it you had there been time. I do not, you see, defend it—I mean I take my own anxiety, not as a proof of caution, but as a foreboding.⌐[2]

Thank Wilson for his letter. ⟨(What [does] Wilson mean by 'putting off' H. W and Manning, when Manning has, and never has had taken from him, what he selected.)⟩ As to H. W. I really know not what to say—and still rather will consider Wilson mistaken than H. W. childish. The latter offered spontaneously to relinquish the Confessions and take the Letters, which he said he preferred—and this more than once before we accepted it—which we did *because* we happened to hit upon a ready made translation—which was a saving of time and expence. I am utterly ignorant *what* the difficulty is; so perhaps cannot answer it. The only additional point is, that while H. W was dilatory, I wrote to him to ask as kindly as I could (*though* he had offered) whether since we wanted it soon he had better not give it up—and at the same time (I think) writing to Wood asked him if he knew of any one who would undertake it, if he did. H. W in his answer assured me I need not have made apology; for I had done nothing but what was kind. After all we did *not* transfer his work to the Letters on that ground but on account of the

---

[1] 'The list of subscribers to the Metropolis Church-building Fund, in our number for October, in which was announced a donation of 1000*l*. from Professor Pusey, and another of 5000*l*. from a "Clergyman seeking Treasure in Heaven," who is generally understood to be Professor Keble will explain the allusion and correct the mistake in our last Number, p. 197.' *The Christian Observer*, 424, 1837 (April), 264. See first note to letter of 7 March to M. R. Giberne. The anonymous donor was Pusey, who gave the £5000 in two installments, and 'was obliged to reduce his servants, to give up his carriage, and to live even more simply than heretofore.' Liddon's *Pusey* I, 331.

[2] See letter of 7 Jan. to F. Rogers about the dedication of *Prophetical Office* to M. J. Routh.

find of a Translation—one should almost think there is some one making mischief—but that I suppose there always is.

We look forward to the great pleasure of seeing you for a week or two— As to my going any where, it is out of prospect at present. ⌜It is a comfort to think that where [sic] I out of health you would let me come to Hursley for a while, as other kind friends elsewhere. But I am rejoiced to say I am better than I have been for years—⌝

Ever Yrs very affly John H Newman

P.S. ⌜Woodgate is Bampton Lecturer which is a good thing⌝

SATURDAY 15 APRIL 1837 dined in rooms

SUNDAY 16 APRIL   3rd Easter   early Communion Pusey assisted   snow all day   did duty morning and afternoon   Pusey preached   buried Bellman's son.   dined with Williams.

MONDAY 17 APRIL   service and lecture in Ad de Br's Chapel—read Number 454 [*Jfc.*]   men to tea in the evening

TUESDAY 18 APRIL   letters from J and Bowden (thro' Johnson)   no c?   walked to Littlemore with Berkeley and Mr Bloxham.   dined with P Claughton

WEDNESDAY 19 APRIL   no l. p.   dined in hall

THURSDAY 20 APRIL   letter from Buller   no s. v. c.   dined with W   early   service and lecture—read Number 455. [*Jfc.*]

FRIDAY 21 APRIL   letter from Grant   no p   J Marriott to breakfast   Woodgate left having taken Bell Broughton   Mrs Champernowne in Oxford   buried Godfrey's child   dined in hall   wrote to Grant, and Rogers on Eden's letter

SATURDAY 22 APRIL   no l and p   walked to Littlemore; back with Williams and Copleston   dined in rooms

SUNDAY 23 APRIL   4th Easter   letters from Bowden and W Pusey   early Communion Pusey assisting   Harrison read for me in morning I in evening   preached Number 459   dined in hall   Trent and Dear in Oxford—and dined in hall

MONDAY 24 APRIL   service in A. d Br's Chapel—read Number 456 [*Jfc.*]   men in the evening

TUESDAY 25 APRIL   St Mark   letters from Woodgate and R Williams and his Mother   no c   service in Chancel—read Number 329[1]   walked with J.M.   dined with Marriott   wrote to R Williams and his Mother, Pope, Bowden, R W[,] J.[,] Mr Richards [of] Bristol and Mr Willis [of] Bath

TO J. W. BOWDEN

Oriel College. St. Mark's [25 April] 1837

My dear Bowden,

Will you let me know, and set Wood or someone or other to tell me, *the hour* when the meeting is on Monday. Dodsworth insists on our coming—so we come.[2] We shall set off in the morning and return in the evening. I fear

---

[1] *U.S.*, 5, 'Personal Influence the Means of Propagating the Truth'.
[2] For a meeting of the S. P. C. K. Newman himself did not go.

we shall bring very few from Oxford—every one is engaged and few feel any interest in the matter. Should not you Londoners take care we have a room *large enough* to hold us   It will be no good, if we stand on the staircase all the while and then return back like the King of France.

I never spoke in my last about your coming here. Ogle wishes to receive you. I trust we should be able to give you a bedroom—but cannot tell till the time comes. There is no doubt either we or Trinity could—so *you may fairly* take your chance. I am rejoiced at your coming, and your Brother's also. The rain is now beginning, as if to make Oxford beautiful by that time.

According to *my own* judgment, I wish my letter to the Christian Observer to appear on all accounts. It floors the Editor—and it is of sufficient length to relieve me of the necessity of writing more on the subject *to him*. It was only what Rogers said which made me right [sic] what I did to you. He thought it would seem arrogant—so and my proper answer would necessarily appear *to those who thought the Observer* in right and who did not see the exceeding absurdity of the Editor.[1] There was a choice between that and what would be in *itself* μικροψυχία[2] and I had rather seem arrogant than be apologetic and cowardly. And I think that [at?] the expense of myself still I shall do the cause good; i.e., if he fairly puts it in (but I now expect it to be cut up into portions κρεουργηδόν[3] like Atreus's sons or nephews)—However, when I found that Wood agreed with me in the main, and had already had your and Pusey's sanction, I am still less reluctant. As to his denial of impugning the Homily of Rebellion, *I have passages* from his worthy Publication ready, which prove my charge—were it worth while to produce them. I am sorry you should have had so much trouble—and thank you for taking it.

I had heard of the Calcutta appointment—alas the labourers are few as yet.[4] Every day shows that the demand exceeds the supply—but every day also gives proof that the seeds are being cast, as we may trust, of a future crop.

I have not yet read the Article you speak of in the British Critic having lent my copy.

Ever yrs affly John H. Newman.

P.S. Is not little John to come this time?

---

[1] The second part of Newman's second letter appeared in *The Christian Observer*, 425, 1837 (May), 317–52. Newman was allowed more space on this occasion, the editor only taking about half the page for his comments. The editor concluded with the remark: 'We await Mr. Newman's remarks upon Justification; far the most important of the questions at issue.' However, no more of the correspondence was published, Newman deciding instead to write *Jfc*.

[2] 'pusillanimity'.

[3] 'like butchers' meat'.

[4] Bowden reported that the S. P. G. were writing to the Vice-Chancellors of Oxford and Cambridge for someone to succeed W. H. Mill as Principal of Bishop's College, Calcutta.

TO MRS JOHN MOZLEY

⌐St Mark's [[April 25]] 1837

What you say about my book is very gratifying [[Prophetical Office]] I hear the same in various other quarters—and it is selling very well. It only shows how deep the absurd notion was in men's minds that I was a Papist; and now they are agreeably surprised. Thus I gain, as commonly happens in the long run, by being misrepresented—thanks to Record and Co. I shall take it out in an attack on popular Protestantism. I call the notion of my being a Papist absurd, for it argues on utter ignorance of theology. We have all fallen back from the Reformation in a wonderful way. Any one who knew any thing of theology would not have confounded me with the Papists; and, if he gave me any credit for knowledge of theology or for clearheadedness, he would not have thought me in danger of becoming one. True it is, any one who by *his own wit* had gone as far as I *from* popular Protestantism, or who had been taught from *without*, not being up to the differences of things, and trained to discrimination, might have been in danger of going further; but no one who either had learned his doctrine *historically*, or had tolerable clearness of mind, could be in more danger than of confusing the Sun and the Moon.

However, I frankly own that in some important points our Anglican ἦθος differs from Popery, in others it is like it—and on the whole far more like it than like Protestantism. So one must expect a revival of the slander or misapprehension in some shape or other—and we shall never be free of it, of course.⌐

TO SIMEON LLOYD POPE

Oriel College. St Mark's [25 April] 1837

My dear Pope,

It is not for not having thought of you that I have not written, but from being busy (as usual) and having nothing to say. I am truly pleased at hearing the comfortable account you give of yourself in your new position—and sincerely trust and wish you may find it all you anticipate. Boodle told me that your alliance was noble—so that your news came too late. It would give me real pleasure to come to see you—but who is to be doing my work in various ways here, and which becomes year after year more intricately twisted around me? I find it never the fit time to go away. Next Tuesday I go to London—but to go and return in one day.

You *should* bring your bride to see the beauties of Oxford. If I came to you, you would only see *me*—if you pressed me ever so much I could not put St Mary's into my pocket to produce it on your tea table—I could not make a balloon of the Radcliffe, or a steam coach of the Bodleian. If you come here, not only shall I have the pleasure of being introduced to your bride, but you can introduce her to Trinity College, Common Room, Gardens, and Hall inclusive—and to the other sights of our University.

By the bye have I ever thanked you for the engraving of your beautiful Church which you sent me—and which everyone admires? The truth is, Short did not give it to me for some months after the time you sent it—and then, when I wrote, I forgot to mention it. It is certainly quite superb.

We are going on peaceably and comfortably here—good seems growing —we hear murmurs from without—rumours of a Commission etc—but I do not see what they can do to *hurt* us—annoy us they can to their heart's content. Vexations they may be—injurious they may be—dangerous they are not and cannot be if we are true to ourselves.

I have not forgotten your hint about wanting Pupils—should I have the opportunity (though I fear that in such matters I am rather on the shelf) I will not fail to speak to you on the subject

Pray convey from me to Mrs Pope as kind a message as a stranger to her has a right to make, stating what extreme pleasure it would give me to make her acquaintance

With every wish for your happiness in the truest sense

Believe me My dear Pope Most sincerely Yours
John H Newman

P.S. I am glad to hear so prosperous an account of your proceedings in your parish. You should come and see Littlemore Chapel.

TO R. I. WILBERFORCE

Oriel College. St Mark's [25 April] 1837

My dear Wilberforce,

I have not yet answered your letter, hoping to have some opportunity of doing so, without any post mark accompanying my acknowledgment—but wish to write to you before Tuesday next, to acquaint you that some from Oxford are going up to London, and therefore delay no longer.

Accept my sincere thanks for the news you gave me—I trust I need not say that you have my warmest good wishes and prayers that the measure you have decided on may be all you can desire.

I fear we shall go in very small force from this place. Every one is busy —some have given up the Society in despair, others have never taken interest in its proceedings. I am writing tonight to Bath and Bristol on the subject, and Pusey to Keble, but the latter doubtless is already up to the whole affair from his proximity to your Brothers

Thanks for your information about the Nonjurors—which Routh was much interested in. Thanks also for your remarks about my new Book. I fancy they advertise books inversely to their chance of selling. At least I find that from the time of publication the sale of mine has hitherto proceeded with a continuous flow.

We hope to begin our Catholic Library in August with the Confessions of St Austin—a volume of Chrysostom or Cyril of Jerusalem, in October— and thenceforward quarterly.

Ever Yrs affectly John H Newman

WEDNESDAY 26 APRIL 1837   no c   walked with J.M. towards Littlemore meeting Williams   dined in Hall

THURSDAY 27 APRIL   letters from Hooker and Mr Roundell   Dear went   Trower of Exeter in Oxford   married James Webb to Susanna Martha Verey   dined with W early service and Lecture read Number 457 [*Jfc.*]

FRIDAY 28 APRIL   letters from Rogers, R. Williams and Bowden   no p and c   anniversary of J and J [Jemima and John Mozley]   walked to Littlemore   The 2 Ms dined with me—W. and Copeland to tea—thence to Pusey's Theological (1st this term) he reading a paper

SATURDAY 29 APRIL   letters from Bowden and Mr Todd[1]   walked with Berkeley to Littlemore   dined in rooms   James of Queen's called.   wrote to Oxenham

SUNDAY 30 APRIL   5th Easter   Pusey assisted me in early Communion   went up to Littlemore with James, and read prayers—Harrison reading at St Mary's   did duty in afternoon and preached Number 460[2]   James, Newman, and Lowe dined with me.   wrote to M. Hudel'eau

MONDAY 1 MAY   St Philip and St James (Rogation)   service in Chancel   read Number [337] ('It sufficeth us')   service in Ad de Br's Chapel   read Number 458 [*Jfc.*]

TUESDAY 2 MAY   (St Athanasius) (Rogation)   went to Littlemore   dined in hall

WEDNESDAY 3 MAY   Rogation   wrote to H, M R G and to Oldham in Eden's letter

TO MISS M. R. GIBERNE

Oriel College. Eve of the Ascension [3 May] 1837

My dear Miss Giberne,

I fear you have thought either your letter lost, or my memory—though both have been safe with me—and I have hoped every day for some leisure time to write. First let me ask—your last packet only contained *one* MS?

[1] James H. Todd wrote from Dublin on 26 April enclosing a printed 'Church Improvement Petition' to the House of Commons for the restoration of the ten suppressed Irish sees. He had read Newman's *Prophetical Office* 'with much pleasure and instruction', but could not agree that there had not been hitherto in England a theology Catholic but not Roman, or that 'the Via Media has NEVER existed except on paper—and that there is nothing to prove that our views if set in motion would not prove self-contradictory, and fall to pieces by their own weight.' He wrote again on 22 May, more reconciled to Newman's words, and admitting that the Church of England, both at the Reformation and at the Revolution, had shown an injurious 'tenderness' towards Protestants at home and abroad. He repeated the charge that Bellarmine and other Romanist writers quoted spurious works of the Fathers when it suited them, and repudiated them when it did not.

[2] *P.S.* IV, 5, 'Reliance on Religious Observances'.

I have had some fidget lest it had *two*, but can only find one with the rest of the foregoing MS. I like it very much but feel I am too little acquainted with children to say how far it is to the life—though I do not in the least doubt it is, and am therefore interested. I suppose even little children *do* give themselves religious airs. One thing I liked much, the two cousins speaking of John and Mary as *children*, and thought it very accurate and amusing. On the whole, I think the effect of the narrative admits of heightening, which you will be able to do as time goes on; that is, when your hand gets in. One bit you must leave out, please—'I think it a sin.'

Jemima writes me good news from you ⌜about my new book⌝—I am amused to hear the same in other quarters. ⌜The truth is, people have been persuading each other that I am a Papist, and wondering what I *can* say for myself, and then when they find I am after all just what they ought from the first to have believed me to be, they are much struck; think it very wonderful; and that there is a great deal in it. However it is good luck for me—and perhaps under cover of this surprise and the relentings attending it, I may be able to discharge some darts against common Protestantism without molestation. Such seems to be the effect here—every one is saying it is so mild a book.

We shall soon have Bishop Cosin on the Canonical Hours⌝[1] in print— and some other works of the same kind. ⌜In the beginning of Queen Elizabeth's reign a private Prayer Book was put out by authority—afterwards it seems to have been suppressed. Pusey has found it in the Bodleian.—Soon too we shall have out a selection of Beveridge's Sermons.[2] I suppose you have seen Vincentius.[3] The Tract on Purgatory is just out,⌝ or ought to be— ⌜that on Tradition (Catena No 3) was out last month. The next Tract will be Catena 4 on the Eucharist, with a most valuable introduction by Pusey.

The Library of the Fathers will commence (we hope) in August with St Austin's Confessions. I trust Froude's works will come out in October—and I *purpose* then, but one must not be over sanguine, to have a new volume of Sermons. Palmer's work on the Church will be out before that time.⌝

You must let me have some more of the Peculiars in your story and soon; I want to see your work figuring in the Catalogue at the end of the Tracts.[4]

I shall like to see your story about Riches—perhaps I do not quite like the names Ath. and Ar.

---

[1] *A Collection of Private Devotions: in the practice of the Ancient Church, called the Hours of Prayer* . . . eleventh edition, London 1838. Compiled by Bishop John Cosin and first published in 1627, the preface to the 1838 edition described the aim of the work as 'to recover or retain, at least in private devotion, a portion of that undoubtedly Catholic and Apostolic system which forms so beautiful a feature in the Breviaries; a portion which had survived the Reformation, forming a conspicuous part of the Primers of Henry VIII. and Edward VI., and which was preserved in that of Elizabeth of 1560, on which this book is professedly founded.'

[2] William Beveridge, *Sermons on the Ministry and Ordinances of the Church of England*, Oxford 1837.

[3] *Vincentius of Lirins' Commonitory*, Oxford 1837.

[4] Some of the *Tracts* had a list of recommended books printed at the end.

On looking at your letter I see it dated April 1. I am quite ashamed indeed—yet am

My dear Miss Giberne Yours very sincerely John H Newman

TO MRS THOMAS MOZLEY

⌐May 3. 1837

I began weekly communion at Easter, and have found the church very well attended. I have it at seven in the morning. Last Sunday I had thirty six communicants. In the course of four Sundays the Alms have amounted to between £19 and £20. I divide them between the Diocesan Fund for increasing small livings and the new London Clergy Aid Society.¬[17]

THURSDAY 4 MAY 1837 Ascension letters from Mr Johnson and Ryder service in Chancel read Number 462 no th. beat bounds of Littlemore on foot—with Williams, Giles (Churchwarden) the 2 Clerks, 2 Spiers (Churchwardens), Hewett, Slatter, Stevens, Standen, Lucas and Wyatt for whom I brought up dinner at William's lodgings. dined in rooms service in Ad de Br's—read Number 461 [*Jfc.*]

FRIDAY 5 MAY Mr Radcliffe (Eyre's friend) and J M to breakfast. not p. s n v c walked to Littlemore dined in hall Archdeacon F came wrote to Ryder

SATURDAY 6 MAY (St John [ante] Portam Latinam) no n and c. walked to Littlemore with Archdeacon F and Williams—round by Iffley to dinner in Common Room Archdeacon F.[,] Woolcombe (Ch Ch) A.F., 2 Champernowne's, Williams and Copeland Marriott and J.M. to tea

SUNDAY 7 MAY After Ascension did duty morning and afternoon at St M's preached Number 464[2] assisted in Communion by Marriott, Berkeley, Spranger—on account of long service dined at Williams's with Archdeacon F.[,] A F.[,] 2 Champernownes, Copeland, Cornish

MONDAY 8 MAY (Apparition of S. Michael) letters from H and W. F. Archdeacon F went dinner hour changed to 4 dined in Hall Keble came service—read Number 448 [*Jfc.*] wrote to Mr Todd—to W F by his Father

TUESDAY 9 MAY (S. Gregor. Naz) about this time I saw J H Standen's death Keble's Lecture walked to Littlemore dined with Williams and Keble at W's Roger's brother came in evening

TO HENRY WILBERFORCE

May 9. In Festo S. Greg. Nazianz. 1837[3]

In my haste in my last I did not mention the *Church* Litany, when I spoke of Bishop Taylor's.

We are going to bring out Bishop Cosin's Hours forthwith—These are but *daily* devotions, I think—not weekly, or yearly. Yet they are excellent

[1] Earlier name of the Additional Curates Society; see note to diary for 9 April.
[2] *P.S.* IV, 17, 'Christ Manifested in Remembrance'.
[3] See letter of 25 March to Wilberforce, to which this is additional.

in themselves, and useful as a beginning. They are taken, I believe, from a manual put out by *authority* in the beginning of Elizabeth's time (which we hope to publish also) and that again from King Henry viiith's Primer.

In the second Edition of the Tract on the Breviary there are considerable additions, which will be useful to any one who wishes to arrange such a system of devotion for him or herself.[1]

While I think of it, I will say, but I do not wished [sic] it mentioned except in confidence, I have at present a considerable intention of bringing out a Quarterly Miscellany, if I can get Ladies to write for it, to be called The Daughters of the Church ⟨Church Gleanings⟩, or some such title. It should be most unrestricted in range and selection of subjects; e.g. one quarter it might be verse, another prose. M R G's story would be one portion (if she would give it) a sketch of some passage of history another etc etc. I am led to think of it by having MS from various ladies put into my hands from various quarters; and I think it would be useful to raise a Standard. The greatest difficulty will be if ever things are sent from persons one does not know much of, which will not do—but of course this is only part of the unavoidable discomfort of Editorship. I hope to be able to get supplies sufficient from persons I or friends of mine know.

To resume the questions. I forget what question I answered last—as to 'the length of time for devotional exercises in a life of leisure,' this is just a question which the Church alone can solve for us. If I refer to the Breviary as a solution, it is because I suppose it is the decision of the Church from very early times. The *principle* seems to be, to sanctify each portion of the day. When we speak of observing *hours*, I suppose it means portions and divisions of the day, not points of time; the third hour extending from 9 A M to 12. etc. It is easy (I suppose) to be 'regular' with this latitude—I think I should be led then to take what I found. Morning and Evening Prayer in Church whenever I had the opportunity, of course—and altogether from three to four hours a day. But it quite distresses me so to define and prescribe in a matter of mere discretion.—If I were a person inquiring, I should get out of the difficulty by *taking* some rule which *came* to me, not forming one for myself—e.g. Bishop Cosin's Devotions—or the Breviary, or those put forth by the Non jurors etc.

(WhitSunday) May 14 'How much to shrink from the habit of retirement being observed by others, not nearest to us'. This of course is a difficulty, yet St Paul and Silas sang praises in prison—and Daniel prayed with windows open. I do not see then that such publicity interferes with the command in Matt vi when it cannot be helped. The only question is whether it is likely to

---

[1] Newman increased the second edition of *Tract* 75 by a further 59 pages. The *Tract* consisted of an historical introduction, an ordinary Sunday's services given at length in English, and two portions of special feast day services. Newman added an abstract of the services for every day in Advent to the second edition, explaining that except '. . . by means of some such extended portion, it is impossible for the reader to understand the general structure, and appreciate the harmony of the Breviary.'

hurt one's own mind; and in such a question it requires far more experience than a Protestant Priest can have to judge—We have no confessions and can give no advice. It is very uncomfortable doubtless it [to] have it known —there is something awkward in the consciousness—but I do not, if I must give an opinion, see that it is dangerous to thoughtful and steadfast minds.

'How to meet dulness of spirits etc'—I think a person must judge for himself here, or rather by making distinctions—but I am so afraid of theorizing or being fanciful that I hardly like to say any thing; and wish what I say to be merely suggestions or rather guessings and questionings than even opinions. I think then that *disinclination* to devotion must *not* be yielded to, is *not* a reason for discontinuing it, *unless* we have reason to suspect it proceeds from bodily indisposition, languor, fatigue etc. Prayer, if not a privilege, let it be to us (to our shame) a penance, if so it must be—we at the same time taking care not to forget *whom* we are before, *who* hears us speak.—Physical cold, if severe, may be a cause of inattention etc, but I believe that cold or other discomfort *in moderation* (like powerful medicines, which are in themselves poisons) is a fit attendance on devotion.—So much for dulness, hardness, disinclination etc. of mind.—But as to inattention, I am not clear what is best. With me inattention chiefly arises when my mind is full of other things and I wish to discharge it[.] I have sometimes thought I will *first* discharge it—but so much depends on the very hour, that I have not found in such cases my mind more collected afterwards. Might it not be well, when in danger of inattention, not to take our ordinary prayers, psalms etc. but others with which one is not so familiar? but I put this as a question. —I think two things contribute much to attention, first to put a certain *space* of time to prayer, that there may be no temptation to hurry—so that if we have done sooner through involuntary hurrying, to remain fixed on our knees to the end of it—or to proceed to other prayers. Next to observe as nearly as possible the right hour. This does not apply so much to devotions *thro'* the day, which are shorter; but *longer* devotions are, I think, difficult to attend to, engage in etc. when out of their due season.—All this shows the morning to be the right time for them, for then we can command our time.

'Whether intermingling some toil, study, education of the poor etc. apply to women.'—Our Saviour so remarkably lays the stress on deeds of selfabasing charity, that I do not think any one is in a comfortable state, who does none such. It were well, if persons who are out of the way of such, were obliged to wash the feet of the poor literally. But no one in this country and age, no woman, but has abundant opportunities. But besides this, I think active duties are incumbent on us all *naturally*, on *the face of the Gospel*.[1]

---

[1] No more of the letter is extant.

WEDNESDAY 10 MAY 1837 letter from R. Williams Rogers made his appearance and breakfasted with Pusey. no s. n. v. c walked to Littlemore with Cornish snow and thunder leaves not out had to dinner Keble, Williams, Rogers, Bloxam, Spranger, Cornish, Claughton, Shepheard, Berkeley, J. M in Common Room (asked Daman, and Harrison)

THURSDAY 11 MAY letter from R Williams Rogers, E Rogers, and J.M. to breakfast walked to Littlemore with Ogle and Rogers. Eyre came dined in hall Service in Ad de Br's read Number 463 [*Jfc.*] Marriott to tea. sent parcel to G and R.

FRIDAY 12 MAY letter from S.W. not p. th. s. n. v and c Rogers went went to Littlemore—wrote to R. Williams and S.W. Theological Pusey and Keble read

TO SAMUEL WILBERFORCE

Oriel College. May 12. 1837

My dear Wilberforce

Your letter of this morning opens a very interesting subject. Doubtless the only right way of missionarising is by Bishops—and the agitation of the question must do good. Perhaps you are hardly called upon even to say *how* it is to be done in the case of a given Society, as the Church Missionary—it being at once a sufficient object at first to make out the *duty*, and when it is made out, to fulfil it being other persons concern quite as much as yours. If you prove your point, others are bound to cooperate with you in acting upon it. At the same time of course it would soften opposition to show that the thing was not only right but practicable.

I suppose in the present state of the Church of England we cannot expect the Bishops to move or follow. I forget how the Law stands—but I *think* the question of Law was made the objection to our Bishops consecrating Bishop Luscombe[1]—not of ecclesiastical order. At the same time it would (would it not?) be an inconsistency in an *English* Society getting Bishops from Scotland? Is there any precedent in the English Church of a Bishop being sent among the heathen? Could not the difficulty be met by getting Daniel Wilson and his Colleagues to consecrate; if the consent of the Calcutta etc Government was requisite, I suppose they might gain it. But one should like to try the power of at least *Colonial* Bishops to do without the State. Is Calcutta a Metropolitan See, or under Canterbury? if the former, it is free to act without the English Church; at least I assume Canterbury would not claim such patriarchal dominion over it.

I am exceedingly glad you are stirring the question, and think it a very happy thought. The very stirring it will be of great use. Any definite questions you send me, I will answer if I can—but I suspect you will want an ecclesiastical *lawyer*.

[1] Michael H. T. Luscombe was appointed Bishop to the scattered English congregations on the Continent in 1825, but he had to be consecrated by the Bishops of the Scottish Episcopal Church. A man of High Church principles, he was one of the founders of the *Christian Remembrancer* in 1841.

I am surprised at what you say about the British Critic. I have heard nothing of the kind before, and do not know to what you allude.

When you wrote to me some time since about the passage in Calvin, I did not know where to look for it—but now I send it you. After quoting a passage from Cyprian's De Unitate in which the connexion between Christ and the Episcopate is enforced, that the Church is set up in Christ etc, he says

'Talem nobis hierarchiam si exhibeant, in qua sic emineant Episcopi, ut Christo subesse non recusent, ut ab illo, tanquam unico capite, pendeant, et ad ipsum referantur; in quâ sic inter se fraternam Societatem colant, ut non alio nodo, quam eius veritate sint colligati, tum vero nullo non anathemate dignos fatear, si qui erunt, qui non eam reverenter summâque obedientiâ observent. Hæc vero mendox [sic] hierarchiæ larva, quâ superbiunt, quid omnino habet simile? Unus principatum, Christi vice, tenet Pontifex Romanus etc' de Necessitate Reformandæ Ecclesiæ p 81 (towards the end of the Treatise)

Yrs very sincerely John H Newman

SATURDAY 13 MAY 1837 letter from Oxenham Keble went walked with Pusey dined in hall 2 Bowdens (*J. and H.*) came J W B lodged at Oriel

SUNDAY 14 MAY Whit Sunday did duty morning and evening at St Mary's preached Number 466[1] Sacrament no one assisting To dinner in rooms—2 Bowdens, Johnson, J.M. and Marriott. wrote to H W and Archdeacon F

MONDAY 15 MAY Whit Monday letter from H W no th s n. v or c but ordination service breakfasted with Johnson. service in chancel—no lecture called on Mrs Lee with Bowden and on Mr Anderdon dined at four with Williams etc Service and Lecture Number 465 [*Jfc.*]

TUESDAY 16 MAY Whit Tuesday letters from C and Boone about a week ago saw J H Standen's death in paper service in Chancel—no lecture walked to Littlemore with Pusey and L.P. 2 Barkers 2 Bowdens and Johnson to dinner with me in Common Room 2 Bowdens Johnson Harrison Copeland Williams, Ogle, J M and Anderdon wrote to W F and H W

TO HENRY WILBERFORCE

Oriel. May 16. 1837

My dear Henry

The University is going to reprint King Edward's two books—*if* it can *buy* a copy to reprint from.[2] Can you put me in the way of getting one?

I have seen Mr Anderdon here before—somehow he did not call on me this time, though he did on Williams etc.—So I called on him—and then he called in the evening, (when I happened to be out) saying he was going

[1] *P.S.* IV, 11, 'The Communion of Saints'.
[2] Edward Cardwell edited *The Two Books of Common Prayer, set forth by Authority of Parliament in the Reign of King Edward the Sixth: compared with each other*, Oxford 1838.

away next morning. I suppose it was accident. Young A. dines with me today, and may throw light on it. Mr Orger (if he is the same man) I have known many years ago—he was Oldham's tutor—and is in the habit of being Mayor's or Sheriff's Chaplain and presenting himself or his book or sermon etc to the King. It makes me laugh to think he should have fired away. He sat under me at St Clement's and perhaps thinks me a renegade. I would not do any thing were I you, *till* the concern appears, and decide by circumstances. Perhaps he then may explain the 'Request'[1]

I will not forget you or Mrs H W or your little boy—nor do I.[2]

Ever Yrs affly John H Newman

P.S. Tomorrow is the anniversary of my loss last year.

WEDNESDAY 17 MAY 1837† Ember f. br. first day of Term University Sacrament in Chancel—I attended and about thirty altogether Bowdens dined at Trinity dined in Hall Bowdens and Johnson to tea

THURSDAY 18 MAY to breakfast in Common Room 2 Bowdens Johnson, Pusey, Hook, Hamilton—afterwards Acland and E. Churton walked to Rose Hill to Mr Slatter's with Bowden and Johnson service in A de Br.s Chapel read Number 252 [452. *Jfc.*] dined after it (i.e. at 8 o'clock nearly) at Ogle's no c. wrote to Johnson of Wadham at Torquay in answer

FRIDAY 19 MAY Ember day breakfasted with Copeland to meet E Churton f d. no c. wrote to Jemima J.M. to tea Bs [Bowdens] and Johnson to tea

TO MRS JOHN MOZLEY

Trinity College. May 19. 1837

My dear Jemima

I do not often write from Trinity—but as yesterday was the anniversary of my getting into a scholarship here, I have some reason for writing in Williams's rooms, though the ink is wretched; not near such as [I] should use in wishing you and John many happy returns of this day in the highest sense of the words—which I do most affectionately. Williams who is sitting with his back to me wishes you the same over his shoulder.

---

[1] William Orger, an evangelical, had matriculated at St Edmund Hall in 1822, B.A. 1826. He acted as private tutor to John Roberts Oldham, who entered Oriel in 1827.

On 25 April he preached at Holy Rhood Church, Southampton, at the Visitation of Archdeacon Hoare. The sermon was published as *The Ministerial Witness to the Gospel*, London 1837. First attacking worldly clergymen, the sermon turned to Tractarian theology, which, Orger thought, took men away from Christ to the Sacraments.

Orger claimed that the sermon was 'published by request'. Wilberforce reported, 'now here is really so glaring a misstatement because it was proposed by Dr Wilson—seconded ironically by one other. Protested against by 2 more when the Archdeacon begged the subject might be dropped and as I said never put to us the subject of printing or not printing'. Wilberforce asked Newman's advice about the best way of contradicting the claim. He was further scandalised because Orger had boasted at a dinner that he had never even read any of the Tractarian publications. See letter of 31 May to Wilberforce.

[2] Wilberforce's young son John had been ill.

I talk of going away from Oxford for 3 weeks at the beginning of June —spending part of the time at Cholderton, and part with T. Keble or Christie. This is to be my holidays for the Vacation. Charles talks of coming to me for a fortnight in the beginning of July—but this is rendered somewhat uncertain by his losing his situation at Stroude which I am very sorry for. It is not his fault at all—his employer makes some excuse—but the truth is this, he never will be settled. People think him eccentric, and will always part with him after a half year or two. Under these circumstances I would gladly give up the whole or any part of my £1000 to get him some situation of permanence; and the only reason I do not propose it at once, is, because I wish to *see* Charles to understand better what his state is—and because I am not unwilling—so that he is not thrown into circumstances disadvantageous to his $\hat{\eta}\theta\sigma s$, that he should do penance some while longer. At the same time I wish you would have a talk with John about it—I mean to this purpose— viz he knows a good deal of business generally, and might suggest the *kind* of thing,—what sort of openings there are etc.—and generally what can be done for him. I do not mean any thing *specific* in the way I lately wrote to you, but general.

I am doubting whether to bring out a new volume of Sermons in the Autumn, or a work on Justification—I have reasons for wishing both—but the former will take me so much less trouble, that I suppose I shall determine upon it. I have *written* enough for the latter, but it would take me a great deal of thought and reading.—It is not quite certain yet whether Froude's papers will or will not be published this Autumn—William Froude comes up next week or the week after—and we shall then settle.

A most absurd panic has risen in London about the Popery of Oxford— whether from the Lyra, or Tracts, or Christian Observer, or Hook's getting in to Coventry[1] or altogether, I do not know. On the other hand, not only have I the most astonishing proofs from very unlikely persons *in Oxford* of their approximation to or adhesion to us in consequence of my last book on Romanism—(which have been very gratifying and comfortable indeed, but do not go to prove to the satisfaction of the London people, that Popery is not in Oxford) but I hear the same kind of thing from *London* people also. —So I suppose persons are both frightened and relieved, as it may be.

I saw by the papers lately J. H. Standen's death—also Miss White's that was—viz Mrs Bissland

Ever yrs affly John H Newman

SATURDAY 20 MAY 1837 Ember day letter from H W University Confirmation —I had not to attend walked to Littlemore with Williams dined in Sheppard's rooms with 2 Bowdens and Johnson Marriott to tea

[1] W. F. Hook had been Vicar of Holy Trinity, Coventry, since 1829. He was elected Vicar of Leeds on 20 March 1837 and took up the living in June. He was in Oxford at this time (see diary entries) to take his D.D.

SUNDAY 21 MAY Trinity Sunday the leaves on the large Elms not appearing even. Cold north east rain, damp all day. did duty morning and afternoon preached Number 468[1] Marriott assisting me in Sacrament m and l to dinner 2 Bowdens, Johnson, Williams, J.M. ⟨?⟩ Berkeley and Courtney in rooms

MONDAY 22 MAY 2 Bs [Bowdens] and Johnson to breakfast. The Bs went. Mrs Pusey went to Guernsey dined in hall service and Lecture in Adam de B's chapel—Number 467 [*ffc.*] Men in evening—Mr Bunsen and Mr Crockenden, J.M.'s pupil

TUESDAY 23 MAY Daman went no m.l.p.th.s.n. v and c. walked to Littlemore dined with Pusey to meet Hook etc. W Froude came

WEDNESDAY 24 MAY W. and A F. to breakfast wind changed to South West dined with Harrison to meet Hook no c

THURSDAY 25 MAY letter from Rickards W F took his M A degree Service and Sermon in afternoon at St Mary's for Schools—Pusey preached—Collection £80 odd dined with Palmer (no service at 6 or Lecture) wrote to Wood no c

TO THOMAS MOZLEY

Oriel May 25. 1837

My dear Tom,

Rickards writes to me by this morning's post for a sketch etc of Littlemore Church. I shall send him dimensions expence etc. as far as I can—but if you could take up your pen and flourish off an outside, ground plan, etc you will be benevolent to him.

Tell Harriett that we are going to set up a Lady's Magazine—and if she can contribute any verses for children etc we shall be glad

The plan is rather a 'Constable's Miscellany' i.e. a set of quarterly little volumes or semi-volumes—verse or prose, as it may happen, for the edification of young persons of the fair sex.

Tell James I have had a talk with Pusey—who as well as Copeland, and in a measure Williams, are for immediately publishing the MSS.[2]—Love to H. James will tell you all the news

Ever Yrs affly John H Newman

FRIDAY 26 MAY 1837 letter from Bowden walked to Littlemore with W F back with Williams and Bloxam. f d Williams, Copeland, Marriott and J M to tea Theological meeting—Harrison read.

SATURDAY 27 MAY letter from Bowden no l and p J M went to Cholderdon. engaged on article for British Critic dined in Hall N B I have to give Littlemore £5 school £5 J W B [Bowden] and £1 from B N C. paid to Bloxam Sept 23 1837

SUNDAY 28 MAY 1st Trinity letter from J early Communion—Williams assisting did duty morning and afternoon preached Number 433 W.F.[,] Williams and Bloxam to dinner Marriott and A.F. to tea W.F. went by mail to London

MONDAY 29 MAY service in Chancel in forenoon—no lecture no th. s. n. dined

---

[1] *P.S.* VI, 23, 'Faith without Demonstration'.
[2] [[Froude's]]

in hall   Keble and his wife came.   service in Ad de Br's Chapel   Lecture Number 469 [*Jfc.*]   to tea Ryder and Mr O Brien and A M

TUESDAY 30 MAY   Daman returned with Ward   no th. s. n.   Keble's Lecture walked with Pusey   dined in hall   wrote to Rickards

TO SAMUEL RICKARDS

Oriel College. May 30. 1837

My dear Rickards,

I hope before you receive this you will have received from T. Mozley a more useful answer to your letter than I can give. He being the Architect, I sent to him forthwith to forward to you a sketch of the Church, which I think he could easily do. What questions can be answered in running hand shall here be attended to. Our Church is fitted up for 210 persons—but we allow nearly a fourth of it for the East end, without any seats in it. The seats are 3 feet apart, which is not at all too much to allow of kneeling. There is no gallery. The fabric and its fitting up were within £800—the stone being found on the spot. This includes extra foundations (£35), which we were tempted to lay by the proximity of the rock—viz. a depth of 8 feet, common foundations being (I believe) not more than 3. Also it includes ornamental work beyond the contract at the East End, which came to £60. And the sum to be gained back for the drawback (not yet received) which we expect will be £50—that is, the cost is or might have been £145 less than I have said; which was about the amount of the original contract—viz. £663—There is no endowment—I wished part of St Mary's endowment to be transferred to Littlemore, which might easily have been done, and suitably, as the original payment to the Vicar comes from Littlemore, but the Provost had some difficulty about it. So the Chapel is but a Chapel of Ease upon St Mary's. Under the particular circumstances, its vicinity to Oxford etc, the Bishop did not hesitate to consecrate without an endowment. I cannot answer your question as to what we saved by the stone being on the spot. I should not suppose a great deal. I may be making a very bad shot—but have some fancy I have heard we might gain about £40 by it.

I have not yet heard of Mr Hull's Second Edition—it was not answered, because the thing was all over a day or two after it came out; and really I do not recollect any thing which was not in other pamphlets, except the lawyer's opinion, if that was in it. However, if it has come to a Second Edition, it certainly would be well to keep one's eye upon it.[1]

I am disposed to agree with what you say about Keble's Sermon.[2] All

[1] William Winstanley Hull published a second revised edition of his *Remarks intended to show how far Dr. Hampden may have been misunderstood and misrepresented*, London 1836. The pamphlet was an answer to the criticisms of Hampden published by H. Wilberforce, Newman, and Pusey. Hull, himself a barrister, wrote 'The law shows them a plain course if they think him heretical; why then do they not follow that course? The law has appointed a proper tribunal for the trial of heresy . . .', p. 43.

[2] His Visitation Sermon of 27 Sept. 1836, preached at Winchester Cathedral, *Primitive Tradition recognised in Holy Scripture*, London 1836.

one can say is, that new ideas *will* startle people—it is like a souse in the water —there must be the contact with the cold. If he had made it a large book, it would not have been read—by giving a little, people are induced to take in enough to get an appetite to take in more. The age is so very sluggish that it will not hear unless you bawl—you must first tread on its toes, and then apologize. What you say about our ancestors' great books is very true. I hope we shall fall back on them and imitate them at last. The Clarendon Press is going to republish Jackson, I hope—and we hope to get out an edition of Patrick.[1] I will recollect what you say about the Traditional Testimonies for certain doctrines—but it is a formidable task.

Some weeks since I had an exceedingly kind and welcome letter from Mrs Rickards on the subject of the Lyra, which I should have acknowledged, could I have got a frank. Will you tell her this and thank her for it?—I cannot account for her not having received the Lyra sooner; I gave orders in November. You give indeed a poor account of the Rectory party. I hope this nice change in the weather has before this set you all to rights

Yrs, my dear Rickards, very affectionately John H Newman

WEDNESDAY 31 MAY 1837   letter from Wood   Ward, Daman, and Orr to breakfast no—1 p   administered Sacrament to T. Cox—Mr Williams of Jesus being there dined in hall?   wrote to H W

TO HENRY WILBERFORCE

Oriel College. ⌜May 31. 1837⌝

My dear Henry,

I would have you, unless you have thought it hopeless to wait to hear from me, write to Mr Orger civilly as you propose.[2] If he evades, I think you may fairly write to the Archdeacon. Somehow I do not think I ought to write to him. I almost doubt whether I would do more—except you had an *opportunity* to make it known. But I would not publish a pamphlet, unless the said effusion had a great sale.

⌜Archdeacon Hodson has just spoken and means to publish his Charge against the Tracts.[3] I wonder how long the powder of the Popery cry will last—they must sooner or later come to the shot of argument. At present they dare not advance beyond common places and declamation.

The Bishop of Salisbury, as you have heard perhaps, has declined ordaining a B N C man, who had not Hampden's testimonial.⌝

---

[1] A twelve volume edition of the complete works of the early seventeenth century divine Thomas Jackson was published at Oxford in 1844. Various of Simon Patrick's works were republished at Oxford around this time, including his *Autobiography* in 1839, and *A Discourse concerning Prayer*, *A Treatise of Repentance and of Fasting*, and *Advice to a Friend* in 1840.

[2] Cf. letter of 16 May to Wilberforce.

[3] George Hodson, *A Charge delivered to the Clergy of the Archdeaconry of Derby at the Primary Visitation of Derby and Cheshire*, Bakewell 1837.

We want to collate the MSS of Editions of the Fathers—Till quite lately, they have been very carelessly collated. In the Vatican there are important MSS of Tertullian, I believe. If James liked a job of this kind, I would tell him more about it. At present we are chock full of Translators.

I am quite sorry this is so late—but if you knew how much I had to do, you would account for it. I have had three or four more-than-Sermons a week, besides other business—and Bowden and his brother here.

There is news I believe of some kind, but I cannot recollect it. I hope to leave this place for 3 weeks next week—chiefly for Cholderdon

⌜At this moment I have four Curates at St Mary's and Littlemore—⌝

Ever Yrs affly John H Newman

P.S. Please to tell Manning, when you write, that Rivington has sent me in a bill for sundry pounds for Tracts etc. sent for by him. I should like at his convenience to receive the money gained by them, or to have them returned to Rivington.

THURSDAY I JUNE 1837 letter from Rogers no—p. th. s. n. v. c dined in hall —Service and Lecture in Ad de Br's Chapel—Number 470 [*Ffc.*]—the last. took tea at Mr B Morrell's wrote to Rogers and sent parcel to Rivington with MS for British Critic

TO FREDERIC ROGERS

Oriel College: June 1, 1837

Your letter of this morning made me very sad indeed.[1] It was exceedingly kind in you to say what you have, and I feel it very much. Ever since I asked you what I did so abruptly, when you were here, not knowing how matters stood, I have borne your sister continually in mind, and was anxious to hear how things were. I am not certain you do not anticipate what is still future *hastily*, but I know I should just do the same in your case. If it is to turn out as you forebode, it is only a fresh instance of what I suppose one must make up one's mind to think, and what is consoling to think, that those who are early taken away are the fittest to be taken, and that it is a privilege so to be taken, and they are in their proper place when taken. Surely God would not separate from us such, except it were best both for them and for us, and

[1] Rogers wrote on 31 May to report that his sister's condition seemed beyond hope. He went on to say:
'Wood has just spoken to me about Froude's remains.—As far as I have an opinion I should say with him, publish them as soon as they are ready: Unless of course there is anything which, on consideration, he as a clergyman of the Church of England had no right to publish.—I cannot help feeling as if his death was a kind of call to publish them now. Perhaps, (or I may say certainly) I should have thought it bad policy to publish them so soon, if circumstances had not pointed that way; for I am not so ready as Wood to throw away your character for judgment and moderation; I hope it may serve you and Oxford many a good turn yet. But, as it is, I should go quo fata vocant.'

that those who are taken away are such as are most acceptable to Him seems proved by what we see; for scarcely do you hear of some especial instance of religious excellence, but you have also cause of apprehension how long such a one is to continue here. I suppose one ought to take it as the rule. We pray daily 'Thy kingdom come'—if we understand our words, we mean it as a privilege to leave the world, and we must not wonder that God grants the privilege to some of those who pray for it. It would be rather wonderful if He did not. When we use the Lord's prayer, we pray not only for our eventual regathering, but our dispersion in the interval. The more we live in the world that is not seen, the more shall we feel that the removal of friends into the unseen world is a bringing them near to us, not a separation. I really do not think this fancifulness. I think it attainable—just as our Saviour's going brought Him nearer, though invisibly, in the Spirit.

You do not say anything about your father and mother. May they, and your sisters, and yourself, and all of you be supported under whatever is to happen, is the earnest and anxious prayer of

Your very affectionate J.H.N.

PS. Keble, Pusey, Williams, Copeland, Wood and you are for the publication of F's Papers. It *is* a leap . . . *Perhaps* I may come to Town just for Dodsworth's Consecration (i.e. his Church's) if he will not think me impertinent—I will write to Rivington about Froude's papers. Unless you find it a trouble I should like you to have a talk with him. Letters are slow work in such a matter.

FRIDAY 2 JUNE 1837 letter from Christie George Waring died this morning f d walked with Keble to Littlemore—his wife and Mrs B Morrell in a fly—round by Iffley. no c

TO J. F. CHRISTIE

Oriel College. June 2. 1837

My dear Christie,

You have really quite a Scottish Second Sight—which is so good as not only to go before but to improve upon the coming event—which I hold to be a great and rare gift. However it was from no wish to put your Scottish descent to trial, that I have not written, but from that truer reason already suggested, that the plan was but inchoate and rudimental which you have at once adorned with the colours of a poetical mind and substantiated into the realities of life. This is fine writing—but one must meet the age—or like a coming event lead the moment. But to business.

We thank you for a knowledge of your plans and will fall into them. We have some notion of going with the Kebles on Thursday hence to Bisley—

whence I shall proceed to you, after two days, for two days—and hence to Mozley. This was *my* plan, should it suit you, agrestissime rerum. I am glad in this way I shall not miss your sisters.

I have no news to tell you—and am stupid—and shall be glad of a *holy* day.

Mrs Pusey is gone to Guernsey to get well—Pusey follows as soon as he can. They say a Committee of Heads of Houses is sitting to digest and reform the Corpus Statutorum—it is to be engaged till this time year.[1]

Ever Yrs affly John H Newman

TO S. F. WOOD

Oriel College. June 2. 1837

Mi Sylvi, seu Sylvani,

seu libentius audis Σίλας, you have made a good shot in what you say about my meaning in my first chapter. After Rose's critique I half thought of writing to you to ask you whether I had made a mares nest, though I thought I had not—and you have hit off pretty nearly what I meant, in your twofold distinction—to which effect I propose to append a note to a Second Edition. Under these circumstances, wishing to have the benefit of your thoughts in the matter, I do propose that your Article should be an exposition, as you offer, of 'the narrow and inadequate notions prevalence [sic] of a Church System'—and we will have the Grotianismus Detectus, or the Calvinus Grotianisans, afterwards. So I reckon you as booked.[2]

I confess I have some fears about dear F's [Froude] papers—but all parties but me are for the immediate publication—and I can not alledge any

---

[1] See note to letter of 13 Nov. to H. Wilberforce.

[2] A review of *Prophetical Office* in *Brit. Mag.*, May 1837, pp. 546–7, expressed a reservation about 'the allegation that the church-of-England system (the Via Media) is only a *theory*, existing in the writings of certain excellent divines, but never tried as a practical system.' The reviewer felt this 'not to be in harmony with history,' and that 'the doctrines and teaching of Sanderson and Hammond, etc., were most widely influential—that perhaps half that part of the nation which attended to religious inquiries was ranged under their banners.' The reviewer's conviction was 'that the real and genuine produce of "Anglicanism" is even now of large extent' but went unnoticed as one of its chief characteristics was retirement.

Wood wrote on 29 May proposing points for an article: '1. There is a life of Grotius advertized; I could take part of his subject, viz: so far as to point out that the Arminianism, or as Coleridge calls it 'Christianity according to Grotius', which succeeded the Calvinism of the Reformation and was its reaction, and which assumes to itself κατ' εξοχην the name of 'Orthodoxy', is just as non-catholic and more Rationalistic, and as far removed from the Mysterious and True system as Calvinism. 2. One might subserve your last book in a small way, thus:—That objection to it which Rose embodies in his notice in the B. M. seems very general. Now allowing for two misapprehensions which they seem to have, (1) that you are speaking of the Church qua Catholic, not (as you are) qua Anglican, and (2) that you speak of its individual religious influence, not (as you do) of it as a scientific Theological edifice, there still I suppose would be a difference at bottom between you as to its realization and completeness. And this arises from their *narrow* and *inadequate notions* of what a Church system *ought* to be. This one might bring out, e.g. by reviewing Mohler, if he treated of Church polity etc. instead of confining himself (as he does) to abstract and isolated dogmas.'

Newman did not append a note to the second edition of *Prophetical Office* but did modify his wording on pp. 20–21.

thing definite—and cannot promise myself the future. The present is my own—so I will publish while I can.[1]

I am going away from Oxford for 3 weeks—and shall be most of my time at Mozley's (Cholderton, Amesbury, Wilts)—I have some thoughts of the possibility of coming up to the consecration of Dodsworth's Church on St Peter's day—Poor D. must learn to act before speaking—at all events to choose his confidants better. I am rejoiced to hear his plans about the new Church—it will be a new era indeed. His 'beadle' ought to be in inferior orders—to discard the gold lace—and cocked hat; and to get a black habit and skull cap. Till then little is done.

I am much distressed to hear how ill Rogers' sister seems to be—but it is our lot.

Ever Yrs affectly John H. Newman.

SATURDAY 3 JUNE 1837 no, th. s. n walked to Littlemore and did duty dined with Copeland in Hall [of] Trinity to meet Kinsey

SUNDAY 4 JUNE 2nd Trinity letter from Harriet m did duty morning and afternoon Keble preached for me Marriott assisting at Sacrament leaves not fully out on the Elms. dined with Williams and Copeland to meet Mr and Mrs Neville and their two sons wrote to H and Mr Willis Dyer went down to his living for good[2]

TO MRS JOHN MOZLEY

Oriel College. June 4. 1837

My dear Jemima,

I wish I could write you a satisfactory letter on the subject of Confirmation. As to books I will mention something before I conclude; as to Sermons, I have none. I shall be writing some soon, perhaps—as a Confirmation is approaching. I will say what strikes me, but it will be difficult to come to the point in a page or two—and I am but partially informed on the subject.

I doubt whether one should look to the Service for the *doctrine* of the Church about Confirmation, though it *might* be there. Prayers are not Sermons, except accidentally. The Puritans etc. wished so to make them. They looked upon Sacraments chiefly *as* Sermons, and thought their grace *lay* in their kindling impressions in the mind. Hence they generally started with a long preachment. In the extreme Protestant (continental) Baptismal Services, e.g., you have a long exhortation. In the same spirit Bucer in King

---

[1] Wood was 'all in favor of your not delaying the Remains [[Froude's]]. It is very well to make use of one[']s character for moderation with other folks, but when they are merely in, (as here) the least accident may any moment undeceive them, and it really does not seem worth while to go out of one[']s way to avoid it.' Wood felt that Froude's views on the Eucharist were unlikely to provoke great opposition as controversial opinions were not very developed on the subject at the time.

[2] Great Waltham, Essex.

Edward's 2nd Book prefixed the Exhortation at the beginning of the Daily Service, which still forms part of the Service. In the primitive way, the worshipper did not think of himself—he came *to* God—God's House and Altar were the Sermon which addressed him and roused him. His Sacraments were the *objects* of his regard. Words were unnecessary. Hence in Ordination the *laying on* of hands is the whole—There are no words necessary—Accordingly in our Service for the Consecration of Bishops the words used in the act of consecrating are not explanatory—the word 'Bishop' is used—but there is no definition etc of the office; any more than of the word 'Confirmation' in the Confirmation Service. It was an objection of the Romans to our Consecration Service that till the Restoration the words did not even contain the word Bishop (? I *think* so.) This is answered by Courayer,[1] who shows that to this day (?) the *same* form is used in the Church of Rome, or used to be. I am not sure of my entire accuracy here—but am right in the outline. Hence in our Confirmation Service the exhortation is an address to those who come, demanding of them *what they have to give*. They give their *word* —the Bishop imposes his hand—such is the interchange.

The *action* speaks. It must be a gift. What else is meant by *laying hands on*? When a person takes an oath, the Magistrate etc administers, and witnesses it. The Bishop would do the same—if it were *merely* a promise on the part of the young. I conceive this is plain to common sense, even if the Bishop said not a word in administering the rite. It must be a peculiar sort of blessing. Every prayer is a sort of blessing; but laying on of hands is evidently a special kind of blessing, before we go on to look into Antiquity, to see the meaning of it. Poor people feel this, as often as they wish, as sometimes happens, to come for confirmation again and again.

Next, *what* is the blessing? The prayer tells us as follows—that those who have been regenerated and pardoned, are to be 'strengthened' by the Holy Ghost, and to have imparted to them the Seven gifts of grace which were poured upon Christ; again that they are to be 'defended', made to 'continue' and 'increase'; lastly that they are to be placed under the protection of God's 'fatherly hand' and to be led forward in obedience. Here we have an 'interpretation' quite sufficient of the word 'Confirmation;' viz as a deep fixing, establishing, rooting in of that grace which was first given in Baptism. These things are *prayed for*, and just *so far* as laying on of hands has somewhat of an *assurance* in it over and above a prayer (in *whatever* measure, more or less,) *so far* are they granted.

[1] Pierre Francois Le Courayer's *Dissertation sur la Validité des Ordinations des Anglais*, Brussels 1723, was a defence of Anglican Orders which caused a great stir when published. One of the objections Courayer answered was that of the Abbé E. Renaudot, who based his charge against English Orders on the fact that the form for Ordination of Bishops had been equivocal, (using only the words 'Take the Holy Ghost'), until the revision at the Restoration, when the qualifying words 'for the Office and Work of a Bishop' were added. Courayer dismissed the objection, firstly because the preceding prayers gave sufficient qualification, and secondly he noted '. . . that the addition in question is unprecedented, and that no trace of it is found in the ancient Pontificals, or even in those which are now in use in the Church of Rome.' *op. cit.*, English Translation, Oxford 1844, p. 107.

In accordance with this the Ancient Church seems to have believed as follows—that the Holy Ghost, who is the present Lord and animating Principle ⟨Power⟩ of the Church, communicates Himself variously to its members;—first in Baptism, in another way in Confirmation, in another way in the Holy Eucharist. His first gift or communication is forgiveness, justification, acceptance—and this is the *distinguishing* gift of Baptism. He is the Spirit of Justification. vid 1 Cor vi. 11. 2 Cor iii. 6–9. This gift He gives complete and whole, and such as is never repeated in this life;—but He also gives the beginnings of other gifts, which are *more fully* given afterwards, viz His sanctifying influences; and since these are those which are more commonly, even in Scripture, called the Spirit, it follows that in *one* sense the Spirit is not given, or hardly given in Baptism. I would have you look to what Jeremy Taylor says on Baptism (I think in his Life of Christ, or Holy Living)[1] and you will find some writers, such as Tertullian,[2] say, that Baptism imparts forgiveness, Confirmation the Spirit; which only means, that confirmation seals in their fulness, winds up and consigns, completes the entire round of those sanctifying gifts which are begun, which are given inchoately in Baptism. If it be said that Confirmation is thus made a Sacrament, I answer that it is properly an integral part of the Baptismal rite; I do not say of the essence, or an essential part, of Baptism, but an integral part, just as a hand is an integral part of our body, yet may be amputated without loss of life. And in ancient times it was administered at the time of Baptism, as its ratification on the part of the Bishop. Even now it is administered at seven years old in the Church of Rome, and it would be well were the custom the same with us—but we, having no rite of penance, seem to substitute this.

If it be asked, what is the *peculiar* grace of Confirmation, I answer it seems as the Greek name implies to be a Perfecting, or man-making. We in it become men in Christ Jesus. The baptismal grace is principally directed towards the abolition of existing guilt, e.g. original sin—the child is comparatively speaking incapable of actual. The grace of Confirmation is directed to arm the Christian against his three great enemies, which, when entering into his field of trial, he at once meets. This is alluded to in Keble's Poem on Confirmation.[3]

This, I know, is but a sketch of what might be said—If you have any other questions you want answered, let me know. I know of no *familiar* book on the subject—Dodsworth ⟨(at Burns's)⟩ has written one which it

[1] Jeremy Taylor, *The Life of Our Blessed Lord and Saviour Jesus Christ*, and *The History of the Life and Death of the Holy Jesus*, first published in 1649; and *The Rule and Exercises of Holy Living*, first published in 1650.

[2] See Tertullian, *De Baptismo*, VII and VIII.

[3] *The Christian Year*, 'Confirmation':
'So should thy champions, ere the strife,
By holy hands o'er-shadowed kneel,
So, fearless for their charmed life,
Bear, to the end, thy Spirit's seal.'

would be as well you should look at[1]—and Eyre of Salisbury ⟨(at Riving-tons)⟩ another.[2] But I should recommend you to read Jeremy Taylor's work on Confirmation—Χρίσις Τελειωτική.[3] Also his remarks on Baptism in either his Holy Living or Life of Christ. ⌜He is a writer essentially untrust-worthy—i.e. if some external attraction meets him, he cannot resist it, he is like an iron vessel navigating between loadstone islands. The necessity, e.g. of seeming an Anti-papist will draw all his nails out.⌝ But, as far as I know, he is correct in these works and gives a good deal of information. It is too difficult however for Eliz-[4]

MONDAY 5 JUNE 1837 no p th s n v c Daman went down walked to Littlemore—reading prayers—dined with Mr B Morrell to meet Keble and his wife

TUESDAY 6 JUNE Radcliffe Service—Bishop of Ripon preached. Dornford in Oxford—(a balloon went up) dined with Copeland wrote to J by A.M. to Bowden by Johnson and to Mr Irons, thanking him for the present of his books.

TO J. W. BOWDEN

⌜Oriel. June 6. 1837.⌝

My dear Bowden,

W. Froude happening to be here when your letter came, I should have commissioned him to get from his Father letters, but for your second. The case was of such a nature, that, even hearing it from any one, a person would wish to be of service in it. It so happened I was confined to my rooms nearly the whole time I was at Malta with a miserable cough, and knew no one. At the same time a place like Malta changes its inhabitants so fast, that I am not certain Archdeacon F. would now know people. So I was glad when your news came about Captain Swinbourne's interposition.

Arvad and Gemaddim are taken from Ezek. XXVII.11 ⌜How very dis-graceful the closing the Abbey was—I hope you had an opportunity of telling your mind to the Bishop of Hereford.[5]

I believe, but you must have heard it if it is true, that on the Bishop elect of Norwich[6] signifying to the Archbishop his intention of proposing

---

[1] William Dodsworth, *Confirmation . . . Scriptural in its Origin and needful to be observed*, London 1835.
[2] Daniel James Eyre, *The Rite of Confirmation explained . . .*, third edition, London 1837.
[3] ['Perfective Anointing'], *A Discourse of Confirmation* in R. Heber (ed.), *The Whole Works . . .*, London 1828, XI, 215–97.
[4] The remainder of the letter is missing.
[5] [[Grey?]] Edward Grey was still Bishop of Hereford, he died later in the month. Bowden had found that there was not the usual service with prayer for the royal family at Westminster Abbey on the afternoon of 24 May, the choir having been given a half holiday for Princess Victoria's coming-of-age. He commented, 'thus one of the modes by which we celebrate this important epoch in a future sovereign's life is the closing of God's temple, and the cessation of the Church's daily prayers for her and her family—This it is to live in a "liberal and enlightened age".'
[6] [[Stanley]] Edward Stanley was to be consecrated on 11 June.

Arnold to preach his Consecration Sermon the Archbishop wrote to him to say *he* had appointed his Chaplain, Mr Rose.

Mr Morris's book is just out.[1] I am told it is a 4s concern, which decides me against buying it. He goes through six heads, Littlemore coming in somehow. The last is the Lyra, which he calls 'Apostolical Hymns'. I have not seen the book—but doubt not it is trash nullo vitio redemptum—for a vitium would make it at least lively. It is dedicated to the King, and has some ancient arms of the University stuck in the Title page—does this represent the Popery times of Oxford?

I am going away on Thursday for Tom Keble's—thence to Christie's: expecting to arrive at T. Mozley's by this day week or tomorrow week; and to return by St John Baptist's day. We have pretty well decided on publishing Froude's remains at once. Harrison's article[2] will become two—one this time, one next. Wood has promised one for October, and I think I shall have one on Hampden. You have done enough for a long while, but should anything come into your head before January or April 1838, it will be acceptable.

I almost incline to publish a volume of Lectures on Justification at Christmas—Pusey wishes it and I see advantages. We hope Keble may be persuaded to expand his Sermon on Tradition into a volume.

Hoping you have moved successfully and are comfortably established.⌉

Ever yrs affly John H. Newman

⌈P.S. I have sent up to the Curate's Fund £20 from our early Communion as a specimen of what would be good to do generally.⌉

WEDNESDAY 7 JUNE 1837 letter from Mrs W W Commemoration—Keble read oration in praise of Founders of Collegiate system dined in Common Room first time—Williams, Copeland, and Harrison with me; besides, Eden, Sheppard, Litton and Stranger. wrote to R W and Christie

THURSDAY 8 JUNE went with Keble and his wife and Williams to Bisley no services[3] but Itinerarium Clericorum[4]

FRIDAY 9 JUNE Williams went to Norman Hill m. but no other Christie came over rainy walked with T. Keble and Christie to Oakridge C. to dinner from Stroude (news that the king was very ill) Christie went back to Badgeworth

---

[1] [[afterwards Dr Morris of New College? a musical man]] Peter Maurice, Chaplain of New College and All Souls, *The Popery of Oxford confronted, disavowed, and repudiated*, London 1837. His other anti-Tractarian and anti-Catholic works included *Popery in Oxford*, Oxford 1833. He also composed several hymn tunes. In a letter of 26 March to B. Harrison, Pusey wrote: 'The walls of Oxford have been placarded for the last week with "Popery of Oxford" and its citizens been edified with the exhibition of Newman's and my name as Papists; all done by Rev. P. Maurice of New C., author of "Popery in Oxford." I have not seen the placard or the pamphlet; Maurice seems an ill-omened name to us. N. only hopes that no one of our friends will answer it, for we ought not to stand upon the defensive.'

[2] [[for the British Critic]] 'Attack upon the Universities-Oxford', *Brit. Crit.*, 22, 1837 (July), 168–215; and 'Universities of England', *Brit. Crit.*, 22, 1837 (Oct.), 397–438.

[3] Newman refers to the Breviary hours as 'services' here and below.

[4] From the Roman Breviary.

SATURDAY 10 JUNE   no services   left T. Keble's for Christie's—Mr Murray Brown to dinner—Copeland and his brother afterwards.

SUNDAY 11 JUNE   3rd after Trinity St Barnabas   preached for Christie morning and afternoon two of F's Sermons, at Shurtington ⟨?⟩[1] and Badgeworth   assisted him in Sacrament   no services   Spranger took my duty at Oxford, as my Curate

MONDAY 12 JUNE   m. nothing else   walked with Christie to Dry hill

TUESDAY 13 JUNE   into Cheltenham with Christie and his sisters, he and I to breakfast with the Copelands—no ss [services]   I set off for Cholderton *T. Mozley's* where arrived about 5

WEDNESDAY 14 JUNE   letter from Rogers   no c   sent parcel to Christie   went with J M in chaise to Amesbury—thence walked to Stonehenge

TO J. F. CHRISTIE

Cholderton. June 14. 1837

My dear Christie,

Fearing you may have inconvenience from the want of your shoes, I send them. Mine, which should have occupied their place, may be sent to Oxford per coach. Since I have this opportunity, I will scribble what comes into my head.

This is an exceedingly pretty village—as far as *near* view goes exceeding yours, and most others. It is rich in chesnuts, elms, limes, and id genus omne—The country about is certainly bare, but good for riding. I was agreeably disappointed in my journey hither—far from the dreariness you foretold, it was beautiful. Little bleakness—and we came between Marlborough and this, through various parks and forests.

I forgot to tell you, which was very stupid in me, for besides other reasons I had beforehand made a point of mentioning it, how extremely useful I have found the Bellarmine you gave me.[2] It has *written* my work just published—and it has written my lectures on Justification. I had kept the Library copy in my rooms till I was ashamed—and, besides there is all the difference, between having *one* volume of a work, not one's own, in one's rooms, and all the volumes ever with liberty to pull about and make marks in. You really could not [have] given me a book which I so needed, have so used, and found so useful; though *why* you gave me any, to this day I have never been able to make out.

I shall book your observation about the increase of Justification, which is important; then I shall add in a note, 'for this further approximation to the Tridentine Council, I am indebted to the Revd J. F. C. Fellow of O.C.'[3]

James, I hope, will write you a line—Harriet is regretting she has nothing

[1] Great Sturdington, near Badgeworth, Glos.
[2] Christie had made Newman a gift of Bellarmine's *Disputationes*, 3 vols, Paris 1608. See Volume V, p. 317.
[3] Among Newman's theological notes there is a slip in Christie's hand giving references about Justification to Pole, Sadoleto, and Contarini. Newman does not seem to have used the references in the *Lectures* and did not insert any acknowledgement to Christie.

to send by way of swelling the value as well as size of my parcel. One thing I forgot, which is irreparable now—I am sure your sisters sing—they seemed so to do, from their mode of singing in Church—and I meant to have got at the truth of it and to have acted accordingly—so this was a floor of mine. Pray give them my kindest remembrances, and tell them I have not yet forgiven myself for making Strawberry so hot yesterday morning.

Ever Yrs affly John H Newman

THURSDAY 15 JUNE 1837 no p s. n. v. c. drove Aunt N. to Andover—report of King's death[1] Two Mr Fawcetts and Mr Overhagen ⟨Vanderhagen⟩ ⟨Vandermuler⟩ [Vandermeulen] to dinner

FRIDAY 16 JUNE parcel from Rivington with proof for British Critic which I revised and returned in evening letter from Bowden almost f. through day not l. p. th. s. n. v. c but m. pen: ps: [penitential psalms] ord. comm. an. [ordo commendationis animae] v. off def. [vesperae officii defunctorum]

SATURDAY 17 JUNE sent letter to Mrs W W m.l. offic. def. pen. ps. nothing else walked with T.M. to Mr Price's Newton Toney

TO MRS JOHN MOZLEY

[17 June 1837][2]

My dear Jemima

Thanks for your tablets which I have already found very useful. You have not told me the name of Mr Mozley's banker, so I assume it is Williams'. and have ordered Rivington to pay into his account £100 now, and £100 in about 2 months time—when it is paid, I will ask about the interest of money. —It seems to me you are quite right in what you do for Aunt[3]—and I have talked to Aunt about it—and she assents. She would quite assent if left alone —and I think the best way will be to drop the subject till her return. I think she would like this. It is quite preposterous that a married woman should have nothing to spend but on herself (I am taking the lowest ground, as if John were out of the question—though you are a Mozley, you are a Christian). Can any husband, who is good for any thing, like his wife only to have so much as she spends on herself? and if you are bound as a Christian to spend on others as well as yourself, who has claims before Aunt? must we not be just before we are generous? is it not a case of justice? Why even as a Governess, to take the very lowest ground, she has earned from our justice what she may claim from our gratitude. And when a certain sum of money has come to you virtually, I cannot see any impropriety. I am writing abruptly

[1] William IV died on 20 June.

[2] The letter is printed in G. Tillotson's *Newman Prose and Poetry*, London 1957, where it is described as 'note on the margins of a letter from Harriett, 17 June 1837'.

[3] Newman added a note, i.e. giving her money; H [Harriett] had said *not*, as it would mean the Mozleys knew of her affair[s]'.

having little room. It comes to this—are you to give nothing to God of what he has given you? I think you quite right.

Ever yrs affly, John H Newman.

SUNDAY 18 JUNE 1837 4th after Trinity did duty at Cholderton in morning preaching Number 471[1] in afternoon at Boscombe preaching Number 7

MONDAY 19 JUNE wrote to Rogers and Spranger letter from W W. Mrs H W still dangerously ill walked to Fyfield calling on Mrs Baynes and Mr Vandermuler off def. m and l Ps: grad: [psalmi graduales] no more

TO FREDERIC ROGERS

June 19. 1837.

. . . Archdeacon F. [Froude] has from the first intended to publish H's papers—only I am trying to *save* him expense. I will not show Rivington one line of the MS.—The idea grows on me which you scouted of publishing one volume first. I have so much to say in favour of it that I cannot do justice to it—First and foremost, the Private Thoughts are so very interesting and instructive that I am sanguine about their selling—i.e. among University men and now 2 or 3 Octavo Volumes is a formidable purchase,—one volume is not. The volume would contain most interesting matter and various— (Private Thoughts, Essay on Poetry, Sermons [,] Essay on Rationalism etc) and would quite stand clear of politics. The Church and State papers would be reserved. Then again the present papers, being more touching as far as they are private would prepare the way for the others—would interest men's sympathies and excite their respect, before their political prejudices were interfered with. Then again J Mozley is idle till Lincoln is decided, he is unsettled, and I believe in *fact* the alternative lies between publishing one volume now, and postponing all till next year. He is not ready. Unless therefore you strongly dissent, you may notice this alternative to Rivington.

Your story about Airy is good:[2] so is Bowden's about Mr Lefevre very good. Is it not curious if the technical eclecticism of Protestant Theology and the arbitrariness of Church of Englandism, has been the *temptation* ⟨trial⟩ against which many liberals have been self-split? so that there is a chance of our being at least *countenanced* by many of them, some from really feeling a relief in our views, others from feeling in them some indulgence[?] of latitudinarianism. Acland's father (if not Acland himself) Mr Stephen—

---

[1] *P.S.* IV, 13, 'The Invisible World'. Preached again on the following Sunday morning.
[2] Rogers wrote on 13 June: 'I was a good deal amused yesterday at hearing your sermons discussed—by Airey (ο μεγας) and an Evangelical—each had read them with the hope and intention of finding something heretical—Airey that he might approve, the other that he might be disgusted—both had been disappointed, Airey took the line of defending you against the bigotry of the English Church . . .'

85

Jacobson—Again Colquhoun, Sir G. Grey, Airey and now Mr Lefevre have all shown symptoms of interest or much more.

P.S. Rivington says the Xtian Observer has increased the sale of the Tracts.

TUESDAY 20 JUNE 1837   news of the King's extreme illness—all but c.   walked with J M caught in rain   news of King's death between 2 and 3 A M

WEDNESDAY 21 JUNE   Eyre called and dined   m. l. p. th. s. and E. P. [Evening Prayer]

THURSDAY 22 JUNE   walked with J M to Quarley   Mrs H W. out of danger   took tea with the Tanners.   m. l. p. lit. [litany]

FRIDAY 23 JUNE   Vigilia S. J. Baptistae   Mr Baynes called as J M. and I were setting off to Salisbury where went over Cathedral, over old Sarum and to Bemerton.   called on Eyre, not at home.   f.d. and thro' day.   v. and nothing more   wrote to G. and R. and to Wilson

SATURDAY 24 JUNE   St John Baptist   letter from H. W.   all but v. c. and E. P.   W W junior went home   walked with T.M.

SUNDAY 25 JUNE   5th after Trinity   letter from Wilson.   did duty morning at Boscombe preaching Number 471 and afternoon at Cholderton preaching Number 472[1]

MONDAY 26 JUNE   parcel from G and R.   walked with J M   all but c. and E. P.

TUESDAY 27 JUNE   sent back parcel to G and R.   wrote to Wilson   T.M. went to Visitation at Salisbury.   walked with J M

WEDNESDAY 28 JUNE   hay making began here   walked with J M   only l. v. c.

THURSDAY 29 JUNE   St Peter's day   m. l. itiner. cler. [itinerarium clericorum]   left for Southampton (W W's)

FRIDAY 30 JUNE   (Aunt N. left for F's Bristol)   W W went to Town.   Wilson took me over to Hursley   Ryder and Wordsworth to dinner.

TO JOHN KEBLE

⌐Hursley[2] June 30/37.⌐

My dear Keble

For many reasons, if you do not object, I think it will be best to publish the first volume of H F's Remains first. The direct reason is that J Mozley ought to have more time for his part—and I am unwilling to put off all for a part. The volume to be published would contain, The Thoughts, Sermons, Essays on Poetry, Liturgies etc, and on Rationalism. This is pretty much in the *order* you mentioned, which on consideration seemed to me best.—⌐I am sanguine that the volume will take with University men⌐ and others—and if so, *one* volume would sell, where two or three would not. Again this volume will interest persons in F's favor, who do not know him; before the publication of the papers about St Thomas, which might offend prejudices, and seem mere ἀγωνίσματα[3] of talent. ⌐I have transcribed the Private

[1] *P.S.* VIII, 4, 'The Call of David'.
[2] Keble was away.
[3] 'displays'.

Thoughts, and am deeply impressed with their *attractive* character⌐ to persons who will read them—⌐they are⌐ very taking, and ⌐full of instruction and interest, as I think all will feel.⌐

These *Thoughts*, (I wish you would think of a good title instead of this) certainly will do a great deal of good; and I wish I could put down half what I feel on the subject. ⌐I have transcribed them for your *imprimatur*. If you say 'Yes' and send them to me, I propose to go to press almost immediately.⌐

My reasons for publishing what I have transcribed are such as the following—

These Thoughts will show people what is the real use of such memoranda, and what is the true character of them, not to ascertain our spiritual state in God's sight, but by way of improving ourselves, discovering our faults etc.

They show *how* a person may indulge *metaphysical* speculations to the utmost extent and yet be *practical*. It might be a good lesson to various Cambridge men and others.

They contain very deep truths and valuable remarks, so as to demand publication in themselves—and useful hints too for the Christian's practice.

⌐They present a remarkable instance of the temptation to rationalism, self-speculation etc. subdued.⌐ When I look around and see others carried away, I sometimes say, 'Well after all, minds are so different—such a one's *talent* lies in a rationalistic line', or 'he has not the *mental power* for what is *called* mysticism—' but now in dear H F's case, we see the strong temptation fairly met and overcome. ⌐We see his mind only breaking out into more original and beautiful discoveries, from that very repression which seemed at first likely to be the utter prohibition of his powers. He used playfully to say 'His highest ambition was to be a humdrum', and by sacrificing the *prospect* of originality he has become in the event more original.⌐ His profound Church views, as brought out in the Becket Papers, have sometimes seemed to me as a sort of gracious reward for his denying himself that vulgar originality which is rationalistic.

Lastly these Thoughts will most powerfully interest the reader in whatever H. F. writes, I am sure—so that it is the best introduction to any thing else. Look at his remarks on Inspiration (p 63 etc)[1]—for (some of) the reasons above mentioned, I am inclined to print them as well as the rest, but I want your opinion.

Please, let me have the MS back, when you have done with it. ⌐Hursley is a most beautiful place⌐

Ever Yrs affly J H N

P.S. Please look at my note on p 19 on a passage in p 20—and correct, re-write, or erase. It is *intended* to meet an objection which I think will be

---

[1] See *Remains* I, 123–7, for Froude's remarks on Inspiration of 1827–28.

raised (that our Saviour's name is not mentioned in these Thoughts) by peculiars etc., but takes the form as it ought to do of mere remark.[1]

I will send you the *proofs* of these Thoughts, if you think you should like to see, as they pass through the Press, whether a sentence here or there should not be cut out.

SATURDAY 1 JULY 1837 went to Winchester with Ryder and thence to Oxford. found letters from Goldsmid, M R G[,] Christie, G. and R.[,] C.

SUNDAY 2 JULY 6th Trinity Spranger read prayers in morning and assisted at Sacrament I read in afternoon and preached Number 319 Vaughan and I dined in Common Room wrote to Mr Goldsmid and Mozley

MONDAY 3 JULY M P E P. no c wrote to Shortland sent parcel to G and R

TUESDAY 4 JULY called on Mrs Trower, H Jenkyns who had left and the Provost who had gone to Bath walked with Copeland to Woodperry calling on Wilson no E P or c. dined with Golightly to meet the Trowers

WEDNESDAY 5 JULY letter from Rogers M P E P *all* services walked to Littlemore—where read prayers Bloxam to dinner—Liddell and S. Denison with Vaughan—Woolcombe [of] Ex. [Exeter College] with Eden Spiers' boy came to be examined for Confirmation

TO FREDERIC ROGERS

July 5, 1837.

I have many things to write about, and hardly know which to begin with.[2]

I send you a number of extracts from Froude's letters to me. It was Isaac Williams's suggestion . . . I propose that a selection of letters, such as this, should follow on the 'Private Thoughts,' as displaying his mind. Read them attentively. If you think there is a chance of their doing, I must apply for yours, Keble's, Williams's, and his home letters. Query to whom did he write when abroad?

My reasons for this selection are such as the following: 1. to show his mind, his unaffectedness, playfulness, brilliancy, which nothing else would show. His letters approach to conversation, to show his delicate mode of

[1] When published, a note was appended to the Journal to explain Froude's reticence about using Christ's name, see *Remains* I, 68–9. The editors explained that Froude, 'though petitioning for the grace of the Third Person in the Blessed Trinity, . . . does not introduce the name of Him, from and by whom the Holy Ghost is vouchsafed to us; and this circumstance may be a comfort to those who cannot bring themselves to assume the tone of many popular writers of this day, yet are discouraged by the peremptoriness with which it is exacted of them. The truth is, that a mind alive to its own real state, often shrinks to utter what it most dwells upon . . . In such a state of mind the appointed prayers of the Church are most valuable, as enabling it to speak its desires without using its own words.'

[2] Copeland's copied extracts preserve the following passage ignored by *Moz.*, which would seem to come from early in the letter:

'. . . You would oblige me if you could undertake yourself or Wood with you the negociations about publishing F's papers, i.e. to propose them first to Rivington, then to Leslie, then to any other who strikes you . . . *If no one will undertake the speculation, then* I have a place in my head for printing and publishing, but the first object is to save Archdeacon F. if possible the expense of publishing,—and this I wish you to try.'

implying, not expressing, sacred thoughts; his utter hatred of pretence and humbug. I have much to say on the danger which (I think) at present besets the Apostolical movement of getting *peculiar* in externals, i.e. formal, manneristic, etc. Now, Froude disdained all *show* of religion. In losing him we have lost an important correction. I fear our fasting, etc., may get ostentatious. His letters are a second-best preventive. 2. To make the work interesting, nothing takes so much as these private things. 3. To show the history of the formation of his opinions. Vaughan was observing the other day that we never have the history of men in the most interesting period of their life, from eighteen to twenty-eight or thirty, when they are *forming*; now this gives Froude's. 4. To show how deliberately and dispassionately he formed his opinions; they were not taken up as mere fancies. This invests them with much consideration. Here his change from Tory to Apostolical is curious. 5. To show the interesting *growth* of his mind, how indolence was overcome etc.; to show his love of mathematics, his remarkable struggle against the lassitude of disease, his working to the *last*. 6. For the intrinsic merit of his remarks.

If you think the notion entertainable, I wish you could put the MS. into the hands of some person who is a good judge, yet more impartial than ourselves, in order to ascertain his *impression* of it. The difficulty is, he ought to have seen the 'Private Thoughts,' of which it is a continuation in fact. I thought of Acland, except that he is a fastidious man. What say you to Hope? But I leave it to your judgment.

If you and the other agree in countenancing the notion, then send down the MS. to Keble with an enumeration of the *reasons* for publishing it which I have given above. You see I have hardly any letters from Barbadoes about the *place*, and none (of course) from Italy. These, when added, will increase and diversify the interest of the whole.

I propose in the preface to say briefly that 'the author had his own opinions about some of the agents in the ecclesiastical revolution of the sixteenth century, which he was as free to hold as the contrary; that we are not bound to individuals, and that the same liberty by which we are able to speak against Henry VIII. may be extended to our judgement of Cranmer.'[1]

I am going to review Lamennais' work in October.[2] It is *most curious*.[3]

[1] The following passage occurs in Copeland's extracts:
'And I mean to cut out (as the red brackets show) all strong *doctrine*, as far as may be, confining his attacks to those which are *historical*, against Protestantism, Jewel etc. etc
What do you mean about my strong meat about the transfer of affections in the British Critic. I have only written about Francké. As to Boone I am perfectly disgusted at his article about Hampden, and have written to tell him so. I should not wonder if it issued in a split, though I should not do it at once of course. Beg Wood to write Boone a line telling him his subject for the October number.'
Newman had written the article 'The Life of Augustus Herman Franké', *Brit. Crit.*, 22, 1837 (July), 94–116. Newman noted in his own copy, 'the last 2½ pages are Pusey's in substance'.
[2] 'Affairs of Rome', *Brit. Crit.*, 22, 1837 (Oct.), 261–83.
[3] The following passage occurs in Copeland's extracts:
'Have you any view about Hampden's Pamphlet? What do people think? I so fear it will be made the excuse for the Bishops ratting—but what to do! I have talked with Sewell and he

As to the statutes,[1] I do not suppose any of us will differ in *principle*, though I have not interchanged a word with any one. *We* are at liberty to alter our statutes, therefore let us *in honorem Dei* alter them. But *what* alterations? As to the *sermo latinus*, I should consent to that being altered; but even here I think it would be most respectful rather to append the alteration as a sort of perpetual suspension than to obliterate it.

My reason for wishing to keep the original text is, that a statute, though obsolete, often lets one into the *spirit* of the foundation, and is, therefore, very important for direction even when not literally obeyed. I should like the alterations to be appended; but this is a matter of expedience.

Next, perhaps some persons would go further than I as to *what* should be repealed. I *would not repeal* the reading Scripture in Hall. Must I then at once return to it? This is not *necessary*, though I should like it. It is sometimes put as a dilemma, you must either repeal your statutes or keep them. I deny it; it is a shrewd argument for a lawyer or politician, not for a divine. Any divine must acknowledge that all of us take a most solemn vow of universal obedience in baptism, which yet we neither attempt to keep nor repeal. I mean that the highest obedience is a *privilege*, and that persons by transgressing lose the privilege, are unworthy of it, and not only do not, but are not allowed to, enjoy it. We are bound to go to church, but a person under an interdict cannot. We are bound to reprove others, but a penitent may not consistently with his fallen state. In like manner we inherit a second best obedience to the statutes; we cannot at will reverse the sins of our forefathers, and retraverse the course of centuries, any more than at will we could repeal the Emancipation Act. We are committed—'go with the men.' It were a privilege to obey the statutes, but our ἦθος is beneath them. We cannot force up our ἦθος; or if this or that person thinks himself equal to certain observances, the majority of fellows may not be. In retaining the statutes, then, not observing them, we are no more breaking our oaths than a statesman breaks his baptismal oath in holding a duty to make the Church dominant, yet not agitating for the reinforcement of the Test Act.

As to the injunctions of Parliament against the praying for the dead, which you say has virtually repealed a portion of our statutes, I agree with you, and, with my views of the omnipotence of Parliament in such a matter, am quite content to urge with you that *nothing more* need be done. The Provost will grant *enough* has been done, and I will allow that *not too much*; he will say Parliament has done good and no harm. From what you say I suppose you will agree with me in all this. Let me know.

was strongly against doing any thing. Such was my leaning at first, Pusey being the other way. Then whether the rising B. As will not be carried away if we are silent. That vile article in the B. C. spoils my purpose of inserting any article in the October against him. Query as far as our Rulers are concerned whether it is not a case of "decipi vult populus"? One is not bound for ever to be blowing life into the cold embers. We have done our part already. They say he is getting popular with the undergraduates. We want a formal treatise on "doctrinal statements." I have thought whether it might make a Tract.

[1] See note to letter of 13 Nov. to Henry Wilberforce.

I saw —— for a day last week,[1] and was as grave (yet natural) as a judge the whole time, except for one instant, when, to try ——, I suddenly on a pause broke out with a sentence like this, turning round sharp: 'So, ——, you wish, it seems, to change the monarchy into a republic?' (this was not it, but like it). —— shrunk up as if twenty thousand pins had been thrust into him; his flesh goosified, his mouth puckered up, and he looked the picture of astonishment, awe, suspicion and horror. After this trial I went back to my grave manner, and all was well. Now don't you see that, for his good and comfort, one must put on one's company coat before him? he cannot bear one's shirt-sleeves.

Stanley attends Sacrament in St. Mary's now.

Cholderton is a very nice place to my fancy; the village itself beautiful.

I see the 'Christian Advocate'[2] at Cambridge has written against the Tracts.

Excuse me if I have not courage to read over this frightful scrawl.

Ever yours affectionately John H. Newman.

P.S. I am told that the 'Christian Observer' has reviewed the 'Lyra,' and in so doing has spoken with interest of Froude as the *most spiritual* and least bigoted, etc., of the whole set.[3]

Keble wants to raise a sum for the endowment of Otterbourn, and I have promised to raise ten pounds. I wish if you see Acland or R. Williams, or any other wealthy friend, you would ask them from me for one pound towards it.

THURSDAY 6 JULY 1837 Trower, his wife, and friend, Golightly, Daman, and Vaughan to breakfast M P E P all services [Hours of the Breviary] in future (unless specified) except on Sundays when those only which *are* specified dined in Common Room

FRIDAY 7 JULY letter from I. Williams Copeland went for week? M P E P f d called on Mrs Hawkins wrote to W.F. [,] Bowden and Sir R Inglis

TO J. S. BOONE

July 7/37

Dear Sir

I propose to send you for the October number of the Review [*Brit. Crit.*] a Paper on La Mennais' new work—one from Mr Wood on I forget

---

[1] This possibly refers to Nathaniel Goldsmid.

[2] George Pearson. See letter of 12 Sept. from Keble, placed before that of 17 Sept. to him.

[3] 'There is a very delightful eclogue by Beta [Froude]—we lament to be informed that the amiable and accomplished writer is no more . . . we turn from doctrinal aberrations to such pieces as these . . . And then to all this there is to be added, what we have too often had to lament in this volume, that there is no thought which is not true, as well as beautiful.' *The Christian Observer*, 427, 1837 (July), 472–3.

what subject, but he shall write to you—and one from Mr Harrison in continuation. Will you allow me to express some disappointment at the article in the July Number on Dr Hampden,[1] as I do not conceive he has given up any thing but *words*, whereas his error was one of things—I cannot but think that most persons who have studied Bull's Defensio Fid[ei] Nic[aenae] will agree with me in this.

Yrs etc. J H N

The Revd J S Boone

TO J. W. BOWDEN

⌐Oriel College. July 7. 1837⌐

My dear Bowden,

Your story was most excellent—it could not be better—it was superb—I have been quite ashamed of myself, however, for laughing—for really I believe the hero of it is a far better fellow inwardly than his outward bearing promises. *I* at least am bound to say so—for the article in the New Church of England Review about me is his: and since it came out, I have felt compunctions at my laughing. It has been a most capital hit in him to *secure a new Review*, one which I verily expected would be against us. The Review is now committed to the Oxford movement. And really the way it is written is like a man who felt what he said—though perhaps I am blinded by his compliments.[2]

⌐I stopped to Cholderton a week longer than I expected, and so missed Johnson, I suppose.⌐ I called on Mr Baynes, and saw his wife, and mother. They are some way off from Cholderton, and not settled yet—but he was kind enough to come over to call. He has been far from well lately.

When do you go to the North? now that the Dutchess (Duchess?) of N.[3] is so important a person, what a thing it would be to be able to cram her! but I believe you are near thirty miles off.

[1] 'Introduction to Dr Hampden's Bampton Lectures', *Brit. Crit.*, 22, 1837 (July), 163–8, reviewed R. D. Hampden's introduction to the newly published second edition of his Bampton Lectures for 1832. The review opened in an irenic tone, claiming that the new introduction 'certainly exhibits Dr. Hampden's system in a more favourable light'. The reviewer went on to make several criticisms, mainly concerning the obscurity of the argument in parts, and the confusingly general way in which Hampden used the term 'facts' to cover doctrines, propositions, events, transactions, or universal truths. The review ended with the recommendation that: 'The use and abuse of technical terms in theology, and the changes of meaning which they have undergone, amidst the fluctuations of thought and language;—the nature and history, the origin and progress of the scholastic philosophy . . . the labours, and errors, of men, who have been equally the subjects of absurd blame and extravagant encomium;—these are the topics on which the Christian divine ought not, surely, to be quite in the dark. It will be a benefit, therefore, to *some* of Dr. Hampden's opponents, if they are induced to read systematically, and to think closely, upon the matters which he has brought under discussion.' See Volume V for the dispute of the previous year about Hampden.

[2] Newman did not keep the letter of Bowden's containing the story, but cf. letter of 23 July to Mrs Bowden. The review was, 'Newman's Romanism and Popular Protestantism', *New Church of England Review*, July 1837, 167–76.

[3] Northumberland. The Duchess had been governess to Princess Victoria. The family lived chiefly at Alnwick, Northumberland.

Your news of the Tracts was good. Pusey cannot at once finish his second Edition of his Baptism—though he is about it. This is, I suppose, what Rivington meant, for no Tracts are out of print besides. I am told the Christian Observer in a review of the Lyra speaks of Froude as the most spiritual of us. Thus at once it displays its usual extreme absurdity, which is thrown out sponte suâ, and will help to puff the Lyra.

I am told Maurice's pamphlet is quite mad, as you say, and too bad to be entertaining.[1]

⌐Cholderdon is an extremely pretty village, and the whole place to me very attractive⌐—ladies indeed like more of trim cultivation—but ⌐an expanse of down ensures a bracing air at all seasons, and the near view is on the contrary quite shrouded with beautiful trees—so it is every thing that is desirable.⌐

We are very barren in news here, as you may suppose. ⌐I hope to hear some account from you about the consecration of Dodsworth's Church.⌐[2] I do not know the formal name of it. You know how anxious the Rogers's are about one of their daughters?—This is a most shabby letter, but I do not like being so long silent.

⌐I am disgusted with Boone's article on Hampden, and have written to say so. Mrs Pusey is not much better yet—they are in Guernsey.⌐

Ever yrs John H. Newman.

SATURDAY 8 JULY 1837   Trower etc went   M P   E P   walked to Littlemore with Berkeley   dined in Common Room   Stanley with Vaughan

SUNDAY 9 JULY   7th Trinity early Sacrament—Berkeley helping me.   m   Assize Sermon (Jacobson preaching) *after* parish morning Service   did duty morning and afternoon   preached afternoon Number 473[3]   baptized afternoon Choules's child dined with Bloxam

MONDAY 10 JULY   Daman went   instituted Mr Payne of New College into Swalcliffe for the Bishop of Oxford   M P   E P   visited T Cox   Mr Parker dined with me Provost returned.   wrote to Church Commission [and?] to Bishop of Oxford about Mr Payne—to Registry Office—and sent two proofs to G and R.

TUESDAY 11 JULY   Acland sent me his address to Electors with a scribble on it.   Mr Dyson, his wife and sister to breakfast in Common Room Eden to meet them   Eden went   M P   E P   no v and c.   went to Littlemore and read   dined in Common Room with Vaughan   began ⟨(or tomorrow?)⟩ examining young Hooper for confirmation

WEDNESDAY 12 JULY   letters from Bowden, S W.[,] Shortland and Church Commission   Vaughan went   M P   E P   went to Littlemore and read   dined in Common Room by myself

[1] See third note to letter of 6 June to J. W. Bowden.
[2] W. Dodsworth moved in 1837 from Margaret Street Chapel, Cavendish Square, to Christ Church, Regents Park.
[3] *P.S.* IV, 1, 'The Strictness of the Law of Christ'.

TO J. W. BOWDEN

⌐Oriel. July 12/37.⌐

My dear Bowden,

I send your gown as you desire. ⌐Did I tell you I had written to Boone in disgust at his review of Hampden? Also I find he allows a Countess of Huntingdon Teacher[1] to write articles in the Review—We must prepare for dropping him⌐

Thanks for what you say about your arrangements—pray convey my best thanks to your Father for his kindness.

Ever yrs affly John H. Newman.

⌐Do you see Acland talks[2] of the '*independence* of the Church'?⌐

THURSDAY 13 JULY 1837 letters from Mr Willis, W F. and book from Registry office went to Littlemore and read M P E P dined in Common Room by myself answered Registry office

FRIDAY 14 JULY letters from Wood and Manning M P E P no prime f d called on Mr Dyson Marriott came into Oxford wrote to Manning and to Williams and Churton on Copeland's letters

TO EDWARD CHURTON

Oriel July 14/37

My dear Churton

You are doomed to be an arbiter and mediator—but I really should like your opinion on the way Boone is conducting the Review.

Of course he has a right to conduct it as he will—but I should say, I want your opinion *what it becomes* us to do.

The name of the schismatical contributor has been sent me—I cannot read it—but he lives at Brighton—and is teacher in the Countess of Huntingdon's Connexion.

Again, is not the article on Hampden most unhappy? especially since he wrote to me to ask *what I would wish done*—He put it into my hands and I had intended to write an article on the subject in October—when out comes this effusion.

Now what do you think best—for I cannot go on when one's subjects are taken out of one's mouth and disposed of just in a reverse way from what one should like. I mean what is the way of proceeding which you, as being Boone's friend, will think kindest to him

Ever Yrs John H Newman

[1] i.e. of the body of Calvinistic Methodists founded by Selina, Countess of Huntingdon, the friend of George Whitefield. The person referred to was probably Joseph Sortain of North Street Chapel, Brighton. See letter of 1 Sept. to Joshua Watson.

[2] [[qu. in the House of Commons?]] See diary for 11 July.

TO H. E. MANNING

Oriel College, July 14/1837.

My dear Manning,

You and yours have been much in my thoughts lately, and I have been continually doing that which you ask of me. It has truly grieved me to hear of the severe trial you are under, though really such trials are our portion.[1] I think one may say it without exaggeration, but they who seek God do (as it were) come for afflictions. It is the way He shews His love, and to keep from so doing is His exception. I suppose we may consider His words to the Sons of Zebedee addressed to us.[2] It often strikes me so when I am partaking the Holy Communion that I am but drinking in (perchance) temporal sorrow, according to His usual Providence. Hence St. Peter tells us not to think affliction a strange thing.[3] Let this then, my dear Manning, be your comfort, —You are called to trouble as we all are, and the severer the more God loves you. He may mercifully consider your present distress and suspense sufficient for His inscrutable purposes—if so it will come to an end with nothing more. But anyhow be sure He does not willingly afflict us, nor will put a single grain's weight more of suffering than it is meet and good for you to bear—and be sure too that with your suffering your support will grow, and that if in His great wisdom and love He take away the desire of your eyes, it will only be to bring her really nearer to you. For those we love are not nearest to us when in the flesh, but they come into our very hearts as being spiritual beings, when they are removed from us. Alas! it is hard to persuade oneself this, when we have the presence and are without experience of the absence of those we love; yet the absence is often more than the presence, even were this all, that our treasure being removed hence, leads us to think more of Heaven and less of earth.

I know all this is scarcely applicable, since you are in the distressing state of suspense, unable to make up your mind to anything, because nothing is definitely determined for you, yet is it wrong to say that one should contemplate and try to reconcile oneself to the worst, so that if anything happier comes it may be so much gain?

However of course the trial is, when anything like amendment comes or respite, as throwing us out of what we had made up our minds to—May Almighty God be with you.

I do not see at first sight any reason why I should not put up prayers as you suggest, and of course I should like to do so, but will ask or enquire on the subject.

Ever yours affectionately, John H. Newman.

[1] Manning's wife was seriously ill. At the end of his letter of 12 July he wrote: 'Do you ever ask the prayers of the Church for a person (without giving the name,) at a distance? If so I should feel much comfort in thinking of another general intercession for her.'
[2] *Matthew*, 20:22.   [3] I *Peter*, 1:6.

SATURDAY 15 JULY 1837 M P E P walked to Littlemore with Marriott dined in Common Room by myself Vaughan returned Provost returned from Delegacy to Queen

SUNDAY 16 JULY 8th Trinity letter from Keble 2 n of m [two nocturns of matins] Marriott assisting in early Sacrament did duty morning and afternoon preached Number 471[1] Copeland, Bloxam, Berkeley, and Balston to dinner

TO JOHN KEBLE

⌐Oriel College. July 16. 1837⌐

My dear Keble,

I am proud at the notion of the Tract on Tradition being useful to you and being bound up with your Sermon.[2] When Wilson proposed it I was somewhat cool about it, merely as thinking it might be an incumbrance to you. We have a good passage from [Jeremy] Taylor in it—but you should look at a letter of Jebb's (or Knox's?) if you have not fallen on it. Mrs Wilberforce Sen. pointed it out to me. It remarks that Bishop Taylor in his Via Intelligentiae (I think) one of his latest works contradicts and unsays his Liberty of Prophesying on this point.[3] I think Hammond in his Work on Heresy or elsewhere asserts that Taylor's Liberty of Prophesying was a mere argumentum ad hominem—or economy—a dangerous one.[4] His Dissuasive, which is quoted in the Tract, is also later than the L[iberty]. of P[rophesying].

I send you H. F's [Froude] paper. But you know it is no novel argument. Dr Brett in the book I also send has it—and [John] Milner the Romanist. Indeed it is a favorite one with the Romanists.

⌐Williams has suggested the publication of extracts from Hurrell's letters. I feared at first they would be too personal towards *others*—but then I came to think that, if they could be given, they would be next best to talking with him and show him in a very different character from any thing else. Then there are so many clever things in those he sent to me—and the first hints of principles etc. which I and others have pursued and of which he ought to have the credit.⌐ Besides, his voyaging in the Mediterranean and Barbadoes

---

[1] *P.S.* IV, 13, 'The Invisible World'.

[2] Keble's Visitation Sermon of 1836, *Primitive Tradition recognised in Holy Scripture.* Keble wrote to ask Newman's permission to include *Tract* 78, the Catena on Tradition, as an appendix to the third edition of the sermon, which was published in 1838.

[3] See *Tract* 78, pp. 112–14, an extract from Jebb which included the quotation: 'that it [the Vincentian Canon] has been unreservedly acknowledged as a just and true guide by Bishop Taylor, in one of his latest works . . . a tribute, this last, the more remarkable, because, in his "Liberty of Prophesying," . . . he had spoken less respectfully of the principle; and his remarkable change of language can be accounted for only by his having undergone a correspondent change of sentiment.'

Following Newman's lead, Keble discussed Jeremy Taylor's later position on Tradition in his Postscript, pp. 68–73. He was anxious to bring in Taylor's work as W. Wilson had used Taylor's earlier work against Keble's argument in his *A Brief Examination of Professor Keble's Visitation Sermon . . .*, Oxford 1837.

[4] 'Dr. Jer. Taylor, in his *Book* of *Liberty* of *Prophesying*, where he hath so *impartially* inforced the *arguments* of his *adversaries* . . .', from 'A Letter of Resolution to Six Quaeres' in *The Works of Henry Hammond*, London 1674, I, 481.

ought to make them interesting. And then moreover, if it could be done salvâ reverentiâ, have we not a certain talent in our hands? ⌜We have often said the movement, if any thing comes of it, must be *enthusiastic*—now here is a character fitted above all others to kindle enthusiasm—⌝ should we not show what he was in himself? With these thoughts and others like I made extracts of his letters to me, (which are the most difficult from the very bold things said and personalities ventured on, and least interesting as his travels barely come in) and sent them to Rogers. He is to send them to you, if he thinks the notion not altogether wrong. ⌜I have written to William F [Froude] about it—who caught at the idea, which he said had already struck him.⌝ If nothing comes of it, no matter. But I am really sanguine any how that the book will be a somewhat romantic one—and therefore do not like to lose the chance of this addition. ⌜Considering the state of the University, everything that can be effected against lowminded Hampdenism will be a gain.⌝ It might show young men there were things extra sterilem hunc orbem.

Will you tell Mrs Keble I have not got over my shame at the impropriety, which did not strike me at the moment, of letting Wilson take me into your house. It was bold enough to go to Hursley, when you were away—but I ought to be contented with that—instead of going prying about, instead of waiting till you were at home. Pray convey my kindest thoughts to her and Miss Keble. I heard from Pusey a day or two since. Mrs P. has not got rid of her cough. I fear Rogers' sister is in a very anxious way.

Pray let me have the proof sheets if I can be of use.

Mr Todd mentioned to me Mr O Brien's work when in Oxford—but said it was out of print.[1] I wanted to get it, if possible, *for myself*—If I get it, you shall have a sight of it. I *suppose* it is Calvinistic. As I am writing on Justification, I am particularly anxious to see it.

Thanks for the Irenaeus.

Will you please put a note such as you speak of about H. F's omission of the sacred names and phrases? The only fear is the seeming apologetic

Ever Yrs affectly John H Newman

P.S. I have looked through H F's papers, and can find no passage but the following—is it what you mean?

'If the Episcopal question terminated in ascertaining whether Episcopacy was conformable to Apostolical practice, the settlement of it one way or other could be of little consequence to us. We have changed many Apostolical practices. We do not consider ourselves bound to a community of goods, yet the Apostolic Church had all things in common. We do not feel obliged to wash one another's feet, yet one of the last commands of Christ obliged the Apostles to do so.'[2]

---

[1] J. T. O'Brien, *An Attempt to explain and establish the Doctrine of Justification by Faith only, in Ten Sermons*, London 1833. See *Jfc.*, p. vii.

[2] From the 'Essay on Rationalism', *Remains* III, 38.

I have found the passage.

'If it was necessary to press this argument, as far as it admits of being pressed, it might with truth be said that the action and words of our Lord here recorded look much more like the institution of a[1]

TO E. B. PUSEY

Oriel College. July 16/37

My dear Pusey

I have from time to time heard accounts of Mrs Pusey and thank you for yours. It would please me more if she made greater advance. I wish you would put your Norman plan into execution. Really there is nothing so good for a troublesome cold or cough as a continual change of air. This I believe medical men acknowledge. Do not come home till it is gone. Now perhaps if you would do this, you would escape a longer tour. Who knows but you may be sent to Rome, if you will not go round Normandy? but perhaps you will say Rome is worth a journey to. I am glad to hear so good an account of the children, who seemed to require a change of air. Barker looked so much better for it, that I please myself with thinking he is a sort of index of your own looks.

Long Vacation in Oxford does not furnish many materials for a letter. I am at my Lectures on Justification—but have hopes they will not take me very long. It is curious, all parties confess it was a new subject at the Reformation—and the Schoolmen scarcely touch upon it. I do not find it form even one head in the four books of the Master of the Sentences—yet respectably sized volumes have been written on it since. It is a very curious phenomenon in the history of the Church. I have long looked in vain for the peculiar or x $\hat{\eta}\theta os$ in antiquity—and this fact just fits in with its absence.

Rogers has sent me a letter in which he says 'I should have said before that I showed your kind letter about Emily to my mother—and part of Pusey's. She mentioned them to my Father, and he wished me very much to say to you both how very deeply he felt your kindness and how gratified he was by it. I never saw him so affected in speaking of any thing. He could hardly speak of them—and he is not apt to lose command of himself in that way. I really do not know how to say these things so, as to make people believe them more than formal and necessary acknowledgements. Will you take on yourself to make Pusey believe that his kindness really is felt? I am so annoyed at my own cold letters on such occasions, that I do not like to write to him again if I can help it.' I fear his sister does not mend. H. Wilberforce's wife is getting well. Manning's is in a serious state indeed. He wrote

---

[1] The extra leaf is missing. The remainder of the sentence: 'Sacramental Rite than any thing does, which we are told respecting the Lord's Supper in either of the four accounts of it.' *Remains* III, 137.

to me so asking for sympathy, and especially since she who was the usual partner of it now gave rise to the need, that a letter from you would I am sure be very acceptable. His direction is Lavington, Petworth, Sussex. From what he says he evidently is bearing the suspense (for that is the worst, the medical men saying that till she gets better they cannot tell whether or not there is a complaint on the lungs) as one should wish, but seems to need comforters.

While *I was away*, I had a letter from Mr Johnson of Torquay, who said that he was provided with a Curate before my letter came to him.

Boone has published so miserable an article on Hampden's Preface, that I have written to him to remonstrate. Besides, it is cutting me out of my own. I spoke to Sewell, who is decidedly against doing any thing. That Hampden's pamphlet will be taken by the Bishops as an excuse for making matters up, I doubt not a bit.[1] Yet is it not a case of decipi vult populus? Non indicente me, hæc fiunt. Really I think no more is required of *us*. Aliorum judicium est—we have passed on the torch—ipsi viderint, if it dies.

What think you of your friend Mr Faber publishing a book under the following or some such precious title? I had seen it for weeks in the Papers and said to myself with some contempt—'Cambridge all over.'—viz 'History of the formation of my opinions—' or 'history of my opinions—' 'by a fellow of a College.'[2]

The Provost returned from London yesterday and is charmed with the Queen, to whom he went up as part of the delegacy. She is short and little, but was perfectly composed, and dignified—and read her speech with a distinctness, emphasis, and propriety which marks her as a person of '*very good* sense'. This is the highest praise the Provost can give any one.

With kindest thoughts of Mrs Pusey

Ever Yrs affly John H Newman

MONDAY 17 JULY 1837   wrote to Pusey by Mr Ashworth   sent parcel to Keble   M P E P   dined in Common Room with Vaughan   no c

TUESDAY 18 JULY   Mr Dyson called   began to pray [in] Church for Mrs Manning M P E P   walked to Littlemore and read   dined with Copeland, where were Wilson, Cartwright, Palmer, and President   no n and c.   parcel came with Mr Church's translations (*of the Fathers*). Mr Goldsmid called—I returned it.

WEDNESDAY 19 JULY   Mr Goldsmid to breakfast   walked to Littlemore and read. dined in Common Room with Vaughan

THURSDAY 20 JULY   St Margaret   letters from Rogers and Mrs W W   dined in Common Room   no c

[1] See letter of 7 July to J. S. Boone.
[2] Capel Lofft the younger, *Self-Formation; or, the History of an Individual Mind . . . By a Fellow of a College*, two volumes, London 1837.

TO FREDERIC ROGERS

July 20. 1837.

. . . I wish you would take a pen with black ink, and mark the passages in the letters you would omit, I marked out the two you mention because Copeland took fright at them.[1] I can quite understand Wood's fears—*but he has not seen the Essays etc.*—they are all of a piece. *Now* let him cease to wonder at my dread of publishing. At the same time I can easily believe that some passages are uneconomical, indeed I transcribed more than I meant to publish in order to allow of cuttings down.

FRIDAY 21 JULY 1837 letters from C and Mrs Bowden—and proof Provost went to Rochester f d sent back proof

SATURDAY 22 JULY St Mary Magdalen letter from James Marriott in Oxford walked part of way to Littlemore—Berkeley going on and reading prayers dined at Magdalen Gaudy no E P no c

SUNDAY 23 JULY 9 Trinity letters from Rogers, Manning and Wood.[2] Berkeley assisted me in early Sacrament did duty morning and afternoon at St Mary's preached Number 299[3] Berkeley and Banister of Wadham—Vaughan and Marriott with strangers one apiece. *my brother* Charles came. wrote to Wood, Manning, and Mrs Bowden.

[1] Rogers wrote on 17 July, 'Froude's letters are *most exceedingly* interesting—and I think must be very much so to any one.—I should have been very sorry to have lost them, and cannot doubt that Keble will give his imprimatur. Can you not put in that passage in some letter where he tells you to go on working though Christie and K. told him you had too much to do.—Allow me to represent however that they do not entirely fulfil that condition of "exciting peoples respect *before their political etc prejudices were interfered with.*—' The tone of *prophecy* and *policy* will tend to harden us into a party (poor Acland!) and such passages as those about his dislike of the niggers—and Socrates' revenge would be stumbling blocks to many people—especially peculiarizers. I think they were (*very* slightly) so to my sister Emily to whom I gave the letters telling her to find fault. I suppose this cannot be helped—as to the attacks on Cranmer etc—I do not see where a more favourable opportunity for throwing off on that line is likely to arise.—It must come, I suppose, and when it does respectable people will be startled—send the letters for *Rickards*'s opinion.) I cannot doubt at all that they will very materially lessen the influence of the Apostolicals over the Clergy—and perplex many friends—think of S. Wilberforce—or of such people as Marriott was while he lectured in "Jewell". I can hardly help laughing while I write ⟨to think how the former will settle it with his peculiar friends. Bp. Winton eg. [C. R. Sumner]⟩.—However all this is merely for finding fault's sake.—And many will be strengthened to see their way clearer.
July 19) I have just (two days since I began this letter) got the papers back from Wood who has been excessively interested—but rather against publishing them as too confidential and uneconomical—I confess I so far agree with him as to doubt about some individual passages —particularly what shews you off as *plotters* . . . I am afraid to shew Hope the papers in their unmitigated form. He has not yet I should think enough knowledge or little enough church feeling to bear such very strong meat.—Should you object to Palmer junior of Magdalen?— He is less likely to be startled at what seems anti-Church of England if he is going on as he was . . . Wood says you should lithograph fifty copies and distribute them among safe hands and do no more.'
[2] Wood wrote on 22 July to say that he had been to see Rivington about the publication of Froude's *Remains*. Rivington had wanted to know whether Newman would put his name to the work as editor and, also, whether they could just commit themselves to the publication of one volume for the time being. Wood was very anxious to have Rivington as publisher. Wood now felt that some passages might be omitted, not from 'any *sentiment* however *strong*, but whatever tends to give an air of individuality or accidentalness to the way in which it was *evolved*. People should not be let behind the scenes too soon . . .'
[3] *S.D.*, 11, 'Christian Nobleness'.

TO ELIZABETH BOWDEN

Oriel College. ⌐July 23.1837.

My dear Mrs Bowden, ⌐

Your letter concerned me very much indeed—but ⌐I am glad to hear from Wood as well as yourself that John is now getting well. I know how any indisposition is apt to pull him down; but the country air will, I trust, restore him fast.⌐ From what you say I suppose he was not able to go up with the address. ⌐All parties speak very strongly of the Queen's self possession and unaffectedness.[1] Many of our friends are in great anxiety and sorrow at this time. You know, I suppose, that one of Rogers' sisters is in a very dangerous way, and that poor Henry Manning is to lose his wife. I had a letter from him this morning, in which he says that a few days will bring his trial to an end. He writes in a very subdued way, but it will be a great blow to him indeed. One cannot help fancying that one's friends have more trouble than other people. I suppose it is because we hear of it more. You know that a month since Mr Rose was quite or almost quite given over—but he is now somewhat better.

Mr Goldsmid called on me a few days since, and breakfasted with me. I really am unfeignedly interested in him—It seems he was born a Jew and professed Judaism till sixteen—when on conviction, against his Father's liking (who was very affectionate however) who is still a Jew, he was baptized —his sisters followed.⌐ One must attribute a great deal that people do not like, to his early years—and ⌐I trust Apostolical principles will mould his mind into more perfect symmetry.⌐ In this way I think one may reconcile oneself to laughing at such adventures, as this late one with Mr Le Fevre, (your continuation of which is very amusing)—that they must tend, one would think, to discipline him. Poor Mr Le F's difficulty however is not a little one for I do not yet see how he will shake off one who perhaps has not over acute observation or over delicate tact.

⌐Mr Churton, as well as myself, are in correspondence with Boone about his vagaries. Mr Ch. pleads hard for him—both for his own sake, and as thinking the Critic will coalesce with the Church of England Magazine or at least become liberal, if we leave it. Certainly by keeping in with it, we, at least muzzle a possible foe, and have an organ. But of course if Boone does not amend a continuation of the alliance is impossible.⌐

I hoped to have seen Manuel [Johnson] here from what he said on leaving —but am sure that Guernsey will do him more good than Oxford air. There is no chance, I fear, of my coming to Town for some months, as you and John kindly propose. Yet I do not like absolutely to give up the chance. There is to be a Confirmation here—till then I am fixed—but we do not know when. I think I must say there is no chance at all—and then take my

[1] [[NB. In receiving the Oxford Address on her Accession.]]

chance. I often, or rather I should say constantly think of my little godson, and should like much to see him. Another business on my hands is the publication of the first volume of my friend Froude's remains—and I am more than meditating a volume of Lectures on Justification; thinking that in many ways this may be useful.

With kindest remembrances to John and the children,

I am, Yours very sincerely, John H. Newman.

TO H. E. MANNING

Oriel College, July 23/1837.

My dear Manning,[1]

I thank you for your welcome tho' sad letter—when I read it, it quite affected me, yet I cannot say why, and it seems almost taking a liberty to say that it did. We must take these things as they are sent; only be sure that you will never pass happier days in your whole life, than this awful and still time, before you lose what is so dear to you. You will feel it to be so in memory, so make much of it, and thank God. We do not feel His Hand while it is upon us, but afterwards. Have you not felt this is the case in the Church Services? These days will make your future life only happier, that is in real happiness, tho' it is so difficult to understand at the time. Everything is good and acceptable, which tends to bring us into the calm expectant state of indifference to the world, which is the perfection of earthly comfort. The thought of the dead is more to us than the sight of the living, tho' it seems a paradox to say so. I mean it has a happiness peculiar to itself, unlike and higher than any other. Do you not recollect the touching words 'Heu quanto minus est cum cæteris versari quam tui meminisse'[2]

I am writing what I know would be quite unworthy your reading were it not that I may thereby shew that I really feel for you—that I trust you do

---

[1] Manning wrote on 21 July: 'Suspense is no longer my trial. A few days will end all her sufferings. I bless God that 'suffering' is hardly true. He has mercifully spared her all acute pain, for a long time—and when it came it was not great. No man knows what it is to watch the desire of his eyes fading away—for such indeed is dying in this most gentle dispensation.

If you could know how much comfort your letter gave me—how much, and how often I have thought of it, you would not find it a trouble to send me what if with me, you would say now that, I am daily, it may be hourly drawing nearer to the last of my trial.'

Manning wrote again on 25 July, the day after his wife's death:

'Many and heartfelt thanks for your kind letter of this morning. I hardly know what has drawn me so closely, and in one way suddenly to your sympathy, but I feel something in the way you deal with my sorrows, particularly soothing and strengthening. Need I tell you why I write again so soon? At least you will rejoice to hear that it has pleased God with a tenderness of hand, I could not have imagined, to fulfil this searching visitation . . .

Many thanks for offering the prayer of the Church. I had already asked my brethren, and several my intimate friends, and it has been to me an unspeakable comfort—and I feel sure God would not have answered us in this way, had He seen that any brighter, and as we say too readily, happier appointment would have wrought His gracious end upon me.'

[2] Epitaph by William Shenstone (1714–63).

believe. I put up prayers in the Church as you desired, and will continue. Marriott who is here desires his kindest thoughts.

God bless and keep you, my dear Manning.

Yours affectionately, John H. Newman.

MONDAY 24 JULY 1837 married [name omitted] to Jane Thomas [at] Littlemore Election for the City[1] M P E P f d no E P [sic] Marriott took tea with us wrote to M R G and James

TO MISS M. R. GIBERNE

Oriel College. July 24. 1837
St James's Eve.

My dear Miss Giberne,

Your two sovereigns and MS were lying on my table on my return, their radiance being concealed in their brown paper envelope. As to the former I have nothing to say but to thank you for them and confess they are of just weight—but the MS demands varied acknowledgments and praise. At the same time I think you succeed far better in your description and dialogues of the children, than of the grown people. Your picture of the two little brother and sister, I really do think quite perfect, and most uncommonly taking— but the 'peculiar' part of it might be improved, though I don't quite see how. I have not a clear view how far in a book written for children, a *mother* (though a peculiar specimen) may allowably be made absurd and faulty— that is, I literally do not see my way.

We have thoughts of starting a quarterly Publication, (did I mention it to you) which will be strictly a Miscellany; taking in whatever comes to hand during the Quarter—verse or prose—story or history—dialogue or Sermon. If we mature our plan, might we appropriate this 'John and Mary' to that purpose?

I am at present busy with my Lectures on Justification, which I am preparing as if for the Press. It strikes me that I have a view which will be useful to many people, yet cannot tell how far it is more than a mere dream or much ado about nothing. Moreover, those persons I have mentioned it to, or who heard them, favor them. Perhaps it will be a volume partly of Lectures partly of Sermons—but all more or less on the same subject.

You must not think I have forgotten to send you the Sermons on Antichrist. I had hoped to have done so before now. I am truly relieved to find H. Wilberforce's wife is convalescent.

---

[1] '. . . in the Oxford *City* election [for 1837], Messrs. Maclean and Wm. Erle (afterwards Judge Erle) were elected, and Mr. Hughes Hughes was thrown out. Mr. Maclean was, after the usual fashion, carried home in a *chair* richly ornamented and borne on men's shoulders; Mr. Erle introduced a novelty (and an improvement), being drawn *in a chariot* by *four white horses* . . .', G. V. Cox, *Recollections of Oxford*, London 1868, pp. 280–1.

As to the translations of the Fathers, there is no reason in the world you should subscribe to them, seeing you can at any time buy such particular volumes as you want. However, I do not think that any decoction, such as even Hooker's can take their place—yet, while I say this, I am unable to anticipate whether a translation can preserve their spirit. I should not wonder if it turned out that they seemed quite flat and insipid. It seems to me the great use of our Library will be to make the clergy read the originals —and it is giving a general *impulse* in a certain direction. However, others think differently, viz that they may become popular reading. I do not deny it—and feel I have no means of judging. The event is the only way of deciding the question.

I do not at all doubt that my correspondence with the Christian Observer has done what I intended it to do—frighten our peculiar brethren. I wish them to be regularly frightened and perplexed. They have been sailing along with all things their own way, and I wish to take them in flank. It is remarkable how plans of altering the Liturgy have died away ever since our movement began. We have given them other things to think about. However, the cry may revive any day—yet the suspension of it is a gain.

I have been agreeably surprised at the mild way in which the Lectures on Romanism have been received. They are said to prove me to be not a Papist. I feel most deeply what you say about the difference between Mary's and Martha's lot—though the former requires strong faith, most especially at this day, when people scoff at the notion—however it has its reward and that not a temporal one

Yours most sincerely John H Newman

TUESDAY 25 JULY 1837 St James letter from Wood. Marriott went Election in Convocation of University members. M P E P Service in Chancel read Number 249 no s. n. v or c. Copeland to dinner

WEDNESDAY 26 JULY letter from Canon Rogers no p walked with C [Charles] to Littlemore—read prayers there dined with C in my rooms (i.e. upstairs)

THURSDAY 27 JULY letter from Manning announcing his wife's death last Monday. Bishop [of] Hereford (Grey's) death in paper dined with C at Copeland's—Mr Norris there. wrote to Wood, Rivington, Mrs W W and T.M. inclosing C's Letter

TO THOMAS MOZLEY

Oriel College. July 27/37

My dear Tom

You must have expected to receive back the letter before this—but C. [Charles Newman] only gave it me this morning. Arthur's letter is a very good one. It is manly and open. I am not at all sorry he should know that some persons know what he was betrayed into. It seems a fitting penance and may be useful to him. He could not have sent you a better letter. As to WW. senior I do not wish to commit him to my *very words*—I gave you but the impression of what he said. As far as I recollect, he *meant* me to tell *you*—and in a good deal of conversation one often brings out a thing which is not intended. Of course it would have been better had he told you.

We are going to publish extracts from Froude's letters. If then you have any, which you would like to be inserted, please send copies to me at once.

I hope my Aunt got down to Bristol safely. Love to H.

Ever Yrs affly John H Newman[1]

FRIDAY 28 JULY 1837   f d   Eden returned

SATURDAY 29 JULY   no m l p v and c.   Lit.   M P   E P   walked to Littlemore dined and C in Common Room with Eden

SUNDAY 30 JULY   10 Trinity   no one to assist me in early Sacrament   did duty morning and afternoon   preached Number 474   dined with C at Berkeley's.

MONDAY 31 JULY   dined with C in rooms.   no E P

TUESDAY 1 AUGUST   S. Petri ad Vincula   County Election: I voted for Lord Norreys   Mr Harcourt   Mr Parker[2]   no v and c   no E P   dined in Common Room with C and Bloxam—and Vaughan and Eden

WEDNESDAY 2 AUGUST   walked to Littlemore—read Services   dined with C in rooms?   no v and c   wrote to H and H W

TO HENRY WILBERFORCE

Oriel College. ⌜Aug. 2. 1837⌝

My dear Henry

I have long wished to write to you, but have delayed, and now am not in a very good humour for it. What a strange thing humour is, and that one should vary about, as one does. Manning wrote me word when all was over, and I have not answered this letter. This is one thing that vexes me. It is no use answering it now, a week after the time. Will you manage to tell him this—for I suppose you will be seeing or hearing from him—I shall like to know how you all bear what God has sent. Of course when reason is allowed to speak, any one must confess what a great, an inexpressible comfort it is to have any one who is dear to us safe lodged beyond the reach of all accidents. Nor does the first sorrow on bereavement exclude this thought in

---

[1] Charles Newman added on the fold: 'Dr Ht [Harriett] John and I have agreed that I should set off this day week 3d august Thursday at 8 oClock by Southampton Coach and get out at Whitchurch and walk to Andover which I believe is 15 miles and stay at any Inn you may appoint till you sent for me by your Phaeton—Pray let me hear whether this suits you. etc etc. I expect to be at Andover by six P.M.

John is very well—I hope you and Tom are the same I am Dr H Yr affte Brother C R Newman'

[2] The Conservative candidates. All three were successfully returned.

religious people. Bystanders think one lamenting and regretting, when what outwardly shows itself is but the natural effect of a definite natural cause, as shadows may attend the Sun, but no measure or index at all of the real state of the heart. So that those who seem to sorrow most, are all the time not sorrowing as those who have no hope. I hope that Manning will brace himself up to whatever duty God calls him to—and not relax in the good fight.[1] The other day I fell in with a neighbour of his who spoke most highly and warmly of what he was doing and the influence he was gaining in his neighbourhood. Poor fellow—it is sad indeed to have to remain among the ghosts of past comfort—but this is a heathen view—they are present comforts still—He must, as he will, realize them as such, and labour as usual, after a little interval. Do try, my dear H. to keep him up to his work, and make him feel that God has called him to be like the great prophet, the desire of whose eyes was taken away, separate, not looking back to the world. How many of God's servants are so introduced to us in fact or in type—Melchizedek, the Levites who knew not their father or mother, Elijah who is only known as the Thesbite, Daniel again, not to say our Blessed Lord. I wish to know how your wife is, and how she bears this blow. She has been continually in my thoughts. I have been glad to hear so good an account of her. I wish there was a chance of you and her coming here. I should like to have a talk about many things— which I cannot cram into a letter, even if I thought of them. I got your Tract, and liked it very much. What should you say if I proposed your publishing a volume of Sermons? You see *we must* provide reading for people. You are abundantly up to this. The simple question is about publishing so soon—that in one respect is a difficulty, but now you are 30 (?)—a considerable age I wish you would think of it. Your name would sell your volume—and your style etc. would phenakize[2] all readers. I think it would do much to diminish prejudice against the views. This only is the difficulty —you ought to take subjects where economy is not necessary—state your *whole* view—but let it be in a matter where it will not offend. I am busy in dear H.F.'s papers. By the bye did he ever write letters to you—for we are giving selections from his Correspondence. If you have any thing to contribute that way, let me have it. And I am busy in a work on Justification—which I have now written nearly twice over—and perhaps shall have to write a third time

Vale dilectissime from Yr affte friend J H N.

[1] Wilberforce wrote on 9 Aug., 'I cannot tell you how dear Manning has risen under this grievous storm—there is no need of any one to stir him up to his work for he is not even for a moment thinking of flagging in it. He told me that he felt this a great trial of those great Catholic truths which he has learned in the last three years—that he had looked into himself to see are there any of them which I have taken up but which seem to me at such a moment fanciful or impractical etc.? and that instead he seemed never before so deeply to have seen their truth and importance. The good he is doing is great indeed. I am quite surprised having been away for a year to see how his influence has grown in the time, the young clergy especially are extensively influenced. His situation here is important, he represents the family and so holds a station which as a mere parish priest he would not . . .'

[2] 'beguile'.

P.S. ⌐I saw your Mother at Southampton, and felt distressed to think that our notions (so to call them) were perhaps perplexing her—she spoke about and against Prayers for the Dead. It is one great distress I feel, the unsettling people, yet I do not know how it is to be helped. It has pained me a good deal. Your sister Mary spoke to me on the same subject,⌐ and I fancy I have contrived to make obscurum obscurius.

THURSDAY 3 AUGUST 1837 letter from Wood and C's friend no m and l dined with C in Common Room as did Marriott, Eden, and Ward of Balliol wrote to Acland, Woodgate, and Perceval no n v or c No E P.

TO T. D. ACLAND

Oriel College, August 3, 1837.

The papers tell me both that you are returned and that the privilege of franking had begun. It will be a nuisance if the papers are wrong in both points; but though wrong in the second, I will not mind, so that they do not make a fool of me by making a mistake in the first. Many thanks for your document, which gave me great pleasure; I thought it the most straightforward sort of thing I had seen for some time.[1] I cannot get myself to wish you joy, for you have great anxieties before you. But I do think it a matter of great congratulation to all friends and servants of Truth, that there will be an accession of sound men to the New House. Anything is better than that superficial way of going on which has been in vogue. Let the House as a whole even be more radical, it will be a great gain if true principles are thrown out more in relief. I do not expect great things—it is, I suppose, impossible to help falling in with Sir R. Peel a very great deal—yet if you were the means of bringing men like Gladstone to act for himself and not by his party, it would be a great thing. You will do much if you make persons of right views feel confidence in *each* other, and *in their* views. And this I should think might be done. Talking of anxieties, I do not forget the announcement[2] I saw in the paper in the midst of your bustle, yet anxiety is not the name for it. Does it not seem like a memento, mercifully intended, that there are higher and more serious things than the whirlpool of politics and ambition!

[1] [[N B April 4. 1876. I have turned up 10 letters of T. D. Acland of 1837 1838 (tho' he has not dated the year)—I have kept some of them. Some are confidential and I have burned them. On his getting into Parliament he says 'I am very glad you thought my address straightforward. You will, I hope, often give me a line when you have a strong opinion on Church matters.']] Acland had just been elected Conservative M.P. for West Somerset.

[2] The death of Acland's two brothers.

Oriel College. Aug. 3. 1837

My Dear Perceval,

We certainly have an old College Account Book of the 16th century, but in the Vacation I cannot find it, nor tell you whether it would help you. But I can tell you, what is much more to your purpose, unless you know of it already—also that our College Book has gone to the making of it—viz that Mr Lloyd of Ch Ch., the Professor of Political Economy has published a pamphlet on 'The Prices of Corn in Oxford' in the 15th and 16th centuries.[1] It is published at Parker's, but doubtless you would get it at Rivington's.

I am glad you are taking up the subject. Also I am glad to think we shall have a resource in you, though I hope we shall not need it, should any atrocious person be fixed on to fill the vacant see.[2] I mean, to give us instructions about the proceedings at the Confirmation.

I do not think you have *published* any account of the said Proceedings. In case there seems occasion, will you be good enough to send me a letter on the subject? I do not think Oxford should directly move—it has done so much lately—but I might easily write to some friends in the country to bestir themselves.

As to the Clause in the Marriage Act, I suppose there are a number of persons who will go on as usual.[3] Considering the Rubric prescribes Banns, has always been acted on, and has not been altered, I shall, unless any new light comes on me, continue to obey it. However if you can strengthen my view here too, I shall be glad.

Yours very truly John H. Newman

FRIDAY 4 AUGUST 1837 letter from A no m l. p v. Lionized C over several places f d no E P

SATURDAY 5 AUGUST letter from Bishop (appointing Sept 5 for Confirmation) J. and Wood no m. l. p. th. n. s. or c. Charles went by Southampton to Cholderton (*the last time I saw him. Aug 24/74*) walked to Littlemore—read Service dined in Common Room sent out all Confirmation notices

SUNDAY 6 AUGUST Transfiguration letters from Harrison and Boone m l p th. s. n. v. c. Sacrament no one helping me did duty morning and afternoon preached Number 475[4] dined with Bloxam as did Copeland. wrote to Bishop

---

[1] William Foster Lloyd, *Prices of Corn in Oxford in the Beginning of the Fourteenth Century, and also from the Year 1583 to the Present Time*, Oxford 1830.

[2] Of Hereford; Edward Grey had died on 24 June and was succeeded later in the year by Thomas Musgrave.

[3] The new Amendment to the Marriage Act of 1836 provided that '. . . . the issue of the superintendent registrar's certificate . . . shall be used and stand instead of the publication of banns to all intents and purposes, when no such publication shall have taken place; and every parson, vicar, etc. in England shall solemnize marriage, after such notice and certificate as aforesaid, in like manner as after due publication of banns.'

[4] *P.S.* IV, 7, 'Chastisement amid Mercy'.

MONDAY 7 AUGUST   Nomen Jesu   read to Chandler   M P   E P   no v. c   called on President of Magdalen   dined in Common Room with Vaughan   examined in Church for Confirmation   wrote to T. Keble in C's letter

TO WILLIAM JACOBSON

Oriel Aug 7. 1837

My dear Jacobson

I have taken up, attracted by the name, the newly published work of (I believe) a friend of yours, Sir F. Palgrave, and cannot help writing you this line in consequence. He has in the course of it quoted from one of my published Sermons in a very flattering way—and what evidently very much enhances the compliment he has not mentioned my name. I assure you I do not recollect having met with any thing more pleasant—for it shows me that people I do not know and in a very different line of life take a real interest in some things I have put into print. And I write this to you, hoping, that if by chance you ever have an opportunity, you will be kind enough to convey my very respectful feelings and best thanks to Sir F.P.[1]

Yours very truly John H Newman

TUESDAY 8 AUGUST 1837   In festo Martyrum Cyriaci Largi et Smaragdi   letter from Archdeacon Wix   no th s n v. c.   M P   E P   read to Chandler   walked to Littlemore, read, thence to Kennington, there dining with Carey, and home in chaise with Mr Carey etc.   wrote to Harrison

WEDNESDAY 9 AUGUST   letter from Perceval   spit blood went to Tuckwell   no m. l. p. th. s. n   no E P   J Marriott to breakfast—went off in mid day   Copeland went to Littlemore for me—dined by myself in Common Room   examined in Church for Confirmation   De Mainbry passed through Oxford the second time

THURSDAY 10 AUGUST   S Laurent: letter from Acland   Copeland read for me—did not go to St Mary's   no M P   no E P   Bloxam, Copeland, Berkeley, and Audland to dinner   Mr Goldsmid called in evening

FRIDAY 11 AUGUST   letters from H and Mr Kilvert   M P   E P   called on Mr Goldsmid   f d   examined in Church for Confirmation   no c

SATURDAY 12 AUGUST   letter from the Bishop changing day of Confirmation   sent out fresh notices for Confirmation   M P   E P   no th s n   walked to Littlemore with Berkeley   dined with Vaughan

[1] Sir Francis Palgrave, *Truths and Fictions of the Middle Ages. The Merchant and the Friar*, London 1837, pp. 370ff., where Palgrave quoted from 'The Religion of the Day', *P.S.* I, 317ff. He introduced the quotation: 'Instead of the Friar in his Study, discoursing with a friend, imagine yourself in the neighbouring Church of St Mary the Virgin. Suppose you have before you a Preacher addressing this University of Oxford, in an age when, by the permission of providence, those sciences which I now recommend, shall be pursued with intoxicating vigour: when the Handmaid, instead of waiting with humility for the commands of her Mistress, shall rudely endeavour to usurp her authority. Consider this Preacher as one, who, never forgetting the prerogative derived from his high and sacred commission as a member of the Apostolical Hierarchy, is equally preserved from the delusions of spiritual pride, and the chill of worldly wisdom, and he might answer arguments like yours with the following words:—' The quotation, in a slightly paraphrased version, begins, 'The heavens do declare the glory of God, but not his will . . .'

SUNDAY 13 AUGUST   12th Trinity   letter from Green and Ward—parcel from Wood with letter from Bowden   no one to help me in early Sacrament   m. l. p th. s. n v.   did duty morning and afternoon   preached Number 476[1]   Copeland dined with me—and Vaughan in Common Room   wrote to the Bishop

MONDAY 14 AUGUST   M P   no p th n s v   no E P   Chandler went to his work again.   instituted Dr Bowles to Noke   called on Mrs Gilbert.   visited T. Cox dined in Common Room with Eden   examined for Confirmation   sent Bishop Dr Bowles's paper.

TUESDAY 15 AUGUST   letters from H W and S.W.   Vaughan went for three weeks M P   E P   walked to Littlemore and read   dined with Audland at Queen's gaudy. in evening to Dr Kidd's to meet Dr Robinson of New York   wrote to Green and Ward   and to S.W.

TO SAMUEL WILBERFORCE

Oriel College. August 15. 1837

My dear Wilberforce,

I was not unmindful of your last letter, but waited for the receipt of your work,[2] which you were kind enough to lead me to expect, to thank you for it as well as to answer the other matters about which you wrote.

Nor was I unmindful of Manning's affliction, but it has been continually in my thoughts.

Nor of Mr Hewett's case either—which has puzzled me and about which I meant to have sent you a message a fortnight since by Henry. You see the only ground on which I could call upon him, in my own heart, would be to attempt to modify his views. But the only reason I could *put forward* without impertinence would be to make him an acquaintance and be civil to him. This involved an inconsistency—and I did not know what to do. If I *sought him* out, I could not at pleasure shake him off. He might well say, Who asked you to come? you knew what I was—now you find out I mean to continue what I am is no reason for your breaking with me. On the other hand I should be very inconsistent if I made friends, of my own accord, with a Dissenting Minister.—It strikes me then it will be best for you to send him a letter of introduction to me—if *he* makes the acquaintance, he cannot complain at my, under circumstances, declining it. I had heard of him before, and doubt not he is a man about whom one must feel great interest.

As to the Tracts, I find we lost so much by the plan of sending them out, and on the other hand they were selling so well in London that I ordered back from various friends the county Copies at the beginning of the year— and am sorry you were not informed of it. I almost suspect I have a small account against you, certainly against Manning. The sum brought in against me by G. and R. [Gilbert and Rivington] was above £70.

I wrote to Boone at once on your intelligence—[or rather] to an intimate

[1] *P.S.* VI, 15, 'Rising with Christ'.
[2] Wilberforce had just published *Journals and Letters of the Rev. Henry Martyn, B.D.*, two volumes, London 1837.

friend of his who wrote to him. Nothing [has] been explained yet—but I
certainly will not go on, unless that sort of thing is given up.

Yours very sincerely John H Newman

P.S. I hope you hear good accounts of Mrs Sargeant, and that Mrs
Wilberforce is as reconciled to her loss as you could expect.[1] I will bear in
mind what you say about the Ad Populum. At present we are straitened for
money. Lately I paid a bill of £330 [for] printing of Tracts for 9 months. As
to the wrappers Rivington negatived the notion—I forget why.

WEDNESDAY 16 AUGUST 1837   packet from Registry office   M P   E P   walked to
Littlemore and read   caught in rain   called on Mrs W Giles   dined in Common
Room with Eden   Pusey returned   examined for Confirmation   called on Pusey
and with him on Dr Robinson   no n. v. c

THURSDAY 17 AUGUST   letter from Green and Ward   none all day [i.e. Breviary]
M P   Dr and Mrs Robinson breakfasted with me—also Pusey and Eden   no E P.
dined with Pusey to meet Dr and Mrs Robinson

FRIDAY 18 AUGUST   letter from C and H   M P   E P   f d   no c   examined for
Confirmation   Cornish came and took tea.   Dr Robinson called.   wrote to Wood,
sent parcel to him, wrote to H.[,] Green and Ward and Mr Kilvert.

TO S. F. WOOD

Oriel. August 18. 1837

My dear Wood,

   Your article is a capital one, and must be useful.[2] You have improved in
writing. I shall mention one or two corrigenda, as I consider, before concluding. Your manner is freer and less constrained than it was—still I think I
desiderate something. Especially I wish you had given us more of your own,
and opened the stores of your mind, instead of cogging from me—though
of course in some places my complaint is but 'that's my thunder.' In the
passage you refer to, you must put in, 'as we have been reminded in a late

---

[1] Wilberforce's wife, Emily, was an elder sister of Caroline Manning, who had just died.

[2] Wood wrote to Newman on 11 Aug. sending the article 'Griffith's *Christian Church*' for
the October number of *Brit. Crit.*, and explaining that it had 'come out differently from what I
meant, and I am very sensible of a consequent floor in it; This is that it treats several important
subjects, each of which require fuller and abler handling, in a jejune and cursory way. The
fact is that I meant it to be chiefly on Spiritualism, and only to treat Mr Griffith by the way,
but I got drawn on to remark on him chapter by chapter, and this makes the bulk of the
Article, and its original point is huddled in at the end.'

He also asked, 'Is my *cogg* from you about Unity at p 25 [*Brit. Crit.*, 22, p. 387] too bare-
faced?' Wood's passage paraphrases Newman's point in *V.M.* I, Lecture VIII, 'The Indefectibility of the Church Catholic'. The words 'by a late writer' were inserted in the article.

For Wood's defence of Newman against Rose see Newman's letter to him of 2 June 1837
and first footnote.

The article was also a review of J. C. Crosthwaite, *The Christian Ministry and the Establishment of Christianity*, London 1835, and W. J. Irons, *On the Holy Catholic Church. Parochial
Lectures*, London 1837. Crosthwaite is only mentioned in a footnote where his advocacy of
the theory of Apostolic Succession is applauded.

work—'or something of the kind, else people will give the article to me, and say I have been cogging from myself. I am not satisfied too at losing what *would* have been a gain—your defence of me against Rose. I know well how little, when one begins, one can tell which way one's pen is going—so I am not surprised at your balk; still so it is, I expected to be saved the trouble of thinking out my own defence, and instead you have made me a present of some things from myself. However it is a shame so to talk—it is a very good article, well put together, and things *brought out* in a way I have not in my book—and so new, as having passed through a new mind. And this is what I have to say. Do not transcribe the article—it is clear enough. You *must* put two or three sentences about Mr Crossthwaite. Send the article to Boone. If he asks alteration, send his letter to me.

I cannot master your objection about that said passage of Hooker's on Justification which you floored in my Sermon. It was, that 'even though we did all that was required of us, we should not approach Justification—which was a mere gratuitous gift—whereas Hooker by saying "*our* little fruit in holiness is etc, we dare not put God's name on our account books etc"[1] implies that our fault is that we do not do *enough*.' This seems to me quite true—but I quote Hooker for quite a different reason, viz to show the *fact*, whatever be the reason, that we are justified *in* Christ, not *by* Him merely—a truth which Hooker brings out most splendidly, as far as words go. It is a passage *so* often quoted by Peculiars, that I confess I long to cite it on my side—and unless you can manage to overpersuade me, the temptation will be too strong.

I have an idea. The mass of the Fathers (Justin, Athenagoras, Irenæus, Clement, Tertullian, Origen, Lactantius, Sulpitius, Ambrose, Nazianzen,) hold that, though the Devil, Satan, fell from the beginning, the *Angels* fell before the deluge falling in love with the daughters of men. This has lately come across me as a remarkable solution of a notion which I cannot help holding. Daniel speaks as if each nation had its guardian Angel. I cannot but think that there are beings with a great deal of good in them, yet with great defects, who are the animating principles of certain institutions, etc etc. I mean, take the case of the Jesuits, a Society in which the highest and the lowest in $\mathring{\eta}\theta o s$ has met together—take England, with many high virtues and yet a low Catholicism. It seems to me that John Bull is a spirit neither of heaven nor of hell. I leave it for you to complete the theory—my practical inference is this. These beings are like loadstones carrying us to the right or left when one would go straight. Has not the Christian Church and its parts ever surrendered itself to one or other of these simulations of the Truth? Is not Mahometanism, nay worse religions, so to be accounted for?

---

[1] 'We see how far we are from the perfect righteousness of the law; the little fruit which we have in holiness, it is, God knoweth, corrupt and unsound: we put not confidence at all in it, we challenge nothing in the world for it, we dare not call God to a reckoning, as if we had him in our debt books . . .', from 'A Learned Discourse of Justification' in J. Keble (ed.), *The Works of Richard Hooker*, Oxford 1836, III, Part II, p. 614.

to come nearer home. That *we* are under the superintendance of some super-natural power, I cannot doubt for an instant—we have a game to play, a course to run. But then comes the question, is it not something short of God? some simulation? How are we to avoid Scylla and Charybdis, and go straight on to the very image of Christ? This is problem—not that we have not much truth—but that our friends may not prove.[1]

I really do *want* Johnson's U.S. analyzed i.e. judiciously—as a Tract nominally against the Romanists—but it need not mention them.[2] Call it the Anglican view. I should *add* to it a sort of analysis of part of Bellarmine—and so leave it. This will be pretty much the character of several of the Series forthcoming, I expect—an analysis of different views. But I *had rather* of all

a precedent. I shall recollect Arthur Collier.[3] At present I want to review La Mennais, and several other works. I have been exceedingly gratified to find Sir F. Palgrave quote me in his new book without my name

Ever Yrs affly J H N.

(Love to R. Williams.)
'Doubt that the stars' is from Hamlet[4] and (I fear) inappropriate. Look.

Some lines ought to be erased p. 27?

I do not like a phrase p. 52

[1] Here, and again below, the rest of the leaf is torn off.
[2] In his letter to Newman of 23 July, Wood had suggested publishing extracts from John Johnson's *The Unbloody Sacrifice*, 1714–18. He felt that there was a confusion of views about the Eucharist, 'whether primitive Roman or Anglican, were agreed as to the Thing therein received, and that the dispute really turned solely upon the *mode and manner* in which It is *conveyed* to us. My idea is, that two very nice Tracts against Romanism (after the manner of No 72) might be made out of Johnson's U. S., the 1st containing the doctrine of the sacrifice as distinguished from the Popish one; the 2d that of the Real Presence as distinguished from Transubstantiation . . . Now would not these prepare peoples minds for Froude's Essay, and your Sacerdotal office? . . . there seems to me a way whereby the inconsistencies of our Doctors may be harmonized or at least accounted for: First, as long as the old belief in the *true corporeal substantial presence* of the Holy Body itself remained, Popish fears forced them to *disconnect* this from the *Elements* . . .'
Wood wrote on 30 July with, '. . . some more crotchets on the subject itself: (1) Have not the extracts from Bishop Cosins exhausted the "against Transubstantiation" side of it? (2) is it really right to go on "cursing and swearing" against the poor Romanists about it? (3) and if so, is it also profitable, I mean, shall one be able to bring out at all appropriately what one wants to say? My present view is that you should start an antagonist series "against Spiritualism or against Rationalism" (whichever you choose to call it) and that a Tract from Johnson with a grand Preface about the Divine mode of conveying invisible blessings under visible forms (or de *Sacramentis* in genere) should commence it.'
Wood did not produce a Tract on the subject but extracts from Johnson were included in Pusey's *Tract 81*.
[3] Wood wrote, 'There is a memoir of Arthur Collier lately publisht, which is most curious. He was the Author of Clavis Universalis, a tract contemporary with Berkeley's Principles of Human Knowledge, and propounding the same theory, only, as it seems to me, with more depth. He was the strangest mixture—an Arian and High Churchman, not to say apostolical, and floors Hoadly in a letter full of dry humour most completely. With your Berkeleian inclinations you might make something of all this . . .' The metaphysician Arthur Collier (1680–1732) attacked Bishop Hoadly on the question of the innocence of sincere errors in letters to *Mist's Journal* in 1719. His 'Clavis Universalis' was reprinted in 1837, along with other of his works, in *Metaphysical Tracts*, edited by Samuel Parr.
[4] 'Doubt thou the stars are fire:
    Doubt that the sun doth move', *Hamlet*, II, ii, 115–6.

SATURDAY 19 AUGUST 1837   letters from J and Mr Irons   walked to Littlemore with Berkeley who and Cornish dined with me   wrote to J

TO MRS JOHN MOZLEY

Oriel College. ⌜August 19. 1837⌝

My dear Jemima

Thank you for your kind letter of this morning, but I rejoice to tell you it is founded on a pure misconception—and except that it annoys me you should have been frightened or made anxious, I should call it ridiculous. I will tell you just what the fact is that you may judge. The other night I spit blood—so I went to Tuckwell. He looked into my throat and found the cause was merely a pimple, or what is called a sore throat. Also by describing to him the appearance of the blood I quite satisfied him that it was no more alarming than a gum bleeding—which would cause a bloodspitting too. Much against my will he made me take physic, keep from going to Littlemore, and not read in St Mary's—he said for two or three days. I obeyed him for one. And then went on as usual. I am perfectly well, thank you— only languid from the heat of the weather somewhat—which I suppose every one is. It is very kind of friends to be anxious—but I am every now and then hearing reports about my health, which are unfounded.

I am busy in various ways—and much as I should like it, cannot afford time to come to Derby. Whenever I come, I will come to be idle. ⌜I am getting through my book on Justification. I have written it twice—and probably shall write it once more. It will be in a style between Sermons and Lectures⌝ —many of them I suppose might be preached; some have been.—Froude's one volume will make two—I had hoped, as I told you, to have it printed at Derby; but Rivington has offered to print and publish it at his own expence, so it would have been unjust to Archdeacon Froude, not to have accepted the offer.

We intend to make the Littlemore Consecration day September 22 a great day. I heartily wish you and John could be here. The Chapel is more furnished than it was—in time it will be quite ornate. Either Anne or Maria Mozley threw out the possibility of their making a cover for the Altar. I heartily wish it would come into their heads, but I cannot ask them, it is so great a work. We have a most splendid Pulpit Cloth, properly belonging to St Mary's but presented by the Vestry to Littlemore. We shall use it for the first time on September 22. Mrs Small is in very weak health—she is in hopes she shall see you in your way to Cholderton.

I was surprised you sent me no answer to my last very long letter, which you sent me word to Cholderton you should. Also I was surprised to hear from Harriet that your servant [had] been baptized—for the last I heard was the question whether *being* baptized by Dissenters she was to be baptized in the Church. And I had hoped you would have told me something about Charles and what John thought of him—but I suppose you had nothing to say. Pusey is just returned from Guernsey with his wife and children. She is not well yet; her cough continues.

Ever yrs affly John H Newman

Love to Aunt—I am glad she is safe back. Thank her for her letter which was very welcome.

SUNDAY 20 AUGUST 1837   13 Trinity   Pusey assisted me in early Sacrament and read morning prayers and preached afternoon   I read afternoon   m. l. p. th.   dined with Copeland

MONDAY 21 AUGUST   letter from R W   M P   administered Sacrament to Thos Cox—his wife ill.   no E P   dined in Common Room with Eden   catechized in evening for Confirmation

TUESDAY 22 AUGUST   Pusey's birthday   rain   Grenfell in Oxford.   M P   E P   went to Littlemore—wet in return.   no n c   dined in Common Room with Ward who was come up into Daman's rooms   Neate came in afterwards

WEDNESDAY 23 AUGUST   letter from Mr Griffin.   parcel from Fulford   Neate breakfasted with me   gift anonymous to St Mary's Altar of Chalice   M P   E P   walked and read at Littlemore—rain in return   f d.   catechized for Confirmation

THURSDAY 24 AUGUST   St Bartholomew   service in Chancel at 11   read Number 356[1]   M P   E P   W Pusey and his wife in Oxford   dined at Vice Chancellor's (Gilbert's) as did Pusey, Jacobson and wife, Mr Bragge, Messrs Stanley and Lonsdell   no c

FRIDAY 25 AUGUST   parcel from W.F. with dear H F's journal—and letters from W.F. and his father.   no l p.   M P   E P   f d   examined for Confirmation   wrote to Bowden, Mr Irons, and Fulford

TO J. W. BOWDEN

⌐Oriel College. St Louis's day Aug. 25/37.⌐

My dear Bowden,

⌐It would have been fittest to have written to you, which for some days I have intended, on St B's Eve[2]—however St Louis and his Oriflamme must do instead. What a long illness you have had. I hope you are quite well now —These rains are very trying to invalids after the heat.⌐ I have several things to say, if I can remember them. First ⌐I have been going again and again to ask you for the exact words to be put on the Littlemore Lagena⌐ I ought to have got you to write them down at once, and have forgotten when I wrote, to ask you.[3] Next ⌐did I tell you that the Lex Divina by which after

[1] P.S. V, 21, 'Affliction, a School of Comfort'.
[2] 'Saint Bartholomew's Eve' was the title of the religious poem which Newman and Bowden had written jointly and published in 1818–19. See Volume I, 56–7.
   The Oriflamme was the sacred banner of France, which the early kings received from the Abbot of St Denis on setting out for war. St Louis IX had received it on 12 June 1248 before going on Crusade.
[3] See Volume V, 329, for the text of the inscription.

60 the Priests ceased to officiate is in the Pentateuch? but I believe I am right in saying there is nothing there about the care of the sacred vessels. By the bye the day before yesterday I had a most splendid present from some lady unknown for St Mary's Altar;—a large Chalice with Leonardo's Last Supper in dead silver—from Randall and Bridges.⌐1

The third thing I had to say, I am sorry I have forgotten. The fourth is, that ⌐the Christian Observer has, I hear, told a lie about me—which they may believe with all my heart, and all those who choose to be gulled by them —but which I should be sorry if my friends believed, seeing it is not the thing that is. The Editor says I used to give Lectures in St Mary's *without the Church Prayers*. I never did.²

About Boone something must be done. Do not let it go the round of our friends, but I am going to write to Joshua Watson, to see if it be impossible quite to dispense with him. We could easily afford to pension him (if he would consent) because if we had it in our hands we might put aside for that purpose part of what Rivington now pays to the writers. But I fear he will stick.

As to the Elections, we may be sure the Whigs will not go out ever— they have resolved, I verily believe, to be kicked out. At present they seem to speak very loudly of the Queen being heart and soul with them—which though true, is little to the purpose in these days. They are more bound to O'Connell than ever, and therefore, one would think, must go further in their reforms; but I have been told, what if true you know doubtless, that the new tail deserves the more honorable name of a Proboscis—being made up of Irish Country Gentlemen, who are not likely to serve under O'Connell— yet I suppose they will be quite as Popish.

If one wished to bring about the repeal of the Præmunire the Bishop of Norwich's Sermon is an ally³—but I am not for touching any of our *forms*. If we can but infuse a new spirit into the Church, these will fall off like the case of a chrysalis—quid leges sine moribus? in like manner quid non mores —where there is a spirit it finds out channels—it creates the external tokens and means of energizing. On the other hand we are not ripe for a change. The peculiars would be for gaining the elections of Bishops to the Church, in hopes of appointing their friends. Better have a liberal for a Bishop who

---

¹ [[Rundell and Bridge's]]

² An article on 'Unauthorized Innovations in Ecclesiastical Vestments and the Administration of Divine Service at Oxford' appeared in *The Christian Observer*, 428, 1837 (Aug.), 502–11. It began with a long letter, signed 'An Afflicted Spectator', consisting of large extracts from P. Maurice's *Popery in Oxford*, to confirm that, 'a confederacy has been organized to innovate upon our established Protestant usages.' The correspondent referred to Newman's Adam de Brome Chapel Lectures, and quoted: 'These lectures are delivered in a chapel, within the walls of St. Mary the Virgin's Church, without any service or preparatory prayer, and I cannot but look upon this as being irregular in the highest degree.' The editor continued: 'Mr. Maurice adds, in a note, that since the above was written Mr. Newman has used the Evening Service of the Church upon these occasions; which is a proof of the previous irregularity.' p. 505.

³ Edward Stanley's Installation Sermon of 17 Aug.; cf. fourth note to letter of 6 Oct. to Edward Churton.

will only be for retaining what is, than a fanatic who will never rest without all sorts of changes.

My best compliments to Hildebrand[1]—I wish there was a likelihood of my coming to Town but I do not see it at present.

Ever yrs affly John H. Newman.

SATURDAY 26 AUGUST 1837 Mr Hope called (*this was the beginning of my intimacy with dear Hope Scott*) walked to Littlemore and read M P E P dined in Common Room with Ward

TO J. R. BLOXAM

Aug 26/37

My dear Bloxam,

The Subscription list[1] stands thus   Nov. 12. 1835—£8.6.0 of this I have no account in detail. Mr Greening gave me *the money*. Yet I think there will be no great difficulty in getting the *names*. £5 was Mr G. himself—The Giles gave something etc.

Then follows what completes the list

Anne Small	James Cordery
John King	Hannah Hurst
William Tombs	Rd Humphries
Sarah Tombs	—— Abel (Christian name?)
James Phipps	Wm Clayden
Henry Parsons	Giles's servant (query name)
Elizabeth Fowler	Widow ⟨Sarah⟩ Bampton
Anne Buck	(Christian name?)
Catherine Price	R Waring
James Carter	Wm Haines
Thos Dover	⟨John⟩ Burrows (Christian name?)
Emma Baker	Children's box

Mrs Tombs will help you to finish it

Ever Yrs J H N

SUNDAY 27 AUGUST 1837   fourteenth Trinity   no one assisting in Sacrament   parcel from Keble   m v   did duty morning and afternoon   preached Number 382[2]   Acland in Oxford   dined with Cornish as did Copeland   sent K [Keble] his proofs—and to R.[Rivington] K's proofs.

[1] Subscriptions from parishioners at Littlemore towards the building of the Church.
[2] *P.S.* IV, 4, 'Acceptance of Religious Privileges Compulsory'.

TO JOHN KEBLE (1)

⌜Oriel. Aug 27/37⌝

My dear Keble,

⌜I do wish *you* would seriously think of the objection which will be made to dear Hurrell's papers,⌝ which the Journal I shall send on Tuesday will confirm. ⌜I will put it as an opponent might.

'In these papers there is much to interest and improve the reader—but the most instructive point of view is the light it casts on a certain school of theology now rising. Here we see ten years since the workings of the minds which have there developed themselves. They are accused of Popery, they deny it; what do we see here? Here is a young man. deeply oppressed by the feelings of his imperfections etc. etc. coming to God for forgiveness, yet not a hint in his most intimate thoughts that he recollected he had a Saviour. His name is not once mentioned. On the contrary what do we hear of? "the holy and great people"—"the Saints—" "the righteous men whom he would imitate;" he expresses his belief in the presence of spirits, of the departed, and Angels—etc. What is his mode of approaching God? by fasting and austerities etc—We do not hesitate [[to say]], here is Dr Pusey's system complete; and what we notice it for is to point out to the [[reader]] that it really does arise from [[is founded on a]] *practical neglect* of our Saviour. We most fully believe the deceased writer to be entirely orthodox—firmly to believe the great doctrine of the Atonement etc. but here is no real *apprehension* of this great truth, no practical adherence to Christ etc etc. —What wonder that in his later papers he actually expresses his leaning to Popery, nay his bitter hatred of our Reformers etc etc. Both then by what he omits and by what he maintains,⌝ by his blindness towards the doctrine of Xt's merits and his attachment to Popery, ⌜he shows us *what is in the mind* of such as Dr Pusey,⌝ much as *they* may disclaim against Popery, much as they may profess to receive the doctrine of justification by faith and Xt's merits.' etc etc

Now, should one in a certain sense admit all this, and say that dear H *felt* (what he did not till afterwards *intellectually know*) that there was but one Baptism for the remission of sins—that our Lord's merits were then *fully* applied—and that, after sin, he *was bound* to go to other subordinate sources for recovering lost ground? I do really think this was in his mind. When he first read the lines in the Lyra called Bondage (vii) there was that in his manner, which showed he felt them more than the writer who ought to have felt them rather.[1] But you know what passed in his mind so much

---

[1] Newman's poem, addressing a 'prophet', ends:
'Then plead for me, thou blessed saint,
    While I in haste begin
All man e'er guessed of work or plaint
    To wash away my sin.'

more than I, that I should like your opinion on the subject. *Some* explanation I think required. I think it was his profound awe and remorse. Is mine too Roman?[1]

Tell Williams there is no occasion for him to come up.

Your brother is with you or you with him—whichever it is, my kindest thoughts to him, and all the Bisley party, if you are at Bisley. ⌐Thank you for wishing me at the Consecration, I should have much liked it. I think I am very cold and reserved to people; but I cannot ever realize to myself that any one loves me. I believe that is partly the reason—or I dare not realize it⌐

Ever Yrs affly J H N

TO JOHN KEBLE (II)

Oriel. Aug 27./37

My dear Keble

I send this back to you, as noting one [thing] in p 94. It is [not ?] R H Froude's remark—but Hickes's and I suppose not original in him.[2] ⌐The *first* sheet goes to Rivington this evening.⌐ The third and fourth, I shall send to you in a parcel on Tuesday morning (so be it)—I was just taking up my pen to write to you when your parcel came. Two days since I received fresh MS of R H F's from the Archdeacon which caused my writing to you. This ⌐I shall send you with the Proofs—and Dr Wiseman's review of you⌐[3]—

[1] Replying on 31 Aug., Keble wrote, 'I have read over all that you have sent, and find little or nothing to wish altered. It being once determined to publish the Journal at all. I do not see that we can be wrong in giving the details of it, startling at first sight as it is to one's mind to think of seeing them in print. I imagine that when we see the proofs we shall be better able to judge of the fitness or unfitness of giving names and other particulars. As it seems to be quite clear that the ArchDeacon does not shrink too painfully from such things, I will look again at the letters about Robert's death, and one or two other points, which I omitted in transcribing on that ground: but I fancy there will be not more but may well be added in correcting the Press. Of course I should think a good deal of what I transcribed was too minute to be inserted: you may *omit* without scruple as far as I am concerned; for my tendency is generally that way. What should you think of omitting, *as a general rule*, those passages which seem at all to reflect on any one . . . If any person when they read the journal gives it the sort of construction which you have imaged out, as to the point of not making more express mention of our LORD and His Mediation, I can only say that I firmly believe it would be a most untrue surmise. Indeed his faith and conduct with regard to the Holy Eucharist appear to me alone sufficient entirely to refute it. I can vouch for this: that he seemed to me to look on the Manifestation of our LORD's Human Nature in the Gospel with more awe and reverence than almost any person I ever knew: and that many years ago. This, and a deep sense of his own (what he calls) imbecillity: and a dread of saying more than he meant, seem to me generally to have been the causes of his instinctively avoiding the Name of our LORD, even when he was most completely talking as it were to himself. This, I believe, comes to much the same account as you have given. I should like it to be put in your words, and make no question but it will reconcile many well-meaning readers who might otherwise be startled at the omission.'

[2] In the 'Essay on Rationalism', *Remains* III, 154, Froude offered a similar paraphrase and eucharistic interpretation of Romans XV, 15–16, as that found in Hickes's *The Christian Priesthood Asserted*. See George Hickes, *Two Treatises, one of Priesthood, the other of the Episcopal Order*, third edition, London 1711, I, 98.

[3] *D.R.*, V, 1837 (July), 43–79, 'The High Church Principle of Dogmatical Authority'. The article was a review of Keble's sermon on Primitive Tradition and the October 1836 number of *Brit. Crit.*, which contained Newman's review of Wiseman's *Lectures on the Catholic Church*. Keble thought the article had 'much more in it than in my Protestant opponents'.

merely that you may see it. Also, ⌐if I get through it,¹ I shall send your MS of his letters with projected omissions. Rivington has consented to take the first volume, and I have told him I am ready for him—but he wishes to delay a short while for the season. The Journal, Private Thoughts, Letters and Essays will form one volume. The Sermons will be a second. ⌐Rivington takes them both.⌐

Curiously enough, you did not date your letter, tho' you noted that dear R H F did not use to date. I have sent to the Coach Office to know if the parcel came from the Bisley Road or Hursley

Ever Yrs affly John H Newman

P.S. If I cannot make out where you are, I shall not send the parcel.

MONDAY 28 AUGUST 1837 St Austin no c M P E P walked with Acland dined in Common Room with Ward Service and lecture Number 255 in Ad. de Br's Chapel for persons to be confirmed.

TUESDAY 29 AUGUST decollatio Ioan Bapt. Letter from Jemima sent parcel to Keble no n v c M P E P walked to Littlemore with Berkeley dined in Common Room with Ward and Eden wrote to W.F.

WEDNESDAY 30 AUGUST letter from H Confirmation—I officiating for Archdeacon M.P. dined in Common Room with Eden and Ward sent parcel off to R.[Rivington] with MS of critique on La Mennais

THURSDAY 31 AUGUST letters from Rogers and Shortland M P E P walked to Littlemore with Cornish dined with Warden of Wadham [B. P. Symons] wrote to Rogers and Shortland no c

TO FREDERIC ROGERS

Oriel: August 31, 1837.

Archdeacon Froude sent up within the last week Hurrell's private journal (1826–1827), of which I did not know the existence before, giving an account of his fastings, etc., and his minute faults and temptations at the time. Also a letter of his mother's, indirectly addressed to him within a year of her death, speaking of his failings and good points. They are more interesting than anything I have seen, except, perhaps, his letters to Keble, which are also come. Does it not seem as if Providence was putting things into our hands for something especial? there is so gradual and unexpected an accumulation. I should be rejoiced at the prospect of your reviewing the volume. I want Rivington to have the volumes purchasable separately; each will have separate interest for a different set of persons—the sermons for parsons, the first volume for young people. You should have the sheets as fast as they come from the press. I doubt whether you know enough at present to begin. These new papers have quite made my head whirl, and have put things quite in a new light.

¹ [[the MS of Froude's Letters?]]

Your judgment about 'The Kingdom of the Saints'[1] is most valuable: first, because it is the first I have had on the subject, certainly the first deliberate one after a perusal of Scripture; next, because it is a very *essential* theory in the Anglican system, indeed it is the heart of it. Further, it fits in to Froude's theory of Church and State; and lastly, not the least, it is valuable for the sake of the person making it.

I wish Wood would put down on paper *where* and *how* he disagrees with me. I see no more than the man in the moon. All I have said is, that the Fathers do appeal in all their controversies to Scripture as a final authority. When this occurs once only it may be an accident. When it occurs again and again uniformly, it does invest Scripture with the character of an exclusive rule of faith. And besides this, they used strong expressions *about* Scripture. Try if you can master his objection. You told me you thought my lecture satisfactory yourself when you read it. Do you mean that the 'Dublin Review' article floors mine or is floored? I do not recollect any arguments it uses against our theory of the Rule of Faith. I fancied the article was Dr Wiseman's, but know no more than you.[2]

I never have had so much important business on my hands at a time as now. The Library of the Fathers, my book on Justification, some Tracts, and Froude's papers.

FRIDAY 1 SEPTEMBER 1837 St Giles's letter (official) from Bishop about Queen Anne's Bounty increasing St Mary's John Philipps called M P E P no p th s n c parcel from Keble with F's papers back answered the Bishop wrote to Mr Watson

TO JOSHUA WATSON

Oriel College. ⌜Sept 1. 1837

My dear Sir,

I am perhaps taking a liberty in addressing you on the subject of my connexion with the British Critic, but as you were acquainted with the

---

[1] *P.S.* II, 20 and 21, 'The Kingdom of the Saints'. Rogers wrote on Aug. 30, 'I have been setting to work . . . to read Isaiah which I mention in order to acknowledge the benefit conferred on all such readers by your Sermons on the Kingdom of the Saints and your view of Prophecy as a record of God's (partly frustrated) intentions. I cannot say how your notions seem to make every thing fall into order to me: and what a meaning they give to what otherwise would have been to me only poetry. They seem to me to grow into a key to every past prophecy.' The theme of the first sermon is God's Providence as seen in the history of the Church. In the second sermon, Newman draws examples of prophecies of the Church, and analogies of her history, from the Old Testament.

[2] *D.R.*, V, 1837 (July), 43–79, 'The High Church Principle of Dogmatical Authority', which included a review of Newman's article on Wiseman's *Lectures on the Catholic Church*. Rogers wrote, 'How kind the Dublin Review is to you "amiable young men," and what a floor it's defence of Dr. Wiseman from your charge of unfairness is.—Wood seems rather penetrated by its (and his own) arguments against Keble's Rule of Faith. He complains that you and K tax his faith too hardly—not merely requiring him to believe *generally that the Fathers assert the subordination of Tradition*; which he would readily do (though his own knowledge went the other way) till he knew as much about them as you do; but also that *this opinion of theirs is proved by certain passages which you adduce*, and from which passages his own reason tells him no such inference can be drawn.'

121

circumstances under which it commenced and have so much right to know what goes on as regards the Review, I am led to think you will let me ask your advice, or even good offices in the matter. I became connected with it last Christmas year under these circumstances;—friends of mine were contemplating, without care for expence, a new Review; I persuaded them to join the British Critic instead. In consequence I am bound to supply Mr Boone with four sheets a quarter free of expence, with the liberty in consequence of being exempt from his Censorship. But at present he has so offended the friends on whom I rely that I am likely to have to write all myself or to end the engagement, which, as it is during pleasure on both sides, will be the result. The great annoyance he has given has been in an Article in the last number on Dr Hampden.[1] Besides, I find he was allowed some Dissenter[2] to contribute to the Review. These two points I have mentioned to Churton, who has very kindly interfered[3]—and there I should have left the matter, hoping better things in future, but for this strike, if it may be so called. Great dissatisfaction too is expressed at the *style* of his Articles, Ecclesiastical Record etc. and all this the more, since Dr Wiseman's Review and others have quoted the British Critic as our organ.

Under these circumstances what would you advise? shall we retire? or (what historical recollections connected with the Review make one desire) is no other plan feasible? May I ask you in confidence, does Mr Boone care for the Editorship? or, to venture on a more delicate, and probably unavailing question, is not the Editorship a property, purchasable of the Editor, as the Review is a property? If it were in our hands, it could well afford a sum in compensation out of the payments at present made to contributors. I am sincerely annoyed at speaking in this blunt way, but wish to put our case frankly and openly before you. I do not see any prospect of compromise, and the question is, what is best under the circumstances. I have not yet said a word to Mr Churton, Mr Boone, or Rivingtons on the subject⌐

Believe me to be, My dear Sir, Very truly Yours ⌐John H. Newman⌐

SATURDAY 2 SEPTEMBER 1837 M P E P walked to Littlemore with Berkeley Palmer dined with me—T. Churton, Bull, and Berkeley with Eden, who did not come to dinner hearing of Herbert's death no c

SUNDAY 3 SEPTEMBER 15 Trinity letters from H W.[,] Wood—J. Marriott m l p did duty morning—afternoon at Littlemore preached Number 304[4] baptized in morning service Hayes' daughter Pusey assisted me in S. Sacramentum Pusey took my duty in afternoon at St Mary's Berkeley dined with me in Common Room

---

[1] 'Introduction to Dr Hampden's Bampton Lectures', *Brit. Crit.*, 22, 1837(July), 163–8. See letter of 7 July to J. S. Boone.

[2] Someone has written above, 'Qu-Mr Sortain'. Possibly referring to Joseph Sortain (1809–60), who was pastor of North Street Chapel, Brighton, from 1832, and author of *Lectures on Romanism and Anglo-Catholicism*, 1841.

[3] [[interposed]] See letter of 14 July to Churton.

[4] *P.S.* VIII, 5, 'Curiosity a Temptation to Sin'.

—Eden—Ward. (*who is this 'Ward', who seems lodged at Oriel?*[1] *'Ward of* Balliol' *is noted on the* 19*th below*—) wrote to J Marriott—Canon Rogers, and Shortland

TO EDWARD CHURTON

Oriel College. September 3. 1837

My dear Churton,

I have been led by circumstances to write to Mr Watson on the subject of my last letter. Copeland showed me yours to him, for the pleasure of reading which I owe you many thanks, and also for the trouble you have taken in the matter.

However, I am now writing to you on a different business. My young friend and relative Mr Phillips,[2] about whom I sent you a letter some months since, has heard that the Undermastership lies between himself and another, and that you have a good deal to do with the decision. In consequence he has wished me to send you a second letter, my first being almost as formal as a Testimonial. I do so accordingly; but wish to be fair to all parties, or rather to himself who would not thank me for sending a mere representation about him for the occasion; so I will write all that occurs to me, if you will let me; and shall send the letter to him, to do what he likes with it.

I do not know a great deal of him personally, nothing has thrown us much together—but I will say what I am persuaded of. You know he has acquitted himself very respectably in the Schools which was the more creditable, considering he has had very uncertain health, and being at All Souls had not the advantage of regular tutorial superintendence during his residence, but had to get it where he could. He is, I fully believe, actuated by the highest principles, and has always been well conducted—and some of his motives for desiring this appointment are most praiseworthy. Considering these motives, I cannot but be desirous he should succeed; though for his own personal improvement, moral and intellectual, it would be better for him to continue in Oxford. He is a young man of gentlemanlike and honorable feelings, with manliness of mind, temper, and good sense; and he would make it his effort, I am sure, to please and satisfy those among whom his duties were cast. In all these respects he would be well fitted for the situation he is seeking.

His deficiencies, as far as I know them, arise from a cause, which such a situation is well adapted to remedy, and at his age one would hope would remedy. For many years he has been left more or less to himself, and one knows the consequence of this at his time of life. It will be a great advantage to him to see more of society, to mix more with and to be thrown more upon other people, to have to submit to the judgment, watch the feelings and

[1] Possibly Richard Ward, M.A. 1837, or W. H. P. Ward, M.A. 1836, the son of the Bishop of Sodor and Man.
[2] John Bartholomew Phillips.

likings, and consult the wishes of superiors, to be carried out of the range of his own thoughts, to have objects set before him to engage his admiration and reverence, and to find himself in circumstances which may exercise his sensibilities, or (what is commonly called) 'tact' in little matters. I am writing to so kind and considerate a person, that I may freely say this to you, and know it will not be taken for more than it means or be viewed more seriously than it deserves.

And now having said my say, I have but to subscribe myself,

My dear Churton Yours most truly John H Newman

MONDAY 4 SEPTEMBER 1837 breakfasted with Acland at All Souls M P E P Berkeley went—I to take his occasional duty walked to Littlemore and read dined with Pusey (Mrs P. not well enough to dine) where W. P. [Pusey] Acland Hussey Hamilton and wrote to Church, J. Philipps inclosing letter to Churton, and to Mr Griffin

TUESDAY 5 SEPTEMBER letters from J Marriott and Ottley Mrs Chandler ill—administered Sacrament to her. M P walked with Pusey Hope, Mr Badeley, Oakeley, Cornish, and Ward dined with me. Mr Watson (junior) called at night.

WEDNESDAY 6 SEPTEMBER went off by Reading Coach to Bradfield Mr Watson and friend also Consecration—22 Clergymen there—about 8 Oriel men. Bishop lunched at Mr Stevens's as did Denison, Archdeacon Berens etc etc. itinerar[ium] no ss.[services] at all. no E P

THURSDAY 7 SEPTEMBER letter from Shortland returned to Oxford early no M P no E P no ss. but v. visited Mrs Chandler dined in Common Room with Eden and Ward

FRIDAY 8 SEPTEMBER letters from Rundell and Bridges and J. James visited Mrs Chandler M P E P f d no c walked to Littlemore with Acland and read Ottley passed through and took tea with me. Bloxam returned wrote to Rundell and Bridges inclosing letter from the Donor of the Chalice

SATURDAY 9 SEPTEMBER letter from H W married Betteris' son to Bayne's daughter M P E P visited Mrs Chandler but did not see her. no th s n or c walked to Littlemore and read dined with [in] Common Room with Ward Eden's Mother etc here. wrote to J. James

SUNDAY 10 SEPTEMBER 16th Trinity v Pusey assisted me in early Sacrament and read morning prayers I read afternoon and preached Number 477[1] dined with Ward in Common Room

TO HENRY WILBERFORCE

Oriel College ⌐Sept 10/37¬

My dear H W

I have a number of things to say to you, if I can recollect them, which I somehow doubt.

While I think of it, I wish you would stimulate Sam. and Archdeacon Hoare, to resolve the Convocation next November in London into a Committee of the whole House, and then to present a protest against the Ecclesi-

---

[1] *P.S.* V, 18, 'Many called, few chosen'.

astical Commission. No Præmunire could hinder this. NB. Since writing this, I hear Archdeacon Hoare is moving. Do not mention *my* name *at all*.

On the 22nd we mean to keep the Festum Dedicationis at Littlemore in a solemn way—with Service—the Holy Communion etc and Sermon—and to observe the whole Octave till the 29th. I wish there was a chance of your being here.

⌜What you have heard about St Andrew's Crosses, I suppose is from Mr Maurice and the Christian Observer;[1] ⟨two Magdalen men have stoles with the cross at the end.⟩ As to the genuflexions I cannot conceive *what* it means. But all sorts of reports are current. I heard the other day 'that I worshipped the Holy Elements in the Service—and what was more strange,'⌝ the oafs proceeded, ⌜'that I did so *before* Consecration.'⌝ So they were actually gulled to believe that I bowed to what I confessed to be mere bread and wine.

⌜Hook has converted 3 Methodist teachers⌝ who 'came to scoff'[2]—⌜and not by conciliation or concession, but, like a mighty man of valour, he slew them by the doctrine of the Apostolical Succession. They are to bring a large body with them, on condition of their still observing their Class meetings, which the Bishop has consented to. They are to attend the Holy Communion in the Church weekly, go to no place of worship except the Church, and Hook is to attend their Class meeting, read the Litany, and a Sermon.

As to Thomas a Kempis, there are other translations.⌝ I wish you would look at *them*. Stanhope is notoriously languid. Your idea about the book is excellent.[3] At all events bear it in mind. The more books of that sort we have, the better. But ⌜we want you to keep the Letters of St A. [Augustine] full before you. A friend of Marriott's has lately been reading them, and is as much struck as you—viz as bringing out Catholicism as a fact. I shall get him to make a selection and send it you to compare with yours—when you have done so, send me your corrected list.

I should like very much indeed the Review of Pashley's Crete—and feel much obliged to you.[4] If you set about it, do not cut up Cramer, for he is coming round. Do not let it be a short review, but justâ magnitudine. It will appear, if nothing happens, in January. I say if nothing happens, for you are aware, *entre nous*, that Sam. has written to me about some Dissenter being a Contributor to the British Critic which makes a difficulty.⌝

[1] [[of New College]] See fourth note to letter of 25 Aug. to J. W. Bowden. Wilberforce reported on 7 Sept. that he had, 'heard the other day from a Priest who is much inclined to Catholicity that you are going great lengths in wearing St Andrews crosses and in some very strange and unwonted genuflections'.

[2] 'And fools, who came to scoff, remain'd to pray.' Oliver Goldsmith, *The Deserted Village*, 180. Hook reported these details to Pusey on 7 Sept., and explained the retention of class-meetings: 'Methodism having got such a hold in this place, being the *traditional* Religion, that the lower class cannot imagine a godly man who does not attend a Class.'

[3] Wilberforce was keen to bring out a translation of a Kempis's *Imitation of Christ*. George Stanhope's translation was published as *The Christian's Pattern*, London 1698. A new edition of an earlier translation was published in Oxford in 1841.

[4] Wilberforce reviewed R. Pashley's *Travels in Crete*, Cambridge 1837, in *Brit. Crit.*, 23, 1838 (Jan.), 225–47. He did not mention any work of J. A. Cramer, the classicist and historian, who had written on Grecian topography.

I fear the Bishop of London will be too much of a mouthful for you. I should be amused to know how you got on with him.[1]

Archdeacon F. [Froude] has sent up papers still more interesting than any I have seen—and dear F's letters to Keble are most striking

Ever Yrs affly John H Newman

P.S. ⌐There is [[are]] still more movements among us here—I mean yearnings and advances towards Catholicism in unlikely quarters.¬ The latest news is Golightly's, who told Acland and others the other day that I had given up Pusey's view on Baptism and had stated so (I believe) in *letter*.

MONDAY 11 SEPTEMBER 1837 (henceforth all Ss [Services] but L [Lauds] from Parv. Off. B M V [Parvum Officium Beatae Mariae Virginis] except M. L. and 1 and 2 v. [1st and 2nd vespers] on Feasts) M P E P walked with Pusey visited Mrs Chandler dined in Common Room with Ward wrote to J and H W J Marriott passing thro' took tea in evening.

TO MRS JOHN MOZLEY

Oriel College. Sept 11/37

My dear Jemima,

We are rather perplexed to get all the *names* of the Littlemore Subscribers to the Chapel. Mr Greening brought me in November 1835 £8. 6. Can you throw any light upon the items of it? He himself and his wife gave £5 of it.

While I think of it, while you are at Cholderton, you will do me an exceeding great favour if you will prevail on H. to send me my letters to my Mother, *including* those I sent to her from the Continent. It disappointed me extremely that I could not have them when I was there. I offered to put them out myself. H. said at the time she did them up, she put them into one box. I shall not rest till I have them.

Will you tell James I am anxious to hear of his having been sedulous in his *Latin and Greek* for Lincoln. They certainly will think of it more than philosophy. I know he thinks Mitchel his friend; I doubt not he is—but he has told a person who has told me that he never could get J. M. to do what *he* (Mitchel) wished, so that James must not take it easy. Besides, I fear that his acquaintance with me will not profit him.

This puts me in mind of what you say about Mrs Latham. You do me injustice in thinking I should not care about it. I am very sorry that my name should be even made the *excuse* of a piece of impertinence, which, little harm as it does to the parties visited, is so disgraceful to the parties offering it. The truth is that wherever the Peculiars are strong they will insult all who stand

---

[1] Bishop Blomfield was staying in the area and was due to dine with Wilberforce. See letter of 6 Oct. to J. W. Bowden.

on the old foundation—and where they are weak, they will cry out with Mr Maurice that they are persecuted. They are indignant beyond measure that their career of innovation is stopped, and they will be impertinent in consequence to all who contribute to stop it. That the Mozleys so contribute in Derby is plain—it ought but to lead them to be more deliberate and resolved in their propagation of Catholic Truth—and this I hold most decidedly, that where Catholic Truth is denied (where it is, when men deny the grace of Baptism) any one, layman, woman, child, has a right to hold up the standard of the faith against Bishops, Archdeacons, and Clergy. It is a mere question of *expediency* how far they should do this—a mere question of the *manner* of doing it, the time, place, towards whom, etc., but they have the right, and are bound, under these discretionary limits, to exercise it.

Hook has converted three Methodist Preachers 'who came to scoff'—and not in any by way, or by concession, but by the doctrine of the Apostolical Succession. He drew his good sword, and forced them to yield—they are to bring or have brought with them a large body of Methodists, on condition they may hold their class meetings weekly—The Bishop has given leave—Hook is to attend the class meeting, read the Litany and a Sermon—and they have promised to receive the Holy Communion weekly in Church, and never to go to any meeting. This gives me hopes for your part of the world—for I have long thought the North was but imperfectly converted, and people had it not in them there to *be* Catholics.

It is quite true that Dr P. Smith has written against the Canticles—this is an old story.[1]

An anonymous lady has sent me from London a most beautiful Chalice for St Mary's Altar. Remind me to show it to you when you come—it is *most* beautiful—and as you may think I have presented it there with great thankfulness and pleasure.

I do not recollect Taylor enough to say how he differs from the view I set down for you on Baptism and Confirmation. [2] Will you when you write state a thing of two?—As to the question of Lay and Dissenting Baptism it is a very difficult one. I inclose a letter on the subject, if you can make it out. Let me have it again. The passage on 'intention to obey God' should have been further explained to avoid liberalism.

I meant to have sent the final account of remainder of Bills at Rose Hill which I settled this Spring, but have no time.

As to Frank it is very sad. He *will* not live with people of intellect and attainment, at least not as regards *religion*. According to all appearances, he is, as regards religious objects, frittering away high talents, and will never have a settled, consistent, comfortable view. As to Hooker, the points in which they think he agrees with them are that the people choose the King—

[1] John Pye Smith, the nonconformist divine, criticised and questioned the canonicity of the Song of Solomon in his *The Scripture Testimony to the Messiah*, second edition, London 1829, I, 46–53.
[2] See letter of 4 June to Mrs Mozley.

and that the State and Church are one and the same. The whole of the 5th Book they would pass over as 'unworthy of Hooker.' Arnold says something of this kind in his Sermons Vol 3.[1]

Ever yrs affly John H Newman

TUESDAY 12 SEPTEMBER 1837   letters from Mr Watson and Lord Lifford   M P   E P Li for La. [Litany for Lauds] no c   walked to Littlemore and read there; Pusey walked part of way. visited Mrs Chandler   dined with Hope [at] Merton as did Ward, T. Churton, Hamilton and Badeley.

TO LORD LIFFORD

To Lord Lifford   Oriel College. Sept 12 1837

My Lord,

No apology was necessary for a letter so considerately and kindly worded as your Lordship's which I received this morning.[2] I only regret that from the importance of the questions it contains I shall be unable to do justice to it in my answer, and may perhaps in satisfying one of them raise another.

I will begin by your surmise that 'possibly I take an impression' concerning the so-called Evangelical body, 'from some 2nd or 3rd rate preacher, which I should modify if I were well acquainted with such writers as Scott and Simeon etc.'

On this I would observe in the first place that I believe I have no where in any thing I have written spoken against *individuals* at least as individuals; I have spoken against a *system* and of individuals only so far as they are identified with it, a system which works its way independently of individuals; which makes use indeed of individuals to advance itself but is not confined within the limits of their personal opinions, which makes them its instruments, outsteps and passes by them, casting them off when it has used them, then in a more developed form takes up others who go further, uses and in

---

[1] Arnold wrote in his Appendix to Sermon XI, 'Christ our only Priest', '. . . Hooker writes, in the fifth book of his Ecclesiastical Polity; a part of his work containing passages so unworthy of all that precedes, and of much that follows it, that nothing but a knowledge of the power of party spirit even over a great mind, could allow us to believe that they were written in honesty.' Thomas Arnold, *Sermons*, fourth edition, London 1853, III, 377.

Arnold was also reported to have said: 'I long to see something which should solve what is to me the great problem of Hooker's mind. He is the only man that I know, who, holding with his whole mind and soul the idea of the eternal distinction between moral and positive laws, holds with it the love for a priestly and ceremonial religion, such as appears in the Fifth Book.' A. P. Stanley, *The Life of Thomas Arnold*, London 1844, II, 64.

[2] Lord Lifford sent Newman a long letter after reading *P.S.* II, 15, 'Self-Contemplation'. He felt that Newman's criticism of Evangelicals for not insisting 'on the objects and fruits of faith' was unfair, and gave many quotations from Scott's Commentary to support them on this point.

Newman draws out the argument of this letter in similar terms and at greater length in *Jfc.*, Lecture XIII, 'On Preaching the Gospel'.

turn discards them, till in the course of generations it arrives at its full dimensions. Hence individual teachers of a doctrine are often far better than it; they do not see its bearings; and though their excellence is always a primâ facie recommmendation of it, nay an evidence for it in *proportion to* the standard to which they rise, yet to estimate it duly we must look at it ⟨beyond and out of them⟩ on a wide field and on what is called the long run. I have never spoken against Mr Milner, Mr Scott, or such as they were; they are the teachers of a past and purer period of that system which in this day outruns them, as being developed by their successors into its legitimate evil results. If I aim at all at individuals, the preface to my Volume[1] will show you I am not aiming at persons *within* the Church.

But next both the writers you mention, Mr Scott and Mr Simeon are, I may say, well known to me. I paid no little attention to Mr Simeon's skeletons[2] when I first went into orders; and in Mr Scott's works I could bear to stand an examination. From the age of 15, when first I knew them, I was attracted by the earnestness, manliness and independence of his character; he seemed to me one who was willing to stand on God's side against the world, and I never have lost this impression of him. He is the fairest specimen that can be taken of the so called Evangelical school, from the very practical character of his works. I am perfectly well acquainted with his Force of Truth, his Essays, his Son's life of him, and above all his Commentary.[3] I will not say I have read it all through, but I cannot recollect the part I have not read, though doubtless in so large a work I am unacquainted with much. His commentaries on the Epistles and Revelations I have read again and again. No, My Lord—in my sermons nothing is written against individuals; but against their system. This is what comes of our living in Colleges, and in our quiet Parishes. Men who are in the world meet with *individuals*—they are caught by their many excellences—and see their system only in them, in the light of their peculiar holiness, amiableness, or depth of character; but we are not under that temptation, we are neither distracted nor drawn aside from viewing things as wholes, and connecting one generation with another. I insist on this, because if your Lordship will bear it in mind in any thing you happen to read of mine or of others' whom I am known to respect, it will clear us of the charge of uncharitableness or party spirit

I will add, as may naturally be surmised from my acquaintance with Mr Scott's writings, that I have not always held my present views. It is now

[1] 'He ventures further to hope, that he may not unnecessarily be supposed in any part of his Volumes, to be hazarding remarks on opinions or practices existing within the Church.' p. ix of 'Advertisement' to the first edition of *P.S.* II, not included in the uniform edition.

[2] Charles Simeon, *Helps to Composition; or Six Hundred Skeletons of Sermons . . .*, five volumes, third edition, London 1815. For Newman's cautious recommendation of the work, see Volume I, 235.

[3] Newman possessed copies of Thomas Scott's *The Force of Truth. An Authentic Narrative*, tenth edition, London 1817; *Essays on the Most Important Subjects in Religion*, seventh edition, London 1814; *A Treatise on Growth in Grace*, sixth edition, London 1824; *The Holy Bible . . . with explanatory notes . . .*, new edition, six volumes, London 1812; and, J. Scott, *The Life of the Rev. Thomas Scott*, London 1822.

above fourteen years since I first *began* to hold them; but they have been the growth of years. They have formed within while I was still a member of religious societies, to which I may now be supposed, and justly supposed, hostile, the Bible and Church Missionary. For a long time I held them while still a member of these Societies, first from not seeing their repugnance to them, then from trying to make the best of things as they were. At last they burst these external bonds from their increase in strength and definite proportions.

I will now go to the Sermon you speak of. I there say that there are two systems of doctrine, the Ancient which insists on the Objects and fruits of faith, and the modern which 'attempts instead to secure *directly and primarily* that "mind of the Spirit" which may savingly receive the truths and fulfil the obedience of the Gospel.' p 186 Now I do not at all deny that the modern system does insist on the fruits and Objects of faith; which you clearly show it does by your quotations from Mr Scott; but I say it does not *directly* or *primarily*. If an awakened sinner asked an ancient believer what he must do to be saved, he would answer (I consider) look to the Word Incarnate, look to the Holy Trinity, look to the Sacraments God's instruments; and break off your sins, do good whereas you have done evil—But I conceive one of the modern school, without denying this would for the most part drop it and say instead, 'Your heart must be changed—till you have faith you have nothing—you must have a spiritual apprehension of Christ—you must utterly renounce yourself and your merits and throw yourself at the foot of the Cross etc' Now the question is not whether this is not *true*. I have said expressly 'That such a spiritual temper is indispensable, is agreed on all hands;' but whether it is *the way to make a man a Christian*. I would maintain, that if we take care of the Objects and works of faith, faith will almost take care of itself. This modern view says take care of the state of heart, and the Objects and works will almost take care of themselves. But I have been stating this modern view as judicious, pious, and moderate men put it forward abstractedly But the mass of men develop it, and then what is in itself (as I conceive) a mistake, becomes a mischief. One says '*Examine* yourselves whether you have this spiritual temper—Without it you are nothing though you abound in good works and are orthodox in creed, you are but a moral man.—do you hate sin? do you love Christ? do you feel that He is the pearl of great price?' etc etc Now such questions are either mere generalisms meaning nothing at all, or they lead to a direct contemplation of our feelings as *the* means, *the* evidence of justification.—

Another goes further, thus; 'As you tell me,' says Newton to Scott in the Cardiphonia, (a work which in its name and contents is an apposite illustration of what I speak against,) 'you *never remember a time* when you were not conscious before God of great unworthiness and intervals of earnest endeavours to serve him, though not with the same success, yet something in the same way as at present, this is but saying in other words *you never remember a time when old things passed away and all things became new.*'[1] Is this insisting on the Objects and fruits of faith 'with a view of ascertaining whether it (the heart) is in a spiritual state or no'? as I word it p. 183. Is it not as I have said, 'examining the heart' itself? *This* is what I mean. Who will say it is uncommon?—As a further illustration let me set down against each other two passages the one of the modern, the other of the Ancient School, being a clergyman's inquiry of a Christian on a deathbed. The first is from the Dairyman's daughter and runs thus:—'My dear Friend, do you not *feel that you are supported*? The Lord deals very gently with me, She replied. Are not His promises *very precious to you*? They are all yea and amen in Christ Jesus. Are you in much bodily pain? So little that I almost forget it. How good the Lord is! And *how unworthy am I . . .* Do you *experience any doubts or temptations* on the subject of your eternal safety? No sir—the Lord deals very gently with me and gives me peace—What *are your views* of the dark valley of death, now that you are passing through it? It is not dark.' etc.[2] Now most of them are *natural* questions and in their place innocent and proper— but here they are evidently used as a *type* or *pattern* of what such examinations should be—next the work being extensively circulated, they have become *practically such* if not so intended by the writer—I consider the popularity of such a work a proof that I am not writing only against some '2nd or 3rd rate preacher' when I say that the so called Evangelical School makes a *certain inward experience*, a certain conscious state of feeling, the *evidence* of justification.' Now take by contrast a Document which is strictly meant as a pattern for a death-bed examination and given as our *rule* by our Church itself. In the Visitation of the Sick[3] the Minister says to the person visited, 'Forasmuch as after this life there is *an account* to be given unto the *righteous Judge* etc., I require you to examine yourself and your estate, both towards God and man; so that etc. Therefore I shall rehearse to you *the Articles of our faith, that you may know whether you do believe* as a Christian man should or no. Dost thou believe in God the Father Almighty etc. And in Jesus Christ His only begotten Son our Lord and that He was conceived etc And dost thou believe in the Holy Ghost, the holy Catholic Church etc.' Here the *Objects* of faith are insisted on—next follows mention of the *fruits*, 'Then shall the Minister examine whether he *repent* him truly of his sins, and be in *charity* with all the world; exhorting him to *forgive* from the bottom of his heart all persons who have offended him; and if he hath offended any other to *ask them forgiveness*; and where he hath done injury or wrong to any man, that he *make amends* to the uttermost of his power. . . . The minister *should not omit* earnestly to move such sick persons as are of ability to be

[1] John Newton, *Cardiphonia; or, the Utterance of the Heart; in the Course of a real Correspondence*, Edinburgh 1819, I, 162. See *Jfc.*, pp. 328–31, where Newman uses this and the following examples.
[2] Legh Richmond, *Annals of the Poor*, fifth edition, London 1826, pp. 214–6. 'The Dairyman's Daughter' was the third of the tales making up the work. It had a vast circulation and was translated into several languages.
[3] In *The Book of Common Prayer*.

liberal to the poor.' Then the sick person is to be 'moved to make a special *confession* of his sins, if he feels his conscience troubled with any weighty matter.' After this follows the most emphatic Absolution in our Ritual. Now without dwelling upon words and phrases, is not the *spirit* of this whole passage quite at variance with that of the Modern School? would not moderns think that if a Minister *confined* himself to such directions, he would leave out *the* most important part of his duty towards a sick person? that is, is it not plain that the Prayer Book has left out *altogether* what *alone* Mr L. Richmond has put in? that in fact the ancient system insists on the Objects and fruits of faith as supplying the direct, natural, and necessary evidence of justification, and the modern on a certain state of inward feeling?—I would almost rest the matter on this instance from the Prayer Book; the feeling of the School in question towards it being a witness sufficient in my favour. On this subject something is said in the Tracts for the Times No 41, which I beg to recommend to your Lordship's notice.[1]

But others of the modern school, nay their principal writers in this day, go or tend to go further still—They almost pursue matters to those consequences which I have hinted at, in a passage on which you thus observe—'I think you must contemplate some other class of religionists, (if religionists they can be called) for you say that with them "the Consubstantiality of the Son or Hypostatic union is scarcely the definition of a spiritual believer," and I am sure you are aware that those who are called Evangelical Clergymen hold and put forth as to the Trinity in Unity etc. to be absolutely and indispensably essential' And then you allude to their feelings about Dr Hampden on a late occasion. I would reply first that I do not speak primarily either of Clergymen or of Churchmen at all[.]   Next I have only said that the maintainers of the Modern System will give up the formal Catholic doctrines in *a choice of difficulties* between doing so and excluding from their society those who seem spiritually minded. Next I by no means mean that all *do*, but that they *tend* to do so, that the Evangelical literature as a whole does, Reviews, Magazines, popular works, that the *more advanced* of their eminent writers do, that they all do *more* than the last generation, that they ought logically to do so according to their system. (vid. the last paragraph of the Sermon.) Further Mrs Hannah More in one of her lately published letters (if I mistake not) speaks most flippantly of the 2nd General Council's settlement of the Nicene Creed.[2] I am pretty sure the word 'Consubstantiality' is one of the words which occur in the passage. Next Mr Erskine's writings, which have been very popular speak out almost as clearly.[3] And lastly Mr Jacob Abbott's

[1] Newman's *Tract* 41, 'Via Media No. II', republished in *V.M.* II, 35–48. See pp. 43–5 on the Visitation of the Sick and Evangelical attitudes.

[2] 'I heartily thank you, dear Sir, for your friendly cautions about what you call the Constantinopolitan jargons, but believe me, I am in no danger; you yourself have hardly a higher disdain of the narrow spirit, the contracting littleness of party in religion. I deplore the separating system and bigotry which has split the Christian world.' W. Roberts, *Memoirs of the Life and Correspondence of Mrs. Hannah More*, third edition, London 1835, II, 191.

[3] For Newman's strictures on the works of Thomas Erskine and J. Abbott, see *Tract* 73, 'On the Introduction of Rationalistic Principles into Religion', republished in *Ess.* I, 30–101.

works, which Sabellianize to the very verge of Socinianism have been edited by Mr Blunt, Mr Cunningham, and Dr Pye Smith; three distinct representatives of the three sections of the great evangelical body.[1] On this subject let me particularly ask your Lordship's attention to Tracts for the Times No 73. As to the affair of Dr Hampden, I do believe this great good will result from it,—that it will alarm pious and serious men (as Erskine has already alarmed some) who have hitherto held what is called the Evangelical System, without seeing the tendency of their opinions. That system has become Rationalistic in Germany, Socinian in Geneva—Socinian among English Presbyterians and Arian among Irish—Latitudinarian in Holland—it tends to Socinianism among our own the Evangelical party. Let us profit by the examples of Watts and Doddridge, and of Dr Hampden himself who though neither Socinian nor Evangelical, speaks like both at once, and is received by both. Dr Pye Smith, Mr Erskine, and Mr Abbott carry it further than the generation before them—their successors will go further still. In consequence the body will split into parts, some will go back to the church's doctrine, others will proceed to an open disavowal of it. The Bible Society has given anticipations of this issue already.—And now My Lord, I will leave off without answering your Lordship's other question, not that I am not fully prepared (as I think) to do so, but because if I am not successful in satisfying your Lordship by the above as regards the point in debate, it is useless to proceed with the discussion

I am etc.

WEDNESDAY 13 SEPTEMBER 1837   M P   E P   walked to Littlemore and read   buried corpse for Berkeley   visited Mrs Chandler   parcel from Keble   wrote to Lord Lifford and I. Williams.

THURSDAY 14 SEPTEMBER   Holy Rood   M P   no E P   visited Mrs Chandler   dined with Vice Chancellor (Gilbert)

FRIDAY 15 SEPTEMBER   Mr and Mrs Neale and their daughters breakfasted with me in Common Room   f d.   M P   E P   visited Mrs Chandler

SATURDAY 16 SEPTEMBER   M P   E P   walked to Littlemore

SUNDAY 17 SEPTEMBER   17 Trinity   letter from Bowden and paper from Churton   Pusey assisted me in Sacrament   took Berkeley's duty in morning preached Number 400 (Pusey taking mine)   did duty in afternoon preaching Number 478   dined in Common Room Cornish with me—and Ward.   wrote to Mr Townsend   in evening introduced to Mrs Eden

FROM JOHN KEBLE
Hursley, Septr. 12. 1837

My dear N.

I have transcribed so much of these letters of H. F as I thought would suit for publication, according to the rules which we seemed to have agreed upon. Indeed

---

[1] J. W. Cunningham published an edition of Abbott's *The Young Christian*, London 1833. J. Pye Smith wrote a preface to *The Cornerstone*, London 1834. Henry Blunt published an abridgement of the work in the same year.

I have put down rather more than I think quite worth publishing: but when you see the originals and all you will be better able to judge for yourself.

I hope I returned to you your proposed sketch of what should be said in the Preface about *the* omission[1] in dear H's journal. I certainly ought to have done so, as most likely you had not a copy: but I do not recollect having sent it, and have been searching for it in vain to put it in this parcel. I do not know that on consideration it requires to be taken up at all with an apologetic air. Perhaps it would be well to observe on it, that since he gave all reasonable evidence of his sincere Faith in the sacred doctrine referred to, his silence is an instructive proof that many words about it are no necessary test of its genuineness. And I am almost certain that there must be many persons to whom it will be a real comfort, as reconciling them to themselves for not being able to assume the tone which some peremptory religionists would exact of them. I think it fair however to tell you that on my mentioning the case to my sister she seemed a little startled, and said she had been so by the like omission in Mrs. Dyson's papers, and had reconciled her mind to it in that case by supposing that many expressions of that kind had been studiously left out in editing her papers.[2]

. . .

I return the Dublin Review with many thanks; some unknown friend has sent me another copy.[3] I see they go upon an absurd notion that the moment Scripture was discerned to have the prerogative we claim for it Tradition was of course discarded: also that no doctrine is worth much which has not a great visible influence: and thirdly that it is an unworthy thing to rest on probable evidence. All which appear to me to be so many foul Ultra Protestant rationalities. However there is certainly a great deal of eloquence and acuteness in the paper, and if one could believe it sincere, a good spirit. I think I must send you Mr. Pearson's letter, in case you should not have seen it, as it is printed not published, and you will see he attacks the Tracts generally.[4] I have written him a long private letter, in which I have especially taxed him with a misquotation of the Tract [73] against Jacob Abbott. The said Pearson is not quite so good reasoner, to my thinking, as his namesake John.[5] By the bye do you know that some young gentleman fresh from Oxford hath been deposing in the neighbourhood of Truro that he went the other day into Littlemoor Chapel and saw wax candles burning before the altar, and understood that there they burned night and day: the which when I heard, I desired the informant to tell the gentleman with my compliments that he is an abominable Liar: should I have spoken more mildly? Wilson has been calling on Rose in the Isle of Wight, and though he did not see him heard a much better account of him. Do you know who is the editor of the B. M. [*Brit. Mag.*] yet?[6] and how does Pusey get on with the Confessions? One word more about H. F. would it be right to point out any where that his great dread of insincerity would naturally make him almost morbidly cautious of using expressions and making allusions which he saw in every quarter so lightly and insincerely employed? I am very anxious to have justice done him in the opinion of good sort of people: there are hundreds to whom he would otherwise be of the greatest use who I fear will not go along with him on this single account—not that we should therefore refrain at all from publishing, but we must be prepared for failure, at least apparent failure, so far.

I cannot light upon Isaac's [Williams] papers, and it makes me sometimes quite uncomfortable. Wilson means to make Cholderton his first stage to Bisley.

yours ever most affly. J. Keble.

Our whole party if awake would desire their kindest remembrances to you. I

[1] i.e. of the name of Our Lord.

[2] Mrs Charles Dyson, *Memorials of a Departed Friend*, London 1833. Edited by her husband, subsequent editions were published in 1835 and 1836.

[3] See second letter of 27 Aug. to Keble.

[4] Most probably George Pearson, the Christian Advocate at Cambridge, who had been attacking the *Tracts* around this time. See letter of 5 July to Rogers.

[5] The seventeenth century divine, author of *An Exposition of Creed*, and Bishop of Chester.

[6] Rose had retained overall control of the *British Magazine* during his illness but S. R. Maitland took on the running editorial work.

have ascertained that Hawkins saw and approved of Arnold's Paper on Malignants[1] before it was printed—and Whately also—I think the blame of it must therefore be put in commission. My new edition will I hope be out this week. Many thanks for your letter and quotations from St Athanasius—I had finished before and shall keep them in reserve. I have fallen in with Daman who seems a nice fellow.

TO JOHN KEBLE

Oriel. ⌜September 17. 1837⌝

My dear Keble,

I should like nothing better than to come to Hursley—and will not give up the notion—I am situated as follows. Till Saturday next I am engaged to the occasional duty at St Aldate's. On Friday is our feast of Dedication at Littlemore—and I should not like to leave before the end of the Octave, i.e. Michaelmas day. Moreover, I should not like to be away on a Sunday. If by Monday October 2 the printer sends me down a sufficient quantity of proof, and nothing occurs here to prevent it, I should rejoice to come to you till the following Saturday—but must let things take their chance. It would be most acceptable indeed if your Brother is still with you. In that case I suppose I had better *lodge* at Wilson's—for you must have a house full.

You returned me all the Papers about H. F. [Froude]—Mr Pearson is very little of a man; thanks for the sight of his pamphlet and for your defence of me to him.—Mr Townsend of Durham has stolen from the Christian Observer some hard words about 'violations of the Rubric,' 'needless bowings,' 'unusual postures' etc in his 'brethren in the South' and has discharged them in a 'Charge' to the Bishop of Durham's 'Peculiars in Allertonshire.' Is not it some thing strong in a dignitary publishing ex cathedrâ on anonymous information, which may be and is mistaken?—The report from Truro certainly is nothing less than a lie—a bare naked lie—but it is odd that within the last week I have heard that a pair of Candlesticks are to be presented to Littlemore in Festo Dedicationis. Did I tell you that I had received from a lady unknown a most splendid Chalice for St Mary's Altar—these things are consolatory—for they show one has unknown friends, who are not the less powerful because one does not happen to know them. I cannot help hoping that the Provost, if he saw, yet did not approve of Arnold's paper. Whately was in a regular fume—but Hawkins, I should have thought, a calmer man—and would do us more justice, much as he might differ.—⌜Mrs Pusey is so far from well, that I think Pusey would like his friends to bear it in mind. I am so glad you like Wood. Do you think you could let me have for the Tracts at once your Papers on Mysticism[2]— We are pressed for materials, since Isaac's [Williams] is not to be put in.⌝

---

[1] Thomas Arnold, 'The Oxford Malignants and Dr Hampden', *Edinburgh Review*, 63, 1836 (April), 225–39.
[2] 'On the Mysticism attributed to the Early Fathers of the Church', later published as *Tract* 89.

They would want no correction; and it would not hinder your working them up for some future purpose. What say you to the following:—

Note [2]

'The foregoing Journal is instructive as regards a point to which it is desirable to draw the reader's attention, viz the (almost) entire absence of our Lord's name in ⟨from⟩ the prayers and meditations therein contained. That the Author's faith in His Grace and merits was implicit ⟨most firm⟩ and most practical when he wrote them, can be amply testified by a friend who was intimately acquainted with him at the time; again there is no reasonable doubt that when addressing Almighty God by name, he was really[1] address-ing Christ also. Moreover from other of his writings as for instance the verses commencing "Lord I have fasted etc" how little [he] rested on any attempts of his own to please God. Yet it is remarkable that no [direct reference to our Lord] occurs; and the circumstance may be a comfort to those who cannot bring themselves to assume the tone of some religionists on the subject, yet are discouraged by the peremptoriness with which it is exacted of them. The truth is that a mind alive to its own real position, often shrinks to utter what it most dwells upon, and is too full of awe and fear to do more than silently hope what it earnestly wishes. The penitent in Luke vii *said not a word*, yet our Lord absolved her from her sins and praised her faith. This reluctance to speak is much increased when, as in the case before us, a person is sensitively alive to the odiousness and the danger of insincerity, and to its actual prevalence in the religious profession of the day. In such a state of mind, the Church Prayers are most valuable, as enabling it to speak its wishes without hazarding its own words; and we have seen our Author most diligent, as this Journal informs us, in attending the morning and evening Service. What he observes somewhere in the Miscellaneous Thoughts which follow is much in point. He there speaks on one occasion of using his own words in prayer, *because* he felt himself unworthy to use those of "wise and holy men"; it follows that all his more hopeful and peaceful addresses would be conceived in the Church's words, and he would use his own only when he felt himself "cast out of the sight of God's eyes." The same remark applies to his sermons: when he would speak upon more intimately Christian subjects, he recurs, from awe, and from dread of insincerity, and as a privilege, to the words of our Services. If there was any deficiency in his religious views at the time of his Journal it was as regards Christ's presence in the Church, which of course is a special ground of peace and encourage-ment to those who receive the doctrine.'[2]

---

[1] Several words are lost here and below.

[2] Keble wrote on 21 Sept.: 'I cordially approve your proposed note with regard to the omission in dear H. F's papers: it says just what is wanted in the tone which is desirable, i.e. not that of apology but of instruction to others.' After suggesting a few minor emendations, he went on to say: 'I do not think I mentioned to you that I was extremely surprised on reading his Journal, to find that he had been so long and so strict in the duty of Fasting. I had not an

As to 'that he may be first etc' if I were to go by my private judgment, I should say as follows—The Jews had accused God's promise of failing—or that he was not δίκαιος. St Paul says ['yea, let God be true'] etc. ['*That thou mightest be justified* in thy sayings'] and asks ['Is God *unrighteous*, who taketh vengeance?'];—After explaining the gospel method, he declares that in this way God was both δίκαιος, free from charge, yet ['the justifier of him which believeth in Jesus'].[1]

As to satisfaction to His *justice*, if we may be said to owe obedience or to be *debtors* to His justice, and Christ therefore as paying the debt *satisfied* His justice, I admit it in this sense. But—I say it is not a manifestation but a mystery

Ever Yrs affly J H Newman

TO GEORGE TOWNSEND

Sept 17. 1837

Revd Sir

I see in the York Chronicle of Sept 13. a paragraph professing to be an extract from your charge which runs as follows. 'I have heard with surprise and grief that several of our brethren in the South, believing themselves to be justified by the customs of a primitive Antiquity, have lately made several alterations which must to the people of their congregations be regarded as innovations; and which have begun a new era of observance of very questionable utility to the Church. Some have added to the surplice a peculiar kind of Cross; others have placed the bread and wine on a small addition[al] table near the Lord's table or altar; others have introduced needless bowings and unusual attitudes of devotion.'

In this passage it is implied that certain clergymen have introduced *alterations* in their *congregations*, and that among those alterations are the adding to the surplice a peculiar kind of Cross—and needless bowings. Other things are said or implied also which I pass by.

As I have reason to suppose that persons well known to me are intended, and am sure of your wish to be accurate in your statements may I request the favor of your informing me by *whom* and in *what* congregations, these 'alterations' and 'innovations' have been introduced?

After receiving your answer, perhaps you will allow me to inform you if I am able how far these statements are correct.

Yr obt Servt J H N.

---

idea of it, that I can remember, for years after the date of that journal.' The substance of Newman's text was incorporated into an editorial note placed at the end of the journal, and a remark included about Froude's secrecy concerning his fasting. See *Remains* I, 68–9.

[1] Newman quoted the bracketed words, *Romans*, 3:4, 5, 26, in Greek.

MONDAY 18 SEPTEMBER 1837   letter from E. Churton   Oakeley called   M P   no E P   dined in Common Room with Eden and Ward   wrote to Keble

TUESDAY 19 SEPTEMBER   letter from C through the Archdeacon   Ward of Balliol called   M P   E P   no s n v c   walked to Littlemore with Cornish—Pusey part of way.   dined with Palmer [at] Magdalen

WEDNESDAY 20 SEPTEMBER   Ember Day   letter from H. W.   f.b.   l. for d at 1   la [lauds]   walked to Littlemore

THURSDAY 21 SEPTEMBER   St Matthew   service in Chancel—read Number   Bloxam to dinner and John Marriott   C Marriott came in evening

FRIDAY 22 SEPTEMBER   Ember Day   letters from Ryder, I Williams, Trower, and Mr Sibthorpe[1]   (anniversary of Consecration of Littlemore Chapel)   full service there morning and afternoon   f d   M P   E P   Bloxam read in morning   I preached ⟨Number 479⟩ in morning—Pusey administered Holy Communion   read in afternoon   collected at offertory about £18 for building schoolroom.   (Rogers' sister died)

FROM GEORGE TOWNSEND

Vicarage. Northallerton. Sept 21st 1837

My dear Sir

Your letter was detained at Durham, or I should have answered it immediately.

The reports to which I alluded have been publicly given to the World in such works, as Maurice's Popery in Oxford, and the Christian Observer.[2] I have heard the rumours in question frequently mentioned also in conversation. I cannot further say by whom, nor in which congregations the innovations in question have been introduced. I have acted only upon wellknown, general, and hitherto uncontradicted affirmations. I am prepared neither to defend, nor to apologize for my noticing the matter. I will not defend it, till I hear I am certainly not mistaken. I will not apologize, for I have done what I believe to be my duty. I shall be most happy to hear from you, and more happy still, if you will honor me, by visiting me, before Christmas at Durham. You are one of the Persons, whom I believed I had occasion to condemn: and I will never shrink from publicly censuring errors, which are more vexatious when they are brought in by our Masters in Israel. Such are you. I thank you for work on Arianism, though there is one paragraph which I much disapprove. I respect your character, I admire your learning, I love your zeal—but it is essential to the good of Christ's Holy Catholic Church, that the Spirits of the Prophets should be subject to the Prophets, and that such valuable men as yourself, if you are wrong, as I have been informed you are, should be reproved by your Brethren. I shall be most gratified by learning from yourself the real state of the case, and making your acquaintance—and I am,

Your friend and Brother Geo Townsend

[1] R. W. Sibthorp wrote on 19 Sept. that he had just come across *Tract* 75 on the Breviary and it had awakened an idea which he had had for some while '. . . that the Roman Breviary might be adapted to the use of Protestants, as an highly valuable Book of Daily Devotion.—I use the word Protestants merely for distinction sake. I have repeatedly, for many years, looked into it . . .'

Newman noted on the letter: 'June 12. 1862. I almost think Sibthorp was one of those who turned me out of the Secretaryship of the Oxford Church Missionary Association in 1830 or 1831, see Volume II, 178, 196–8. But I recollect I always said and thought that he acted as a gentleman, when others did not. J H N'

[2] See third note to letter of 6 June to Bowden and fourth note to letter of 25 Aug. to him.

TO GEORGE TOWNSEND (1)

not sent   [22? September 1837]

Revd Sir

I am indebted to you for the complimentary language of your reply to my letter, and wish it was as apposite, as it is in your mouth flattering. I had hoped to have learned from you the particular 'innovations' which you considered were indulged by several of your brethren in the South, in order, as I said in my letter, to inform you, if possible, how far you were correct; but though you express your wish to know the real state of the case, you do not give to your charges that precision and definiteness which are a preliminary to my gratifying it. Since however, as you observe, you alluded among others to myself, I have ascertained at least what you did *not* mean, when you spoke of innovations, though you do not favor me with what you *did*. With your permission then I will state what you did *not* mean when in your official character of Master Keeper of the Peculiar[1] of Allerton and Allertonshire you spoke of alterations of the Rubric, introductions, innovations, needless bowings, unusual attitudes, and the like general terms, as indulged by several of your brethren in the south.

The formal occasion on which you thus spoke would impose the duty of silence not of reply, were your brethren of the South or their Congregations within that Peculiar; since they are not, it becomes their justification.

In saying then, that 'some have added to the Surplice a peculiar kind of Cross,' you did not mean that any professor, fellow of a College, or Member of Convocation, that any of our parochial Ministers, that any one who has taken part in any theological discussion or controversy here or elsewhere, has added any Cross whatever to surplice, gown, or any part of his dress.

In saying that 'others have introduced needless bowings,' you did not speak of bowing to the Altar, for at the Cathedral, where *alone* (I believe) this laudable practice exists, it is no *introduction*, nor of doing obeisance to the Holy Elements in the Eucharist, for I have heard of no one any where who does so; nor of bowing at the Name of Jesus, for you would not call that 'needless.'

Nor by 'introducing unusual attitudes of devotion', did you mean turning to the East in prayer, because there is no service, no congregation in Oxford in which the received custom has been changed, though so edifying and highly sanctioned a usage might suitably be even now introduced where it has been neglected.

Nor by the 'alterations' which you say they justify 'by the customs of a primitive antiquity,' did you mean any of those particulars (such as 'the peculiar kind of Cross,' 'the additional table,' and the rest,) which you

---

[1] i.e. a parish or place exempt from the jurisdiction of the Bishop whose diocese they lie in, due to their having been granted to a different authority before the Reformation.

happen to mention, because your brethren in the South do *not* in matter of fact appeal to antiquity in justification, though they might so appeal.

Nor by innovations on the Rubric, did you mean the 'placing the Bread and Wine on a small additional table', though you said it, because the Rubric prefixed to the Prayer for the Church Militant expressly bids us '*then*' to 'place' them 'on the Table', which implies they were not there, but somewhere else, before.

Nor by the said innovations did you mean turning to the East in Prayer, not only because this has ever been the custom in our more solemn places of worship as Cathedrals, but because the Rubric implies it in speaking of the reader of the Lessons 'so standing and *turning himself* as he may best be heard of all such as are present.'

Do me the justice to confess that I have taken some pains to show what your words did *not* mean; will you not now at least tell me in turn what they *did*?

Your obt Servt J H N.

TO GEORGE TOWNSEND (II)

sent   [22? September 1837]

Revd Sir

I return you my best acknowledgments for the courtesy of your reply, and feel the force of the terms of compliment in which it is couched. I am only sorry that you should feel unwilling to comply with my request which gave occasion to it, by informing me what you mean by 'needless bowings' and the other assumed alterations and innovations on the rubric which in your charge you attribute to certain clergymen including myself. You do not wish to say any thing but what is substantially not to say strictly correct, I am sure; had you favored me with the particulars to which you allude, perhaps I could have shown you that you have done so. As it is, nothing remains but to leave you in the state of misapprehension as to facts, which it is too plain you are in at present.[1]

Yr obt Servt J H N

E. B. PUSEY TO RICHARD BAGOT, BISHOP OF OXFORD

September 26, 1837.

My dear Lord Bishop,

As they have troubled your lordship with those strange statements of what some of the clergy in Oxford are supposed to have done, it seems due from us to inform your lordship what the real state of the case is.

The reports began with a Mr. Maurice, a chaplain of New College, who seems a very excited and vain and half-bewildered person, who seems to think that he is

---

[1] See further the letter of 6 Oct. to E. Churton, and that of 13 Oct. to Townsend.

called by God to oppose what he calls the Popery of Oxford. He published a heavy pamphlet, which would have died a natural death had not the *Christian Observer* wished to have a blow at Mr. Newman and the 'High Church,'[1] and so taken it up though with a sort of protest against identifying itself with Mr. Maurice's language; and thence, I am sorry to say, Mr. Townsend, Prebendary of Durham, has repeated it in a 'Charge to the Clergy of the Peculiar of N. Allerton and Allertonshire.'

The charges made have been 'needless bowings, unusual attitudes in prayers, the addition of a peculiar kind of cross to the surplice, and the placing the Bread and Wine on a small additional table near the Lord's Table or Altar.' These are, at least, what Mr. Townsend repeats.

With regard to the 'needless bowings,' I cannot imagine the origin of the report: there have been no bowings, except at the Name of our Lord.

The 'unusual attitudes in prayer,' I suppose, refer to the new chapel at Little-more, where there is, as in old times, an eagle instead of reading-desk, and the minister during the prayers kneels towards the East, the same way as the congregation, turning to the congregation in the parts addressed to them in the way recommended by Bp. Sparrow in his 'Rationale of the Common Prayer,' and which Bp. S. doubts not is implied by our rubric before the Te Deum, which speaks of the minister's '*turning* himself as he may best be heard,' which implies, he says, that before, he was turned some other way. And he speaks of this practice as still existing about his time.[2] Mr. Newman does the same in his Morning Daily Service in the chancel of St. Mary's, when he has a congregation in many respects different from that which attends the Sunday Service; but in the Sunday Service he has introduced no change whatever. In the Daily Service, being a new service to a new congregation, he thought himself free to follow what seemed to him the meaning of our rubric, according, as it does, with primitive usage and that of our own Church, sanctioned by Bp. Sparrow (whose comment on the rubric has been reprinted by Bp. Mant in the Christian Knowledge Common Prayer-book)[3] and by the practice in Cathedrals in the Litany and Ordination Services, as your lordship well knows.

The 'additional cross' was, as I mentioned to your lordship, worn by one individual only; but I had not time to explain that this was no device of his own, but according to one interpretation of the rubric prefixed to the Morning Service about the 'Orna-ments of the Church and the Minister' being 'the same as in the 2nd year of Edw. VI.' . . . I am content with that explanation of the rubric which dispenses with our observing it; we have too much to do to keep sound doctrine and the privileges of the Church to be able to afford to go into the question about dresses . . .

With regard to the remaining charge I need not say anything to your lordship. The innovation clearly is with those who allow the Bread and Wine to be placed upon the Altar by clerks or sextons; only I would say that the 'small additional table' has not been unnecessarily introduced. In St. Mary's and St. Aldate's the Elements have been placed in a recess already existing near the Altar; in St. Michael's the old custom has never been disused; in St. Paul's and Littlemore only, there being no other provision, since the Elements must be placed somewhere, a small neat table has been used as being the more decent way.

. . .

[1] See third note to letter of 6 June to Bowden and fourth note to letter of 25 August to him. The editor of the *Christian Observer* attempted to keep a distance from Maurice in his remarks, but commented: 'We cannot hear without just alarm of Fellows of Colleges crossing themselves at particular parts of the service, as if they were in a mass-house, instead of a Protestant academical chapel, of the ostentatious display, inside and outside of churches, of crosses, triangles, doves, and decorations, of a manner unusual in protestant places of worship, of clergymen forsaking the reading-desk, to kneel, like Popish priests, before an "altar" sur-mounted with a cross, and with their back to the people while reading the daily service; of side tables introduced into chancels . . . of Mr. Newman's accompanying the administration of the Lord's Supper with unprescribed bowings, approachings, and retirings . . .' *The Christian Observer*, 428, 1837 (Aug.), 505–6.

[2] Anthony Sparrow, *A Rationale upon the Book of Common Prayer of the Church of England*, Oxford 1839, pp. 20 and 34–5.

[3] Richard Mant published an annotated Book of Common Prayer in 1820, for which the S. P. C. K. bore the expense.

Mr. Newman as well as myself much regrets that these idle reports have caused these explanations to be made to your lordship. We would have contradicted them sooner had there seemed any sufficient reason, such as this. I join myself, because these papers always join Mr. Newman and myself, although we maintain no one doctrine or practice which has not the sanction of the great divines of our Church . . .

I have the honour to remain, Your lordship's faithful and obedient servant,

E. B. Pusey.

SATURDAY 23 SEPTEMBER 1837   Ember Day   letters from Keble and Ward of Sodor and Man[1]   M P   E P   f d   Berkeley returned   wrote to I. W. [Williams] Trower and Mr Sibthorpe

TO ISAAC WILLIAMS

Oriel September 23. 1837

My dear Williams,

I do not think it at all necessary or even expedient you should bring in the Fathers—and though I am sorry what you took so much pains with should be lost, we can do without it.[2] The great thing is to bring out the ἦθος. So I shall expect you to set about the rest, if you can conveniently. As far as I recollect the third part was what *seemed* to me to require most correction.

I expect to go to Hursley Oct 2 for a week to consult with J.K. about dear H.F.'s papers.

The anniversary yesterday went off most delightfully. The people of their own heads ornamented the Church most tastefully with flowers. Bloxam's brother has given two Candlesticks and an Offertory Bowl—and we have got a list of Benefactors. I preached, and Pusey (as representing the Chapter of the Diocese,) divina fecit. Bloxam read. The Collection at the Offertory was made for building a School House, and amounted to above £18. Some people from Oxford expressing a wish there might be evening service too, we had it. I have some curious things to tell you about an occurrence there—also a number of little gossipings about our progress, unless I forget them. The best is, that the Bishop of Lincoln (if one dare believe the report) has in a charge recommended the Tracts.[3] And the most absurd that our neighbour

[1] W. H. P. Ward of Oriel, son of the Bishop of Sodor and Man.

[2] Williams was preparing his papers 'On Reserve in communicating Religious Knowledge' for publication as *Tract* 80. The *Tract* aroused a good deal of controversy and he published further material on the subject, partly by way of elucidation, as *Tract* 87. He included his paper on 'The Testimony of the Early Church' in the second tract.

[3] In his 'Charge delivered at the Triennial Visitation in 1837', Bishop Kaye alluded '. . . to the tracts published by a society of learned and pious men connected with the University of Oxford, whose object is to recall the minds of men to the contemplation of primitive Christianity, and to bring back the Church to a closer resemblance to the form which it bore in its earliest ages.—It may be that they have in some instances exposed themselves to the charge of being influenced by too indiscriminate an admiration of antiquity, and of endeavouring to revive practices which the Reformers wisely relinquished, because experience had shown that they were liable to be perverted to the purposes of superstition. If, however, in

of Kennington[1] is preaching against us, saying to his people that he is raised up for the purpose.

Another year we must (so be it) make the Anniversary more known. People in Oxford are disappointed they did not hear of it. But I did not like to make a fuss.

As there is an omen in our rebuilding a Church on old foundations, is there not another in this, that we have been tempted to go deeper and put *extra* foundations in *order* that we might get *to the rock*?

Mr Sibthorp has been writing to me to urge us to publish an Anglican Breviary

Could you be so good as to send a line to Bisley to *Wilson* who is there to tell him I shall be here till October 2nd, and should be rejoiced if he would come. I have not enough to say to put him to the expence of a letter from this place

Ever Yrs Carissime Most affly John H Newman

P.S. We have lost our School Room—Mr Towsey the preacher has got it.

SUNDAY 24 SEPTEMBER 1837   18th Trinity   letters from Rogers (with account of his sister's death) I. W. [Williams] and Mr Townsend.   parcel from Rivn [Rivington] with first sheet of F's remains   Pusey assisted me in Sacrament   Pusey read morning and preached   I read evening   dined in Common Room   Carey in Oxford and dined in Common Room

MONDAY 25 SEPTEMBER   administered Sacrament to Mrs Penny [?]   M P   no E P dined in Common Room?   wrote to Rogers and Wilson   no c

TO FREDERIC ROGERS

Oriel: September 25, 1837.

My first feeling on receiving your letter was to think how great a privilege I had lost, by not taking advantage of the leave you gave me some weeks since, to come to Blackheath for a day. But then it struck me that *I* had not lost it; there are things only allowed one under circumstances, and though, as far as my own gratification went, I would have gone from Oxford on purpose, yet that in many ways would have been outstepping duty and propriety, and so I comfort myself that under things as they were, leave was not given me providentially, though by you.

Also, I felt great relief in your letter from finding, not only that the worst was over, but that it was over so happily.

the pursuit of a favourite object they have run into excess, let us not, on that account, overlook the good which may be derived from their labours. While we read their writings, our attention can scarcely fail to be directed to certain subjects especially deserving it at the present juncture —to the unity, for instance, and to the authority of the Church . . .' John Kaye, *Nine Charges delivered to the Clergy and Diocese of Lincoln . . .*, edited by his son, London 1854, pp. 145–6.

[1] The Curate of Kennington, Berks., near Oxford, was Peter Maurice, who was causing such a stir about what he termed the 'Popery of Oxford'. See letter of 6 June to Bowden.

You have, in every way of viewing her memory, nothing but pleasant thoughts about your sister.

We are celebrating the anniversary of the Consecration at Littlemore the day you lost her, the 22nd. I like such coincidences, there is something very pleasant in them. We had a most delightful day in every way. The weather was most lovely, and the people, out of their own head, ornamented the chapel with flowers. I preached, and Pusey administered the Sacrament. We were *asked* to have Afternoon Service when Morning Service was over, and complied. The Offertory collection was for a school-room, and we got above £18. It was a most pleasant day, and all this while your sister was leaving you. Well, if anything which has been done in Oxford, whether in prayer or other way, has been useful to her, I hope she will not forget us now.

TUESDAY 26 SEPTEMBER 1837 St Cyprian administered Sacrament to Thomas Cox M P E P walked to Littlemore to dinner Mr Maguire, Mr Davenport, Pusey, Copeland—Mr Hewett with Ward, Carey and Eden (*who is 'Ward'?*) no v c wrote to Mr Townsend

WEDNESDAY 27 SEPTEMBER breakfasted with Ward ⟨[?]⟩ to meet General and Mrs Carey etc. M P E P walked to Littlemore no s n v c dined in Common Room went to I. Williams in evening who had just returned wrote to H

THURSDAY 28 SEPTEMBER letters from Trower and Shortland M P E P dined at Trinity Ward ill

FRIDAY 29 SEPTEMBER St Michael Archangel and Octave of Dedication letter from W.F. Service in Chancel—read Number M P E P f d

SATURDAY 30 SEPTEMBER M P E P walked to Littlemore no s n v c dined at Trinity wrote to Keble

TO JOHN KEBLE

Trinity College. Sept 30/37

My dear Keble

I have delayed writing that, if so be, I might not disappoint myself or you. It is my hope to leave this famous University for you on Tuesday October 3 by the Southampton Coach and get to you in due time.

Williams is here, and I trust, flourishing—though somewhat tired by his journey. He has nothing to say.

I say Tuesday rather than Monday in order to finish some things I am doing here, so that I may come to you with a safe conscience.

Of course you know long before this that dear Rogers has lost his sister. —Mrs Pusey is better

Ever Yrs affly John H Newman

P.S. Rivington on seeing the first sheet of R H F's papers, wrote to propose to print 1000 instead of 750 copies.

SUNDAY 1 OCTOBER 1837   19th Trinity   did duty morning and afternoon   preached Number 351   Pusey took north side in Sacrament   dined with Berkeley

MONDAY 2 OCTOBER   Angeli Custodes   prepared Wood's translation of Galatians for the press   M P   no E P   dined in my rooms   Williams took tea with me.   Ward getting well (*who is Ward?*)   *Can he be 'Canon Ward'?*   sent parcel to Rivington

TUESDAY 3 OCTOBER   letters from Rogers and J   itinerar.   nothing else   went off by Southampton Coach for Hursley   (*was this for the consecration of Amfield?*)[1]   no M P   E P   Evening Service in Cathedral Winton.   dined at Mr Yonge's—

FRIDAY 6 OCTOBER   wrote to J., Rogers, R W.[,] E Churton, W F. and Bowden

TO J. W. BOWDEN

⌐Hursley. Oct. 6. 1837.⌐

My dear Bowden,

⌐I am here for a week to consult with Keble about Froude's papers, which are now in the Press, and require a good deal of attention.⌐ This visit, I suppose, quite destroys the chance of my coming to Town at present; according to the Proverb that 'you cannot keep your cake and eat it'. I ought to be very thankful in having such kind friends, that in spite of the Proverb, I have a cake in store, though I am already eating one.

⌐You will, I think, be deeply interested in Froude's papers. His Father has put some into my hands of a most private nature. They are quite new even to Keble, who knew more about him than any one. His letters too to Keble are most exceedingly striking. What a marvel it is! but I really do think that a fresh instrument of influence is being opened to us in these Papers. They do certainly portray a saint. They bring out, in the most natural way, an ἦθος as different from what is now set up as perfection as the East from the West. All persons of unhacknied feelings and youthful minds must be taken by them—others will think them romantic, scrupulous, over refined etc., etc.,⌐

I am sorry to hear that Johnson is still ailing—Some one, I forget who, spoke to me of him the other day, having met him in Normandy. Do not forget the paper you are to send by him—we want sadly some publication on the plan of the first Tracts. ⌐Mr Townsend of Durham has been in the most silly way firing off against us in a charge. Truro people told Keble that they had it from an Oxford man, that he (the Oxford man) had gone into Littlemore Chapel and found lights burning there, and was told they burned day and night. Daman (our fellow) was told at Ilfracombe by the clergyman that I wore on my surplice a rich illuminated Cross. We had a most happy Anniversary of the Dedication of Littlemore—the people out of their own heads ornamented the Chapel with flowers—I preached and Pusey administered the Holy Communion. You know I suppose, that C. Thornton is to be married to Harrison's sister. They say that Mr Gathercole? ought to

---

[1] See next letter. The consecration of the chapel at Ampfield, which was within Hursley parish, was not until 1841.

be supported, but I do not know the rights of the matter.[1] They say he is coming down to Oxford when term begins. Have you seen Manning's address to the Archbishop about Convocation etc., it is most capital—quite splendid.[2] I have had an interesting letter from Mr Sibthorp about putting out an Anglican Breviary. Mr Brown of Cheltenham has been preaching against Oxford views as alarmingly increasing.[3] Also I have heard of sermons in the Isle of Wight and at Brighton. In return for yours, I will give you another epos of the Bishop of London   At his table H. Wilberforce said in answer to a question, that in case of a demand for marriage without banns or licence (according to the New Act) he should consult his Bishop; on which the Bishop of L. said 'Were I asked, I should give no answer. I should say You and I must both obey the Law—and if we do not choose to obey the Law, we must go out of the Establishment'. There is nothing to hope from him. By the bye the Bishop of Lincoln has spoken in favour of the Tracts in a charge. This is capital.⌐

I think I have told you all the news. With kindest remembrances to Mrs Bowden and the children, who I hope are now all comfortably settled.

Ever My dear Bowden, Yrs affly John H. Newman

⌐P.S. I heard the other day of a young man in an office being led to Apostolical views by the Record—Then he bought Pusey's Tracts—and he now lends them about and has become a propagandist. Hook has converted three Wesleyan preachers.⌐

TO EDWARD CHURTON

Hursley. October 6. 1837

My dear Churton,

Your letter and papers were very kindly purposed and very acceptable. I wrote to Mr Townsend at once to ask him *whom* he meant and *what* practices in particular. The first question he answered candidly enough—

---

[1] Michael Augustus Gathercole, Curate of Cleasby, Yorks., was an anti-Roman journalist, who was imprisoned in 1838 for publishing a libel in the *Watchman*, imputing improper practices to the nuns of Darlington. He edited the *Church Magazine* from 1839–44.

S. F. Wood had written on 23 July: 'As to Gathercole—he is the Author of Letters (or something) once a Dissenter—once one himself, now an Anglican clergyman; editor of a penny magazine called the Churchman—which has an immense sale in the manufacturing North, and puts forward good views very strongly and soundly. He is now trying to set up . . . a Church paper . . .' He was hoping to try and recruit Oxford support for the project. Newman noted on the letter: 'I think Mr Gathercole is still alive, I did not see an amiable side of him. JHN March 26/78'.

[2] Manning had been elected proctor of the Archdeaconry of Chichester for the forthcoming Convocation. It had been agreed that the Address which he had drawn up should be presented to the Archbishop. It was hoped that an amendment would be made to Convocation's Address to the Queen, asking that the Church should be allowed some form of check upon the recommendations of the Ecclesiastical Commission before their submission to Parliament. See letter of 28 Oct. from Manning.

[3] John Browne was Minister of Holy Trinity, Cheltenham.

he said he meant among others myself—The second he did not answer, and for this plain reason, that he has not the means of answering. He has taken his information (as indeed he told me) from the Christian Observer etc using (I am told) the C.O.'s very words, and he does not literally know *what* the 'needless bowings etc. etc. *mean*. What could he do then poor man, but refuse to explain? I said in my letter, that if he told me what he meant, I would inform him how far he was correctly informed. Since he would not tell me, nothing remained but to express my regret that he precluded me from setting him right—which I did in a second letter.

Pusey, however, being not immediately concerned, has taken up the matter—and has written at length to Mr T. requesting him, on receiving the information given, to retract what he has said. If he declines, he ⟨(P.)⟩ means to send his letter to the British Magazine.[1]—I should express my warm thanks, which I feel sincerely, for your kind alertness in this matter, and your letter to the Paper,[2] except that I recollect we are engaged in a common cause, which makes such acknowledgments officious.

As to Boone, things are in a new position. But first I will say that he put *into my* hands Hampden's Pamphlet—I answered in the Letter you saw, that I thought nothing need be done *immediately*—and why? my reason was that our Articles that quarter were all supplied. However I had intended in the following number to insert one on the subject, and had put down notes for it—when, behold, out comes the immediate Number with the obnoxious paper.[3]—Then as to the Dissenter, if one could trust Boone, I see no abstract difficulty in a Dissenting writing—but I do not give B. as Editor credit for discrimination enough to decide fairly whether a Dissenter's Article is or not Dissenting.

Now however things are changed since I wrote to you. My friends have almost to a man, and independent of each other, struck, or what is the same as striking. I *cannot* go on with Boone, if I would—I should have to write all the Articles myself.—And what I have this morning read in the new Number upon Dr Stanley[4] is so very exceptionable, that, if *they* did not strike, I think I should myself strike with myself, against myself.—The

<hr>

[1] Pusey's long letter of 28 Oct. to Townsend was published in *Brit. Mag.*, 12, 1837 (Dec.), 637–42. Pusey expanded the points which he had made in his letter of 26 Sept. to the Bishop of Oxford. He explained in a prefatory note that the letter was published with the entire concurrence of Townsend, whom he quoted as saying 'The authorities on which I depended, and the exaggerated reports I heard, certainly misled me.'

[2] Newman preserved two anonymous letters to the *Durham Advertiser* entitled 'Ultra-Protestantism', simply labelling them '1838'. The letters, which may well have been written by Churton, attempted to explain the real nature of the *Tracts* against the misrepresentations of P. Maurice.

[3] See letter of 7 July to Boone and that of 1 Sept. to Joshua Watson.

[4] Edward Stanley's Sermon at his Installation as Bishop of Norwich was reviewed in *Brit. Crit.*, 22, 1837 (Oct.), 446–52. The review opened with a glowing commendation of Stanley's suitability for the office. The section which certainly would have annoyed Newman followed a quotation from Stanley: 'that conscientious difference from another form of Christianity does not imply the guilt of schism.' While the reviewer did not entirely concur with the Bishop, he agreed in insisting 'upon the *higher* necessity of agreement in Christian spirit' to strict ecclesiastical conformity.

upshot is this, which I will communicate to Boone and Rivington, how you think best, and as soon as you will—that I am ready to send the 4 sheets for the January Number—but not beyond. This is final.

It is now, I suppose, six weeks since I wrote to Mr Watson to tell him this—he having been a witness in a way to my engagement with Boone[.] I told him I had mentioned the matter to no one else not to you, Boone, or Rivington; and that I would proceed, as he advised, except that my retirement was a settled thing. He wrote back to advise me to wait till he could see and communicate with our friends—and hoping things might be made up. So the matter stands. I do not like to annoy him with letters, yet, since I have spoken to him, I must write again to tell him that the January Number is our last, if not the present.

I mentioned also to Mr W. that if the Editorship was purchaseable, as property, we should be glad to treat for it.

Since neither Boone nor Rivington have heard from me, pray do not let any one know about it *before they do*. I will communicate it to them in the way you think best.

Many thanks for what you have done about Philipps.—Berkeley I suppose has told you about *our real* doings. As to the additional table, it is implied in the Rubric prefixed to the Church Militant Prayer, unless the Bread and Wine are to be on the ground before it. I suspect it would not please Mr T. a bit better, and it would quite satisfy us for the Clerk *to bring them then* from the Vestry and give them the Clergyman, only it would not be so convenient—As far as I understand, I suppose Mr Gathercole ought to be supported.

Yours most sincerely John H Newman

P.S. Keble desires kind remembrances.

TO MRS JOHN MOZLEY

Hursley. October 6. 1837

My dear Jemima,

I am here for a day or two to look over Froude's papers with Keble—so that there is no chance of my going to Cholderton, as H. kindly proposed— (will you tell her?) They are in the press. Rivington on seeing the first sheet increased the impression from 750 to 1000 copies, which is a good sign. I am very sanguine of the effect of them. The first volume will consist of Private Memoranda and his letters. I think I asked Tom, if he had any letters of Froude's he should like to appear, to send them.

I rejoice to find you purpose to come through Oxford on your return. Williams is taking my place in my absence—he gives up the Curacy now definitely.

As to the Dissenters' Baptism, I should myself advise re-baptism (i.e. with the conditional form), I doubt not, in the *particular case*; but I wish it to stand *on* the particular case. I do not like to lay down a general rule on so delicate a matter. I would not urge it on persons—but I should not be contented with such Baptism, if the responsibility lay with me. What I meant by our *intentions* being taken, though there were some incorrectness in *form*, was this—that, if persons did all they *could*, one might trust the intention would be taken. Now the *opportunity* of Church Baptism is something they can avail themselves of—so that their foreseen coming in after life to Church Baptism may have been a condition, of regeneration being conveyed to them as children in Dissenting Baptism. A person who being baptized by Dissenters, and *hearing* the question raised, sits still and does not inquire, *has not* done all he can.

Do you recollect a Mr Macguire who came and bullied me last year?—well, he has turned round this year. I am not confident of his remaining fixed in any thing. He is an Irishman.[1]

One has every reason to trust that Church views are spreading in various quarters in the way you give one instance of, which is very satisfactory. The great clamour which is being raised is a proof of it—and the grotesque reports. The Kebles heard from Truro of an Oxford man who deposed he went into Littlemore Chapel, found lights burning, and was told they burned day and night. Daman (our fellow) was told by the clergyman at Ilfracombe (an Oxford man and pupil of mine)[2] that I wore on my surplice a rich illuminated cross. The Coachman of the Coach which passes Littlemore at three when the bell is ringing seems regularly to give the passengers an account of us about as veracious I suppose, as those of Oxford guides generally are. We were told from a passenger one day that they crossexamined little Baker who got up to lock and unlock the wheel. I see the said Coachman touch his companion and turn to the passengers behind him when I meet them—so he is a regular herald like the Record and Christian Observer, 'whether in pretence or in truth.'[3]

We have been too kind to Charles, that is the long and the short of it—I cannot say I am surprised, though I am much hurt at his way of going on. He never has felt as a penitent yet—and I told him so last winter, when he began to receive the Sacrament. I said he was going too fast—and so he was.

Every thing seems to have been most consoling about Emily Rogers' death.—The Tom Kebles are here—

Love to Tom & H and believe me, My dear Jemima

Very affly Yrs John H Newman

[1] This may have been the Catholic priest who visited Newman on 30 July 1835. Newman was visited by G. Errington, another Catholic priest, in July 1836. See letter of 26 Oct. to Keble.
[2] John Mill Chanter.
[3] *Philippians* 1:18.

P.S. I have lately been reading a novel you spoke of, I Promessi Sposi, and am quite delighted with it. It has not the vigour or richness of Walter Scott, but it seems to me full of nature, and displays a depth of religious feeling, which never approaches W. S.'s compositions, beautiful as they are. It is most inspiring—it quite transported me in parts.

TO FREDERIC ROGERS

Oct 6. 1837.

I think you will be much struck with Froude's journal, Rivington even on seeing the first pages proposed at once to increase the impression from 750 to 1000 copies. W. F. [Froude] wants some light thrown on the difference between HF[']s and Whewell[']s view of Architecture.[1]

TO R. I. WILBERFORCE

Hursley. October 6. 1837

My dear Wilberforce,

I am here on the business of Froude's papers, which are now in the press —and write thinking there may be letters of his to yourself or Samuel, which you might like to be inserted among those which we are about to publish. If so, and you would send them, we should see whether they would fit into the rest. I return to Oxford within the week—but it is no matter whether Keble and I are together or not—you can direct to either. Perhaps however you had better to me for I am going to ask another favor—viz. a copy of the character which Rickards gave of him.[2] He alludes to it in a letter —and I should like to see what light is thrown upon it by what has now come to light. You will, I am sure, be much interested in these Papers. The first volume is to consist of Journal, Memoranda, and Letters—The second of Sermons and Essays. No more will be published at first. The third will consist of his Becket Papers, etc. and *may* run into a fourth.

Thank you for your kind proposal about the Critic which would be very acceptable indeed—and a subject such as Goldsmith's life would do uncommonly well. At this very moment, however, I do not know how we stand as to Articles etc.—You shall hear from me again—and then I will take my chance of your willingness continuing, and your time serving, which I hope they will.

We have the most gratifying news in every direction of the spreading of

[1] See letters of 4 and 7 Jan. 1838 to Rogers.
[2] S. Rickards read characters from handwriting, and his assessment of Froude in 1829 had been: 'This fellow has a great deal of imagination, but not the imagination of a poet. So it leads him into all sorts of fanciful conceptions, making him eccentric, and often sillyish', *Remains* I, 236.

Church principles. Indeed I think nothing but a Star Chamber or Court of High Commission can (humanly speaking) hinder it—and these expedients are not to be thought of in the 19th century. I heard of a youth in a Wine Merchant's office the other day being converted to them by the Record. Then he bought Pusey's Tracts—which he proceeded to lend to the servants in the family. He was *discovered* by my informant in a controversial attitude with another youth, and was defending the good cause very skilfully. They say he is a wellconducted person and attends to his business. What takes place in one instance, will in others, so be it. Hook has brought over three Westleyan Ministers by the doctrine of the Apostolical Succession—they came to criticize and caught a Tartar. Sermons have been preached at Cheltenham, Brighton, and other places for the benefit of the said Church principles by Messrs Brown, Maitland, etc. The general cry seems to be, these principles are very dangerous, subtle, persuasive, and far spreading—and by all means do not *examine* into them. Again, I ask, is this language for the 19th century?

With kind remembrances of both Kebles

Ever Yrs most sincerely John H Newman

SATURDAY 7 OCTOBER 1837   letter from Pusey

TO ISAAC WILLIAMS

Hursley Oct 7/37

My dear Williams

I think it would be a satisfaction to people here, if you could by return of post put down on paper your thoughts about the 'P—t' in Froude's journal. In saying this, do not take me as implying *what* J. or T. K.'s feeling is on the subject—but merely as asking for yours. Especially consider whether it is too plain as it stands, and whether Pxxxxxx would be better—or whether there is any other way of keeping people from running upon *Pusey's* name; such as Pr. or G.P. etc Also consider *what weight* you think should be given to Prevost's not liking his name to appear.

Will you tear off and send the accompanying to Pusey and tell him you are going to write to me and will convey any message. It is only a message he has to send.—

No news here—except that Daman was told by the Clergyman of Ilfracombe that I wore a rich illuminated Cross on the sleeve of my Surplice

Ever Yrs affly John H Newman

P.S. Would it not be worth while for you to call on Bliss to see if your MS was sent by Keble there?

SUNDAY 8 OCTOBER 1837 Williams and Pusey took my duty   I preached twice for Keble morning Number 473[1] afternoon Number 400

MONDAY 9 OCTOBER   letters from Williams and Pusey, from H, and from Mr Wade sent parcel to G and R. with proofs

TUESDAY 10 OCTOBER   letters from Pusey and Rogers

THURSDAY 12 OCTOBER   returned to Oxford and the T K's [Keble] to Bisley Rogers and brother just arrived—dined with them   found letters on return?

FRIDAY 13 OCTOBER   first day of Audit   Daman came   Provost dined in Common Room   about 6 or 7 to dine—Neate Denison—

TO GEORGE TOWNSEND

Oriel College. October 13. 1837

Revd Sir,

I beg to thank you most sincerely for your very kind note received this morning, with the copy of your important Petition.[2] What you said about me to Dr Pusey did not give me a moment's pain, for I felt most convinced that a mind so generous and open as yours could not retain upon it, what I trust I may call without self deception, an untrue impression concerning me. If my letter was fairly the cause of that impression, I am very sorry for it, and hope you will consider it unwritten.

As to the subject which led to it, excuse me if I think you hardly see the difference, which really exists, between statements put forward by yourself and by persons of no authority and name in the Church. I am sincerely sorry, if our silence towards objectors of the latter class, has involuntarily led you to a misapprehension of the real state of the case; and, without implying that the silence was an error, I most readily grant that it occasioned the misapprehension. Still, since it has taken place, it is plain it ought to be removed; and since we have had the disadvantage of your disapprobation, it is natural I should think it fair, as far as we have succeeded in removing it, to have the benefit of our success. It seems fair that in some way or other it should be signified that your Charge does not allude to myself or friends of mine, so far as it does not allude to us, and so far as its meaning has been modified by our explanations, even though you censure us the while, that such explanations were not sooner given.

Might not the difficulty be adjusted without compromising the feelings of either party, if you sent to the York or other Newspaper in the North such extracts from Dr Pusey's letter as directly bear upon the particular points animadverted on in your Charge, as from yourself, yet without expressing

---

[1] *P.S.* IV, 1, 'The Strictness of the Law of Christ'.

[2] Townsend had issued a printed Declaration 'against the interference of the State with the Church in the Marriage and Registration Act, against the Praemunire and for Convocation'. Townsend wrote on 10 Oct. to explain that he had misunderstood Newman's intentions in his letter of 22 Sept., and to apologise for the strong language he had consequently used about Newman in a note to Pusey.

your opinion upon them? but I would gladly leave this matter to your better judgment, having stated the *end* which is to be consulted.

Let me thank you very warmly for your kind invitation of me to Durham, and beg in return to offer to you, should you come into the South, such hospitality as our Common Room can give, which at least shall not be behind Durham in heartiness.

I have talked with Dr Pusey on the subject of your petition, in which I cordially concur, and wish it all the success which I trust sooner or later must attend it.

I am, Revd Sir, Yours very faithfully John H Newman

SATURDAY 14 OCTOBER 1837 second day of Audit Provost dined in Common Room same number [at dinner]

SUNDAY 15 OCTOBER 21 Trinity Pusey assisted me in early Communion Spranger read in morning I in afternoon Woodgate preached

MONDAY 16 OCTOBER no v Christie came we all dined with the Provost

TUESDAY 17 OCTOBER letter from Boone no v c Gaudy dinner—I presiding, the Dean [W. J. Copleston] not making his appearance in Oxford till the evening wrote to J M and Boone

TO J. B. MOZLEY

Oriel. St Luke's Eve (not Vigil) [17 October] 1837

My dear James

Extract from Saturday's Paper—

'Lincoln College. Two Fellowships, one Exhibition and one Scholarship, are now vacant and will be filled up on Monday the 6th of November next.

The Fellowships are confined to the county of Lincoln. Candidates for the Exhibition etc etc . . . Candidates must present to the Rector testimonials of good conduct on or before Monday the 1st of November. Candidates for the Fellowships and the Exhibition must at the same time produce certificates of the place of their birth.'[1]

You will meet John and Jemima here, I suppose—With kindest remembrances to your Derby circle

Ever Yrs affly John H Newman

WEDNESDAY 18 OCTOBER St Luke no p. th. s. n. v. c. did duty in Chancel read Number 267 Vaughan came? Statute reading dined with Bloxam wrote to Mr Irons Marriott went

THURSDAY 19 OCTOBER Christie went no. th. s. n. c College meeting Audit continued dined with Williams as did Rogers and Jeffreys

[1] James Mozley tried for a fellowship at Lincoln College but was unsuccessful. See diary for 6 Nov. and letter of 12 Dec. to Bowden.

FRIDAY 20 OCTOBER   College meeting continued   wrote to Mr Joshua Watson in parcel to Rivington

TO JOSHUA WATSON

Oriel Oct 20/37

My dear Sir,

I happened to be writing to Churton the other day, and mentioned to him I had communicated with you on the subject of the British Critic. Since I wrote to you, another number has appeared—which contains a Review of Bishop Stanley's Sermon so very unsatisfactory, as to destroy whatever remaining wish I might have personally of cooperating longer with Mr Boone. Accordingly I told Churton that after the January Number, I should be unable to send any additional contributions—what he has done upon this information I have not heard.

This is all, I believe, I have to say on this most unpleasant business— Thanking you for the kindness of your reply, I am,

My dear Sir, Most truly Yours John H Newman

SATURDAY 21 OCTOBER 1837   wrote to Hook, Shortland, Audland and Mr Wade

SUNDAY 22 OCTOBER   22 Trinity   Spranger assisted me in Morning Communion and read morning prayer   I read afternoon and preached Number 480[1]   W.F., R. [Rogers] and Williams [,] Copeland and Mr Goldsmid to dine with me in Common Room

MONDAY 23 OCTOBER   walked with Rogers and Hope   dined in Hall

TUESDAY 24 OCTOBER   Rogers went   dined at Dr Kidd's

TO E. B. PUSEY

[24 October 1837]

My dear P.

It is difficult to recollect one's reasons all at once—but, as far as I understand, we are bound by the Ordination Service to administer 'the discipline of Christ (I am not sure I am right in my wording) as this *Church and Realm* hath received it.' If this keeps me in captivity in many points, surely it also secures a certain liberty (in mentioning the *Church*) which it is my privilege to be bound to, as much as it is my disadvantage to be tied to the State. So much for the Major Premiss—for the Minor, the *Church* has not yet received this Parliamentary enactment and the Rubric and I believe Canons are against it. If it be said that on authority of Parliament we give out banns after second Lesson instead of after Nicene Creed, as the Church directs, I answer, that this was done before our time; we have received it, and no

_____
[1] *P.S.* IV, 12, 'The Church a Home for the Lonely'.

principle being involved in it continue it. — As to the present innovation, it promises to be the first of many following.

On these grounds, as far as I see, I should decline to marry on the License of a Superintendant Registrar.[1]

As to Rose's saying 'yes' — he is a timid waverer — I do not trust him one bit.

But Hook also is for marrying on such License — and there have been so many irregularities before now, that it may seem a slight thing — and one hopes the matter will be set right in the next Parliament.

Therefore I do not think I should go to the lengths of *recommending* a man to resist; though at present I am disposed to do so, myself; I would put the case before him and leave it.

At the same time would it not be well to have a fund against such emergencies (which we could easily get together) — and to tell Mr Irons, that however he makes up his mind, yet at least a fund is ready to pay the expense of fines etc, incurred by those who are willing to suffer in a good cause?

Ever Yrs affly J H N

P.S. I want *of all things* some of Manning's petitions. Will you tell him so well you right [sic]. It is quite wrong he has not sent us up some.

WEDNESDAY 25 OCTOBER 1837 letters from Hook, Pope, and Sir R Inglis M P E P walked to Littlemore and read parcel from Rivn [Rivington] dined at Palmer's [of] Worcester to meet Mr Maitland J Mozley returned sent parcel to Rivington THURSDAY 26 OCTOBER sent parcel to Keble Sir R Inglis called on me dined at Palmer's [of] Magdalen to meet Mr Roufsem the Chaldee sent parcel to Rivington [23–26 October] very irregular and defective these days [in recitation of the Breviary]

TO JOHN KEBLE

┌Oriel Oct 26/37┐

My dear K

I send you a shabby parcel — but Rivington is so pressing that I cannot help it. The sooner you return the proofs I send the better. I was blind to let the 'showed' for 'shd' pass.

As to Wilson I have mislaid or in other words 'cannot put my hand upon' his letter — but the purpose is to make me send him Fosbrooke's British Monachism — which, were it not a library book, I would do gladly.

┌Sir R Inglis has been to the Isle of Man and tells me the *clergy* there have substituted a petition *for* instead of a petition *against* the suppression

[1] See third note to letter of 3 Aug. to A. P. Perceval about the Amendment to the Marriage Act.

of their see—being tempted by the spoils. The laity are getting up a petition against.

A Roman Priest is here with whose appearance all who have seen him are in great admiration. I have not yet been exposed to the temptation. Claughton says he was the only gentleman of the whole party when he dined at Trinity. Pusey says he puts us to shame by the ascetic appearance of his face; and Palmer calls him 'a fellow sitting like a rabbit in the Bodleian'—He has been feasted by Short, and *lionized by Hughes*—but as he came recommended by Mr Vigors, the stream was quite as high as the fountain.⌐1

I am much fussed with proofs MS etc of the Fathers as well as dear H's. ⌐Palmer of Magdalen has with him a Chaldee, and a French (converted) Priest—Palmer of W. has Mr Maitland—⌐

Ever Yrs affly J H N

⌐Mrs Pusey is *not better*⌐

P.S. The *pencil marks* on the Proof are for you. Could you not put in some initials?

FRIDAY 27 OCTOBER 1837   letters from J and Homfrey   ½ f b   f d   all but c

SATURDAY 28 OCTOBER   St S and J [Simon and Jude]   Williams went or yesterday to Norman Hill   did duty in Chancel   read Number 215[2]   J and J [John Mozley] came and dined in my rooms with me and J. and A.M [James and Arthur Mozley]

SUNDAY 29 OCTOBER   23 Trinity   letters from Mr Banister and anonymous   J and J went to Littlemore in morning   Spranger assisted me in early Communion and read prayers in morning   did duty in afternoon and preached Number 481[3]   dined with me in Common Room J. and J. [,] J M. [,] Harrison, Cornish, and Marriott. A M [Mozley] in evening   answered Mr Banister and anonymous

MONDAY 30 OCTOBER   letters from Manning and parcel from G and R with letter from R   walked with John M. [;] J. and J. [,] Copeland and J M dined with me in my rooms   [30 October–4 November] very irregular or worse this week, in [Breviary] offices.

FROM H. E. MANNING

Oct. 26 [Oct. 28. 1837]

My dear Newman,

Hy Wilberforce gave me some months ago your kind message. I will do no more than thank you for it. One great thought is before me night and day, but I have long since been unable either to speak or write of it.—I feel what passed between us then has given me a privilege in your friendship, which perhaps nothing else could.

All I can do now is to keep at work. There is a sort of rush into my mind, when unoccupied, I can hardly bear.

I write to you now to ask you to be so kind as to send me word in what way you appropriated your offertory to the additional Curates Fund. I am not without hope that the Bp of C[Chichester] may adopt the plan, and make a Diocesan fund from the

[1] [[could it be Dr Russell?]] Hughes and Vigors were probably those of Trinity.
[2] *P.S.* VII, 17, 'The Unity of the Church'.
[3] *P.S.* VI, 22, 'The Weapons of Saints'.

collected offertory of his whole flock. This would be very primitive, and encouraging to Catholic practices.

I am in communication with him about it—and have been desired by him to consider of a plan for a Diocesan Society for Church building. Perhaps the two objects (Curates and Churches) might be combined so as to have *one Fund* instead of *two Societies*. The Committee having power to vary the respective grants according to the needs of the Diocese.

The next point on which I wish to hear from you is about Convocation.[1] An amendment will be moved if not by Mozley's Proctor, by somebody. But what should be its nature? Should it be for a dissolution of the Commission. 2. for a reconstruction of the commission. 3. for License to debate in Convocation. 4. or for a Provincial Council—*stare super vias antiquas*. Pray let me know your mind about it. I wish you would come to London at the time Convocation meets. I am very much afraid of some serious committal of the Convocation to a false principle. The Dean of Chichester (the last prolocutor) told me that two years ago, that is *before the Commission*, the lower house almost clashed with the Bishops in an amendment on the Address which was too *liberal*, and *reforming*. And he expects a thorough collision this time. Write to me as soon as you can about this.

The Address is working well here.[2]

Out of 31 replies 27 *heartily* consenting. There are 100 Clergy (incumbents) in the Archdeaconry. If nothing else comes of it, at least a greater measure of agreement on one Church principle than we have yet seen here, will be gained. It is also going through the other Archdeaconry (Lewes)—the Proctor being active, and for the most part agreeing.

Would it not be well to reprint Leslie's Regale?[3] I have been very much interested with your papers in the B. M. about Convocation.[4] I wish you would reprint them in any cheap shape, or print a pamphlet about it just *now*. The idea of the development of the Church principle by the Civil power I never saw put so clearly—I am only sorry it is so short. Can you find time to put together precedents of the changes proposed by the Ecclesiastical Commission being effected by canonical means—before Henry VIII as an act of the Church, and since by her consent. How used they to carry out such alterations?

I hope you will excuse this illegible letter, as I am writing on my knees with a heavy cold—Believe me,

My dear Newman, Ever yours affectionately H. E. Manning

TUESDAY 31 OCTOBER 1837   fast   letter from Christie   J. and J.M. [Mozley] went to Derby ½ f b?   f d

[1] The Convocation of the Province of Canterbury was to meet 'in pursuance of the writ of her Majesty' on 16 and 23 Nov. It was only a formal meeting, to draw up an Address from the clergy of 'loyalty and affection' to the new monarch, since the synodical powers of Convocation had been suspended since 1717. For an account of the proceedings see *Brit. Mag.*, 12, 1837 (Dec.), 712: 'A large number of the members of the Lower House of Convocation, deeply feeling the responsibility resting upon them at this first meeting of the constitutional representatives of the clergy, since the establishment of the perpetual Ecclesiastical Commission, were anxious humbly to propose to the upper house that a clause should be inserted in the address, praying that henceforth the deliberation and sanction of the whole body of prelates might be required as a condition to any changes in the institions and administration of the church. Two amendments were proposed respecting the commission, but were ultimately suffered to drop.' See letters of 2 Nov. and 22 Nov. from Manning.

[2] See letter of 6 Oct. to J. W. Bowden and note there.

[3] Manning and S. F. Wood brought out a new edition of Charles Leslie, *The Case of the Regale and the Pontificat stated. . .* London 1838.

[4] 'The Convocation of the Province of Canterbury', *Brit. Mag.*, 6, 1834 (Nov. and Dec.), 517–24, 637–47; 7, 1835 (Jan. and Feb.), 33–41, 145–54. *H.S.* III, 337–421.

TO JOHN KEBLE

[end of October 1837]

My dear Keble

I have first to inform you, if you do not know it, of my having disgraced myself most exceedingly and eat dirt so much that even an enemy (as the Poet says) οἰκτίσειεν ἂν[1]. I have had Williams' books all this while. So, please, without more ado gratify my great disgust by putting some penance upon me.

Next, there is another cancel which with your leave I wish to make—in one place H. F speaks of 'Mr—'s humbug about the Vaudois,'[2] Every one will know it is Mr now Dr Gilly—so, if you do not object, I earnestly desire to leave out the words 'Mr—'s humbug.'

Also, I have taken the liberty in the Sayings to leave out the bit about the British Critic and Boone. Rogers thought I might do so without writing for your leave.

Also look at p 30 of what I now send line 11, after 'reading' in the MS follows the word 'sermons—'this seemed to me disrespectful to religious writings—there being a great difference between reading good books (and a sermon is a good book) and running after preachers. Nor did I think *reading* sermons was a failure of the Peculiars. If however you think I am biassed by having written Sermons myself, and that the word is well placed, pray insert it.

p 56 it seems some word should go before 'consider' or the word 'consider' be changed. As it stands, it seems as if he was going to treat the subject.

Ever Yrs affly J H Newman

WEDNESDAY 1 NOVEMBER 1837   All Saints   letter from Audland   service in Chancel   read F's [Hurrell Froude's]   dined in hall   wrote to Archdeacon F. [Froude] [,] Manning and L A T[3] (or yesterday)

THURSDAY 2 NOVEMBER   letter from Shortland   Acland in Oxford   dined at Trinity

FRIDAY 3 NOVEMBER   letter from Joshua Watson   ½ f d   theological meeting at P's [Pusey]—I read Apollinarism [sic][4]

---

[1] 'would pity me'; cf. Euripides, *Orestes*, 784.

[2] William Stephen Gilly's *Narrative of an Excursion to the Mountains of Piedmont, and Researches among the Vaudois, or Waldenses*, London 1824, had aroused much sympathetic interest. The phrase was printed as 'much disgusted at —— about Vaudois', *Remains* I, 218.

[3] Probably an anonymous correspondent.

[4] Newman worked on the Apollinarian heresy, leaving notes, in 1835 and again in 1839. In August 1835 he had some of his material on the subject privately printed, and this may have formed the text for this talk. These notes were later used for 'The Heresy of Apollinaris', *T.T.*, pp. 301–27.

TO JOHN KEBLE

⌐Oriel Nov 3 [1837]¬

My dear Keble

Will you send on the accompanying proofs to G. and R?

It is not 'Brougham and the Whigs' you want inserted but 'Bishop of Landaff and the Sumners.' Unhappily I forgot to strike out a Provost; but if you think it worth while, a note on the proofs you are sending up might be in time.

On the whole I was afraid of adding the C. R. [Common Room] initials. I was not certain how far Pusey would like it—and neither Tyler nor Hawkins would be flattered by their share.

I have heard from Mr Watson this morning of Boone's resignation.

Mozley *will* have a vacancy next Easter.

The letters to R W [Wilberforce] are valuable. The story of the Bishop the Whig governor and the money, however, is contained in another, and less offensively to the Whigs etc.[1] At least this is my impression. I agree with you that, as it stands, it commits the Bishop.

I should somehow be afraid, at least at present, of publishing any thing about Mrs Spedding. Would not it tell vastly more to the public than it would set right to friends?

As to your German, Pusey thinks him nothing above a literary beggar. He does not tell me to represent him favorably. Mrs P. [Pusey] is about the same.

⌐Your news about the Bishop of W is good—In return I have to present you with two rumours; one that the Somersetshire peculiars [[Evangelicals]] are to get up a petition signed by 2000 against I don't know what—perhaps all candles, postures, and vestments which imagination ever pictured—next that 200 and more of the Winchester clergy are petitioning the Archbishop to call a Provincial Council to censure the Revd J Keble for laying waste the Diocese by his Sermon on Tradition—also that there is a great desire to make the said J. K commit himself on some point which will set him wrong with the majority¬—and that justification is thought the best subject to use for the purpose. ⌐Therefore bear in your mouth the tongue of the wise and put a βοῦς ἐπὶ γλώσσᾳ.¬[2]

Ever Yrs affly J H N

P.S. I cannot find that any part of the 5th Novr Service has ever had the sanction of Convocation

---

[1] See Volume IV, 216. The story was omitted in *Remains* I, 334.
[2] 'ox on your tongue', said of those who keep silence for weighty reasons.

TO JOSHUA WATSON

Oriel College Nov 3. 1837

My dear Sir

I am relieved to find you agree with me in thinking it would have been an inconsistency to have continued taking part in what was conducted on views so different from those which I should wish to see advocated in the British Critic.

The four sheets shall certainly be forthcoming from us for the January Number—I wrote word to Boone to that effect about ten days since.

No one could doubt that Boone would behave handsomely in this matter. I have had no correspondence with him about it—but should be glad if there was any way in which I could show my own good feeling towards him.

Believe me, My dear Sir, Yours with great respect John H Newman

SATURDAY 4 NOVEMBER 1837 letters from J.[,] Manning and Mant walked with Daman to Littlemore but not to Service dined in hall

FROM H. E. MANNING

Nov. 2. [1837]

My dear Newman,

I trouble you again with a letter, but pray send your answer thro' Harrison as you are busy. But first let me say the thing in your letter that most of all burdens my conscience is the thought that I should have so insufficiently expressed myself to Harrison as to lead you to think that, I wished for any aid in printing the *Address* —or that as many copies as could be of any use were not at the service of everybody. I wrote about a pamphlet from Archbishop Wake—of which I already had 500, and kept the press standing in case H. should like any more—so if a parcel of either or both would be acceptable to you let him tell me.

I will now only add something on one point. Mozley has pledged the Wiltshire Proctors to move an amendment praying for leave to do business in Convocation.[1] This will not only be refused by the Crown, but rejected in limine by the Bishops— and the collision will be of infinite mischief. I wrote to Mozley yesterday suggesting either 1. to substitute a request for a Provincial Council, the consent of which should be necessary as a previous condition to all recommendations of the Ecclesiastical Commission before they can be proposed to Parliament or 2. this and Mozley's as an alternative.

This would probably pass the Bishops, because it is no more than the Bishops of Exeter, Winchester, Rochester and others have already in substance contended for.

In this way the lower house would only be throwing their weight into the opposition already existing among the Bishops to the Ecclesiastical Commission.

It is in fact only asking that the consent of the whole Episcopate should be canonically ascertained—and the *Bishops* cannot object to that. Indeed we know many of them demand it.

It will then remain for the Presbyters in every Diocese to make fully known by address to their respective Bishops their detailed feelings, and opinions about the several

[1] See T. Mozley, *Reminiscences chiefly of Oriel College and the Oxford Movement*, London 1882, I, 426–9.

recommendations. And so each Bishop would not only act for, but *if he were wise* (Remember Hy W's story of the Cows) *represent* his Church in a Provincial Council, which Provincial Council might be convened with no more pomp than a common meeting at Lambeth.

Also I do not think Mozley's amendment would pass the lower House, which, I believe, consists of,

1. Z's [High and Dry] who would do nothing.
2. X's [Evangelicals] hot for Convocation.
3. A few against Convocation, and the Commission equally.

Any two of these parties would outvote the 3rd. and Mozley's amendment would unite 1. and 3. But the alternative would unite 2 and 3. And so in all probability pass both houses, and for once unite Convocation. It would be all over with Ecclesiastical assemblies should the two houses fall out, or the Commission continue unchecked.

If our address is signed by 2/3 of the Incumbents, I am thinking of putting out another (if Convocation should expire without effect) praying the Queen to issue a mandate to the Archbishop to convene his suffragans and obtain their consent to the Ecclesiastical Commissioners recommendations before proposing to Parliament, the Address to be presented by our *Bishop*, who I am sure would heartily concur, though he has not *said* so. I believe our present recusants would sign such an address. We have 46 answers, and only 5 refusals. Harrison will send me your opinion, and Pusey's about this.

Believe me, my dear Newman, Yours ever affectionately H E M

SUNDAY 5 NOVEMBER 1837   24 Trinity   letters from Mr Davenport and Wood. Pusey preached University Sermon   Spranger read morning—but no time for any but proper Psalms and Lessons—not proper prayers   Five Ministers to assist me in Holy Communion   read evening and preached Number 482   began catechisings in Church   dined in hall

MONDAY 6 NOVEMBER   J.M. [James Mozley] failed at Lincoln   wrote to T [Mozley]

TUESDAY 7 NOVEMBER   letter from Mr Watson of Gilsborough[1]   dined in hall and Stevens and John Froude[2]   wrote to W F.

WEDNESDAY 8 NOVEMBER   breakfasted with Copleston and John F and Stevens John Champernowne died   curtain put up in inner room   Mr Maitland, Acland, Copeland, Williams, Copleston, J.M. [,] Cornish and Bloxam to dinner   wrote to Wood

THURSDAY 9 NOVEMBER   letter from Mr Roberts of Monmouth   began [Breviary] Services regularly   all   dined with Berkeley   wrote to Manning, Mr Roberts and Mr Watson of Guilsborough

FRIDAY 10 NOVEMBER   all [Breviary hours]   f.d   called on Mrs Gilbert   wrote to A Buller by H Champernowne.

SATURDAY 11 NOVEMBER   Letter from W F.   all   walked with Daman   dined in hall

SUNDAY 12 NOVEMBER   25 Trinity   m l no more   Spranger assisted me in morning breakfasted with Daman to meet his brother and sister   Spranger read in morning   I in afternoon reading Number 483[3]   dined in hall   J.M. took tea with me.   wrote to Mr Poole and Archdeacon Mant

MONDAY 13 NOVEMBER   a cold all this week and no Services   dined in rooms

---

[1] J. D. Watson, Vicar of Guilsborough, Northants.
[2] The Vicar of Knowstone, Devon, 'who was such a thorn in the ample flesh of Bishop Phillpotts of Exeter'. See Piers Brendon, *Hurrell Froude and the Oxford Movement*, London 1974, pp. 6–7.
[3] *P.S.* VI, 9, 'The Gospel Sign addressed to Faith'.

161

TO HENRY WILBERFORCE

Oriel College. ⌜Nov 13/37⌝

My dear Henry

The sooner the Article is done, the better—of course. ⌜Boone has given up the Review⌝—*this is a secret*—but you know nothing of the circumstances, nor does Sam, else you would not talk about it as you do. Hitherto every thing has gone as I could expect it, or anticipated.

I shall be rejoiced at your coming up. The measles are in College, but I suppose you have had them. I have a cold today, but it will doubtless be gone in a day or two. ⌜On Friday next Marriott reads a paper at Pusey's—there will be none the week after. Pusey preaches at Ch Ch both next Sunday and Sunday week.⌝ Thursday week the 23rd the new Statute (a most atrocious one) about alterations of Statutes comes on—but we hope to settle its business by ourselves.[1] Under these circumstances I had rather you would *not* be here *on* that day—lest you should seem to have come up for the purpose. And now I have told you all about all—I *hope* you will get a bed in College.

I will have a talk about St Austin with you then. I shall rejoice to see you. ⌜Last Sunday Mr Menzies of C C C preached (I am told) against Pusey and me, not to say Keble;⌝—i.e. his words *need* not mean any thing, only he meant *what* his hearers understood him to mean. This is the way people get off. ⌜I am told he warned the young men against going to hear *preachers*—Capital in an x. [Evangelical] Well, if we teach them generally that 'two can play' at their game, we shall have done well.

Ever Yrs most affly John H Newman

P.S. Report says Manning is coming up—you should come together. You were away, when I was at Hursley.

TUESDAY 14 NOVEMBER 1837   letter from Dodsworth   Williams dined with me in my rooms   men in Common Room in evening

---

[1] Earlier in the year some Whig politicians had made attacks upon the Oxford Colleges, claiming that their Ancient Statutes were redundant and due for revision, and that they misapplied endowments intended for poor scholars. A Universities Commission had been threatened but then dropped, and Wellington had given assurances that the University and Colleges would undertake reform themselves.

The Hebdomadal Board had advised the Colleges to go through their Statutes, and had appointed a committee of its own to go through the University Statutes and prepare a systematic revision. At the end of October the committee had produced suggested amendments to the first three titles of the Statutes, and a meeting of Convocation was scheduled for 23 Nov. in order to discuss them. Uproar broke out because members of Convocation felt that the Board had gone beyond its powers in determining that a revision was to be undertaken without consulting them. The Vice-Chancellor's summons of Convocation simply announced that 'A General Revision of the Statutes of the University having been for some time in progress . . .'. See W. R. Ward, *Victorian Oxford*, London 1965, pp. 104–8.

WEDNESDAY 15 NOVEMBER[1]   letters from Mr Roberts and R W

FRIDAY 17 NOVEMBER   letters from Mr Davison (about Churchbuilding)[2] and Mr Poole[3]   f d   theological meeting Marriott reading   afterwards a talk about University Statutes   wrote to Mr Goldsmid and to

SATURDAY 18 NOVEMBER   meeting in Common Room of M As from all Colleges about the Statutes

SUNDAY 19 NOVEMBER 26 Trinity   letter from Mr Goldsmid   Spranger assisted me in early communion   Read prayers morning and afternoon   preached number 484 Pusey preached University Sermon   dined in hall

MONDAY 20 NOVEMBER   no th s n   dined with Copleston to meet his Father

J. F. RUSSELL TO A FRIEND

Nov. 18, 1837

. . . How you will envy me when you hear that I have just returned from a most delightful visit to Oxford. Irons and I left London at ten o'clock on Monday, and reached the University about five. On Tuesday morning I was dressed by eight, and hastened down to Oriel, which stands in a narrow street, facing great St Mary's. Having surveyed the great court, I retraced my steps, and finding that great St Mary's Church was open, I entered. An open screen, surmounted by the organ, separated the nave from the chancel. I looked through the glass doors and beheld Newman kneeling before the altar with his face towards it. A few people were kneeling with him: this was his regular morning service. I returned to Queen's, where one Pocock (a man of note and worth in the University) met us at breakfast. We soon completed our repast, and Irons and I hastened to Christ Church. I left my card at Linwood's, and Irons was soon closeted with Dr Pusey. Irons rejoined me about two, and said that Pusey had enquired about me and would see me at three. At three, accordingly, we found ourselves in the innermost cell, the central chamber of the 'Popery of the kingdom.' I should say, first, that we passed through a hall, and a large room well furnished with books, before we entered the sanctuary. This was a large chamber of some height and nearly square. There were two lofty Gothic windows, at one of which was placed a standing-desk. There were also two or three tables, a sofa, and sundry chairs in the room, all more or less laden with books. The Doctor was seated in an armed and cushioned chair, and received us with much kindness. He is a young-looking man, about my height, very pale and careworn, with a slight impediment in his speech. Irons put some erudite questions to him about the Canons of Nice and the celibacy of the clergy, and the Doctor laughed at Irons' plausible argument that, under existing circumstances, it was better for the clergy to marry as fast as possible! Pusey soon alluded to my brother. He said he had received two letters from him, but he thought it useless to argue with him on paper. The question at issue between them was a simple matter of fact. I might tell my brother that Mr Newman never intended to deny that the Atonement satisfied God's justice; and that the very words of the tract [No. 73] could not be wrenched so as to warrant so grave an accusation as my brother's. I said that he had made up his mind that the words of the heading of the passage—'The Atonement not an exhibition ['manifestation'] of God's Justice', must be taken as an epitome of the contents of the page. Pusey said that the emphasis ought to be laid on the word 'exhibition', and that he was sorry that more care had not been taken with the heading so as to avoid its being misunderstood. The bell of Christ Church now struck four, and Pusey put on his surplice, and we followed him into the cathedral. Before we parted he invited us both to dine with him on the following day. Service ended we returned to Queen's,

---

[1] On this day J. F. Russell and W. J. Irons met Newman and dined with him at Pusey's. Russell's account of the visit (Liddon's *Pusey* I, 405–8) is printed below for the vividness of the picture.

[2] W. Davison, of Worthing. Like several others during these years, he asked for plans and details of Littlemore Church.

[3] Reginald Chandos Pole.

and presently dined at the Fellows' table. Dinner over we adjourned to the 'Common-room', and sat there until nine. The talk naturally fell upon Pusey, etc. It was allowed that the Doctor and Newman *governed the University*, and that nothing could withstand the influence of themselves and their friends. Every man of talent who during the last six years has come to Oxford has joined Newman, and when he preaches at St Mary's (on every Sunday afternoon) all the men of talent in the University come to hear him, although at the loss of their dinner. His triumph over the *mental* empire of Oxford was said to be complete! Pusey is considered the great benefactor of *Oxford*; he supports five divinity students in his own house, and his benefactions to the poor are very great. He had preached a sermon (to a crowded congregation) in St Mary's Church, on the 5th November, which had occasioned immense excitement, and he was engaged to preach on the two following Sundays. It was said that he possessed an indirect but great influence over the whole clergy of Oxford, and that even those who did not openly profess themselves 'on his side', were imperceptibly adopting his sentiments . . . On Wednesday, after breakfast, Irons and I called on Newman. He was seated at a small desk in a comfortable room, stored with books. He is a dark, middle-aged, middle-sized man, with lanky black hair and large spectacles, thin, gentlemanly, and very insinuating. He received us with the greatest kindness, and said he had been invited to meet us at Pusey's, but had so 'grievous a cold' that he feared he could not come. Irons, however, overruled all objections, and when we left him he gave us to understand that we should meet him. The hour of five found us at Christ Church. When we entered Pusey's sanctum we found him and [Benjamin] Harrison, Student of Christ Church, by the feeble light of bedchamber-candlestick candle brooding over the last sheet of Pusey's fifth of November sermon. Presently an argand lamp threw its mild lustre over the room, and Newman was announced. Pusey seemed delighted to see him. He asked me how I liked Oxford. I discoursed on its superiority over Cambridge, and added that it reminded me of a city of the middle ages. We then had a little talk about sundry old customs which were still observed in the city. Harrison departed with the sermon, and we went into the dining-room. There were two other guests besides ourselves, and we were soon seated at table. Newman was opposite me, Irons at my right, and Pusey at the head of the board. The conversation was chiefly between Irons and Newman (Pusey is a man of few words). It referred to the heresy of Irving and his followers, and Dr Pusey observed that miracles had [might have] been performed by that party, if always considered as the rewards of *personal faith* and not as wrought in confirmation of any particular and uncatholic views of doctrine. The question how far we receive the authority of the first four General Councils was also broached. Newman and Pusey seemed to know less about them than Irons. I suggested that we only received their decisions so far as the great verities of the Faith were concerned, and Newman and Pusey agreed with me. Newman suggested that the distinction to be made between matters of doctrine and matters of discipline was this, i.e. that matters of doctrine are those which have been *universally* received, as are the Trinity, Incarnation, Episcopal Succession, Baptismal Regeneration, and the like. Irons made some observations on the Atonement. He said that every other act of our Saviour's life was, in its own place, of equal value with His last sacrificial one. Newman strongly insisted, on the contrary, that the Atonement *alone* was the grand procuring and meritorious cause of our pardon, and quoted sundry texts in proof of it. In reference to the text, 'He died for our sins, and rose again for our justification', he commented on the errors of those who, resting on the first part of it, 'He died for our sins', think that their salvation is secure without the Church, forgetting and overlooking altogether the latter clause of the verse, 'He rose again for our justification', that is, He rose that He might send the gift of His spirit upon the Church, and through her clergy and sacraments, through all ages, dispense the means of grace and justification. Pusey had not gone into the question of the succession, but he thought the only point in it which required guarding was that respecting the consecration of Parker, etc. Auricular confession, he feared, was a grace which had been lost to the Church and could not be restored. Presently, after dinner, Dr Pusey's children ran into the room. One climbed Newman's knee and hugged him. Newman put his spectacles on him, and next on his sister, and great was the merriment of the Puseyan progeny.

Newman, it is said, hates ecclesiastical conversation. He writes so much that when in society he seems always inclined to talk on light, amusing subjects. He told them a story of an old woman who had a broomstick which would go to the well, draw water, and do many other things for her; how the old woman got tired of the broomstick, and wishing to destroy it broke it in twain, and how, to the old woman's great chagrin and disappointment, *two* live broomsticks grew from the broken parts of the old one! We quitted Christ Church about nine, highly delighted with our visit. It was esteemed the highest honour that could have been paid us . . .

TO JOHN KEBLE

Oriel Nov 20/37

My dear Keble

Will you please return these four Revises as soon as you can, with the two inclosed letters.

In p 326 (line 5 from bottom) I have altered 'creating' into 'making', doubting whether H F could be borne out in the use of the word.

In p 328 line 3, what is the antecedent to '*that* tyrant'?

In p 348 I have left out a bit at the earnest wish of several, even Williams. Yet I do not like again to disarrange the type, and have an affection for the phrase 'holy humble etc.' Utere judicio tuo.

Do not forget when it comes, the bit, 'Do not trust —— He is a humbug and no high Church man.'

Pusey's dedication was the result of sheer gratitude—and, I know, more pleasant to the giver than to the receiver. But I suppose it is a duty to receive such tributes, and there is an end of it. I allow it is not pleasant.[1]

I was amused at Mr Norris's account. Rivington wrote me word a London Clergyman was to have the Review, on which I answered, we would have all or none

Ever Yrs affly John H Newman

P.S. We are at feud with the Hebdomadal Board about the Statutes.
P.S. It is so simple a thing to have the page cancelled, that I wish Heathcote was with you to put 'a Provost' before. Is there no indifferent person (Moberly?) who could decide? If you cannot find any one at once, never mind.

TO JOHN KEBLE

[[about Nov 20. 1837?]]

Postscript—p 104 [[to Keble's Sermon on Tradition?]][2]
1. I would not say 'hurried'—it will be taken up—'inadequate,' 'insufficient,' etc etc.

[1] Pusey's 5 November Sermon *Patience and Confidence the Strength of the Church*, Oxford 1837, was dedicated to Keble. The dedication spoke of Keble as one 'who in years past unconsciously implanted a truth which was afterwards to take root'.
[2] The 89 page Postscript to the third edition of Keble's Visitation Sermon *Primitive Tradition recognized in Holy Scripture*, London 1838.

p 108 third line from end.

2. Might the word 'Manifestation' be in italics? What I have said is that men are not content to take the reasons for the Atonement as a mystery, but are determined it shall *manifest to them* God's justice.

This is all I have *said*; at the same time I candidly confess that I see nothing in Scripture or Antiquity to make me think that it was a satisfaction to God's *justice*—or to what attribute it *was* a satisfaction. It was a satisfaction for sin, but *how* is the very point which seems to me a profound mystery. *If* it *be* any where said to be a satisfaction to God's justice, it is neither more nor less than a mystery than otherwise. I only say I do not *in matter of fact* find authority. I will submit at once when it is shown me; the case is quite unaltered whether this be part of the doctrine or not. But *before* authority it seems as officious to say it as a satisfaction to God's *justice*, as if one said that the creation of the world was a proof of God's prescience. It may be so—if it be said so, I believe it—but I should take it on *faith*—it would not be *manifest* to me. The Atonement *manifests* holiness and love, but not justice in our sense of the word, any more than the preservation of Moses manifests God's eternity etc etc yet God is eternal. The only text I know of which seems that way is ['that he might be just, and the justifier'],[1] which I believe the Fathers interpret to mean that He who is perfection in righteousness Himself should impart of His fulness to believers.

p 110 line 2

3. 'the reason added,' *has* it been added, or is it to come in what follows?

p 115

4. 'So far *incautious*.' I would not confess so much—people take one's admissions for so much more than is meant, in an uncandid rhetorical way.

p 118

5. 'not as altogether accurate.' duriusculi dictum? 'not as coinciding in every point with what I have said' etc etc.

p 121

6. 'Not set down in so many words—circumstantial evidence' etc—too apologetic. I certainly do not recollect, however, (as you say) that it *is* said any where in so many words. Look however at the first of these references, whether it is to your purpose—the following are not so strong but look the same way

       Athan [asius] de Syn 9 throughout
            ad Afros init
            ad Episc 13 init
            Encycl i fin
            de Decr 4 fin 27[2]

['not using their own wording, but taking it from the Fathers'][3] etc. Athan

---

[1] *Romans* 3:26. Newman quoted the words in Greek.

[2] *Epistola de Synodis Arimini et Seleuciae; Epistola ad Afros; Epistola ad Episcopos Aegypti et Libyiae; Encyclica ad Episcopos Littera; Epistola de Nicaenis Decreta.*

[3] Theodoret, *Ecclesiastical History*, I, 7. Newman quoted the words in Greek.

ap Theodor Hist i. 8. [7] Surely this is the nutshell of the matter—does Dr Wilson[1] mean to say that (historically) they *invented* the ὁμοούσιον etc. If not they must have had it from Tradition, which is all you say. A dilemma might be formed thus:— the Nicene Creed is either from the Fathers or actually deduced from Scripture—if it is from Fathers, it is a Tradition— if from Scripture, he maintains the incredible nonsense that the Fathers framed out of their own minds a form of words which by accident is nearly phrase by phrase the same as one in Irenæus—Tertullian etc etc. writers which they were already acquainted with. Is there not an ambiguity in the word *deduced*, and hence the confusion? i.e. it either means argumentatively inferred or actually received—but this is a maresnest.

I like your P S very much—it is quite sufficient for all who will attend, and for those you write—and there are scattered through it many choice hints which might be developed to great profit.—I trust it is all working up *towards* a book—for I do not like these unsystematic productions; they do not last. Who reads Horsley against Priestley?—I am sanguine, the theological papers, this, etc. are to combine into a whole some day. N.B. Should not the P.S. be sold separately, for those who have bought the Sermon?

You have certainly been most exceedingly diligent about R H F's papers. I must try to recollect what I have to say.

1. I propose to send all the proofs from myself to you, that you may send them back to Rivington—and I shall write to him to urge him to begin at once.

2. I propose to arrange the letters written to whomsoever chronologically. This will not inconveniently distract from each other those written to *one* person—his early ones to you will be all together—I shall come in about 1828—but sparingly at first, so as not to hurt yours—Archdeacon F. comes in quite late. I propose not to give dates of *months*, unless there be some particular reason, for fear of seeming minute and pompous; but to *number* the extracts as you have done; and to add to the general number (A1. B.5. C.3. D.20) as it may be—A meaning 'addressed to his Father'—B to his brothers —C to you—D to me—and the number annexed being the number of *A's* extracts etc.—In this way the letters will be kept *distinct*, yet *names* not mentioned. In that case the extracts would run—e.g. thus

      25. (C.20) (without explanation, which the
      26. (A.2)   reader's sense may find out)
      27 (C.21)
      28. (D.3)
      29. (B.1)   etc

But I submit all this of course to your better judgment—but propose it, for you to strike out something better.

3. I advise, or suggest rather, putting in initials or names wherever possible.

---

[1] William Wilson, *A Brief Examination of Professor Keble's Visitation Sermon*, Oxford 1837.

Dashes put a reader out and are like contractions in Greek. Though x be an unknown quantity, it makes a sentence luminous. I do not think that his Father will be pained by any allusions—the contrary—that it will console and sooth him. You see he has transcribed all the touching part of what I sent you. Perhaps it might be well to ask William, which I will do, but I cannot help thinking he would like his name to appear. You will see he has sent me up a letter of Mrs Froude's, which will (I suppose) be prefixed to the whole. As to other names W. for Wilberforce etc are often quite innocent. I. for Isaac etc. I should even be inclined, unless it were very odd, to put X. instead of—where the name ought to be concealed.[1]

TO JOHN KEBLE

[[After 'about Nov 20'?]]

My dear Keble,

There are one or two passages in the Letters, (in the sheets I now send) which I cannot correct for want of the copy. I have marked them for you. And if and where you think you can, I really should like initials instead of dashes. I mentioned to Rogers, that you thought it did not matter, and he was quite surprised. He said a dash was always unpleasant and put him out. By the bye the said R is for keeping the 'Schola Ph Sp' passage.

I came away from you without calling on Mr Lovell, which I had fully intended to do, and which it annoyed me to have omitted. Also I did not take any note of Judge C.'s remarks about Statutes. Some curious things have turned up (entre nous) about ours.[2] It would appear that the Lincoln Statutes are binding. They were *not* set aside by decision of Law in 1726— they have been acted upon at times *since*. The first and, I believe, greater portion of them was enacted in Adam de Brome's Provostship;[3] and all that can be said is that there have been *instances* in the first 400 years in which they were not acted upon.

William Froude has been here for two days—he went down last night.

Mr Townsend has quite made the amende, and I hope will take measures for setting matters right. He said some most exceedingly strong things in the letter P [Pusey] had received in my absence—and then got ashamed and has

[1] The last part of the letter is missing.
[2] The original Statutes of Oriel dated from January 1326, but new Statutes were drawn up in that May. They were known as the 'Lincoln Statutes' because they appointed the Bishop of Lincoln as Visitor of the College, rather than the King.
A dispute arose in the early eighteenth century about which Statutes were binding. Provost Carter had three times used his 'negative voice' to oppose the decision of the fellows in elections to fellowships, and the Bishop of Lincoln had upheld his decision. On the final occasion, in 1726, Edmunds, who had been rejected each time by the veto, appealed to court to try and get the authority of the January 1326 Statutes upheld. He was successful. The King was recognised as Visitor of the College, and the Provost's veto was rescinded. See D. W. Rannie, *Oriel College*, London 1900, pp. 6–13, 134–40.
[3] 1325–32.

168

retracted all. Mrs Pusey is rather worse than better. John Champernowne, who is just come up, is in a most dangerous way with some kind of fever. His Mother has been summoned here, and arrived 2 or 3 days since. Today is supposed to be the crisis—he is rather better. The Vice Chancellor has booked you for the first Tuesday in December. Pusey would have been gratified had you sent him your Postscript

Ever Yrs affly J H Newman

TUESDAY 21 NOVEMBER 1837   letter from Churton   no th s n c   meeting in Common Room about the Statutes?

TO EDWARD CHURTON

Oriel College. Nov 21. 1837

My dear Churton,

I am exceedingly obliged to you for your kind and friendly letter just received, and since we both have one end, and that I trust, not abstract and distant, but real, immediate and so identical, I will say as near as I can all I feel on the subject of it, and we will try to settle matters as we can.

Take the first view of the case—there are a certain number of men of principle and ability, in and out of Oxford, whom I think I can worry and torment into writing periodically for the B.C.—Some I have succeeded with, others (and the more powerful) not yet. They have their own employments, and enough to do in them. Yet I tease them. They are not paid for their articles;—*money* then is not their motive. But men *will* have a quid pro quo—Do not you see at once, how things are? I assure you within this year letters have come again and again, 'Why will not some [one] of you become Editor of the B.C. (as if it lay in *our* power by willing it!) we would write for *you*.'—To be sure, Boone has been a difficulty, and that is over— if a man like Miller were Editor, I could still get some of them to write— one (I suppose) would who has not yet,—Keble—but still I could not for a continuance rely on my powers of persuasion, and I do not see how I could pleasantly go on asking the favor. Men do nothing for *nothing*—what these men want, is, an organ. They have hitherto interested themselves in the B.C. from *hope*—provisionally. I cannot yet say whether I would or not *venture* to attempt going on as before. I do not say I would not—let us hear who the Editor is—but I fear any how I could not.

But again, some of these men, who care not for expence, this time two years, as I told Mr Watson, wished to set up a Theological Journal. They said, 'We want to see the high Catholic ἦθος developed, as far as may be, in *all* departments and modes of showing it. We do not mean *we* have it—but we have an *idea* of it—We want a Review *conducted*, i.e. morally conducted, on the Catholic temper—we want all subjects treated on one and the same principle or basis—not the contributions of a board of men, who do not know each other, pared down into harmony by an external Editor, but our Editor must be the principle, the internal idea of Catholicism itself, pouring itself outwards, not trimming and shaping from without—' Now this is all very fine language, but perhaps you see the sense of it. They wanted *one* witness—a defective witness, if one, is better than the abstract and generalized testimony of even good men, if strangers to each other—All great things are done by concentration and individuality. We have been ruined by coalitions —if we are saved, it must be by God's single instrument, though defective, and though (when His purpose is answered) broken by Himself. Such was the state of things two years since—I persuaded them, to save expence and from deference and respect for the B.C., to attempt to join it—and in consequence applied to Mr Watson, who was not a party, but a witness to all that went on between Boone and me.

Now please, My dear C., on what conceivable ground can you talk of Rehoboam and the elders,[1] when the long and the short is this, that a number of men, lay and cleric, will not consent to write without being paid for it (I do not speak of *money* payments) and when the elders are surprised they will not—this in the 19th century and in commercial England!—proh pudor—

As to Miller, his name is very taking—qu: between ourselves—does he hold the doctrine of the Apostolical Succession?—Nov 22. We should be quite satisfied, *if you were Editor*. Please to make this to the proper quarters as our proposal—and give into it yourself as a public spirited man. At this minute I cannot think of the man out of Oxford (who has any chance of being able to take it) but yourself whom I could thoroughly trust. The result of our correspondence with Mr Townsend you will see in the next B. Mag.[2] Your observations about Justin are important. I have not had time yet to refer, but hope soon

Ever Yrs most sincerely John H Newman

WEDNESDAY 22 NOVEMBER 1837   letters from Acland and Mr Hale[3]   instituted Mr White   no c   to Littlemore—back with Bloxam and Mr Sibthorp   Williams and Fulford to dinner   wrote to Churton and Bowden—sent Mr Herbert White's papers to the Bishop

[1] I *Kings*, 12. Rehoboam ignored the advice of the elders and listened to the opinion of the young men about how the people of Israel should be treated.

[2] *Brit. Mag.*, 12, 1837 (Dec.), 637–42. See letter of 9 Oct. to Churton.

[3] Francis Rivington wrote on 18 Nov. that W. H. Hale had accidentally seen a proof sheet of Froude's *Remains* when visiting the printing office, his attention having been caught by the word 'humbug'. Hale himself wrote on 21 Nov. that he did not think it right that such an intimate document should be published so soon after the author's death. He had written to Keble about the matter, hoping that the publication would be reconsidered.

TO J. W. BOWDEN

[[Oriel College—Novr 22. 1837]]

My dear Bowden,

I was quite startled by Johnson telling me I had nearly edged upon your last day in Town—which I was not aware of. ⌐Jenkyns is a very amiable good tempered man, but a thorough going Conservative—very sensible, *not* enthusiastic—and very influential in Durham.[1] He has edited Cranmer for the Clarendon and done it in style.⌐ His wife was a Cousin, a Hobhouse I think—of the Under-Secretary's family.

⌐So the two parties of the Aristocracy are to join—and the Church, as distinct from the Establishment, to be quietly dropped⌐—this, or something of the kind seems likely. ⌐As to our Statutes[2] it is a long business—I will get you some papers on the subject. The Revision is quite a *new* question without precedent since the Laudian Code—The Heads [[of Houses]] wish to bring it into the ordinary business of the University as *their* concern—the Convocation as if sui generis to judge it by antecedent[3] precedents, i.e., precedent of a revision. Much may be said on both sides—but we give in a Protest to-morrow to save our right and negative the whole—but how it will go I know not—as I hear to-day the Master of Balliol[4] has been bringing up men. You know Boone has given up—but this is, I suppose, a secret.⌐

Ever yrs affly John H. Newman

FROM H. E. MANNING

[[Nov 22/37]] 7. York Terrace Regt's Park

My dear Newman,

I write one line to tell Pusey and yourself the end of Convocation.

Two or three amendments proposed by Archdeacon Hoare—Sydney Smith— etc. The last wearied and worried the Convocation and disinclined it for better matter. Almost everybody present expressed himself against the Commission. But fear of Collision, respect for the Archbishop, doubt about technicalities etc., and the decided opposition of the Prolocutor to admit, what I think was within our Privilege prevailed so far as that the amendment was negatived by consent of mover etc. On the whole this is perhaps best. I think much strength has been gained to the main question against the Commission. And we are going immediately to try, and inculcate printed addresses throughout every Archdeaconry praying for the *Royal Mandate for a Provincial Council*[5]—This the Archbishop.

I write in immense haste—write and tell me what you advise.

Kindest regards to Pusey and Harrison.

Ever yrs affectly H E M

[1] Henry Jenkyns, who had been a Fellow of Oriel from 1818–35, was Professor of Greek at Durham. He edited *The Remains of Thomas Cranmer*, four volumes, Oxford 1833.
[2] See note to letter of 13 Nov. to H. Wilberforce.
[3] [[qu. omit?]]
[4] Richard Jenkyns, the brother of Henry, who was an advocate of College and University reform.
[5] Pusey underlined the words 'Royal Mandate for a Provincial Council', and noted in pencil, 'to have our own Rubrics or the Catechism repealed or altered?'

THURSDAY 23 NOVEMBER 1837   letters from Manning and Archdeacon Froude   sent letter to Hale in a parcel   Convocation for Revision of University Statutes—   dined at Magdalen to meet Mr Sibthorp   no c

FRIDAY 24 NOVEMBER   letters from Mr Pole and Hook with one from Mr Norris   instituted Mr Judge   f d   no c   wrote to Mr Davison, Dodsworth, and sent Mr Judge's paper to the Bishop

SUNDAY 26 NOVEMBER   27 Trinity   letter from W F and remainder of Hurrell's Journal from Archdeacon Froude   Spranger assisted me in early Communion   did duty morning and afternoon   preached Number 485[1]   Pusey preached University Sermon   dined in hall   J M to tea in evening

MONDAY 27 NOVEMBER   letter from John M [Mozley]   no c   dined in hall   H W came   Ryder took tea with us

TUESDAY 28 NOVEMBER   letters from Rogers Dodsworth and Goldsmith   dined in hall—and H W.   no c   men to tea in Common Room in evening (*this went on every week, being my soirée*)

WEDNESDAY 29 NOVEMBER   fast   letter from R Williams   administered Sacrament to Thomas Cox   f b   l   f d   walked to Littlemore with H W and Berkeley—and with Williams back   Manning came   wrote to Rogers, Dodsworth, and Goldsmid.

TO FREDERIC ROGERS

Oriel College: St. Andrew's Eve, [29 November] 1837.

Certainly I should like your article soon, and doubt not it will do very well.[2] But I am very sorry to hear about your headaches, and hope you have not been distressing yourself. It is certainly strange that any one like yourself should be so withheld from usefulness, but depend on it there is a reason for it. We all need some sharp bond [?]—though you, one should say, less than others: we *see* yours; in the case of others the hair-shirt is hidden. So much for moralising.

Your news about your law plans quite delighted me.[3] We talk (*entre nous*) of setting up some halls here, making men stay instead of going into the country, and getting W. Froude and Johnson to set up a school of science. The said W.F. wishes you to come down to him to Dartington at Christmas.

As to your criticism on R.H.F.'s text, some of the things you object to were already altered in the proof. The 'Dome of St Peter's' was written out by W. Froude himself. Why might not St Peter's dome be like a geometrical staircase? You need not make your review a mere panegyric.[4]

The Lincoln men seem to have thought James Mozley a Puseyite. They confessed he was the best man, and elected instead a nephew of Arnold's,[5] which, to their horror, they discovered too late.

[1] *P.S.* VI, 9, 'The Gospel Sign addressed to Faith'. The sermon seems to have been preached in two separate parts.
[2] 'Froude's *Remains*', *Brit. Crit.*, 23, 1838 (Jan.), 200–25.
[3] Rogers had been considering plans for starting a Law School, and had been discussing the matter with J. R. Hope.
[4] Copeland's copied extracts include the following as part of this sentence: 'as to Bunsen it is too late but not I hope of consequence, I will think about "promiscuous intercourse." '
[5] John Penrose of Balliol.

THURSDAY 30 NOVEMBER 1837   St Andrew   Manning, Marriott and H W to break-fast   service in chancel—read a Lecture to be published   no c   dined with Browell to meet Mr Maitland   H W, Manning and Williams with Pusey

TO AN UNKNOWN CORRESPONDENT

Oriel St Andrews' Day [30 November] [1837]

My dear Sir,

I have just received and heartily thank you for your Sermon and the kind way in which you have given it to me.

I assure you I feel it very much and am,

My dear Sir, Yours most truly John H Newman

FRIDAY 1 DECEMBER 1837   letters from R. Williams, Goldsmid, and Churton   f c walked with Manning and H W to Littlemore   no v and c   wrote to Painter about Church of England Gazette

SATURDAY 2 DECEMBER   H W went   no m l p   Thomas Cox died   dined in hall

SUNDAY 3 DECEMBER   Advent 1   all [Breviary hours]   did duty morning and after-noon   preached Number 486[1]   Marriott assisted me at Communion   dined in hall   sent parcel and letter to M R G

TO MISS M. R. GIBERNE

⌜Oriel College. Dec 3. 1837⌝

My dear Miss Giberne,

I have long been intending to acknowledge your last packet—but as excuses will only make my neglect worse, I will say nothing.

First then did you give me any sum lately in a parcel? I have got down £4 in April last!—if you did, it is all safe, but I wish to know. There is no mention of it in your letter.

Next I like your new story Paulus and Julian very much indeed—except the first scene which might be worked up more. Pray go on with it. I send it to you—also the latter part of Little Mary—which I hope you will not alter a great deal. ⌜Mr Walker came with your parcel, but gave me no opportunity of being civil to him—and while in the room did nothing but caper about and grin—whether he thought me an unsafe person to sit in a room with, the grandfather of Jesuits (as the Persians say) or however else you explain it,⌝ so it was.

I had hoped Little Mary would have been in the press before now—but it shall before long. Consider however whether you approve of the plan. ⌜I propose to bring out a series of small books—some verse, some prose—not periodically but occasionally like a Library. Yours would come in here and there⌝—and might all be collected together into one volume or volumes,

[1] P.S. IV, 22, 'Watching'.

without any difference from what they would be if published not in a series. If you approve, I shall commence at once.

The first volume of my friend Froude's Remains is through the Press—the second will be finished by Christmas—and the work out I suppose by New Year's day—My own work is not in Press yet. Two volumes of the Fathers are passing through the Press—and half a volume of the Tracts, to complete vol 4.—I confess we are behind hand in every thing—but then we have so much on hand. *Perhaps* we may soon have the British Critic on our hands—but this is a secret. Also we are setting up a normal monastery here, which is to affiliate itself through England, but this too is a secret.[1]

We have nothing to hope or fear from Whig or Conservative Governments—or from Bishops, or from Peers, or from Court, or from other visible power. We must trust our own ἦθος (ethos) that is, what is unseen, our unseen gifts and their unseen Author. I do hope we shall be strengthened to develop in new ways, since the ordinary ways are stopped up. Some of the Bishops, as Norwich, are driving fast at a denial of the Creed, which is heresy—and when a bishop is heretical, man, woman, or child has licence to oppose him. The faith is prior and dearer to us than the visible framework which is built upon it. And if we so account it, we shall perchance be blessed to preserve the framework too. It was a worse time after all, when Athanasius was against the whole world, and the whole world against Athanasius—

It is an old story that the witch of Endor was a ventriloquist—certainly in this day it sounds rationalistic.

Pray tell any one to call on me you like.

Williams writes in the Lyra,[2] under no signature, I believe—he writes Breviaries, and verses about Churches, Churchyards and Gravestones—Who is to be your new Incumbent?

Ever yours most sincerely John H Newman

I send the 4 Sermons.

P.S. I fear I have mislaid the part of little Mary in which her Aunt and Cousins first make their appearances. I must have put it into some safe place.

MONDAY 4 DECEMBER 1837   walked with Manning   dined in hall   Keble came wrote to Churton

---

[1] Newman noted in his collection of 'Stray Facts': '1837. Decr 21. It appears from Bowden's letter of this date that, as early as this, we had a plan for a house of young Apostolicals, such as we had afterwards at St Aldate's   He says "Johnson intimates that you have some scheme like the setting up of a house for young *monks*. Tell me therefore in confidence. As you know, I subscribed £200 for the Bishops' Churches . . . If you have any scheme which £100 next Easter would in any way forward etc etc" From 2 letters of James Mozley's Aug 26 Septr 2/38 it seems as if the "Hall" was to begin in Octr 1838'
'Easter 1838 Wood speaks of the chance of setting up a house for 10 [?] clerics at £50 apiece at Manchester'.

[2] [[qu. 'in the British Magazine'?]] Isaac Williams contributed five poems to the *Lyra Apostolica*, nuder the signature *zeta*. Most of his works, such as *The Cathedral*, were published anonymously.

TO EDWARD CHURTON

Oriel College. Dec 4. 1837

My dear Churton,

I hope we do indeed approximate to an arrangement—and now I will tell you what I have to propose. Miller, it seems, declines—and you will not come forward, unless it is absolutely necessary. What think you then of Manning of Merton? perhaps you do not know him—but I should think Mr Watson must, at least by name, and when you write, you can ask him what he has to say to him. He is an exceedingly sound man—a clever man— with some time his own. He lives in Sussex near Petworth, but has friends in London, and is not unfrequently there. He has been a conspicious person in the late Convocation, and was opposed to its being allowed liberty of debate. I know him very well, and he agrees with me in views—but he is no Pupil of mine—he came ex officinâ de Balliolo, and was transplanted to Merton. Since that he has been in the country. He is, in no conceivable sense, of the Oxford school (to use a wrong word)—Pusey knows him now, being drawn to him by congeniality of opinions—but he is Pusey's, only so far as Pusey is Truth's, and Manning also—and as you are Manning's or Pusey's, which is not at all.

I conceive we cannot get on without a responsible Editor—what is every one's business, is no one's.

Till this preliminary point is settled, it is useless to go further. But perhaps I may as well say here, that when I wrote the famous Cæsar aut nullus sentence, I meant by nullus, merely to express a discontinuance of our present plan of gratuitous articles—There was an object for them, if thereby we were keeping alive the Review for better things than the then Editor; but none, if it is for good in the hands of an Editor we do not know.

Also let me say by way of explanation that in the said Cæsar aut nullus note, so far from overlooking the fact of Mr Watson having the choice of Editor, and not showing confidence in him, I said expressly to Rivington that nothing could be *so far* more satisfactory—the unsatisfactory thing being his being *confined to London* on his selection. For even he cannot make a silk purse out of etc.

As to Mr Le Bas, do you think then he would not write for us?

Ever Yrs most sincerely John H Newman

P.S. I am very glad to hear you have got hold of the Jesuits.[1] Where is an article I heard of about the Fathers? I did not hear the exact subject.

---

[1] Churton contributed an article to the Jan. 1839 number of *Brit. Crit.* on 'The Revival of Jesuitism' (reviewing a new English edition of the Jesuit Constitutions), and an article to the Jan. 1838 number on the 'Use of the Fathers'.

TUESDAY 5 DECEMBER 1837 letter with Mr Goldsmids MS no m l no E.P. dined with Pusey to meet Keble. men in the evening

WEDNESDAY 6 DECEMBER dined at Mr Morrell's to meet Keble

THURSDAY 7 DECEMBER Rogers came? dined with Harrison to meet Mr Maitland

FRIDAY 8 DECEMBER no v and c Mr Gibbins called from Dublin[1] f d Theological meeting at Pusey's—Keble reader Mysticism of Fathers

SATURDAY 9 DECEMBER Mr Gibbins to breakfast Keble went no c Dr Gilly called on me with Palmer Mr Gibbins (*T.C.D.* [Trinity College Dublin]) dined with me

SUNDAY 10 DECEMBER 2 Advent candles for first time? Spranger assisted me in early Sacrament no th s n v c Spranger did duty morning, I in afternoon I preached Number 487[2] dined at Trinity with Williams, as did Rogers.

MONDAY 11 DECEMBER no th n s v. c dined with Hamilton to meet his Father

TUESDAY 12 DECEMBER letter from Churton wrote to Bowden by Johnson dined with Palmer at Magdalen, as did Rogers men in the evening in Common Room

TO J. W. BOWDEN

⌜Oriel Dec 12/37.⌝

My dear Bowden,

My hand is so cold I shall write you a poor note.

⌜As to the Statutes, the Heads of Houses hurried things on so indecently, there was no time for any thing. We had several meetings but could not agree. At first only 16 signed the Protest, in the course of three weeks it has increased to between 30 and 40—but that is a small number. The majorities were so large it was not possible we could bring up on a sudden sufficient men; and as the questions were intricate and time was requisite to come to a fair judgment, it would have looked like party spirit. I am told the Sheffield Clergy are going to send a remonstrance to the Heads of Houses. It would be well if more residents in various places did so—but they should first wait for V. [[Vaughan]] Thomas's pamphlet[3] which I suppose will give information—and read Greswell's; who however unluckily gives in to the Edinburgh's clamour for the Professorial System.[4] Is it not curious we should be pulling with the Edinburgh, and the extreme Whigs? the Heads are geese indeed.

[1] J. H. Todd sent a letter of introduction with Richard Gibbings of Trinity College, Dublin, who had just produced an edition of the Roman *Index Expurgatorius*.

[2] *P.S.* IV, 15, 'Moral Effects of Communion with God'.

[3] *Reasons for protesting against the Principle upon which a General Revision of the Statutes of the University has been undertaken* . . ., Oxford 1838. Thomas also produced 'Thirteen Objections', for private circulation.

[4] Edward Greswell, *A Letter to his Grace the Duke of Wellington . . . on the Proceedings in the House of Convocation* . . ., Oxford 1837. Greswell called for a restoration of Oxford 'to what she once was, and what she is supposed by her Statutes still to be; not an aggregate assembly of Colleges and Halls, . . . but an University of Faculties . . . with a Professorial system.' (p. 34) A similar point had been made by Sir William Hamilton in a series of critical articles on Oxford and the Universities which he contributed to the *Edinburgh Review* between 1831 and 1834. See W. R. Ward, *Victorian Oxford*, London 1965, pp. 82–3.

Entre nous, I think the Editorship of the B.C. will be offered to *Manning* —but this is *quite* a secret—Then I shall try to get Wood as his Sub-Editor.

Mr Atkinson fellow of Lincoln has been rejected for a school at York on the ground of his holding Oxford opinions—he was asked totidem verbis if he held the opinions of the Tracts. James Mozley has suffered *at* Lincoln for the same reason.

I am very anxious now about Froude's remains they will arrest and bring forward very many, I doubt not, but they will much scandalize and I fear throw back some persons by their uncompromising Anti-protestantism —and they do tend to make people disloyal towards the Establishment—I *hope* not, to make them Romanists. He is very severe on the Romanists.[1]

With kindest thoughts of Mrs Bowden and the little children.

Ever yrs affly John H. Newman.

WEDNESDAY 13 DECEMBER 1837   dined in Hall?   no c
THURSDAY 14 DECEMBER   letter from M R G   Manning went   walked with R. to Littlemore   first day in Common Room dined with me W. Harris, Mr Bekker [,] Copeland and Harrison.   Williams with Rogers—etc.   no c
FRIDAY 15 DECEMBER   no v and c   f d

TO HENRY WILBERFORCE

Oriel Dec 15/37

My dear Henry

I have only time to say that I have just heard from Rivington that he has not received your Article.[1] They are in sad want of it. I conjecture some stoppage on the road. I hope you booked it—pray inquire at once. If it is not sent directly, it stands a chance of not appearing, or rather the certainty

Ever Yrs affly John H Newman

SATURDAY 16 DECEMBER 1837   no th s n   dined in Common Room   Mr Bekker with Rogers

TO WILLIAM B. PUSEY

Oriel Saturday Dec 16/37

My dear William

Is it consistent with your plans for tomorrow to read prayers for me at 4 o'clock at St Mary's? Your brother so entered on his ministerial duties[2]

Ever Yrs affly John H Newman

[1] 'Pashley's *Travels in Crete*', *Brit. Crit.*, 23, 1838 (Jan.), 225–47.
[2] cf. diary for 1 June 1828.

SUNDAY 17 DECEMBER 1837 3rd Advent early Sacrament—Spranger assisting m l p th s Spranger did duty morning—I preached Number 189[1] W Pusey ordained, and read prayers for me in afternoon I baptized in service London's son and Frances Mills dined in Common Room

MONDAY 18 DECEMBER letter from Pope no th s n v c Rogers, Daman, Greswell, Marriott and Eden went M.M. [Maria Mozley] came here from Cholderton wrote to Pope

TO S. L. POPE

Oriel College. Dec 18. 1837

My dear Pope

Pray accept for yourself and Mrs Pope my very best and kindest congratulations on the event in which you have been so much interested and of which your letter this morning informs me—I sincerely trust that, as all things have been so prospered hitherto, they will so continue. As to your kind proposal, I should be highly pleased, but there is one difficulty—Do you in your parts allow of a sponsor standing by proxy? I do not see any objection to it myself. I fear it is quite impossible my leaving Oxford for some time to come. If the matter could be so arranged, I should be most willing.

There is no great news here—The two first volumes of my dear friend Froude's Remains will be out in a week or two, and will give rise to so much criticism, that unless I was pretty well used to it by this time, I would have enough to annoy me. My Lectures on Justification are on the brink of the Press. The Library of the Fathers is going on slowly, but well. An interesting series of little books is coming out from Parker of Oxford and Combe of Leicester, the two first of which are [Jeremy] Taylor's Golden Grove and [Simon] Patrick's Hearts Ease.[2] Also Hooker's Treatise on the Sacraments is to be published separately out of his fifth Book.[3]

Your friend Boodle was talking of you yesterday—what makes you say that Dodsworth is cross?

I hope this late event will make you view every thing in rose colour—your last letter was jaundiced, or blue or black; which will you have?

Ever Yrs most sincerely John H Newman

TUESDAY 19 DECEMBER 1837 letters from Rose and John M [Mozley] Copleston went M. M. and J. M. to breakfasted [sic] no c raining—else was to have gone with M M to Littlemore dined with Provost Acland in Oxford wrote to Rose and Wood and to John M by J M.

[1] P.S. VII, 3, 'The World our Enemy'.
[2] Jeremy Taylor, The Golden Grove. A Choice Manual, containing what is to be believed, practised, and desired or prayed for . . ., Oxford 1836. S. Patrick, Heart's Ease, or a Remedy against all Troubles . . ., Oxford 1837.
[3] Keble edited Selections from the Fifth Book of Hooker's Ecclesiastical Polity, Oxford 1839.

TO E. B. PUSEY

[19 December 1837]

My dear P

I propose to write to Rose 1. that nothing can be better than Maitland's having the British Critic. 2 that I know my friends respect him, but I cannot say any thing about their entering into any formal *agreement* with him   3 that I will gladly write for him myself. 4 that, at the same time, I consider the whole arrangement with Boone under Rivington (i.e. about four sheets for nothing) at an end.

and I suppose I had better *not* call on Maitland.

I wish I could propose to walk with you today but I cannot

Ever Yrs affly J H N.

or should we join Maitland with all our hearts?

WEDNESDAY 20 DECEMBER 1837   Ember Day   J M and M M went   f d   no th s n c

THURSDAY 21 DECEMBER   St Thomas   Service in Chancel   read Number 185   no c   dined with Copeland

FRIDAY 22 DECEMBER   Ember Day ½ f b   f d   Spranger went   wrote to Mr Powell, sent answers to the Questions to the Bishop—and proof to Rogers   Sent up first Lecture to G and R. (*on Justification*)

SATURDAY 23 DECEMBER   Ember Day   letters from Wood, Manning, and Shortland   f d   Eden returned   walked to Littlemore

SUNDAY 24 DECEMBER   4th Advent   no one to help me in early Sacrament—9 communicants   no c   did duty in morning   Pusey took my duty in evening   dined in midday   I went to Littlemore where read and preached Number 488[1] and baptized child

MONDAY 25 DECEMBER   Christmas Day   did duty morning and afternoon Provost assisting in Chancel   preached Number 488   no c   dined at Provost's

TO JOHN HENRY PARKER

Christmas Day [1837]

My dear Mr Parker

I am very sorry to have delayed answering you so long. As far as I can make out, James's book is not one it would be worth while to publish

Yours very truly John H Newman

The best compliments of the Season to you.

[1] *P.S.* IV, 16, 'Christ Hidden from the World', preached again the following day.

TUESDAY 26 DECEMBER 1837   St Stephen   service in Chancel   read Number 325   no p th s n c   very wet   dined at Mr Parker's

WEDNESDAY 27 DECEMBER   Service in Chancel   read Number 278   no p th s n c   wet dined in Common Room by myself   sent up my Second Lecture on Justification

THURSDAY 28 DECEMBER   letter from Bliss   service in Chancel   read Number 7   no th s n c   Maitland called   wrote to Dodsworth [,] Bishop of O [Oxford] and Mr Todd

FRIDAY 29 DECEMBER   letter from Rogers   no ths n s c   called on Maitland   wrote to J and Utterton

TO MRS JOHN MOZLEY

Oriel. In Festo S Th. Cant [29 December] 1837

My dear Jemima

I ought to have written before this and now am so hurried I do not know how I shall say what is to be said. There are two additional Poems to insert in the Lyra—The Thrush—and the call of David—The latter I cannot put my hand upon, but it is in the Lyra in the B.M. [*Brit. Mag.*] somewhere —and I should like a proof of it, as I suspect a word or two must be altered. The Thrush I believe is in the B M of Spring 1833 and is by Keble. Before I end the letter, I must decide *where* they are to go. Also have you a list of the errata of the last Edition? One or two were rather bad ones—e.g. in Williams's Clement etc, which I noticed to you during the printing, but I suppose they came too late. Could you contrive to tell me *what* errata you have. I sent a number at various times.

My Lectures are in the Press—and I am too full of business. We have all sorts of matters on hand—and I do not know how to make my way through all. A little time will do it, I suppose.

I went to the Kings' Arms the morning James and his Sister left for Derby and found they were just gone.

When you write to Maria Giberne, please tell her which I forgot to do in answer to a question of hers, that Williams writes in the B M now but no other writer of the Lyra I know of.

We are full of negociations about the B.C.—I am much perplexed how to conclude Froude's second volume—there is not room for the Essays in it and it is short without.

I had hoped to have written to Harriet on her birthday but doubt whether I shall be able. When you write, will you say, I did not forget it.

I am acting as Editor to two or three little books published by Combe [of] Leicester. The Breviary Hymns is one of them.[1]

[1] *Hymni Ecclesiae, excerpti e Breviariis Romano, Sarisburiensi, Eboracensi, et aliunde,* Oxonii 1838; and *Hymni Ecclesiae e Breviaro Parisiensi,* Oxonii 1838. Newman also edited around this time: Christopher Sutton, *Godly Meditations upon the most holy Sacrament of the Lord's Supper,* 1838, and *Disce Vivere,* 1839; Anthony Sparrow, *A Rationale upon the Book of Common Prayer,* 1839; Edward Wells, *The Rich Man's Duty,* 1840; and Thomas Wilson, *Sacra Privata,* 1840. All of these were published at Oxford by Parker, and printed by T. Combe.

My best thoughts of you and John this season—and of Aunt,—and of all at the Friary

and believe me My dear Jemima Ever Yrs affly John H Newman

89 The Winter Thrush—(B.M. first half of 1833 p. 420) (to come after 'Vexations in Loneliness')

57 David Youngest born of Jesse's race (to come after Isaac in Hidden Saints)

SATURDAY 30 DECEMBER 1837 no p th s n c

SUNDAY 31 DECEMBER letters from Utterton and Mr Wilks (of the C. O. [Christian Observer]) did duty morning and afternoon Pusey (?) assisting me at Sacrament preached Number 181

TO WILLIAM DOWDING

Oriel College Tuesday [1837?]

My dear Sir,

Will you give me the pleasure of your company at breakfast tomorrow morning in our Common Room at 9 o'clock

Yours very truly John H Newman

TO T. D. RYDER

Oriel Thursday. [1837?]

My dear Ryder,

My reason for putting you off, was that Pusey supposed I had engaged myself last week to him for today, and had made a party in consequence. Pusey now says *will you dine with him today at six*?

Ever Yrs J. H. Newman

MONDAY 1 JANUARY 1838 letter from Keble Service in Chancel read Number 53[1] dined with Ogle wrote to Keble[2] [1 to 3 January, Breviary] irregular these days

TUESDAY 2 JANUARY letter from Williams

WEDNESDAY 3 JANUARY wrote to Williams and Mr Russell

[1] *P.S.* VII, 5, 'Temporal Advantages'.

[2] Newman noted in 1875: 'By my letter to Keble of Jany 1. 1838, it seems that, when I began daily Service at St Mary's, I borrowed an Eagle as a reading desk which was doing nothing from time immemorial in the Oriel ante-chapel; and the Provost bade me return it. However, by this move I got him to obtain from the University the reading desk for St Mary's which they had since 1827 promised the Parish and never given. All this I tell Keble apropos of *his* wanting the said Eagle for Hursley

In the same letter are my suggestions for a Preface to Froude's Remains.' Keble thought the College authorities might be willing to give the eagle 'for Heathcote's new Chapel at Ampfield'.

Oriel College. Jan 3. 1838

Dear Sir,

I meant before this to have troubled you with a few lines respecting your book, which I was very glad to see.[1] Such books are especially wanted in this day. It is not to be expected that the multitude even of Clergymen, when they get into active employment, will set to upon the works of our Divines, and the only thing that can be done by way of making an impression upon their opinions is to collect testimonies from them. One must hope that theological acquirements will be more an object provided for in the next generation, but I speak of the Church as it is.

Your volume is a book rather to consult than to read through, except where persons have *their minds to make up* on the subject; therefore I do not profess to have done more than dip into it—but always with pleasure. I sincerely hope that it will be as extensively read as it will be beneficial when read—and that you may be encouraged to proceed in similar undertakings.

I heartily wish it had so happened I had been able to be more attentive to you than I was when you were in Oxford—and hope that next time you come I shall neither be so devoured with business or made so stupid with a cold as I was on that occasion[2]

I am, My dear Sir, Yours very faithfully John H Newman

P.S. I hardly know how to direct—but think myself safe in directing to your Publishers'

Oriel College. Jan. 3. 1838

My dear Williams

All that is kind for the New Year to you, Prevost, and all yours. I envy you your pilgrimage to Dartington—but I am on pilgrimage among dear H F's *works*—which are shrines too. I am very anxious indeed at present— so much so that unless I was afraid of seeming too serious, I would beg you to think of me at serious times—You see, two works are coming out, this of dear H F's and my Justification, which at present quite frighten me. 'Before[3] of a dreadful thing etc.' You recollect.—I am so afraid of [making] some floors in my Lectures—and I know not whom to ask. It seems as if I must

---

[1] *The Judgement of the Anglican Church (posterior to the Reformation) on the Sufficiency of Holy Scripture, and the Authority of the Holy Catholic Church in matters of Faith . . .*, London 1838. An anthology of texts on Tradition taken from the Anglican Divines, with a lengthy introduction where Russell quoted approvingly from *V.M.* I.

[2] For Russell's description of the visit, see at 15 Nov. 1837.

[3] A word or so is lost here and below.

venture, and depend on myself and my good luck—and I only trust that I may be carried through as heretofore. Yet I so fear this is presumption—at least I have an indefinite sort of evil conscience on the subject. I shall be easy when it is all out.

I sent to Baxter forthwith, and he said the proofs had already gone to you.

You can read my letter to the Archdeacon if you think it will give you any information

Ever Yrs most affly John H Newman

THURSDAY 4 JANUARY 1838 letters from the Bishop[1] [,] Christie[2] and Mr Todd [Breviary] none

TO FREDERIC ROGERS

Jan. 4. 1838.

W. F. [Froude] can give me no help about the papers on Architecture in B. M. [*Brit. Mag.*] Decr. 32 and Jan. 33.[3] Look at them and write a short note to be put at the bottom of the pages, stating whether *they* were written before Whewell and *how* they differ. I am confident he thought them out before Whewell appeared but am startled to see him in the rough draught allude to Wh. Do this at once for the printers are in haste. The work must not be long behind your article.

I have had talk with Maitland and shall have more. We are on most easy terms, however it ends. I want him to take the responsibility and let us have our swing, he demurs.

FRIDAY 5 JANUARY 1838 pamphlet from Perceval no th s n v c
SATURDAY 6 JANUARY letter from Rogers Service in Chancel read Number 164 no p th v. c.

[1] Bishop Bagot wrote on 3 Jan., 'I am gratified by your wish to dedicate your lectures to me, and willingly accede to your request. You speak too favorably of my kindness, for I fear but little has been in my powers'. The dedication, to *Jfc.*, spoke of 'veneration for his sacred order, of dutiful submission to his diocesan authority, and of gratitude for kindnesses received . . .'

[2] J. F. Christie wrote on 2 Jan. concerning Froude's *Remains*, 'Gilbertson who has now come to me tells me Prevost is sorry you are publishing as much as you are doing. He thinks people will catch hold of passages. I suppose that letter to me is an instance of what he means, and I confess I think it is possible enough—though still as people are sure enough to carp at something, you will I suppose answer that the question is—will there be enough elsewhere to make Froude understood and to give those who do *not* wish to carp the clue to his character and opinions. For myself I do not profess to decide.'

[3] The two papers were republished as 'Church Architecture' in *Remains* II, 335–74. For the point in question see next letter and note in *Remains* II, 335. Whewell had published his opinion in his *Architectural Notes on German Churches, with Remarks on the Origin of Gothic Architecture*, London 1830.

SUNDAY 7 JANUARY   1st Epiphany   letters from Rogers and Pope   did duty morning and afternoon Pusey (?) assisting at Sacrament   preached Number 114

TO FREDERIC ROGERS

Jany 7. 1838

. . . If I understand you right the point is this—Whewell thought the *Roman* Architects not the Middle Age Architects only could not construct a certain vaulting. Froude thought no such thing, but that the Middle Age Architects could *not* construct such arches as the Romans *could*—I think I heard Froude say even the curve of an ellipse—consequently at Iffley etc. you have two broken segments of circles meeting together. If this is right I think I understand you perfectly and feel obliged.

The Bishop has in the kindest and most cordial manner assented to my request.[1] Will the following do. Answer *this question* some time. To the R. Rev. Father in God Richard,/ by divine permission, ⟨is this right for another to say or only a Bishop himself?⟩/Lord Bishop of Oxford, Dean of Canterbury and Chancellor of the most Noble Order of the Garter [,] this volume is inscribed in a feeling of veneration for his sacred order, of dutiful submission to his Diocesan authority, and of gratitude for his condescending ⟨favourable⟩ notice/.—

Maitland and I have had most amicable confabs and he is in a not unpleasant state of half fidget, half satisfaction—soothed and then suddenly frightened. To show him how far we were from *obtruding our* notions on the Review I showed him the conclusion of your Article, where you say 'We do not pledge ourselves.' Somehow or other it had the reverse effect (whether as showing there might be things, which *we* held tho *we* did not pledge ourselves) and he looked queer and shivered all over. He has undertaken to edit the next number and we to help him but what will be the issue I cannot say. In order to break him in Pusey is to come out with one of *his Κατ' ἐξοχὴν*[2] articles on the Church Commission. By the bye the said Pusey is uncommonly taken with your article—and begins to smell a rat in dear F. himself. I have looked on gravely as having baited a trap.—

I should add out of my own head that I have read your article several times over and like it more and more every time.

Rivington wishes me to enlarge the second volume. F has left some very neat analyses of Butler (apparently written in 1828) with a few original notes—would it be absurd to print them. I so wish you were here. I have no one to consult. And now Carissime.

Vale memento mei Tui Tuissimi J. H. N.

[1] See first note to diary for 4 Jan.
[2] 'great man'.

TO HENRY WILBERFORCE

Oriel ⌜Jan 7/38⌝

My dear Henry

I am so very busy I have hardly time to acknowledge the receipt of the other half of the 5£ note—for which thanks. I send the volume of Sermons.

⌜As to the Candlesticks, I shall receive any gift most thankfully, but I doubt about them. First I have some for the *mere use* of the Church, very plain, but able to hold a candle in the dark morning. Next £5 won't buy candlesticks such as you have in your eye. Thirdly I so fear getting into trouble at St Mary's—though in time I might venture.

I suppose a gift to Littlemore would not be the same thing to the giver?⌝ Yet what do we want *there*? ⌜A Christmas or Whitsuntide Altar cloth—£5 would be enough—or a[1] pulpit Cloth—Friends are at work at a splendid *Easter* Altar Cloth which will not be finished till Easter year—we have £10 for the *material* but that is not thought enough—might the £5 go towards *it*? Or at St *Mary's* we want a Linen Table Cloth.⌝ One might be worked in the loom on purpose to any pattern—and I believe *within* 5£. ⌜It might have the pattern of a Cross etc.⌝ This seems to me a good idea—Might it not have ⌜a rich (damask worked) border⌝ approximating to a fringe. The difficulty of keeping it clean and the trouble of washing would be the difficulty. Can you suggest?

As to the Article for the British Critic the time has passed by for the subject—so please *forthwith* send me back *all* the books—I say all and forthwith, because I suspect I want some of them

Ever Yrs affly J H N.

P.S. ⌜I have heard from Marriott at Rome dated St Thomas day—not a very good account of himself—very good of Manning—tolerable of A. Harrison.⌝ All kind thoughts for the New Year.

P.S. G. Ryder has asked me to be sponsor to his child. Entre nous, I am very anxious what to do. I do not like to refuse people, but I have had three new Godchildren in the course of a year. It seems unkind to decline, but what can one do? I wish one could sell one's compliance. People either wish it or they do not. I should like to put some work upon a man, or make him give some sum to an object—It would try his wish and do a benefit else-where. Do not say all this—I suppose I shall say yes in the particular case—but not as freely as I should like.[2] And as to the future I really am quite anxious—I *have* refused one about a year ago. I should have liked to [have] stopped with such as your little boy. You had claims on me which G. Ryder has not.

[1] Illegible word, omitted by Newman in copying.
[2] It is not known what Newman replied to Ryder at this time. Next year on the birth of his second child he took up the matter again, see letter of 7 Jan. 1839 to him.

MONDAY 8 JANUARY 1838   East wind   frost

TUESDAY 9 JANUARY   letter from Marriott and proof from Sewell [?]   frost—a little sun   returned proof and wrote to H

TO MRS THOMAS MOZLEY

Jany 9. 1838.

My book[1] is now in press, and in a very unfinished state yet, so I have to work like a horse. I am very anxious about the *unity* of the composition. One always exaggerates what is in hand—or I should say for certain that nothing I have done has given me such anxious thought and so much time and labour. I have written it over, and recast parts, so often that I cannot count them. Now as I print, I am rewriting it in fact—only two sheets have come down yet—and I cannot help hoping, that, if all that is to come is like them, my trouble will be repaid—but, since an Author always has an affection for his worst productions, perhaps this is a bad sign.

WEDNESDAY 10 JANUARY 1838   parcel from J and J M. [John Mozley]   letter from Dodsworth   proof of Fs [Fathers] from G and R   began to snow   went to Littlemore in snow to read   dined with Bloxam [at] Magdalen   wrote to Bliss   sent proof to Keble

THURSDAY 11 JANUARY   proof   sent proof to Keble

FRIDAY 12 JANUARY   letters from Daman and C   parcel from Manning and proof   meeting at Archdeacon's about Mrs A Smith's charity   f d   sent back parcel to Manning—wrote to Daman, Pope, and sent proof to Keble

TO H. E. MANNING

Oriel Jan 12/38

My dear Manning

I like your pamphlet much, as does Pusey, and trust and believe it will be useful.[2] I have nothing to find fault with but a few grammatical or other points, which I have marked.

Entre nous, Maitland only takes the British Critic for the next number on trial. However, I suppose he will continue it. You allude, I guess, to the passage in the Record about the British Critic[3]—They are determined we should be Crœsuses, and will not give Pusey's £1000 to the Churches the

---

[1] [[Lectures on Justification]]

[2] *The Principle of the Ecclesiastical Commission examined, in a Letter to the Lord Bishop of Chichester*, London 1838.

[3] 'We state it as a fact, which we have received, on what we deem undoubted authority, that the *Puseyite* party have bought up the BRITISH CRITIC, which publication accordingly will from henceforth be dedicated to the promulgation of their principles.' *The Record*, 1045, 1 Jan. 1838.

credit of selfdenial.[1] Lately they have proclaimed our buying a column in Mr Gathercole for a £1000. It is amusing what bugaboos we are—they see us in every bush, like the Hammersmith ghost the Papers are full of. Yet it is curious they should be so near the mark—we have just 'stolen away' as they come to find a maresnest.

However, things stand thus;—but it must not be talked about—Mr M. [Maitland] and I are going to try each other—Himself I like much—he is honest and straightforward—but I fear Rose's influence—So we are going to break him in thus:—Pusey is in the next number to write a strong article on the Church Commission[2]—By the bye I rely on your article too on H. Martyn—It must be ready by the end of February at latest.[3] Maitland begins to see our position, and (as it affects the British Critic) is in a state half pleasurable half nervous—alternately soothed and startled, as a little boy being ducked in the sea, or a horse brought up to a post he shies at.

NB. I see no *notes* to your pamphlet, except one or two shabby little ones at the foot of the page

Your parcel has been three days coming—I send it back at once. I suspect [E.] Churton wrote the article you speak of.[4] I cannot read what you say about Misopapisticus—who and where is he?[5]

Ever Yrs affly J H Newman

P.S Why do not you *date* your letter?

SATURDAY 13 JANUARY 1838   Latin Sermon and Sacrament which I attended.   Marriott in Oxford

SUNDAY 14 JANUARY   2 Epiphany   early Communion   did duty morning and afternoon   preached Number 381   Eden's brother to dine with him

MONDAY 15 JANUARY   letter from Buller and Williams   very cold night   no c

TUESDAY 16 JANUARY   letter from Bliss   dined with the Provost to meet Ottley, as did Pusey and Eden   sent to Town 5th Lecture   [16 to 29 January, Breviary] very irregular this fortnight

WEDNESDAY 17 JANUARY   letter from Rivington and anon   wrote to Bowden and Rivington   about this time the glass down at 10° Fahrenheit in my inner room

---

[1] *The Record*, 1029, 6 Nov. 1837, attacked those who had given up the Church Pastoral-Aid Society and joined the Additional Curates Society, claiming that the latter was manipulated by a small clique. It had actually been the heavily Evangelical influence in the Pastoral-Aid Society which had caused many to quit it. *The Record* went on to suggest that Pusey had offered £100 a year to the Pastoral-Aid Society if it would alter its constitution according to his suggestions, and that he now contributed the money to the Additional Curates Fund.

[2] 'The Royal and Parliamentary Ecclesiastical Commissions', *Brit. Crit.*, 23, 1838 (April), 455–562.

[3] 'Memoirs and Journals of the Rev. Henry Martyn', *Brit. Crit.*, 24, 1838 (July), 120–33.

[4] 'Use of the Fathers', *Brit. Crit.*, 23, 1838 (Jan.), 24–47.

[5] *Letters on the Writings of the Fathers of the first two Centuries, with Reflections on the Oxford Tracts . . .*, by Misopapisticus, London 1838. The letters were appearing separately in *The Record* at this time.

TO JOHN EDWARD BOWDEN

> Oriel College. (In my rooms, sitting opposite
> the windows looking into the Quadrangle)
> Jan. 17. 1838[1]

My dear John

This is not so large a letter as yours, but by writing smaller perhaps I may make it as long. Did you write the Greek word in your letter? I dare say you find Greek harder to pronounce than Latin, and the words are often longer. I shall so like to hear how you get on—but I fear you will find the irregular verbs difficult.

Love to your sisters and brother,

> Yrs affly John H Newman

TO J. W. BOWDEN

> ⌜Oriel College. Jan. 17. 1838⌝

My dear Bowden,

First let me, though the season is some what over, tender my kindest thoughts to all your party upon it. Such an interchange is, I believe, the only remains we have now (is not it?) of the primitive salutations, such as the 'Christus resurrexit'—The Invitatory in the Breviary seems to constitute a most suitable greeting all through the year.[2] Yet ⌜to me, I am sorry to say, this Christmas has been very little of a leisure time. I have been quite overwhelmed with business, though I am thankful to say, not overpowered—for I am particularly well—whatever comes. Anxious I have been, and am very, about several things. Froude's volumes will open upon me a flood of criticism, and from all quarters. It is just a case where no two persons have the same judgment about particulars, and I am fully conscious that even those who know one will say 'what *could* he mean by putting *this* in? what is the use of that? how silly this! how trifling that! what is it to the world if so and so? how injudicious he is cutting his own throat⌝—quem Deus vult perdere' etc ⌜but on the whole I trust it will present, as far as it goes, a picture of a mind, and that being gained as a scope the details must be left to take their chance. Then about by own work I am a good deal fussed. It is the first voyage I have yet made proprio marte, with sun, stars, compass and a sounding line, but with very insufficient charts.[3] It is a terra incognita in our Church, and

---

[1] The copy gives the year 1835, probably a misreading of 1838. John Edward Bowden was at this time aged eight. His father wrote on 21 Dec. 1837, 'John insists on sending you a line—which I enclose—but you need not trouble yourself to read it, much less to acknowledge it—'

[2] The Invitatorium, a brief versicle, varied with the season of the year; at this time it was 'Adoremus Dominum, qui fecit nos'.

[3] *Lectures on Justification*. [[N.B. It so happens that I use the same metaphor, as well as express the same feeling in my last Discourse on University Education.]] See *Idea*, p. 213.

I am so afraid, not of saying things wrong so much, as queer and crotchety —and of misunderstanding other writers for really the Lutherans etc. as divines are so shallow and inconsequent, that I can hardly believe my own impressions about them. We have three volumes of the Library of the Fathers in the Press, but Baxter is so miserably slow, I think we shall have to take another Printer. This again, is a very anxious business,⌐ especially as having other things to do.

⌐Maitland has taken the British Critic with a promise of our assistance— when I know more, you shall hear more. Nothing could be better *unless* he were under Rose's eye—for he is going to live in Town—but we must be quite decided, and if he will not put in our strong articles, we must retire. Your offer towards the young Monks was just like yourself, and I cannot pay it a better compliment.[1] It will be most welcome. As you may suppose, we have nothing settled, but are feeling our way. We shall begin next term, but since however secret one might wish to keep it, things get out, we do not wish to commit James Mozley to any thing which may hurt his chance of success at any College, if any where he stands for a fellowship—though *I* have given up the notion of his doing so. After Easter will be a better time so far as this, that there may be some eligible man among those who stand for our Fellowships unsuccessfully. I trust the plan will answer *when* begun —but do not know how to start and fear wasting money through clumsiness. During this next term, with Johnson's help, I hope to concoct something, and you shall hear from me. I am told Pusey has got off very well in the Edinburgh but have not seen it.[2] I suppose they wish to play the peculiars and us against each other. As to the Statute business,⌐ it is too long to put down on paper—but ⌐I do not see one could have acted differently.⌐[3]

With kindest remembrances to Mrs Bowden and Johnson, and best compliments to the Swinburnes.

Ever yrs affly John H Newman

THURSDAY 18 JANUARY 1838   letter from Rivington (about British Critic)   wrote to Dodsworth

FRIDAY 19 JANUARY   letter from Manning   f d   wrote to Rivington

SATURDAY 20 JANUARY   letters from John M [Mozley] and Goldsmid   Acland in Oxford

[1] [[qu. offering?]] See first note to letter of 3 Dec. 1837 to M. R. Giberne.
[2] See letter of 30 Jan. to E. Churton and note there.
[3] See note to letter of 13 Nov. to H. Wilberforce. For a detailed account of the Oxford Convocation of 23 Nov. 1837 and the minor changes which were made in the University Statutes, see *Brit. Mag.*, 12, 1837 (Dec.), 704–5.

TO JOHN KEBLE

⌐Jany 20. [[1838]]⌐

My dear Keble

I have not had time to correct these sheets properly. I shall verify the references to Whitby and Hickes, and Johnson.[1] Very likely I have been over anxious (you will judge) in my notes—if so, of course cut out. ⌐I hope to have a few extracts from the Tracts etc. [[against Rome]] made an advertisement⌐ of and put as a leaf into the British Magazine. I think it necessary to quiet people by showing them there are two sides to a question

Ever Yrs affly J H N

P.S. ⌐If you have any choice sentences against Rome⌐ in any thing *you* have published, ⌐will you (if you wish) have it sent up⌐ to Rivington ⌐for insertion⌐ in the list. I shall put some sentences from my Romanism and from the Remains. Do you object? I propose doing it thus:—

Extracts

from

Tracts for the Times

To speak against Ultra Protestantism is not to favor Popery

Extract

1. (extract one—)

2 etc

3.

Tuesday Evening ⌐Pusey approves of the Advertisement,⌐ but I doubt whether it will be well to extend it beyond the Tracts and shall ask him tomorrow.[2]

SUNDAY 21 JANUARY 1838   3rd Epiphany   early Sacrament   did duty morning and afternoon   preached Number 385   Fulford to dinner—with Eden, Brown, Mr Calcott, and Berkeley   thaw began

MONDAY 22 JANUARY   letter from H   thaw   walked to Littlemore

TUESDAY 23 JANUARY   wrote to J M. [John Mozley] Wood and L.M.N. Post Office Oxford

TO JOHN MOZLEY

Oriel College ⌐Jan 23/38⌐

My dear John M.

Perhaps your Father would like to know (unless he has seen it in the Papers) that Dr Mavor is dead. Please, ask Jemima for my brother Charles's

[1] References in Froude's 'Essay on Rationalism' to D. Whitby, *Paraphrase and Commentary on the New Testament*; J. Johnson, *Unbloody Sacrifice*; and G. Hickes, *The Christian Priesthood Asserted*. See *Remains* III, 106 and 154.

[2] See letter of 28 Feb. to Keble.

direction. Since I wrote (thank Jemima and you for your letters) ⌐I have become Editor of the British Critic, much against my will¬—(this had better not be mentioned) ⌐this will put an end to my scheme of being Editor of a Miscellany,¬ and I am sorry I have given you any trouble about it. I agree with you in thinking Southey vastly superficial, but the tone on the whole good, except that he is sometimes irreverent.[1] While [will] you give Jemima this message for Harriet (Tom must[2] a little)

Ever Yrs affly J H N

WEDNESDAY 24 JANUARY 1838 freezing again walked to Littlemore Cornish, Fulford, Bloxam to dinner—with Eden, Hussey, Ward, Williams of Jesus and Christie wrote to Keble

TO JOHN KEBLE

Oriel College ⌐Jan 24. (1838¬

My dear Keble

I send you what in point of matter and size, I fear, is not worth the postage, first to say (lest you should be expectant,) that I have not had a proof for 10 days—and have written about it—I fear there is some mistake about Rogers determining something. It seems to me very important the book should be out by February 1.—Would it not be desirable if you could send the preface at once? but perhaps you have sent it up to London.—

⌐Will you think of a motto?—You have black balled what comes home to me, as best—'so many tokens of a frail love lost etc'

What think you of this from the Paris Breviary?

Se sub serenis vultibus
Austera virtus occulit,
Timens videri, ne suum,
Dum prodit, amittat decus.¬[3]

I am Editor of the British Critic—but do not tell this. It will be known fast enough, and I am sick at the thought.—The Lyra has come to a third Edition.

I hope you will give a good account of Mrs Keble this severe weather, when you write—My kindest regards to her and to your sister if with you and believe me

Yours ever affly John H Newman

[1] Robert Southey, *The Book of the Church*, fourth edition, London 1837.
[2] Illegible word.
[3] *Hymni Ecclesiæ, e Brevario Parisiensi*, edited by Newman, Oxonii 1838, p. 192. The stanza, taken from Matins of the Office *Sanctarum Mulierum*, was adopted for the titlepages of the volumes of *Remains*.

THURSDAY 25 JANUARY 1838 Conversion of St Paul Service in Chancel—read Number 360 Williams returned? dined in Common Room with Eden Copleston came

FRIDAY 26 JANUARY Copeland returned? f d Marriott came

SATURDAY 27 JANUARY fire at Printing Office first day of term Daman came Spranger returned wrote to Keble

SUNDAY 28 JANUARY 4 Epiphany m letter from Wood and Rogers[1]—from J with part of proof of third edition of Lyra by A.M. [Arthur Mozley] and from Keble with Preface to Froude's volumes Sacrament in morning Spranger assisting (last time of candles?) Spranger read morning Service I afternoon and preached Number 132 with Queen's Letter for National Society[2] dined in rooms sent off MS of Lecture 7

MONDAY 29 JANUARY 1838 walked to Littlemore dined in Hall [Breviary] very irregular this week

TO MRS JOHN MOZLEY

O. C. ⌈Jan 29/38⌉

My dear Jemima

I have very little to say except to thank you for your letters. Mrs Small is so much better that for weeks she has not been prayed for, and I suppose is counted well. ⌈The glass in my inner room has stood at 10°—22° below the freezing point. I have never had it so cold for a continuance, or at all, since I have been in them⌉

As to M R G.'s [Giberne] MS, since this engagement with the British Critic has destroyed the possibility of my undertaking any thing else, I have not (being busy) looked into it.

⌈I am quite sick at the thoughts of having the British Critic but there was no one else, and I did not like so important a work to get into hands I could not trust. I do not begin with it till the July Number.

My book on Justification has taken incredible time. I am quite worn out with correcting. I do really think that every correction I make is for the better, and that I am not wasting time in an overfastidious way, or making it worse than it was,—but I can only say the means [[openings]] of correcting are

---

[1] Rogers wrote on 26 Jan., 'Has Wood told you that he and R.W. [Williams] talk of publishing a translation of the Breviary (or greater part of it) in monthly (?) numbers by subscription. He wishes to do it in an independent way without committing you or anybody else so perhaps he has not . . .'

Newman seems to have written a cautionary letter to Wood and he replied on 5 Feb. to explain his plans: 'Robert Williams has been translating since last summer, and on his showing me a specimen I found it quite well and closely enough done to form a good basis for correction, and undertook to take the Commons and otherwise to help him. Supposing us to finish this summer what we think of is this: Two months before the Church-year begins to bring out, first the Psaltery, next the Commons, and then on the 1st. of each month to bring out all the festivals *retained in our Calendar* both in red and black, for the month. At the end of the year this would make a thick volume.' They were only planning to print it privately and circulate it to subscribers.

The plan was abandoned after causing alarm among some Tractarians, even though part of it had been printed. See letter of 2 Nov. from G. Prevost and the ensuing correspondence with Keble.

[2] The National Society for promoting the Education of the Poor in the Principles of the Established Church, founded in 1811.

inexhaustible. I write—I write again—I write a third time, in the course of six months—then I take the third—I literally fill the paper with corrections so that another person could not read it—I then write it out fair for the printer—I put it by—I take it up—I begin to correct again—it will not do —alterations multiply—pages are re-written—little lines sneak in and crawl about—the whole page is disfigured—I write again. I cannot count how many times this process goes on.[1]—I can but compare the whole business to a very homely undertaking—perhaps you never had it—washing a sponge of the sea gravel and sea smell. Well—as many fresh *waters* have I taken to my book. I heartily wish it were done. Seven Lectures out of 15 (say) are in the Printer's hands—Two more nearly finished. I have to write at the end a sort of Essay as an Appendix on the Formal Cause of Justification which will cost me some thought and reading.

Thank John for his letter. I suppose the *first* sheet of Lyra[1] has passed the Press.

Ever Yrs affly J H N

Love to Aunt

TUESDAY 30 JANUARY 1838   In Festo S C. [Caroli] Martyr   f.m   f d.   service in Chancel   read Number 332   meeting of Diocesan Committee of S.P.C.K.   wrote to Churton, Manning, and Wood.   all but c

TO EDWARD CHURTON

Oriel College. In Festo S. Car. Martyr. [30 January] 1838

My dear Churton,

I have intended to write to you before now, not to inform you of what so well informed a person has long known, but 'to sollicit your vote and interest' for the most unwilling Editor of the B.C. who has been caught in his own trap. I wished a *friend* to be Editor, but had no intention of being nabbed myself. I do not commence till July, but have told Rivington I will find him an Article which is wanting to make up the next; and as you said you had the Jesuits in hand, I write to know whether you can let him have it for the April Number.[2] It will be a great accomodation if you can. Please let me know.

Also, will you kindly undertake, as you proposed, a series of Articles on the Fathers? Please, let me know this also.

I have got all your hints and hope to profit by them. As to the men you mention, I will keep them by me, but will not apply to them at once. Young Mr Whytehead is the only exception—as it might be nailing him. If you had

[1] The third edition of *Lyra Apostolica* was being printed by Henry Mozley and Sons at Derby.
[2] Churton's 'Revival of Jesuitism' appeared in *Brit. Crit.*, 25, 1839 (Jan.), 143–86.

an opportunity of getting from him a good Article, I should be grateful. The delicate thing is, that I suppose we should be rather intolerant of bad doctrine, and if he is only a beginner, or (what Dr Whitaker calls) a semi-coctus tyro, there might be some collision.

How long is the present fair wind and smooth current to last? I do not see at all what the issue is to be—our good friends on the Protestant basis *must* plunge deeper if they would make any fight against us—and both Christian Observer and Record, I am told, show signs of doing so. But if so, there is no chance of schism *in* the Church, for they cannot plunge Liturgy and Articles with them.

On the Committee of 12 Laymen for the Curates' Fund are placed the names of Gladstone, Acland, Bowden, and Wood—this is good.[1]

Is not the Pusey Article in the Edinburgh a *very* great εὕρημα?[2] to be acknowledged, and to be argued with, is certainly much, foreby being puffed. Pusey is going into the subject of the 'glorious' in an Appendix to his Second Edition, which will be sold separate—it is very good.[3]

The Fathers lag through the exceeding dilatoriness of our Printer—whom, I fear, we must leave—Friend Copeland is just returned—I am sorry to say his eyes are not so well as one could wish

Ever Yrs most sincerely John H Newman

TO H. E. MANNING

Oriel College. In festo S. Car. [30 January] 1838

My dear Manning,

Things are, as you may know, in a new posture. I am Editor of the British Critic, to my disgust, to come into play in July. Now first, please, send me back my 50 names, of which I have no copy. Next, may I look on you as a *regular* contributor? I hope so. I shall expect your Articles with the seasons, something sharp in winter, promising in Spring, flourishing in summer, and fruitful in Autumn. Answer me about this. Is there any line or department of writing you would like to monopolize? answer this too. Of course you will let me have your Review of Martyn by the middle of February. When I come in, we shall pay 7 guineas a sheet; which will be all gain to the Apostolical cause, for we may be sure that it will go towards agitation in *one shape or other*.

I congratulate you on your success in Church Building matters—and hope you will get as tight hold of your Diocesan as you can, and make him

---

[1] See note to diary for 9 April 1837.
[2] 'Dr. Pusey's *Sermon on the Fifth of November*', *Edinburgh Review*, 66, 1838 (Jan.), 396–415. The article was by Herman Merivale.
[3] Pusey published separately three appendices to his sermon *Patience and Confidence the Strength of the Church* The second was entitled 'Remarks on the Revolution of 1688, and the Principles involved or not involved in its Condemnation'.

take a line, ut decet Episcopum.[1] You know, I suppose, that Pusey's projected review of your Pamphlet has blown Maitland out of the Review to my great sorrow.[2] But no wonder—he was setting out on a voyage of adventure with a rum crew and thought twice before he cut cable.

I am glad the Regale[3] is coming out—and altogether prospects are fair. The Archbishop has put on the Lay Committee of 12 of the Curates' Fund, Acland, Gladstone, Bowden, and Wood. This shows how the current is setting.

Please to send me forthwith certain papers of Wood on the subject of Justification and the Council of Trent, if you can spare them

And now Vive Valeque My dear Manning

As wishes and prays Yrs affly John H Newman

WEDNESDAY 31 JANUARY 1838   College meeting about Aberford[4]   walked to Littlemore—with the 2 Morrises back   dined in Hall

THURSDAY 1 FEBRUARY   f d   Daman went away suddenly

FRIDAY 2 FEBRUARY   Service in Chancel   read Number 37   Mr May passing through Oxford   Quarter Account Day   Gaudy Dinner—Provost, Dean, I, Greswell, and Marriott—Eden did not dine   no n v c

SATURDAY 3 FEBRUARY   letters from Rose and Manning   Philip Pusey very ill   dined in hall—Mr Tate and Mrs Hodson with Marriott

SUNDAY 4 FEBRUARY   5 Epiphany did duty morning ⟨?⟩ and afternoon   four ministers at Communion   preached Number 30

TO JOHN KEBLE

Oriel Febr 4/38

My dear Keble

I hope I was not impatient in writing to you. G. and R. *sent to me* for the Preface.[5] Now they say they are waiting for the wood cuts belonging to the Articles on Architecture.

I liked the Preface much, as did Williams. With his sanction, I corrected one or two grammatical errors—but you will be able to do it better, if you

[1] See letter of 28 Oct. 1837 from Manning.

[2] Pusey wrote to B. Harrison on 21 Jan. about Maitland's withdrawal from the editorship of *Brit. Crit.*: '. . . Mr Maitland not liking to undertake, with an article against the Commission in it as neither could he well, being at Lambeth, lest the Abp should be supposed to be secretly attacking it, or else it would be disrespectful to him.' S. R. Maitland was Librarian and Keeper of Manuscripts at Lambeth.

Manning's *The Principle of the Ecclesiastical Commission examined* was one of fifteen works reviewed by Pusey in his long article 'The Royal and Parliamentary Ecclesiastical Commissions', *Brit. Crit.*, 23, 1838 (April), 455–562.

[3] Charles Leslie, *The Case of the Regale and the Pontificat stated . . .*, London 1838. Manning and S. F. Wood were the editors.

[4] An Oriel living in Yorkshire.

[5] To the first part of Froude's *Remains*. In a letter to Sir John Taylor Coleridge of 7 Feb. 1869, Newman explained that the 'Preface to Froude's Remains, consisting of 22 pages, is certainly Keble's, not mine, except the portion about 'Romanism' from p ix to p xv.' See Volume XXXI, 87*.

will. In p. xv last line you will find an addition you should look to—*self-righteousness* is what most men mean by Popery. Also you will see an addition in the same page, which correct, cut out, or supersede, as you will. It is intended to meet a misunderstanding of Marriott's who on reading the passage, asked if we were cutting at the Articles.

You will see in the end of page iii 'high but not the highest—' cut them out if you do not like. I wished duly to state the fact—if you say 'high' only, you seem to panegyrize—if 'not the highest' only, it is unfair to him. Men will think of double thirds.[1] If you alter, please alter also 'having obtained' into 'obtaining' which is neater, but not worth while *by itself* altering for. This opening sketch (which in its matter came from the Archdeacon) was sent down to him a week since, begging him to write up at once if he had any fault to find.

In the proof of the *text* of Vol 2 you will find I have added some extracts from Milton[2]—cut them out or not as you will. (You will receive this some days hence.)

I grieve to say little Philip Pusey is in a very alarming way. He has had a fever on him for some weeks, which has determined to his lungs—at first they thought something immediate was to happen—Now Dr W says that he *may* with care in course of time recover.

Ever Yrs affly John H Newman

P.S. Will you not pronounce, we *must* be going wrong since the Edinburgh is for us? I was struck the other day with the words in the Lesson, 'the *world* shall fight with him against the unwise[3]—' is not this an excuse for being apparently mixed up with secular influences?

Bloxam is busy about the Eagle.[4] By the bye there is to be sold a brass Eagle in Wardour Street London at (I believe) Poole's—but will not be sure of the name.

P.S. There is no hurry about your coming up—so I consider it *not fixed*

Williams and I thought it best not to give any *instances* of trivial passages being important.

TO R. F. WILSON

⌈February 4. 1838

I may well address you as an ancient shepherd doth a more fortunate one, 'Tityre tu patulæ'. Do you really think I have time to meditate verses to

---

[1] Hurrell Froude obtained double second class honours in his B.A. examination. The Preface refers to this with the words, 'after having obtained on his examination, high, though not the highest honours', pp. iii–iv.

[2] Froude discussed Milton in his essay on 'Causes of the Superior Excellence of the Poetry of Rude Ages', and several excerpts from the *Treatise on Christian Doctrine* were included in the annotation. See *Remains* II, 322–4.

[3] *Wisdom*, 5:20.

[4] See note to diary for 1 Jan.

Amaryllis? that is, you are a country swain and have the choicest [[gifts]] which Hursley can give, but I assure you that for me, to go to the point, I have not written a letter except on business, I do not know when. Do come here some time, and we will have some quiet talk together; . . . my hand is too tired to write letters, unless I am forced; literally my hand is in a continual ache.

. . . Sewell has done us good service in the Quarterly; certainly his article is a very kind one.[1] How is it that Sewell, Jewell, Whewell, rhyme?

. . . Rogers's article is admirable.[2] Pusey is quite astonished. I believe he took him for a good-natured, sharp schoolboy; but he has gone about muttering 'We have a giant.'

. . . Will you, My dear fellow, promise me two articles a year for the British Critic? I will pay you seven gold sovereigns (guineas would sound better) for every sheet⌉

MONDAY 5 FEBRUARY 1838 letter from Miss Holdsworth breakfasted with Mr Hall dined with Fulford at Exeter who goes away tomorrow (*he had been my private pupil*)

TO E. B. PUSEY

Febr 5 [1838]

My dear P.

Many thanks for your news about Mrs P. for which one ought to give thanks elsewhere. Certainly it is very gracious. I hardly know whether one should offer any expression of joy to herself, considering that the gain, if granted, is not to be hers.

May it all be what is best for you and for her, however it is.

Ever yours most affly J H N.

TUESDAY 6 FEBRUARY 1838 letters from Churton and Mr Kilvert dined in hall wrote to Miss Holdsworth

TO MISS HOLDSWORTH

Oriel College. Feb 6. 1838

Dear Miss Holdsworth,

I was very much pleased at receiving your letter, as containing the news of the progress of the inquiry into Church principles in your neighbourhood. One really trusts the inquiry cannot proceed without what one considers

---

[1] 'Memorials of Oxford', *Quarterly Review*, 61, 1838 (Jan.), 203–38.
[2] 'Froude's *Remains*', *Brit. Crit.*, 23, 1838 (Jan.), 200–25.

truth prevailing among good kind of people; because they have hitherto been bound up in a cramped unnatural attitude neither standing or sitting. The only safety many people find against Catholic truth is *not inquiring*, but that cannot last in the 19th century.

As to the question which has led to your letter, I am glad to say you will find an elaborate answer in the next Tract Number 81 which ought to have been out long ago, but will by the first of March if not before. It is upon the Sacrifice in the Eucharist, and consists of an historical sketch of the variations of doctrine in our Church and a Catena of English divines upon it. It runs to near 250 pages; so it is as long as any one can wish. I think it will answer all your questions—As to the word Sacrifice, it occurs two or three times in the Prayer after the Lord's Prayer, which prayer is part of the ancient Sacrificial rite—whoever then puts any other but the Sacrificial sense upon the word, is putting a new sense, and must be put on the defensive. As to the word 'oblations', I believe it is historically certain that it was put in by the Revisers of 1662 with a *view to introduce* the ancient doctrine —(as they introduced in the Rubric the word 'Consecration' soon after). The word oblation is only left out when there is no oblation of Bread and Wine—vid Rubric before Prayer for Church Militant—On this subject you will find some interesting matter in Knox's Essay on the Eucharist.[1] Altar occurs no where, thanks to the zeal of the innovators—however, *custom* has sanctioned it. If any word has a prescriptive right, it has. 'Companion to the Altar' is the usual title of the books of Preparation for the Holy Sacrament; and if there be a sacrifice, and a Priest, I do not see how any one can deny there is an Altar.

I believe the Church Catholic has ever considered the Holy Eucharist not only a sacramental representation, and also a real and proper sacrifice of bread and wine, but a sacramental presence of Christ Crucified—the shadow, as it were, of the Cross on Calvary being continued on to the end of the world;—or, again, the worshippers being carried back as if to the very foot of the Cross. In Hebrews 10, it is said typical sacrifices are at an end. This is not a typical sacrifice. As a Sacrament is not a mere type, but an outward form of Christ's exalted, so the Sacrifice is not a type, has nothing substantive, but is the offstreaming of that which it represents.—I fear I am not as clear as I should be. After you have seen the Tract which is publishing, if you would let me know any difficulties you still have, I would try to satisfy them. Johnson's Unbloody Sacrifice[2] in 2 Volumes small octavo is a standard work on the subject, but badly put together. My volume on Justification is passing through the Press, and a great anxiety to me—I have spent incredible

---

[1] The 'Treatise on the Use and Import of Eucharistic Symbols' of 1826, together with the prefatory 'Letter to J. S. Harford' and a Postscript, appeared in *The Remains of Alexander Knox, Esq.*, London 1834, I, 138–255. It was later reprinted in *The Doctrine of the Sacraments*, London 1838.

[2] John Johnson, *The Unbloody Sacrifice, and Altar, Unvail'd and Supported*, two volumes, London 1714–18.

pains upon it, but am very diffident how it will turn out. Not that I have not my own determinate view, but I fear it will be hard and laboured to read.

Hurrell Froude has an essay on the Eucharistic Sacrifice, but it will not appear in his present Volumes.[1]

I was much interested in a MS. which I was allowed to see some time since, and was told was yours. How I wish there was a way to avail ourselves of assistance which would be most valuable to the cause. I have had several schemes about setting up a sort of Magazine—but have had difficulties I have no room to recount

Yours most truly John H. Newman

WEDNESDAY 7 FEBRUARY 1838   letter from Wood and proof of third edition of Lyra dined at Trinity   wrote to Rose and sent back proof   letter in parcel from Rivington proposing 2nd edition of Romanism[2]

TO THOMAS LATHBURY

[7 February 1838]

Sir,

I have just received and perused your Paper on Mr Price's history of Nonconformity—and feel I have to thank you, which I do very heartily for your offer of allowing me to insert it in the B.C.

It will be well for that Review if it can command Articles written with so much learning and in so interesting a style. As however I do not go along with the general line of opinion upon which it is written, I think it best with much regret, and great respect for the author to decline it. If it is not a liberty to state my difference from it, I should say I view the church less in the light of an Establishment. The former paper you speak of has not reached me[3]

Yr obt Servt J H N

TO HUGH JAMES ROSE

Oriel College. Febr 7. 1838

My Dear Rose,

I wish I could send you a more satisfactory answer to your question than this will be—by more satisfactory I mean something more than you can provide without going beyond the Principal's House, which I know is not

[1] See *Remains* III, 132–64.
[2] The second edition of *Lectures on the Prophetical Office of the Church* was published later in the year.
[3] Lathbury wrote on 26 Jan., explaining that he had sent an article on various works concerning Church Reform and Unity to Boone for *Brit. Crit.*, and Boone had undertaken to recommend it to his successors. He now enclosed a further article reviewing Thomas Price, *The History of Protestant Nonconformity in England from the Reformation under Henry VIII*, two volumes, London 1836–38.

easy for any one to do. As far as I can judge of the very interesting case you mention, I should think the person in question cannot properly be under any sort of uneasiness.[1] To put the case in the strongest light possible against him, stronger than the truth, one might say that he was baptized against the will of the Bishop. It does not seem to me that such circumstances have any tendency to invalidate his Baptism.—In the case of Lay baptism, the Bishop's implied permission has been considered necessary, as every one knows, by high authority; but I conceive the Sacerdotal powers of the second order are as substantive as those of the first. The Bishop is the sole principle of jurisdiction, and the sole fount of orders but not the sole principle. A Presbyter acting in disobedience cannot be in worse case than Bishops and Presbyters in a state of heresy or in schism—yet surely the Primitive Church admitted the acts of such clergy as valid, though the grace attending them be suspended till the subjects of them conform and are reconciled. The great Baptismal controversy is in point, as treated in the time of Cyprian, and by Augustine in controversy with the Donatists. It was determined that the Baptism of heretical and schismatical Clergy (the matter and form being duly observed) were real—and that all that was to be done to bring them into effect, that is to realize their *spiritual* benefits, was for the baptized to be reconciled to the Church by imposition of hands, or rather confirmed, for about the meaning of the imposition there is some controversy.—To go into authorities would be more than could be done in a *letter*, but if it would be any satisfaction to your friend, if he thinks this line of argument to the point, I will most gladly do so, if you will send me a note to that effect. I should say then, that though for his own comfort he might obtain, if he has not already, the Bishop's ex post facto sanction, yet he has as distinct a reason for saying he *is* baptized now, as for saying *he was not* as a Presbyterian—

As to your other question[2], the longest list of instances I know from the Fathers on the subject of lying is to be found in Gataker on Antoninus xi §18 Page 400.[3] (My reference is from Mosheim.) he gives, Origen in one or

[1] Rose wrote on 2 Feb. about the difficulty of a person who had been born a Scottish Presbyterian but had come to Episcopalian views when at college. The question of his baptism had perplexed him but at first he had been satisfied with the arguments in favour of the validity of lay baptism. When going to Rose to be examined for orders he had explained the problem and they had decided that he should apply for baptism to the chaplain of the Bishop he was to go to. The Bishop, however, felt that this was wholly unnecessary. His perplexity continued and so he was baptised by a clergyman, and had since been ordained. His scruples became more intense and he sent Rose some questions which Rose now passed on to Newman. The main question was whether a priest was ever meant to act as anything other than the delegate of the Bishop, and, therefore, whether a baptism without the Bishop's sanction was valid?

Rose sent Newman's letter on to the enquirer, who was the Rev. Francis Garden, later editor of the *Christian Remembrancer*.

[2] Rose asked, 'will you kindly tell me where I can find references to the passages on which Mosheim found his charges against Ambrose, Hilary, Augustin, Nazianzen and Jerome as to inculcating the duty of *lying* for the good of religion. He gives no references (see Cent. IV. Pt II. Ch. III, §16) and I do not know where to turn'.

[3] Thomas Gataker, *Marci Antonini de Rebus Suis*, Utrecht 1697, pp. 330–1. Newman's reference was from J. L. Mosheim, *An Ecclesiastical History, Ancient and Modern . . .*, London 1825, I, 282.

two places—Clement—Augustine, and Lactantius. And Dallaeus de Usu P.[1] ch vi p 159 etc. gives Jerome—Dionysius Al. ap. Athan.—and Greg. Neocaes. ap. Basil.—These are cut and dried passages which every one knows.

I am exceedingly glad to hear of your progress towards health—Harrison tells me you have got into King's College. The Record is an unwilling messenger of good in stating the fact that you are giving Lectures.

With every kind and sincere wish for your health, and (what then cannot but be) usefulness

I am My dear Rose Yours very sincerely John H Newman

THURSDAY 8 FEBRUARY 1838   dined with Spranger

FRIDAY 9 FEBRUARY   letter from Ryder   f d

SATURDAY 10 FEBRUARY   dined in hall

SUNDAY 11 FEBRUARY   Septuagesima   letter from Mr Trail   early Communion Spranger read morning—I afternoon   preached Number 489[2]

TUESDAY 13 FEBRUARY   letters from H W and Goldsmid

WEDNESDAY 14 FEBRUARY   Pusey went to Town about Mr Davenport[3]

MEMORANDUM. THE IRISH ESTABLISHMENT

July 6. 1875.

It seems from the answers I made to the following letters of Mr Trail,[4] that I had at this time, 1838, a great distrust of the soundness of the Irish Establishment—and thought its clergy radically Evangelical and did not much care to undertake their cause. vid. on the state of things a letter of Dr Todd's, and unluckily destroyed one of Archdeacon Mant's.

And I said to Mr Trail, or seemed to say, 'The sees were suppressed by the fault of the Irish Bishops and clergy—I will go so far as to join a petition

---

[1] J. Dallaeus, *De Usu Patrum*, Geneva 1656, pp. 159 ff.

[2] *P.S.* V, 8, 'The State of Innocence'.

[3] James Mozley wrote to his brother Tom on 21 Feb.: 'Pusey himself has been up to London just now to be a witness for Mr. Davenport, whose case you may have seen in the papers. His relatives choose to think him mad because he has given away £40,000 for charitable and religious purposes. Pusey met him at dinner in the Long: and went to testify to his sanity, as far as he could judge at the time. He was examined an hour and a half in rather a bullying way, and had seriously to give his opinion that the clergyman, seeking treasure in heaven, who gave £5000 to the London churches, was not mad. By the way, I strongly suspect this clergyman to be Pusey himself . . .' *Letters of the Rev. J. B. Mozley, D.D.*, London 1885, p. 72. Pusey had contributed £5000 to the Metropolis Churches' Fund about a year previously. See Liddon's *Pusey* I, 331.

[4] Newman received a letter from William Trail, of Bushmills, Co. Antrim, dated 5 Feb., enclosing a petition. He noted on the letter, 'answered Feb 28/38', 'answered to this effect, that we would petition for a restoration of what things were—*not* for any organic change. We were in captivity, and till God gave a signal, must so remain. I would not even agitate for the repeal of the Praemunire, tho' I might sign with others; and will not pronounce what a *Bishop's* duty may be about it and similar points.' See also letter of 20 July to Trail.

for their restoration, but for nothing more. I do not understand your new "organizations".

'And further I think you are political, and it is a great principle with me to take things as they are, and work them as they are—if we succeed in working with what we have, political changes will of course follow—but I will not directly agitate against that captivity in which the Church lies—Let us rather enforce baptismal regeneration and its developments, apostolical succession etc etc.' and this in my secret heart I thought the Irish Establishment would *not* do.

TO G. D. RYDER

Feb 14/38

My dear Ryder

I had already made sundry inquiries for you of Eden at Keble's bidding —but elicited nothing

The Butler has now submitted the following statement:—viz. that of the £30 of which consisted your Undergraduate caution money, £10 was reserved, ut moris est, for M.A. caution money,—that near £16 was owing at the time of your M.A. degree for Battles [sic] etc.—which leaves rather more than £4 unaccounted for; which sum I suppose you either received back at the time or it went towards the liquidation of the College fees for the M A degree; but you can tell me this perhaps. Well—the £10 which remained in the College's hands as Caution Money is now more than exceeded, and you must therefore renew your deposit, or advance, of the same sum. It stands thus—University and College fees up to St Thomas Quarter 1837 £10. 10. 9—Common Room Account £1. 10. 5. making a total of £12. 1. 2 against which setting the old £10—reduces it to £2. 1. 2 and against that the *new* £10 which you have to send, you will then have left £7. 18. 10 in our hands to run out before you are dunned again.

Many thanks for the Paper, which made me marvel—I neither recollect writing it nor lending it to you; but I doubt not I did. You see it cannot possibly have put me to any inconvenience.

Your contribution to Froude's Remains is very important. It has been put into the Preface, the only place that was open. I mean the passage about Popery[1]—the rest is pretty much contained in other letters

Ever Yrs very sincerely John H Newman

TUESDAY 15 FEBRUARY 1838 sent up the last proof of F's Remains volume 2 Ashworth dined with me in hall

---

[1] See *Remains* I, xiii–iv. The editors quoted a passage from a letter of Froude to Ryder which highlighted Froude's anti-Roman feelings, 'Since I have been out here [Naples], I have got a worse notion of the Roman Catholics than I had. I really do think them idolaters . . .'.

FRIDAY 16 FEBRUARY letters from R Williams, Goldsmid, and Mr Werter [J. W. Warter]

SUNDAY 18 FEBRUARY Sexagesima Spranger assisting in early Sacrament Spranger did duty in morning did duty in afternoon and preached Number 490[1] (S. Wilberforce preached University Sermon against Pusey)[2] baptized Chadwell's child dined in rooms

WEDNESDAY 21 FEBRUARY dined with Copeland

THURSDAY 22 FEBRUARY letter from Woodgate 5 Lectures (Bamptons) from Woodgate Ashworth dined with me in Hall?

FRIDAY 23 FEBRUARY buried Mr Piniger at Littlemore—very rainy f d wrote to Woodgate

TO H. A. WOODGATE

Oriel. Febr 23/38 Eve of St M. [Matthias]

My dear W

I like your first lecture very much—though there is not quite matter enough to please me.[3] I have nothing particular to observe, except that if you choose you might attenuate your Socinian, into a Quaker-socinian or something less. Milton's Treatise on Christian Doctrine[4] is a curious specimen how far the process can be carried. It advocates Divorce and Polygamy—as to the former, it parries the argument 'They two shall be one flesh' *quite* in the received Protestant style by referring to the use of it in 1 Cor. vi—*therefore* in the other passage it has nothing to do necessarily with *religious* union. By the bye Luther and Co are believed (I think) to have been on the point of publishing their approval of Polygamy—You know they actually did allow it in the case of a Rheingrave, Luther Melanchthon, and 5 or 6 others, and that under their handwriting. Again how little is in Scripture for Public Worship—Accordingly Milton gave it up. Indeed is there any one precept or doctrine, which 'want of clearness' and 'change of times' will not wash away? *Some* are in the future when they should be imperative—therefore (says Mr Basil Montague)[5] 'Whoso sheddeth man's blood etc' is not binding on us now. Others are Jewish—others are addressed to *individuals* and *therefore* mere argumenta ad hominem, etc etc. I suppose in one of your later Lectures you may be writing expressly on this subject—if so, I hope you will work it up richly with examples. So much for the first—By the way you should *in the*

---

[1] *P.S.* VIII, 18, 'Ignorance of Evil'.

[2] Samuel Wilberforce '. . . felt very strongly the practical danger of the unexplained sternness of the view of post-baptismal sin set forth in No. 67 of the 'Tracts for the Times.' This, of course, was an eminently practical subject, and three . . . sermons . . . were devoted to the subject of sin and its consequences, with a tacit but well-understood reference to the teaching of the Tract above named.'

See S. Wilberforce, *Sermons preached before the University of Oxford, . . . in the Years 1837, 1838, 1839*, London 1839, Sermon I, 'The Moral Consequences of permitted Sin'.

[3] His Bampton Lectures of 1838 on *The Authoritative Teaching of the Church shewn to be in Conformity with Scripture, Analogy, and the Moral Constitution of Man.*

[4] See J. Milton, *De Doctrina Christiana*, ed. C. R. Sumner, Brunswick 1827, pp. 179–86.

[5] Basil Montagu, miscellaneous and legal writer, who specialised in bankruptcy. His edition of Bacon's *Works*, which was published in sixteen volumes between 1825 and 1837, was heavily criticised by Macaulay in a celebrated article in the *Edinburgh Review* of 1837.

text make your apology for the phrase Bible Christian, or people will think it satirical.

The second is clear and good—from whom comes the quotation at the end?—I still say that there is not matter enough—but this is your taste, which you have a right to, and I do not wish any thing altered.

The third is far too important to be left for the first Sunday in term. THIS MUST NOT BE. You *must* preach it in full term. It is the best of the three. I observe however 1st. you should notice that the Jews *had* tradition, first in Moses' words about writing on their foreheads, teaching their children, etc. vid Ps 79.1. etc. next there was the great post-captivity Tradition as evidenced first in the interpretations of the Septuagint—next by the Apocrypha—third by the Rabbinical and Christian writers—the doctrines of the atonement, our Lord's divinity etc. seem to be thus clearly handed down. Secondly I observe, you must not say the Apostles were quite ignorant till the day of Pentecost—Our Lord spent 40 days teaching them the things which belong to the Kingdom of God—moreover before the end of the 40 days, they chose another Apostle, (whose Eve this is) which implies a good deal. Thirdly you all along assume that Scripture is the standard of appeal but do not prove it. Have you any where said, 'I shall take this for granted and *prove it elsewhere*?' It ought to be proved somewhere or other.—However on the whole this is a capital sermon—and I do not think it needs the fourth to follow at once.

What can you mean by saying you differ from Keble and me? I do not discover it.

Thanks to the fair hands of your Deaconesses,[1] they certainly have boiled the peas, on which otherwise I should have had a dreary penance   And now farewell. If you knew how busy I was at this moment, you would give me credit for having got up this letter

Ever Yrs affectly John H Newman

SATURDAY 24 FEBRUARY 1838   Service in Chancel   preached Number 217[2]
SUNDAY 25 FEBRUARY   Quinquagesima letter from Rogers   Spranger assisted me at early Sacrament   Spranger read in morning I in afternoon preaching Number 491[3]   dined in rooms   wrote to Rogers (or tomorrow?)

TO FREDERIC ROGERS

Febr. 25. 38.

I am vexed at the mistake and were it not too late would cancel the leaf. As it is concoct a short 'erratum' and let Rivington have it *forthwith*. I can

[1] Woodgate, whose handwriting was difficult to read, had had his lectures transcribed.
[2] *P.S.* VII, 17, 'The Unity of the Church'.
[3] *P.S*. IV, 21, 'Faith and Love'.

only account for their delay by supposing they have other work in hand. By the bye Keble found some apparent false point or other in the Architecture Article and that [?] he wrote down to Archdeacon Froude to enquire about it.—It is pleasant to find you approve the Preface, every one will be struck by it in his own way. It is just the kind of thing to make a hundred varying impressions.

Is it impossible for you to undertake a mission to Dublin forthwith? I am justified by Froude's known wishes to assign you your expenses out of his Fund. I want Mr Todd as a permanent contributor to the B. C. but want to know more about his opinions. He is a very frank pleasant man. I am precluded from going to Dublin by Whately being there. I would send a letter to Mr Todd saying you were visiting the place, and would be obliged for civilities. It would give us so much more confidence in our dealings with each other, if you could thus smooth matters.

. . . It was curious the passage in the Preface you allude to originally stood without the instances of the Praemunire and Marriott said on seeing it 'Here is an attack on the Articles!' So I being exceedingly shocked put in the instances.[1]

Acland I suppose would have us pull with Rose. Lately one or two sermons every Sunday, and sometimes a Saint's Day, are attacks on Pusey. I Williams came in for it yesterday (his Tract No 80) hitherto I escape—

MONDAY 26 FEBRUARY 1838   letter from H   went to Littlemore   R H F's books out in Oxford

TO JOHN KEBLE

Oriel ⌈Febr 26/38⌉

My dear Keble,

At last I send you a precious book. It was published in London on St Matthias's day—and came down here this evening.

⌈No news—except that it is the fashion now to preach against people. S. Wilberforce took Pusey in hand yesterday week—Mr Hill of St. E. H. [[Edmund Hall]] took to task Pusey and Williams on Saturday. There was a touch too in both afternoon Sermons yesterday and yesterday week.⌉

I am sorry to say Rogers has made a mistake in his note on the Architecture Paper—I sent it him in proof, but he did not discover it. But his

---

[1] It was explained in the Preface that Froude had considered himself 'a minister not of any human *establishment*, but of the one Holy Catholic Church, which, among other places, is allowed by her Divine Master to manifest herself locally in England, and has in former times been endowed by the piety of her members: that the State has but secured by law those endowments which it could not seize without sacrilege, and . . . has encumbered the rightful possession of them by various conditions calculated to bring the Church into bondage', *Remains* I, xiv–xv. Various examples of the means by which the Church was kept in bondage were given, such as the suspension of her synodal powers and power of excommunication.

eyes, poor fellow, were in fault. Is not Hurrell's book a good present for Lent?

I hope you will send us a better account of Mrs Keble and your sister next time. ⌜The winter seems now over⌝

Ever Yrs affly John H Newman

TO MR STONE

(Copy)   Febr 26. 1838

The Editor of the British Critic presents his Compliments to Mr Stone,[1] and desires to express his obligation to him for his offer of Articles for it.

He is sensible of the value of Mr Stone's assistance, but under present circumstances he does not feel the necessity of going beyond the circle of persons on whom he already depends for contributions.

TUESDAY 27 FEBRUARY 1838   Shrove   letter from Woodgate   Williams and Copeland to dinner   men in Common Room in evening
WEDNESDAY 28 FEBRUARY   In festo S.H.[2]   Ash Wednesday   f b and d till t   service at 11   wrote to Woodgate and Mr Trail   [Breviary] all

TO JOHN KEBLE

Oriel ⌜February 28. [[1838]]⌝

My dear Keble

⌜Pusey bids me say that he is going to affix to his pamphlet the list of passages against Popery which have already been stitched into the British Magazine.[3] If then you think of giving your own extracts, he would be very much pleased to receive them, and that at once⌝

Ever Yrs affly John H Newman

TO H. A. WOODGATE

Oriel. Febr 28. 1838

My dear W

You have made a floor. Forster tells me that it is unlawful for a Bampton to exchange with a Select—Item, that Short of Bloomsbury, who is preacher,

[1] Probably Thomas Stone, of St John's College, Cambridge, author of *Sermons, preached in the Parish Church of Prestwich*, London 1835. Stone had written to Pusey on 13 Jan. to say how much he valued the *Tracts*, which he had just come across, and how much he agreed with their teaching.
[2] The anniversary of Hurrell Froude's death.
[3] The extracts were appended to Pusey's *A Letter to . . . Richard Lord Bishop of Oxford, on the Tendency to Romanism imputed to Doctrines held of old, as now, in the English Church*, Oxford 1839.

has made a great point to get that Sunday, so that, if he could, yet he would not change with you. So you must be content to be as you are. You do not tell me if I shall send you the Lectures back. Unless I hear from you, I shall send you back the three first. The 1st of April is in Term time, but all your questions are superseded by the University Rule about exchanges. I think your proposed alteration in the beginning of Number 1 an improvement. As to your taking for granted Article vi[1] as an axiom, you are a pretty fellow —This is putting salt upon the bird's tail indeed. What? have Romanists nothing to say for themselves? are they to be set down by a self evident proposition? They will agree with you in saying that the Doctrines of the Gospel cannot in any part be contrary to the Apostles' teaching in Scripture —only they say there *are* doctrines, which are *not* in Scripture, which the Apostles spoke but did not happen to write. I wish you joy of your εὐηθία.[2]

Also I wish you joy of your improved handwriting, which in your last letter was so marked as to seem to indicate a desire on your part to approach a lady's hand.

I am not very much in favor of your St Paul and St James τόπος[3]. The weather is now mending and I hope your cold will go

Yrs affectly John H Newman

THURSDAY 1 MARCH 1838   Assize Sermon   Baptized Jubber's child   wrote to Mr Merewether   all but c

TO W. F. HOOK

[Oriel College, Spring 1838]

You are, indeed, in the thickest fire of the enemy; and I often think how easy it is for us to sit quietly here sheltered from bullets, while you often get what is meant to hit us.[4]

FRIDAY 2 MARCH 1838   letter from Wood   H. Westmacott in Oxford   f b till d [Breviary] all   H Westmacott dined with me and went to the Theological in evening, where Marriott read—wrote to Wood and Mathison and to [R.] Westmacott by his brother

[1] 'Of the Sufficiency of the Holy Scriptures for Salvation'.
[2] 'simplicity'.
[3] 'line'.
[4] W. F. Hook was being frequently attacked by Evangelicals and Dissenters in Leeds as a friend of the Tractarians. See W. R. W. Stephens, *The Life and Letters of W. F. Hook*, London 1880, II, 1–9.

TO S. F. WOOD

[2 March 1838]

Now, for your friend Milnes—I assure you I am puzzled—I know he would be a great accession to us, but have not a grain of confidence in him. I think him a man who can admire what is beautiful, but who has not got the root of the matter in him—that is, he is not in earnest. Now can I consistently ask him to do what will only give him an opportunity for more talk? Besides, I never could be sure he would not be saying something I did not like—and I have no right to expect that he would allow me to find fault with what he sent me at my own (as he would call it) fancy. I think then I must give up the notion—therefore do not ask him.

J.H.N.[1]

SATURDAY 3 MARCH 1838   walked with Daman   Williams dined with me in hall   all but c

SUNDAY 4 MARCH   1st Lent   Letter anon: from Welshpool[2]   Spranger read in morning   I in afternoon and preached Number 492[3]   Spranger, Cornish, and Marriott assisted me in Communion   dined in Rooms

TO MRS JOHN MOZLEY

Oriel College March 4. 1838

My dear Jemima,

I send a card which Clough of Jesus is anxious to get circulated and its object promoted. If you or Harriet (to whom perhaps you will send the names etc) can do any thing, I think the case will speak for itself.

My book is nearly out of hand. I suppose it will be published in another fortnight. I referred to your passage in Milner from Luther on the Galatians[4]; but it seemed to me so very mild and sober compared with other parts, that I could hardly think that I had found what you meant. My book at first sight will seem not a popular one, from the Latin and Greek in it—but this does not interfere with the *reading*. It is only in notes. Yet I fear it will be dry and hard in parts.

---

[1] Wood wrote on 1 March to report that Richard Monckton Milnes, author of the recently published *Poems of Many Years*, had offered to write for *Brit. Crit.* Although Wood seems to have been friendly with Milnes, he had reservations about his suitability.

[2] The correspondent, giving the direction, 'B.D., Post Office, Welshpool', asked how 'a young couple of small independent fortune' could best observe the fasts of Lent according to the discipline of the Church of England, within their own family. The correspondent had formerly heard Newman preach at St Mary's.

[3] *P.S.* VI, 1, 'Fasting a Source of Trial'.

[4] Joseph Milner, *The History of the Church of Christ*, London 1819, IV, 508–24.

You have seen perhaps by the papers that we have an accession to our family in Oriel.

Love to John and Aunt and believe me,

My dear Jemima Ever Yrs affectly John H Newman

P.S. I wish I could get Charles's direction. All this time I have not been able to write to him.

MONDAY 5 MARCH 1838   walked to Littlemore and did duty

TUESDAY 6 MARCH   received present of Paten and Offertory Dish for St Mary's from London.   dined in Hall   wrote to Lambert and Rawlings acknowledging the Plate and to Manning   sent parcel with Manning's Article   Undergraduates in evening

FROM H. E. MANNING

Lavington, March 2. 1838.

My dear Newman,

I have fulfilled to the best of my power the promise I gave about Martyn—but with a difficulty I can hardly tell you. So many personal, and family feelings hampered me that, I have altogether failed. Many things I think I ought to have said, I felt unable to say, and many things I have said ought perhaps to be omitted. I would gladly have escaped it, but having pledged myself I would not fail if I could help it. I have only to beg that you will unsparingly handle it—and if you find yourself able to do without it that you will keep it back. The more closely I have read his journals the more I have felt the miserable state, to which the Church was then reduced. I was altogether afraid of touching the school of Theology, for there seems an unfeelingness, and profaneness in raising a strife over the relics of the Saints, which reminds me of a passage in St. Jude's Epistle. So much with the article, which you will use as you think best.[1]

I have got a case of the τοπος ἀργυρόσταυρος. My Bishop excessively wishes to establish in Chichester a college for candidates for Holy Orders—to take them for 6, or 12 months, and indoctrinate, and break them in. He has begged me to think of some scheme—I can only think of a lease of a house, and a few sets of rooms, and some good Catholic who will live on £100 a year to poison them up to the crown of their heads. I have a promise from a friend of such a sum for 5 years. The Bishop is ready for any reasonable scheme—and would lend his best aid, and countenance, even to requiring candidates to attend, and having greater regard to them afterwards, if worthy, in the Diocese.

This is one project.

Now for another—Leslie is hankering after a reprint of Brett's work on Liturgies.[2] He wrote to Palmer, who dissuades, saying there are ἀδιάφορα? in it—would raise questions—divide clergy etc, etc. What do you think of it? And what should you advise about a reprint of Brett's collected works—I think I could get Leslie in motion, and would take your trouble on myself. Pray answer me this as soon as you can, as he is waiting for advice.

Poor Rose has been ill again—I have not heard of him this last week—I shall hope to hear from you, and when you write tell me how Pusey, and his two invalids are—I do indeed feel for him.

Believe me, my dear Newman, Ever yours affectionately, H E M.

[1] 'Memoirs and Journals of the Rev. Henry Martyn', Brit. Crit., 24, 1838 (July), 120–33.
[2] The Collection of the Principal Liturgies of Thomas Brett, the non-juror, was reprinted by Rivington later in the year.

P.S. I have forgotten to say that, I have read Froude's Remains with exceeding interest, and pleasure—I had little idea of what he was till now. The preface is as bold as it is good. The Record has been remotely insinuating some heresy against you, arising, I think, from your '*Arianism*'.[1]

I am afraid the article is a specimen of the ἐξ ὧν μή ἔχει—something like the posthumous praises of the Egyptian Kings.

At first I intended to put in many passages about the heathenism of the European Government etc in India and have got some stuff ready for it—I left it out, because it would not come in without breaking up the rest, so I will look out for some text hereafter.

TO H. E. MANNING

Oriel College. March 6. 1838

My dear Manning

I feel very much obliged by your article, which came quite safe. I send it tonight to the press. You will have a proof of it; I only regret it is so short, for it is very good and impressive. One or two words I have left out, but *very* few. The only observation I have to make on it, is that it has somewhat too many quotations for a review. Two I have thought you would let me omit— one is A Kempis's, not that I did not like it, but because I thought it could be easier spared—the other the lines from the Lyra, as having appeared in the last Number. There is a quotation from St Austin, which will not come down to you but which perhaps you will be so kind as to put in in proof. I thought it had better be in *English* since there was a piece of Latin before. This, I believe, is all I have to say.

Your College scheme is good. As to a head to it, Pusey suggests Ward the Bishop of S and M's [Sodor and Man] son—which I do not much fancy —as I told him. I suggested Seager, which he seems to think plausible. He also suggests *your Dean himself*, if you can trust him[2]—what say you to this? it would be a means of strengthening Cathedrals.

You say our Preface to the Remains is bold—is it near so bold as the publishing itself is? I sit prepared but not comfortable in expectation of the first report of the explosion in the Observer etc. having applied the match.

There is no news here—I am sorry to say that not only Rivington pays nothing under the present Interregnum in the Review, which [but?] he scruples at paying any thing under my management—which I demur at. I

---

[1] 'Now, Mr *Newman*, one of the writers of the Oxford Tracts, according to what is reported, in his Lectures in "The Prophetic Office of the Church," would have us believe that what is called the Apostles' Creed came from the Apostles, at least substantially and nearly in the form we now have it. If there was such a creed in Irenaeus's time how came he not to use it . . . ?' The writer, signing himself 'Misopapisticus', went on to draw up a definition of tradition from Irenaeus that was 'traditioned and taught by all Protestants deemed orthodox throughout the world.' 'But this declaration of Irenaeus has often been perverted in the same way as he tells that passages of Scripture were perverted by the heretics. It has been separated from its "context," and been made to apply not only to *all* the doctrines of Scripture, but also to all matters of Church order and discipline. This is an heretical work.' *The Record*, 1058, 15 Feb. 1838.

[2] George Chandler, D.C.L., Dean of Chichester.

think I shall stickle for 5 guineas a sheet,—indeed I have. I have this morning received a present of plate for St Mary's Altar. Mrs Pusey is decidedly better and has come downstairs—and the little boy is rather better. She has lost her sister—and there is no hope of her brother.

Brett's works would be valuable, when collected, though I believe they are unequal. His Tradition[1] and Liturgies are the two I know to be good. If you think about it, Copeland's bookseller here, I forget his name ⟨Gooch⟩, would give us some information. Now *in confidence* I just throw out something. Goldsmid of Exeter (a lawyer in town, nosti,) is very hungry for articles to write etc etc.—he has married a descendent of Brett and is proud of it—If you think his want of judgment would not spoil all I wish you could make him Editor—it would give him something useful and sobering to do, and he is (I think) a good fellow. Think of this and please *burn this side the letter*.

Therefore, I shall say nothing more upon it of a more valuable nature. —(Is my 'heresy' in the Record a real live heresy or a Record-heresy)

Ever Yrs affly John H Newman

WEDNESDAY 7 MARCH 1838 f b and d wrote to Wood on hearing of fire in Paper Buildings *news of Badely's and Wood's loss in fire at Paper Buildings*[2]

THURSDAY 8 MARCH no s and n walked with J.M. called on Mrs B Morrell sent Woodgate his three first Lectures

FRIDAY 9 MARCH letter from Wood f b and d no s. n very busy today with Appendix to book (*Justification*) in evening administered oath to Mr Norris of C C C about a will

SATURDAY 10 MARCH no n c.

SUNDAY 11 MARCH 2nd Lent Spranger assisted me in early Communion and read in morning I read in evening and Copeland preached for me dined at Berkeley's.

MONDAY 12 MARCH had a cough and cold all this week no Services Daman went for me to Littlemore Mr Sherlock called with letter from Mr Todd[3] dined *yearly dinner* with the Iffley and Littlemore trustees at the King's Arms—Provost, President C C C, Vaughan Thomas, Archdeacon, Marshall Hacker, and I. Sent up last MS to Town J and T. Keble called

---

[1] Thomas Brett, *Tradition Necessary*, London 1718.

[2] Wood wrote on 8 March, 'I have had a most narrow escape of having my chambers burnt, and all my poor books . . . The fire, which was truly devouring reached within *one* room's width of me, and for some time there seemed no chance of our being spared. At last the means of our being so were a party-wall, and the enormous hose of the Floating Engine, which was trailed up my staircase and into my attics like a great serpent, and thence exspuebat upon the fire.' He went on to report that Badeley had lost his fine library, and that the cause of the fire had been '. . . Mr [William Henry] Maule's setting his bed on fire; if common fame speaks true he is a very bad fellow, and his chambers had been the scene of all sorts of abomination'.

[3] James H. Todd wrote on 27 Feb. to introduce Rev. H. Sherlock, who was hoping to be admitted M.A. *ad eundem* at Oxford. Todd invited Newman to visit Ireland in the summer: 'Until you come to Ireland therefore you will never thoroughly understand Popery—not even the Tracts for the Times themselves, which some people think certainly the very quintessence of Popery, will give you such a knowledge of the working of that system as a trip of a week into the mountains of Connemara or the Joyce country . . .' Newman wrote on the letter long afterwards: 'This letter shows the fears he had lest, taking a theoretical view of Catholicism, not a real and practical, I should move in a direction adverse to the Anglican interest.'

TUESDAY 13 MARCH Mr Sherlock to breakfast Keble's Lecture Undergraduates in Common Room in evening as usual

WEDNESDAY 14 MARCH f b and d. Anderdon called on me

THURSDAY 15 MARCH did preface to Sutton's book[1] walked with J.M.

TO HENRY WILBERFORCE

Oriel College, ⌈March 15. 1838⌉

My dear Henry,

I was not neglectful of your kind letters, though my great press of employment kept me silent. As to your commission there was nothing to do, as Miller was out of print and Justin not in the Library. Would it not be well if you gave instructions to your London Booksellers to try to pick up Miller[2], if it could be done without any great expence? The first Editions of such books, though often not so valuable in themselves as the subsequent, yet have a value as being the first, and a College Library is a place where such circumstances may be suitably regarded.

I have now done my book and have no proof even left except a note at the end and the Advertisement. It has taken me much more time than any other book, if I can fairly compute, and am not influenced by the urgency of present over past impressions. It is a subject which ought to have taken less as having been in my thoughts, of course years and years before a scientific treatment of either Church Authority or the Arian Question could be, and continually before me as being the matter of Sermons, and yet I had nothing produceable scientifically. I do not think I have altered my opinion since this time year, except in those very minor matters in which one says this or that indifferently, according to the exigencies of the system, as Calvinists decide the question of God's willing the Salvation of all men this way or that according as best to strengthen their position. I cannot count how many times I have written the greater part of it, if not all—yet there is just one passage of a few pages which, though a ticklish one, is just as I first wrote it—but I am not over pleased with it—there are two or three other *rhetorical* bits which remain. What has taken me so much time is first the adjustment of the ideas into a system, next their adjustment in the Lectures, and thirdly and not the least the avoiding all technicalities and all but the simplest and broadest reasonings. As to what I read you, or what you heard on St Andrew's day, it is partly cut out, partly re-written—but in one way or other swept away bodily. Now after all this, you will expect a most splendid affair—I

[1] Newman edited Christopher Sutton, *Godly Meditations upon the most Holy Sacrament of the Lord's Supper*, Oxford 1838. In the Preface, Newman cautioned: 'If any one be disposed to censure [the language of the work] as too glowing, or what may be called rapturous, let him rather consider whether his own estimate of its sacred subject itself be not inadequate . . .'

[2] Possibly John Miller's 1817 Bampton Lectures, *The Divine Authority of Holy Scripture asserted*, a third edition of which was published later in the year.

cannot at all tell, how it will take as a whole—that there are good bits, I am aware.

Now ⌜as to the British Critic⌝ to which I have forthwith begun to turn my thoughts, ⌜I want your assistance by all means⌝—and four times a year, if you can let me. ⌜I fear you will find the pay very bad, only 5£ or guineas a sheet.⌝ You have shown yourself so perfect a Jack the Giant Killer in re Pashley,[1] whose recent misfortune I hope I may without ἐπιχαιρεκακία[2], rejoice over, that I should like you to take that line, as indeed you seem willing to do. By ill-fate I have put your letter on the subject of the Critic in so safe a place that I cannot find it—I know you proposed something which seemed to promise,—something about some Society. What say you to a series of articles on the Societies? excepting the S.P.C.K. which is taken. Let me know. Do you think you could let me have an article by the middle of May?

As to the proposal of the lady you speak of, I smiled at the notion of *my* writing books for girls—have I yet been Father Confessor to a boarding School? but it is a most desirable thing. You know I have wished a series of books and to get women to write them who would do them best. The British Critic has dissipated that plan, but I trust it is being taken up in London. Would not the Lady *in question attempt it*? The subject of Confirmation is one I had actually proposed to some female friends, but it will not be done I see.

⌜Froude's remains will be like the frost he describes, which, by its rigor hardens their roots.[3] I do not wish the Truth to spread too fast and this check seems (if one may say so) providential. Bold hearts will stand the gust, but the reeds are bending, and the shallow [[trees]] may be uprooted.⌝ Vale, Sir Henry, Knight of the most pungent order of Giant Killers, be severe, be cautious, be fortunate.

Ever Yrs affly J H N.

FRIDAY 16 MARCH 1838   f b and d   Woodgate in Oxford   Keble read at Pusey's
SATURDAY 17 MARCH   letters from C. and Bowden   at St Mary's at 7 AM[4]   called on Miss Edwards   walked with Pusey   Berkeley lost his brother.

[1] Wilberforce reviewed Robert Pashley's *Travels in Crete*, two volumes, Cambridge 1837, in *Brit. Crit.*, 23, 1838 (Jan.). Wilberforce was very critical of Pashley, acknowledging his learning and detail, but regretting his 'irreverent and supercilious spirit' and his 'delight . . . in gross and sensual images'. Wilberforce attacked the tendency of the book to degrade Christianity from the rank of divine revelation.
[2] 'spitefulness'. Pashley's library and collection of Cretan antiquities, as well as a great many copies of *Travels in Crete*, had been destroyed in the recent fire at the Temple.
[3] [[the roots of plants]]
[4] '(This is the first instance of my hearing a confession) March 18.—On Wednesday Evening March 15, as I was sitting in my rooms, a young (person) man came in, and (in the course of conversation) by degrees said he wished to confess to me previously to receiving the Sacrament of the Holy Eucharist on Sunday next (today) and asked if I should object to receive his Confession. I said I should feel it painful, both from the responsibility and the distressing trial of hearing it; and that I would think of it. He said he should go elsewhere, if I would not—yet he wished me rather, and yet should be sorry to pain me. I saw him again the next

SUNDAY 18 MARCH   3rd Lent   letter from Manning   early Communion Spranger assisting who read prayers in morning—I afternoon and preached Number 493[1] dined with Bloxam, as did Wms [Williams], Copeland, and Cornish

MONDAY 19 MARCH   my cold not gone   [19 and 20 March] in consequence no Services Mr Sherlock to dinner   wrote to Bowden, Todd, R.W. and Wood enclosing Bowden's MS.

TO J. W. BOWDEN

⌐Oriel College. March 19. 1838.⌐

My dear Bowden,

I have been many days meaning to write to you, but first was hindered by hearing you had not returned, then by the press of employment which finishing my Lectures gave me. I hope they will be out in the course of this week. ⌐The British Critic upset my plan of a Library opusculorum—but I had gone so far as to send one to press. Wood has sent down (with your leave, I presume) for yours, which I am sending up to him.⌐ I think it likely to prove useful—⌐it has some very good hits in it. If I were to criticize, I should say it is wanting in ease, in places, which I thought was the fault of Dr Spencer[2] in its original state. I mean, it is rather abstract objections and answers, than people speaking.

Many thanks for your most welcome and munificent offer of a quarterly article for the B.C.—but I must not be too grasping—⌐ if you can do it and without trouble, it will delight me. I talked to [Manuel] Johnson, and he seemed to fear such thing was almost too much. ⌐I like your subjects too—We will have the British Association by all means in July, and I deliver it to your mercies

day, when he said his reason was to gain peace of mind and that he had thought of it for two years and more, and latterly from reading Bishop Taylor.—and when I reminded him that if he began he must tell me *all*, he (assented as being) said he was aware of it. Then I told him that I felt that Confession could not be separated from Absolution, referring to the Exhortation to the Communion—and while I thought it would be well for many of us at least in certain seasons of our lives, if we were in the practice of *Confession*, that I was thus far decided as to the use of *Absolution*, that it was a removal of the disabilities and bar which sin put in the way of our profiting by the Ordinances of the Church—that I did not see it was more than this, though I had not a clear view of the subject, that if it was more I trusted I should be guided to see it—but that any how the act was *God's*, and He could as really use me as His instrument, though ignorant, as He could the inanimate element in Baptism. This was the *substance* of what I said, and I added I should be ready to receive him at seven o'clock on Saturday morning in the Chancel of St Mary's.

So yesterday the 17th at the time appointed I was there, and sat down against the rails at the Altar at the North end to get out of view from chance intrusion—I sat in my Surplice—and he came and knelt before me.' *A.W.*, p. 214. The note goes on to describe the form used, followed by the prayer for guidance which Newman had drawn up for himself on 15 March.

[1] *P.S.* V, 13, 'The State of Salvation'.

[2] Wood had written to ask Newman's opinion about publishing Bowden's small tracts, both those which had appeared as *Tracts for the Times* and others. He felt there was 'a great want of such things for our poor in town'. Bowden had contributed *Tracts* 5, 29, 30, 56, and 58. *Tracts* 29 and 30, 'Christian Liberty', took the form of a dialogue between a fictitious parishioner, John Evans, and his rector, Dr Spencer.

joyfully.⌐1 It is an anxious thing how we shall *go on*, but I trust we shall start well. ⌐I hope in the July Number we shall have a paper of Keble's on Walter Scott,2 of Harrison's on Professor Lee's Job3 of Copeland's on Bishop Kenn,⌐4 besides articles from H. Wilberforce etc., ⌐and (I hope) Mr Todd of Dublin.⌐ But keep all this a secret even from our circle of friends—because else I shall get into a scrape.

Pusey is writing a most elaborate article on the Church Commission which (as far as I have seen it) is a most overpowering and melancholy exposure of it by a mere statement of facts.5 I wish it were not quite so long but it is a very large subject; and I certainly find every thing most concisely put, as far as I have read.

In reviewing the British Association, do not forget the first Report. There is a splendid oration there in praise of Priestley with choice bits about his theological opinions—⌐6 Certainly I seem to have made a considerable floor in the 'jube'7—but I leave it to you and Wood. Du Cange explains it thus, which equally puts me in the wrong. 'Jubere Dignare, velle: . . . eadem notione Lector in Officiis Divinis a Præside Chori postulans benedictionem ait, "Jube domne benedicere" '

⌐I have not seen Williams's Cathedral8—but I fear it will be obscure. However every one has his line and his victims. To be sure what a mass of Catholic Literature is now being poured upon the public. Have you seen Palmer's Book?9 It is quite overcoming, his reading—and makes one feel quite ashamed. It will do a great deal of good, for just at this moment we need ballast. Then again Froude's, in an opposite direction, as if marking out the broad limits of Anglicanism, and the differences of opinion which are allowable in it. Then Woodgate's Sermons,10 which began yesterday, with a bold uncompromising statement of the doctrine of Tradition, and of the difference between the Catholic and Rationalistic spirit, which comes from a

---

1 Bowden had offered to try and produce a *Brit. Crit.* article every quarter and 'wanted to take up the British Association proceedings first'. The article appeared as 'The British Association for Advancement of Science', *Brit. Crit.*, 25, 1839 (Jan.), 1–48. Newman wrote in 1874, 'old Tractarians 30 or 40 years ago, were the first to protest against the British Association then beginning. My dear friend, the late Mr Bowden, wrote a strong article against it . . . Our deep suspicion of it was, because, in spite of its being a scientific Society, it would meddle with religion. It then undertook the office of patronizing it by a mild, cold, Deism', Volume XXVII, 43. See also Volume XXVIII, 267.

2 'Life and Writings of Sir Walter Scott', *Brit. Crit.*, 24, 1838 (Oct.), 423–83.

3 Samuel Lee, *The Book of the Patriarch Job, translated . . . to which is appended a Commentary*, London 1837. The proposed article did not appear.

4 'Life and Works of Bishop Ken', *Brit. Crit.*, 24, 1838 (July), 167–90.

5 'The Royal and Parliamentary Ecclesiastical Commissions', *Brit. Crit.*, 23, 1838 (April), 455–562.

6 See *Brit. Crit.*, 25, 1839 (Jan.), 33–5, about Priestley.

7 The words in the Breviary, 'Jube domne benedicere', usually translated, 'Pray, sir, a blessing'. Newman seems to have suggested a translation of 'Sir, pray for a blessing', which Bowden queried, giving a reference from St Peter Damian about its place in the office.

8 [Isaac Williams], *The Cathedral*, Oxford 1838.

9 [[on the Church]] William Palmer, *A Treatise on the Church of Christ*, two volumes, London 1838.

10 [[Bamptons]] *The Authoritative Teaching of the Church shewn to be in Conformity with Scripture, Analogy, and the Moral Constitution of Man.*

certain Pamphlet.[1] I hope to do something with my forthcoming lectures—and there are to come Keble's papers on Mysticism (read at the Theological) in the next (5th) volume of Tracts[2]—(By the bye have you seen Williams's most valuable Tract 80?) Then Pusey's Lectures on Mysticism[3]—then your Hildebrand—then Froude's Becket etc., which is now ready, and all besides this the B.C.—But one must not exult too much. What I fear is the *now* rising generation at Oxford, Arnold's youths—much depends on how they turn out.⌉

Thank John for his note duly and with kindest thoughts of you all.

Ever yrs affly John H. Newman

TO JAMES HENTHORN TODD

Oriel College. March 19. 1838

My dear Mr Todd,

I have long been meditating a letter to you, first to thank you for a Sermon you sent me of yours[4]—but chiefly for a more selfish reason.—I believe that in the course of a few months I shall have the management of the British Critic, and I am looking about for writers—it struck me that you and Mr Crosthwaite would not be unwilling to assist, if you liked our ways of going on; and then I thought that, if so, perchance the department of Romanism was one which you would not object to engage in. But I am reckoning without my host in all this, and so I will rather go back to the previous question.

It is best in all these arrangements to be very candid, and I know I can be so with you without being thought impertinent; and I will try to say what I mean as simply as I can. We wish of course that the Review should speak with one voice, and not write against itself in its separate articles—Now as far as I know, I really do not think you would disapprove of any thing we are likely to say. The point on which, judging at a distance, disapproval on your part was most likely, was the Revolution question; but from what I have read or heard you say, I think you are not bigotted to King William. We are as strongly opposed to the Romanists as an *existing system* in these countries, as you can be; though we do not like abusing them. I am not aware that you are especially attached to Luther either.—as we are not. We do not praise Cranmer, or Jewell; but we keep silent; and I think ever should. We have perhaps very high views of the abstract power and position of the Church as a ruling body—but then, considering it to be in captivity, we hold it a

---

[1] Bowden's *A Religious Reason . . . for the Subscription to the Articles*, Oxford 1835, pp. 11–19, describes the contrast of the catholic and rationalist spirit.

[2] *Tract* 89, 'On the Mysticism attributed to the early Fathers of the Church'.

[3] Presumably Pusey's 'Lectures on Types and Prophecies', which were written in 1836 but never published.

[4] *The Restoration of the Kingdom to Israel, a Sermon, preached in the Chapel of the Molyneux Asylum . . .*, Dublin 1837.

Christian duty to obey our Masters, as the Jews obeyed Nebuchadnezzar. Is there any point, will you let me ask, on which there is likely to be any serious difference between us?—And now pray pardon me if I have gone beyond the limits of candour.

Your friend Mr Sherlock is a very pleasing man indeed, and I have got a good deal of information from him. I wish there was any chance at present of my availing myself of your kind proposal to visit you—which would be a great treat. I do not like to give up the notion of doing so some time or other —but see no prospect at present—my engagements are so numerous.—It is indeed a very tempting offer; but we are short of hands here as yet. Is there any chance of your passing through this place at any time to London? Always in Vacation time, and sometimes in Term time, I could give you a bed.

I keep by me your valuable notes about the corruptions of the Fathers by Romanists for future use. Some friends of mine are sceptical on the point; i.e. that Romanists have done more (which is enough in all conscience) than the Tract Society does with Milner's works etc etc. Would you think of a paper on this subject for the British Critic, reviewing Mr Gibbings' book?[1] —Could Mr Crosthwaite be tempted to take Palmer's new work on the Church as the subject of an Article?—I think if we disagree on any point, perhaps it is (you see I am doing my utmost to find some ground of quarrel) about the Church *Establishment*—Certainly some of us have gone lengths on this subject.

Yours most sincerely John H Newman

TO S. F. WOOD

Oriel March 19/38

My dear Wood,

I have nothing to say except to wonder at Rogers's inexplicable silence. Have you seen Palmer's book? it is a stupendous magazine of learning and has quite made me feel ashamed. It will be good ballast at this moment, for he professes to consider the later Anglican Church infallible, which will be a proper antidote to Froude's παρρησία.[2] His treatment of the Lutherans etc. is characteristic. He takes hold of them as gently and tenderly as if he was ipsissimus Luther—and when he has got them safe on his knee, he fetches them the most cruel and malicious blows. The utmost he says for them is that 'they most probably were not heretics.' It put me in mind of the conduct

---

[1] Richard Gibbings of Trinity College, Dublin, had edited *An Exact Reprint of the Roman Index Expurgatorius*, Dublin 1837. Newman noted, 'March 30. letters from Mr Todd and Crosthwaite', but they do not seem to have contributed any articles. Newman himself reviewed Palmer's *Treatise on the Church* for the October number.

[2] 'outspokenness'.

of Petit André in Quinten [Quentin] Durward.[1] Or Isaac Walton and the trout.[2]

Woodgate's Sermons have opened well.

Love to all friends Ever Yrs affly J H N

TUESDAY 20 MARCH 1838   dined with Copeland   wrote to C and W.F.   men in Common Room

WEDNESDAY 21 MARCH   f b and d   letter from Wilson inclosing letters to him from Wood   sent up last proof of Lectures on Justification

THURSDAY 22 MARCH   letter from Rogers   put room to right   sent back books to Library   dined in hall, Williams with me

FRIDAY 23 MARCH   f b and d—m l th s n   sent to the Bishop Visitation Paper—and wrote to Wood inclosing letter to Wilson.

TO S. F. WOOD

Oriel College. March 23. 1838

Carissime,

First I am glad to tell you I am getting on very fairly with the translation of the Hymns[3]—but I am now writing on a different matter.

Wilson has sent me some letters of you to him, which act implies some perplexity on his part about remarks made in them—and certainly there are one or two in them which at first reading startled me, and I think are open to misconstruction. Therefore, My dear W., I will tell you just what I think.[4]

You say 'In Him they lived and breathed—He was their very self—*but* what they wanted was something *exterior* to themselves, some sweet friend on whom to rest, and so they betook themselves to the spirits of Saints departed.' Now has not this a Pantheistic tone? for what is Pantheism, but *so* to consider God within us, as to deny He is without us? He is as fully without us, as fully an *object* of our worship, as if He were not within us; and, though I would not willingly theorize on such high points, this for what we know may be one of the reasons why we are not told to address our ordinary supplications to the Blessed Spirit, because He has taken the office of God within us—but if so, is not Christ altogether 'exterior' to us, and a 'friend' whom we may approach and rest on?

[1] The hangman in Walter Scott's novel who always greeted his victims cheerily, e.g. the incident in Chapter VI.

[2] Isaak Walton, *The Complete Angler*, Chapter V.

[3] Newman had promised some translations of hymns for Wood and R. Williams's projected translation of the Breviary.

[4] Wood had mentioned in his letter of 8 March that he had 'had a rowing from old Wilson . . . for talking disparagingly of Anglicanism'. It is not clear which Wilson was involved, it may have been R. F. Wilson. Wood sent a long reply on 24 March to explain the main points at issue.

Again you say—'In fact there is no immediate access to Him'. This too seems to me to go beyond our knowledge. In the Lord's prayer the words 'Forgive us etc' are considered by St Austin, the Church of Rome and (for what I know) the Church Catholic to be the means of pardon for venial sins —is not this an approach without the ordinances of the Church, except prayer altogether be considered such? yet you say the ordinances 'are the *sole* channel wherein Christ's merits can flow.' The Roman Church herself all but allows this, if she does not altogether—certainly her members do. Bellarmine says, in the often quoted passage, that on account of our ignorance of our moral state, and the danger of vain glory it is best to trust,—he does not say in the Church, but—the misericordia Dei. Certainly all those who hold that there is no remedy like Baptism for mortal sin after Baptism, *are* thrown upon the (what may be called) uncovenanted mercies of God—on the depths of that treasure of grace which is hid in Christ, not deposited in His Church.

Then again, I hardly know whether you did not without intending it, disparage the Apostles. Though they as others owed all they were to the grace of God, have we not reason for thinking that they who lay on Christ's breast, saw Him revealed from heaven, and were taken up into Paradise had *more* grace, and so are inwardly as they were outwardly cut off from other men as being better than they? I am not saying this against the honoring other saints, but as preserving to them a prerogative of honor.

Next in your first letter you seem to draw a distinction which I cannot master between the Establishment and the Church of England. The Ch of E. *is* the Establishment—besides this there is the Church *in* England—I know of no third. The Holy Church no where, whether in England or elsewhere, can do wrong—she is the immaculate Spouse—then only can you say the Church has gone wrong when every where and in Council assembled she has done it. Else it is but the deed of her children here or there.—The Articles etc were inflicted on her in this country by the State—you say she *at least willingly* retains them and so is partaker of the sin. It is impossible —the Church in England is identically the very same Church as in France —she is a whole Church and entire, as being a spiritual presence in every place—To say she does here what she does not in France is a contradiction in terms. Her retaining them is about the same as St Paul retaining his bonds at Philippi—she is like Paul the Prisoner, ruling her children though in prison, and not more willingly there than St Paul when he waited for the magistrates to come. She waits God's good time as Daniel in Babylon, but is as guiltless of her captivity as Daniel. Evil men, false sons, have enslaved her—The collection of Christians in England no more *constitute the Church* than the corporate body of the S.P.C.K—they are not an integer, or one— they are but members of the Church. A bishop, presbyters etc. in Synod are but a *type* of the Church; a type for certain purposes, one of which is the communication of grace, another the securing of order.

But you will say, 'at least I may speak against Bishop and presbyters etc of one Diocese—and therefore of united Dioceses etc etc'—I think not—i.e. *not* so far as they are *types* of the Church invisible, for they are sacred *as* types—and though they consent to the bad deeds in question (never mind whether faultily or not, which is not to the point) yet as *called* after *her* of whom they are a type I think they may not be spoken against. They are an appointed image, or sacrament of something beyond them, and it is not reverent to speak against them—Or to say the same thing in the way of precept 'Thou shalt not speak evil of the ruler of thy people—' It is only when they are *out of* that connexion, *not* as a Church, but as an Establishment, as tyrants, as the world, as religious Societies, as Peers of Parliament, that we may censure them. The genii I speak of are genii of nations or places, not of Churches for there is but one Church, and the outward visible Churches in every place are as little substantive (so as to have genii) as the ever recurring and perishing elements in the Eucharist—they are the continual evanescent offstreaming of the invisible glory.

And it seems to me, it is as inadvisable as it is unallowable to speak against 'the Church—' ([I?] will grant that 'the Church of England' or National Church, as the Kirk, may abstractedly be spoken against, as being the same thing as the Establishment—but not *in fact*, because the word Church is homonymous, and no one would understand one aright.) Human nature wants *an authority*—God has supplied the need—to speak as if the *visible authority* which God has given—(for if the collective Bishops Priests and Deacons whom we see are not that authority none *is* given,) was wrong is to undo God's mercy. Hence though I have full liberty abstractedly to speak against individual heretical Bishops, yet I should be very cautious of even doing that; because men have not subtle minds enough to make the distinction;—the only way (I conceive) in which it is allowable is in the *way of appeals to the Body of the Church to disown those* individuals; thus you uphold the Church (viz the body) while you censure what at first sight seems identical with it. Of course I do not exclude the lawfulness of all speaking and writing which though not directly yet ultimately go to the same aim. As to the existing evils, I think it more religious and expedient to attack men like Cranmer (who in fact deserve it far more) than our good Archbishop.—Should you not be shocked at falling in with Roman Catholics speaking against their Church?—If we are to do any good we must keep together—this perhaps makes me alarmed at every symptom of unsettlement; for words tell *on others*.

Excuse this long affair.

Will you please get the inclosed forwarded to Wilson. My book has been some time out of hand, except a note at the end, but that is out of hand now. I have returned all books to Library, and my room is decent, as it should be in Lent. I so wish you and Williams could come down on Saturday in Easter Week—No one hardly will be here. Your hint about the notice of the Regale

in the B.C. came too late.[1] Maitland had finished it—but we will see next time.
I am sorry for it. I send back your MS with thanks—Moehler's work,[2]
translated into French, has just come to me, too late! Who is Hunter Gordon
Esqr who has just sent me a little book? let me know, for I have to acknowledge it[3] Sad news indeed about poor M.[4]

Ever Yrs affly J H N

P.S. By the bye is there not some danger of persons like yourself, who are
not (or only in a degree) engaged in direct religious duties, pastoral and the
like, letting your theories run too far; letting your activity of mind expand
itself in theories?

SATURDAY 24 MARCH 1838 Vigil l. no d. still engaged in putting rooms books
papers etc to rights.

SUNDAY 25 MARCH 4th Lent Annunciation m l. letter from Wood early
Communion—Spranger assisting who read prayers in morning—when Provost
baptized his 4th child—and I in afternoon and preached Number 494[5] dined in
Hall Ryder and Anderdon to tea sent up last revise (of title page)

MONDAY 26 MARCH Collections began in College

TUESDAY 27 MARCH letter from Mr Rodber Curates' Fund no c about this time
E Churton in Oxford

WEDNESDAY 28 MARCH[6] letters from Dean of Chichester and W F no c f b.d.
Spranger left Oxford wrote to Dean of Chichester—Mr Goldsmid, Mr Rodber,
Mr Kilvert and (by A.M.) to H inclosing £10

TO MRS THOMAS MOZLEY

⌐March 28. 1838

It is now nearly a week that I have been at liberty from my book; and now
I am clearing decks for my new employments as Editor of the British Critic

[1] Wood had asked Newman to insert a notice about the new edition of Charles Leslie's
The Case of the Regale and the Pontificat stated, which he and Manning were editing, in the
April number of *Brit. Crit.* The notice appeared in the July number.

[2] J. A. Moehler, *La Symbolique ou exposition des contrariétés dogmatiques*, trans. F. Lachat,
two volumes, Besançon 1836.

[3] Hunter Gordon (of Lincoln's Inn), *The Present State of the Controversy between the
Protestant and Roman Catholic Churches*, London 1837. Wood replied that he knew nothing
of Gordon. Newman noticed the work in his article 'State of the Religious Parties', *Brit. Crit.*,
25, 1839 (April), 395–426; *Ess.* I, 263–308.

[4] G. F. G. Mathison, who had recently been deeply involved with plans for the establishment of colleges for the training of schoolmasters in connection with diocesan authorities,
had just undergone a serious breakdown of health. Wood, Acland, and Gladstone were the
most active of a group of friends who continued his work during his recovery.

[5] *P.S.* V, 14, 'Transgressions and Infirmities'.

[6] William Palmer, of Worcester College, wrote to Newman at about this time concerning
Froude's *Remains*: 'As to Froude, I should have been glad that some passages had been
omitted; but I think all sensible people will see that it was a mind of uncommon candour,
which exposed all its workings to friends, and was feeling its way—and that nothing there said
is fixed, but merely thrown out for consideration.'

and of the Library of the Fathers. My book is rather longer than I expected
—it has taken me more pains and thought than any book I have done—at
least, I think so. The great difficulty was to avoid *being* difficult—which, on
the subject of Justification, is not a slight one—It is so entangled and mysti-
fied by irrelevant and refined questions.⌐

THURSDAY 29 MARCH 1838   letter from Robert Wilberforce   Woodgate to breakfast?
or last Thursday   no p and c

TO JOHN KEBLE

Oriel ⌐March 29. 1838⌐

My dear Keble,

⌐You must not be vexed,⌐ as you will not be, ⌐to have a somewhat excited
letter from Edward Churton on the subject of dear H's Remains.⌐ I should
not think it worth while to apprise you, or to anticipate the possibility of
others too, except perhaps from anxiety, lest you *should* be vexed—but ⌐I
doubt not you really will not be so.—All persons whose hearts have been
with Cranmer and Jewell are naturally pained, and one must honor them for
it.—⌐ E. C. has been so over excited here, that it is difficult to put his protest
into mere words.[1] I am glad to say that ⌐it seems a general opinion here that
the Journal [[The Thoughts]] ought to have been published, and is full of
instruction⌐ etc—but our friends fear (not for themselves but for others) the
Anti-reformation bits. ⌐Yesterday morning, I had the following pleasant
announcement from William F [[Froude]] 'My Father is *much* ⟨(sic)⟩ pleased
with Hurrell's Book. He had been rather alarmed by some comments made
on it in a letter from Sir J. C. [[John Coleridge]] but the book itself has quite
re assured him. The preface says exactly what one wished to have said.'⌐

It is an officious thing in me perhaps attempting thus to write—but I
(from my absurdities) have been in many more scrapes than you, and may
perhaps be somewhat more callous

Ever Yrs affly J H Hewman

FRIDAY 30 MARCH 1838   letters from Mr Todd and Crosthwaite, Goldsmid, and
Dean of Chichester   my book on Justification came out   f.b.d.   sent beginning of
Cyril to Baxter (*printer*)   [Breviary] none
SATURDAY 31 MARCH   letters from C and Wilson   Williams went

[1] Churton wrote to Pusey on 21 Sept.: 'If, in the strong feeling of regret which the first
reading of poor Froude's Remains excited, I expressed myself beyond the license of a friend,
let it be considered unsaid. I must still own that there are sentences and even pages of that
book, which I could wish almost to have lost my right hand sooner than have seen published.
But I think I see something of the false principles and wide ramifications of false principles,
by which this age is misguided; and I wish to be more and more in heart and hand with those
who are applying the true corrective.'

TO H. A. WOODGATE

[April 1838]

My dear Woodgate

On the other side I have transcribed the passage you want. I like your fifth and sixth Sermons very much indeed.—Is it impossible to change the places of third and fourth—so as to have the latter on the fifth Sunday in term?

If you can be in Lincoln's Inn Fields[1] next Tuesday, or on May 1st you will be doing an essential service to the cause of order.

Ever Yrs John H Newman

SUNDAY 1 APRIL 1838   Passion Sunday   letter from Mr Roberts of Monmouth   all but c   did duty morning and afternoon   Cornish, Berkeley and Morris assisted me in Communion   preached Number 495[2]   dined in Common Room and Bloxam and Berkeley with me

MONDAY 2 APRIL   Daman went   all but c   Eden and I left alone.   Mrs Pusey went to Town   b. and w. [bread and water?] in morning   walked to Littlemore   dined in Common Room by myself?   wrote to Wood with M R G's MS.

TUESDAY 3 APRIL   all but c   b and w in morning   dined with Woodgate   wrote to Archdeacon F and W F by Champernowne to C with draft for £5 and to Rivington inclosing note to Maitland

WEDNESDAY 4 APRIL   f b.d.   all but c   Goldsmid called.   wrote to Todd

TO H. E. MANNING

Oriel College. April 4. 1838

My dear Manning,

So after all Pusey swelled out to such an unconscionable size, insanae magnitudinis, as his German friends say, that you were fairly jostled over the side of the nest. However, for one reason I am glad of it, though it was a surprise to me on the appearance of the Number, (else I should have let you know—I *offered* to postpone your Article, but Rivington did not seem to accept it)—I am glad of it, because I wish you to add to it, the matter that still remains in your Portfolio. So, please, unless inconvenient to you, write Roworth the Printer for a proof, and tack on dexterously a second fitte.[3]

Mr Goldsmid, to whom I mentioned the notion of editing Brett,[4] without consulting any one, has caught at it. If you see no reason against it, pray write to Leslie about it—and I will recommend G. to call on him. The only

---

[1] Where the S. P. C. K. met.

[2] *P.S.* V, 15, 'Sins of Infirmity'.

[3] 'canto of a poem'. Manning's article on Henry Martyn had to be postponed to the July number of *Brit. Crit.* due to the length of Pusey's article on the Ecclesiastical Commission, which ran to 107 pages.

[4] See letter of 6 March to Manning and that of 2 March from him.

fear is lest he should be rhetorical—but I hope we shall be able to keep this under.

You know of course from the Dean of Ch. [Chichester] that the first of May is to be desecrated to a row in Lincoln's Inn Fields. It is so very important that I am writing in all directions, if possible to bring people up. You will not be slack in the work yourself, therefore I shall not write to Henry Wilberforce about it.[1]

We are getting into considerable hot water in some places about the Remains—but it was to be expected—if we can but turn it into steam, and direct it aright, it may accelerate our motion towards desirable objects. Archbishop Laurence in republishing his Tracts on Baptism has spoken kindly but disapprovingly of the Baptismal views of the Tracts for the Times.[2]

Yrs ever affly John H Newman

P.S. If you happen to be writing to H.W. tell him that Miller's Bamptons[3] are in Number 6175 in Lumley's Catalogue 56 Chancery Lane

THURSDAY 5 APRIL 1838   letters from Miss Holdsworth and   baptized Emily Lucas (or yesterday?)   all but v and c   Mr Goldsmid to dinner in Common Room and Nevil   wrote to Manning and Wood
FRIDAY 6 APRIL   letters from Mr Leger of Darlington and H.   f b. and d.   [Breviary] all   wrote to J. [,] Mr Leger and Mr Roberts   burnt some papers on Justification— above 600 pages i.e. above 400 pages of print octavo

TO MRS JOHN MOZLEY

Oriel College. April 6. 1838

My dear Jemima,

I heard from Harriet this morning news about you, which rejoiced me very much—I will say no more except that you are ever in my prayers.

I have got my book off my hands some time; indeed I hope you will have

---

[1] Manning wrote to Newman on 16 March about possible ways of reforming the S. P. C. K. The Society's Tracts were approved by the committee, and by Bishops appointed for the purpose, but they could then be rejected by ballot at the monthly meetings. The Dean of Chichester, George Chandler, was introducing a motion at the May meeting to abolish this power, and hoped that a good number of Oxford men would attend. Manning himself felt '. . . that the Bishops only are the consecrated Guardians, and dispensers of the Faith, and that we teach in their stead, that whether our teaching be oral, or written . . . all ought to be "permissu Superiorum" . . .'

[2] Richard Laurence, *The Doctrine of the Church of England upon the Efficacy of Baptism vindicated from misrepresentation*, third edition, Oxford 1838. The Archbishop of Cashel wrote in his Preface: 'Lately, however, and that in the place where I now write, men of talent, learning, and piety, have advocated from the pulpit and the press, among other things, the doctrine of Regeneration in Baptism, which I have myself maintained; but have encumbered it with opinions and appendages with which, if I do not misconceive them, I cannot coincide. In their zeal against *Rationalism*, they appear to me too much to decry the use of Reason in explaining the language of Scripture . . .' He went on to criticise various particular points from *Tract 67*.

[3] John Miller's 1817 Bampton Lectures, *The Divine Authority of Holy Scripture asserted . . .*, third edition, Oxford 1838.

a copy, or have had. I am now at our Translation of Cyril which is passing through the press, at a new Edition of the Lectures on Romanism, and on the British Critic. I have been putting my rooms to rights, and am getting quite decent.

Poor Mrs Quarterman is dead. She went on month after month in the sad, uncomfortable, distressed way you recollect, always behind hand in her rent etc. At length I spoke to Pusey and he without my meaning it put her on his list of regular almswomen. This was a most exceeding great relief to her, and she was full of happiness and thanks; this was about a month since. Shortly after a place in the St Clement's Almshouses fell vacant, and the Master of University put her in. They say good fortune never comes single, but it was too much for her—she seems to have died of joy.

Old Carr the butcher came to me to be paid some months ago. I stared and said, he had been paid by me a year and a half since. He then explained by saying—'then it must have been his son'—which it was. It seems he has quarrelled with his friends, scraped together all the money he could, gone off to America, and been made bankrupt, leaving his wife, I believe. His father spoke very tenderly of him, and said no one could make out what the matter was; he had always been a wellconditioned youth. I cannot help suspecting that, as it was, I paid him too much, but it is lucky I have not to pay it twice over.

Mrs Pusey is a great deal better. They are going away (or rather she) for six months—first to Clifton. Philip is in a very precarious state—and Lucy has been seriously indisposed and I fear is still very delicate.

There is, I believe, to be a great gathering at the Christian Knowledge meeting on May 1—I suppose a large party of us from Oxford will have to go up to it.

And now, I believe I have told you all the news, and so with best love to John and Aunt, and kind remembrances to all at the Friary

Yrs ever affly John H Newman

SATURDAY 7 APRIL 1838 letters from Wood and Henderson all but p dined in Common Room with Eden and J.M. Mrs Pusey returned from Town

SUNDAY 8 APRIL Palm Sunday letter from Wood m and l Berkeley helped me in early Communion did duty morning and afternoon Churched Mrs Feldon[?] preached Number 265(?) no—Number 19 Goldsmid and Berkeley and A.F. to dinner—Bridges with J.M. wrote to Wood and Henderson

TO THOMAS HENDERSON

Oriel College. April 8. 1838

My dear Henderson,

I felt much obliged by your kind and friendly letter, and the sight of Mr Coffin's very interesting letter. If he would not be afraid to know me, I could explain by word of mouth his difficulties as to Froude's Book much better than by writing. But any how, if I say a word or two to you, you will catch my meaning, and if you see him at any time, can explain instead of me. It is impossible not to be much interested with such a letter as you have sent me.

1. 'our Communion Service replaced by a good translation etc—' The *Canon* of the Mass, or St Peter's Liturgy (vid Tract on Liturgies in vol 2)[1] as distinguished from the *Ordinary*, is, as there is every reason for believing, from the Apostles, as are the Liturgies of St James, St Mark, and St John; —our Service contains a part of it—to restore St Peter's Liturgy, i.e. the said Canon, would not take out one word of our Service—It would merely put together the separate portions, part of which are scattered about the Service, part left out.—⟨(I beg to add that I am decidedly against any alteration myself—I am sure we do not deserve it—on this subject vid Froude's Remains vol ii. p 382)[2]⟩ To say that the Reformers have so treated the Primitive Communion Service, does not tend to diminish our reverence for the *remains* of it, which we have—any more than our Lord's being crucified, spit upon, and killed, would lead us to be disrespectful to His sacred remains—rather the contrary.—The remains we have of the Primitive Service are the Church Militant Prayer in the beginning, the Consecration Prayer in the middle, and the Eucharistic Prayer at the end—besides other fragments. If he reads the Tract on Liturgies, he will find all cleared up. There is a passage in vol i p 410[3] to the effect of what has been said, viz that the mutilations at the Reformation do not hurt our reverence for what is left.

2. 'Really I hate the Reformation etc.—' He meant Luther, Calvin etc, and our Reformers such as Cranmer, *so far* as they gave in to that rationalist spirit. If Mr C. wishes specimens of this spirit he may refer to the comparison of Calvinists and Socinians in the Notes to Pusey on Baptism.[4] If he wishes some hints on its workings in this day, he may consult Tracts for the Times Number 73 (I think) on Erskine and Abbot.[5]

3. 'I am more and more indignant etc' The Protestant doctrine spoken of is, that in the Holy Communion there is no communication of a heavenly gift —but that the elements are (as some say) merely commemorative—or (as others) intended to impress our minds—or (as others) means of interesting ourselves in the *benefits* of Christ's death—and that there can be nothing

---

[1] *Tract* 63, 'The Antiquity of the existing Liturgies', reprinted in *Remains* II, 383–411.

[2] 'I very much doubt whether in these days the spirit of true devotion is at all understood, and whether an attempt either to go forward or backward, may not lead our innovations to the same result.'

[3] 'By the bye, the more I think over that view of yours about regarding our present Communion Service, etc. as a judgement on the Church, and taking it as the crumbs from the Apostles' table, the more I am struck with its fitness to be dwelt upon as tending to check the intrusion of irreverent thoughts without in any way interfering with one's just indignation.' *Remains* I, 410, from a letter to Newman of 11 June 1835, see Volume V, 77.

[4] *Tract* 69, pp. 281–95. A two column parallel of texts from Zwinglian or Calvinist authors and Socinian authors on the interpretation of baptism.

[5] Newman's 'On the Introduction of Rationalistic Principles into Religion', reprinted in *Ess.* I, 30–101.

more than bread and wine, because we see nothing more;—or, as F. has elsewhere expressed it, that there is nothing supernatural and unearthly in it. 4. 'Pour moi etc'[1]—He names Cranmer, Peter Martyr, Bucer, Luther, Melancthon etc as a *set*—but not Ridley, who he says was 'the associate' of that set, which is just so much against him.—The rest he certainly did think had set afloat that rationalistic spirit which is now sapping and withering every thing.

And now in ending this letter, I cannot help repeating, what I wish I could find fitting terms to express, that I am *very* much obliged by your kindness in consulting me about dear F's book, and much pleased with your amiable young friend, and will most readily write or say any thing more on the subject, if necessary. I wish there was a chance of you coming here yourself.

My Lectures on Justification have been a most arduous and anxious business—and I am quite enjoying myself at having got them off my hands and mind—

Yrs most truly John H Newman

MONDAY 9 APRIL 1838 Passion Week letter from Mr Hornby f b. l. at 1 [Breviary] all service in Chancel at 11 and 6 PM through this week except Friday when at 4 as usual wrote to Mr LeBas in parcel to G and R.

TUESDAY 10 APRIL f b l. at 1 all Rogers came. R. and J M to tea wrote to Williams, Wilson, and Mr Hornby

TO JAMES J. HORNBY

Oriel College. April 10. 1838

Dear Sir,

I felt the kindness of your letter, and particularly that part of it in which you are good enough to make some remarks on a passage in your Preface to the last Volumes of Mr Knox's Remains, which I spoke of to Mr Sherlock.[2] I should be very sorry if you considered I mentioned the subject to him except in course of conversation or with any serious feeling; yet I hardly can be sorry he has mentioned it to you, seeing I have gained the gratification of the remarks you make on it. What I thought of it, was just this—and in the main it is borne out by what you have said—that you felt interested

[1] 'Also why do you praise Ridley? Do you know sufficient good about him to counterbalance the fact that he was the associate of Cranmer, Peter Martyr, and Bucer? . . . *Pour moi*, I never mean, if I can help it, to use any phrases even, which can connect me with such a set.' *Remains* I, 393–4.

[2] Hornby wrote on 7 April to thank Newman for sending him a copy of *Jfc*. Newman had explained to Sherlock, a friend of Hornby, his dissatisfaction with certain expressions in Hornby's preface to Volumes III and IV of the *Remains of Alexander Knox*, London 1837. Hornby felt that Newman had misconstrued his words by attributing more of a meaning to them than they contained. He does not specify the passages in question or what their subject was.

enough in what was doing here to be anxious—On the other hand perhaps it was not altogether unnatural that persons such as we, with very little encouragement from any quarter, what we do well not understood, what we do ill well understood, should feel sorry not to meet with encouragement where we had reason to think we had in the main gained approbation.

I assure you I shall value most highly any remarks you take the trouble to make on my volume, which Mr Sherlock said I might take the liberty to send you. At the same time I am sanguine that you will not find fault with the general drift—At least I think I agree with Mr Knox in the main—though I think his view of the doctrine may be presented more in verbal accordance with the formularies of our Church than he has done

Believe me, My dear Sir, Yours very respectfully John H Newman

TO ISAAC WILLIAMS

Oriel College. April 10/38

Carissime

First I ought to thank you for the very pleasant gift I have had from you —and which I was rejoiced to find so considerable in size. I expect to find in it food for a long while.

But this does not lead me to write—but this—viz Hewett, whom you know, is going to be married to Miss Edwards next Tuesday—and asked if there was a chance of your being in Oxford. I am to marry them, but they wish to receive the Sacrament afterwards—and they had a great desire, if so be, of your presence. I said you were out of Oxford. So I write thinking you might like to send him a line, since you are not to be here—and also it struck me, what you might not think of yourself, that *your own* book[1] might be a very acceptable present.

Rogers comes down here today. As to dear F's book, I feel more and more, it is a call on the Church to repentance, (not to change) and, as Jonah's coming would be exciting to the Ninevites, or the child Samuel's oracle to Eli, in such sense it is exciting, but in no other. And there I shall let the matter rest. I so wish I knew how Keble felt—I have heard from C. of T. K's judgment.[2]

There is an account in today's paper of the Queen asking the Primate to dinner, and then letting him find his way to the dinner table as he could, quite dropping him out of his rank by precedence—and he in consequence next day protesting and saying he would not go again unless things were different—The tone of both him and the Bishop of London in the Scotch

---

[1] *The Cathedral*, Oxford 1838.
[2] Probably J. F. Christie and Thomas Keble.

Established Church question, shows there is the worst possible understanding between the Church and Government—[1]

Next first of May recollect is to be a very important day in Lincoln's Inn Fields—I hope a large party will go up from this place

With kindest thoughts of your party at Stinchcombe

Ever, My dear W, Yrs affly John H Newman

WEDNESDAY 11 APRIL 1838   letters from Mr Faber, Ellison, Dr Evans, and Wood   f b and d   all   wrote to Mr Faber   R and J M to tea

FROM GEORGE STANLEY FABER

289 Regent Street, London, April 9. 1838

Dear Sir,

A letter from my chaplain Mr Richardson informs me, that you have been so good as to send me a copy of your Work on Justification. For this I beg to thank you: but you will not wonder, that I had *already* secured a copy from Mr Rivington since my arrival in town.

I read the first four Lectures yesterday; and rather looked into, than read, the Appendix—London is not the best place in the world for any thing that requires attention, at least for a sojourner like myself: and I doubt not, that, either to this, or to my own want of clear-headedness, or to both conjointly, I ought to ascribe the difficulty which I felt in gaining a distinct apprehension of your views. I dare say, the difficulty will vanish, at all events when I read the Work a second time: but, at present, I am unable to say, *whether* or *how far* I agree or disagree with you; because in truth, I do not understand *what* your precise system is. Sometimes you seem to agree with Mr Knox[2] and the Council of Trent; sometimes, with myself[3]; sometimes, with neither—From the *mode*, in which you wish to do away with the force of the passage cited by me from Clement of Rome, I conclude, that you *mainly* agree with Knox and the Council—I think you have been unsuccessful in your attempt to nullify the passage from Clement.[4] Should I, upon more mature consideration, see any reason to change my sentiments relative to the amount of Clement's evidence, I hope I shall have grace enough to confess it. Such, however, is not the case at present: nor do I see, how your proposed construction is admissible for a moment, save on the principles of Pelagianism. No doubt, *a Pelagian* would find no difficulty in your construction: but, as you are no more an admirer of that heresy than *myself*, I do not find it easy to account for your criticism. Should my own work pass into another edition, I shall not fail to notice your remarks upon me or rather upon my witnesses: and I shall beg your acceptance of a copy. I trust, that my spirits in the reply will be as good as your own in the criticism.

You and I quite agree in rejecting that modern absurdity, Insulated Private Judgement. I have been on its back, in sundry publications of my own, any time these dozen years: and it is truly marvellous, how difficult it is to make modern

[1] Many in the Church of Scotland had complained for a long while about the right of lay patronage and wished for the introduction of some means of popular control over the appointment of ministers. The General Assembly had passed a Veto Act in 1834 and this led to several conflicts in these years over the cases of appointed ministers who were rejected by the local people. The famous Auchterarder case was still proceeding. See J. H. S. Burleigh, *A Church History of Scotland*, Oxford 1960, pp. 334–48.

[2] Alexander Knox's 'Treatise on Justification' and 'The Doctrine respecting Baptism held by the Church of England' were published in the first volume of his *Remains*, London 1834.

[3] In his *The Primitive Doctrine of Justification investigated . . .*, London 1837. Faber discussed *Jfc.* in appendices to the second edition of 1839.

[4] See *Jfc.*, pp. 396–9.

good men understand the very simple principle of *an historical appeal to the unanimous consent of Antiquity as to the true meaning of Scripture*. As we all like our own modification the best, and as I happen to have the somewhat ambiguous advantage of being your senior by many a long year, I cannot help expressing a hope, that you do not go *beyond* me. I restrict the use of the Fathers purely to the point of *interpretation* of the Written Word. If we advance a step beyond: we take the first step into Popery. Thus, on all the *really* catholic doctrines, we have our witnesses *unanimous* and *express*: but, as for prayers for the dead and such like gear, where is there a word about them in the Bible?

I may just as well say: that, on p. 4, you would prove the Church of England, to deem Baptism the *instrument* of Justification, by the adduction of an Article, which absolutely says *nothing* of the sort.[1] On the contrary, you *omit* the striking passage in the second part of the Homily on the Passion, where faith is declared to be the *only instrument* of our salvation: as also the passage in Dean Noel's *recognised* catechism,[2] in which faith is similarly declared to be the *instrument* of our justification —I think you should correct this oversight—and I would rather *you* would do it your self, than leave *me* to do it.

Believe me, with much respect, yours very truly, G. S. Faber

I specially mention the Homily and Noel's Catechism, because they use the precise *word* INSTRUMENT; the former excluding *any other* instrument, and therefore obviously excluding Baptism: but the same *idea* occurs again and again in other documents of our Church, where, relatively to Justification, faith is described as *a mean* or *a hand*. Whence and how you are to prove, that our Church deems *Baptism* the *instrument* of Justification, I confess I see not. *Baptism*, as the Article, to which you refer, justly says, is the *instrument* whereby we are brought within the pale of the Church Catholic: but *faith*, in the judgement of our Church, is the *instrument*, nay (says the Homily) the ONLY *instrument*, of our salvation, which of course subincludes the first step toward it, our justification—I really wish you would reconsider your perplexing reference to Art. xxvii at p. 4.

TO GEORGE STANLEY FABER

Oriel College. April 11. 1838

Dear Sir,

I beg to return you my best thanks for the kind and candid way in which you have received what I should have been wanting in respect, if I had not presented to you, my volume on Justification.[3] It would be a great satisfaction to me, could I hope you would approve of it in all its parts; though I trust there is much from which you will find no reason to differ. Being composed without reference to the pending controversy between yourself and Mr Hornby,[4] it is not surprising you should be unable, as you observe, to say

[1] Article XXVII 'Of Baptism': 'Baptism . . . is also a sign of Regeneration or new Birth, whereby, as by an instrument, they that receive Baptism rightly are grafted into the Church; . . .'

[2] Alexander Nowell's 'Larger Catechism' was presented to Convocation in 1563. The first translation, by T. Norton, was published in 1570.

[3] Newman stated in his advertisement that his *Lectures* had been written without reference to the works of 'those respected authors' Knox and Faber, and explained '. . . but while the points from which he [Newman] starts are different, so too are his arguments, as being drawn not from Primitive Christianity but from Scripture.' *Jfc.*, p. vii.

[4] James J. Hornby was the editor of Knox's *Remains*, who, in the preface to the third and fourth volumes, had called upon Faber to produce a work on the doctrine of Justification by Faith, and to show that it was in accordance with the teaching of the Primitive Church.

how far you agree with it, and how far not. Perhaps I can hardly say myself; for words are used by different writers so variously, that often to attempt to adjust them is but a source of greater confusion. I think however you are right in saying that I partly agree with you, partly with Mr Knox, and partly with neither. As to the passage in the 27th Article, I conceive that a state of union with the Church *is* a state of justification; as is taught among other places in the Baptismal Service, 'that he being delivered from *Thy wrath* may be received into the ark of Christ's Church;' and in the Collect in the Visitation of the Sick 'Preserve and continue this sick member in the unity of the Church.' Moreover, that the Church, into which Baptism grafts us as an instrument, is not merely the *visible* Church is to me evident from the Baptismal Service speaking of incorporation into God's '*Holy* Church,' which the mere visible Church is not; whereas the formal incorporation into the mere visible congregation is effected not by Baptism but after it in the words, 'We receive etc'—which are declaratory of what has already been done invisibly.

This I would say about the sense of Article 27. As to the Homily on the Passion I *have* spoken of it in a note on the foregoing page (p 3) and considered it at length in Lecture 10; however, I am not the less obliged by your friendly offer to allow me to correct the suffered omission instead of yourself.

You seem to ask me whether I am an advocate for prayers for the dead in Christ; and say 'As far as such like gear where is there a word about them in the Bible?'—I am sure you would not thus speak, if you knew there were persons to whom such expressions gave great pain. Why may I not believe a thing not in the Bible, if I do not force the belief on others? This *forcing* is the 'first step into Popery' of which you speak. The 6th Article says that Scripture contains all that is to be '*required* that it should be believed as an article of *the Faith*,' and 'thought requisite or *necessary to salvation*.' I claim the right of private judgment in matters *not* of 'the Faith'. Things may be true, [though] not declared in Scripture, e.g. the canonicity and inspiration of its books as they have come down to us. Again, I conceive that though the whole *faith* is in Scripture, yet *ordinances* need not [be] shown to be there. Now Prayer for the Dead in Christ is an ordinance; and Catholic Tradition may as suitably sanction it as it sanctions the change of the day of rest from the seventh to the first, or teaches us that washing one another's feet is not literally binding on us. For myself I do not believe it *is* commended in Scripture, being included in such general expressions as 'for all the Saints—' Eph vi. 18. But I would willingly pass by, if you would allow me, points in which I may be unable to follow you, in grateful acknowledgment of what you so truly state, the length of time, and (if I may venture to add) the important service of your exertions in the cause of the just Catholic principle of Quod Semper etc.[1]

Believe me, Dear Sir, Yours very respectfully

John H Newman

[1] The Canon of Vincent of Lerins, *quod ubique, quod semper, quod ab omnibus creditum est.*

FROM GEORGE STANLEY FABER

289 Regent Street April 12. 1836 [Postmark: 1838]

Dear Sir,

I should not have troubled you with a second letter, had I not perceived, with regret, that I had hurt your feelings by an inadvertent expression, though pilfered from King Lear, relative to prayers for the dead—I wrote with great rapidity and with the everlasting noise of London ringing in my ears: but most sorry should I be to say any thing painful to one whom I so highly respect as yourself. It certainly makes a difference, whether a point of unscriptural belief be, or be not, *forced* upon another: yet I cannot help thinking, that such points, if we hold them, ought to be carefully kept within our own bosoms. I did not mean to say, as I had no right to say, that *you* advocated prayers for the dead: I simply took the practice, as illustrating what I meant by a scrupulous adherence to Scripture *alone*, though to Scripture *as interpreted* by the unanimous consent of the Primitive Church. Different minds are differently constituted: and, though *I* cannot believe any doctrine save on the authority of Scripture, I feel that I have no warrant for requiring that the faith of *another* should be marked out with equal simplicity, provided he does not force it upon his neighbour. *Thus far* I admit what you say: but, *in principle*, I still think, though I mean no offence, that the belief of any doctrine *not* in Scripture is the first step into Popery.

You will, I am sure, pardon me, if I say, that the defence, which you offer for prayers for the dead, strikes me as inconclusive.

Prayer for the dead, you say, is an ordinance: and Catholic Tradition may as suitably sanction *it*, as the change of the day of rest and worship.

Here you would assimilate two matters which are entirely dissimilar. Prayer for the dead, if made an ordinance, involves the imperative belief of a *doctrine*: but the change of a sacred day involves *no* doctrinal belief. Nor is this all. I have ever contended, and still contend, that the change of the day may be distinctly established from Scripture *itself*; when Scripture is *interpreted*, as [I] maintain it *ought* to be interpreted, by the unanimity of Antiquity. On *this* point, of course I need not refer *you* to the primitive attestation of Justin Martyr. As for *mere* ordinances in general, I look upon them as a matter of perfect indifference which every Church may lay down at its own pleasure. The apostolic canon is open to *any* grave and decorous modification: *Let all things be done decently and in order*. Prayer for the dead, if an ordinance, bears no analogy to the colour of the gown in which a clergyman is directed to officiate. I could not pray for the dead, without belief of a *doctrine*, which is *not* revealed in Scripture, and which *without* revelation we *cannot* know to be true: but it would be a matter of the most profound indifference to *my* conscience, whether the Church directed me to officiate in white or in black or in doctorial crimson. The same remark applies to all the other *material* of public worship. I would not wish an iota of our admirable liturgy to be changed: but still, if any other equally sound form were imposed upon me by the Church, I should in conscience feel myself bound to obey.

You do not satisfy me as to what you say, touching our Church's teaching Baptism to be the instrument of Justification—It goes upon the assumption, that all persons, admitted by Baptism into the pale of the visible Church, are in a justified state. Of *this*, I have have [sic] never yet seen any proof. I observe, that you purpose at p. 3 to notice hereafter the Homily on the passion: but you do not seem to notice the strong passage in Noel's Catechism. As I happen to have it with me, I transcribe it.

Fidem, igitur, non *causam*, sed *instrumentum*, esse justitiae dicis: quod, scilicet, Christum, qui est justitia nostra, amplectitur; tam arcta nos conjunctione cum illo copulans, ut omnium eius bonorum participes faciat? SIC EST.[1]

This is *my* doctrine, with which I cannot reconcile *yours*.

I have, in common justice, deferred reading your very important volume, until I am fairly lodged in the country. The perpetual interruptions and noise of London

---

[1] G. E. Currie (ed.), *Nowell's Catechism*, (Parker Society), Cambridge 1853, p.61.

quite distract me: and I should act, both most improperly and most disrespectfully to you, were I to form any judgement upon it from a metropolitan perusal—Least of all would I form any judgement, save from an *entire* perusal—We go together so far, that I shall be really sorry if we cannot go together to the end. I mean the end *speculatively*: as far as the end in its *better* sense, I only wish, from all that I have heard of your truly christian character, that I was as certain of *my own* travelling toward it, as I am strongly inclined to a full assurance respecting *your* travelling thitherward.

I suppose I need scarcely say, that I have read, with utter disgust, and I fear I must confess with not the most christian feeling of hearty contempt, the sundry offensive and deplorably *ignorant* attacks which have been made upon you. You and I may not always agree: but I think I can insure you from *any* such attacks, so far as *I* am concerned.[1]

Believe me, my dear Sir, with great respect, your sincere brother in Christ,

G. S. Faber

THURSDAY 12 APRIL 1838   letter from Mr Merest of Darlington   f d   all   Vaughan [,] Shepherd[,] Dean and Greswell came   wrote to Dr Evans

TO MISS M. R. GIBERNE

⌐Oriel College.⌐ April 12/38

My dear Miss Giberne,

I am beginning a letter now which I ought to have sent long ago, and which now I shall not send for a day or two, considering the season. I have delayed hoping to give you some information of the printing of your little story—but now I have come to the conclusion that it had better be part of a *volume*, and not printed by itself—so, please, your pen must move quickly. My reason is this—you know I have long attempted, in vain, to bring out or set on foot a *series*. My taking the B.C. put an end to the notion of my doing it myself—Then I had hoped people in Town would—but they will not— so please let me have some other stories. I sent 'little Mary' to a friend in Town to print, and asked his candid opinion; he says 'I think the story a capital one, lively, natural, and effective'.

And now having got as far as this, and people coming in, I shall stop.

⌐Easter Tuesday. [[17 April]]⌐ Froude has not said that *all* the Clergy, or Clergy in England should follow a trade. He only says that in *founding* a Church, as in the West Indies, or in our great Towns, one ought not to be bound by the *same rules* by which the Church is governed *when* settled—but is thrown back upon a strictly apostolic state. I think this is what he says.[2] Any questions you choose to ask, I will gladly answer according to my ability.

All you say about Mr Wilson is very encouraging. Things certainly seem

[1] See letter of 16 May to Faber and that of 1 May from Faber placed before it.

[2] 'Also it might be advantageous to point out by the way, that in a missionary church, such as that in Yankee land, it is very stupid to insist on the clergy having no secular avocations: honest tradesmen, who earn their livelihood, would be far more independent and respectable presbyters than a fat fellow who preaches himself into opulence.' *Remains* I, 366.

improving every where—and it is most pleasant to hear proofs of it as I do continually. ⌐To day a pleasant thing happened to me. Two parishioners, who were [[to be]] married, begged to be allowed to receive the Holy Communion at the time of their marriage. It was quite their own thoughts¬—I had not said a word to them, or any where, about it. ⌐I have had a second anonymous present of plate for St Mary's Altar. The Parishioners received it in Vestry in silence, and then began disputing about the expence of repairing a pinnacle of the Church.¬ What an irreclaimable spirit Mammon is.

I hope I may have the chance of seeing you in your passage through Oxford. I shall probably or certainly be here. You ask what I am doing— editing the Fathers, editing the British Critic, (which I begin next Number) and publishing a new edition of my Romanism. All this involves business enough.

I have had exceedingly nice and kind letters both from Mr Hornby and Mr Faber on the subject of my Lectures on Justification—though, as was to be expected, the latter will reply to me, I suppose, on a second edition of his work.

⌐I have had an organ given to Littlemore from an unknown hand. Nothing like raising up Treasure Houses—money flows in by a natural law—the law of faith and its reward. Ask much, and you gain much¬

I suppose I had best direct to you at home now

Believe me, My dear Miss Giberne, Most sincerely yours

John H Newman.

FRIDAY 13 APRIL 1838   Good   letters from Mr Faber, Manning and Goldsmid   did duty morning and afternoon   preached Number 74   f d   all   Morris assisted me in Sacrament

TO MRS E. B. PUSEY

Good Friday April 13/38

My dear Mrs Pusey

I feel much obliged indeed by your wish to entrust me with the disposal of the £50—and will gladly take charge of it.[1] Your letter is altogether most kind, far more so than I deserve. Pray believe you have been constantly in my prayers night and morning, and particularly this week again and again. Let me in turn beg you, as I do most sincerely, to forgive me if I have at any time been rude or cold to you.

Ever Yrs affectionately My dear Mrs Pusey John H Newman

---

[1] The £50 was a legacy which Mrs Pusey had received at the time that she first heard about the possibility of a conditional baptism. Her relief was so great that she set it aside for the time. She wrote to Newman, 'I venture to ask you to employ it, in any way you prefer, that may be to the glory of God.' See note to diary for the next day, and that for 19 June.

SATURDAY 14 APRIL 1838 Easter Eve letters from Le Bas and H W f d all Acland in Oxford Daman came between 5 and 6 baptized[1]—then v. then evening service had meat at tea.

SUNDAY 15 APRIL Easter Day letter from Bowden inclosing £100 did duty morning and afternoon preached Number 496[2] Pusey administered Sacrament— I assisting Rogers and I dined with Pusey wrote to Bowden

TO J. W. BOWDEN

⌐Easter Day [[15 April]] 1838.¬

My dear Bowden,

⌐I received duly this morning your most munificent gift, which I am answering on a shabby bit of paper for want of a better. I trust I shall be a faithful steward for so large a sum.[3] The day before yesterday (Good Friday) I received a promise of £50 and other promises have been made. We only want to start well, which I hope we shall do.¬ As to the article on the Br. Association, I should have *liked* it for next number[4]—but perhaps it will be *still more* acceptable in October, since in the Long Vacation other contributors may be tempted to idleness; and I trust we shall any how do well in July. So let the Article stand over. ⌐I like your idea about the Cathedral, but had given the book to Rogers to review.¬[5] I will bear it in mind—since the

[1] One of these was Mrs Pusey who for some years had been worried about the validity of her baptism as she had been baptised by a dissenter. Her scruples had prevented her from receiving Communion for some months. The possibility of conditional baptism had been discussed but Pusey had hesitated about it for two years. Newman had suggested asking for the Bishop's sanction and had now obtained it.

To mark the occasion, Pusey presented Newman with the four volume Benedictine edition of St Gregory the Great's *Opera Omnia*, Paris 1705. The following note is pasted inside the cover of the first volume:

'My dear Friend,

I know not how to thank you for all your gentle tender kindness to me and mine, especially for yesterday, which, also, perhaps but for you, had never been to us, what I trust it is and will be. I can only say with S. Aug. Retribues illi, Domine, in resurrectione justorum.

The accompanying book, which is meant as a sort of outward memorial, was Bp Lloyd's, and has been mine for nearly nine years, and been used by me during the latter part of the time, and so seemed, amid other things to be the best sort of token. And if sending this book of our "Cognomenti Magni" and a confessor be an omen, though one may not wish the days of confessors to return, yet if they do come, there is only one higher wish
ever your very affectionate and grateful friend
E B Pusey

Dominicâ Resurrectionis A. S. 1838

The book, you will see, belonged once to the "Bibliotheca Scholarum Piarum", perhaps it may, when God wills, to some "school of the prophets" in our own land.'

[2] *P.S.* IV, 23, 'Keeping Fast and Festival'.

[3] £100 towards the 'house for young writers' which Newman was planning. See letter of 24 April to Pusey.

[4] The article appeared in Jan. 1839. See letter of 19 March to Bowden.

[5] Bowden had suggested a review of the volume in connection with the parliamentary attacks on cathedral establishments. He wrote on 14 April, 'an article on the *poetry* of Cathedrals should come out *now*, on Williams's poem—while in all probability the battle on those foundations will be fighting?—If so, and if no poet—like Keble—would undertake it, I would do my best . . .'. The work was not one of those reviewed by Rogers in the Oct. number. A brief notice of it in July remarked that the 'Poems have obscurities, as a great deal of poetry must have . . . but we are greatly mistaken if they have not a long course of prospective influence in store for them.' *Brit. Crit.*, 24, 231.

Session will be over by July I do not suppose there is any reason for its being reviewed in the number then to issue.

I heard that [Manuel] Johnson was not well—is this so? I am very sorry. I wish you had mentioned the subject. ⌐I have had very pleasant and kind letters from Mr Hornby and Mr Faber on the subject of my lectures which I sent to both.

I wish some of you in London would set up a series of light works such as you speak of. Had not the B.C. come in the way, I had proposed to do so.⌐ Kindly thoughts of Mrs J.W.B. and all yours at this season.

Ever yrs affly John H. Newman.

⌐P.S.⌐ I very much desire to see Hildebrand, and rejoice at the prospect of seeing yourself here at Whitsuntide. ⌐As to May 1. my notion was to go up and down in the day, unless some reason came in the way.⌐

MONDAY 16 APRIL 1838 Easter Monday very inclement weather much snow service in Chancel no lecture (no evening service) first day of examination for fellowships went with Pusey about House Christie came Provost to dine with us in Common Room

TUESDAY 17 APRIL Easter Tuesday married Mr Hewett to Miss Edwards administered to the party the Sacrament—(10 without me) breakfasted at Edwards's attended Vestry for Churchwardens. Pusey and family went to Clifton. walked with Rogers. Neate came. wrote to Wood, H by Golightly and Miss Giberne

WEDNESDAY 18 APRIL first day of Viva voce

THURSDAY 19 APRIL second day of viva voce dined with the Provost election in evening

FRIDAY 20 APRIL day of election. Pritchard and Church elected[1] stood besides, Woolcombe, Pattison, Utterton, Crawford, Street, Salmon, and Haddan gaudy dinner

SATURDAY 21 APRIL letter from Mr ⟨J.F.⟩ Russell of Cambridge

SUNDAY 22 APRIL 1st Easter early Sacrament did duty morning and afternoon preached Number 497[2] dined in Common room

MONDAY 23 APRIL Acland went wrote to Ellison

TUESDAY 24 APRIL University Litany—Sacrament dined with Dr Kidd

TO E. B. PUSEY

Oriel April 24/38

My dear Pusey

I was truly obliged by your notes, though the news was sad.[3]

I have decided to keep in the Austin the two notes you speak of—but perhaps I do not enter into your reasons, I will see about the verses.

[1] See M. C. Church (ed.), *The Life and Letters of Dean Church*, London 1895, pp. 18–21, for Church's account of the Oriel examination.
[2] *P.S.* IV, 18, 'The Gainsaying of Korah'.
[3] The Puseys had just received the report that their son, Philip, could not be expected to live very much longer. He did live until 1880, though a permanent invalid.

I have delayed writing, in order to tell you about the house. I have concluded the bargain to-day. To begin ab ovo, I must say that our Election might have been better, might have been worse—and it is *most lucky* J M[1] did *not* stand. Directly after the Election (and then after Merton) he went to four or five of the parties, and got a great deal to encourage him as to our plan, but nothing of *immediate* success. J.M. can get *no* one to join at once. Till men despair of gaining fellowships, much as they may like it, they will not join. Moreover it has got wind over Oxford that you are buying a house —we were seen in it, and Mr West has proclaimed it to all comers at Carfax. Further, the charge of Puseyism has (I will not say, told) but been made at the Merton Election. Lastly Hope has been most urgent with me to abandon the plan altogether. I will tell you all when we meet. To be brief, for reasons which I will also tell then, I have taken the house from Midsummer—it is meanwhile to be painted as far as necessary. The whole expense with taxes etc and rent of fixtures will be £65 to £70 a year—on a lease for seven years with the option of relinguishing it for a forfeit of £10 at the end of the first year, and a promise of then putting in the sash windows if we continue.

Thus there is no hurry in deciding on any thing.—

Mr Whitford sends a letter to you—and begged me to say something or other which I forget—he will attack you in Lincoln's Inn Fields on Tuesday. There is good about him.

With kindest thoughts of Mrs Pusey

Ever Yrs affly J H Newman

WEDNESDAY 25 APRIL 1838   St Mark's   letters from Mr Roberts of Monmouth, Mr G.A.Poole, Dr Evans and Goldsmid   service in Chancel   read Number 235 wrote to Goldsmid

THURSDAY 26 APRIL   letters from Christie, Marriott, Wilson, Porcher, Sir F Palgrave, Mr Bayne and one without signature.   wrote to Wilson[,] Wood Mr Richards and Mr Willis

FRIDAY 27 APRIL   letters from J Marriott[,] Pusey inclosing Chandler's and Bowden f d

TO MISS HOLDSWORTH

Oriel College. April 27/38

Dear Miss Holdsworth,

I am very much ashamed at my delay in answering you—but have been very busy since Easter—and not being obliged to answer one day more than

---

[1] J. B. Mozley was put in charge of the 'house for young writers', and some of his letters describe the scheme. On 15 April he wrote to Newman's sister Harriett, 'we are commencing our plan of a Society in real earnest, and are already in treaty for a house opposite Pusey's . . . your brother is to order furniture forthwith . . . no sofas or arm-chairs.' *Letters of the Rev. J. B. Mozley*, London 1885, p. 76. On 27 April he wrote to his own sister, 'Newman has taken a house, to be formed into a reading and collating establishment, to help in editing the Fathers. We have no prospect of any number joining us just at present. Men are willing, but they have Fellowships in prospect . . . which would be interfered with by joining us, for we shall of course be marked men. It would, I have no doubt, seriously injure any one's chance at any College now being connected so openly with Newman and Pusey.' *ibid.*, p. 78.

another, have let time slip away. Yet I hope you will have conjectured, without my writing, that any person you are acquainted with, will be most welcome here, as far as I can welcome him—and I feel much obliged to you for the projected visit from Mr Tracey.

As to your declining the undertaking which I was bold enough to suggest through Miss Froude, I can say nothing more of course; but I still have a right to my private opinion, and do maintain it, that you could, I feel sure, be of use to the cause of Catholic Truth in the way I mentioned—though I am far from daring to say that there is no other way in which you will be of as much or more. Certainly we do want tales on our side very much—to take people's imagination—as such works as Geraldine on the one side and Father Clement on the other show[1]—and I should much rejoice if persons such as yourself gave the composition of them a fair trial.

I am sorry the Tract on the Eucharistic Offering is not out yet—but it does not depend on me.

As to Du Pin[2] I am not particularly fond of him—yet he contains a good deal of useful information. I prefer Tillemont as far as his Memoirs[3] go. Du Pin was a sort of semi-dissenter from his Church—and a man of lax views on many points, I should fear. Yet I suppose you may trust him.

It is certainly very lamentable that the Bishops should be chosen as they are, but I do not see that it touches the question of the validity of their Ordination. They come before the existing Bishops for consecration, and, as you observe, the consecration is *their* act—But again, if we turn to history of the Jews we find far more flagrant anomalies compatible with the continuance of the Sacerdotal powers. If the history of the High Priesthood be traced, Caiphas's was a far more irregular appointment (High Priest *that same year*) than that of any Bishop now; yet he prophesied, *as* High Priest.

Pray excuse my delay, and do not suffer it to be the cause of my losing the pleasure of hearing from you, if you have any question to ask.

Believe me, dear Miss Holdsworth, Yours very truly John H. Newman

P.S. But after all, is there *no* line of subject which you will think of undertaking, though the poor novel is put aside?

SATURDAY 28 APRIL 1838   letter from Mr Hornby   term began   Mr Westmacott

---

[1] [Emily C. Agnew], *Geraldine—A Tale of Conscience*, two volumes, London 1837. It was reviewed by Newman in *Brit. Crit.*, 24, 1837 (July), 61–82: 'its object . . . to recommend the Roman Catholic religion to the favourable notice of the English Protestant'. *Father Clement: a Roman Catholic Story*, Edinburgh 1823. Published anonymously, it was a popular anti-Catholic novel by Grace Kennedy, a Scottish Presbyterian.
[2] Louis Ellies Dupin (1657–1719), a French patristic scholar and ecclesiastical historian who was accused of Gallican leanings. His *Nouvelle Bibliothèque des auteurs ecclésiastiques*, six volumes, Paris 1686–91, was criticised by Bossuet, received official censure, and later volumes were placed on the Index.
[3] L. S. Le Nain de Tillemont, *Mémoires pour servir à l'histoire ecclésiastiques des six premiers siècles*, sixteen volumes, Paris 1693–1712.

called   letters from Archdeacon Froude and Henderson by private hands   dined in hall

SUNDAY 29 APRIL   2nd Easter   letters from Bowden, J.[,] Mr Morris, Mr Willis and Mr Maitland.   Williams assisted me in early Sacrament   did duty morning and afternoon   Woodgate preached   to dinner in Rogers' rooms, Bloxam, Berkeley with us.   W. Newman came in the evening

MONDAY 30 APRIL   Rogers went to Town   I followed him an hour or two afterwards and went down to Blackheath

TUESDAY 1 MAY   St P and J [Philip and James]   Daman took my duty   came up from Blackheath with R.   went *with Rogers* to service at St James's.—saw Gladstone, Acland, etc.   met Pusey.   meeting in Lincoln's Inn fields.   took up my lodgings at Mr Bowden's 17 Grosvenor Place where dined with Bowden and his wife

WEDNESDAY 2 MAY   St Athan.[Athanasius]   breakfasted at Bowden's   (my godson Herbert Newman Mozley born)   called on Acland   went to service at St James's   walked with Wood, Manning, and Copeland.   called on Mrs Goldsmid   went down to Hackney to dine with Mr Norris—with Keble, Copeland, Bloxam, Berkeley, Wilson, Archdeacon Watson, Dr Spry, Mr Irwin, Mr Parkinson, Mr Powell and Mr Norris junior.[1]   returned to Bowden's

THURSDAY 3 MAY   breakfasted at the Swinburne's   came off to Oxford   dined in rooms   on my return found letters from Mr Faber, C, Anonymous, Mr Sibthorp, Brewer, and E.Q.V.[2]

FRIDAY 4 MAY   f d

SATURDAY 5 MAY   Mr Graves came—I asked him to dinner for tomorrow but he could not.   dined in hall

SUNDAY 6 MAY   3rd Easter   letter from Mant   did duty morning and afternoon   preached Number 499[3]   Sewell, Marriott and Morris assisted me in Sacrament   Woodgate preached Bampton Lecture   Brewer dined with me in Hall

MONDAY 7 MAY   letter from John M [Mozley]   Coffin, Newman and Bunsen to breakfast   dined early   walked to Littlemore—back with Bloxam and Morris   Mr Bowyer sent painted glass for Littlemore Chapel   wrote to John M.[,] C and Keble   Rogers returned

TO JOHN KEBLE

Oriel. May 7/38

My dear Keble

I think it worth while to scribble a line or two to say that the Vice Chancellor has booked you for 2 o'clock on Tuesday the 15th—and that your notices are being printed. Pusey *will* be here according to his present arrangements.

Dr Wiseman in my opinion is certainly the writer of the Article in the Dublin Review—and it is a remarkable article because he is to assail or something like assail the Apostolical Succession in our Church;[4] which is better than the patronizing air he has of late adopted, and argues his feeling of the seriousness of the combat

Ever Yrs affly J H Newman

[1] See Volume XXV, 88, for Newman's recollection of this 'sort of fraternization'.
[2] An anonymous correspondent.
[3] *P.S.* VI, 10, 'The Spiritual Presence of Christ in the Church'.
[4] The first three collected volumes of the *Tracts* were reviewed in 'Tracts for the Times', *D.R.*, IV, No. 8, 1838 (April), 307–35. A further article, dealing specifically with the Anglican claim of Apostolical Succession, appeared in October.

TO JOHN MOZLEY

Oriel College. May 7. 1838

My dear John

You have my best congratulations, and Jemima. It was very kind in her to write. I rejoiced to see her handwriting. I had not received your letter (nor have—how did you direct it?) but Arthur told me. I write at once, but hope soon to write Jemima a longer letter.

With the greatest pleasure will I stand sponsor—I wish I knew the day and hour. It is very pleasant to have Harriet and James as fellows. As to the name, since the remonstrance of Elizabeth's friends 'there is none of thy kindred that is called by that name,' I suppose all similar questions are silenced. As Jemima has a memory for days, let her know that the 2nd of May (which Arthur said was the day) is the feast of St Athanasius. I therefore propose he should be called Athanasius Mozley—Also tell her the 2nd[1] of May was the day (I believe) I went to school—And the day on which I was knocked up 5 years ago at Leonforte in Sicily, where I remained three days helpless.

Our town expedition was very fortunate. I dined with Mr Norris at Hackney on the Wednesday and came down next day

Excuse haste—with kindest remembrances and congratulations to all your party

Ever Yrs affly John H Newman

TO HENRY WILBERFORCE

[7 May 1838]

My dear Henry

If you do not think it too late, I would send you at once books for an article in the British Critic of this sort

very	'Cummins as you name
short	Pratt on Scotch Episcopacy
works	Vaughan state of religious parties
all	Irons on Apostolical Succession' etc[2]

Let me know *at once* if you will attempt it, and I will at once send you the books. Tell me how to direct my parcel. I must have the review at latest in

---

[1] Newman went to Dr Nicholas's school at Ealing on 1 May 1808.

[2] John Cumming, *An Apology for the Church of Scotland; or, an Explanation of its Constitution and Character*, London 1837. J. B. Pratt, *Scottish Episcopacy and Scottish Episcopalians. Three Sermons*, Aberdeen 1838. Robert Vaughan, *Thoughts on the past and present State of the Religious Parties in England*, London 1838. W. J. Irons, *On the Apostolical Succession. Parochial Lectures*, London 1838.

3 weeks. After many promises, I fear I may be in want of Articles. The review should be on the state of parties and the rising of the waters[1]

Ever Yrs affly J H N

TUESDAY 8 MAY 1838   walked early to Littlemore to meet Bloxam about ground for school house   dined in Hall   first (*yearly*) service and Lecture in Adam de B's Chapel   read Number 498[2]

WEDNESDAY 9 MAY   letter from Mr Faucett[3]   walked with Pusey   dined in Hall— Williams and Bowles my strangers.

THURSDAY 10 MAY   letter from Bowden   walked with Pusey and Rogers   dined and Rogers at Trinity

FRIDAY 11 MAY   letters from Miss Holdsworth, John M. [Mozley] and Wood and Williams   Pusey came with news about J.M. and the Bishop of O [Oxford][4]   f d walked to Littlemore with Rogers and Anderdon   wrote to Wood and Mr Bowyer

SUNDAY 13 MAY   4 Easter   did duty morning and afternoon   preached Number 505[5] Woodgate still going on with Bampton Lectures[6]   Mr Wackerbarth (Henderson's friend) to dinner, Rogers, Cornish, and Marriott—Anderdon and E Rogers in evening

TUESDAY 15 MAY   dined in hall   service in A de B's Chapel   read Number 500   men in Common Room in evening   wrote to T.M. inclosing draft from Eden for £40

WEDNESDAY 16 MAY   letters from Bowden and E.Q.V.   wrote to Bowden[,] E.Q.V. [,] Keble and Mr Faber

FROM GEORGE STANLEY FABER

Clapham Common May 1. 1838

Dear Sir,

Your letter followed me to this place, where I am, for a few days, on a visit to a friend and connection of mine—Were envy a disposition in which the Christian might indulge, I should envy the beautiful spirit in which it is written: but, as it is not, I may, at all events, both safely and beneficially, hope, in my own particular, to profit by it, through at least an *attempt* at imitation—My pugnacious propensities are, I trust, a good deal softened down by age, if not by anything better. Hence, with this disclaimer, you will not, I am sure, think any worse of me, if I venture to doubt the correctness of your averment, that the *practice* of Prayer for the dead does *not* involve *doctrine*. You yourself advocate it, on the ground, that the Primitive Church deemed it *pleasing to God and in some unknown way useful to the dead*. Now, if we teach that *any practice is pleasing to God and in some unknown way useful to the dead*; we teach, I should incline to say, a *doctrine*. I do not see, how this inference from your statement can be avoided.

While we are on the subject, have you any *evidence* to shew, that the Primitive

[1] Wilberforce did not produce the proposed article. Newman wrote an article on the 'State of Religious Parties' for the April 1839 number of *Brit. Crit.*, but did not review any of the works mentioned here.

[2] This was the first of the twelve 'Lectures on the Scripture Proof of the Doctrines of the Church' which Newman delivered on consecutive Tuesdays between this date and 7 Aug., excepting 10 and 17 July, when he was in London. Eight of the Lectures were published as *Tract* 85, though termed 'Part I'. They were republished in *D.A.*, pp. 109–253.

[3] Joshua Fawcett. See letter of 30 May to him.

[4] Probably in connection with J. B. Mozley's coming ordination.

[5] *P.S.* VI, 11, 'The Eucharistic Presence'.

[6] Newman preserved a fragment of a letter which he sent to T. Mozley on 15 May: 'Woodgate is preaching a capital set of Bampton Lectures, which I am told make Keble and me appear moderate men.'

Church recommended the practice in question on the ground whereon you make it repose?

I do not recollect that any writer before Tertullian ever *mentions* the practice: and the impression upon my *memory* is (for *here* I have not the book before me), that he simply recommends, *from his own private judgement*, the use of prayer, for her deceased husband, to a bereaved widow. Nor yet does he *vaguely* recommend it, as in some *unknown* way useful to the dead. On the contrary, its *purposed utility* is distinctly avowed to be, that *the departed individual might partake of the first resurrection, instead of waiting for the second*. This cannot be designated as an *unknown* way. It is some years since I read the passage: but the impression upon my memory is *not*, that Tertullian recommends the practice, *as familiarly recognised and adopted in the Church*. To make good the statement in your letter, you ought, I think, to have distinct historical evidence to *this* effect: and I do not *remember*, though very possibly I may be mistaken, that the practice is ever mentioned or recommended *at all* anterior to Tertullian; still less, that it is so recommended as the practice of *the Church from the beginning*. I do not say, that I should receive it *even then*: but your statement of *a fact* must obviously be made good by *testimony*, before the fact can be deemed substantiated. *Downward* from Tertullian, you may find the practice gradually creeping into the Church: and Augustine, though with much backward and forward writing, might seem *hesitatingly* to base it upon a purgatory. But have we any evidence *upward* from Tertullian; whose bare *personal* recommendation does not strike upon my apprehension as any evidence at all? We have such strong warnings in Athanasius and Cyril of Jerusalem and others to receive nothing *doctrinal* or *doctrinally practical* save what can be established from Scripture, that I shrink with a sort of horror from admitting any such thing without distinct scriptural warrant: and I must fairly tell you, that your deduction from the scriptural charge, that 'we should pray for *all* saints' works no conviction in my mind. You will, I am sure, pardon this freedom in an old, though (I hope) not an obstinate, man.

I cannot acquire any clear and distinct idea of your view of Justification, either from your elaborate work or from the brief statement in your letter. The assertion, that Inherent Righteousness is a formal cause of Justification, while Faith, which *precedes* and is the *seed* of Inherent Righteousness, is the instrumental cause, strikes me, as something very like a contradiction in terms. I can *understand*, though I cannot *receive*, Bp. Bull's system, that we are forensically, as by an instrument, justified through what he calls *Fides Formata*; because he makes *Faith and the Produce of Faith* to be *one* complex matter, and through this *one* matter he supposes us to be justified *on account of* Christ's merits. But, in your system, so far as I can form any idea of it, we are *first* instrumentally justified through Faith; and *then*, when we are *already* justified, justified *again* by our Inherent Righteousness as a causa formalis. This process, if it *be* the process for which you contend, I have vain [ms torn] to understand. I can form no idea, how a person who is *already* justified forensically or made rectus in curia through the instrumentality of Faith, can *again* be justified by any *subsequent* process. Of course you know, that Bull advocates the forensic idea quite as much as I do—It strikes me, that you *confound* together the two ideas of Justification and Sanctification, the cause and the effect; while Bull so *amalgamates* them, as, by a sort of theological fiction, to make the two *distinct* ideas a *single compound* idea. With neither system can I agree: nor do I think it possible, that the correct idea (or, at least, what I *deem* the correct idea) can be better or more clearly expressed than in our old homily. I will give the passage, that you may understand what I allude to.

'Faith doth not shut out repentance, hope, love, dread, and the fear of God, to be *joined with* Faith in every man that is justified: but it shutteth them out from *the office of justifying*.'

So far as I can understand this passage, it directly contradicts both Bull and yourself.

Possibly it may be a touch of the amour propre, but, in your remarks upon my own Work in your appendix, you do not seem to have made good your point either grammatically or evidentially or argumentatively. But this is too long a matter to enter upon in a letter.

Should you honour me with an answer to this, if you deem it necessary, have the goodness to direct to me at Robert Welbank Esqr., Tandridge Priory, Godstone. After a short intermediate visit, we purpose going thither on the 7th and of staying there about a fortnight.

Believe me, my dear Sir, with real respect and regard, your obliged humble servant G. S. Faber

TO GEORGE STANLEY FABER

Oriel College. May 16. 1838

Dear Sir,

I hope you will allow me to plead my engagements in this place as an apology for delaying my answer to a letter which was quite as kind as your former one,—and I cannot say more to express my thanks to you for it. I will say now what I have to observe in reply as briefly as I can.

You observe that if, as I consider, the Primitive Church deemed Prayer for the Faithful Departed 'pleasing to God and in some unknown way useful to the dead,' this is to make it involve doctrine. Certainly it is, so far—but in this way all ceremonies involve doctrine; for rites and ceremonies are not practised except as being pleasing to God. This doctrine is an inference *involved*, and which cannot be helped—it is not the direct view or the essence of the thing in question, which is essentially a point of practice not of faith. There is nothing in Scripture about using the Cross in Baptism— so that, if your way of viewing the matter were correct, one might say 'No one can use the Cross, without thinking such a usage pleasing to God—but *that* is a doctrine—and it is not in Scripture that the use of the Cross is pleasing to God—therefore it is unlawful—for no doctrine is lawful which is not in Scripture.' I on the other hand should urge that it is a Catholic usage, accidentally involving doctrine.

As to the evidence, I consider there is evidence enough that the Church prayed for the dead in Christ, but not evidence that they knew *why*—for they give *various* reasons. Tertullian in the passage you refer to, gives as a reason that the departed may have part in the first Resurrection—but other petitions offered referred to their having rest and peace now, and a merciful trial at the last day. Ussher seems to me to bring this out satisfactorily in his chapter on the subject in his answer to a Jesuit.[1]

As to the *date* of the evidence, I would only suggest this—that as far as I know, there is as good evidence for this usage as for the genuineness and authenticity of many books of the New Testament; which are received on the custom of reading them in some Churches from the beginning, the testimony of one or two Fathers to one or two *verses* in them, and the fiat of the 4th century which formed the Canon. E.g. I speak without accurate investigation, but I believe St Paul to Philemon is received on a reference to

[1] James Ussher, *An Answer to a Challenge made by a Jesuite in Ireland*, London 1625, (reprinted at Cambridge in 1825), Chapter VII, 'Of Prayer for the Dead'.

it in Tertullian, (though I do not find it noticed in the Index in my own edition) on a passage in Caius, and then by Origen and Eusebius. This is a favorable specimen—I think I am right in saying that not a single Latin Father for 3 centuries quotes the Epistle to the Hebrews, but Tertullian who gives it to S. Barnabas, Irenæus and Hippolytus seem to have thought it not St Paul's, or not canonical—at all events it was not, I believe, received by the Roman Church in early times. I may be incorrect in these particular instances, but they serve as illustrations of what I think will be found to hold, viz that we receive great part of the Canon on less evidence than that produceable for prayers for the dead in Christ. The main evidence for both is the *reading* of the one and the *use* of the other in the Church from the beginning. Mr Palmer, I think, has shown in his Origines Liturgicæ that the 4 Liturgiæ are of such high Antiquity that no date can be assigned for them short of the Apostles—and they all contain these prayers.[1]

As to my considering that 'faith which precedes inherent righteousness and is its seed is the instrumental cause of justification, and inherent righteousness its formal cause,' I should explain myself thus:—I do not consider that lively faith *is* the primary seed of inherent righteousness, but that the indwelling Spirit is. Faith may exist in the unregenerate, but it is dead. The indwelling Spirit enters through Baptism, and henceforth faith is both lively and the instrument of justification. Baptism is the original instrument and issues in the entrance of the Spirit—*in* which, not as by a second process, consists our justification. E.g. supposing animal life to consist in a certain organization, that part of it which is called the lungs might be considered the *instrument* of life, as enabling us to breathe.—This organization as a whole would depend on the presence of the soul, and the presence of the soul would be referrible to God's original breathing it into our body. Hence the Spirit and the soul are the corresponding formal causes proper, inherent righteousness and organization the formal causes improper, God's Baptism and God's breath the primary instruments, faith and breathing of the lungs the secondary instruments. This is not a correct illustration in all points, but so far.

I heard a report last Term on your being in Oxford. Should that ever occur again, I hope you will allow me the gratification of waiting upon you[2]

I am, Dear Sir Very respectfully Yours John H Newman

THURSDAY 17 MAY 1838   letters from W.F. [,] J M and Mr Goldsmid
FRIDAY 18 MAY   letter from Anderson   f d

[1] See William Palmer, *Origines Liturgicae, or Antiquities of the English Ritual, and a Dissertation on Primitive Ritual*, Oxford 1832, I, 5ff.
[2] Faber replied on 7 June: 'I am not perfectly clear, that I *understand* your system of Justification. Each *separate* proposition, whether I admit it or not, I can at least *comprehend*: but, when I attempt to *combine* your several propositions into *one distinct and compact system*, I will honestly confess to you that I am foiled.' The correspondence continued but no more of Newman's letters have survived.

SATURDAY 19 MAY letter from Bowden Bowles of St John's and Merewether to breakfast dined in Hall

TO HENRY WILBERFORCE

Oriel—May 19/38

My dear Henry,

Chalmers' Lectures ought to have been added to the List—and Chalmers has not yet finished his say—so I have changed my mind[1]—We will postpone it till next time, and it shall be your next subject. Now I propose one which if it takes you, will be a very good one. It is to take Tract Number 80[2] and illustrate it negatively, i.e. by its breach, out of the modern books for children —*Their* faults might be brought out effectively and you need not pledge yourself to the views of the Tract if there are parts of it you have not considered yet. You might begin by saying 'This Tract takes a large subject, of which we here mean to take part.' And after sketching its contents, pounce upon the unfortunate victims which you select. I send you some I *happen* to have—but you will find much better doubtless. One great peculiarity of modern Tracts for children [is] that they teach children *how they ought to be educated*. If you could make some observations on Mrs Barbauld and Miss Edgeworth etc[3] it might be good but perhaps these might stand over for a separate number. A simple and easy way of taking the subject would be simply to take the separate *Canons* of teaching given in the Tract, and illustrate them successively by modern Books; adding any other instances out of Meetings of Societies, modern Churches, etc. which occur. And I would have the whole article bear upon the necessity of *a library* for children being set about—here you may cut at the Christian Knowledge Society's books— bring out the case of Lord Brougham's knowledge under difficulties put on or taken off—also others, of which I send you one—'Travels in Palestine.' Mrs Sherwood is another I should *principally* attack, were I you[4]—both because her works are so popular, and because she has turned Universalist. Write at once to Rivington for any books you want in my name.—And, charissime, be quick—which I know you will be, unless you think me unreasonable.

I had a nice little note from your wife, for which pray thank her kindly

Ever Yrs affly John H Newman

[1] Thomas Chalmers, *Lectures on the Establishment and Extension of National Churches*, London 1838. The Lectures were delivered in London between 25 April and 12 May and created great interest, drawing large and distinguished audiences. Wilberforce reviewed the work in *Brit. Crit.*, 26, 1839 (July), 228–44.

[2] [[Isaac Williams on Reserve]] 'On Reserve in communicating Religious Knowledge'.

[3] Anna Letitia Barbauld (1743–1825), wrote poetry and various prose works such as *Early Lessons* and *Hymns in Prose for Children*.

Maria Edgeworth (1767–1849), a novelist, who was greatly admired by Walter Scott, she also wrote moral tales. Her most famous novel was *Castle Rackrent*.

[4] Mary Martha Sherwood (1775–1851), a prolific writer of religious stories and popular books for children, all of an evangelical slant.

P.S. Rogers well suggests that St Aug's account of St Ambrose's conduct to him, (sitting still and reading a book) is a remarkable and happy specimen by way of contrast of the Catholic mode of effecting conversions.[1]

I should like to have the books back. After all I have sent but a few shabby ones.

I am in fact sending you no books at all—except to swell Williams' Tract into a parcel—Send to Town for the last Publications of the Tract or any other Society at random.

SUNDAY 20 MAY 1838   5 Easter   letters from Pusey and H   did duty morning and afternoon   preached Number 506[2]   called on Tinney   Fausett preached against us[3]   dined in rooms.   wrote to Pusey J M Mr Hornby Goldsmid and Mr Roberts of Monmouth

TO E. B. PUSEY

Oriel College. May 20. 1838

My dearest Pusey

I am so very much grieved at what I hear of your indisposition that I cannot but write a few lines. Of course you will not be so imprudent as to travel back unnecessarily. Do stop at Weymouth. Barnes has sent this message. And it will be quite necessary for Mrs Pusey—I do hope you will stop.— Really I am so very much distressed for her too—for of course yours increases her illness. Yet it is a great comfort that dear little Philip is not to have that accumulation which very much shocked me to hear reported. May God grant, since it is inevitable, that you may have the privilege of seeing him '*fall asleep*' in the Lord. That pain should accompany his leaving you would indeed be an aggravation.

James Mozley wrote to me full of delight—not knowing where to direct to you, and desiring me to say so to you.[4] He purposes being got ready for his Examination by his brother who, he says, is a good hand at it. I wrote to the Archdeacon at once.

Fausett to-day has fired off a sermon against us, as leading to Popery; strong and severe with one or two compliments. The time was now come to speak out A great deal, against what he considered a quasi Transubstantiation —he took a miserably low view. A great deal about Rome being Antichrist— against an enthusiastic mind (meaning Froude) against publishing private correspondence—in favour of the Reformation—against insidiousness. This

[1] St Augustine, *Confessions*, VI, 3. St Ambrose sat silently studying, while enquiring visitors, Augustine among them, came and went freely.
[2] *P.S.* VII, 12, 'The Gospel Feast'.
[3] Godfrey Faussett, *The Revival of Popery: a Sermon preached before the University of Oxford, at St Mary's . . .*, Oxford 1838.
[4] In his letter of 14 Aug. to Keble, Newman implied that the ordination of James Mozley had been a special favour from the Bishop at Pusey's request.

is all I have heard of it. Rogers' article in the B.C.[1] came in for it—and he spoke of *Reviews* being enlisted—and a pushing party etc.[2]

I had heard you were to preach

With kindest and affectionate thoughts of Mrs Pusey

Ever Yrs affly John H Newman

MONDAY 21 MAY 1838   Rogation   Mr Dolfee called.   f d   Keble came
TUESDAY 22 MAY   Rogation   Die Av.[3]   letter from Lebas   Keble read his Lecture and went directly afterwards   f d   but 1   service and Lecture read Number 50 1 men in evening in Common Room

TO J. W. BOWDEN

⌜Oriel College. May 22. 1838⌝

My dear Bowden,

I regret to send you so shabby a letter, expecially since it is to convey a disappointment. ⌜Smith has been persuaded by his Magdalen friends not to leave Oxford—they think that he will gain more good here during the year.⌝ This has vexed me very much. ⌜I hear of two other men as *possible*—but do not know whether the chance is such as to make it worth while for Mr Robinson to come down.[4] The two men are Seager, a friend of Pusey's and a considerable Eastern Scholar—and a Mr Hill of New College, who (they say) is a very nice sort of man; but whose name I never heard of before.

You know Fausett has been firing away at us in gallant style.

I fear I shall be hard pressed for Articles for the B.C.⌝ but cannot tell yet.

Ever yrs affly John H. Newman.

P.S. I am sorry we are full here as to beds but Johnson has, I understand, provided.

[1] His review of Froude's *Remains*, Jan. 1838.
[2] Faussett exclaimed that, 'when . . . the marks of deliberation and design, the evidence of numbers and of combination . . . find their way into the periodical and popular and most widely disseminated literature of the day;—when the wild and visionary sentiments of an enthusiastic mind, involving in their unguarded expression an undisguised preference for a portion at least of Papal superstition, and occasionally even a wanton outrage on the cherished feelings of the sincere Protestant . . . and this too under circumstances which imply the concurrence and approval, and responsibility too, of an indefinite and apparently numerous body of friends and correspondents and editors and reviewers;—who shall any longer deny the imperative necessity which exists for the most decisive language . . .' *The Revival of Popery*, Oxford 1838, pp. 13–15.
[3] For 'Dies Aviae'. Newman's paternal grandmother died 22 May 1825.
[4] [[qu. as Curates to Mr Robinson in a new Chapel?]] Bowden, who was on the Additional Curate's Fund Committee, had set up a separate Fund at Roehampton to subsidise a curate for his hamlet. He was looking for somebody who would introduce 'catholicity'. Newman seems to have suggested Bernard Smith of Magdalen, but he remained there as a probationer fellow until his appointment to the Rectory of Leadenham in May 1839. C. F. Robinson, as Perpetual Curate of Putney, was responsible for any appointment. David Lewis went to Roehampton as Curate about a month later.

⌐P.S. I shall expect you and Mr Robinson at dinner on Saturday at 6,⌐ if I do not hear from Johnson or in other way to the contrary.[1]

WEDNESDAY 23 MAY 1838 Rogation f b f d wrote to Mr Bayne, Woodgate (in parcel) H W. [,] W F and Bowden

TO HENRY WILBERFORCE

[23 May 1838]

My dear H W

Will you, please, *forthwith*, send me the *name* and *direction* of the person from whom I forwarded you a letter the other day. One came to me also from the same, and by ill luck I have mislaid it and cannot answer it. I am much vexed at this, and I wish no longer to delay.

Keble told me something or other about your not writing your Article— Of course I have no right or wish to perplex or hurry you.

Fausett has been firing off against the Remains, more suo. I suppose he will do us some damage. If I can, I shall try to get all of us to observe King Hezechiah's orders to the men on the wall about Rabshakeh.[2]

Ever Yrs affly John H Newman

TO H. A. WOODGATE

Oriel May 23/38

My dear W

Your sermon abounds in important matter, ill put together. I conceive you are right in what you say of the Church Catholic never having been in any essential error.

As to tradition, I should speak thus:—*facts* of whatever kind are only known (except by miracle) in two ways—by senses and by testimony. Past facts cannot be known by senses and therefore are by testimony. Tradition resolves itself into testimony. A written or printed book is the testimony of a stranger—and believed because others bear witness to its trustworthiness. Tradition is the succession of testimonies, of each age to the next, of which the last link touches *you*. To say we believe by tradition is only to say we are

---

[1] [[N.B. Just at this time, June 1838, was the zenith of the Tract movement—it was at this Commemoration my answer to Faussett came out. The next letter 17 Aug. 1838 is the beginning of a change of fortune]]

[2] 'Do not answer him', 2 *Kings*, 18:36. Newman did answer him, but explained: '. . . I cannot conceal from myself that I am one of those against whom your recent Publication is directed. My first impulse . . . was to resolve not to answer it, and to recommend the same course to others. I have changed my mind at the suggestion of friends . . .' *Letter to the Rev. Godfrey Faussett . . . on Certain Points of Faith and Practice*, Oxford 1838, p. 3.

told by persons *who* have been told by others who etc—Josiah would not have known the book of the Law to be divine by himself. He found it in a miraculous place, or the priests etc or Jeremiah would inform him. I do not think the difference of oral or written tradition alters the case—in either case it is testimony of a particular person, in oral, of the person who speaks to you—in written, of the person who wrote (i.e. perhaps some hundred years before) or (if you resolve this again) of the persons you have known, who testify to the supposed date of the writer. Tradition is often used in quite a different sense for the res tradita—but here I take it for the *mode*—i.e. for a chain of successive testimonies. And I agree with you that (*sense* being put out of question) we know facts by miracle or tradition, i.e. *including* in tradition its last link, *testimony made to us* personally, which last link often is *all*, i.e. in cases where the witness has *seen* the facts and does not take his account from a prior witness.

Ever Yrs J H N

THURSDAY 24 MAY 1838 Ascension Service in Chancel—read Number 507[1] Communion Service—no assistance saw Mr Prior Mr Merewether and son, Faber, Church, 2 Marriotts and Rogers to dinner in Common Room with me

FRIDAY 25 MAY Rogers went to Cambridge dined in hall—and J Marriott

SATURDAY 26 MAY Neville[,] Prior and Phillips to breakfasted [sic] in Common Room with me—several with Marriott dined in hall. H. Shepheard returned Bowden and his son came took tea at Johnson's—

SUNDAY 27 MAY After Ascension letters from Mr Lebas, H W and E.Q.V. Williams (?) assisted me in Sacrament Williams did duty in morning I in afternoon and preached Number 508[2] Bowden, Johnson, and dined with me in rooms

MONDAY 28 MAY went with Bowden etc to Magd. Chapel. Bowden, Johnson, Lewis, Harrison, Woolcombe, Newman and Anderdon to dinner

TUESDAY 29 MAY Bowden, Johnson, Bloxam, Berkeley, Williams, Copeland to breakfast walked with Bowden and J B [his son] and Johnson to Littlemore, but not to service dined with Williams at 4, as did Bowden, Nevil and Prior service in A de B's Chapel—read Number 502 wrote to Mr Fausett [Fawcett] men in evening Pusey returned

WEDNESDAY 30 MAY letter from R Williams Bowden and J.B. went dined in hall wrote to H W

TO JOSHUA FAWCETT

Oriel College. May 30. 1837 [1838]

Dear Sir,

I very much regret that the accident of mislaying your obliging note has occasioned a delay in my answering it. In consequence I have written to Mr Wilberforce for your direction, to whom a letter came from you with mine.

[1] *P.S.* VI, 16, 'Warfare the Condition of Victory'.
[2] *P.S.* VII, 12, 'The Gospel Feast'. Newman had preached a different part of the sermon on 20 May.

In reply I need scarcely say I feel much flattered by your good opinion, as implied in your request, though I fear I must ask your leave to answer it in the negative—When you have so valuable a list of contributors to your volume, of course it can matter little whether you have my own name or not; but it seems disrespectful and so to require an apology, to decline helping so very excellent an object as liquidating a debt incurred in Church building.[1]

If I were to give reasons, which perhaps it is impertinent to do, I would say that I have not sufficient respect for Lord Morpeth to unite with him in a literary work[2]—and that I am not friendly to the principle of holding Bazaars for sacred objects.

I am, Dear Sir, Your faithful Servant John H Newman

THURSDAY 31 MAY 1838 letter from Mr Todd (or Tuesday?) Woodgate married walked to Littlemore—back with Bloxam dined at Mr Parker's

TO HENRY WILBERFORCE

Oriel College. May 31/38

My dear Henry,

I will tell you just what I think about your prize money—Pusey returned the evening before last, and I have waited for my answer till then.[3]—To tell you the truth, people here were much offended at the announcement in the Papers signifying your good luck—and that not our friends exactly, but persons more exoteric also. They thought it was countenancing a very vicious system. This being the case, certainly as far as Oxford is concerned, I think that to give the 200 guineas *openly* will be so far from an act of ostentation, it will but be righting yourself with persons you would not wish to be wrong with. If you were to ask me, certainly I do think it would be a reparation, and that a reparation is called for. I say this with the less reluctance, because

---

[1] Joshua Fawcett wrote from Low Moor near Bradford, Yorks., on 5 May that he was assembling a volume of 'original Literary Fragments from the pens of Eminent Authors' for the benefit of his Church, which had a debt of £500. Contributors to the volume included 'Lord Morpeth, Revd Dr Hook, Revds W. S. Gilly, George Townsend, Henry Melville, Archdeacon Wrangham, Chancellor Raikes etc etc etc'. Hook had suggested Newman's name.

[2] Lord Morpeth was Chief Secretary for Ireland from 1835–41. He had introduced three unsuccessful Irish Tithe Bills between 1835 and 1837, all of which would have diverted part of the Church's revenue 'to the purposes of general education'. He was to vehemently denounce both Froude's *Remains* and *Tract* 90 in the House of Commons.

[3] A prize of 200 guineas awarded by the Christian Influence Society for his essay on 'The Parochial System', which was published later in the year. Wilberforce wrote on 6 July that he had given the money to the Winchester Diocesan Church Building Society. Newman's opinion of the Christian Influence Society is reflected in a brief notice in *Brit. Crit.*, 24, 1838 (Oct.), 489: 'Little as we like the principle of that Society, we find much satisfaction in finding it recognizing . . . the . . . most impressive appeal of a sound Churchman to Englishmen to exert themselves for the increase of the Parochial System up to the present state of our population.' The notice went on to point out that two works which had been recently awarded by the Society had contained instances of Apollinarianism and Nestorianism.

it quite takes away, as far as those whose principles you like best are concerned, all fear of ostentation. On the other hand not to do it openly, and at once, I do think would have a very sad effect on the Philistines and the daughters of the uncircumcised.—As to the object you have no need to ask me that—you know of plenty—but as open and as speedy as possible, should the offering be made. Of course what strikes one is the Curates' Fund.[1]

As to the Article for the Critic, I really am in want—nearly all who promised, ever so faithfully, have fallen off like leaves in Autumn, when they should be budding. I should like of all things if you would do Chalmers and Cumming, if you could do a *careful* one—(i.e. if you have *time* for a careful one)—but Chalmers[2] is too precious a morsel not to do justice to. I wish you could continue it with the Debate on the Scotch Church Extension—If you will, I will send you two reviews on the subject in the Eclectic and Westminster.[3] I ought to have the Article by the 20th at *latest*—Your Father's book[4] will not be reviewed this number.—Send at once for Chalmers, and I will settle with you. I have a copy—Also write by return of post—

Ever Yrs affly J H N

FRIDAY I JUNE 1838   Mrs Whitehead to breakfast   began Article for B.C. on Oxford Memorials[5]   f d

TO J. C. WIGRAM

Oriel College. June 1. 1838

Dear Sir,

I have just received and read an Article which you have been so obliging as to send me for the British Critic—and, in requesting some alterations in it (if I may ask such a favor) I think it better, and hope you will allow me, to use my name and address you frankly, though I have not the pleasure of your acquaintance.

My difficulty arises in no small degree from the work you have undertaken to review. I fear it would be very inconsistent in me to imply such a

---

[1] See note to diary for 9 April 1837.

[2] See first note to letter of 19 May to Wilberforce.

[3] 'The Scottish Church Extension Scheme', *Eclectic Review*, new series, 3, 1838 (April), 432–458. [John Robertson], 'Extension of the Church of Scotland', *London and Westminster Review*, 1838 (April), 98–118.
Recent investigation had shown that church accommodation in the Scottish cities was gravely inadequate for the needs of the population. Plans for church building, or extension, caused friction in some quarters. The Government was naturally reluctant to upset dissenters, because their support was needed. Evangelicals were worried about the rights of patronage, and moderates equally worried about a possible influx of evangelicals.

[4] R. I. and S. Wilberforce, *The Life of William Wilberforce*, five volumes, London 1838. The work was reviewed by C. W. Le Bas in October.

[5] 'Memorials of Oxford', *Brit. Crit.*, 24, 1838 (July); H.S., III, 315–35. A review of James Ingram, *Memorials of Oxford*, three volumes, Oxford 1837.

251

good understanding between the British Critic and the Scotch Establishment, as the tone of your remarks on the Glasgow System and Mr Stow convey.[1] I feel just the same aversion to the idea of seeming to fraternize with the Kirk Schools as we are accustomed to feel towards that of fraternizing with Roman Catholic Schools. Under these circumstances perhaps some other book might occur to you to prefix to your Article.

I fear too I should be very inconsistent, and should surprise all who know me, if I were the Editor of a work which implied praise of Mr [John] Hey, Archbishop Tillotson, and Dr [I.] Watts.[2] It seems disrespectful to urge such a request; yet under the circumstances I think you will allow me to ask that the passages which relate to them may be omitted.

There is another request, which I have to ask—that you would omit the reference in the last page to the Schoolmaster's Manual,[3] and the passage connected with it.

One or two verbal alterations perhaps you will allow me to add—such as, that the word *science* p 3 should be in italics—that in p 19 the word *Lord's-Day* should stand for *Sabbath*, and for *intelligence* some such word as *seriousness*. Also might I request that in p 8 the clause which implies that reading the Bible with prayer is the appointed way of arriving at religious truth be omitted.

Trusting you will excuse the freedom of this communication,

I am Dear Sir Yr faithful Servt J H N

SATURDAY 2 JUNE 1838 Vigil Pentecost ½ f.b f.d Bowden, wife, and wife's sister came (*partly by railroad—a new thing*) Acland came Wood and Williams came, and Rogers from Cambridge—to tea-supper.

SUNDAY 3 JUNE Pentecost did duty morning and afternoon—preached Number 339 Williams, Cornish, and Marriott assisted me in Sacrament I, Rogers, Wood, and Williams dined together

MONDAY 4 JUNE Whit Monday Service in Chancel no lecture went to Magdalen to Chapel Wilson came to dinner, two American Clergymen (Walters and Smeads) W. Harris, I. Williams, Bloxam; Rogers had Faber and Whitehead, and besides Wood, Wilson, and R Williams Acland and Mr Cavendish in evening. wrote to Anderson and Mr Bayne of Warrington

TUESDAY 5 JUNE Whit Tuesday Service in Chancel—Wilson took the duty Wood, Williams and I, and Bowden etc. went to Service at Littlemore, Williams reading

---

[1] David Stow (1793–1864), educational writer and founder of the Glasgow Normal School, which was in a sense the first full teacher training establishment in the country. Of evangelical leanings, Stow was an elder of Thomas Chalmers's Church in Glasgow. Here in the draft Newman cancelled: 'We all know how most persons in England feel towards Romanists—and how far they would be from praising a Romanist School—I do not wish to have towards the Kirk or any body of Christians the popular feeling towards the Romanists; but'.

[2] All three writers were of rationalist or latitudinarian tendencies.

[3] Wigram, who was Secretary to the National Society for promoting the Education of the Poor in the Principles of the Established Church, had recently published the *Schoolmaster's Manual* as 'a collection of Practical Hints for the information of National Schoolmaster's. The revised article appeared as 'The Training System of the Model Schools of Glasgow', *Brit. Crit.*, 24, 1838 (July), 212–29.

and preaching thence all to Iffley. dined in hall Service in Ad de Br. read Number 503 Wood and Wilson dined with Acland went to Acland's to tea wrote to J and Mr Todd and Mr Crosthwaite men in evening

TO MRS JOHN MOZLEY

Oriel College. ⌐June 5. 1838¬

My dear Jemima,

I intended long before this to write—and was yesterday concerned to hear from Mrs Bowden, who is here, that your little boy has got the hooping cough—I hope there is nothing serious in the case, but it seems formidable in so young a child. ⌐I am full of work and shall be till July. All my writers for the British Critic almost have in the last moment deserted me—and it seemed as if I should have to write half the Review myself. But things now look better¬—Sewell has descended as a Deus è machinâ, if you understand what that is—in the shape of an article on Plato[1]—and Harrison has kindly set to work. ⌐I gave¬ (entre nous) Mr Le bas ⌐the choice of 6 articles;—he *chose*, having *already* read it, my Lectures on Justification—and has sent me an unfavorable and very puzzleheaded critique upon it.[2] Of course it is sent to the press—but I am in this absurd dilemma, that the more perplexed it is, or the less perplexed, the better it is for me and the worse for the Review, or the better for the Review and the reverse for me. It seems to me a very cool thing in the said Le bas;¬ but all this is among the secrets of the Review, except so far as the Review itself will show it.

On the whole I am rather at ease about my Lectures—at first I thought I should be very obscure—but am satisfied from what people say that I am not, except so far as the subject obliges me. As to your question I think John is right, not you. If you can put your question in a fuller form, I will answer it precisely. None of the peculiars will willingly admit a formal cause[3]— indeed to do so is to cut their own throats—and yet it is so very absurd to say there is none, that the question seems to me the very joint of the controversy and a complete overthrow of them. Their only chance is to mystify the matter, which Luther, Calvin and the later writers have done in different ways—though for the bulk of their people, the simplest way is to represent it as a refined, difficult, subtle, or (as they speak) 'sophistical' question. I feel certain it is the right way of taking the question—and that it will (at least I trust so) if so taken now, introduce the same confusion into their ranks, as

[1] 'Plato', *Brit. Crit.*, 24, 1838 (July), 1–60. Harrison did not make any further contributions to *Brit. Crit.*

[2] C. W. Le Bas, 'Newman and Faber on Justification', *Brit. Crit.*, 24, 1838 (July), 82–119. While Le Bas commended the learning and eloquence of *Jfc.*, he wrote that '. . . desperately hard reading we have found it! . . . He has delved deeply into the bowels of the matter; and has, consequently, provided a pretty severe trial of strength and endurance . . . And, once or twice, his imagination seems to have seduced him a little way into the realm of shadowy and mystical fancies.'

[3] Of Justification.

an ambush rising up would. It is curious to me to see how very dull in understanding the notion, your old veterans are, as Mr [G. S.] Faber or Mr Le Bas, who have accustomed their minds to one certain view, and who cannot right-about and form against the enemy, and how simple the subject appears to those who take it up for the first time. A lady wrote me word the other day, whom I had damped before the book came out with the warning that it would be an abstruse subject, that she had not found any difficulty in the subject from beginning to end, not denying of course that it requires attention —and she is far too clever a person and clearheaded to think she understands what she does not. It is curious to see how warmly women take up the whole Catholic system and how intelligently, when they do—I have just seen this lady, nothing more.

We have gained this year one most capital Fellow, in Church—he is in every respect a desirable man, as far as one can judge—and of a true and understanding Apostolical ἦθος. I am sorry John should have had such unpleasant business connected with St Werburgh's,[1] but I do not see what else he could have done. It shocked me very much to hear the details of Frank's [Newman] wife's accident.—We have formed a large party here this Whitsuntide. Wood, Wilson, and R. Williams, and Acland are here—two Cambridge men—two United States Churchmen—and a French Roman Catholic[2] is expected today, who is writing a history of Catholicism in England, and is very much struck with our divines of the end of the 17th and beginning of the 18th century—and quite idolizes Bishop Ken. His wife is an Englishwoman, I hear. You know we have an organ at Littlemore. All are well there—we hope to begin building the School House at once

Ever Yrs affly J H N

P.S. Old Faussett has been firing off at us. He is like an old piece of ordnance, which can do nothing but fire—or like an old macaw with one speech. He fired off at Milman, and against Hampden—and now at us.[3] He can do nothing but fire, fire.

WEDNESDAY 6 JUNE 1838 ember Williams went in middle of day letter from Manning f b f d. first day of term—University Service Sacrament walked with Wood etc wrote to Manning, Pope, Westmacott, and Lancaster

[1] At Derby.

[2] Alexis-François Rio, religious writer and art critic, and a friend and sympathiser of Montalembert. After holding posts at Vannes, Tours, and Paris, he married the heiress of an English Catholic family, and this enabled him to give up teaching in order to pursue his literary interests. He travelled in England a good deal during these years, preparing a projected work on the English Catholic question. He was introduced to the London literary, religious, and political circles by his friend Richard Monckton Milnes. His *La Petite Chouannerie* was favourably reviewed in *Brit. Crit.*, 32, 1842 (Oct.), 261–99. See M. C. Bowe, *Francois Rio, sa place dans le renouveau catholique en Europe (1797–1874)*, Paris 1939.

[3] Faussett attacked H. H. Milman's *History of the Jews* in his *Jewish History vindicated from the unscriptural view of it displayed in the History of the Jews . . . in a Sermon preached before the University of Oxford . . . Feb. 28, 1830*, Oxford 1830. He seems to have preached against Hampden in Dec. 1835 or Jan. 1836, see Volume V, 188.

Oriel. June 6. 1838

My dear Manning

My idea is this that the Apostles, without any reference to system, put down the *heads* of what they taught and called it the Creed. Their wording of it might vary at different times and places as our Lord varied His Prayer —but taken as a whole it was the same every where. It was as if the outline of some figure, one person fixed and perpetuated by points in certain definite places, and others in others; e.g. .·˙·. or . ˙ . The descent into hell might have been an *original* article of the Creed of Aquileia. Accordingly I take the doctrine guaranteed by the Consensus omnium in early times to be the matter of which the Creed is a kind of form—and as to the doctrine of the Eucharist, I conceive it is maintained under 'the Church' or 'the Communion of Saints' —i.e. I conceive that the Creed was a help to the memory—and that when primitive teachers came to that Article 'the Church' or 'the Communion of Saints', *then* they brought in the Eucharist. At the same time, if any one maintains that the doctrine of the Eucharist was sui generis, a profound and awful secret not to be talked of, not included in the Creed, non valdè repugnor.

I conceive the Church cannot insert a new article in the Creed. The tone of the Athanasian Creed seems to me decisive of this—'*This* is the Catholic Faith etc etc.'

I wish we could get you a Principal[1]—*Do* write me an article for the British Critic by September 1. and choose your subject quickly.

Ever yrs affly J H Newman

P.S. Why cannot you be Principal for a year or two yourself? When will you send me yours or Dodsworth's account of the S.P.C.K—I look to *you* to send it, whoever writes.

THURSDAY 7 JUNE 1838 Wood went walked with Wilson went with R. and W. [Rogers and Wilson] to New College to service dined, as did R. and W. at Trinity

FRIDAY 8 JUNE ember letters from R Williams inclosing £50[2] and Sir W Heathcote ½ f b f d G Ryder and wife etc. came Stevens, J Marriott [,] C Marriott [,] J M. [,] Rogers, Copeland, G. Ryder and Mr Durnford to tea wrote to R Williams and R Wilberforce

SATURDAY 9 JUNE ember letter from Mr Faber Mr Anderdon called f d Dr Mcbride asked me to dinner to meet S. Wilberforce

[1] For the proposed Chichester Theological College. See letter of 6 March to Manning and that of 2 March from him placed before it.
[2] For the new house for young writers; cf. fourth note to diary for 16 Oct.

TO J. R. BLOXAM

Oriel June 9. [1838]

My dear Bloxam

You doubtless have before this discovered that I took you and myself in, in saying tomorrow was a Vigil. I was misled by the Tempus Paschale being past.

Ever Yrs John H Newman

TO R. I. WILBERFORCE

[9 June 1838]

My dear Wilberforce

Excuse great haste and ½ a sheet of paper—I do not like a post to pass without acknowledging your most acceptable article[1]—which I send up to the press tonight. It seemed to me very effective and likely to take people. I wish you would think of some other subject.—There was ½ a sentence which in proof I think I should like you to doctor—it was to the effect of implying that clergy should not depend on the contributions of their people. I am sure *each* clergyman should[2] [be a charge on] his own people—but the early Church was a voluntary one, so far as the laity *as a body* supporting the clergy *as a body*. The insertion of one word will make the difference.

I do not know enough of [Alexander] Knox to speak—He seems to say dangerous things, but then his works are *private letters*, and his *words* can hardly fairly be taken by the inch. I should be unwilling to think him more than eclectic, though that is bad enough. Froude did not like him. I think his works on the Eucharist have done much good. Mr Durnford of Magdalen has called this evening and introduced himself. He is now in the room, and begs to be remembered. G. Ryder is here.

Ever Yrs most sincerely John H Newman

P.S. What a *permanent* work you had [have] made of the most important Life[3] you have just published. I have had little time however to look into it.

SUNDAY 10 JUNE 1838   Trinity Sunday   J M ordained deacon   did duty morning J M read afternoon   preached Number 300[4]

---

[1] 'Life of John Jay, Chief Justice of the United States.', *Brit. Crit.*, 24, 1838 (July), 146–66.
[2] Paper torn.
[3] Robert and Samuel Wilberforce's *The Life of William Wilberforce*, five volumes, London 1838.
[4] *P.S.* VI, 24, 'The Mystery of the Holy Trinity'.

TO JAMES BOWLING MOZLEY

In fest. SS. Trin. [10 June] 1838

Charissime,

I send you my Surplice not knowing whether or not you want it. It is that in which I was ordained Deacon and Priest. With every kind thought

Ever yrs affly John H. Newman

MONDAY 11 JUNE 1838 St Barnabas Service in Chancel—read Number 302 School Service in afternoon—the Bishop preaching

TUESDAY 12 JUNE service in A. de B's Chapel—read Number 504 went to Kinsey to wine—came afterwards to men in Common Room

WEDNESDAY 13 JUNE dined with Bloxam to meet his brother and Mr Walsh—as did Rogers

THURSDAY 14 JUNE Keble came? dined with Dr Kidd

FRIDAY 15 JUNE f d

SATURDAY 16 JUNE Rogers' party in Common Room, Bloxam, Williams, Harrison, Copeland, and Keble and I with Anderdon (any more?)

SUNDAY 17 JUNE 1st Trinity early Sacrament—Williams assisting did duty in morning Keble read and preached in afternoon dined with Pusey to meet Keble as did Rogers (*during these years there were great gatherings, dinners etc at Easter, Whitsuntide etc. or if some stranger, as an American Bishop came*)

TO T. D. ACLAND

Oriel, June 17, 1838

There is nothing which right principled men have more to dread in these days than a certain kind of fallacy, which may be called Argumentum à Calculo. When such a man for some reason or other wishes to adopt a plan put before him by Liberals, peculiars, etc., he says to himself, 'How may a Churchman *cast it* into his own theory?' and by some ingenuity he is sure to be able, by modifying this or omitting that, to express it in his own calculus, just as you would throw an algebraic problem into geometrical expressions. Having then granted it *geometrically*, he proceeds to allow his Liberal friends to use it algebraically—I mean, with all its original unqualified and objection-able peculiarities.

I feel very much the painful situation of a Member of Parliament wishing to do right, yet finding, if so, he does nothing. But I would ask by way of suggestion, whether, if all M.P.s who dislike Liberalism, could get them-selves to dissent and stand aloof, rather than try to squeeze objectionable measures into their conscience by the Argumentum à Calculo, whether this great advantage would not result—that they would *know each other* and strengthen their own views, till they would be and would show themselves a formidable body.[1]

MONDAY 18 JUNE 1838   dined in hall   went to Pusey's in evening

TUESDAY 19 JUNE   began pamphlet in answer to Faussett or rather yesterday evening (*before his sermon had been published*—)   *continued it*—*went to Press with it*   public meeting about St Ebbe's new church[2]   dined with Copeland at 4 as did Keble, Williams etc.   service in A de B's Chapel—read Number 509   men in evening Pope came

WEDNESDAY 20 JUNE   Accession   Keble went   Service in middle of day   no Lecture   Provost preached University Service   dined in hall—Pope dined with me.

THURSDAY 21 JUNE   Pope. Lewis. Seager. Johnson to breakfast   Rogers went Faussett's Sermon published   walked with Pope   dined in rooms   sat up all night writing *my answer* [to Faussett][3]

FRIDAY 22 JUNE   letters from Mr Hadfield and   finished pamphlet in morning (*the meaning of this is, that, Faussett, tho' he had preached against us on May 20, kept back the publication of it for Commemoration, thinking that then it would remain unanswered —all who came up for the Commemoration buying it, and then going down before there could be time for me to answer. So I wrote and printed the greater part of my answer before his Sermon came out, and was able to bring out my pamphlet a day or two after his, to his great surprise, and before Commemoration.*) Pope went   walked to Littlemore   dined in rooms

SATURDAY 23 JUNE   letters from Ottley and Rivington   Mr Bayne to breakfast   f d went in evening to Short's to meet Phillipps and wife

SUNDAY 24 JUNE   2nd Trinity   letters from Wood and Mr Walter of America   Marriott assisted me in morning Sacrament   did duty morning and preached Number 389 afternoon   J.M. read for me in afternoon   went to wine to Common Room to meet Trower   took tea with Woodgate and wife

MONDAY 25 JUNE   wrote to Mr Banister about Gordon—to Gordon—to Accountant of S.P.C.K.   my pamphlet ⟨against Faussett⟩ came out last at night [sic]   Ottley past thro' but I missed him

TUESDAY 26 JUNE   Radcliffe Sermon—Bishop of Salisbury—left card on Bishop of Salisbury   dined with Williams solus   service in Ad de B's—read Number 510 last evening party

WEDNESDAY 27 JUNE   Commemoration   laid first stone of Littlemore School House; I, Williams, and Bloxam—Copeland, J M, Smith [of] Magd.   Ryder, Morris etc were there. I preached sermon after service   dined with Provost to meet Dornford

[1] Acland wrote on 10 June: 'There is considerable excitement on the subject of education among liberals particularly among those who are radical on principle, and not merely compromisers with the feeling of the moment.—They are driving after some plan by which the state shall educate the poor, without leaving it to the chance of the poor themselves or chance benefactors paying for it; of course they do not consider that the Church is a system for national education, nor do they think it capable of being made the vehicle or administrator of national education . . .' Acland asked Newman's advice about possible plans, to which he and others could subscribe, which would make some allowance for the Church's interest in education, it being taken for granted that it was impossible to establish the ideal of a fully Church supervised system.

[2] Newman subscribed £50 to it which, considering the sum, may have been Mrs Pusey's gift, see letter of 13 April to her. The (nearly) £50 which she subscribed to the 'house for young writers' later in the year (see at 16 Oct.) would then have been a further gift.

[3] *A Letter to the Rev. Godfrey Faussett, D.D., Margaret Professor of Divinity, on Certain Points of Faith and Practice*, Oxford 1838. Newman concludes: 'I am quite aware that some of the subjects I have treated might be treated more fully and clearly. But neither the limits of a pamphlet, nor the time allotted me, admit it. Yours did not appear till yesterday, and the Term ends in a very few days.' pp. 98–9.

THURSDAY 28 JUNE   Harrison breakfasted with Marriott   Manning came in   (Coronation Day)   walked about with Manning   f d.

TO THE EDITOR OF THE BRITISH MAGAZINE (H. J. ROSE)[1]

Oriel College June 28/38

My Dear Sir,

It has annoyed me very much to find that quite against my wish mention of the British Magazine has crept into the Article on Bishop Kenn in this present British Critic.[2] The words slipped past my eye in proof or would certainly have been struck out. I should like very much to be able to repair this most involuntary offence—an offence both against the kind understanding which ought ever to exist between the British Magazine and Critic, and against the claims which the Magazine has upon our gratitude for its services to the Church and on my own personal acknowledgements in particular for its uniform kindness towards me. I am very seriously sorry, and wish I could show it otherwise than by word

Yours very faithfully John H Newman

FRIDAY 29 JUNE 1838   St Peter   Service in Chancel   read Number 216   Bloxam went   Harrison, and Manning to dinner with me—Marriott had the 2 Trowers—

SATURDAY 30 JUNE   Marriott went   walked to Littlemore with Manning.   Copeland to dinner with me and Eden.

SUNDAY 1 JULY   3 Trinity   letter from Mr Lebas   did duty morning and afternoon   Cornish assisting me in Sacrament   J M preached his first Sermon in afternoon   dined with Copeland to meet Mr and Mrs Mitchell [,] Luttman Johnson   wrote to Mr Le bas

MONDAY 2 JULY   at Magdalen Chapel   Copeland went   dined with Hamilton and Manning

TUESDAY 3 JULY   letters from Mr Lebas and J   Seager and Manning to dinner with me.   Barker [?] with JM.   Service and lecture in Ad de B's Chapel—read Number 512   wrote to Mr Le Bas

WEDNESDAY 4 JULY   Manning went   [A.P.] Stanley elected at University   walked with Spranger to Littlemore   dined by myself in Common Room   wrote to J and to Mr Faber   Keble in Oxford

[1] Rose was still officially editor of *Brit. Mag.* In replying on 7 July he wrote, 'Maitland is kind enough, during my present infirmity, to take the burthen of the thing off my shoulders, leaving me now only to do what I like or can with ease.'

[2] A *Brit. Mag.* review of *The Prose Works of Bishop Ken*, London 1838, contained the remark: 'Surely those things are lessons for us to profit by in these days, when division for nothing seems one of our dangers and one of our sins', *Brit. Mag.*, 13, 1838 (March), 313. Copeland took this up in his article on the 'Life and Works of Bishop Ken', '. . . the assumption which is made in the salutary caution of the reviewer of Ken's works, in the British Magazine, to us of these latter days, to beware of "*division for nothing*," is very gratuitous. It is a strange thing to assume, that the distressing schism which, at that time, rent the Church, was "*division for nothing*," in any stage of it; or that the Non Jurors were schismatics; which this language might seem half to imply." *Brit. Crit.*, 24, 1838 (July), 179.
Rose replied that he had been grieved because 'the B. C. under *your* hands is no ordinary matter and of course will be read'. He felt that Copeland had misconstrued the argument.

TO F. W. FABER

Oriel. July 4/38

Dear Faber

The above[1] has been lying by me some days, and should have gone to you. It seems to me unadvisable to translate the documents, as you think also. I should like you to let me have the benefit of your judgment, if you look into the works of St Austin I have set down—but I *think* they ought to be translated. They are all against the Donatists. I am not aware of anyone else who has written against them.

Yrs very truly John H Newman

TO MRS JOHN MOZLEY

(July 4. 1838)[2]

My dear Jemima

I am much obliged by your reminding me about Aunt. I had quite forgot. I will take care to pay in the whole sum for this year (except the October dividend) to Williams's to John's name at once. You say she is not well. I am very sorry to hear it; you do not say whether by rheumatism.

I am sorry too I am unable to come to you; but at present it is not possible. I go away at considerable inconvenience on account of my teeth—I broke one the other day—and I have long owed the man a final visit. At present I have weekly lectures in Adam de Brome's Chapel going on—so that it is a real trouble to go up at all—and I should not without cause. Landzelle said he should keep me a whole fortnight—else, had I any days over, I would come round by Derby. Also it is the *print*[ing] the Fathers that keeps me here—Baxter is tiresome enough as it is—but at 100 miles distance, he would not get on at all.

I have just published a letter to that goose Faussett, who literally knowing nothing at all on the subject has thought fit to publish his Sermon. It is an act of madness, if he knew his position; for though he may raise a cry, every body sees he exposes himself.[3] . . . some more plate (a Paten and Offertory Dish) was sent from other (anonymous) quarters?

[1] A list:
   'Optatus—de Schismate Donatistarum—AD. 370
   Augustine—Contr. Ep. Parmeniani. libb. 3.
          de Baptismo. libb. 7
          contr. litt. Pelitiani libb. 3
          ad Donatistas post collationem lib 1.—a.d. 412.
          contra Gaudentium libb. 2 A.D 420
   August. or Anon—Ep. cont. Donatistas, 5. de Unitate Eccles:—lib 1. AD. 402'
[2] The date appears to have been added later by Newman.
[3] Conclusion and signature have been cut off on the verso, with the loss of three or four lines here.

People are going to set up an Architectural Society here—Mr Parker and [Manuel] Johnson have much to do with it.

THURSDAY 5 JULY 1838   Keble went   letters from Landzelle and Bowden   Mr Faber called   called on Miss Keble   took luncheon with James Mozley to meet Mr and Mrs Bainbrigge   dined with Spranger

TO HENRY WILBERFORCE

O.C. July 5/38

My dear H W

I forget whether you said you had Cumming's—I have not. As I am going away to Bowden's in a day or two, I have not time to get it you. You had better send for it through your publisher, and since you have read it you need not wait for it to begin your article.

Do your article as soon as you conveniently can. It is very desirable, as you suggest, to get up a pond or vivarium, from which one can produce and serve up a dish of fish at a minute's notice. So be quick, if you can.

What I should like, would be a lively article on the Scotch Establishment, or the miserable town Church extension system such as both Dr C. [Chalmers] and the Bishop of London advocate it.[1] If you could show up the evils of this or of any part of our present anti-church system, it will do. Do not scruple to quote good bits and to cut them up, salvâ modestiâ tuâ. I must, if I can manage it, have a number of articles good humouredly exposing things as they are. The article on Exeter Hall in the present number is a specimen of what I *aim* at, such as it is.[2]

If I can find the Church extension debate in the Mirror of Parliament I will send it; but[3]—and let me have it as soon as you can

Ever Yrs affly J H N

The books I send are as follows:—
Vaughan Pratt Chalmers Irons
Eclectic Number 4 ⎫ I send these, in case they may direct you to
Westminster Number 60 ⎬ *documents* etc. If so, write to Rivington for
⎭ them in my name.[4]
I cannot find the Mirrors of Parliament. I should like all the books back some time or other.

FRIDAY 6 JULY 1838   letter from Marriott   f d   called on Mr Faber   walked to Littlemore (and read) with J.M.

[1] See respectively letters of 19 and 31 May and that of 11 July to Wilberforce.
[2] Newman's 'Exeter Hall', *Brit. Crit.*, 24, 1838, 190–211.
[3] A line has been scratched out, and another half line lost where the paper has been torn.
[4] See notes to letters of 7 and 31 May to Wilberforce for the details of these works.

SATURDAY 7 JULY   walked to Littlemore—back with Morris   Ryder and Pattison to dinner

SUNDAY 8 JULY   4th Trinity   letters from Rose, Palmer, and Hodgson auctioneer James Mozley assisted at Sacrament   did duty morning and afternoon at St Mary's preached Number 263[1]   Assize Sermon—prayers at ½ past 10   dined in Common Room   took tea at Woodgate's lodgings   wrote to Rose and Landzelle

TO HUGH JAMES ROSE

Oriel College. July 8. 1838

My dear Rose,

I am exceedingly obliged to you for your kind letter just received—Had I known you still took so much part in the B.M. I would have written to you at once—but I heard you were at Ramsgate, and wrote to your brother or Maitland as it might be. Really the passage in the Article of the B.C. vexed me extremely. It was owing to the Coronation[2] cutting off my time—I was obliged to send back the proofs in a great hurry, and merely skimmed over the Article, knowing I could trust the principles of the writer and not suspecting the possibility of any other anxiety on such a subject. At the same time though it was most miserably inconsiderate and stupid to say what he did, I am sure it was nothing more—there was no bitterness in it; but he alluded to what he had happened last to read which fretted him. I at once taxed him with it, and he woke as out of a dream, and was much annoyed—he is away now. I cannot conceive what made him so stupid—but I am sure there was no design or premeditation in it.

You make me anxious by what you say about the B.C. as 'conducted by me.' I took it, because there was no one else who would please all parties, very unwillingly—and I feel that there will be many things in it I do not like—Indeed I ought to be the last person, living in such a house of glass, to amuse my time with flinging at my next door neighbours. I trust in time to get a number of persons to write regularly, but it is uphill work at first.

I felt very grateful for the review of my Lectures on Justification in the B.M. and have so longed for an opportunity to say so, that I will not let this slip.[3] I mean, it was the review of a person who had done justice to them. A man may agree with one or not; but it is a much higher *personal* gratification to find one has been fairly considered and entered into. And I felt this of that review. When a reviewer *agrees* with one, it ought not to be a personal gratification—certainly, I feel the other a much *greater* one. I wish I could say the same of the article on the subject in the B.C.[4]—not that I am speaking against it editorially (of course), but personally—But I put it in quite de-

[1] *P.S.* VIII, 13, 'Truth hidden when not sought after'.
[2] Of Queen Victoria on 28 June. See the letter of that day to Rose.
[3] *Brit. Mag.*, 13, 1838 (June) 669–71. The reviewer felt that even those 'who disagree with its opinions must allow that in compass of learning in fixedness of view and in maturity of thought, it brings to their minds the writings of our old divines . . .'
[4] C. W. Le Bas, 'Newman and Faber on Justification', *Brit. Crit.*, 24, 1838 (July), 82–119. See second note to letter of 5 June to Mrs J. Mozley.

liberately and am answerable for it, as an Editor is answerable. But this I say in confidence.

Your remark about our Communion Service seems to me very important and is much on my mind.[1] I have heard this said, which may be insisted on that, while parts of the Service are lowered by such an analysis as you allude to, others are indefinitely raised. The run of men do not fancy anything *literally Apostolic* in the Service—Does it not add a most considerable awe to consider the Prayer upon the Offering etc etc. Apostolic and fraught with that deep meaning which such an examination assigns them? Can you prove to me these portions *have* such a deep meaning, *without* letting out the fact that innovations and omissions have been made? do we not gain more on the whole? ⟨again, what you say about 'Disciplina Arcani' is most important— —but one is in this dilemma, *either* one is rash *or* one is *keeping back* things. What is to be done when questions are raised? Does it not become expedient to *begin* with being open?⟩ Again after all the changes are rather in arrangement and in omission than otherwise. When we know what the Service means, we recognize in the disjecta membra, in the solemn words as 'sacrifice', 'memory', all that we need, and we can put a spirit into what before was almost lifeless. Nay may we not love the service more for its very misfortunes? as we should be more tender of a persecuted and mutilated brother? —I have said just a word on the subject in a Letter I have just published to Faussett, but wish much to treat the subject at length. The Romanists, refusing the Cup to the Laity, put their own Service into a parallel difficulty.

Should it suit your purpose, I should *rejoice* to see any portion of the Review of Geraldine in the B.M.[2]—but, if you did, you would fairly put me in the wrong, after my slip in the Bishop Ken.

I have long hoped to set about some Churches of the Fathers, on Julian's conduct about education—but have been altogether prevented. I hoped to begin directly the B.C. came out—but at present see no great chance.

Believe me, My dear Rose, if you will let me say it, that you are ever in my prayers morning and evening, knowing your value, and loving you

Yrs most sincerely John H Newman

P.S. You do not say *when* you go, so I[3] direct to King's College

[1] Rose wrote on 7 July, probably with Froude's *Remains* in mind: 'May I ask whether considering it as allowed that the *truth* is in our Communion Service altho' too timidly brought forward, it is safe to put forward to an ignorant and selfsufficient public such severe reflexions on our Communion Service—Would not the '*Disciplina arcani*' be advisable there? If *they* are taught to consider this most awful of all our services as so grievously imperfect, whither may we expect them to go? And Low Churchmen again, who make so little of the Sacraments, may *they* not use this as an argument in reply to our urgency "At least get a Service which you respect yourselves and which you do not hold up to public censure; and in which the truth, as you think it, shall be faithfully and duly taught, before you insist on *our* making so much of it" . . . If, generally speaking, we unsettle half taught men as to the Prayer Book what anchor have they? I say this, not dogmatically, nor even *more Socratico*, but sincerely in doubt, and wishing to see more clearly.'

[2] Newman's article 'Geraldine—a Tale of Conscience,' *Brit. Crit.*, 24, 1838 (July), 61–82. Rose had asked if he could reprint a passage from the article 'in order to shew the calmness and moderate views of those who conduct the British Critic.' The passage appeared in *Brit. Mag.*, 14, 1838 (Aug.), 219–20.   [3] To the Isle of Wight for his health.

MONDAY 9 JULY 1838 dined in Common Room with Copleston, Eden, and J M wrote to Archdeacon Wix and to Copeland and sent to Rogers proof of Latin Preface[1] J M to tea with me.

TUESDAY 10 JULY came to town by Tring, thence by railroad—J M taking both Sunday and Tuesday, and weekday and occasional duty in my absence, leaving it to Berkeley after him called on Wood—came down with Bowden to Roehampton called on Landzelle

WEDNESDAY 11 JULY letters from H W and Rogers went to Town with B. called on Wood—thence to Landzelle—then to B. again—sent letters to H W., and Henderson, and proof of Latin Preface to Combe [of] Leicester—went to Diorama and to Dodsworth's Church to Service came back and dined by self at Roehampton B and his wife at Sion House

TO HENRY WILBERFORCE

Wood's. July 11/38

My dear Henry

I will tell Rivington to send you Cummins—On the whole I think you have settled rightly about the £200[2]—You see you are setting an *example*. It is not a personal thing alone—people now cannot appeal to you one way, but must the other. The Bishop of London, joined by York, Salisbury, Litchfield [,] Chester, Winchester etc is introducing into the London Church Committee a *rule* or *principle* that each individual poor person should purchase his seat in order that he may be 'independent' and be able to say 'I have a right to that seat—' this cuts at so many principles at once, as it [is] evident, that I hope it will be resisted by Pusey and others.[3] Perhaps there will be an article in the B.C. against it.

I rejoice to find you and Mrs W. talk of coming to Oxford—Come, if you can to the anniversary of our Littlemore consecration September 22— But any time, I shall be there, as I expect, after Saturday week next. Coming to you is quite impossible on my part, thank you—

Ever Yrs affly John H Newman

P.S. The Edinburgh, I see, advertises an article on 'Whitfield and Froude.' Wood wants to know whether you have ultimately and finally given up any idea of having his Altar.

---

[1] To the second volume of Latin hymns which Newman had edited, *Hymni Ecclesiae, excerpti e Breviariis Romano, Sarisburiensi, Eboracensi, et aliunde*, Oxonii 1838. The first volume, *Hymni Ecclesiae, e Breviario Parisiensi*, Oxonii 1838, had an English preface.

[2] See letter of 31 May to Wilberforce.

[3] J. W. Bowden wrote on 4 July: 'We had a *sad* meeting of the Church building Committee the other day—The Bishop of L—— sported anew his celebrated ἔπος about independence and a plan for modifying the laws of the Society in accordance with it past a *first reading*, after a long discussion, by 9 to 7, the nine including 6 prelates, the 7 being *all laymen*. However, the scheme is not to be definitely adopted till March—so something may yet be done.' The article 'The Bishop of London and New Churches', *Brit. Crit.*, 20, 1836 (July), 199–208, had expressed worries that churches built with the aid of the Metropolis Churches Fund would be gradually allowed to introduce pew rents.

THURSDAY 12 JULY 1838 went to Town with Bowden wrote to Rogers and Gold-smid went to Landzelle then back with B H.B. [Henry Bowden] to dinner

FRIDAY 13 JULY did not go to Town ½ f b ¾ f.d. ½ f t. called on Jeffreys who was out, being driven by Mrs Bowden evening chapel began at Roehampton.[1] Lewis came in evening

SATURDAY 14 JULY letters from H W, Sewell, Henderson, and Gordon went to Town with B. Dodsworth asked B. and me to dinner on Monday, and me to preach tomorrow—declined both. went to Landzelle returned with B. Wood came to dinner wrote to H W and Sewell Wood went back

TO WILLIAM SEWELL

Rivingtons' July 14. 1838

My dear Sewell,

I happen to be in Town for a day or two and have got your letter. Nothing can be a better subject than Animal Magnetism—I have already been think-ing how desirable it was. And should be truly glad to receive a Review from you about it. The first of September is the day I should like it by for the next number of the B.C.[2]

Yours most sincerely John H Newman

TO HENRY WILBERFORCE

[14 July 1838][3]

My dear H

Your note seems very good as far as I can judge—as to the *reasons* you give and argue against, I suppose they are some of them gained not from my report—but they seem all matter of fact. One additional reason I have heard given is that the poor are *unwilling*, experience proves it, to sit in free seats, feeling it to be a degradation.

As to your article, I did not understand I was to cram you—and I am in a bustle. Let me see. You see, I have not read Dr C's [Chalmers] Lectures. I think you *must* find them suggest views. What I should *like*, would be for you to *analyze their faultiness*, and trace them up to πρῶτα ψεύδη.[4] If you could show the inherent viciousness of the Scotch Kirk, and how both Dr C and Mr Cummins in distinct ways try to overcome it, it would do. I hardly know what to advise not knowing your data. But I should like a *statement* of the *facts of the case* in Scotland as regards the extension of the Church in great Towns[5]

Ever Yrs J H N.

---

[1] There was only a proprietary chapel in the village of Roehampton until the building of a church in 1842–3. See first note to letter of 22 May to J. W. Bowden.
[2] William Sewell, 'Animal Magnetism', *Brit. Crit.*, 24, 1838 (Oct.), 301–47.
[3] Dated from postmark.
[4] 'primary fallacies'.
[5] See fourth note to letter of 31 May to Wilberforce.

SUNDAY 15 JULY 1838   5 Trinity   J.M. did duty for me at Oxford   preached in morning at Putney Number 473[1] afternoon at Roehampton Number 472[2]   Johnson came to dinner

MONDAY 16 JULY   letters from Le Bas, Philipps and Goldsmid   went to town with B   called on Wood and Badeley   went to Landzelle   J.M. left Oxford Berkeley takes my duty   Bloxam returned   back by myself   wrote to Le Bas, Philipps and Sammons   F. Marriott, Lewis and Mr Curry to dinner

TUESDAY 17 JULY   letter from J M   Edinburgh Review just out with review of Froude's Remains[3]   went to Town with B.   called on Joshua Watson—went to National Gallery where met Harrison and Thornton   called on Dodsworth.   went to Landzelle   returned with B.   Wood, Acland, R Williams, Johnson, Lewis, and Mr Swinburne to dinner

WEDNESDAY 18 JULY   letters from R W. [,] S W. [,] Williams and Mr Trail.   went to Town with B.   called on Westmacott for two or three hours—thence to Somerset House—met Rogers, with him to Straker's, where chose H.B.'s books[4]—thence to (Smith's) Silversmith's   by myself to Landzelle—and down again by ½ past 7   wrote to R W and S.W.

TO R. I. WILBERFORCE

London. July 18. 1838

My dear Wilberforce,

I have just got your letter. The Prussian Schools is a subject I should of all things like an article on—but take what comes in your way, when you get abroad.[5] I should say, however, as to the Archbishop of Cologne, that the subject is engaged, though I suppose nothing will come out at once. And besides it is so very tickling a subject that I am not quite certain whether you would approve of the view I should be disposed to take. Facts are facts, and if the Archbishop has broken engagements or done any thing else immoral I would not attempt to defend him—but I confess I like his *side* as far as I understand his principles—and though I do not suppose you are for the King of Prussia, yet I should not be surprised at any one whatever being not for the Archbishop.[6] If this is a misapprehension on my part and loses me a

---

[1] *P.S.* IV, 1, 'The Strictness of the Law of Christ'.

[2] *P.S.* VIII, 4, 'The Call of David'.

[3] James Stephen's article 'The Lives of Whitfield and Froude—Oxford Catholicism', *Edinburgh Review*, 67, 1838 (July), 500–35, the hostile part on Froude beginning on p. 525. Stephen was particularly critical of Froude's self-scrutiny and fasting: 'It is no part of the economy of our nature, or of the will of our Maker, that we should so cunningly unravel the subtle filaments of which our moves are composed . . . It is not by these nice self-observers that the creeds of hoar antiquity, and the habits of centuries are to be shaken; nor is such high emprize reserved for ascetics who can pause to enumerate the slices of bread and butter from which they have abstained. When Whitfield would mortify his body, he set about it like a man.' The article was republished as 'The Evangelical Succession' in *Essays in Ecclesiastical Biography*, London 1849.

[4] A present, it would seem, to Newman for officiating at Henry Bowden's second marriage; see diary for 19 June and postscript to letter of 2 Aug. to J. B. Mozley.

[5] Wilberforce's article 'Prussian Schools' appeared in *Brit. Crit.*, 25, 1839 (Jan.).

[6] See the article 'Observations on Prussian Official Papers respecting the Conduct of the Archbishop of Cologne', *Brit. Mag.*, 14, 1838 (Sept. and Oct.), 249–57, 378–83. The Prussian Government had negotiated with the Vatican between 1828 and 1830 in an attempt to gain ecclesiastical toleration of mixed marriages in Prussia's Rhine territories. The Pope issued a

good article, and particularly if I am disappointed in other quarters, the greater bore for me.

Wishing you a pleasant time of it

Ever Yrs most sincerely John H Newman

P.S. I hope long before this Rivington has sent you the poor acknowledgment for your last article which is due to you.[1]

FROM SAMUEL WILBERFORCE

Brighstone Rectory July 13. 1838.

My dear Newman:

Would you like a review for the British Critic on 'The White Man's Grave.'[2] It is a graphic description of Sierra Leone and the very curious state of society there— The line of the Review would be 1. a slight sketch of the History of Sierra Leone; which might be made I think very interesting; 2. a view of the present state of Society there; which would be at first interesting at times it might even be amusing; and then would open the very important point of making our Missions more really episcopal than they have ever been yet. The state of Sierra Leone divided into every stage of religious fervor and apathy strikingly shews the effect of our present system; and the circumstances which the Coloniae gave peculiars opportunity for; while the character of the blacks peculiarly needed the active development of Church Principles—

If you would like such a Review I will set about it directly and send it for your observations:

Believe me my dear Newman to remain ever most sincerely yours

Saml Wilberforce.

P.S. Are you going to publish another set of Hymni Ecclesiae from the Roman Breviary? Can you mention to me the title of the best collection of them[.]
I am trying to move in a memorial to the Church Missionary Society to send out Missionary Bishops. I am met by an objection that the Archbishop will not consecrate any who are to be paid by Societies and has refused to consecrate one for the Canadas to be paid by the S. P. G.[3] Can you give me or tell me where I may find any hints of the [one or two words missing]

TO SAMUEL WILBERFORCE

London, July 18, 1838.

My dear Wilberforce,

I felt the kindness of your offer, and certainly it seems like folly to hesitate about accepting it, considering who offers it; yet, on the whole, I think it

brief which tolerated the marriages 'to avert greater injuries to the catholic interest'. This in itself appeared hypocritical to the reviewer: 'the papal doctrine of the nineteenth century is, that the pope can dispense with the law of God, and that the means sanctify the end.' The Government obtained a more specific agreement about the matter from the Archbishop of Cologne in 1834. When the Archbishop died, enquiries were made about the attitude of his proposed successor. Despite his initial assurances of toleration, the new Archbishop had been taking the strongest measures he could to discourage the marriage of Catholics to Protestants.

[1] 'Life of John Jay, Chief Justice of the United States', *Brit. Crit.*, 24, 1838 (July).
[2] The reputation which the colony acquired after the seventeen changes of governor which took place, mostly due to death, between 1792 and 1814.
[3] The Society for the Propagation of the Gospel.

best to do so. I have just got your letter, and feel that I ought to answer it at once, though I would rather do so in a less hurry.

To say frankly what I feel—I am not confident enough in your general approval of the body of opinions which Pusey and myself hold, to consider it advisable that we should cooperate very closely. The land is before us, and each in our own way may, through God's blessing, be useful; but a difference of view, which, whether you meant it or not, has shown itself to others in your sermons before the University, may show itself in your writings also; and, though I feel we ought to bear differences of opinion in matters of detail, and work together in spite of them, it does not seem to me possible at once to *oppose* and to co-operate; and the less intentional your opposition to Pusey on a late occasion, the more impracticable does co-operation appear.[1]

While I feel, then, what I lose, and not the least on the particular subject you have selected, I think it best to conclude as I have expressed above. With kindest thoughts I am my dear Wilberforce,

Yours very truly John H. Newman.

THURSDAY 19 JULY 1838   letters from HW.[,] H and J   went to Town with Bowden and his wife   married H Bowden to Miss Burgoyne at St George's.[2]   went to Lady B's to breakfast   went with B to Somerset House.   took place,[3] went to Landzelle walked down by 9 o'clock   wrote to H.W.

TO HENRY WILBERFORCE

July 19/38

My dear H W

My first feeling about your question, has reference to the dibs, and reasonably—£300 per annum is a small sum to pay Curates out of.[4] It is no good being in a large parish without having money to spend. I should, as far as I see, make it turn on this. I do not see any other objection. It is most important to strengthen Dodsworth's hands, and to conglomerate about the metropolis. I have nothing more to say on the subject. It does seem a call. I do not think I have more to say

Ever Yrs affly J H N

[1] See note to diary for 18 Feb. J. B. Mozley wrote to T. Mozley on 13 June, '. . . Sam Wilberforce preached at St. Mary's on Sunday afternoon [10 June] . . . People say there were hits in it at Newman.' T. Mozley replied: 'From what I hear, S. Wilberforce does not confine himself to preaching in St. Mary's. He goes about talking against Newman and Pusey's views. It is to be hoped that he will publish, and so give N. and P. an opportunity of answering him. He taunts his brothers with being ridden by Newman, and boasts of his own liberty.' *Letters of the Rev. J. B. Mozley, D.D.*, London 1885, pp. 80–1.
[2] Henry Bowden's second marriage.
[3] i.e. booked a place in the coach.
[4] Henry Wilberforce wrote the previous day that '[W.] Dodsworth has written . . . almost to offer me a Church in Chelsea'. It was a new church, 'the income from pew rents, (supposing it to fill) about [£]300 per annum.' He asked Newman's advice.

FRIDAY 20 JULY 1838   did not go to Town   ½ f b   f l   ¾ f d   f t   Marriott and Lewis called   called on Mrs Thompson with Mrs B.   in evening at Chapel   Johnson at dinner, who went off in evening to London to embark at Ostend   wrote to Mr Trail, Wood, and Westmacott[1]

TO WILLIAM TRAIL[2]

answered July 20/38

1. that I had a great objection, in a matter affecting so nearly the Church, to overlooking our Bishops. It was *their* business. If it ought to be done and they did not do it—we ought to petition them, not the Queen.

2. As a private individual I will not undertake the responsibility of great changes—we are in captivity—I have no call to agitate for freedom. Bishops perhaps have such a call, and if so they must [decide] whether or not they will incur the responsibility of conducting measures. For us to do so, is to put ourselves out of the way, and to incur responsibility uncalled   And even to petition the Bishops, being an initiation of measures, is to incur responsibility   Did Bishops begin, I might be bound in duty to follow. If it is right, they should begin, not we, then it is want of faith not to sit still and wait ⟨these topics [1. and 2.] were hardly touched on⟩

3. I cannot trust the present body of the Irish Church—and would rather trust liberals as Bishops viewed as they would be by the Church with great jealousy by the body than Evangelicals, who would be backed by the body. ⟨this was not introduced⟩

   The bulk of the letter was urging that till we agreed more together, till we *repented* as a Church, till we gave up politics, till we acted under our Bishops quietly, all attempts at outward reformation, but [were] but rebellion against God who had put us under oppression as a judgment. I said we had better have a general fast to ask *what* our sins were, then petition for relief.

   Then I answered his separate observations.

   I said I would, without Bishops, only petition for a restoration. If a restoration were litterally impossible, I would petition for nothing. This is not inconsistent with protesting etc. and asking the Bishops to petition;

SATURDAY 21 JULY 1838   left Roehampton with B. for London—set off by railroad coach to Maidenhead, thence to Oxford   The Provost gone 2 hours before—Eden gone—no one in College   had some dinner   Berkeley and Bloxam called   found letters from Dr Heberden, Eden, and Pusey. Faussett's preface to his second edition[3] came out about last Wednesday

[1] In connexion with the monument to Newman's mother in Littlemore church, which Westmacott was to execute.

[2] William Trail, a layman, wrote from Bushmills, Co. Antrim on 13 July commenting on Newman's reply of 28 Feb., see note to diary for 11 Feb. Newman's present reply sufficiently indicates Trail's position, which he had already brought forward in long letters to the *Dublin Record* in Dec. 1837 and Jan. 1838.

[3] Of his sermon, *The Revival of Popery*. Faussett added a nine page preface in reply to Newman's *Letter*. He began by questioning the validity of Newman's *Letter* as a reply, '. . . the letter is anything but a regular answer to the sermon, and should seem to have been

SUNDAY 22 JULY   6th Trinity   St M.M. [Mary Magdalen]   letter from C   Berkeley helped me in early Sacrament   did duty morning and afternoon   preached Number 401[1]   dined with Berkeley, where Mr Sibthorp, Palmer [of] Worc. 2 Morrises, Bloxam

MONDAY 23 JULY   called on the Misses Gutch   Church in Oxford   Moberley and his wife in Oxford   dined at Magdalen Gaudy with Bloxam   made notes to my second Edition of Letter on Dr F's Preface[2]

TUESDAY 24 JULY   letter from Archdeacon Wilkins   called on Moberley f d. service in Ad de B's Chapel read Number 513   Church to tea   wrote to Archdeacon Wilkins and to Heberden

WEDNESDAY 25 JULY   St James   letter from S.W. and proof sheet from Pusey   did duty in Chancel   read Number 232[3]   walked by myself.   Mr Sibthorp, 2 Morrises, and Berkeley to dine with me.   Smith with Church

TO FREDERIC ROGERS

July 25th. 1838.

—As to the Sacrament Plate I had no wish it should be up to £10. I wish it handsome, that is all. Smith said they rarely made any up to that sum. I have no wish he should add a price in order to gratify me. As to the monument at Westmacotts, my *idea* was this—a female figure interchanging with an Angel a measuring line, plan, (or any thing which matched a building begun,) for a crown.[4] I wished it to be very subdued . . .

Faussett in his Preface to his second Edition[5] says at the Reformation era almost all the Protestant world were all but Consubstantialists and that the English Divines of the Laudian era were no better—he gives up by name Laud, Cosin, Bramhall, Andrewes and Bilson, and by implication Hooker— and says he does not swear by Hooker or by the rhetorical figures of Chrysostom or superstitious credulity of Cyprian, quotes Field to find fault with him. Is he not a bold fellow to stand upon his ipse dixit against the world, and abuse all as innovators who do not agree with him?—Then, he talks of my hastiness, unseemly triumph, mystifying his language, feeling or want of feeling which he shrinks from characterizing, infelicity, flippant suggestion, being utterly uncandid, reluctant admission, singular and instinctive coincidence with Dr Wiseman, constant appeal to a confused and wearisome medley of human and traditional authority and inveterate habit of mind.—On the other hand I have the satisfaction of finding as far as I can ascertain that I have sold 750 copies to his 500.—

written without any complete perusal of it, including of course the Notes and Appendix.' The preface was chiefly concerned with the antiquity of the term 'altar', and the nature of Christ's presence in the Eucharist.

[1] *P.S.* IV, 3, 'Moral Consequences of Single Sins'.

[2] Newman took up Faussett's points in footnotes to the second edition of his *Letter to the Rev. Godfrey Faussett . . . on Certain Points of Faith and Practice*, which he expanded by five pages.

[3] *P.S.* VII, 7, 'The Duty of Self-Denial'.

[4] The memorial to Newman's mother which Richard Westmacott was executing for Littlemore Chapel.

[5] See note to diary for 21 July.

THURSDAY 26 JULY   letters from H., Williams, Mr Faber, and Pope   went over to Littlemore with Berkeley and read service   dined by myself   wrote to H and Rogers

TO ISAAC WILLIAMS

Oriel College. July 26/38

My dear W

Bloxam is to all appearance quite well—he has thrown off his languor, and uncomfortable looks and feelings. I suppose he is very delicate—but so far is good. The School House is rising rapidly, and, I trust, will be finished by Sept 22. Shuttleworth, I hear, is writing something against Tradition[1]—item that worthy person has taken lately literally to cut me. Archdeacon Browne of Ely has charged against the Oxford Tracts, and is publishing appendixes against my letter to Faussett; so I hear.[2] The last worthy has published a preface to his Second Edition, *iracundius paulo*. On the other hand I have sold 750 to his 500; and come to a second Edition as soon as he. As to the question you ask me, I should really conceive that Judas *did* forfeit his Apostleship on his betraying our Lord—'from which Judas by transgression fell.' It has always been held in the Church that there *are* heresies etc. which forfeit the apostolical gift. Palmer seems to show in his last work that it is doubful whether orders even in schism are valid—so I think he says—i.e. valid till the Church formally recognises them.[3] However, this is going to another subject. I should have thought that antichrist was some one far more heinously wicked than the scribes and Pharisees. I shall be here the whole vacation. I am glad you are going on with a second volume to the Cathedral.[4]

I saw Harrison for a minute in London—I wish he did not look so pale and thin.—I shall delay this letter till tomorrow to answer your inquiry about Walker;—when I hope to say something about St Basil also. Rose has sent me a letter showing himself so much hurt about the allusion to the B.M. in Copeland's article, that I at once wrote a letter to C., hoping he

---

[1] P. N. Shuttleworth, *Not Tradition, but Revelation*, London 1838. Confusion was caused because some advertisements, and even the titlepages of some copies, gave the title of the work as *Not Tradition, but Scripture*. A brief notice, probably written by Newman, stated 'we are not uncandid to Dr. Shuttleworth, when we say, that this ambiguity at starting is no unfair symbol of the whole production. For instance, he says, that "the great leading principle of Protestantism" is "the entire *sufficiency* of Scripture, independently of tradition, as a rule of faith and doctrine." Sufficiency for what? teaching or proving? for the persons Dr. Shuttleworth writes against do not dispute the proposition as he words it.' *Brit. Crit.*, 24, 1838 (Oct.), 486–7.

[2] J. H. Browne, *Strictures on some Parts of the Oxford Tracts. A Charge delivered to the Clergy of the Archdeaconry of Ely . . . on June the 7th, 1838*, London 1838. The Charge was published together with a 146 page Appendix which consisted of an examination of points from the *Tracts* against extracts from the leading Protestant divines. Browne mentioned Faussett's Sermon but not Newman's *Letter*.

[3] W. Palmer, *A Treatise on the Church of Christ*, London 1838, II, 411–12.

[4] *Thoughts in Past Years*, Oxford 1838.

might soften things to him, but being unable to get his direction, it lies on my mantlepiece.[1]

July 27. Walker is much better. His wife tells me he has been out of Oxford some days for his health and Wingfield recommends his being out for a month or two

I put down some Epistles of St Basil's for translation.

Ed. Bened. Ep. 14 22 74 90 92 93 94 99 138 150 297
I send some longish ones. *Use your judgment however*

The Bishop of O. [Oxford] is delivering a charge in favour of the Oxford Tracts, I hear. Saying he does not fear the Masters, but he does the disciples

Ever Yrs affly J H N

P S Kindest remembrances to Neville

FRIDAY 27 JULY 1838   H. Cornish called   went over to Littlemore and read   called on Mrs Honey   Dr Evans of M. [Market] Bosworth called but I was out.   wrote to Williams
SATURDAY 28 JULY   letters from Mr Le Bas, W. F.[,] Henderson and proof from Marriott   baptized George Horn Standen   dined by myself in Common Room   M R G came into Oxford—walked with her to Littlemore   wrote to W F.
SUNDAY 29 JULY   7th Trinity   by myself in early Communion   married Benjamin Waite to Anne Paine   did duty morning and afternoon   preached Number 428[2] walked about with M R G   dined at Exeter with Morris to meet Mr Hall of St Mary Magd.
MONDAY 30 JULY   my second Edition of Letter to Dr F. came out.   M R G's brother and sister came and they went   dined by myself in Common Room

TO E. B. PUSEY

Oriel July 30/38

My dear P

You and yours are much in my thoughts. I do trust you will get on during the summer. I returned from Town a week since—Landzelle, as usual, gave me a good deal of pain, though not so much as before. He has attempted to fill up a decayed tooth which as yet gives me so much pain in eating that I think I must live on broth and soup for a while. However, on the whole, he has been very successful. Mr Le Bas, who poor man lost a daughter a day or two since, comes down to see me to-morrow. It is his own invitation—why he comes and how long he stays, I cannot make out. The Bishop of O. [Oxford] is delivering a charge in favor of the Tracts etc. Mr Browne Archdeacon of Ely is publishing a charge against them with appendixes containing strictures (I hear) on my letter to Faussett. Before your letter

[1] See letter of 28 June to H. J. Rose.
[2] *P.S.* IV, 14, 'The Greatness and Littleness of Human Life'.

came, I had written very brief notes in answer to his [Faussett's] preface. My second edition has kept pace with his, though he printed in his first only 500 to my 750. I have had a letter from Henderson inclosing an undergraduate's letter giving a lively, painful and (I hope) exaggerated account of the excitement Catholic views are exciting among the young men.[1] Have you seen the Bishop of Ex's [Exeter] speech on the Church Discipline Bill against the poor Archbishop? He says if it had passed he would not obey it and a bill of pains and penalties might have, for him, deprived him of his see.[2] I hope James M. sent you Mr Middleton's Charges.[3] They were 'on the primitive mode of spreading Christianity from centres—' I speak from memory. I must let you off the Article. I have declined S. Wilberforce's offer of assistance. Sewell is to write on Animal Magnetism—do not mention this—There is no news here. Let Seager have S. Greg. Nyss.[4] The British Critic is full of typographical errors—I *must* have some friend (from the hall)[5] to correct the press, at hand. If Mr Tuson wants the plans etc of Littlemore, let him speak positively, and I will set Underwood about it— else it is not worth while the expense. The school house (we trust) will be finished by September 22. We cannot get *ready* men for the Hall—all in promise only. I am solus—and am somewhat teased at the notion of Mr Le Bas' coming. I have only seen him once—and he is deaf.

With kindest thoughts of Mrs P and the children

Ever Yrs affly J H N

TUESDAY 31 JULY 1838   letter from Mr LeBas   dined by myself   service in Chancel read Number 514   Mr LeBas came

WEDNESDAY 1 AUGUST   letter from Rogers   Bloxam to breakfast   lionized Mr Le Bas rainy   Marriott passed through   to dinner Mr Le Bas, Bloxam, Morris, and Marriott

THURSDAY 2 AUGUST   letters from Rogers, J M and Mr Plunkett   Berkeley to breakfast   Marriott went   LeBas went   Mr Herbert Evans passed through Oxford, and left me a letter of Bishop Butler's (*I have since given this to Dr Hawkins*) and Waterland's History   dined by myself   wrote to J M and Pope and by parcel to Henderson, Goldsmid, Harrison, Rivington, and G and R.

---

[1] See letters of 8 April and 2 Aug. to Henderson.

[2] 'Over the clergyman's civil state he had no power, but he had power over him in a spiritual point of view; and . . . before his Master and my Master, I will remind this erring clergyman of his folly or his vice. I will reprimand him for it. If he will not obey the remonstrance, I shall proceed to that sentence, which this bill tells me I shall not pass: *I shall proceed to excommunicate him.* Then if this be done, your lordships in parliament may pass a bill of pains and penalties against me—*you may deprive me of the seat which I now hold* (but of which I shall never make myself unworthy)—you may rob me of my see—you may take from me my robes—but my integrity to heaven I shall maintain inviolate.' H. Phillpotts, *The Church Discipline Bill. Speech in the House of Lords on the 26th July 1838* . . ., London 1838, pp. 7–8.

[3] Probably the *Sermons and Charges* . . ., London 1824, of Thomas Fanshaw Middleton, Bishop of Calcutta.

[4] Seager did not contribute to the Library of the Fathers, nor did any work of Gregory of Nyssa appear in the Library.

[5] 'house for young writers'.

TO THOMAS HENDERSON

Oriel College. Aug 2. 1838

My dear Henderson,

I think your Catechism likely to serve well its purpose[1]—We want such works and the more we have of them the better. I had no remarks to make on its contents, except the following. 1—It is very true that Baptism is admission into a Covenant—nothing can be truer. Yet I do not think this is the primary and best way of viewing it—or our Church's way, and it has been adopted by our writers especially since 1688 (as I believe) to avoid the difficulties connected with the higher way; which is, to consider it admission into *the Church*—Such is the language of our Baptismal Service, which speaks of incorporation etc continually, but scarcely at all, if at all, of the covenant—though that it is also a covenant is plain from the questions to the Sponsors. When it is considered as admission into the Church, then at once the Christian is viewed as one of a *body*—but when as admission into a Covenant, this is consistent with the independence of the soul of every thing here below, rite, minister, body, teaching etc. and readily leads to the independent, calvinistic, private judgment, liberty of conscience, voluntary system, which in one shape or other is now in fashion. 2. I conceive that the Church into which the catechumen is baptized is, not the Visible, but the Invisible—'that he being delivered from Thy *wrath* may be received into the Ark of Christ's Church' 'incorporated into Thy Holy Church.' certainly is something more than the Visible Church. And surely 'Thy faithful and elect children' is synonymous with the Communion of Saints. 3. People will differ in opinion, but still, since I so think, I will say, that I conceive Confirmation is not a Sacrament as Baptism and the Lord's Supper chiefly because it is not 'generally necessary to salvation.' It may be startling to affirm but I do not think our Church claims there are more than two sacraments, but only two *such as* Baptism and the Lord's Supper, only two necessary to Salvation. In the Catechism it gives a definition of a Sacrament which applies to (e.g.) Orders—'I mean an outward etc—' And to the former question it merely answers 'Two only as *generally necessary* etc—' In the Articles it says there are but two sacraments *of the Gospel*—and says that the 5 Roman Sacraments in addition are, as they exist in Rome, corruptions etc. but any how have not *like* nature of Sacraments with Baptism and Lord's Supper and then gives an additional reason that their outward Sign is not given by God. On the other hand the Homilies in one place speak of the Sacrament of Matrimony, and in another speak of *other* Sacraments or in some such way.—And now you have all my criticisms. I shall be much pleased to find you publish.

The extracts of letters you send me are very interesting, and thank you

[1] Thomas Henderson, *The Catechist; or, the Church Catechism explained*, Colchester n.d Second edition, London 1840.

for the sight. I would do any thing I could—I have always given men who were 'perplexed' the very same advice which you have, viz to keep to their Prayer Book—both as being put into their hands by God's Providence and as being allowed on all hands (except indeed by far gone Evangelicals as they are called) to be the substance of the Apostolical Tradition—I willingly talk to young men on Church subjects and often check talking. But the truth is, they are most elevating and striking and therefore from their novelty most exciting subjects—*I* did not make these truths—and they will excite when preached just in proportion to the degree in which they have beforehand been neglected. I think I should have advised your friends certainly not to have attended my Lectures—I never have tried to proselyte—but when persons *are* perplexed and come to me for information, then I am induced to write Lectures to meet that existing perplexity. I will say too that those Summer Lectures (which by the bye are going on *now*, out of Terms,) are the only compositions in Church in which I have had any regard to any but my own Parishioners—My Sermons are the same in Vacation as Term Time—and even as to the Summer Lectures in question, I am continually asking such of my Parishioners as attend if they understand them, and not unfrequently am asked for them by them to read and lend afterwards. It is within this week that a woman in the very lowest rank spoke to me about a Sermon of mine 3 years since on Antichrist, as having instructed her. I certainly do write for my own people—but University men attend—I cannot say I am sorry—but I would do any thing I could to keep them from being excited

Yrs most truly J H Newman

TO J. B. MOZLEY

Oriel College. Aug 2. 1838

My dear James,

I do not at once send the books, as I suspect, much as I should like it, the two works will not coalesce. I wish you would get up Sir F. P. and see, if you have any view about it or if you *think* he will coalesce with Tyler.[1] If so I would send him and a volume of Collier for the general history, if you wanted him. Write again to me at once, if you see your way enough *really* to want him.

Rivington has declined Froude's new volumes[2]—I shall write to Keble and to W. F. to see what they wish. It seems to *me* best you should get the Becket off your hands at once, and I should like you when you leave Cholderdon to come here, and superintend the printing at once. But you shall hear again from me.

You see Lord Morpeth has been upon me in the House as Editor of the

[1] J. B. Mozley reviewed Sir Francis Palgrave's *Truths and Fictions of the Middle Ages. The Merchant and the Friar*, London 1837, in *Brit. Crit.*, 24, 1838 (Oct.), 372–99. He wrote a separate article on 'Tyler's Memoirs of Henry V', *Brit. Crit.*, 25, 1839 (Jan.), 96–124.
[2] The second two volume part of the *Remains*.

Remains.[1] Gladstone has defended me—Sir R. Inglis the University—O'Connell has patronized the Tracts. The Bishop of Oxford is delivering a charge in our favor. Archdeacon Browne of Ely against us. The Bishop of Exeter has been making a remarkable speech in the House, saying that, though their Lordships etc. passed a certain Bill, *he would not obey it*—and they might eject him first. The Archbishop very much excited on the other side. Rogers is to be in Derby in about 10 days time. I heartily wish Tom may make a Book of his Sermon—encourage him in it—I will when I write. Mr Le Bas has been paying me a visit. He went today. [Charles] Marriott is negociating with a view of going to Chichester.[2] Faussett's and my Pamphlets have come to a second edition. I have sold *in the same time* 750 to his 500. Who would have thought persons would buy an *answer* without the *question*. He is very angry in Preface to his second Edition talks of my 'flippant suggestion'[3] etc etc I have answered his Preface in a few notes.—Rogers reports an amusing saying of a Lady whom he knows about my Letter—'Now Dr F. will be quite pleased and convinced by this, and obliged to Mr N. if he is a nice kind of man.' As to your preaching distinctly, the art consists in not *dropping your words*—which is very difficult. I have not attained to it from want of strength. You must not glibly run over bits of sentences but enunciate and enucleate every word. The want of this is what the Provost found fault with so malignantly. Vaughan Thomas is very angry with Faussett

I have not time to read this over

Ever yrs affly John H Newman

P.S. The Puseys about the same. I have had in Town a very nice present of books from some one.

You must not speak against Dodsworth

[1] In the debate of 30 July on the Maynooth Grant, Lord Morpeth asked the Commons, 'Could they now be so ungracious as to refuse 8,900*l.* for the education of their Roman Catholic brethren? If they were to be always talking of the objectionable doctrines taught at Maynooth, they must not be surprised if they sometimes heard of the not very satisfactory doctrines which had recently become fashionable at Oxford. A book had been published lately, which certainly would be likely to make disciples of a new school, and which he was given to understand proceeded from that university. It was a work called "The Remains of the Reverend R. H. Froude," and was published, he believed, by Mr. Newman, who was the principal of one of the colleges in Oxford.' He went on to quote some passages from the *Remains*, and 'therefore called upon hon. Gentleman to look at home before they threw their missiles of invective abroad in future'.

Gladstone replied that he 'had never heard a speech more cruelly unjust than that made by the noble Lord. Even if Roman Catholic principles were inculcated in the University of Oxford, that fact had properly no relation to the question; but he had no hesitation in characterizing the assertion as a mere vulgar calumny. If the noble Lord would read the preface of the book he had quoted, he would find that the editor expressly guarded himself against being supposed to entertain the opinions of the author, and stated, that he gave it to the world as the singular production of a remarkable mind.' *Hansard* XLIV, 817–9.

[2] As principal of the new theological college.

[3] Newman had suggested that the Babylon of the Apocalypse might just as well be applied to London as to Rome. Faussett called this 'Mr. Newman's flippant suggestion', *The Revival of Popery*, second edition, p. viii. Newman appended a note to the second edition of his *Letter* to explain that he had not been jesting but 'that London has, at this moment, many of the tokens of the Apocalyptic Babylon', p. 40.

FRIDAY 3 AUGUST 1838   letter from B   walked to Littlemore—read   f d   wrote to K and to Mr Plunkett

TO JOHN KEBLE

Oriel. ⌐Aug 3. 1838¬

My dear Keble

⌐Rivington has declined publishing any more of the Remains—i.e. volumes 3 and 4.¬ His reason is, it has not sold so well as he expected.[1] It came out in March—i.e. 5 months since—360 copies are sold. This, considering it consists of 2 volumes, seems to me very good and promising—that is, for the sale of volumes 3 and 4, if they are to be undertaken.

⌐Archdeacon F. [[Froude]] offered to print the first two,¬ and would have, had I not managed to get Rivington to print them. ⌐There will be no difficulty then on that score. Also, I shall write at once to William to ask his and his Father's wishes about publishing at once—but let me have your thoughts.

I am for it,¬ but have no strong wishes. James Mozley has got it all ready. It will be an advantage to have it pass through the press *while* it is fresh in his mind—and a good thing for him to discharge his mind of it, and turn to other things.

The Volumes will contain the Becket, and the Essays—the Becket being the chief part of them. It struck me that if the title ran 'Times (etc) of Thomas B. Archbishop of C. (or the like) by the late Revd R H F' we should avoid clashing with the former title or seeming advertising the same work, while we gave a more attractive title. But this is a matter of detail.

I hope your journey into Devonshire has been all you wished it to be, and that Mrs K's health has been benefitted by it. ⌐I hear the Bishop of O [[Oxford]] is delivering a charge in favor of our proceedings.¬ He has not yet come to us. ⌐Archdeacon Browne of Ely is publishing something against us.¬ You see what Lord Morpeth has been saying in the House. ⌐O'Connell, I am sorry to hear, has in the same worthy company been patronizing the Tracts¬—Faussett has got angry in his second edition. T. Mozley talks of publishing his Sermon as a book on the Poor Laws. Mr ⌐Le Bas has been stopping with me a day or two—and been very easy and unaffected.¬ The news from the Puseys does not say much—they seem neither better nor worse. ⌐Bowden is in the North¬—but his plans for establishing an Apostolical fort at Roehampton have hitherto answered very well. I am by myself here absolutely.

Ever Yrs affly John H Newman

[1] John Keble replied on 7 Aug. that the sale of the first two volumes of Froude's *Remains* had been less than he had expected; 'But I am nevertheless for publishing the remainder with all speed.' He added that Archdeacon Froude did not mind what had been written about the work; his sister, Miss Froude, spoke of it 'as if it was the greatest comfort to them'. On the other hand, '[Charles] Miller has taken regular fright and declines having any thing to do with us at present; [George] Moberly likewise disappoints us', having given up translating St Ambrose in favour of editing Bishop Cosin: 'I suppose he thinks it would hardly suit his present position to embark so openly (so people might represent it) in our boat.' George Cornish and his neighbours did not pretend to approve of the *Remains*, but they had not been set back by it, and were 'on their way to good principles'.

SATURDAY 4 AUGUST 1838   letters from Christie and W F.   walked to Littlemore and read   dined by myself in Common Room

SUNDAY 5 AUGUST 8th Trinity   did duty morning and afternoon   preached Number 402[1]   by myself at Communion   Bloxam, Berkeley, and 2 Morrises to dinner   wrote to Christie and T. Keble

TO J. F. CHRISTIE

Oriel. Aug 5/38

My dear Christie,

I write on this paper, for the want of any other. You do not say what your anxiety is, I am truly sorry for it. I had not heard that T.M. came round by you.

You are hard on me about the passage in my Letter to F. [Faussett][2]. Why not say at once that T.K. [Keble] thought the Pope Antichrist, and then leave it to my common sense to be sorry, if I ought to be sorry?—instead of making a parode from my Letter, and quoting me as an argumentum ad hominem against myself, and filling up two pages of your letter? If it had been any one but you, I should have called this pomp, that is, a little.

I did not know that T.K. considered that the communion of Rome was the Babylon of the Revelations. And I do not believe he does. I do not believe any one does (to speak generally) who holds the Apostolical Succession. I do not believe you do. I do not believe you hold that Cardinal Fisher was in communion with the Mother of harlots and the habitation of every unclean and hateful bird.

But if he was in your opinion, then I must say with St Paul 'Are not they who eat the sacrifices partakers of the Altar?' I must hold it is impossible that our orders can be other than the orders of the Mother of Abominations. I believe it has always been held in the Church that there are heresies which annul orders—and if so, what heresy can be so bad as that of the seat of Antichrist?

However, as to the practical point of my withdrawing what I have said —first the second edition has been out this week past. Next, though I might

---

[1] *P.S.* IV, 6, 'The Individuality of the Soul'.

[2] Newman had written in his *Letter to Faussett*: 'Another question on which we may be fairly indulged in a liberty of opinion is, whether or not the Church of Rome is "the mother of harlots," and the Pope St. Paul's "man of sin." . . . How those divines who hold the Apostolical Succession can maintain the affirmative, passes my comprehension; for in holding the one and other point at once, they are in fact proclaiming to the world that they come from "the synagogue of Satan," and (if I may so speak) have the devil's orders.' p. 31.

Christie wrote on 2 Aug., 'If I hold the Apostolical Succession—I believe that my orders came from Christ and his Apostles in a direct line—and—that for a time they underwent pollution as it were in the Church of Rome, does not affect their present authority. You would not deny that a wicked bishop is in some sense Antichrist but you would not therefore call his orders the devil's orders—and I see no inconsistency in holding that the Church of Rome was in certain respects AntiChrist and yet not in all—and not in those affecting our descent from her.' He hoped that Newman would make alterations in a second edition out of deference to those who differed from him and to whom Christie thought he had been hard and inconsiderate. He named T. Keble as an example.

forbear to say what I thought true from proper deference to others (which I would have done in this case), I do not see how I could *withdraw* it, without implying I had changed my mind. However, I shall write to T.K. and am much obliged to you.[1]

Do you know there is a chance of Marriott leaving Oxford for a year or so? You see Lord Morpeth has taken to task Froude and me. The B.C. was pretty well for a first Number—not so well as I hope hereafter. I have had a present made me of an Autograph letter of Bishop Butler's dated Oriel . . . Copeland is with Bishop Lowe[2] on his Visitation—but has left no direction behind him. I am solus here. Rogers comes up on the 25th *Do come up for a day.*

Ever Yrs affly John H Newman

MONDAY 6 AUGUST 1838 Transfiguration proof from Pusey walked with Ogle dined with Hamilton at Merton sent proof to Pusey

TUESDAY 7 AUGUST Nomen Jesu letter from Mr Le Bas called on President [of] Magdalen and Mrs Kidd. expected Westmacott but he did not come dined by myself in Common Room service in Ad de Br's Chapel—read Number 515—last Lecture and Service sent proof of Preface to Breviary Hymns to Rogers at Derby

WEDNESDAY 8 AUGUST letters from Keble and Marriott dined by myself in Common Room sent proof of Cyril to Church

THURSDAY 9 AUGUST Dr Potter (Bishop of Massachusetts Sect, or coadjutor) called on me. dined by myself in Common Room

TO JOHN KEBLE

[August 1838]

My dear Keble,

I was stupid not to send you the inclosed book in my last letter, or the letter in a parcel—one of the two. H. Cornish left it with me some ten days since. *He* had heard the Bishop's charge, and reported that it was the best expressed thing on the subject, according to his views, he had met with, he could not wish, (to his feelings,) a word altered. It said, it did not fear about the Masters, but had some apprehension of the disciples. Of course any caution the Bishop gives about people going too far, is the kindest office he can do us; for, I suppose, we are all anxious lest persons should not *reason on* with us, but deviate off the high road. The weight of authority then just does what is wanted. I rejoice to hear from Pusey that the Psalms are progressing

[1] T. Keble wrote on 24 Aug. that he found Newman's manner of expressing himself on the subject too rhetorical, and, that even if belief in the Apostolical Succession and in Rome as Antichrist were not reconcilable, 'yet neither possibly may be altogether incorrect, as is allowed to be the case (is it not?) in the high points of free-will etc.' See letters of 28 Aug. and 21 Nov. to J. Keble.
[2] David Low of the Scottish Episcopal Church.

so well. When I see them dedicated to the Bishop, it will be a very pleasant day.[1]

Thank you for your very nice account of your Devonshire visit—Your account too of Mrs Keble's improvement is very pleasant;—and of Archdeacon F [Froude] being so well and hearty. That article in the E R is not by Merivale.[2] It could not be—He knew Hurrell—but by a Mr Empson, I believe, a friend of Spring Rice's, a professor at the East India College, and a great liberal though very amiable man.

W. Froude was coming here last week, but hindered—I hope to see him in the course of the Vacation. I shall write to him at once about the printing —telling him particulars of expence as far as I can.

Copeland has not yet returned from his rambles. He got me in to a sad scrape by his hit at the B.M. [British Magazine] for which I was truly sorry.[3] And the wretch has run off without giving his direction, so I cannot pursue him with my vituperations. Your news about [C.] Miller is bad.[4] I wish I may come down to you for a day some time. I should like it but can't say. The loss of two days on the road is the evil

Ever Yrs affly J H Newman

TO H. E. MANNING

Oriel. August 9. 1838

My dear Manning

I am much concerned to hear of your late indisposition. It has not arisen, I trust, from your neglecting yourself? Do get well, and in a little while let me hear from you, if you have five minutes, how you are.

I like your Sermon and thank you for the sight.[5] The part about the Creeds p 33 seems to me particularly useful. It was much wanted   Are you quite safe in the Note on p 28? If the Canon of Scripture was formed in the second century, how could the Roman Church doubt of the Epistle to the Hebrews up to Jerome's time—and the Greeks of the 10th century keep a most pregnant silence as regards the Apocalypse? Is not some word wanting p 51, note, to show that the passage in B [Blanco] White's note *is* a quotation and not his? His own remark that follows, telling us so, comes somewhat abrupt.

I am not quite certain that I enter into your third head p 36. Is it that the

---

[1] Keble was working on his metrical version of *The Psalter, or Psalms of David*, London 1839. The volume was published anonymously and dedicated to the Bishop of Oxford.
[2] 'The Lives of Whitfield and Froude—Oxford Catholicism', *Edinburgh Review*, 67, 1838 (July), 500–35. The article was by James Stephen. See note to diary at 17th July.
[3] See letter of 28 June to H. J. Rose.
[4] See note to letter of 3 Aug. to Keble.
[5] *The Rule of Faith . . .*, London 1838. The sermon was preached on 13 June in Chichester Cathedral, at the Episcopal Visitation. A 136 page Appendix was published separately later in the year.

doctrine of original sin is important but not fundamental? this seems a delicate thing to say? unless you explain what you mean by fundamental. If it ['fundamental'] means that confession *on which* a man is admitted into the Church,' and 'important' that confession 'which he must add *when in*, else he will be put out again,' I suppose it is safe. But then comes the difficulty, *why* may not these be made fundamental, if heresy requires it? and if so, *how many* of these are, and where do you draw the line against the Romanist? I almost like rather to bring in original sin under Baptism, and the Eucharist under the Incarnation.

I see you have adopted the old style—it takes off somewhat from perspicuity, though it is fuller

Ever Yrs affly John H Newman

P.S. Remember me very kindly to Harrison.

FRIDAY 10 AUGUST 1838   St Laurence   proof of Cyril from Church   f d   walked to Littlemore and read.   letter etc from Pusey   wrote to W F. [,] J M and Smith the Silversmith

TO J. B. MOZLEY

Oriel. August 10. 1838

My dear James,

I hope you are not over solitary at Cholderton. I have little to say, but I write lest you should be, to provoke an answer. A letter just now came to me from Pusey.—I grieve to say Mrs P. is not so well, and has been confined to her bed for a day or so; but do not say this, for people exaggerate things, when they hear them.

I have looked into Tyler—don't tell, but it is tylerissimum. If you *could* combine it with Sir F. P., I should be glad, to save me the trouble.[1] You would have much to say in its praise, 'research etc' and one or two good bits might be taken. Let me know how Sir F. P. gets on—In what you write, do not be too essayish; i.e. do not begin 'Of all the virtues which adorn the human breast etc'—be somewhat conversational and take a jump into your subject. But, on the other hand, avoid abruptness, or pertness. *Be easy*—and take the mean—and now you have full directions how to write.

A ragged paper came to me this morning, with great portions cut out—parts however remained, else it could not have some. I will extract for your edification a sentence or two—'The Debate was rendered remarkable for bringing before the notice of the country, through Lord Morpeth, a sect of damnable and detestable heretics, of late sprung up at Oxford,—a sect which evidently affects Popery and merits the heartiest condemnation of all

[1] See first note to letter of 2 Aug. to Mozley.

true Christians. We have paid a good deal of attention to these gentry, and by the grace of God we shall show them up, and demonstrate that they are a people to be abhorred of all faithful men. We do not hesitate to say that they are criminally heterodox' etc etc that they are *what?*—Do you know that Lord M. went out of his way to bring in my name?[1] The paper in question is the Dublin Record.

Bliss, in the Oxford Herald has called us all, Froude inclusive, 'amiable and fanciful men'—The Bishop delivers his charge next Tuesday. Frazer's Magazine, I am told, has opened on us.[2] We must expect a volley from the whole Conservative Press. I can fancy the Old Duke sending down to ask the Heads of Houses whether we cannot be silenced.

Rivington declines printing any more of the Remains—saying they do not sell well enough. Keble advises the publication at once, and I am writing to W. Froude on the subject. So you must prepare to come up here for the rest of the Vacation, and superintend the business. Rogers comes here on the 25th. He is now at Derby.

I have sent my Sermons on Antichrist to the Press as a Tract, to commence Volume 5 with.[3] I have finished my Lectures in Adam de B's Chapel; and am looking out Sermons for my New Volume. Jacobson's volumes are come out.[4] I am most happily quite solus—you cannot think what a relief it is

Ever yrs affly John H Newman

SATURDAY 11 AUGUST 1838   M R G and her sister passed through Oxford—   dined by myself in Common Room

SUNDAY 12 AUGUST   9th Trinity   early Sacrament by myself.   did duty morning and afternoon   preached Number 475[5]

MONDAY 13 AUGUST[6]   wrote to Anderdon

---

[1] See second note to letter of 2 Aug.
[2] 'Treason within the Church', *Fraser's Magazine*, 1838 (Aug.), 187–95. The extremely hostile reviewer thought that the Tractarians were '. . . doing the work of the apostate church, and of her most subtle missionaries, the followers of Ignatius Loyola . . . as a settled plan and design, they aim at some great change and alteration in the church.' A letter of reply, together with an editorial rejoinder, was published in December, and a third installment included in March 1839.
[3] *Tract* 83, 'Advent Sermons on Antichrist'; *D.A.*, pp. 44–108.
[4] W. Jacobson's Latin edition of *Patres Apostolici*, two volumes, Oxford 1838.
[5] *P.S.* IV, 7, 'Chastisement amid Mercy'.
[6] Pusey wrote to B. Harrison on this day: 'For myself, I am very glad of the publication of the "Remains"; they may very likely be a check: but that in itself may be the very best thing for us, and prevent a too rapid and weakening growth: it may cast people back upon themselves, and make them think more deeply of the principle, which they had half taken up; his careful self-discipline is, of course, calculated in this self-indulgent age, to do much immediate good, as will his protest against change both upon his own friends and others: and his views will get sifted ut alteri prosuit saeculo.' (Pusey House Mss)

TO E. B. PUSEY

Oriel College. Aug 13/38

My dear Pusey,

I am concerned you do not give an improved account of Mrs Pusey. Are you quite sure that the South might not be expedient for her? If you went to Malta, you could have all your books with you—a steamer carries any quantity of luggage. In the winter you would have hardly any fellow passengers to incommode you—and would hardly lose a day's work. When there, you would be settled quite as much as in England. You would find probably Rose there—and you might instil good principles into Queen Adelaide, who deserves them. I am quite sure that in point of usefulness, you would lose no time at all. They have a superb library attached to St John's Church—and I doubt not the MSS are well worth inspecting. They come from Vienne.

As to the Preface, I think it very likely to be useful, and I hope you will finish it and send it at once to press.[1] I think I would have it as a Preface to *the Confessions*, though on a more general subject, because (I feel) we shall have occasion for many such, pro re natâ—and shall be doing more good, and make a greater impression, by a repetition of the same thing in different lights and by different hands, than by one treatise. A perfect discussion would be too long, and require a greater knowledge of the objections to be made than we can have at present, at least this is what I throw out.

Shuttleworth has just brought out his attack on Tradition in a 3/6 duodecimo.[2] Is it or not worth while to have an Article on it and other works in the B. C.? It contains the usual τόποι. I do not suppose it will sell. Or should it be a preface to Cyril?

As to the Manchester plan,[3] I am suspicious of *endowments*. Somehow, in this day, I do think we ought to live for the day—and rather generate an ἦθος than a system. £1000 can be spent more to advantage as ready money.

[1] The first 19 pages of Pusey's preface to his translation of St Augustine's *Confessions* took the nature of a general preface to the Library of the Fathers. He wrote on 9 Aug., 'It was written, on the Abps plan of having a sensible preface, as to the value of the Fathers as living in earlier times, and being witnesses etc.; and some to satisfy fear and stop excitement.'

[2] P. N. Shuttleworth, *Not Tradition but Revelation*, London 1838. See first note to letter of 26 July to I. Williams.

[3] Pusey wrote on 9 Aug., 'Robert Williams called here. I talked with him about the Colleges for manufacturing towns; I have opportunely enough received a book from Mr. Parkinson at Manchester, which makes an opening there. The more I think of Froude's plan, the more it seems to me the only one, if any thing is to be done for our large towns. I had come to the same conclusion for missionaries, that they ought not to be married men. As he says, the exhibition of the domestic graces, is not enough to make an impression upon persons in such a state.

Now perhaps it might make least splash if it were connected somehow with the existing College at Manchester, and it would be a good hint to the Bp of London to begin endowing Colleges, while he is proposing to pull them to pieces. It might show what might be made of St Paul's. What I should like then would be a place for (ultimately) 12 Fellows, but beginning with not less than 2, with an endowment of £1000 for each, which would give a permanency to the plan, and so enable one to make rules for them. The Bp might be visitor, which would place it under proper sanction; and they might be self-elective, like other colleges, so that there would be no difficulty about patronage.' See Liddon's *Pusey* II, 36–40.

Combe does not come till October. Copeland has not yet returned from the North. H. Cornish has done ½ his Chrysostom and I have sent it to Keble. H Wilberforce, I believe, has the plan of Littlemore, but I will enquire.

It is not for want of thought, but I *cannot* think of a Frontpiece.[1] I can think of nothing better than a Dove over a Cross—which is too vague, and too bold.

Ever Yrs affly J H Newman

TO H. A. WOODGATE

Oriel College. Aug 13. 1838

My dear Woodgate,

As I do not know, nor can learn, your direction in full, I do not put this into the box, but send it separate, that you may know that a little deal box will come to you by coach with the imperfect direction contained on this. It contains a small sacrament case, so small that I am ashamed of the poorness of the present. I can only say that when in London I rejected what was shown me, as being not good enough, though they said it was the usual fashion, and this is made on purpose as an improvement. You must not be angry with me for this earnestness about it. The truth is this, that the subject of our never having in any way shown our sense of your kindness really was on my Mother's mind—it was much her wish to show it in some way or other, and my sister's too, that I am only fulfilling what is almost as strict as a bequest. And you must take it as if from her.

I am vexed your Sermons[2] are not out. Shuttleworth has already answered them, with an express allusion to them, in a little work on Tradition just out.[3] I should like to have reviewed them in the B.C. and have anticipated objections. As it is they will come out *under* a volley, which is like setting off on a journey in the rain. Do, my dear fellow, set to work at once, and bring them out in no time—write at once to the University Press on the subject. And do, please, ask Mrs Woodgate with my best and kindest regards to make you set to work, and despatch a Lecture a week—this is easy work indeed —you might easily have them out by October.

The Bishop delivers his charge here tomorrow—in which he speaks favorably, I am told, of the Tracts for the Times. As I know you like frankness and modesty, I will quote you a passage from the Dublin Record[4] which has been sent me by some one.

---

[1] For the Library of the Fathers. The emblem finally chosen was 'St. John the Baptist seated on a rock in the wilderness, and pointing with his left hand to heaven, while his right holds a rude cross, with a pendant scroll inscribed "Vox clamantis in deserto." ' See Liddon's *Pusey* II, 442–4.

[2] His Bampton Lectures on *The Authoritative Teaching of the Church . . .*, Oxford 1839.

[3] P. N. Shuttleworth, *Not Tradition, but Revelation*, London 1838, p. 70, alludes to Woodgate's Lectures.

[4] For 4 Aug.

'The debate was rendered remarkable for bringing before the notice of the country, through Lord Morpeth, a sect of damnable and detestable heretics, of late sprung up in Oxford—a sect which evidently affects Popery and merits the heartiest condemnation of all true Christians. We have paid a good deal of attention to these gentry, and by the grace of God we shall show them up, and demonstrate that they are people to be abhorred of all faithful men. We do not hesitate to say that they are criminally heterodox; but wherefore should Lord Morpeth act so unworthily as to build an argument upon the eccentricities of the Puseyites? etc etc.'

Ever Yrs John H Newman

TUESDAY 14 AUGUST 1838 sent parcel to Woodgate with Sacrament instruments Bliss's relation called on me wrote to Pusey in parcel Service at 11 when the Bishop's Charge Parker of Bicester preached Visitation Sermon news of Rector of Ex's [Exeter][1] death just about now. dined at the Visitation dinner wrote to Keble walked with Berkeley in evening

BISHOP OF OXFORD'S CHARGE

[14 August 1838]

. . . .

2. I have spoken of increased exertions among us, and of an increasing sense of our Christian responsibilities; and therefore you will probably expect that I should say something of that peculiar development of religious feeling in one part of the Diocese, of which so much has been said, and which has been *supposed* to *tend* immediately to a Revival of several of the Errors of Romanism. In point of fact, I have been continually (though anonymously) appealed to in my official capacity to check breaches both of doctrine and discipline, through the growth of Popery among us.

Now, as regards the latter point, breaches of discipline namely, on points connected with the public services of the Church, I really am unable, after diligent inquiry, to find any thing which can be so interpreted. I am given to understand, that an injudicious attempt was made in one instance, to adopt some forgotten portion of the ancient Clerical dress; but I believe it was speedily abandoned, and do not think it likely we shall hear of a repetition of this, or similar indiscretions. At the same time, so much of what has been objected to, has arisen from minute attention to the Rubric; and I esteem uniformity so highly, (and uniformity can never be obtained without strict attention to the Rubric,) that I confess I would rather follow an antiquated custom (even were it so designated) *with* the Rubric, than be entangled with the modern confusions which ensue from the neglect of it.

With reference to errors *in doctrine*, which have been imputed to the series of publications called the *Tracts for the Times*, it can hardly be expected that, on an occasion like the present, I should enter, or give a handle to any thing, which might hereafter tend to controversial discussion. Into controversy I will not enter, But, generally speaking, I may say, that in these days of lax and spurious liberality, any thing which tends to recall forgotten truths, is *valuable*: and where these publications have directed men's minds to such important subjects as the union, the discipline, and the authority of the Church, I think they have done good service: but there may be some points in which, perhaps, from ambiguity of expression, or similar causes, it is not impossible, but that evil rather than the intended good, may be produced on minds of a peculiar temperament. I have more fear of the Disciples than

[1] John Collier Jones died on 7 Aug.

of the Teachers. In speaking therefore of the Authors of the Tracts in question, I would say, that I think their desire to restore the ancient discipline of the Church most praiseworthy; I rejoice in their attempts to secure a stricter attention to the Rubrical directions in the Book of Common Prayer; and I heartily approve the spirit which would restore a due observance of the Fasts and Festivals of the Church: *but* I would implore them, by the purity of their intentions, to be cautious, both in their writings and actions, to take heed lest their good be evil spoken of; lest in their exertions to re-establish unity, they unhappily create fresh schism; lest in their admiration of antiquity, they revert to practices which heretofore have ended in superstition.[1]

TO JOHN KEBLE (I)

Oriel. ⌐Aug 14/38¬

My dear Keble,

I write to you partly for instruction, and partly as a relief—⌐I am just come away from hearing the Bishop's charge—and certainly I am disappointed in the part in which he alluded to us. He said he must allude to a remarkable development both in matters of discipline and doctrine in one part of his Diocese—that he had had many anonymous letters, charging us with Romanism—that he had made inquiries;—that as far as discipline went,¬ (by which he meant *acts* as opposed to *writings*) ⌐he found nothing to find fault with—one addition of a clerical vestment there had been, but that had been discontinued—(alluding to Seager;¬[2] though many persons, I doubt not, thought it meant me,) ⌐but this he would say that in the *choice* of alternatives, he had rather go back to what was obsolete in order to enforce the Rubric, than break it in order to follow the motley fashions now prevailing. Next as to doctrine (i.e. writings) he had found many most excellent things in the Tracts for the Times (this was the only book he referred to) and most opportune and serviceable—but for other words and expressions he was sorry, as likely to lead *others* into error—he feared more for the disciples than the Masters, and he conjured those who were concerned in them to beware lest etc etc.

Now does it not seem rather hard that he should publickly attack things in the Tracts without speaking to me about them privately¬ and hearing what had to be said for them? I suppose it is such expressions as 'making the Bread etc.'[3]—else, I know not what it *can* be—⌐What good then does it do to fling an indefinite suspicion over them, when the things alluded to may be orthodox?¬[4] Perhaps I may recollect in time, but I literally do not know

---

[1] For the bishop's footnote to this passage in the charge as published, see note to letter of 21 Aug. to him.

[2] Charles Seager had worn a cross on his stole for a time.

[3] The first edition of Newman's *Tract* 10 contained the words, '. . . as intrusted with the awful and mysterious gift of making the bread and wine Christ's Body and Blood', which some had read as equivalent to transubstantiation. In later editions the words were softened to 'the awful and mysterious privilege of dispensing Christ's Body and Blood'.

[4] [[when (in the main) they be orthodox?]]

what he alludes to. ⌐Then again, it seems hard that those who work and who *therefore*, as men, *must* mistake, should not have those mistakes put to the score of their workings, and be thanked for that work which others do not. It is very comfortable to do nothing and criticize.⌐ It is easy to sit as many a clergyman does and shake his head and find fault—and I suppose it is wise. However, one has nothing to do with this.

What I write to you about is for advice—The Bishop means every thing that is kind, and I dare say I am making too much of it—And this is the point I am coming to.

My first impression was to take it seriously, and to write to the Arch-deacon if he would wish the Tracts stopped—for if so, they should be. Then I thought, that I should be writing something else; so that that would do no good; and I did not see my way to promise to write nothing, at a time when the Faith is in jeopardy; though I confess nothing would be more pleasant to my feelings if it was right to do it, than to retire into myself and to set about reading without writing. I have long wished it. Then I thought whether I should ask him what the things were he objected to in the Tracts—but my difficulty there was, what if it was the phrase I have above alluded to—*could* I, salvâ integritate fidei, withdraw it—and if I could not, should I not have made matters worse? then again supposing it was Pusey's remarks about exorcism, or penance etc? or supposing he were to turn round and say, 'Well then, discontinue turning to the East' etc etc?—or 'do not publish more of the remains'? and moreover might I not oblige him against his will to say more and command more than he intended, *in order* to give his words a definite and consistent meaning?

I am led then secondly to treat the matter *not* seriously—to consider that the Bishop having several times done Pusey marked favours, ordaining James Mozley etc and letting me dedicate my book to him, has been *forced* to say something, conniving at us all the while—and that it is unkind and unwise to make him commit himself to a meaning—that all I have to do therefore is to go on just as usual—and to take it as one of those rebukes one reads of in history, which are like a smack in the face and nothing more. Other persons probably would be disappointed the other way. If Cornish thought it for us, how much more open enemies? (At the same time, I saw by their faces our men were disappointed.) The Bishop having given us a hit, now the debt is on his side—and on the strength of it he may be kind to us again.

These are the thoughts which have passed through my mind—I dare say I shall be well tomorrow—but it is disheartening to be snubbed, while persons who do nothing, may look wise and say 'Yes, that's it—you go *too far*—the Bishop has just hit the thing—we approve of a great deal etc—' without being able to point out what they *mean*, or knowing more how to go *any* 'far,' 'too' or not, than to command a squadron of horse.

Ever Yrs affly John H Newman

P.S. A stranger has made me a present of an autograph letter of Butler to Clarke dated Oriel

TO JOHN KEBLE (II)

⌜Aug 14/38⌝

My dear Keble

⌜You will perhaps think me fidgetty not to wait for your answer to my letter of today, but as despatch will be requisite if I adopt the following plan, I write at once by coach.

If seems to me that my course is to send the Archdeacon [[Clerke]] a short note to the following effect—that I was glad to find he approved of some things in the Tracts [;] I am sorry to hear for the first time that the Bishop thinks some parts of the Tracts for the Times of unsafe tendency— that I do not ask which parts he means, because in his Charge he pointedly declined any thing like controversy to which such a question might lead— that he gave his opinion as a judgment and as such I take it—that under such circumstances it would be very inconsistent in me to continue the publication of these Volumes with this general suspicion thrown over them by my Bishop—accordingly I now wrote to say that if he would specify any Tracts which he wished withdrawn from publication, nay if he said all of them, I would do so forthwith—that I should not like to suppress *parts* of Tracts, that might be unfair to the writers—however, that I must except numbers 67 and following and number 82 [81] (they are Pusey's) over which I had no control. Also, that there were a few others which⌝ were published in another shape, and so far ⌜were not my property—but which should not be published in the Tracts,⌝ if they were in the number of those objected to.'

⌜By doing this I think I set myself right [[with him]]. I really cannot go on publishing with this censure against them.⌝ I do not think the pecuniary loss will be great, ⟨(could we not ship them off to America?)⟩ except in the Tract on the Breviary which I fear would be one of those selected. ⌜And if he ordered some to be suppressed, the *example and precedent* I am sure would be worth ten times the value of the Tracts [[suppressed.]]⌝ likely to be selected. ⌜Unless you think this quixotic, I am disposed very much to do it⌝

Ever Yrs affly John H Newman

⌜P.S. Since writing this the idea so grows on me of the absolute impossibility of going on with the Tracts with the Bishop saying parts are dangerous⌝ as received by others, ⌜that if I do *not* write thus to the Bishop, I certainly *must* cease them.⌝

P.S. I suspect it is a general impression that it is a snub.

FROM JOHN KEBLE

Hursley, Aug. 15. 1838.

My dear Newman,

Before I got your second note, I was going to write to you to say that I thought the chief thing was to ascertain if you possibly could what was the Bishop's real meaning, for I quite agree with you that it would be *impossible* to go on with this kind of indefinite censure upon the Tracts. Yet I cannot conceal it from myself that your second theory is a very probable one, viz. that the Bishop spoke in that tone without any very distinct meaning, and so far it seems a pity to make him commit himself. Therefore if any way could be found of ascertaining his exact wishes without the result aforesaid, I should think it most desirable and fair. The less official and formal in short the channel by which you communicate with him, the better, I should think, on sundry grounds. You see he will hate to be driven into responsibility, at least if he is like most of his station, and the benefit and satisfaction of obedience to a suppressing order will be sadly marred, should he feel himself baited as it were into giving that order, contrary to his better judgement. But if you could get any friend whom the Bishop would trust to get from him privately the particulars with which he is disgusted, you might defer to him and deny yourself without at all forcing him into what he is sure to find one day a false position. Very likely the Archdeacon may be such a friend as I now speak of and in that case the course you point out is a clear one. Otherwise could not Pusey do you think communicate with his Lordship confidentially? always provided that you do not think it proper yourself to seek an interview with him: against which indeed I can imagine sundry very good reasons. Such a course will I think be attended with this very great benefit; that it must convince him you *bona fide* mean obedience, (which any kind of official application would not so certainly mean: it might be a sort of challenge) and I should not wonder if it set him on thinking twice on the things themselves and ended in his withdrawing his censure altogether. Anyhow I come back to what I began with: that it will be impossible to go on with an indefinite censure from one's own Bishop on the publication. Whichever way it turns out one may see advantages—if he continues silent, i.e. virtually prohibits, there is the precedent of obedience which you will set: if he relaxes, you may go on comfortably: and doubt not but a door will be opened for you in any case. At the same time I must own your complaint against those who sit still to find fault is too just. But you had counted the cost before, and knew it would be so . . .

WEDNESDAY 15 AUGUST 1838   wrote to Keble in parcel   dined at Queen's Gaudy

THURSDAY 16 AUGUST   letters from Keble, J M[,] Perceval and Eyre   went over St Peter le Bailey as Rural Dean   dined with Bloxam   wrote to Archdeacon

TO ARCHDEACON CLERKE

Oriel College, August 16. 1838.

My dear Archdeacon,

If there was any one else I could write to, I would do so; as I am unwilling that this letter should have at all a formal air, or be a call for a formal answer. I would not have written it to one like yourself officially attached to the Bishop; but I know no one else near enough to him to be of service to me; and therefore I must trouble you against my will.

In his Charge the other day he said, that there were things in the Tracts for the Times, of which I am Editor, which might do harm to certain minds.

He did not specify what things; in consequence, as you will easily perceive, a general suspicion is made to attach to them as containing something dangerous in one part or another. There is no part of the work from beginning to end which escapes such suspicion.

I do not write this on the spur of the moment, but have thought over what I am going to say. As far then as I can at present judge, I say with great sorrow that it is quite impossible for me to continue the Tracts with this indefinite censure upon them from my own Bishop. It is repugnant to my feelings, as well as to my principles, to do so. Considering what the subjects discussed in the Tracts are, I feel it to be clearly my duty to withdraw from the position in which I now find myself,—that of being the author of works which have attracted the public notice of the Bishop. As matters stand at present, I think it my duty, much against my will, to discontinue the Tracts and to withdraw, as soon as may be, the existing volumes from circulation.

I do not think that in so acting I am influenced by any undue sensitiveness; I do not rely on my own view of the case only. A Bishop's lightest word ex cathedrâ is heavy. His judgment on a book cannot be light. It is a rare occurrence.

It has struck me, (and this causes me to write to you) that there is one way in which I may escape what is very disagreeable to me. I do not ask to know any particular passage which the Bishop disapproves; because he said he did not wish to be supposed entering into the controversy, which I take to be an intimation that he wishes to avoid discussion. But if I could learn from you, as a friend, not as Archdeacon, which are the Tracts which he disapproves, (which I most honesly say that I do not know) I will at once withdraw them without a word, and shall be saved the necessity of suppressing the rest;—that is, I will withdraw any of them, except two over which I have no control, the Tract on Baptism and No. 81.

With the best expressions of my gratitude to the Bishop for the kindness he has so often shown me, not without some feeling of pain also, now expressed for the first and last time, that the first notice I should have of his dissatisfaction with any part of my writings, should be on so solemn and public an occasion,

I am, etc. J.H.N.[1]

FRIDAY 17 AUGUST 1838   letter from Le Bas   wrote to Bowden

[1] Archdeacon Clerke replied on 18 Aug. that he did not know what details of the *Tracts* the Bishop had in mind. He wrote that his 'own impression is that the Bishop does not wish the withdrawal of the tracts at all and that the misconstruction which may have been put on them or on any parts of them arises from the misconception of the reader as much as from the ambiguity of the writer, but if there be a probability that time will remove these misconceptions there will not remain sufficient reason for the step which you at present feel inclined to take.
I write what I think because I do not know more of the Bishop's wishes on this subject than yourself. He never discussed the subject of the tracts with me before he composed his charge nor has he stated to me since any particulars . . .' He advised Newman to call on the Bishop and discuss the matter.

TO J. W. BOWDEN

⌐Oriel. August 17. 1838⌐

My dear Bowden,

⌐I delayed writing⌐ in answer to your very acceptable letter, ⌐in order to give you an account of our Bishop's Charge, which an ear witness told me was favorable by name to the Tracts for the Times. He has been here, but alas! it is the other way. This is too strong a way of putting it, but my impression of it is this—he has acted towards our *objects* and at the same time given *us* more or less of a slap; which, by the bye, is what I have always predicted will be our fate. What he said was very slight indeed, but a Bishop's lightest word ex Cathedra is heavy. The whole effect too was cold towards us, in this way, 'that he had had anonymous letters saying we were going into Romanism—that he had made inquiries of our way of conducting the service etc., and had found nothing'. Thus it was negative; there was no praise. Then as to the Tracts he said that we were sincere—and that certain objects recommended in them such as keeping fasts and festivals were highly desirable, but that there were expressions in them which might be injurious to particular minds, and he conjured us not to go too far etc. Now here as far as the cause goes is abundant gain. He spoke strongly in favor of observing the Rubric, of recurring to antiquity, of Saints Days, and he by implication allowed of turning to the East, the πρόθεσις[1] etc., etc. but what has he done to us? Why we stand thus—How many times in a century is a book, and that principally the writing of a person in a Bishop's diocese, noticed in a Bishop's charge? it is not usual. Next it is said [[by him]] to contain exceptionable expressions. Is it possible that any work in the world of 4 thick volumes should not? certainly not. The *truth* then of the remark is not enough to account for what a Bishop says, unless it is *important* to say it. Nothing but important truth will enter into a Bishop's charge—and, since he has not said *what* the exceptionable things are, he has thrown a general suspicion all over the volumes.

Under these circumstances I felt that it was impossible for me to continue the Tracts—and wrote to Keble on the subject. He, without knowing my opinion took the same view, stating it very strongly; and I feel whatever difference of opinion there may be about it, *I* cannot do otherwise—it would be against my feelings. Pusey is at Weighmouth and knows nothing yet what has happened—nor does any one else; so do not talk of it to any one. Accordingly I have written to the Archdeacon, not as Archdeacon but as a friend, to say that I propose to stop the Tracts and withdraw the existing ones from circulation; that this is very unpleasant to me—that the only way I can see to hinder it, is, if I could learn privately from the Bishop any particular Tracts he disapproved which I would at once suppress, and carry on the rest. I have not had his answer.

[1] The side table for the eucharistic bread and wine.

Well, my dear B. has not this come suddenly and taken away your breath? it nearly has mine. But I do not think I can be wrong. One of our Marriotts passed through to-day. (F.M.[1] has quarrelled with Lady Ripon and left) and I was telling him what was in the Charge—and it at once struck him, before I spoke, that the Tracts must come to an end—And I think good may come out of it—it will be a considerable loss of money, I fear—and the fifth volume is almost ready for publication—(the first Tract is in the press) but I think the precedent will be very good and it [[will]] make people see we are sincere and not ambitious. I am fancying what the Bishop will answer. Unless I thought he would dread committing himself, I should fancy he would *in* his Charge, which is to be printed, insert in general terms the *kind* of fault he meant in the Tracts leaving *me* to apply it—but I doubt whether any thing so vague will save me the necessity of withdrawing them. —It was an exceedingly strong and bold charge; and if *I* suffered, the Archbishop of C. [[Canterbury]] and the rest of the Commission did not suffer less.[2]

The Rector of Exeter [[Jones]] is dead—we are very anxious about his successor—the Election is Sept. 1. I fear I shall in consequence any how lose Sewell's article.[3] I have not a single article for the B.C. nor yet had *any* time to write one. I am sure I ought not to be sorry if the Bishop lessens my work. Shuttleworth has published a little book against Tradition very superficial, retailing old objections, but specious and perhaps mischievous.

C. Marriott is going to Chichester.⌐ M. is settled I believe. ⌐Manning has been very unwell. Le Bas has been paying me a visit—⌐he too has been very unwell since ⌐he had just lost a daughter.⌐ H.W. declined that offer— it was too poor a thing.[4] Best and kindest thoughts to Mrs B. and the children —and compliments to your host's circle.

Yrs ever affectly John H. Newman.[5]

[1] Fitzherbert Adams Marriott, of Oriel, M.A. 1836.

[2] The Bishop used the Charge as an occasion to record his protest against the Ecclesiastical Commission, which he termed 'a power as irresponsible as it is gigantic'. He went on to 'disapprove the Commission, as utterly unconstitutional in its *permanency*, in the *extent* of its *powers*, and in the obstacles which it throws in the way of fair and open discussion,—in the limited selection of its Clerical members, taken from one rank of the Ministry only,—in the exclusion of four-fifths of the Bishops from all participation in the consultation on Church measures . . . and, lastly, I disapprove this Commission, as being under the controlling influence of the Government for the time being, and therefore not altogether likely to remain unbiassed by the force of political claims . . .', Richard Bagot, *A Charge delivered at . . . his Third Visitation*, Oxford 1838, pp. 7–8.

[3] William Sewell was Sub-Rector of Exeter College. His article on 'Animal Magnetism' did appear in October.

[4] See letter of 19 July to Henry Wilberforce.

[5] In a postscript, Newman copied out again the extract which he gave at the end of the letter of 13 Aug. to H. A. Woodgate.

Bowden replied, 'I cannot help expressing my feeling that the *withdrawal of the existing tracts from circulation* would . . . be a most fatal measure—Discontinuing them is another matter—but the withdrawal of a book by the author is in people's eyes equivalent to a recantation by him of the principles which it asserted.—No one would dream that you really did it in deference to episcopal authority, but all would imagine that you had seized on the excuse to call in things of which you were ashamed'. Bowden urged Newman not to act except upon a very clear directive from the Bishop as the expressions of the Charge had only been general and the Bishop probably did not attach to them 'a tythe of the weight which you do'.

TO R. W. CHURCH

Oriel ⌜Aug 17/38⌝

My dear Church,

I trust we are at last moving. I send you two—and two more are in the press.[1]

I will say two or three things which strike me, and some of them fidget me. First bear in mind, please, about the possible cancels—viz 1. the place with Veil for Seal. 2. I am not satisfied with '*tribe* of heretics' for παῖδες it is perhaps too contemptuous—'school' is meant—'heretic people' is not bad but inadmissible. 3. In one of the headings 'Manichism' stands for 'Manicheism'—will you see if there are any other instances of the same mistake? —4. I have by mistake uniformly written Mills for Milles. 5. We have got into a sad mess between Greek and Hebrew forms of proper names—Esaias, Noah, Hezekiah, Hosea, etc. I can suggest nothing, try to make things as uniform as you can in these last sheets. 6. I am much afraid we have not been *consistent* in our *mode* of *expressing* in the margin this formula—Ps 21(22)6. or Ps 22(21)6 or Ps 21.6 (22.6) or Ps 22.6. 21.6 Sept. 7. I hope our little letters for note indexes are consecutive. 8. and that the numbers for sections of Milles' edition are consecutive and continuous.

I suspect just as it is on the point of finishing I shall have to turn aside to the British Critic, and leave it all in suspence.

If possible, let me have the first sheet (K) back by the first post, i.e. to receive on Monday morning

⌜All the Exeter men are in great commotion here. Cornish is sent for from Switzerland. The Rector died of a cold. The election is on September 1.

The Bishop has been delivering a charge in which he countenances the objects and subjects of the Tracts, and snubs somewhat the Tracts themselves.

C. Marriott comes through on Saturday—it is arranged that he goes to Chichester⌝

Ever Yrs John H Newman

P.S. There is another thing on my mind. I have not read the Benedictine Admonitiones to the Separate Lectures as I ought. Will you tell me if I omit any thing.

In the two sheets I send you have only to verify marginal references and to read them through.

⌜ἐν εὐαγγελίοις I conceive to be 'in the Gospel *readings*' or 'lessons' 'in Gospel passages—'but am not sure⌝ enough to say.

---

[1] Sections of Church's translation of *The Catechetical Lectures of S. Cyril . . . of Jerusalem*, Oxford 1838, in the Library of the Fathers, Newman wrote the preface and assisted with the editing.

SATURDAY 18 AUGUST 1838   letter from Mr Goldsmid   C. Marriott came into Oxford   Bloxam dined with me   wrote to the Bishop

SUNDAY 19 AUGUST   10 Trinity   by myself early Sacrament   did duty morning and afternoon   preached Number 237[1] ⟨1 of Samuel⟩   baptized Ward's child in Afternoon Service?   Mr Garden called on me   dined at Berkeley's   wrote to the Bishop [,] H W and Goldsmid

TO RICHARD BAGOT, BISHOP OF OXFORD

Aug 19/38

My dear Lord

I wrote the other day to the Archdeacon on a subject which I think it likely he has mentioned to your Lordship. He thought it better, however, that I should at once address myself to you. In any way your Lordship thinks best either by letter or by waiting on you, I shall be much obliged by being allowed the opportunity of stating what I have already mentioned to him

I am etc.

TO HENRY WILBERFORCE

O C Aug 19. 1838

My dear H.W.

Had I a good memory, I should know as well as be conscious of a number of things I had to say—but I feel sure I shall miss half. This is to ask for the Littlemore Plans which you have kept an unreasonable time, and to the great inconvenience of many parties—so, please, send them back forthwith. Next how does the Article for the B.C. do? I have not *one* Article yet for October. If this goes on, I must give up. You have heard C. Marriott is going to be Manning's Principal at Chichester.[2] C. Greswell, I am concerned to say, has had something like an attack of brain fever; and is not yet convalescent. We are all in anxiety here about the Election at Exeter—it does not take place till Sept 1. The Fellows are all scattered—Cornish is in Switzerland. This is an anxious thing. I heard from Anderdon this morning—he had it on his conscience he had not written to you. ⌐I will tell you a secret— it is more than likely the Tracts will be suppressed. The Bishop has been delivering a very strong and good charge, but, while taking a number of good things *from the Tracts*, as *we* should say, he has given the said Tracts a leetle, a very leetle wipe.[3] He has said there are expressions in them which may be of disservice to certain minds—and by not saying what, has thrown

---

[1] *P.S.* III, 2, 'Wilfulness of Israel in Rejecting Samuel'.
[2] Charles Marriott was principal of the new Diocesan Theological College at Chichester from 1839–41. Bishop Otter had entrusted Manning with much of the planning of the College.
[3] 'blow'.

a vague suspicion over them all. Now I doubt not he thought this is a most mild course—and that it would be merely a *check* to them—and does not seem to consider that by my principles, and still more my professions, as exhibited in the said Tracts, I cannot be party to any thing which he censures ex cathedrâ ever so slightly. So I have written to demand satisfaction on these terms—if he will be kind enough to say *what* the Tracts are which he thinks exceptionable, I will withdraw them without a word—If he does not, I shall suppress the whole with as much speed as is convenient.⌐ Keep this quiet. Probably I shall not have time to write to you the sequel—but I imagine that Keble will know in 10 days time.

⌐I have been solus in College a long while. You cannot think what a lounge it is to be rid of Eden—but I fear he will be soon returning.⌐ By the bye what a state the College Tuition will be in, Copleston, Greswell, and Marriott retiring—and I hear of other retirements in project. Raro antecedentem.[1] Dear F. used always to say that he wished to see the P. [Provost] eat humble pie—The present state of things at this distance of time is owing to what then took place.

Ever Yrs affectionately John H Newman

P.S. ⌐Your Father's life is to be reviewed by Le Bas.⌐ Rivington has spoken strongly about Biography being his forte. I have not seen the Article yet, and am of course anxious about it.

MONDAY 20 AUGUST 1838 Sir W Heathcote called Mr Garden to breakfast and Marriott went out with Berkeley to dine at Carey's letter from Pusey in parcel

TUESDAY 21 AUGUST letters from Wood (inclosing £40 which I paid into J M's account at Parsons at once) and from the Bishop of O. [Oxford] Marriott went? dined with Morris at Exeter Le Bas's Article came[2] news of Harrison's being appointed at Lambeth[3] wrote to the Bishop and to Le Bas.

FROM RICHARD BAGOT, BISHOP OF OXFORD

Cuddesdon, August 20, 1838.

My Dear Sir,

I thank you for your letter this morning: the Archdeacon had shown, or rather had sent me yours to him; and I can with truth say I have been much distressed ever since—not with the tone of your letter or complaint, for that corresponds with all I have ever met with from you, and tends only to increase the respect and regard I have ever felt for you since our first acquaintance,—but my distress has been in having given pain where I so little intended to do so, and I thought such a feeling could not have been caused.

I really think you cannot have fully or accurately heard what I did say on the subject—for, be assured, had I meant in any way to *censure* I should neither have taken that line nor adopted so strong a measure without previously conferring with you.

[1] cf. Horace, *Odes*, III, 2, 31–2.
[2] 'Life of Wilberforce', *Brit. Crit.*, 24, 1838 (Oct.), 239–71.
[3] See note to diary for 22 Aug.

Having been myself repeatedly appealed to (anonymously) to check and notice what I felt sure were exaggerated or unfounded charges, and knowing how much misrepresentation was going forward on the subject, I thought (especially as I believe the subject had been touched upon by other Bishops) I could not, in the position I held as Bishop of *Oxford*, avoid alluding to it,—or, in point of fact, giving an opinion between your adherents and your adversaries. And when I approved so much, *censured* nothing, and only lamented things which from ambiguity of expression might, I feared, by others be misunderstood or misrepresented, I own—although I should not have been surprised at dissatisfaction expressed by those who differ widely from the Tracts at my *approbation of so much*—I little thought I could have given pain to the other side by the caution I gave them to avoid the possibility of misrepresentation.

I repeat, my dear Sir, my belief that you did not hear accurately what I said. Wait then, I entreat you, till my Charge is printed before you act upon any judgement you may, as I now think erroneously, have formed.

A hasty withdrawal would undo much good which has been done by those Tracts, and therefore lead to harm; nor would it be quite fair to me, as it would make me appear to have said or done that which I really have not. I can assure you I could mention names of persons whom you would respect, and who are great admirers of the authors, and approvers generally of the Tracts themselves, who have regretted to me the occasional use of expressions of being capable of misrepresentation, or of being understood by some in a way and to an extent not felt nor intended by the authors: and to this I alluded in the caution (for *caution* only it was) which I gave.

I shall be in Oxford ere long, and will call upon you, when I trust we shall meet as we ever have done, feeling sure you will not think that I ever intentionally at least gave you pain, or acted unopenly towards you.

In the meantime I shall be obliged to you to state to me by letter your impressions of what I did say,—but let me repeat my hope that you will not hastily take any steps founded on your present feeling.

Certainly no person whom *I* have met, or who heard my Charge, viewed that part of it in the light in which it appears to have struck you.

Believe me, my dear Sir, Faithfully yours,
R. Oxford.

TO RICHARD BAGOT, BISHOP OF OXFORD

Oriel College. Aug 21/38

My dear Lord,

I am very much obliged by your Lordship's kind letter, and will most certainly take the course you recommend, of waiting till the Charge is printed.[1]

It has ever been my wish to approve my words and acts to your Lordship's judgment. I know indeed that, among any persons whatever there must always be differences of view in minor matters, whether relating to points of

---

[1] In the Charge as printed, p. 21, the Bishop added this footnote to his remarks about the *Tracts*:

'As I have been led to suppose that the above passage has been misunderstood, I take this opportunity of stating, that it never was my intention therein to pass any *general censure* on the Tracts for the Times. There must always be allowable points of difference in the opinions of good men, and it is only where such opinions are carried into extremes, or are mooted in a spirit which tends to schism, that the interference of those in authority in the Church is called for. The authors of the Tracts in question have laid no such painful necessity on me, nor have I to fear that they will ever do so. I have the best reasons for knowing, that they will be the first to submit themselves to that authority, which it has been their constant exertion to uphold and defend. And I feel sure, that they will receive my friendly suggestions in the spirit in which I have here offered them.'

expedience, or of opinion, or to modes of speech; and I have interpreted your Lordship's ordinary silence, as regards the Clergy generally, as an intimation that you allowed that difference, and that, whether in such details your judgment lay this way or that, you did not think them of importance enough to prescribe to us any particular course respecting them. But I have ever considered also, that you had at any moment the power of setting bounds to this liberty; and that the formal expression of your feelings in any matter ought to be my rule. As to the Tracts, in so large a work, there must be, I am quite sure, very much of human infirmity, much incorrectness both of thought and expression. This must be the case any how, whatever was the nature of such imperfections but your Lordship's alluding to them in your charge has of course pronounced upon their importance,—and for that reason, and because it is my duty to obey you, and from a reluctance to appear to others, particularly to those who differ from me, to be transgressing the bounds of speech which you prescribe, and from a feeling of the inconsistency there would be between such conduct and the professions of the very Tracts which would give rise to it, I felt it impossible to entertain the idea of allowing them to continue the object of your Lordship's remarks if I could hinder it. A withdrawal of them in whole or part seemed both to observe my duty to you and to avoid discussion. And I hope you will believe what I trust I may say quite sincerely, that I shall feel a more lively pleasure in knowing that I am submitting myself to your Lordship's expressed judgment, in a matter of this kind, than I could have even in the widest circulation of the volumes in question.

I will not but answer your Lordship's question. The impression that I carried off from the Charge was this:—'that as to the Tracts for the Times, fully believing the sincerity of the writers, your Lordship still thought they contained expressions which in the case of minds peculiarly constituted might produce injurious effects; that you were apprehensive of the scholars more than of the masters; but that the chance of the effects alluded to led you seriously to warn the latter to weigh their words and to consider what might come of them.'—

Let me express once more my sense of the kind anxiety which your Lordship shows in your letter to consult my feelings and let me assure you that I am, with great sincerity

Your Lordship's faithful and obliged Servt J H N

TO E. B. PUSEY

Oriel Aug 21. 1838

My dear Pusey

Your letter has made me very seriously uneasy as regards Mrs Pusey. I have had a talk with Dr W. I do not know how he has decided. Malta is a very comfortable place—magnificent houses and rents very low—a place used to the English, and to invalids. Froude *quite* lost his cough when there —he always said it was the only time during his illness that he was free from it—and his notion was that, had he stayed there, he should have got well.

I have this day received from another quarter an additional £40 for the Hall—but no inmates!—I will think about the endowment plan.

Richards, they say, is likely to be head of Exeter.[1] Our Greswell has had something like a brain fever, and, I suppose, must give up the Tuition. Palmer of Worcester is going to be married. Acland is just come, but I have not seen him. Hamilton has begun afternoon service daily. William's [Pusey] little boy is to be baptized next Sunday.

And now I must tell you about the Bishop's Charge and the Tracts—it has all been the wrong way. He said in it that having been troubled with anonymous letters, he felt it right to speak about a particular development of opinion etc in one part of his Diocese—Then after speaking about observances etc. in Church and saying he could find nothing to censure, he went on to speak of the Tracts—and said that in them were expressions which might be dangerous to certain minds—that he feared more for the scholars than the Masters—but this being so he conjured the latter to mind what they were about. It was extremely mild, and he has allowed us turning to the East etc etc (implicitly)—and recommended Saints Days, fasting etc. It was altogether very good—but it did the very thing I have always reckoned on, took our suggestions, but (as far as it went) threw us overboard.

After thinking about it, I thought that, since the 'expressions' in question were not mentioned, an indefinite censure was passed *over* the Tracts; and that I could not continue them under it. I wrote to Keble—and he, apart from me, agreed in this opinion. Accordingly I wrote to the Archdeacon stating this, and saying that Bishop's lightest word ex Cathedrâ was heavy —and that judgment on a Book was a rare occurrence. Therefore under the circumstances I must stop the Tracts, and recall those which were in circulation. However, if the Bishop would be kind enough privately to tell him what *Tracts* he objected to, I would withdraw them without a word, and the rest would be saved. He said he had not seen the Charge before it was delivered, and referred me to the Bishop. I have had an answer from the Bishop this morning—very kind, as you would expect. I think (between ourselves), the case is as I thought. He did not fully consider the power of a Bishop's word—nor fancy we are so bound by professions (to say nothing else) to obey it. He meant to *check* us merely, not having a distinct view of *what* the 'expressions' were, and not duly understanding he has a *jurisdiction* over me. If he says one thing, I another, we cannot remain *parallel* to each other, he merely indirectly influencing me. He cannot but *act upon* me. His word is a deed. I am very sorry, but I see no alternative yet, between his telling me to withdraw some, and my withdrawing all—I suppose he will

[1] Joseph Loscombe Richards was elected.

put something into his *printed* charge to soften matters—but I do not see how. He is, as you know particularly kind, and I am quite pained to think that I have put him (apparently) into a difficulty, but I do not see how I could help it. ⟨(Keep all this quite secret)⟩ *You* are quite out of it—first because your *name* is to the Baptism, and he did not mean you; next because I have excepted the Tract on Baptism in my letter.[1] So Harrison goes to Lambeth

Ever Yrs affectly John H Newman

P.S. Your account of the children is very good. Give my best and kindest thoughts to Mrs P.

WEDNESDAY 22 AUGUST 1838   letters from Wood, Harrison,[2] and Tyler.   sent Le Bas' article to Roworth   Spranger, Bloxam, and Marshall to dinner   wrote to Keble, Perceval, Harrison, and Tyler

TO JOHN KEBLE

Oriel College. ⌜Aug 22. 1838⌝

My dear Keble,

So little has yet passed that this is not worth the postage, and I should not write, did I not want advice prospectively. So I will say where I stand.

⌜I did not write to Pusey for many reasons—he had enough to think about[3]—and might seem in a measure *particeps criminis*, and unfit to mediate, though I suppose that his Tracts are not in fault. And he was at a distance—so I wrote to the Archdeacon stating pretty much what passed between you and me—that I had recourse to him, though in an official capacity, when I had rather have chosen another, because there was no other—that I neither wrote formally myself, nor wanted a formal answer; that the Bishop by

---

[1] Pusey remarked in an undated note: 'I have seen the Bp of Os charge but lost it; I think it leaves, or rather compels us to be free, since he appeals to us to take it well: but it is not what I should have wished.' He wrote to Keble on 23 Aug., 'One must expect principles to cost something, but the withdrawal of the Tracts from circulation, and that in consequence of a Bishop's disapprobation, is a tremendous blow, which one should be glad to avoid if possible . . . The act of obedience ought to produce a good effect upon people. But it seems a gratuitous infliction, not upon us, but upon principles.' Liddon's *Pusey* II, 57.

[2] B. Harrison wrote on 20 Aug. to inform Newman of his appointment as Chaplain to the Archbishop of Canterbury. He wrote that the Archbishop 'at Lambeth: he expressed himself in the highest terms of regard for "the Oxford Divines", to whose views, it was a great satisfaction to me to find, he seemed fully aware that he should be regarded as giving his unqualified sanction by this appointment; and at the same time, without seeming to wish me to express an opinion upon a single point, he stated, in the most unreserved way, wherein he could not go along altogether with the views of those for whom he had so great a respect.' In a letter of 11 Aug. to Pusey, asking his advice about accepting the appointment, Harrison mentioned that the Archbishop had expressed great regret at the publication of Froude's *Remains*.

Pusey thought that the appointment opened up a 'happy prospect', but Harrison soon grew far less sympathetic to the Movement.

[3] [[Mrs P.'s illness?]]

saying there were ambiguous and unsafe expressions in the Tracts (by the bye the Charge itself is very good and strong—and speaks out more than any Bishop has done perhaps, except the Bishop of E [[Exeter]]) had thrown a suspicion over the whole—and that under the circumstances I seemed to have no course but to remove them out of his way;—that a Bishop's word was not a light one, and could not be—that it was rare;—that it struck me I might be saved a very disagreeable measure, if he would kindly get from the Bishop, not as Archdeacon but as a friend, not the expressions, because I gathered from his Charge he did not wish to get into discussion, but the Tracts which contain them—on which I would withdraw such Tracts without a word, and the rest would be saved. I ended by thanking the Bishop for the kindness he had so often shown me and by hinting my pain that the notice I should have of any part of my writings being under his disapprobation should be on so public and solemn an occasion. I was not pleased with my letter, but it was the best I could write, and the Bishop seems to have taken it, as I meant, which is enough.

The Archdeacon answered that he had not seen the Charge before he heard it, that the Bishop had not consulted him, and that he thought I had better think nothing of him and address the Bishop. This made me suppose that Spry is at the bottom of the Charge, which the Bishop's letter somewhat confirms.

I then wrote to the Bishop, (who [[(had)]] received my letter to the Archdeacon from him) merely asking whether I should call or write to him.

I received his answer yesterday morning. He begins by saying that he has been pained ever since he received my letter, not with me, because I had perfectly satisfied him in my own demeanour etc but at the idea of having pained me; that I must have misunderstood him, and he intreated me to wait at least till the Charge was printed—that to withdraw the Tracts, at least at once, would be unfair to him as making him seem to say more than he meant—that he had been forced to give judgment on account of anonymous letters and other Bishops having spoken—that he had in his Charge approved very much of what we had done—censured nothing—only warned—that he considered that the opposite party had rather cause to complain he had gone so far—that my impression was not the general one—that he assured me that persons who thought the Tracts were doing good and had a great respect for me yet lamented expressions etc in them, and that he would call on me when next he came into Oxford and hoped to meet me on the same terms as ever, and that he wished to know *my impression* of what he had said. Nothing could be kinder or more feeling than this letter.—

It seems to me plain from it that the Bishop thought a great deal in the Tracts very good, but would not commit himself in any way to them. Accordingly (as far as I remember) there is not a word of praise bestowed on *them* but on the otherhand to balance *his own* adoption of what they recommended, a slight discredit cast about them,—that he has not read them, that he goes by what he hears said, has seen extracts perhaps etc—and (not thinking of our feelings at all any more than if we were the very paper Tracts) he propitiates the popular cry with a vague disapprobation, just as men revile Popery in order to say strong Catholic things. Of course this is entre nous— I have expressed myself much more strongly than would be right, were I not putting you in possession of my thoughts with reference to forming a judgment. Also, I am not sure if he was not rather annoyed with me when he delivered his Charge, whether on account of the Remains, or other reason. —I think he has not considered that a Bishop's word is an act—that I am under his jurisdiction—that he cannot *criticize* [[but commands only.]]¹— that his word would not act as a damper merely but as a command.

⌐I answered last night to this effect—that I would certainly wait till his Charge came out—that I had ever studied to please him in word and act —that no two persons agree in minor matters, viz of expediency, opinion or in expressions—that his ordinary silence, as regards his Clergy, I had interpreted to mean, that in such matters, whichever way his own judgment was, he allowed such differences—but that I had ever felt that he could withdraw his permission and that when he spoke, his word was my rule;—that, as to the Tracts, they were a large work and but a human production and doubtless full of imperfections—I knew this any how—but his formal noticing the faults made them *important*—that for this reason, and to obey him, and lest the world and my opponents should find me in the false position of being in opposition to him, and in order that the *doctrine* of the Tracts might not be inconsistent with my *conduct* as to them, I had felt to withdraw them in whole or part was my only course, and I intreated him to believe I should find real pleasure in submitting myself to his expressed judgment. Then I told him what my impression was of what he had said. He would get this letter this morning.

Now qu. 1 am I driving him into committing himself about [[to *name*]] certain expressions etc? You see I have distinctly waived all wish to know them. but 2. In my first letter I professed to wish to go by *what he really wished* i.e. 'if I privately learned what Tracts he disapproved etc.'⌐ Now qu. am I to take in to account the τόπος πρὸς δόξαν¹? e.g. ⌐suppose he tells me in speech or conversation 'Go on with the Tracts'—and yet prints the Charge (N.B. I think he will print as he read it.⌐ I cannot help thinking he has a dread of seeming inconsistent. He *may* put a *note* about the Tracts) ⌐with the critique on them, what am I to do?⌐ Is or is it not the consideration of 'scandal', 'example' etc to go for nothing? ⌐am I to appear to be undutiful when I am not? I have no view, but will do what you advise. I wish to be *prepared* with my ⟨(a)⟩ view.

Ever Yrs affectly John H Newman

P.S. Harrison is Chaplain at Lambeth in place of Ogilvie, and in the best

¹ 'consideration of appearances'.

way—the Archbishop confessing it would look like patronising 'the Oxford Divines.' Richards is likely to be head of Exeter. I have very uncomfortable accounts about Mrs Pusey. W. Palmer (of Worcester) is going to be married. Our Greswell has been most dangerously ill, and it is feared must leave Oxford.

FROM JOHN KEBLE

Hursley, Eve of St. Bartholomew 23 Aug. 1838.

My very dear N.

I have considered your letter as well as I could and think it on the whole very encouraging. The Bishop has clearly fallen into the error of which you suspected him—using words of course without any definite application; and, moreover, seeing how little most of us care for the sentiments of our Diocesans, he has naturally assumed that his words would not be taken as they were uttered, and is now startled to find that they are so. In the end this must do him and the cause too a great deal of good; not least if it prevents his taking counsel chiefly of the men whom mortals call High and Dry. But to the immediate point: you have probably seen him before now—or at any rate your course has opened you more clearly than I can see it at this distance. As far as I do see, I think I should do this. In your conversation or correspondence, the Tracts at least if not the very expressions will probably come out to which he refers. You may fairly represent your own dilemma and submit to him different ways of proceeding which occur to you and take his pleasure upon them. He must, I think, feel what you say, that it will not do to go on pressing the high claims of one's Diocesan, and afterwards go on taking no notice of a censure from him, however indefinite. He will therefore probably give *permission* at least to proceed in some one of the ways which you suggest to him—or he will leave you to your choice among them. He has said he does not wish to have the Tracts suppressed *generally*: if he chooses to name any particular ones, or any expressions, all you have to ask is, would he have them suppressed *sub silentio*, or with some sort of explanation: e.g. a little Tract on the Difficulties of the Tracts: giving briefly the authority for each expression, so as to justify it in point of Faith, but stating that it is withdrawn in obedience to those who have a right to command, and who think it not prudent. Should he decline giving any particulars (which I hardly expect) what if you proposed to him to make out yourself a list of the Tracts or expressions you supposed him to mean: and proceed in like manner with them, as if he had stated them in the first instance himself? I do not see you *could* go further than this in the way of submission: and the example of that will do infinite good, especially if it be clearly understood that nothing is censured as heretical but merely as indiscreet. I do not know that any other way of proceeding occurs to me. I am not at present prepared to say that you should go on in obedience to his private command, supposing it really contrary to his public one. But I dare say he will modify his printed charge in some degree, so as to square with your proceedings . . .

TO A. P. PERCEVAL

Oriel College. August 22. 1838

My dear Perceval,

I have this evening received the answers to your questions. They come from a Roman Catholic Priest of name, and, if he is an honest man, are sure to be correct. 1. 'The Edition of the Vulgate practically adopted by us

302

Catholics is that of Clement 8, printed by Platina; or reprints of that impression. There is however nothing *materially* different in the *old* copies of the Vulgate in the MS or the printed edition of Sixtus 5.—2. The Profession of Faith drawn up by Pope Pius 4th is required from every one who takes Holy Orders, and is repeated at every promotion; secondly all Professors in public schools whether clerical or secular are required to make it; thirdly it is required whenever any degree is conferred in Divinity and on the presentation to any benefice; fourthly all who have the cure of souls undergo an examination in moral and dogmatic divinity, and then make the above Profession of Faith.'

As to your proposal for the B.C. any thing from you would be highly prized by the Editor, and I hope you will bear it in mind. I doubt however whether the very plan you propose would not suit a Magazine better than a Review. The name of a writer could not be given, I think—and I should hardly think the Dublin R. [Review] long enough established to honor it with notice *by name* in the B. C. I could give two or three pages of the small type at the end to an answer to it, speaking of the Dublin as 'a late critique on Mr P.'s book,' if that would do—but that would not give room for reprinting the text of that critique.[1]

You have heard, I suppose, of Palmer's proposed marriage, and of Harrison's appointment to be Chaplain to the Archbishop vice Ogilvie.

Yours very sincerely John H. Newman

TO JOHN KEBLE

[late August 1838]

My dear Keble

James M. [Mozley] and I looked through the Appendix to A [Arnold]'s 3rd volume of Sermons; his Pamphlet on Church Reform; and his Pamphlet on the Roman Catholic claims but in vain. There are some words *very like* those used by H. F. [Froude] in the 'Church Reform'—but not the same.[2] I sent the sheet to Derby, saying that, if I found any thing, they should hear from me—but I had nothing to write.[3]

On the receipt of your last note, finding the reason why you were anxious, I wrote at once to say that a note must be appended to the words of this sort—'(These words occur in substance in a recent publication.)' I hope the letter has got in time, before the sheet was printed off.

I wish you would think of some good title to the Volumes—e.g. (by way

[1] Perceval's *The Christian Peace Offering*, London 1829, and *The Roman Schism illustrated*, London 1836, were reviewed in an article in *D.R.*, 6, 1837 (Oct.), 468–525. The author was John Maguire, of St Edmund's College, Ware, later Wiseman's Vicar General in London.

[2] See *Remains* III, 361, where Froude refers to the passage from Arnold about Hooker which Newman alludes to in letter of 11 Sept. 1837 to Mrs J. Mozley (see note there).

[3] Henry Mozley and Sons of Derby were printing the second part of *Remains*.

of supplying an ἀφορμή[1]) 'Essays and Notices ⟨Sketches⟩ ecclesiastical and historical by etc.' with the *particular* titles separately as they come—or with a subdivision following thus 'Part i containing Essay on Rationalism and other Papers—' 'Part ii containing an account of the attempt to unite Church and State in the reign of King Henry ii'—

Will you let the inclosed go to Moberly the first opportunity—but there is no immediate hurry[2]

THURSDAY 23 AUGUST 1838   letter from Le Bas   f d   Eden returned   wrote to Wood and Daman

TO S. F. WOOD

Oriel. Aug 23. 1838 St B. E. [Bartholomew's Eve]

My dear Wood,

You are a very good fellow by the measure and weight of £40. I hope, however, you duly recollected the increased expence of the Breviary, before you sent it—If not, you shall have it back, e.g. supposing the expence is greater than you expect. I shall be truly glad to see Carey and will lodge him in College—I am sorry to say the Hall has not started, for want of men. It is not that men are not willing, but difficulties are in their way of coming at once.

Thanks for the German Review, which is very nice and has gone to press.[3] I should gladly receive others. As to the Article I will not encroach on your Holiday now, which may be needlessly. Supposing I settled on coming to you at the last moment if I am in great distress? Would this annoy you? I am exceedingly sorry to hear the account you give of yourself. Really you were not well, when I saw you in Town. I was sure you were not. Why do you not take more holiday? you said you were going to Germany some time since. Supposing you have back your money and go off by the first Rotterdam Steamer.

And now if my hand were not so tired, I would give you a sketch of our matters here—but it is weary—and there is the chance, though I hope not to be fulfilled, (I mean as a possibility in idea) of my ceasing to write from my wrist paining me. It has for some time been an effort to write letters for this reason. As a prolusion to my main subject I advertise you, that in return for your excellent news about Harrison, that I fear Sewell somehow will not be Head of Exeter, and that W. Palmer of Worcester is going to be married. We have very unsatisfactory accounts of Mrs Pusey.

[1] 'starting point'.
[2] The remainder is missing.
[3] A brief piece on the state of theological literature in Germany which was printed in *Brit. Crit.*, 24, 1838 (Oct.), 490–2. It concentrated on Strauss's *Polemical Tracts*.

Now to proceed. What think you if the Tracts are all to be withdrawn? I cannot tell. But be mum, and do not let the matter run the round of our friends, though I suppose a many know it in some way or other.

Our Bishop has been pestered with anonymous letters—(now I am going to be free, when perhaps I ought not—but it is between ourselves—and writing it down tends to clear my own ideas on the subject) begging him to condemn the Tracts. He approves of their matter, and he means to recommend them in a Charge. Yet what will the anonymous letters say?—2do He is told by various people, for what I know Spry, that the Tracts contain injudicious expressions—and, for what I know, the Remains lead him to think I want a check or set down. His way then is apparently clear before him —he recommends a number of good things in a visitation Charge, which the Tracts had advocated, not however as in them, and has a slight slap at the said Tracts, as containing unadvisable expressions and as obliging him to warn the writers.

Now comes my side. I say, if my zeal were running riot the way to check me was to tell me so in private—not to hit me indirectly in public with a view of sobering me. Next, a Bishop cannot *criticize* ex-cathedrâ those under him. His word is law. I am under his jurisdiction; I cannot for ten thousand reasons go on circulating matter which he has ever so lightly animadverted on. It is putting myself in a false position.

So a correspondence has ensued—he is very kind, and I like him personally so much that I trust it will be, as it had begun, nothing but cordial;— but I say this,—I do not ask to *know* the *expressions* in fault, but tell me privately (I wrote to the Archdeacon first to be still more indirect) *what* Tracts you wish withdrawn, and I will withdraw them without a word—and so I shall save the rest—for, if I do not know which, I must suppress all. He on the contrary says that I must have misconceived his words and that by so acting I shall be putting a comment on them which is unfair.—In my own opinion he has no definite passages from the Tracts in his mind—I consider that when he wrote he had an eye *solely* to what our enemies would say—and it did not occur to him to consider about us—and I *think* he is (naturally) annoyed about the Remains. I have promised to do nothing till the Charge is printed which it is to be. If you have any wise suggestion to make under the circumstances, I shall be glad to hear it.

Ever Yrs affectly John H Newman

P.S. As to the Breviary, is not this the way? whether people believe it or not, say in the Preface what is the fact that a friend has given you leave to use his translations and is not answerable for any thing. In this way I am clear of all but the abstract idea of translating from the Breviary Services. I think translating *all*, will diminish the attack on you from Protestants, as including the legends on Saintsdays.'

FRIDAY 24 AUGUST 1838 St Bartholomew's letters from Keble and Bowden. Service in Chancel read Number 270 f d

TO R. W. CHURCH

Oriel St B's [Bartholomew] day [24 August].

My dear Church,

Baxter has not done more than two—but he makes some excuse about Pusey's Preface.—⌈I wish I could think of something good for κατ' οἰκονομίαν. I doubt whether in a new Father I shall not introduce the word 'economically.' I consider it to mean a representation or scene, only a true one.– E.g. the traveller and ewe-lamb are *represented* in word, and are not real—but the Apostles asked Christ about the End of the World by God's bringing together *facts* as Nathan did *words*. It is a *true fable*.

Harrison is appointed Archbishop's Chaplain in the place of Ogilvie. Palmer of Worcester is going to be married. Dr Kidd tells me Richards is to be Head of Exeter, if he will consent.—Thus I have given you three Ecclesiastical Promotions.⌉

I am grieved to hear a very bad account of Greswell. It is very doubtful if he can return to Oxford. If so, I suppose, Tutors must be sought among the Juniors

Yrs affly John H Newman

* E.g. Hos. li 2. etc. Ezek. 4.–5.–24.[1]

SATURDAY 25 AUGUST 1838 breakfasted with Acland Rogers came and dined in Common Room with Eden and me

SUNDAY 26 AUGUST 11 Trinity letters from Pusey, Manning and Harrison. by myself in early communion married waiter at Star to Mrs Barton's daughter did morning duty went over with Acland to Garsington and stood sponsor for W P's [Pusey] child and preached for him Number 304[2] Spranger did duty for me dined with Eden and Rogers in Common Room

TO E. B. PUSEY

Oriel. Aug 26. 1838

My dear Pusey

I send you what has passed between the Bishop and me—here things will stop, I suppose till the Charge appears.

I am sorry you are so concerned—depend upon it, without reason. Nothing can stop the course of things, but our acting against God's Will. I *could* not have acted otherwise than I have.

[1] The holograph extract gives, 'Hos. i. 2. etc Ezek. [chapters] 4, 5. 24.'
[2] *P.S.* VIII, 5, 'Curiosity a Temptation to Sin'.

I do not mean to say at all that my motives and feelings are what they should be—but my reason sees clear that I ought to do what I have done, though it were well if I could do so with a more single mind.

And I do not think you enter into my situation, nor can any one. I have for several years been working against all sorts of opposition, and with hardly a friendly voice. Consider how few persons have said a word in favor of me. Do you think the thought never comes across me, that I am putting myself out of my place? what warrant have I for putting myself so forward against the world? am I bishop or professor, or in any station which gives me right to speak? I have nothing to appeal to in justification, but my feeling that I am in the main right in my opinions and that I am able to recommend them. My sole comfort has been that my Bishop has not spoken against me—in a certain sense I can depend and lean as it were on him. Yet, I say it sorrow-fully, though you are the only person I say it to, he has never been my *friend*—he has never supported me—His letting me dedicating that book to him was the only thing he have [sic] done for me, and very grateful I feel. I can truly say that I would do any thing to serve him. Sometimes as I have stood by as he put on his robes, I felt as if it would be such a relief if I could have fallen at his feet and kissed them—but on the contrary, though from the kindness of his nature he has been ever kind to me, yet he has shewn me, *as me*, no favor—unless being made Rural Dean was such, which under the circumstances I do not think was much. When that unpleasant Jubber business took place, and I needed a great deal to cheer me, he wrote an answer to the Dissenting Minister, but not a line in answer to my long letter.[1] I do not say think [sic] in complaint, but to express my position. If he breathes *but* one word against the Tracts, it is more than he has said out in their favor—for he does not expressly give them his approbation, as far as I recollect his Charge. I *cannot* stand, if he joins against me. Here is Faussett but yesterday writing against me—well now the Bishop says a word—is not that taking Faussett's part? is it not by implication assenting to what he says and deciding between him and me?—What is it to me, though friends of mine, or though strangers think well of what I have written? I feel I have no business to be writing—I want some excuse for doing so, and instead of giving it to me, my Bishop turns against me. I cannot stand against this. Even if I do not withdraw the Tracts, I see I cannot continue them—The next volume is begun—and I suppose must be finished; but I suppose they will then stop. And I do not see how I shall have heart with [out] special encouragement from the Bishop, to write any thing more on strictly Church subjects. His kindness to me, which has always been great, is from the kindness of his nature.

It is very well for people at a distance, looking *at* me, to say (as they will) I am betraying a cause and unsettling people. My good fellows, *you* make me the head *of a party*—that is *your external* view—but I know what I am, I

[1] See Volume IV, 297–8.

am a clergyman under the Bishop of Oxford and any thing more is accidental.

August 28. On reading this over, I fear you will think me in a fume—but I am not. I have written the above rapidly, and it reads abrupt. Every thing seems likely to be satisfactory.

August 28. (In festo S. August.) Yesterday Acland who had been at Cuddesden brought back the news that the Bishop was uncommonly pleased with my letters, and would do any thing we wanted about his Charge—This entre nous. I had copied out for you the correspondence, and had intended to send it. You now will know *all* that has passed, and if you choose to write as a mediator, you can. (but you should not speak as from me.) The said Acland has given me several thoughts for a device for the Title page. First (which will not do) the Cœtus Doctorum (Raffaelle's) commonly called the de Sacramento, I think. Next Raffaelle's Cartoon Pasce oves meos. Thirdly (which I like) a picture ⟨lithograph⟩ of Jacobson's—a figure of theology with two children, one reading the other looking in her face—and doctors on each side. The only fear is the size of them. He says that in the Mosaic in the Testudos at Rome there generally is a vine which springs up at the foot and curls round the whole design—he suggested that it might form the margin. I shall go to Parker to-day about it, to consult his wood engraver.

As to endowments, I have no strong opinion. If they are to be endowments, they ought to be migratory of course. E.g. if a new rector of Manchester disapproved, they ought to be able to set off for Birmingham or Sheffield.[1]

As to S. Sp. and M. If I had my *choice* I should say Seager; but then you hinted something about Morris needing something in order to remain in Oxford. Sp. is an excellent fellow and very sound—but I should think S. much preferable.[2]

I am much annoyed at some hints of the Archbishop's conversation with Harrison having got out here through me. I told one person who happened to be in the room at the time *as* a great secret—It has been very unfortunate; but I have done all I can to stop it, and I hope, it being vacation time, to do so. I should be very sorry if it got to Harrison.[3]

Ever Yrs affly J H Newman

P.S. I send the Littlemore plans—let me have them back. The Bishop spoke

[1] Pusey had been proposing a College of Clergy at Manchester (which would act as a model for other Colleges to 'ameliorate the heathenish state of our great towns'). He wished it funded by endowment but Newman was critical of the idea (see letter of 13 Aug.). Pusey had replied on 15 Aug., pressing the plan of endowment as the easiest basis for maintaining a fixed set of regulations in the institutions. He wrote again on 21 Aug., 'I have been thinking that if you decidedly think that one ought not to attempt a foundaton, that the only way will be to return to the original plan of assisting Hook at Leeds . . . for your end of producing an ἦθος, are not large plans, as being action, the very way to do? One College of Clergy founded for a large town is a great speaking fact'. See Liddon's *Pusey* II, 36–40.
[2] Harrison's departure for Lambeth had left Pusey without an assistant lecturer in Hebrew. He had considered C. Seager and J. B. Morris but Harrison had suggested R. J. Spranger. He consulted Newman as knowing Spranger better.
[3] See note to diary for 22 Aug.

so strongly about observing the Rubric, that two grave middle aged clergymen have come into Oxford to enquire of Bloxam how to get copes made, one saying his father etc. etc had one. The little child was baptized 'Edward Boverie' on Sunday, Acland standing for you.

MONDAY 27 AUGUST 1838 letter from W.F. Joseph Fourdrinier and his wife in Oxford   walked to Littlemore with Rogers and read   dined and Rogers with Bloxam
TUESDAY 28 AUGUST letters from J M. and Mr Cooper. admitted Steven's two little children into the Church Westmacott came—and dined with me in my rooms. Rogers went The Whatelys in Oxford went up in fly to Littlemore in evening Sir R. Westmacott in Oxford

TO JOHN KEBLE

Oriel ⌈Aug 28/38⌉

My dear Keble

Having a stranger in Oxford, I write in a hurry. The prospect of my being able to come to you is less just now than it was.—When you next write to your brother, will you give him this message,—'that I thank him much for his MS, which is gone to press, but that there are many sentences in his letter which I cannot construe.'[1]

⌈The Bishop, you will be glad to hear, is very much pleased with my letter and wishes that nothing should appear in his Charge which may give any pain—[this] comes indirectly through Acland, and must not be mentioned;—so every thing is as well as it can be. This is a great comfort to me, since your brother speaks about it in a way I do not like, and both Pusey and Bowden are annoyed. Thanks for your letters, both as advice and encouragement—Your quotation from Virgil brought tears into my eyes[2]—No one has encouraged me but you—Pusey was so cast down when he heard it, that he himself needed comfort. I have no cough, thank you—it is always voluntary, arising not from the lungs but from a feeling of weakness in my muscles of utterance.⌉

Ever Yrs affly J H N

[1] T. Keble wrote on 24 Aug., 'I am *very* sorry to hear that you have some scruples about continuing the publication of the Tracts. Surely the expression of some doubt or slight disapprobation on the part of the Bp. could not be considered as a Veto—unless he himself on being applied to, should say that he wishes you so to understand it . . . I send you this impertinent message from Mr. Burke. "You never give yourself time to cool—You cannot survey, from its proper point of sight, the work you have finished, before you decree its final execution—You never go into the country, soberly and dispassionately to observe the effect of your measures on their objects. You cannot etc. etc. etc."

In good earnest I wish you would go to Hursley or any where else, to be a little while out of the way of your Faussetts, Shuttleworths. etc.'

For Newman's reaction to this letter see that of 21 Nov. to J. Keble.

[2] Keble ended his letter of 15 Aug. with the quotation, 'O passi graviora, dabit Deus his quoque finem', *Aeneid* I, 199. He added, 'I will not change Virgil's plural, though you *say* you are absolutely alone'.

309

WEDNESDAY 29 AUGUST 1838   Bloxam to breakfast to meet W. [Westmacott].   went with W. to Blenheim   to dinner to meet W., Bloxam, Spranger, and Berkeley   wrote to Marriott, Manning, and Wood

TO H. E. MANNING

Oriel College. Aug 29/38

My dear Manning,

I am very much concerned indeed to hear of your new attack—do let your first business be to get strong. Had I not had a friend stopping with me, I should have answered yours before this, to beg you to give up all thoughts of any article. I do so now. There is every reason for thinking I shall have quite enough without you—and you will write more to your own satisfaction and that of your readers when you are better.

I have no news to tell you. The Exeter Election is to be settled on Saturday. Men talk as if Richards was to get it. W. Palmer of Worcester is going to be married. How good Harrison's appointment is. We have been very empty here—but some few men are now making their appearance—Our school room at Littlemore is going on well

Ever Yrs affectly John H Newman

THURSDAY 30 AUGUST 1838   letter from Daman   W and I breakfasted with Bloxam Westmacott went.   wrote to J.M.

TO J. B. MOZLEY

Oriel Aug 30/38

My dear James,

I am truly pleased to find you have got ready the article on Sir F. P. [Palgrave] and expect it with interest. I shall be at Bradfield the whole of Wednesday next and a bit of Thursday—else I shall be here.

As to your absence from Oxford, I am not able to say that your absence this week or that week has been a loss—but I am sure your being away all the time has been. I doubt not that persons would now be in the House, if it were but open. Indeed I know of one. It seems to me to be a point now to get it into habitable condition—and I have other things to do myself.

Greswell has had so bad an illness, he is not returning to Oxford. Palmer of Worcester is going to be married. Rogers was here for two days lately. The Littlemore School House is rising fast, but, alas, will not be a pretty building. The news from Weymouth is not satisfactory—they[1] all return about the 12th and *perhaps* go to Malta. The Exeter Election is on Saturday next. Dr Kidd told me that Richards is to be head. You know that Harrison

[1] The Puseys.

is gone to Lambeth vice Ogilvie. Archdeacon F. is doubting about the immediate publication of the new volumes of the Remains. Eden is returned

Ever yours affly John H Newman

FRIDAY 31 AUGUST 1838   f d   wrote to Jemima

TO R. W. CHURCH

Oriel ⌐Aug 31/38⌐

My dear Church,

I find I have omitted to read, as I ought, the Benedictine Monita before the separate Catecheses[1]—are you aware whether I have floored in consequence?

C. Marriott is here for the day. ⌐Greswell has written to resign the Tuition⌐ —Rogers was here for 2 days—Eden is returned —⌐The common notion here is that Richards will be elected at Exeter tomorrow⌐

Ever Yrs John H Newman
Turn over

P.S. I thought I mentioned to you that an index of Texts would be wanted. I had put in some half sentences omitted before; I am glad you found those besides.

TO MRS JOHN MOZLEY

Oriel College. ⌐Aug 31. 1838⌐

My dear Jemima,

I have been wishing to write to you for several weeks, but have been expecting daily a letter which I wished to receive first from a friend. It has not come, and so you must be content with this mysterious *explanation*, which is something like darkness visible, by way of accounting for my silence. And the worst of it is, I have had many things to say in the interval which I now have forgotten.

Tom has never sent any message about Archdeacon Wilkins. I want to know something about him—Harrison's appointment is capital. Palmer of Worcester is going to be married. Our Greswell has had a most dangerous fever, and is giving up all his College duties and retiring from residence at once. Mrs Pusey comes back about the 12th. If there is any hope, she will go to Malta for the winter—but this is not to be told.

[1] Church was translating St Cyril of Jerusalem's *Catechetical Lectures* and was using the Benedictine edition of the *Opera Omnia*, Paris 1720. In the edition each Catechesis was prefaced by a brief introductory 'monitum' or 'praeloquium'.

I hope St Cyril will be finished in the course of a fortnight—if so, and if (as I hope) the October Number of the B. C. is off my hands by that time, and if it is convenient to John and you, I have thought of coming to you after the 22nd (the Anniversary of Littlemore Consecration) for ten days or so—but my plans are so little formed, that you will not at all disarrange them by saying you are engaged—so pray do not scruple to say how things stand exactly. It is never the right time to leave Oxford—so many things start up the last moment, that I cannot answer for myself beforehand. I hope T. and H. will come through going back.

I should like to have the account of the third Edition of the Lyra some time—and will pay it at once. I believe I have not yet. Thank John for the Wogan.[1]

Our School House at Littlemore is getting on. I am sorry to say it is not a handsome building. I left the matter too much to others; Underwood has so much business, *through* the Chapel, that, I suspect, he has not attended to it as he ought.

⌐My hand has got so tired with writing, it is quite an effort to me to write a letter. My teeth plagued me a good deal for a month after I left Town, but they are very well now—except that there are so few of them.⌐

Maria Giberne has been in, or passed through Oxford several times. She is stopping at Mr Wilson's. The Exeter Election is decided tomorrow morning. The general impression seems to be that Richards will get it. The difficulty was whether he would take it, the Rectorship being very poor, and his living a good one. Mr Le Bas was with me for two or three days, and Westmacott left yesterday, after being here for several days. His brother's living is near 30 miles from this place, though in this County.[2]

I am glad to have so good an account of the baby, and that an alliance has been struck up between him and my Aunt. I shall be truly glad to see them; but I must not promise I shall come.—Joseph Fourdrinier has passed through here—but out of consideration, it being Saturday evening when he came in, he did not find me out till Monday, when I was engaged to go to Littlemore and to dinner. I offered them luncheon but they would not have it. I am glad to hear that M. Mozley is better. Love to H. J. T. [Harriett, John, Tom] and my Aunt and kind remembrances to the rest, and believe me, My dear Jemima

Ever yrs affectly John H Newman

SATURDAY 1 SEPTEMBER 1838   letter from R Williams[3]   Marriott in Oxford   Exeter

[1] William Wogan, *An Essay on the Proper Lessons appointed by the Liturgy of the Church of England*, London 1753, was reprinted in two volumes in 1838 by Henry Mozley at Derby.
[2] Horatio Westmacott was Rector of Chastleton, Oxon.
[3] Robert Williams wrote, doubtful about going on with the translation of the Breviary because of the opposition: 'My view shortly is, and it is what has made me give the pains to it I have, that for the *good of the Church*, as a thing which will Catholicise our friends in all

Election—Richards elected Rector. walked with Marriott to Littlemore—thence he to Bradfield.

SUNDAY 2 SEPTEMBER 12 Trinity letter from Woodgate did duty morning and afternoon Hawkins of Exeter assisted me in Sacrament preached afternoon Number 101 ⟨conscience⟩ Cornish ill—called on him dined in Common Room with Eden.

MONDAY 3 SEPTEMBER called on Cornish who better. sent up first Sermons of volume 4 for the Press

TUESDAY 4 SEPTEMBER letters from R. [,] J.M. [,] Mr Sparks and parcel from Bowden with his Article Copeland returned dined with Eden in Common Room? wrote to Bowden

TO J. W. BOWDEN

⌜Oriel College. Sept. 4. 1838.⌝

My dear Bowden,

⌜Many thanks indeed for your Article⌝ which has just arrived, which I have read with great interest.[1] I sincerely hope it has not annoyed you to have had to write it—I trust that in a short time I shall so be *stocked* with Articles as not to take any one in a hurry. ⌜It is a very instructive paper,⌝ and I hope, will do much good—the extracts, and remarks on them are very striking. ⌜If I have a criticism, I should say that the first part might have been somewhat condensed.⌝ I shall send you a proof; it can go by post in two sheets. ⌜There is a bit in sheet 46, which I think had best be left out. It is where⌝ *after* speaking of the members of both Universities *together* who at once were Associationists and Agitators for liberalizing the places, ⌜you go to speak of *each* University *separately*. The truth is I am so uncomfortably situated as to some of these persons among us, that I should not like to seem to be attacking them. Baden Powell has lately commenced cutting me—why I know not—ditto Shuttleworth. So has Daubeny, though I believe in him it is mere awkwardness. I think the sense will run clear after this omission; about 3 of your pages are omitted by it.—Also when you speak against Dr Lloyd,⌝[2] instead of saying 'singular that a *clergyman* should in the above passage,' put some periphrasis or milder word for clergyman. ⌜I suspect he was a friend of Mr Todd's of Dublin and I should not like to disgust him. In the next page for 'Indeed, *it appears*,⌝ that it was a single professor and he *happily* a layman', I propose to word it 'Indeed as far as the Report

ways, the Breviary ought to be translated. The longer it is put off the more row it will make'. He left the matter to Newman's judgment.

Pusey wrote to Newman about this time: 'Will you caution Williams, who will perhaps be in Oxford before this, about the Breviary, as far as you think right; your extracts [*Tract* 75] have been the subject of a great deal of attack here, in part from what you do say, in part from what you do not.'

[1] 'The British Association for Advancement of Science', *Brit. Crit.*, 25, 1839 (Jan.), 1–48.
[2] [[qu. of Dublin?]] Bartholomew Lloyd, Provost of Trinity College, Dublin, see *art. cit.* p. 38.

shows, it was a single professor, and he a layman etc.,' ⌐not to offend Daubeny. I must look about the 4 men who had degrees—Brewster, Faraday, and Dalton were three, but what persuasion was the fourth? D'Israeli[1] had his degree subsequently. I have left out the names in pencil. The *facts* are so severe, I was afraid to add them. Priestley was not a Clergyman—but I will refer.⌐ And now let me repeat my thanks for a very seasonable article.

⌐As to the Bishop and me I have little to tell you. I have written 2 letters and he one. I have promised not to do any thing till the Charge is printed. I have heard indirectly, what is very good news, but of course secret, that he is much pleased with my letters, and that he is desirous to make any alteration in his Charge which may relieve me. I am quite certain that in my position I could do nothing else. To suffer my Bishop to breathe a word against me, would be to put myself in a false position. Depend upon it, our strength, (as to every thing, or person, political, religious, philosophical) is *consistency*. If we show we are not afraid of carrying out our principles in whatever direction, humanly speaking, nothing can hurt us—And it seems the most likely way to obtain a blessing. I do not think it would have been volunteering a persecution. Observe, I do not think I am out of the wood yet—for I do not see how the Bishop can materially alter his Charge, or how I can bear any blow whatever. However, I am sanguine it will end well—at the same time I am bound to say that Pusey in the main seemed to agree with you, as did Thomas Keble.

⌐I am concerned to say there are very anxious accounts of Mrs Pusey. They return here in the course of ten days and then perhaps go to Malta.⌐ Your news about Johnson was very good. ⌐It is a floor Sewell not being Head of Exeter—tho' I never expected he would. The existing Heads here seem to chuckle over it much. I must not boast before it is out, but I expect [[suspect]] this B.C. will be a good one. Two of our Translations of the Fathers will greet you on your return to the South. I think they will do us harm at first. We shall see choice bits of bigotry, fancifulness, superstition etc., etc., strung together in the Record etc. etc. as F's remains have been treated. I talk of going to Derby on the 24th for a fortnight.⌐ What a sad account you give of the children. I hope poor John is by this time set up. ⌐We have had a very nice Summer here.⌐ Kindest remembrances to Mrs Bowden.

Ever yrs affectly John H. Newman.

⌐P.S. My fourth volume of Sermons has gone to Press. And we are advancing into the third Tract of volume 5.

P.S. Hale of Charter House tells me that 'the Institution of a Christian

---

[1] [[the Father?]] Bowden's article protested against the role which the British Association took in encouraging the granting of honorary degrees to non-Anglicans. Benjamin Disraeli's father Isaac, author of *The Curiosities of Literature*, was granted an honorary Oxford D.C.L. in 1832 for his *Commentaries on the Life and Reign of Charles I*.

man'[1] has lately been republished with other Tracts, and he does not recommend the publication.⌐

WEDNESDAY 5 SEPTEMBER 1838 dined early walked to Littlemore to prayers with Copeland—then by coach to Bradfield wrote to Mr Faber

TO JOHN KEBLE

⌐Sept 5. 1838⌐

My dear Keble

I am very much obliged by the trouble you are taking about the Article. It will be quite in time. ⌐As to Archdeacon F [[Froude]] William wrote me the same thing. He is going to see W. and I am to write to W. particulars of the volumes. You see most of them have been *already* published in the B. C. and B. M. and the Essay on Rationalism will rather explain than make difficulties.⌐

You have not said lately how your sister was. ⌐As to my coming to Hursley, I think, if I come, it must be after our audit [[Oct 17 etc]]. I have not been at Derby for two years,⌐ and I talk at the end of this month going to see my sister. Indeed I ought. I shall be here till then. I am very much grieved about the state of Bisley. ⌐The Puseys come home in a week⌐

Ever Yrs affly J H N

P S. ⌐Sewell seems in most trying circumstances to have acquitted himself very well. I wish one could be kind to him.⌐

THURSDAY 6 SEPTEMBER 1838 commemoration Service at Bradfield—preached Number 516[2] tried to get back to Oxford—coach full

FRIDAY 7 SEPTEMBER came back to Oxford on my return letters from Wood and Mr Parry f d wrote to Mr Sparkes, Mr Parry, R Williams, C. [,] J.M. [,] Tyler and W.F.

TO J. B. MOZLEY

Oriel College. Sept 7. 1838

My dear James,

I have just returned from Bradfield—but for this I should have answered you by return of post:—to wit, that you must not think of giving up your

---

[1] After the issue of his 'Articles' of 1836, Henry VIII called on Convocation 'to set forth a plain and sincere exposition of doctrine', and 'The Godly and Pious Institution of a Christian Man' was produced the following year. Published as *The Institucion of a Gentleman*, London 1555, it was reprinted in 1839.

[2] *P.S.* V, 6, 'Remembrance of Past Mercies'. J. Marriott was a curate at Bradfield, near Reading, Berks.

visit to Derby. You do not see my reason for anxiety about the Hall. It is that we *are spending* other people's money *on rent*, yet doing nothing;—but now, I think it matters not whether you come a week earlier or later. If I can get my business all over, I propose to go to Jemima for 10 days on the 24th and wrote some days ago to that effect.—I shall be glad to see you on Monday next and shall order dinner at ½ past 5 for you. Eden is here (quod absit!) or rather (qui abesset!). You can have Rogers' room to sleep in. Pusey comes back on this day week. Mrs P. is rather better—

I have no news to tell you. I *hope* we shall have a brilliant Number of the Critic, but cannot tell yet. Berkeley is busily engaged editing Sparrow,[1] and is full of Bibliothecae Patrum and Collections of Councils. We hope to have a splendid day at Littlemore on the 22nd I wish it were not Ember Day. I am very sorry to hear your Father is unwell. Your letter gave me the first hint of it. Some of the Heads (as you would expect) are crowing over Sewell's non-election. You see the University is not our field of eminence. Manning has been very ill a second time, I am concerned to say.

There being no news I sign myself

My dear J Yours very affectly John H Newman

SATURDAY 8 SEPTEMBER 1838[2] dined by myself in Common Room Sewell's article came.

SUNDAY 9 SEPTEMBER 13 Trinity by myself in morning communion read prayers morning and afternoon preached Number 257[3] ⟨Josiah⟩ dined with Morris in Common Room Exeter

MONDAY 10 SEPTEMBER J M. came into Oxford in Common Room to dinner he, I and with me Berkeley and Bloxam

TUESDAY 11 SEPTEMBER dined in Common Room, where Eden had a number to dinner, J. M had Smith

WEDNESDAY 12 SEPTEMBER J.M. went to Derby?

TO JOHN KEBLE

Oriel ⌐Sept 13/38⌐

My dear Keble,

Many thanks indeed for your most acceptable MS—which will do us good service; good service to the Review and good service to its readers. It certainly is very interesting.[4] I will not fail at once to propose some other

---

[1] Berkeley assisted Newman in editing Bishop Anthony Sparrow's *A Rationale upon the Book of Common Prayer*, Oxford 1839.

[2] Keble wrote to Pusey about the matter of the Bishop's Charge on this day: 'I congratulate you on the lowering cloud from Cuddesdon having passed off so comfortably. I thought it impossible the Bp. could mean so much as N. at first seemed to think. I wish it may teach one to avoid using words at random of course.' For Pusey's continuing correspondence with the Bishop about the Charge, see Liddon's *Pusey* II, 59–64.

[3] *P.S.* VIII, 7, 'Josiah, a Pattern for the Ignorant'.

[4] 'Life and Writings of Sir Walter Scott', *Brit. Crit.*, 24, 1838 (Oct.), 423–83.

subjects to you—and had in mind, since you mention it, to send you Shuttleworth's book etc. But a thought just struck me—viz do you think Dr M [Moberly] could be persuaded to undertake the 'perfection of weakness'[1] together with Woodgate's B. L. [Bampton Lectures] when published? Could you sound him?

⌐I think it will be a brilliant number, thanks to my friends. There are only seven articles—Le Bas—Rogers—I—Sewell—J. Mozley—Bowden,[2] and you. I doubt whether I have put them in the right order.⌐ I suppose the names should be secret.

Pusey etc returns tomorrow—Mrs P. has caught a fresh cold. From what Dr W [Wootten] says, I am very desponding.

⌐I have proposed to W. F. [Froude],⌐ subject of course to a reference to you, ⌐to meet me at Hursley after St Luke, when he will have seen his Father.[3] The *preface* to the Becket papers might frighten people considerably —on Church and State—and, as far as I am concerned I [[could]][4] consent to its being unpublished. It never has been. I am told Mrs D's letter has got into the Times.⌐[5] It is very good news that the Translation of the Psalms is coming out. Do not sacrifice your 'turns' too much—I fear it.

I have nothing more to say, except that Pusey is going to publish his Society for the Propagation of the Gospel Sermons, which he has preached at Weymouth[6]

Ever Yrs affly John H Newman

FRIDAY 14 SEPTEMBER 1838 letter from Mr Leger R Williams came into Oxford The Puseys came into Oxford wrote to Mr Leger and Thornton R W took tea with me

SATURDAY 15 SEPTEMBER R Williams went

SUNDAY 16 SEPTEMBER 14th Trinity letter from Eyre early Communion by myself did duty morning and afternoon read Number [265] ⟨obedience the way to Thou art not far from etc⟩[7] dined with Bloxam?

[1] Keble wrote on 8 Sept., 'Moberley is going to write us a paper at Winchester on the Relation of the Doctrine of the Eucharist to that of the Resurrection of the Body . . . He spoke of Shuttleworth's book as the very perfection of weakness.' George Moberly included both Shuttleworth and Woodgate in the collection of books which he reviewed in his article 'Catholic Tradition', *Brit. Crit.*, 25, 1839 (April), 450–79.

[2] Bowden's article was deferred to January and Charles Thornton's 'The State of the Church in Upper Canada' appeared in October.

[3] Keble was surprised that the *Remains* had not sold better and wondered about the effect of the adverse criticism of Faussett and others. He was concerned about Archdeacon Froude's scruples about continuing with the *Remains* and wrote, 'I should be very sorry for the Essay on Rationalism not to come out.' For publication, the 'Essay on Rationalism' was placed in the first volume of the second part of the *Remains*, and the Becket papers in the second volume.

[4] A further word or two lost.

[5] A letter of Mary Davison, widow of John, was in circulation. She categorically denied a claim of R. D. Hampden that her husband had 'both read and expressly approved his Bampton Lectures'. See *Brit. Crit.*, 24, 490.

[6] Two sermons, *The Church the Converter of the Heathen*, Oxford 1838. The sermons were strongly in support of the Society and criticised the Church Missionary Society, chiefly for placing neither its constitution nor its missionaries under the Bishops.

[7] *P.S.* VIII, 14, 'Obedience to God the Way to Faith in Christ'. Preached on the text *Mark* 12:34, 'Thou art not far from the Kingdom of God.'

MONDAY 17 SEPTEMBER   letter from H Eyre came into Oxford I dined with him at one o'clock   walked with Pusey   wrote to H and T. Keble

TUESDAY 18 SEPTEMBER   letters from Ullerton [Utterton?] and Thornton

WEDNESDAY 19 SEPTEMBER   ember day   letters from Mr Scott and H   ½ f b   f d

THURSDAY 20 SEPTEMBER   Vigil   letters from Bridges junior and Wilson   f d   wrote to Wilson

FRIDAY 21 SEPTEMBER   ember day St Matthew   letter from Faber   service in Chancel read Number 259   f d but l.   wrote to Bowden and H   Marriott came into Oxford

TO J. W. BOWDEN

⌐Oriel College. Sept. 21. St. Matthew's 1838.⌐

My dear Bowden,

I hope you will not think I treat you shabbily, when I say, that I shall reserve your article for the January Number of the Critic, —for if you hurried or inconvenienced yourself to do it, it does seem ungrateful. However, I shall not bore you for another Article so soon as I else should have. Why I have done so would take too long to tell. First I found that as matters stood I should have no theological article at all, unless I inserted my Palmer, which at first I thought of reserving.[1] Then again I found that yours, Sewell's and Mozley's were too much the same kind of article—and there are a number of reasons too many and little to mention why I could not postpone M's or S's—I think it will be a very good number—so that I can afford to keep yours back; and it will be a [2] of reserve for January, which will be no little ease to my mind. For it is miserable to begin with nothing.

⌐To-morrow we celebrate the Anniversary of the Dedication at Littlemore. Pusey is here, but⌐ I regret to say ⌐cannot come.⌐ I regret especially, as you will, for the cause. ⌐I grieve to say that there seems no hope whatever of Mrs Pusey. Some London Physician is coming down to-morrow. He does not realize the truth yet—but is sanguine and desponding by turns—so perhaps it had better not be talked about. This is a very great blow indeed.⌐

⌐The Bishop's charge is to appear soon,⌐ to-morrow perhaps curious,[3] if it does. ⌐I met him in the street the other day, and thanked him for his kindness. 'No' he said, 'do not thank me—wait till you see'. These are ominous words—but from what he has written to Pusey, I cannot think he *means* to put me in an awkward situation

The Archbishop of Dublin [[Whately]] is here, and is just what he was in manner etc. At first I was afraid to call, knowing how annoyed he had been; but I got him sounded, and found he was pretty tame, and called in consequence. He is so good hearted a man, that it passed off well. I set him

[1] 'Palmer's *Treatise on the Church of Christ*', *Brit. Crit.*, 24, 1838 (Oct.), 347–72; *Ess.* I, 179–215.
[2] A word or two illegible to the copyist.
[3] See previous pararaph.

upon Political Economy and the Irish Poor Law—listened for half an hour, and came away.⌐

Of course you know long and long ago, that ⌐Richards is head of Exeter. He is a very good fellow, but I cannot deny that it is a floor.[1] Perhaps it will throw Sewell more upon us. David had with him every one that was discontented etc., so may we.⌐

We are getting on through the Third Tract of Volume 5. My new Volume of Sermons is in press. I fear St Austin will be delayed for the Table of Contents. How is your brother and his wife? you have not mentioned anything about them. I hope your children got quite well soon.

Ever yrs affly John H. Newman.

TO R. W. CHURCH

⌐St Matthew's Day⌐ [21 September] 1838

My dear Church,

As soon as you can, the index—as I know you will without my fidgetting. As many *facts* as you can verify in my Preface, verify.[2]

I am aware of the following false prints[3]—add any more you can ⌐Marriott is here, come up for our Feast of the Dedication tomorrow⌐

Ever Yrs J H N

SATURDAY 22 SEPTEMBER 1838 Littlemore day ember day Sir J Clerke [Clarke] *M D* to see Mrs Pusey went up to Littlemore with Marriott Service twice—I preaching in morning Number 516[4]—and performing Holy Communion f d Bishop's charge out Marriott went back

SUNDAY 23 SEPTEMBER 15th Trinity early Communion by myself did duty morning and afternoon read Number 124[5] dined in Common Room by myself?

MONDAY 24 SEPTEMBER was to have breakfasted with Garden and his wife, but did not. Archbishop of Dublin called on me Mr Parker, Copeland, Bloxam, Smith and Berkeley to dinner

TUESDAY 25 SEPTEMBER walked with Copeland dined with Copeland wrote to F., R.W., Faber [of] Univ., Woodgate, Mr Scott, and Mr Leger. T and H came into Oxford to Ogle's

---

[1] 'blow'.
[2] To *The Catechetical Lectures of S. Cyril . . . of Jerusalem* in the Library of the Fathers.
[3] Newman added a list.
[4] *P.S.* V, 6, 'Remembrance of Past Mercies'.
[5] *P.S.* VIII, 8, 'Inward Witness to the Truth of the Gospel'.

TO F. W. FABER

Oriel College. Sept 25. 1838

Dear Faber,

Never mind about the Optatus—it will be welcome when it comes, but we have enough to go on with.[1] S. Cyril and the Confessions (Latin and English) are now finished. S. Cyprian's Treatises are going to press. At Christmas we proceed with S. Chrysostom on the Ephesians. The original of Cyril is also going to press directly.

Mr Townsend's friends certainly, as you seem to think, have more to fear from him than his opponents: I think however you will be relieved when you see the Charge. He quotes, or rather refers to you very fairly—merely as coinciding with him generally in Reformation principles.[2] I am not surprised at the misconceptions which have attended you in the North. It must be so for a time. Dr Pusey several months since preached at Clifton. He told the congregation that, if they were men of large sorts, they would have completed Bristol Cathedral. I believe an aisle is wanting. It got about, avouched by ear witnesses, that he had called on them to subscribe to a Popish Chapel or Cathedral, building in the place. Of course a person must always aim at truth, and if he cannot feel himself safe in saying more than this or that, he must not say it;—but, to state a matter of fact, of this I am sure, that the more you say and the further you go, the further people will follow. They will always lag a little behind in order to be safe and moderate, and to have the satisfaction of abusing you. They will any how make unfortunate you, a sacrifice to their self importance—and will criticize and disown you in order that they may with a good grace adopt (in substance) what you say. I have no doubt in the world that you are doing good by what you have been preaching, in spite of all apparent scandal and temporary misconception.

You will be much concerned to hear that Mrs Pusey is given over—but I should not like this to be said about, as from me

Yours very truly John H Newman

TO R. I. WILBERFORCE

Oriel College. Sept 25. 1838

My dear Wilberforce,

I felt very much obliged by your Article—of course it is too late for this month, but shall appear in January.[3] I have no wish to break with Bunsen

---

[1] Faber did not complete anything for the Library of the Fathers.

[2] George Townsend had recently delivered a Charge attacking the principle of reserve or economy in religious matters.

[3] 'Prussian Schools', *Brit. Crit.*, 25, 1839 (Jan.), 76–95.

whom I know—but I suspect he has no smack of Apostolicity about him. Your article does not seem, however, to commit the B.C. at all, as far as I see at first sight. It is very interesting and, I hope, will be useful. I shall propose a word or two (no more) of emendation in the passage about Lord Melbourne and Hampden.[1] The allusion is so apropos, it cannot be omitted —and yet in my situation here, it is difficult. There are one or two words besides, I shall ask your indulgence about. But the article is a capital one.

I hope you will think our October number a good one—there is one floor. Keble and Rogers[2] have written too much on the same subject.

You will be much concerned to hear that Mrs Pusey lies without any hope of recovery. When God will please to remove her, is of course uncertain. There is no doubt about it, yet I should not like to be the means of putting it about.

When do you mean to pay this place your promised visit. The Archbishop of Dublin is here, and just what he was.

Ever yrs affectly John H Newman

P.S. I do not see that we differ in our views about the Archbishop of Cologne at all. Wilson and Wood both, I think, separately undertook the subject. Wilson has given it up. I do not know how Wood stands—but if you have got it up and he not, I should be obliged much by an article on the subject from you.[3] As to the Archbishop I am for 'measures not men'—he represents a *principle*, whether he individually be right or wrong.

TO H. A. WOODGATE

Oriel College. Sept 25/38

My dear Woodgate,

I believe nothing hinders your going to press at once; though formally the Delegates' leave should be asked to use the University Types.[4] You have nothing to do then, but to send up your MS to Parker for the purpose. The Preface and Notes of course will come last. When you send them up, you can tell Parker that, if there is any difficulty about beginning printing at once, it is the same to you—you can print elsewhere. I will gladly look over them, but I should prefer doing so, when they are in proof. On Monday next, I propose going to Derby for a fortnight—afterwards I shall be here,

---

[1] See *Brit. Crit.*, 25, 80–81, where Wilberforce draws an analogy between Melbourne's appointment of Hampden to the Regius Professorship of Divinity and the equally controversial appointment of Vatke to the Chair of Divinity at Berlin.

[2] Rogers wrote on 'Poems by Trench and Milnes', and Keble on the 'Life and Writings of Sir Walter Scott'.

[3] See letter of 18 July to Wilberforce.

[4] For the printing of his Bampton Lectures on *The Authoritative Teaching of the Church shewn to be in Conformity with Scripture, Analogy, and the Moral Constitution of Man*, Oxford 1839.

if you want to send them to me. Thanks for your kind invite—but I have not been in Derby for two years.

Kindest compliments to Mrs Woodgate and believe me

Yrs ever affectly John H Newman

WEDNESDAY 26 SEPTEMBER 1838 breakfasted with Ogle walked to Littlemore and read; back, from Iffley with T and H, calling on Mrs Slatter dined at Ogle's where also Bloxam.

THURSDAY 27 SEPTEMBER breakfasted with Ogle walked to Littlemore and read—back with Bloxam. Ogle, T and H. to dinner with me in Common Room Berkeley afterwards.

FRIDAY 28 SEPTEMBER Miss Homfray went made Mrs Edmonds' will walked with H to Littlemore f d back by myself called with H on Mrs Whately went to Ogle's to tea

SATURDAY 29 SEPTEMBER St Michael letter from Mr Scott Service in Chancel in morning read Number 517 and part of 471[1] called on H Bishop dined with Ogle

SUNDAY 30 SEPTEMBER 16th Trinity letter from Bowden by myself at Sacrament in morning H went to Littlemore in morning did duty morning and afternoon preached Number 269 dined with Ogle

TO JOHN KEBLE

⌐Sept 30/38¬

My dear Keble

I ought to have written to you several days since—and now, as ⌐I go to Derby tomorrow, please to direct your answer to Pusey¬—and if not inconvenient to you, at once. ⌐It is as to the *Dedication*.[2] We wish to have your critical judgment on every word; it is Pusey's writing, and I have not yet undertaken to think about it—for I want your thoughts about it first.¬

As to your own concerns, many thanks for your Article, which must be serviceable. It struck me a good article might be written [on] 'the Cathedral' contrasted with a number of other poems, e.g. Mr Moultrie's[3]—on this subject, viz that nothing but Apostolicity is poetical—that religious poets are forced to go *out of* their religion, (e.g. into domestic matters etc) for poetry when their religion is Peculiarity etc. The idea is Williams'. Would this fall in with any floating matter you have? Or what think you to taking Southey's Poems, (e.g. Thalaba etc) just published?[4]

⌐There is no change, or prospect of change, as to Mrs Pusey. Do you

---

[1] *P.S.* IV, 13, 'The Invisible World'.
[2] [[of Library of the Fathers to the Archbishop?]]
[3] John Moultrie, *Poems*, London 1837. A second edition appeared in 1838.
[4] Robert Southey, *Thalaba, the Destroyer*, London 1838. This was a new edition of the poem which Southey wrote in 1800.

know a good London Physician has been down, and pronounced her case, humanly speaking, hopeless?⌐

E. Churton is mollifying, and has written me a letter, half penitential, and half nouthetetic.[1] It strikes me, if you are clear for it, it would be a good thing for you to go to press with Cornish's Chrysostom.[2] What I sent you was about half—Unless we get one under another, we shall never get on. Will you mention the subject to Pusey.

Ever Yrs affly John H Newman

P.S. ⌐Our Bishop's charge is out—I should like to know what you think of it.⌐

To the Most Reverend/ Father in God/ William Lord Archbishop of Canterbury/ Primate of all England/ and formerly Regius Professor of Divinity/ in the University of Oxford/ This Library/ of ancient Bishops, Fathers, Doctors/ Martyrs and Confessors/ of Christ's Holy Catholic Church/ is inscribed/ in token of reverence/ for His Grace's high office/ and of affectionate gratitude/ for his Episcopal kindness./

MONDAY I OCTOBER 1838 Spranger took my duty in my absence came away by 2 o'clock coach *in afternoon* for Birmingham—lay down to sleep *for an hour or two* at Coach and Horses—at ½ past 3 on

TO J. R. HOPE

Oriel Sunday night [October 1838][3]

Dear Hope,

I have had a note from Oakeley to say that he is ready to preach on any of the three next Sundays, not afterwards for a month. He adds 'I shall be very glad to do so any where on the Queen's Letter'[4]—

Yrs most truly John H Newman

TUESDAY 2 OCTOBER 1838 Tuesday morning by Leeds mail to Derby—where arrived at 8 A M walked into the Town with A [Arthur Mozley]—who dined with us wrote a word to Bowden in J M's letter to [Manuel] Johnson into the Friary[5] in the evening as afterwards

---

[1] 'admonitory'. See letter of 3 Oct. to Churton.
[2] H. K. Cornish and J. Medley's translation of St John Chrysostom's *Homilies on I Corinthians* appeared in 1839 as volumes four and five of the Library of the Fathers, Keble wrote the preface.
[3] Dated by Hope.
[4] Hope noted, 'i.e. for the S. P. G.', Society for the Propagation of the Gospel.
[5] The Mozley family home.

TO J. W. BOWDEN

Derby Oct 2/38

My dear Bowden,

I have nothing to say but to thank you for your letter; but should be much obliged if you would mention to Rivington about the non-printing off of the Article on the B. A.[1] However, there is no chance of its being printed till I return the proof, which I have not done. And any how I shall write to Roworth.[2] Your news about all your party is excellent indeed—I had forgotten your voyage was to be before the end of September. James M. has written to Johnson about the Aula;[3] give my kindest remembrances to him. Mrs Pusey is about the same, but, I suppose, there is no kind of hope.

My sister Jemima desires her kind remembrances to you and Mrs Bowden.

Ever Yrs affly J H Newman

P.S. I am glad you like the Tract 83

WEDNESDAY 3 OCTOBER 1838 walked with J and Ja [James Mozley] *to see the railroad making* A M to dinner wrote to C. [,] Bridges, Mr Ball (for Treasurer) to Churton and to Rogers

TO EDWARD CHURTON

Derby. Oct 3. 1838

My dear Churton,[4]

I shall at any time be much pleased to receive any communications from you for the British Critic—indeed I had expected some, since you were so good as almost to promise—but since you did not send, I thought you had

---

[1] 'British Association for the Advancement of Science'.
[2] The usual printer for *Brit. Crit.*
[3] Manuel Johnson was considering taking up residence in the 'house for young writers'.
[4] Churton wrote on 18 Sept. to apologise for his delay in finishing his article for *Brit. Crit.* on the 'Revival of Jesuitism', and explaining that he was having difficulty in finding any recent information on the subject.

He went on to say, with regard to Newman's *Letter to Faussett* and Froude's *Remains*, 'I have read your controversy with Il Dottore *Falsetto*. Bating that I heartily wish that you had never given him the opportunity, you have answered him exceedingly well . . . I do not at all sympathise with your lament over our Communion Service: for how can you justify it, when you confess that all that is of vital consequence has been retained. No! I ever shall regret that the pruning knife was not far more extensively used in the preparation of those extraordinary papers. I could hardly have expected that you would defend them with less zeal;—but they have sadly encumbered a plain good cause.—Hook has his late Visitation Sermon in the press. It will be accompanied with an Appendix, in which I believe he means to say something of this indecorous attack of the Margaret Professor. We have great reason to be thankful for the remarkable success which continues to attend his efforts. Your opponents will never find ground to stand upon, *unless you are so kind as to give it to them* . . . you must perceive that, since the appearance of Frowde's Remains, your friends are perplexed, and some who were neuters have declared against you . . . indeed I have not found one, who defends that publication, except Dr. Pusey . . . pray think of the peril of new divisions, and on points confessedly unnecessary.'

some good reason. You are very kind to be so frank in the expression of your opinion about me. I hope never to be distressed at it, except what must arise from differing in any matter from any one like yourself. While we hold the same faith, I should be a fool if I did not allow you to have your own opinion about matters which are not of faith, about historical events and characters, and the train of circumstances which have resulted in those conclusions which we both accept as true and obligatory. Still less have I any right to complain of your censuring me in matters of conduct and judgment, when I claim a right to censure our predecessors in the Church. It would be very inconsistent.

As to the passages in the Remains you speak of, I never have repented publishing them one single moment, and though I cannot imitate your language and say 'I *never* shall regret', yet I have no reason to suppose I ever shall. As a matter of honesty I never shall, I think, I am so constituted, other persons are so also, that I do dislike uncommonly to keep things in, and seem to be playing a double part. There are persons who are much easier, after they have told another that they differ from him. This is the kind of feeling I mean. While the world thought, I liked Jewell etc. or rather while any of my friends thought it, I was uncomfortable. I am glad an opportunity has been given me to show them what I am. You know your bargain now; at least I am no hypocrite. I cannot help fancying that you were easier after speaking out in my room; give me credit for the same state of mind.

I do detest the talk that is made, to me the odious hypocritical talk, (*not to others* for they believe) about certain things and persons—and if I did not try to rule myself, I could say very violent things, and astonish you as much perhaps as you astonished me when I last saw you. And this consideration, while it quite removes (I trust) all pain from my mind at any thing you said, may perhaps tend to soften you towards me. Is all the strong feeling, all the expression of it, to be on one side only? why should we not bear with each other, agreeing so clearly in main matters as we do.

I have said *honesty* itself would urge me not to play the hypocrite with kind persons like yourself, who would give me credit for an agreement with them which did not exist; but I do fully believe that Keble and I have acted on the truest and wisest view of what is *expedient*. On this subject I will say nothing, lest I should vex you; yet the pain persons feel is no proof we are not right. Operations which save life are often painful—But the upshot is this, as I have said—we have on certain points very strong feelings different ways. I as *strong as you* yet I am willing to act with you, as far as we go together, not withstanding; I trust you will on the other side also.

As to the alterations in the Communion Service, I only mean that if our Reformers had cut out parts of the (e.g.) first chapter of St John which were not fundamental or quite essential,—and forbidden us to read or use the rest, I should be indignant, though I was forced to agree that they were not fundamental.

I have not yet seen, but will certainly get your 'Letters of a Reformed Catholic.'[1] I have a friend who knows well the capabilities of Newcastle upon Tyne—and will ask him your question—[2]

With the kindest thoughts and feelings

Yours most truly John H Newman

P.S. You understand your Article will be most welcome, whenever it comes.

TO FREDERIC ROGERS

Oct. 3. 1838

—I like your Article very much and think there is a good deal in it.[3] It remarkably agrees with Keble's. It is hard somewhat—and I do not quite see the connection of parts of your dissertation—at least it is not brought out enough—and I do not see the intimate bearing of it on the instances of Milnes and Trench which follow—but on the whole it is very successful. It would improve you much if you would try to write silly articles. As a specimen of what I mean take James M's, which is clever but somewhat boyish and diffuse; too much so to be allowable more than once, but he can always, I know, *condense*, and put in matter [,] and his danger was dryness. Let him once get a copia verborum etc and then he may relapse into philosophy. I should say something of the kind of you. I have as yet praised, not criticized the said J. M. in consequence of a hint of yours.

What think you of my dedicating my new Volume of Sermons to Rose? view it on my side and his side. I should not be sorry if you wrote to me here about it, before my return to Oxford. Pusey seemed to think he would take it very kind; and would not hear of my writing to Harrison first to sound Rose—also he seemed suprised at my first mentioning the idea,—but then said, when I asked him why, 'Oh no, I think it a very good idea, and will diminish the Cambridge jealousy about us, only it would not have struck me.'—I am trying to make out whether it is inconsiderate to Pusey, considering the Rose and Pusey controversy.

... I think the number of the B. C. a capital one there is not one bad article.—

THURSDAY 4 OCTOBER 1838 letter from Manning walked with Jo and Ja [John and James Mozley] to Morley to call on Mr Fox, who was not at home. M M [Maria Mozley] to dinner received and sent back proofs to G and R

[1] *Letters of a Reformed Catholic*, London 1839. They were two separate pamphlets, 'Nos. I. & II. On the leading Principle of the Reformation: and on Private Judgement and Authority in Matters of Faith', and 'No. III. On Apostolical Succession.'

[2] Churton wrote that at Newcastle, 'a gentleman is writing pamphlets addressed to Bp. Maltby against you. *Do you know of any zealous Clergyman of right principles in that neighbourhood?*'

[3] 'Poems by Trench and Milnes', *Brit. Crit.*, 24, 1838 (Oct.), 271–301. Newman also mentions Keble's 'Life and Writings of Sir Walter Scott', and James Mozley's 'Palgrave-Truths and Fictions of the Middle Ages', both of which appeared in the same number.

FRIDAY 5 OCTOBER   called on Mr Dean, Dr Baker, and H M. [Henry Mozley]   ½ f b ½ f d   received and sent back proofs to G and R. and letter to R.   J M to dinner

SATURDAY 6 OCTOBER   letters from Rogers, Mr Waller [Walter], Hook inclosing letter from Mr Nevins, and proofs from Baxter and Pusey   sent back proofs from Baxter and Pusey

MONDAY 8 OCTOBER   letter from R Williams   wrote to Spranger

TUESDAY 9 OCTOBER   to dinner, Mrs M. Mr and Mrs S. Fox, Mr, Mrs and Miss Cox   wrote to R Williams [,] Herbert Corn Market and Conservative Journal, sending subscription

WEDNESDAY 10 OCTOBER   letters from Spranger and Pusey (proof)   to dinner A. —A.M. and J.M. and Miss Spaldin

THURSDAY 11 OCTOBER   wrote to Pusey (proof) Rose, and Wilson

TO R. F. WILSON

[Derby 11 October 1838][1]

Also please tell Keble that I should of all things like a Review of Mansoni's Promessi Sposi, if he feels inclined—I have long wished it for the B.C. and he could make it fit on beautifully to his last Article. Or what would he think of developing explaining and defending his view about primary and and secondary poets—which (or course) at first startles people?—e.g. why is not Dryden though he wrote for money, able, though not in degree yet in kind, to ra[nk] with Scott who wrote for money?—[2]

I have no news to tell you here—I go back to Oxford, so be it, on Monday next. I should rejoice to see you at any time good luck allows of

Ever Yrs affly John H Newman

FRIDAY 12 OCTOBER 1838   ½ f b   ½ f d

SATURDAY 13 OCTOBER   letters from Rose[3] and H.W.   A M and A [Arthur Mozley and Anne] to dinner

SUNDAY 14 OCTOBER   went over (with Mr and Mrs M) to Mickleover to do duty for Mr F. Curzon, who is in prison.   In afternoon at St Werburgh's—very rainy   wrote to H W and to Mr Waller [Walter] of Bideford

MONDAY 15 OCTOBER   set out with J. and A.M. [James and Arthur Mozley] to Oxford by Northampton   Daman ill in bed   on my return found letters from Hicks, Pope, Bowden, R Wilberforce, Rose—and Mr Kilvert with book

TUESDAY 16 OCTOBER   letters from R Williams and Mrs W W.   with J M chosing furniture etc for the House (*this was, I suppose, the house for students etc that Pusey*

---

[1] Dated from the postmark, the first part of the letter is missing.
[2] Keble wrote on 15 Oct., 'As to Dryden, the reason why I put him where I do is not his writing for money, but because I cannot detect [in] him any pervading feeling to urge him any how into writing—I should be glad if I could, because I admire his energy and ability extremely.'
[3] H. J. Rose wrote on 11 Oct. to announce his departure for Rome for the winter, on account of his poor health. He wrote again next day, gratefully accepting Newman's offer to dedicate *P.S.* IV to him, '. . . as a very great *honour* publicly—and privately a *very very* high gratification indeed.' See letter of 9 Jan. 1839 to Mrs J. Mozley.

and I set up opposite Ch Ch[1]   Christie not up this audit   plan on foot about the monument to Cranmer etc.   dined with the Provost—James there.   Eden made Dean, I Junior Treasurer.

WEDNESDAY 17 OCTOBER   letters from Keble and Wilson (by Williams) W.F. [,] J. [,] and E Churton   H Westmacott and his wife to breakfast   Daman ill in bed all through the week   went with Mr Hornby (*of Winwick*) to Littlemore   Gaudy dinner   wrote to Hicks, Keble, R Williams and R Wilberforce

TO JOHN KEBLE

Oriel instauro[2] Oct 17/38

My dear Keble

I have received your letter by Williams and this letter from W. F. [Froude] at the same time. I propose, with your leave, setting off for Hursley next Monday; W. F. does not say how long he shall be with you; for myself I ought to be back here as soon as my business with you and with him lets me—for there is plenty to do here.

Thanks for your hints about the irregularities in Church Service, your plan is much better. I had thought, however, of your objections, and thought somehow they would not apply—but I dare say they would.[3] I congratulate you on the state of the Psalms etc. I *suppose* it would be more respectful to write to the Bishop of O [Oxford]—but shall see Pusey tomorrow, and will

[1] The Chronological Notes refer to a small account book. The account covered 7 July 1838 to 6 March 1840, taking only one page of the book, and balanced at £462. 19s. At the head of the page are two notes: 'We took the House in St Aldate's from June 24. 1838—and the agreement I made with J. M. [James Mozley] was, that I would supply Rent, Taxes, Rates, and keep two servants at £30 a year each—besides buying furniture, kitchen utensils etc.'— and those who occupied the house their board, coals, candles, etc. The following is the account.' 'In the House were J. M.[,] [M.] Pattison, [A.J.] Christie, his brother [C. H. Christie], [F. M. R.] Barker and [C.] Seager.'

The credit side of the account is made up mainly of gifts from friends. A balance due of £119. 9s. is marked 'Fund', i.e., money funded for the *Tracts* and similar purposes since 1833, with the note in pencil, 'this is still to pay'. The list of benefactions reads: 'July 6/38 NB I have £100 from J W B [Bowden] 50 from R W [Williams] The promise of £50 from M P [Maria Pusey] £48 odd paid[;] £30 from E B P never paid[;] £90 a year from R W and £50 a year perhaps through B H [Benjamin Harrison?] and maintenance for one (say £100 ⟨£50⟩) from C. M. [Marriott] £40 donation paid from S F W [Wood] Mr L promise yearly of £100 from Fellowship for two scholars in divinity'. Mr L, never named, was a stranger to Newman.

Though the house was not the success that Newman had hoped, he noted that three of its residents obtained fellowships, Pattison, Christie, Mozley.

[2] 'back again at Oriel'.

[3] It would seem that in the missing part of his letter of 11 Oct. to R. F. Wilson, Newman had thrown out the suggestion of inviting communications to himself, as editor of *Brit. Crit.*, about irregularities in Church services. Keble wrote on 15 Oct., 'I cannot think the way you mention either right or expedient—not right, because it seems so like what we charge on the Record, setting one's self up to be a kind of Bishop: not expedient, because the chief practical result it would have will be the cramming of your letter box with insulting anonymous letters from peculiars etc. complaining of our own friends. These are my rough ideas on that proposition—but could not the object be in some measure attained by a striking sentence or two, repeated in various forms, and illustrated by cases as they happen to come to your knowledge, in your Ecclesiastical Record? setting forth the duty of *well informed* Laymen especially to inform their Bishops of such things . . . If we can get the Bishops remonstrated with, the matter will be much mended.'

ask.[1] Today is so busy a day, and Mr Hornby of Winwick is into the bargain here, to be disabused about 10,000 reports of us, that I fear I shall not have time to see Pusey.

I am *quite sure* that our readers will not be tired with more Poetry—I do so wish you would undertake Mansoni—As to Romanism, we all know but a little—but still the contrast with our own way of going on is so striking that a person may know much negatively.[2] There is a notion here of building a 'Church of the Reformers', on order to force your humble servant either to subscribe to it *or* not. I do not mean to say so worthy an object was the motive principle.[3] Thanks to Wilson for his letter

Ever Yrs affly John H Newman

TO R. I. WILBERFORCE

Oriel College. Oct. 17. 1838

My dear Wilberforce

I inquired, as far as I could, when you wrote. Young Bunsen was away. Pusey now tells me he has undertaken to answer Tholuck, though he cannot without first writing to him for further information.

Your article will be most valuable for the next number.[4] I aim at having almost a number in advance; unless I do this I shall be never comfortable —nor will any thing go on well. Do not undertake the Archbishop of Cologne[5]—if for no other reason, there have been so many articles lately on the subject in various reviews,—that unless a person felt almost impelled to write by his subject, I would not desire it done.

I have little news to tell you—How long your letter has been here I know not. I found it on my table on my return from Derby the day before yesterday. I am in the Tower—the Statute about elections reading—and the elections of officers for the year impending. Eden is Dean, and I Junior Treasurer; for we have hardly Tutor or officer in the body. Greswell has had so severe an illness that he has given up all duties—Marriott is going either to Chichester or Rome—and Daman, whom you know not, is ill a bed—Copleston is gone to Exeter—Mr Hornby of Winwick is here today, and very kind—so was Mr [G. S.] Faber who was here several months since. I am going to Keble's next Monday for a few days to meet William Froude. Rogers is Senior Treasurer—

Ever Yrs most sincerely John H Newman

P.S. James is flitting about the room like the ghost of a Senior Treasurer[6]—

[1] Keble asked whether it would be best to write to the Bishop of Oxford to ask for permission to dedicate his forthcoming *Psalter* to him.

[2] Keble wrote, 'I should like Manzoni, but don't feel up to it; amongst other reasons, for want of practical experience of the R. C. System: which seems to me a sine qua non for doing that book well.'

[3] See letter of 22 Oct. to Mrs J. Mozley and note there.

[4] 'Prussian Schools', *Brit. Crit.*, 25, 1839 (Jan.).

[5] See second note to letter of 18 July to Wilberforce.

[6] William James, Fellow of Oriel until 1837, had been Senior Treasurer many years before.

THURSDAY 18 OCTOBER 1838 St Luke's Statutes read College meeting greater part of day Service in Chancel read Number 261 dined with the Provost to meet [W.] James

TO H. E. MANNING

[18 October 1838]

My dear Manning,

I add to Marriott's letter a brief note to say first how I rejoice you are going abroad—next how I envy your going to Rome—thirdly how I hope you will thoroughly convert Rose whom you will meet there—fourthly to say that Marriott *must not* be kept in suspense. It is a most miserable thing for his health, I assure you—and I shall recommend him forthwith to write to the Bishop and withdraw proprio motu, unless the Bishop decides one way or the other.[1] It is very cruel indeed, though it is not meant to be so. If there is any thing more than another likely to do M. harm, it is this shilly shally way of going on

So with very affectionate thoughts, Yours John H Newman

P.S. Mrs Pusey's case has been pronounced hopeless, as far as man goes, this 5 weeks—but it is as well not to make a talk about it—P. does not give up hope, knowing there are efforts made other than those which medicine reaches. Thank you, I am very well. I rejoice in the prospect of your coming here (I am only going away *next* week ⟨from the 22nd to 27th⟩) and will gladly look over any thing—

FRIDAY 19 OCTOBER 1838 letters from Acland and Wilson (or rather yesterday) College meeting continued f d

SATURDAY 20 OCTOBER first day of term—Eden and Daman Tutors, Daman ill. Everal ill—visited first time. dined in hall

SUNDAY 21 OCTOBER 19th Trinity early Sacrament—Williams assisting me. read prayers morning J.M. preached

TO MRS E. B. PUSEY

Oriel Oct 21/38

My dear Mrs Pusey

I am much affected by your very kind note, which I shall make much of. God grant you still, and for ever and ever, and more abundantly, the peace and confidence with which He blesses you are present[2]

Ever Yrs affectionately John H Newman

[1] See letter of 2 Nov. to Mrs Thomas Mozley.
[2] Mrs Pusey wrote earlier the same day:
'My dear Mr Newman
Thank you for all your "kind thoughts" and words of and about me. You comfort me more than you know of, and at Weymouth where my bodily discomforts were greater and my

MONDAY 22 OCTOBER 1838 *went somewhere—to London?* [Hursley] Williams
visited Everall in my absence

TO MRS JOHN MOZLEY

Oriel Oct 22 [1838]

My dear Jemima

This is a most shabby letter, but I am just setting off to Keble's, and can
find no paper.

Keble is well inclined to take Mansoni, but I find both he and others think
it expedient not to have more poetry for some time in the B. C. Every one
thinks it a very brilliant number. Sir F. Palgrave is highly pleased with
James's [Mozley] article.[1] Others have spoken in great praise of it. ⟨J's
article⟩. I am glad to find Sir F. P. is author of a most favorable and friendly
review of Froude's Remains in the Gentleman's Magazine.[2]

I send you the nutmegs. On Saturday I had the present of a rich Cross
embossed antique offertory dish for Littlemore.—Thanks for Harriett's
intelligence, which Pusey. was tempted with, but I fear has difficulties in it.
We know Mr Werter [Warter]—though I have not seen him. They are
getting up a sort of Cranmer and Latimer testimonial here; whether it is to be
a Church or a Cross or a monument is undecided. They told the President
of Magd (so it is said) that it was for the *Primitive* Martyrs and so got his
name—they told the Vice Chancellor[3] it was done against me, and he
withdrew his; so they say.[4]

With kindest remembrances to your whole party, and love to J.[,]A. and
H. [Herbert]

Ever yrs affly John H Newman

faith weaker I felt it was invaluable to me, to know your sermon on a Particular Providence
[*P.S.* III, 9]; *it* has cheered and calmed a sick bed, and will doubtless (if such be God's will)
do the same when my latter hours approach. For that, and much beside, *especially* for *one*
act, most gratefully, affectionately and humbly yours Maria'.

The last sentence undoubtedly refers to Mrs Pusey's baptism, see note to diary for
14 April.

[1] The article reviewed Palgrave's *Truths and Fictions of the Middle Ages. The Merchant
and the Friar*, London 1837.

[2] Palgrave wrote that he was 'very grateful to the editor for having in so judicious and
affectionate a manner performed his act of duty to his friend's memory, and given us so true
and lively a picture of his profound piety, his brilliant talents, and his accurate and varied
knowledge . . . It was impossible that the editor could pass over unnoticed the probable
expression of a feeling, that many of the sentiments and expressions encouraged a dangerous
tendency to Romanism; and he has successfully met it, from the author's own repeated
declarations.' See the *Gentleman's Magazine*, 10, 1838 (July), 49-54.

[3] A. T. Gilbert.

[4] It was widely believed that a Martyr's Memorial would be a test to Newman and Pusey,
and the plan was drawn up at a meeting at Golightly's house. Froude's *Remains* seem to have
been a catalyst. Harrison wrote to Pusey, 'I heard . . . its first origination to have been called
forth by the publication of Froude's "Remains" . . .'. As time went on there were attempts to
turn the Memorial into an anti-Roman demonstration, and it was hoped that this would unite
more people like Newman to the project. See the following letter from Pusey and the letter
of 28 Dec. to T. Henderson.

FROM E. B. PUSEY

Oct. 23. 1838.

My dear Newman

. . . . . .

The object of this parcel is, however, not the dedication, but that you and Keble may talk over this Church of the Martyrs. Yesterday Harrison and Sewell, today [W.] Churton, called upon me about it. Among other things, C. says, that he or they thought in the first instance that you had been consulted about it, and that they mistook what had been said to and by T. Mozley for what had been said to and by you. However, it seems that they are very anxious that it should not be a source of discord, and that we should join.

I told both that I would do nothing without you, for that since it had been spoken of as a hit against you, even if I should be satisfied with any plan myself, I would not join in any thing which did not satisfy you. Further, that a plan to commemorate the Reformers now, was at all events suspicious, but that as certain things had been said, of course we could not join unless right principles were somehow expressed and embodied in the very monument itself; that mere general terms would not do; thus Sewell talked of their being 'martyrs for the truth' I said it must be said somehow 'Catholic and primitive truth' as opposed to 'Neoteric.'

Sewell talked of a cross in Broad St, which would be in many ways a good, besides that it is not respectful that carts should drive over the place, where they yielded up their souls; Churton of a Church (which plan is not yet given up.) I said in addition that it must not be the Martyr's Church, canonizing them, that there might be no objection to a cenotaph, provided the inscription were a sound one, but that the Church must be called after someone already canonized, not by individuals.

Both I put off by saying the inscription must first be agreed upon. I half referred Sewell to Routh for an inscription, but withdrew, fearing that unless someone were at hand to suggest to him what these people were about, he might not see through it.

Churton's plan, which he had called to show you, was for a Church on the site already purchased for the new district Church of St Ebbe's, which by pulling down a few houses (which the corporation talked of taking down) might be laid open to the end of Queen St. and that it might be made a little Cathedral with cenotaphs. Certainly splendid notions for these people to have lighted upon, one, a cross in the midst of the broadest street in the city; the other, a Cathedral with shrines!

Churton's prospectus also was altogether sound, except that the first sentence spoke of 'pure and Scriptural truth' instead of Catholic; but then the next had Catholic.

Now what I want you to consider, is whether, we should say that we would have nothing to do with the plan, (in which case it *might* fall to the ground, if we were united, or it *might* be carried on by the Recordites out of the University, (which would do no harm) or it might be done by weak persons in the University who did not see what was meant), or should we capitulate, making our own terms. The Record may have its triumph for the time, and we might have the precedent for setting up crosses, instead of digging them out on Whit-Mondays . . .[1]

WEDNESDAY 24 OCTOBER 1838   wrote to Mrs W W

---

[1] Pusey soon became more decided, writing on 5 Nov. to B. Harrison, 'My final conclusion about the monument is, that *I* had rather not have anything to do with it. Three years ago I printed . . . that the great mercy in our Reformation was that we had no human founder: we were not identified with men, or any set of men: it was God's mercy that we had so little of human influence'. He wrote to the Bishop of Oxford on 12 Nov., 'I fear lest this plan should tend to increase the vulgar impression that we were a new Church at the Reformation, instead of being the old one purified.' See Liddon's *Pusey* II, 64ff.

TO H. E. MANNING

Hursley, 24th October 1838.
(I go back on the 26th.)

I return through G. and R. the two first sheets of your postscript.[1] The beginning is rather hard, e.g. I do not see how Paley's Evidences have to do with the 'rule of faith,' in any sense in which the words are or can fairly be used, i.e. I do not see the meaning or drift of calling 'the grounds and proofs of revelation' the rule of faith. Nor do I think it subserves the part of exhausting the divisions of the subject which seems to have led to your noticing it. Again, I think this obscure.

Bating this objection in the outset, I think all that follows very good; the twenty objections are valuable and happy, particularly the last,[2] and the whole is clearly and well worked out. As to Chillingworth, I should consider him a shuffler; but I do not see why we should not use the better sayings of shufflers against their worse.[3] It is a homage they pay to truth, and both exposes them and stultifies their admirers—two worthy ends.

FRIDAY 26 OCTOBER 1838 on my return found proofs from R Williams letters from Carey, Manning, Mr Burder, the Bishop[,] Mr Bridgford, Perceval, Mrs Jones, and Mr Brown sent back 2 proofs to R Williams

SATURDAY 27 OCTOBER letter from Undergraduate anon. visited Everall twice

SUNDAY 28 OCTOBER letters from H and proof from Williams called on Everall— who could not see me preached Number 518

MONDAY 29 OCTOBER Everall died dined with Copeland to meet Williams' brother wrote to the Bishop

TO RICHARD BAGOT, BISHOP OF OXFORD

Oriel College Oct 29. 1838.

My dear Lord,

I was out of Oxford for several days when your Lordship's note with its enclosures arrived, and since my return it has been with Dr Pusey, who has just sent it back. I believe it is his intention to write a note of acknowledgment and for the perusal, perhaps before I close this.

[1] Manning's separately published *Appendix* to his sermon *The Rule of Faith* . . ., London 1838.

[2] Manning formulated twenty popular objections, which he attempted to answer in the main part of his *Appendix*. The last of these was: '20. That the rule of faith above given cannot be proved to be the rule of primitive times.'

[3] William Chillingworth, the seventeenth century divine, who, after a brief spell in the Roman Catholic Church, became a strong anti-Roman controversialist, denying the notion of a gift of infallibility in any Church. Manning explained that for Chillingworth, 'the one great principle of his reasoning is *universal tradition*, to the exclusion of the living infallible judge . . .' p. 26.

In returning Dr Spry's letters, I beg to express my great gratitude to your Lordship for the very kind consideration which has led to your allowing me the sight of them. In that kindness I have an abundant compensation for any remarks in your Charge which I may have misinterpreted to mean more than their fair import.[1]

It was my intention before this to have thanked your Lordship for the note which you have added to it concerning the Tracts for the Times. I did not do so at once, wishing to go by the judgment of others who were likely to take a more dispassionate view of the matter than I could. I now beg to offer my best acknowledgments for expressions which they consider enable me to proceed with the Tracts without inconsistency.

TUESDAY 30 OCTOBER 1838   letter from Anon:

WEDNESDAY 31 OCTOBER   All Hallow Even   letters from Goldsmid and (proof) from Williams   breakfasted by myself   quarterly meeting of County Schools   Mr Merewether called   walked with Pusey   f d   wrote to Mr Browne, Mr Danson, Mr Bridgford, and proof to R Williams

THURSDAY 1 NOVEMBER   letter (proof) from Williams   read Number 266   sent back proof to W.

FRIDAY 2 NOVEMBER   proof from W and letter from Westmacott   buried Everall wrote to Westmacott, Mr Jones, H, Carey, the Bishop, and proof to Williams

TO EDWARD CHURTON

Oriel College. Nov 2. 1838[2]

My dear Churton,

I have nothing to say except what I have said before, that it will please me much to have your article on the Jesuits, whenever you send it. And I should not write except that I fear you may be in suspence.

Copeland, instead of gaining, has lost time by going to Begbroke—he has to come in to Oxford continually, and spends a certain portion of his day on the road. Perhaps his health may gain by it, which it certainly did by his going to the North.

[1] The Bishop of Oxford sent two letters from Dr J. H. Spry, rector of St Marylebone, for Newman to read, as showing that a 'warm and sincere friend' of Newman did not find anything discouraging to the *Tracts* in his recent Charge. Newman, however, had for some time considered Dr Spry more of an 'Establishment man' than a friend of the Tractarians, cf. Volume IV, p. 302, note 4.

[2] Churton wrote on 15 Oct. to thank Newman for his letter of 6 Oct., and went on to say: 'You say, alluding as it seems to the Editorial responsibility for poor Froude's Remains, "The pain persons feel is no proof we are not right. Operations which save life are often painful." If the pain that has been felt were confined to persons opposed to your principles, I would allow the force of such an argument: but when you cannot but be aware that the pain is felt by those, who would give up everything but a good conscience to approve of *every thing* you do, it seems to me quite inapplicable. Do not think that the good old men whom I could name, feel towards you as Fabius was accused of feeling towards Scipio. You could not think so, if you had heard or known what pleasure they felt in the revival of that spirit which you have done so much to restore.'

Your brother Whittaker and others are busily engaged in erecting a Church or Cross to the Reformers, which they hope to do without including Ultra Protestant associates. It is satisfactory to know that their plan has not the slightest reference to any thing that has been said in this place lately against the Reformers, but is quite independent of it. I hear a report, which I will not vouch for, that there is to be a public meeting with speeches, the Bishop in the Chair.

Yours very truly John H. Newman.

P.S. Many thanks by your transcript of the Breviary Hymn[1]—I am much gratified by your approval of the last B.C. The Article on Sir W.S. is by Keble, but I suppose the Editor ought not to tell.

TO MRS THOMAS MOZLEY

Novr 2. 1838[2]

Marriott is to go to Chichester after all[3]—but not till after Christmas—meanwhile he goes with Manning to Rome.

People are busy here in getting up a Memorial to the Reformers, but whether it is to be an Ultra Protestant or an Anglican testimony—whether a Church or a Cross—whether with Reformers' names mentioned or not—whether to be set up here and [or] elsewhere—and whether to be supported by Oxford people or strangers, does not appear. There are the most opposite plans. Three prospectuses have come out, or at least three plans, independent of each other and independent of the Committee. I suppose they will manage to put it into shape at last. They say that they got the President of Magdalen's name, by saying it was intended to commemorate the primitive Martyrs—and lost the Vice Chancellor's by saying it was intended as a hit at me.

If Tom wants to come, or will come, to Oxford by January 13, I can give him a turn in St Mary's pulpit which will pay his expenses.

I knew there was something I should forget, and so I have. I leave the turnings for James [Mozley].

Ever Yrs affly John H Newman

SATURDAY 3 NOVEMBER 1838   proof from Williams and letter from Prevost   dined at Trinity with Williams   wrote to Prevost, Mr Faber, and E Churton

[1] Churton sent a less known Latin version of the Breviary hymn for the feast of the Ascension, *Salutis Humanae Sator*, which he had found in a Franciscan Breviary.
[2] The date apparently added later by Newman. The first sheet is missing.
[3] To be principal of the new Diocesan College.

Bisley. November 2—1838

My dear Newman,

Every body, whom I have yet seen, of those who used to sympathise with us, is greatly distressed at the intended publication of this translation of the Roman Breviary—

If the authors could be persuaded on our earnest entreaty to suppress it, I will be ready to be answerable for all the expence incurred thereby.

Only please to write me word as soon as possible whether this request (which I write with the entire concurrence of [T.] Keble and Jeffreys) can be complied with.

Believe me, My dear Newman, Yours very faithfully George Prevost.

I am just going away, in a great hurry,—

TO GEORGE PREVOST

(answer)

Oriel. Nov 3/38

My dear Prevost

I at first intended to do what doubtless you meant me to do—to convey your letter to the Translators and Editors of the Breviary. You must have wished me to do so, because the simple reason you use against their undertaking is that you and others dislike it. This, I feel, to be a strong one—but it could not weigh with persons, till they knew who the parties were.

But when I came to think, I determined to wait for a second letter from you for this reason—because I feel sure that the one I have received will appear to strangers peremptory. It would give me greater satisfaction in informing the parties in question of your wishes, if they had not been conveyed with the request to return an answer 'as soon as possible'. This will appear to strangers like summoning a town to capitulate. Depend upon it, such a course is not persuasive. You say you write in a hurry, which doubtless accounts for your *apparently* abrupt and positive tone

Yrs very truly J H N

P.S. Thank you for your addition to Tract 84, which you will see I have used.[1]

FROM GEORGE PREVOST

Stinchcombe November 7—1838

My dear Newman,

Your letter of the 3d, which was forwarded to me from Bisley, did not reach this place till yesterday, and I was out all day at Badgeworth.

I am very sorry that I should have seemed to have written in a peremptory or

---

[1] Prevost contributed the pages of explanation, from p. 35 onwards, to T. Keble's *Tract* 84, 'Whether a Clergyman of the Church of England be bound to have Morning and Evening Prayers daily in his Church'.

uncourteous manner, but I was in fact in a hurry both because I was just going from Bisley, and because we all thought no time should be lost in making the proposal known to the Editors.

I hope therefore you will forgive whatever may have seemed uncourteous or positive—I never thought of my letter being forwarded to the Editors, but rather that you should understand it as a request for you to communicate the proposal if you thought good.

The entreaty to have an answer as soon as possible arose from our very earnest desire to know, (as soon as might be) what has been determined. Indeed if you knew in how much distress of mind I, or (I might say) we wrote that letter, I do not think you would take our expressions much amiss—Besides the very fact of writing for one or two others besides oneself, makes one's style seem constrained and perhaps abrupt.

I remain My dear Newman yours very faithfully George Prevost.

SUNDAY 4 NOVEMBER 1838 proof from Williams, letter from Mant   preached Number 519[1]   Copeland and his friend Dr Monro dined with me in Hall   2 proofs to Williams

MONDAY 5 NOVEMBER   dined at Bloxam's with Rogers, where Parker, Combe, Pickering, and Willemot   wrote to Denison as Junior Treasurer

TUESDAY 6 NOVEMBER   letters from Wood, proof from R Williams, Westmacott, W.F. and by parcel from Bowden, and Keble inclosing from Archdeacon Froude   Daman's sister came up about now.   wrote to Bowden, Wood—proofs to Williams, and to Keble and Wilson in parcel

TO J. W. BOWDEN

⌐Oriel. Nov. 6. 1838.⌐

My dear Bowden,

I have long wished to write, but am so very full of business. Will you, please, correct what remains to be corrected (as you mentioned) in your article, and then despatch the inclosed to Messrs Roworth, which contains directions to them to print it off at once as the first article of the January number. ⌐I will attend to your Hildebrand directly. Your news about Lewis is most encouraging. I lament about Palmer,[2] but, good fellow as he is, he never has been one of our own. Samuel W. [Wilberforce] is so far from anything higher than a dish of skimmed milk, that we must hope nothing from him. What think you of his deterring men from going in to the House[3]? I had written to Wood as a lawyer about the case.[4] It comes on in London. An incumbent has, I suppose, a right without reason assigned to object to

---

[1] *P.S.* V, 2, 'Reverence, a Belief in God's Presence'.
[2] [[qu. his marriage? vid. Jany 3. 1839]]
[3] [[This was the House opposite Ch Ch. vid letter of Jan 17.]]
[4] [[qu. is this the Wolfrey case?]] Mary Woolfrey, a Roman Catholic, of Carisbrooke, Hants., was cited before the Court of Arches on 19 Nov. by the vicar, George Breeks, for placing on her husband's tombstone in the parish churchyard the inscription, 'Pray for the soul of Joseph Woolfrey'. Judgement was given on 12 Dec. that it had not been proven in court that the inscription was illegal or contrary to the doctrine or discipline of the Church of England.

inscriptions. They say the lady is a R. Catholic. I am sure I wish the Breviary done in the best way. W and W¹ are not to commit me, stating in the Preface etc. Dr Rock Lord Shrewsbury's Chaplain tells us the R.C's in England *are about to adopt* the Sarum Breviary. I cannot conceive by a flight of fancy its being a prejudice to Johnson, his being in the House.⌐

Ever yrs affly, J. H. Newman.

TO JOHN KEBLE (I)

Oriel ⌐Nov 6/38⌐

My dear Keble

⌐On Saturday Morning I had a letter from Prevost, protesting in strong terms against the Breviary being published. I wished to send it to Wood and Williams but felt that some explanation was necessary to send them so need-lessly abrupt a letter. Wood sends me back the answer I inclose, which you will see, implies (what I had told him) that though I did not feel that Prevost's opposition was an insurmountable objection, I would translate no more hymns without your leave. Your letter has saved me the awkwardness of writing to you on the subject. What I proposed to Wood was to correct the Breviary by *some standard*. I confess I much dislike correcting it by my private judgment or the vague opinions of the day, or by 'what people will think.' I mentioned to him the 39 Articles—calling it 'The Breviary reformed according to 39 Articles'⌐ I do not see that his objection is a good one—⌐but⌐ *this* seems a strong one, viz ⌐the 39 Articles would not cut out the Legends.² Then I thought of the Preface to the Prayer Book. What would you say to 'according to both together?'—But after all is there any of our standards which would cut out such as the following:—'Let St Mary and all Saints intercede for us to the Lord, [[etc]]⌐ that we may be worthy to be aided and saved by Him who liveth etc'? ⌐Are we bound to cut out what is of unknown antiquity and not forbidden by our Church?⌐†

---

¹ [[Wood and Williams]] Bowden wrote on 5 Nov., 'I find that Wood and Williams have changed their plans and are going to publish the *whole* Breviary—is not this wrong?—taking into view their way of talking about it, I cannot but rather fear for the consequences—the issue of fact, as it seems to me, between your friends and their impugners is, whether you are leading them to what Rome is or to what Rome was—and this being so I cannot but deprecate any movement which seems to imply a wish to mix ourselves up with the modern inventions legends and the like of the Southern Church—not that I should much mind any thing which those men, of themselves, did, but I dislike the connection of your name with it, thro' the hymns—I suppose you will cause them to insert, in their preface, a disclaimer of any general responsibility of yours for the publication—I wish instead of the present Breviary, they had thought of some thing in use in ante-Tridentine times.—some MS. of the Use of Sarum etc etc—'. He wrote again on 23 Nov. pressing for the translation of a medieval Breviary, and pointing out: 'The grand manoeuvre which is in truth to be executed is a general falling back, from the different posts occupied by a divided Church, upon the ground occupied by it before its division'.

² Brief lives of the Saints, sometimes legendary, in the Breviary. Only a fragment of Wood's letter survives, and this just reports that Williams was unlikely to agree to revising the translation of the Breviary according to the Articles.

Of course ⌐the sooner I can have your answer⌐ conveniently to yourself ⌐the better. They go printing on, but this at present will involve very little cancelling,⌐ for scarcely more than the 'Ave Maria' occurs in the Psalter which they are doing

Thanks for your good news from Dartington.

Ever Yrs affly John H Newman

† ⌐I do not think it will do to attempt to correct it by *history*. None of the parties concerned are strong enough in facts to do so.⌐

P.S. I will let you know at once about the Vice Chancellor

FROM S. F. WOOD

Temple Tuesday Novr. 6/38.

My dear Newman.

Since my hurried note of last night an idea has occurred to me, which, in case of Keble's giving judgement against the entire Breviary coming out, I should wish you to have without delay.

Robt. Williams's repugnance to undertaking any retrenchment *himself* is so strong that this is out of the question; and my own opinion is as decided as to the impropriety of a young layman's doing it. But *if you and I wish it*, he will agree to devote the time and money which has been and has to be expended on it to such an expurgate Edition undertaken by a person who likes and feels competent to make the omissions. In other words, if you will write a Preface with your name or initials saying that some friends of yours have put a Translation of the Breviary into your hands, and that you have undertaken to give it to the world with such omissions as bring it into harmony with the English Church, he will go on with me translating, preparing and correcting for the press, and bearing the expense. Now under the circumstances I think I may say I *do* wish this very much, and it does not at first sight seem to involve you in any more than No 75 has already. All the *trouble* you need have about it, will be the Preface, which may be as short as you like, and deciding on the omissions. You may say that your friends have undertaken all the mechanical labor, and so not be answerable for blunders. In this case we would send you the Psalter in sheets, to direct what cancels need be made, (I don't think if the initial Hail Mary etc is cancelled, the references need be) and then as each proof of the Proprium came out you should have it to omit or modify. Long before the Proprium was out, you would make up your mind what course to pursue as to the Saints days, and direct us accordingly.

Should you like this, and it proceed well, all that has happened may bring out more good, and so bring a greater blessing on all of us. So be it.

yrs very affly SFW.

It will be well, if only as regards the Printers, to decide as soon as may be.

TO JOHN KEBLE (II)

Tuesday Night [6 November 1838][1]

My dear Keble

I have just received this, and am disposed to think that, if they sacrifice their plan to me, they have some call on me to do what they here suggest

Ever Yrs J H N

[1] Newman wrote this note at the top of Wood's letter of 6 Nov., given above.

Hursley, Novr 7. 1838.

My dear Newman,[1]

I feel that we are got rather into a difficulty owing to the overhasty proceedings of the two Ws [Wood and R. Williams]; though one feels the greatest respect for their motives and the energy with which they have undertaken this work, I cannot understand their not bearing the responsibility of selection when they are willing to bear that of the whole work—it seems like straining at a gnat and swallowing a camel. Neither do I quite see what Wood takes for granted, that the row occasioned by the publication will of course be more some time hence. I should rather expect the contrary. I confess therefore, I could find it in my heart, considering the feelings of such people as Prevost, my brother, Harrison and Isaac Williams, to wish that their work might be suspended for the present. I do not see that it is such a pressing duty, and now that so many minds are turned to the subject, we shall all by degrees come to see our way more clearly. I think that Prevost etc are just now a little more alarmed than usual at the Remains, and when that has spent itself, and they find no particular harm come of it, they will be more ready to consider whether some good use may not be made of the Breviary. And I suppose what has been printed off may be considered as so much forward to the publication whenever it may seem desirable. I should hope, that even the third volume of the Remains, with such a Preface as we must try to prefix to it, accompanied also by Isaac Williams's new Tract [No. 86], will tend in some measure to compose and quiet people. If however it is thought best under all circumstances to proceed, I do not see how they could do better than make their own corrections and submit them to you: the submission will take away whatever might be presumptuous in the effort as a *Lay* Effort. And it seems to me that the best rule of correction would be to give themselves time to go through the matter historically: failing that, to take care to abide by the Articles and Liturgy *to which they are pledged*, and to err on the safe side, i.e. rather to leave out what you would wish to insert, than *vice versa*: taking care to announce in the Preface, that one is not to be understood as condemning all that one omits. The more I think on it, the more impossible it seems to me to be right in translating the whole—Is it not disrespectful towards those to whom they most wish to show respect: remembering such texts as, 'I also am a man', and 'see thou do it not'? Again, as to those many legends which to ordinary readers must appear more or less ludicrous, is it dealing reverently with the Saints to place them unnecessarily in the way of such a 'public' as ours? For instance, in St Patrick, where according to the custom of Rome they have made definite and expressed by numbers the general fact of his being unwearied in prayer, I have myself heard a very good sort of person talk of St Patrick on account of it in a way which made one feel how unjust it is to the Saints to give currency to such histories concerning them. I feel this so strongly, as well as the danger of captivating imaginative persons by such hymns and prayers as Ave Maris Stella, that were the book merely to be published as a document I should think some very express deprecation on these points necessary—how much more when intended for devotional purposes. And all this seems so obvious that one cannot but think Wood and Williams ought to suspect their own judgment for its not having occurred to them: as Williams in particular ought, if as I understand he allows himself to speak lightly and disrespectfully of the English Church Services: saying (e.g.) 'it is too ridiculous, to see one's mother wearing her cap awry'; and again that he 'thinks it right to go to Church constantly, but cannot help feeling it wearisome'. I think it rather hard that the whole burthen should be thrown upon you: but I suppose it is what in your position you must expect. Of course you will make use of me, if I can be of any use, in the revising. I think the Preface should take notice of the objection, 'Will not any book of the kind interfere with the Prayer Book?' . . .

[1] Written before receiving Newman's letter of 6 Nov.

WEDNESDAY 7 NOVEMBER 1838   letter from Mr Watson—proof from R Williams
visited Mrs Edmonds

TO JOHN KEBLE

Oriel. ⌜Nov 7. 1838⌝

My dear Keble,

I pester you with letters, and you snubbed me for paying postage—so I
can do nothing but own that I pester.

First the Vice Chancellor has written to fix Tuesday the 20th at 2 o'clock
for your Lecture.

Next ⌜I conceive that you will quite approve of Wood's proposal in his
second letter—since it involves me in no greater responsibility than you
consider I already incur, while it gives me control. So I have written to tell
Wood that, *as so* conceiving, I will accept his offer.⌝[1]

Next the University Press for want of type cannot begin S. Cyprian at
once. Pusey therefore wishes me to ask whether you and Cornish are in a
state to go to press with the translation of Chrysostom in 1 Cor.—You have
half the MS—and, if it is feasible, you had better send up some copy at once
for Baxter, and write to Cornish to get on with the rest.[2]

We ought, I suppose, to go to press at once with the Remains. Would
you take the Essays chronologically or not? if chronologically, the Hooker,
State Interference, etc etc will come *before* Rationalism; or rather Rationalism
will be nearly the last. Does Archdeacon F's [Froude] assent *go to* these
Essays at all? or only to Becket?

I mentioned to you a thought I had about printing it at the Mozleys'.
Of course *I* should like this—but in proportion as I liked it, I should wish
to be cautious about deciding on it, even if you were willing. I suppose it
would be cheaper—but I am not sure that they could put it out of hand so
well and so quickly as a town Printer. Of course I would have specimens sent
first which you should see. I mentioned it to Wm Froude. James M. [Mozley]
has taken such pains with the Becket, that an attention like this is fairly his
due, if it be on other grounds right.

Ever Yrs affly John H Newman

P.S. Mrs Pusey much the same. Mrs Richards (Exeter) is nearly given over.
Greswell (our) is in an alarming state.

---

[1] Wood wrote on 8 Nov. that he was rejoiced that Newman agreed to undertake the revision
of the Breviary, though he still thought the original plan would have been best. He wrote:
'Still I quite sympathize in your not "liking" what fate has forced upon you, and am very
sorry for it'. He went on to outline plans for speedy revision so that the first parts could still
be published in Advent.

[2] Charles Thornton's translation of St Cyprian formed the third volume of the Library of
the Fathers, and H. K. Cornish and J. Medley's translation of St John Chrysostom's Homilies
on I Corinthians formed the fifth and sixth. Newman wrote the preface to the former and
Keble to the latter.

THURSDAY 8 NOVEMBER 1838 visited Mrs Edmonds

FRIDAY 9 NOVEMBER [letters from] Keble Prevost called on Mrs Edmonds

SATURDAY 10 NOVEMBER [letters from] Denison[,] Hicks

SUNDAY 11 NOVEMBER [letters from] Wood[,] Street visited Mrs Edmonds baptized between services Godfrey's and Bellman's children preached Number 411 in type[1] dined with Berkeley to meet Mr Dukes

MONDAY 12 NOVEMBER dined in hall went after dinner to tea to Mrs Horseman's. wrote to Hook, Watson, and Mant.

TUESDAY 13 NOVEMBER Mant of N.I.[New Inn] Hall to breakfast Christie came walked with Christie and Browell Laprimaudaye, Cotton [of] Ch Ch and Bridges to dinner—P. Claughton with Christie—Fox with J M men in evening wrote to John Mozley?

WEDNESDAY 14 NOVEMBER letters from Williams and Ryder audit walked with Rogers dined in Hall. Williams with Christie

THURSDAY 15 NOVEMBER Audit in tower settled about Oriel Scholarships[2] dined with Fox at Pembroke, as did J M

FRIDAY 16 NOVEMBER audit—elected Robinson Exhibitioner and Dudley f d tea in Common Room—Copeland, Christie, J M.[,] R and I

SATURDAY 17 NOVEMBER letters from H and R Williams breakfasted with Bridges Christie went called on Mrs Gilbert and Miss Gutch advertisement of Cranmer Memorial came out walked with Cornish answer from delegates against printing translations[3]

TO JOHN KEBLE

Oriel ⌐Nov 17/38⌐

My dear Keble

⌐On receipt of your last I wrote at once to W. and W. [[Wood and Williams]], undoing what I had done, and stopping the cancelling etc. What Williams says, I will extract. However, he begged very hard to be allowed to go on printing, on the full understanding that I was to have entire command over its publication and the direction of all cancels and alterations—on the ground that they had made engagements with a printer, ordered new type etc and would incur a most considerable expense for nothing unless they printed now. On these considerations and conditions I allowed as much as this. But the publication of course is absolutely suspended.⌐

I send St Cyril—and what has been done of St Chrysostom; the latter perhaps will guide you better of the two.

[1] *P.S.* IV, 19, 'The Mysteriousness of our Present Being'.
[2] 'The time had now arrived when Oriel was to follow the lead of other colleges, and add Scholars to the various classes of her membership. The change in the value of money had seriously hindered the fulfilment of Richard Dudley's intentions, and the conscience of the Society was troubled. Accordingly on October 17, 1838, six Exhibitions or Scholarships were founded, with the express object of satisfying the supposed obligation; and at the same time a Scholarship to be held by an undergraduate of the college was created out of a bequest of £700 left for that purpose to the college by Richard Twopeny, Fellow from 1779 to 1787. The Scholarship was to be called the Rutland Exhibition'. D. W. Rannie, *Oriel College*, London 1900, pp. 213–4.
[3] T. Combe, University Printer, sent Newman a minute from the Delegates of the University Press, explaining that they were only willing to print texts of the Fathers, not translations.

Will you tell Wilson that if he wants me to continue his name on the College Books he must pay to Messrs Hoares or Hammersley's £10 into the Treasurer's account instanter.

Ever Yrs affly John H Newman

Extract from Williams' letter[1]

⌐'Wood has asked me to write etc etc. which I am the more ready to do as I have confessions to make and sorrow to express for the rash talking which Mr Keble speaks of. I have only to mend for the future—for the past pain I have given him and other friends, I will beg you, if you will, to express my sorrow. I am disappointed at the decision against immediate printing, but we both acquiesce as in duty bound . . .

If you can, do palliate my foolish and rash talking, which is what *I* will not attempt, and if I have caused pain to any, ask them to forgive me.'[2]

SUNDAY 18 NOVEMBER 1838 letters from Goldsmid and Jones—and from Marriott preached Number 520[3] wrote to R Williams

MONDAY 19 NOVEMBER read to Mrs Edmonds dined in hall read in Chapel Keble came

TUESDAY 20 NOVEMBER visited Mrs Ivory for first time. Keble's Lecture walked with him—called on Mr and Mrs Palmer. dined in hall read in Chapel men in evening sent up parcel to Rivingtons

WEDNESDAY 21 NOVEMBER letters from R Williams and W Froude Keble went and T. Keble junior letter from Woodgate with his Sermons. Johnson to breakfast visited Mrs Ivory walked about with Williams read to Mrs Edmonds paid into bank Wilson's Junior Treasurer £10 and Keble's £20. dined in hall wrote to Williams and Goldsmid

TO J. W. BOWDEN

Oriel. Nov. 21. 1838.

My dear Bowden,

⌐Your Introduction[4] seems to me very apposite, lucid, and cogent. Perhaps it requires some touching up in style. As to the text Heb. VI, would it not be enough to refer in the note to Pusey on Baptism, or to *Bishop Taylor*? As to your statements about corruptions etc., really I do not like to give my

[1] Postmarked 10 Nov.

[2] See end of John Keble's letter of 7 Nov. above. R. Williams wrote again on 16 Nov.: 'We are anxiously looking for your answer, being wholly at a stand, till we receive it; from the delay I augur well, as a proof that at least you have not thought the proposition to our friends of publishing the whole as a mere document, altogether hopeless.

It is perhaps worth your knowing, that all the persons to whom I have mentioned this question, not only now, but all through the past year, I mean, particularly those who do not feel with you on Church matters, have been strong in advising an *entire* publication, as the only course that can save us from responsibility; and generally, they advise no preface, though they ask for a statement concerning the "errors of Popery". This we should give them by quoting the articles.'

[3] *S.D.*, 7, 'Faith and the World'.

[4] [[qu. to Hildebrand?]] Bowden's *The Life and Pontificate of Gregory the Seventh*, two volumes, London 1840. It would seem that Bowden had sent Newman a draft of the first chapter, which dealt with the origin of papal claims.

opinion, and wish you to follow your own judgment. It seems to me, if I must speak, that Saint worship as it practically prevailed in the middle ages, is a very great corruption—but how far the formal acts of the Church involve such worship, and what its limits, I cannot say, and I am so bothered and attacked on all sides by friends and foes, that I had much rather say nothing, and had I my own wish, I certainly should say nothing and write nothing more. I mean, I distrust my judgment, and am getting afraid to speak. It is just like walking on treacherous ice—one cannot say a thing but one offends some one or other. I don't mean foe, for that one could bear, but friend. You cannot conceive what unpleasant tendencies to split are developing themselves on all sides—and how one suffers, because one wishes to keep well with all, or at least because one cannot go wholly with this man or that. About the Canon at Ephesus, Palmer says in the Tracts you know what. Froude and the Dublin Review attack him.[1] I am inclined to side with them; —but it seems one of those points in which different persons will take different sides.⌉

There is no chance of my being in London at Christmas, thanks for your question—unless I run up for one single day to complete the affair of my teeth.

I hope Johnson may be persuaded to remain here for some time.

⌈Your S.P.C.K. motion is a very important one, and I will mention it about.[2] We have a Scholarship examination on the very day which will keep me here.

O course you must reckon on your Hildebrand being much attacked. Yet I do not see how you could guard yourself better than you have.⌉

With kindest thoughts of all yours.

Ever yrs affly John H. Newman.

⌈P.S. Should not Dr Adams know, if he does not, that the present Bishop of Bath and Wells[3] in his funeral Sermon for the Princess Charlotte prayed for her soul?

I rejoice at your news about Lewis.⌉

[1] Palmer tried to use the Canon of Ephesus to refute papal claims of jurisdiction over the English Church. He wrote, 'the Patriarch of Antioch . . . attempted against the Cyprian Churches what the Pope had since attempted against us; viz. took measures to reduce them under his dominion. And . . . he claimed to consecrate their Bishops. Upon which the Great Council of the whole Christian world assembled at Ephesus, A.D. 431, made the following decree, which you will find is a defence of England and Ireland against the Papacy, as well as of Cyprus against Antioch . . . ". . . no Bishop shall interfere in another province, which has not from the very first been under himself and his predecessors".' *Tract* 15, 'On the Apostolical Succession in the English Church', p. 7.

For Wiseman's criticisms, see *D.R.*, 5, 1838 (Oct.), 291ff. Froude explained his strictures on the argument in his letter of 27 Jan. 1836 to Newman, Volume V, 203.

[2] Newman did not keep the part of Bowden's letter which referred to this.

[3] 'We commend too, as far as we may, and as it becometh us, into thy hands, the soul of her who is departed. We pray, we humbly pray, that she be received into the mansions of the blessed: that she exchange a corruptible crown for one that is incorruptible . . .', George Henry Law, *A Sermon preached at the Cathedral Church of Chester . . . the Sunday after the Interment of her late Royal Highness the Princess Charlotte Augusta*, second edition, London 1818, pp. 18–19.

FROM S. F. WOOD

Grosvenor Square Novr. 20/38

My dear Newman.

I am very glad that you have sent us these specimens of the way in which you would modify the Breviary, as it enables us to realize it more than we had before done. What occurs to both of us upon it is this: 1st. that it will take up a great deal more of your *time and thoughts* than it is fair to do upon the mere *contingency* of a future publication: 2d as to the alterations themselves; I must tell you honestly we don't like them, and should be unwilling to see you hastily committed to them. And this leads us to ask ourselves, "Are we not involving Newman, by the relations in which he has stood to us, in an act which he would not naturally have taken—which we do not desire to see him take—and which, when the time comes may prove neither satisfactory to himself, nor really expedient? And if so, what is there to be set on the other side to counterbalance all this? "Nothing but our convenience in proceeding with a task in which we are at present engaged."

These considerations have made us determine to suspend the printing for the present altogether, and to pay off the printer as if we had done with him, and to lay up our clean sheets upon a shelf. Should the day come when the whole Breviary is called for as a Document or otherwise we may take up our work where we left off. Or, should you, when the time arrives when Keble and others think such a publication advantageous, choose to undertake, on fuller consideration and unbiassed by any wish not to baulk preconceived plans, a Revised and Re-modelled Breviary, we will put our Mss into your hands to deal with as you like.

And now having finished the business part of my letter, you must let me tell you my dear Newman how very sensible we have been of your tender kindness towards us, and which has been no small consolation under the feeling that others would be thinking us rash and selfwilled, and also under the first disappointment of having to abandon what we were going along with, full swing. Having got past this, I do not feel that we have any thing to regret either in the course we took or what has happened. We went to the farthest verge in not consulting people in order to do them a benefit unawares; and then the explosion came just in time to avert what the event proves they would not have borne. I must own all that has come out has only convinced me of this, and not changed my mind as to the matter itself. Also, I cannot but think that both you and Williams are very heterodox in your notions about the propriety of bringing out such a sacred Book as the Breviary as a mere Document. I should tell you why we do not (at first sight) like your suggested emendations; it is chiefly that they are not mere omissions, but substitutions: perhaps one might do this not to leave a service incomplete by a single Antiphon, but to do it in extenso—surely one great part of the Breviary is that its forms have become Sacramental, but why should a person feel obliged to use *your* form or *mine*, it becomes a matter of taste whether he think it a *nice* one or no.

Now that the Breviary is off my hands I mean to try to get up an Article or two for the Critic in the English History line, which is lying unappropriated at present; of course I am too late for the January No. but I think I may undertake to have one ready for April; and you will use it or no according as it is wanted. What a thing it is to be a learned man! where *did* you get all that learning you stuff into those notes to Cyril? Williams, who is poorly, sends his love.

Ever your affectionate S F Wood.

TO JOHN KEBLE

Oriel College. ⌜November 21. 1838⌝

My dear Keble

⌜You seemed to me so uncomfortable yesterday, that I write this. You will see it requires no immediate answer.

First I will tell you that Wood informs me by a letter received this morning that they have determined 'to suspend the printing (of the Breviary) altogether, and to pay off the Printer as if they had done with him and to lay up their clean sheets on a shelf.' I think all persons should remember that they have done this at a pecuniary sacrifice, besides the disappointment.

And now to my subject. I will first give you an unpleasant sketch of things, being sorry so to trouble you. Some months since [[J.F.]] Christie wrote me word that your brother was one of the persons included in my remark in my Letter to Faussett as holding at once the Apostolical Succession, and that the Pope was Antichrist;⌐ and therefore that I might have expressed myself in a better way concerning such persons. ⌐I had already modified the passage in the 2nd edition somewhat, from a hint that Williams had given me; and on receipt of this [[Christie's]] letter I wrote to your brother to express my sorrow for what was quite unintentional, and to say that in truth I still did not think that he held the Pope to be *the* Antichrist. He answered that he did not wish to argue the matter, that he heartily wished I would go out [of] Oxford some where or other for a time, and forget Faussett etc and that he was sorry to hear that I was proposing hastily to give up the Tracts. The tone of his letter, of which I forget the rest, hurt me a good deal, the more so as being quite unexpected.[1] However, I said nothing except conveying a message through you, to the effect that I could not construe parts of it. I then sent to ask him if I might make a collection for the poor of Bisley on our anniversary at Littlemore, which in consequence of his assent I did and sent it him. — About the same time he sent me his Tract, as I certainly thought, for publication.[2] Accordingly, I had it printed and sent him the proof. He in answer expressed himself perplexed at my having acted so hastily. About the same time Pusey wrote to Jeffreys to know if he would take part in the scheme of a College of Priests for a large town. Jeffreys, scarcely giving a direct answer to the question asked him, went into a long argument against the idea itself, to Pusey his senior who had not asked his advice; proposing instead a mode which he preferred and suggesting how I could give advice to Christie in furtherance of it. Then lately came Prevost's letter about the Breviary; which, in telling me for the first time of his objection to the plan, said that he, Jeffreys, and your brother were much distressed at it; spoke of those 'who *used*' to sympathise with us — offered to pay expences if it were stopped at once, and begged an immediate answer. I thought this an abrupt and positive letter⌐ in one who is not my senior; I thought it ⌐a continuation of former occurrences which I have detailed. I recollected, little as I know of Prevost, two instances witnessed by myself, in which his manner had dis-

---

[1] T. Keble's letter of 24 Aug. See notes to letters of 5 Aug. to Christie and of 28 Aug. to Keble.

[2] T. Keble wrote in his letter of 24 Aug., 'I have lately met with "extracts" from different quarters relative to the daily service, which I made many years ago, before I was in Orders. Perhaps with additions and re-arrangement an useful Tract might some time or other be made from them or others to the same purpose — so I forward them herewith to you to be dealt with as you shall think best . . .'. Newman published them, together with explanatory material by Prevost, as *Tract 84*.

concerted persons he spoke to; and I thought it right that he should be told what I thought and still think a fault in him. Whether I did this in the best manner is another question; though I see no reason yet to think it was not,⌉ other than that nothing one does is best.

⌈Now I write this for two purposes; first I put myself entirely into your hands. I will do whatever you suggest. I really do hope I have no wish but that of peace with all parties, and of satisfying you. If you tell me to make any submission to any one, I will do it. Indeed, I am determined, if I can, that no charge should lie against me, beyond that of being myself, that is, of having certain opinions and certain ways of expressing them.

And next about these opinions and their expression; here too I give myself up to your judgment. If you will tell me what not to do, I will not do it. I wish parties would seriously ask themselves *what* they desire of me. Is it to stop writing? I will stop any thing you advise. Is it to show what I write to others before publishing? it is my rule. Pusey saw my letter to Faussett; Williams and others heard and recommended the publishing of my Lectures. Is it to stop my weekly parties or any thing else? I will gladly do so. Now this being understood, may I not fairly ask for some little confidence in me as to what, under these voluntary restrictions, I do? People really should put themselves into my place, and consider how the appearance of suspicion, jealousy, and discontent is likely to affect one, who is most conscious that every thing he does is imperfect, and therefore soon begins so to suspect every thing that he does as to have no heart and little power remaining to do any thing at all. Any one can fancy the effect which the presence of ill-disposed spectators would have on some artist or operator engaged in a delicate experiment? Is such conduct kind towards me? is it feeling? If I ought to stop, I am ready to stop; but do not in the same breath, chide me, for instance, for thinking of stopping the Tracts, and then be severe on the Tracts which appear. If I am to proceed, I must be taken for what I am; not agreeing perhaps altogether with those who criticize me, but still (I suppose) on the whole more subserving than not, what they consider right ends. This I feel, that if I am met with loud remonstrances before gentle hints are tried, and suspicions before proof, I shall very soon be silenced, whether persons wish it or no. To the Library of the Fathers I am pledged. To the British Critic only to the end of this year; and to nothing else besides the Remains. If such a result takes place, if persons force me by their criticisms into that state of disgust which the steady contemplation of his own doings is sure to create in any one [[serious man]], they will have done a work which may cause them some sorrow, perhaps some selfreproach⌉

Ever Yrs affly John H Newman[1]

P.S. W. F's [Froude] marriage is settled.

[1] [[This was the last occasion on which I could prefer a claim for *confidence*. The very next autumn (1839) my misgivings began, which led me in 1840 to write a very different letter to Keble. July 10. 1885 J H N]]

Hursley 26 Novr/38.

My very dear Newman,

Before I say any thing else, I must say what I meant to have said at Oxford and do not know how I forgot it—how very much I admired Wood and Williams' way of giving up their project, and Williams's confession, and what a good omen I thought it for future goings on. I say this now to satisfy my conscience, feeling that I ought to have said it before. Next with reference to you and my brother—all that has passed has impressed my mind rather painfully with the extreme difficulty of really understanding one another, and entering into one another's feelings: so that every line I write, I write with misgiving, fearing to do more harm than good. I am sure as I can be of any thing in another person's mind that Tom and you are substantially agreed: I think the amount of his scruples, when he has been most alarmed, was this; that he considered you as going on too fast, and with too little regard to the feelings and wants and state of information of persons in general: and that being his impression, I suppose he considered it his duty when he had opportunity[,] to act as a *drag*, and try to make us more suspicious of ourselves than we seemed to him to be. I rather take shame to myself for two things in the business: first that I have been used to *whiffle* off his objections and scruples with too little respect, which has made him shy of at all *arguing* them: (and to this I attribute his passing over the point about the Antichrist, when you addressed him about it;) the other that I did not press him more when I gave him your message about not being able to construe some parts of his letter: I remember when I told him he said he merely meant to express a friendly anxiety about your health and comfort. He does not, I think, sufficiently enter either into the difficulties of the position into which you have been called, or into the keenness of your feelings—(for you know, my dear N. you are a very sensitive person—)and again I do not think he has an adequate sense of the claims of the 4th and 5th centuries in points wherein the English Church has varied from them. But I cannot bear you to regard him as unkind or unfriendly, I do not think it is in his nature. As to your leaving off writing, he has told you himself what he would think of that; and although I can in some sort understand, how very painful, nay bitter at times must be the sensation, when you are blamed by those from whom you looked for support, I suppose it was a kind of thing on which you must have counted when you devoted yourself to this cause, and that as you did not begin for their approbation, so neither will you leave off for their blame, except you really see reason to acquiesce in it. I fear I seem to be writing in an unfeeling way, but cannot tell how I have felt since I had your letter. I am sure not like one who cared little for your comfort. I did not know that I had seemed uneasy in Oxford. I was harassed by some thoughts about other things, and I was in my own mind rather vexed that I could not make Tom see things more as you and I do: but I was not aware of your being so uneasy on this point, or I would have entered into it more at large viva voce. I am not in the least prepared to say, 'do not do such and such things'. I asked Rogers and Williams[1]

THURSDAY 22 NOVEMBER 1838   E Rogers Coffin Haddan and Woolcombe to breakfast   visited Mrs Ivory   baptized Robert Charles Broadhurst (Coles's daughter)   walked with Miller to Littlemore and read prayers   Browell, Miller, and Spranger to dinner with me   wrote to Woodgate, and to Keble by Baxter

[1] The rest is missing.

TO H. A. WOODGATE

Oriel College. Nov 22. 1838
St Cecilia's Day

My dear Woodgate,

I write a hasty note, rather than not acknowledge your parcel. You will receive the first proof in the course of a week. The type taken will be the same as Chandler's Lectures. They will send you the proof by post—but if you want the copy also, you must let me know and then both will come to you in a parcel. As to your queries on passages in the Lectures, there was nothing which could not be altered in type—I thought the wording of one or two admitted of modifying, nothing more. As to your Title, I like best, if you think it sufficiently suits your subject, 'the Rule of Faith in the Christian Church illustrated by analogy etc'—or some such title. Let me know your resolve soon as I cannot have them advertised till the title is settled.[1]

Miller who is in the room wishes you to know that Nelson of St John's has a living, Gilston in Hertfordshire

Ever Yrs affly John H Newman

FRIDAY 23 NOVEMBER 1838 letters from Marriott (from Paris) and Mr Fourdrinier read to Mrs Edmonds walked with Pusey early visited Mrs Ivory f d

SATURDAY 24 NOVEMBER breakfasted with J M as did Rogers and Church called on Mrs Ivory who could not see me walked to Littlemore with Ryder—Williams reading—dined with Spranger J. Froude in Oxford

SUNDAY 25 NOVEMBER last Trinity letter from Bowden and proof from G. and Riv[ingto]n—parcel from Derby with specimen proofs early communion Williams helping me (S.W. there) S.W. preached University Sermon visited Mrs Ivory Spranger read prayers in morning I in evening preached Number 521[2] dined in hall

MONDAY 26 NOVEMBER visited Mrs Ivory

TUESDAY 27 NOVEMBER visited Mrs Ivory Class List out—W. Newman in the first class dined in hall—Rogers had strangers. men in evening

WEDNESDAY 28 NOVEMBER visited Mrs Ivory walked to Littlemore and read for Williams—very rainy and windy dined at Trinity

TO JOHN KEBLE

Oriel ⌐Nov 28/38⌐

My dear Keble

⌐Thank you for your kind letter. I will but observe it

1 that your Brother knows the *country* clergy and makes their feelings his standard, I do not deny, for I have no means of knowing, that it is as he says

---

[1] The title chosen for his Bampton Lectures was *The Authoritative Teaching of the Church shewn to be in Conformity with Scripture, Analogy, and the Moral Constitution of Man.*
[2] *S.D.*, 6, 'Faith and Experience'.

—but I do not write for them. Of course, as is natural, I write for those I do see, viz the generation, lay or clerical, rising into active life, particularly at Oxford. That I am useful to them, by the way things which may be injudicious towards the Clergy, I am certain, whatever ultimately comes of it. I do not consider that for them I am going too fast. The character of a place of this kind must be considered, before persons can fairly undertake to judge about what is best or not. One cannot stop still. Shrewd minds anticipate views [[conclusions]], anticipate objections, oblige one to say yes or no—oblige one to defend oneself, oblige one to anticipate *their objections*—What your brother calls 'unsettling' is not *mine* but *others*' here—who must be anticipated and treated, lest *they* do harm. It is better surely to refute objections than to let others be the prey of them. In fact, in a place of this kind, if one *is* to speak (which is another matter) one must be prepared to pursue things, and admit or deny inferences.

2. Then comes the question, *ought* one to speak, though one *may* be making way here, if it is at the expence of the country clergy. And this is the point on which I spoke before and perhaps not clearly enough. I have *no call*—I am not in station—Is it not natural that the questions should rise in my mind 'What business is it of yours? and are you doing it in the best way?' When then a man like your brother *does* object, he has my own latent feelings on his side—and he goes just the way, whether he wishes it or not, to reduce me to silence.

3. But, though silent, it never entered into my head to be [[that I need or should ⟨ought to⟩ be]] doing nothing. It is still a great question with me whether I should not be doing better by reading and preparing *for future* writing on the Fathers, than by offhand works; and with this view giving up the Tracts, the B.C. and preaching at St Mary's. At the same time, did I do so, many things would occur, which one should wish otherwise and which would pain me—and I should be blamed by those who now, without knowing it, are certainly going the way to bring it about.[1]

Ever Yrs affly John H Newman

THURSDAY 29 NOVEMBER 1838   Vigil   letter from Archdeacon Wilkins   f b   f d   did not visit Mrs Ivory

TO JOHN KEBLE

Oriel. Vigil of St Andrew [29 November] 1838.

My dear Keble

I send John Mozley's specimens which I told him to make after G. and R.'s copy, which I also send.[1] It seems to me the large letters in the Title

[1] Henry Mozley and Sons were printing the second part of *Remains*, the first part had been published by Gilbert and Rivington.

Page are too narrow, and the lines in the text sometimes not quite parallel. Could these faults be corrected, I do not see others. Will you give your opinion on the whole subject. I suppose it is much cheaper than G. and R.

I send you again Hurrell's letter to Bishop Jebb about Mr Knox—with my proposed edition of it. I extricate the Bishop, but Mr Knox remains—and what say you to offending Mr Hornby?[1] could one have a deprecatory note?—will you think about it? and, if you think it feasible, make one. Also I send a Tract of his about Archdeacon Berens, which does not seem to me *tanti* to publish; but I leave it to you. Also will you cast in your mind *in what order* the Papers should come. You seemed to think the Essays should come before the Becket History. If so, in what order should the Essays stand? chronologically? This seems to me best; but let me hear your opinion. I inclose a list of them, as nearly as possible, chronological

Ever Yrs affly John H Newman

FRIDAY 30 NOVEMBER 1838 St Andrews Record paper sent me. news of Mr Woolcombe's death—our incumbent[2] did duty in chancel read Number 354 visited Mrs Ivory my fourth volume of Sermons in Oxford f d wrote to Bishops of Chester and Winchester and to G Ryder in T R's [Ryder] letter

TO J. B. SUMNER, BISHOP OF CHESTER AND C. R. SUMNER, BISHOP OF WINCHESTER

Oriel College, November 30th, 1838.

My Lord,

I have just received by post a number of *The Record* newspaper,[3] containing a report of my having expressed myself to the following effect, with relation to the sees of Chester and Winchester: 'that the sees of Chester and Winchester are, from the unfitness of those who occupy them, *ipso facto* void, and that the clergy of the dioceses cannot be justly called to render their nominal diocesans canonical obedience.'

I am perhaps unnecessarily intruding myself and the paper in question on your Lordship's notice, when I briefly state, which I beg leave to do, that the above report is untrue in all its parts, and that I deny it as thoroughly as I can deny anything. Nor can I fancy any conversation of mine which has given rise to it. As far as I can recollect, I have not been expressing any judgment at all about any bishop whatever. And I think I may add, I have thought no opinion about any; except indeed such opinion about conduct

[1] 'On Mr. Knox's Views of Church Discipline', *Remains* III, 299–314. J. J. Hornby was the editor of Knox's *Remains*.
[2] John Woollcombe, rector of Cromhall, Glos., an Oriel living.
[3] *The Record*, 1140, 29 Nov., stated: 'We think it due to the Rev. Mr. Newman, of Oxford, to state that reports are current in the metropolis that he has expressed himself to the following effect, with relation to the sees of Winchester and Chester: . . .'

as we spontaneously form concerning whatever comes before us. The idea expressed in the report above given is to me quite a new one. I have addressed a copy of this to the Bishop of Chester.

I am, My Lord, Your Lordship's obedient servant,
John H. Newman.[1]

TO G. D. RYDER

Oriel. St Andrew's Day [30 November] 1838.

My dear Ryder,

I am very sorry to say that I have, not lost, but what is as bad at this moment, mislaid or hid your letter amid a heap of others—but I recollect the upshot of it.

As to the question of fundamentals, I have sufficiently declared my opinion in my book on Romanism—and in my own mind am very sorry indeed that Palmer should have taken a line, not against mine, but against the current of English Divines. His is the first real nearing to Romanism which has in *principle* been made.[2] But since he has only assumed it and half stated it [while] chiefly occupied in detail, all halfthinkers and moderate men go about puffing the judgment and moderation of his work, having not a dream of what they are doing. His book certainly is most admirable in *details*, in which (i.e. in the minor premiss) he finds his difference from Rome— but as to his major, I heartily wish it could be proved to go against our formularies, and I half suspect it could. But this is not lightly to be said, and therefore I have no right to say it.

As to your Article then, I would gladly take any one, which took the view of Fundamentals, without dogmatizing in their favor—and again without severe *expressions* against Cranmer. Facts cannot be altered—but we can spare words.

Was there not some other subject you wrote to me about? There is a great fat lie, a lie to the back bone, and in all its component parts, and in its soul and body, inside and out, in all sides of it, and in its very origin, in the Record of yesterday evening. It has no element of truth in it—it is born of a lie—its father and mother are lies and all its ancestry—and to complete it, it is about me.

Yours most sincerely John H Newman

---

[1] In their replies, J. B. Sumner called the paragraph 'manifestly absurd'; C. R. Sumner, 'worse than absurd'.

[2] William Palmer, *A Treatise on the Church of Christ*, two volumes, London 1838, Appendix to Chapter V, 'On the Doctrine of Fundamentals.' Palmer wrote of the term 'Fundamental': 'As an ambiguous term, as conveying no one definite notion, it seems unqualified to be of any practical utility in questions of controversy.' *op. cit.*, I, 122. Newman attached importance to the definition of fundamentals (see *V.M.* I, 216ff.), and was critical of Palmer's opinion in his review of the work, see *Brit. Crit.*, 24, 1838 (Oct.), 363ff.; *Ess.* I, 203ff.

SATURDAY 1 DECEMBER 1838   letter from Goldsmid   visited Mrs Ivory   dined in hall

SUNDAY 2 DECEMBER   Advent Sunday   Mr Gleed preached in the University pulpit   did duty morning   J M assisted me in Sacrament   did not visit Mrs Ivory   did duty afternoon   preached Number 522[1]   dined in hall   Seager with J M.

MONDAY 3 DECEMBER   letter from Bishop of Chester   began to visit Bliss's son   first day of viva voce examination for Candidates for Scholarships   dined with Cornish   wrote to Westmacott

TUESDAY 4 DECEMBER   letter from Bishop of Winchester   visited Bliss's son   second day of viva voce   dined in hall   did not have men in evening

WEDNESDAY 5 DECEMBER   letters from Goldsmid, Keble and Wilson, and Fox— elected Mr Hayter and Pritchard's brother[2] scholars.   visited Bliss's son and Mrs Ivory   walked with Carey   dined in hall   sent letter to Keble by Baxter

TO JOHN KEBLE

Oriel ⌈Dec 5/38⌉

My dear Keble,

Thank Wilson for his offer about the Roman Catholic Priest's book. I have managed to mislay his note and forget the name. It promises well, but till he can make out whether or not like Courayer and Bl. [Blanco] White he turned liberal, I do not see one could move—Thank him also about Moberly —I will write to M. by this parcel.

⌈As to my last note, I had not the most distant thought of speaking disrespectfully of the Country Clergy. Indeed my saying that 'my own secret feelings were on your brother's side' showed it. I assure you these feelings are so strong, that it is with great scruple and much uneasiness that I published the Tract in question (the last)[3] and I may say the same of what I said to Faussett about Antichrist. To read and otherwise employ myself on the Fathers, without venturing any thing of my own, is what would give me most peace of *conscience*. What I do is done under the stimulus of external things which I witness—and therefore if on the other hand I see externally any one like your brother throwing cold water, both the *stimulus* is gone, and I have an *excuse* for what I *like* better than Tract and Pamphlet writing. I do not think I have the fidget you speak of (as far as I can make out) from seeing things clearly and decidedly and not getting others to see them too —but when others [[protest]] resist (I do not mean peculiars [[Low Church]] but persons like your brother) I feel a sort of bad conscience and disgust with what I have done—and this I tried to say in my first letter. And yet, if *I am* to speak, I cannot speak otherwise than I do. I can be silent, but I cannot speak as Harrison etc. My constant feeling when I write is, that I do

---

[1] *P.S.* V, I, 'Worship, a Preparation for Christ's Coming'.
[2] T. J. Prichard, brother of J. C. Prichard, who had been elected Fellow of Oriel earlier in the year.
[3] *Tract* 85, 'Lectures on the Scripture Proof of the Doctrines of the Church.'

not realize things, but am merely drawing out intellectual conclusions—[1]
which, I need not say, is very uncomfortable.⌉

I will bear your advertisement for Curates in mind. Names *can* be put down to the Fathers still. I send Wilson his MSs, if it is any use—but he asked for it

Ever Yrs affly John H Newman[2]

P.S. Will you give Wilson the inclosed.

THURSDAY 6 DECEMBER 1838 Carey, Seager, A F. and Bunsen breakfasted with me. visited Mrs Ivory and Bliss's son walked with Cornish, Williams and Copeland dined in hall. wrote to Goldsmid—and to T and H in parcel send Woodgate proofs of his Lectures.

FRIDAY 7 DECEMBER visited Mrs Ivory called on Bliss who could not see me f d walked to Littlemore sent parcel with F's MS to Derby

SATURDAY 8 DECEMBER visited Mrs Ivory walked with Pusey Ingham the American dined with me in hall

SUNDAY 9 DECEMBER 2 Advent Spranger assisted in early Communion read prayers morning and evening read Number 523[3] dined in my rooms

MONDAY 10 DECEMBER visited Bliss's son and Mrs Ivory

TUESDAY 11 DECEMBER letters from Wood and Henderson walked with R to Littlemore dined with Short [at] Trinity wrote to Wood and to Keble in parcel

WEDNESDAY 12 DECEMBER called on Mrs Ivory visited Bliss's son dined in hall wrote to Churton

TO EDWARD CHURTON

Oriel College. Dec 12 1838

My dear Churton,

Let me thank you very warmly for your truly valuable article, which I have just received and read with much interest. It is in every point of view valuable—as regards its matter, and its bearing upon the B.C., to which it cannot fail to be of service.[4] I have waited for it with much earnestness—but it has more than fulfilled any expectation I could form of it. It goes up to Roworths tonight, and you will have it in proof. Please put the foreign languages into the note, and put *translations* of them in the text. I fear this

---

[1] [[vid a passage in my account of my Sicilian illness. J H N July 10/85]]. 'I seemed to see more and more my utter hollowness. I began to think of all my professed principles, and felt that they were mere intellectual deductions from one or two admitted truths . . .' *A.W.*, p. 125.

[2] For Keble's reply see the next letter from him.

[3] *P.S.* V, 17, The Testimony of Conscience'.

[4] 'Revival of Jesuitism', *Brit. Crit.*, 25, 1839 (Jan.) 143–86. Churton replied on 20 Dec. concerning the details of the suggested amendments. Newman noted on the letter: 'July 15. 1875 . . . it shows my disagreement with the tone of Churton's article on the Jesuits, and my disinclination (Decr 1839 [1838]) to oppose the devotions of the Immaculate Conception and the Sacred Heart'. Churton wrote unsympathetically about both devotions.

will give you some little trouble—but I have already exacted it in this number in another article.

There is one passage in it, which I think is not expressed in guarded terms enough, and which I should be obliged by your correcting in proof. It is about the Eutychianism of the Roman system. The whole controversy is so delicate a one that one has need of especial care. I think some of your phrases or sentences may be taken as Nestorianizing. I suppose it correct to speak of all the adjuncts of our Lord's *human* nature, as *His* adjuncts—i.e. the properties etc of *God* the Son. 'The heart of God' is as correct an expression in theory as the 'blood of God'—or the 'body'. The fault lies in the irreverence principally. I have not time here of course to say all I would, but will briefly note down the things I wish you to be so good to think of, when the proof comes to you.

p 54 'fulness of Godhead which dwelt in its fleshly tabernacle—'should not some words like 'took unto Itself' or 'was one with' or 'made its fleshly tabernacle instinct with itself'—all these are cumbrous—(but I wish to save the post) The *Fathers* say '*deified*—'I say this merely to explain myself, *not* recommending it. The Nestorians' *favorite* phrase was that the manhood was the *tabernacle* of the Word.

ibid. 'heavenly virtue—' Surely the human nature has the *virtue of the* Godhead.

'Thus the Immaculate conception'—I wish this sentence could be omitted.

ibid. end. ⟨and p 55⟩ I wish the passage from Massillon could be omitted —since I think it *will admit* of a Catholic sense.

And now with renewed thanks, I am, Yours most sincerely

John H Newman

P.S. I am sorry that so beautifully written an MS should go into printers' hands.

LORD BLACHFORD (FREDERIC ROGERS) TO ANNE MOZLEY

March 5, 1886.

. . . Curiously enough I see by an old diary, under date December 12, an account of—I am at a loss for a substantive—not quarrel, not exactly difference, but a kind of stern alienation for a fornight, ending in tender reconciliation, which was due to this difference between himself as supporter of (S.) Wood, and (R.) Williams and Oakeley, who were pressing the publication of the 'Breviary' on one side, and T. Keble and Prevost on the other. I seem to have objected to some actual or intended letter to Keble, and I certainly in my mind, and probably in the tone of my conversation, sided on the whole with the Prevost side rather than the Wood and Williams side. This made me a disagreeable confidant to him, and this again he took as very unkind, and showed it in a certain flinty way which he had at command on great emergencies. But then, you occasionally saw what this flintiness cost him. And when you came to frank explanation, there came from the rock a gush of overpowering tenderness.

THURSDAY 13 DECEMBER 1838   visited Mrs Ivory   dined in hall   wrote to Prevost by W., to Keble in parcel and to Mr Merewether and his son

FROM JOHN KEBLE

Hursley Decr 8/38.

My dear Newman,

I am very glad of your last note not that *I* had any doubt of your meaning, but people are so easily misunderstood—and of this your construction of Prevost's note is a remarkable instance. I venture to say this without having seen it, in consequence of a detailed account which Tom has sent me of the manner in which it was written. Among other things Tom says 'He (P.) proposed writing a longer letter, and entering more into particulars—especially because it would seem more courteous and kind: but this (I think I distinctly remember) I overruled, and urged him only to say as briefly as possible what we had agreed on, and seal the letter and be gone, as he was considerably later than he had intended to be "for a Church Building Meeting at Gloucester." If there was any thing in any way uncourteous in the letter, I am to blame; and I should be glad for Newman to know this. But it must be considered that the matter was a very serious one, and that it is far better that we should appear rude, officious, and absurd, than that an irremediable evil (for if it were an evil it would have been irremediable) should have been inflicted on the Church by the publication of a work professedly devotional yet scandalous in some respects'. It seems therefore plain that whatever may have been the case in former instances Prevost really did not deserve snubbing on this occasion. And do you not think that he is the last person whom Hurrell if he could know would wish one to snub? I set this down as much for my own sake as yours—feeling sometimes inclined to deal rather rudely with him and such as he is, and always feeling afterwards that I was wrong. And now my hand is in, I think I will go on quoting: although I am sure Tom would be angry if he knew it. But I cannot help thinking that any thing but unfriendliness was intended. 'I will say nothing of Newman's answer to Prevost, (which being directed to Bisley was many days before it reached him) nor of Prevost's —or rather our—apologetic reply' (of which I never heard before. Ed.) 'But while we were thus sore, came out the Tract [No. 85] which has since, amongst us privately, caused a good deal of discussion and uneasiness: because as it seems to us, being written hastily and printed as it was written, many passages occur which may too easily be made a very bad use of—though (possibly) not one which may not admit of a plausible explanation. This made me say (to I. W.) that I could greatly wish that all the Tracts should be revised by 2 persons besides the Author. Isaac's *hearing* some (or all) of the Lectures, and admiring them (as how could he do otherwise) cannot I think be considered as what you call an Imprimatur. But the truth is, you clever men hate to revise your own writings, much less to let any one else do it.' (I know in this he writes in some ignorance of your practice, in your sermons especially) 'Therefore I do not at all wonder that Newman says to us "you must take my Lectures as they are or not at all". Nevertheless I stick to my[1] and should be glad to have all pass through two minds at least. Of course I say this with reference to the Tracts only, whatever my opinion might be to the benefit of extending the rule to all your publications. I will only further say that the thought of having lost in any degree the confidence of Newman and yourself, (which naturally must have crept into our minds since the affair of the publication of the Remains) has occasioned us unknown, I don't know what—uneasiness. That evening and another since at Stinchcombe, Prevost cried like a child about it. But I am got too old for such ebullitions, and do not I think trouble so much as I ought about the whole matter. However, 'I beg on ye', as the people say, don't imagine that we[2]

[1] Word illegible.
[2] The rest is missing.

[[Autumn [December] 1838]]

My dear Keble

⌐Will you give me your opinion, if you see any reason against inserting the inclosed in the forthcoming B C.⌐ I should like it again soon.

⌐I feel the kindness of your sending me the extract from your brother's letter. If I say that my view about Prevost's letter is *substantially* what it was, I do so only for the sake of honesty. Any thing I can do, to smooth matters I gladly will. I only hope that Prevost has got over the annoyance of my letter (for which⌐ annoyance ⌐I am truly sorry⌐ and for having caused it) ⌐as I have, I trust, the annoyance of his. As to the Duumvirate of Revision I have no objection to it. But the question will rise *who* are to be they? will your brother allow more than one or two out of all our friends? and again how is time to be found for it? It's with difficulty one get[s] one revisor. Are all the articles in the B. C. to have a second revisor after myself?—I repeat I have no objection except what seems the impracticability of it. It is virtually injoining silence, which had better be done openly, if it is to be done. Hurrell's papers *have* had two revisors.⌐

If I can hit on any one for the Heathcote Prize examination I will tell you

Ever Yrs affly John H Newman

Oriel ⌐Dec 13. 1838⌐

My dear Keble

⌐As you have not seen what passed between Prevost and me, I send it you. Since your last letter I have written to him by [[Isaac?]] Williams. Please let me have the letters back.⌐

I should add one thing that ⌐after all I *did* let Wood and [[Robert?]] Williams see Prevost's first letter. I⌐ had mentioned it to them—and ⌐thought they would be fancying something worse than it was,⌐ unless I showed it— and I thought that for other reasons it was right.

Ever Yrs affly John H Newman.[1]

---

[1] Keble replied the next day: 'About the revision of the Tracts etc. I suppose Tom would say where there is a will there is a way: but I grant it would be inconvenient in many ways, and time would be lost. Also it would not get over the difference about the Reformation which lies at the bottom of all this. I think we must rub on as well as we can, only trying to bear one another in mind.

About Prevost's letter I say no more than that I cannot at all comprehend your view: and so e'en let it pass.'

See note to letter of 23 Dec. to Keble for Keble's later feelings about this letter.

TO GEORGE PREVOST

Oriel Dec 13. 1838

My dear Prevost

I take the opportunity of Williams's leaving Oxford to send you a line to thank you for your last letter and to assure you that I am exceedingly sorry that my letter gave you pain, and heartily wish any thing in it unwritten which ought not to have been written, I hope you will kindly recollect that I considered myself defending dear friends whom I thought attacked without reasons assigned. I can only hope that the annoyance of my letter has as completely passed from your mind as I trust that the annoyance caused by yours has passed from mine.[1]

With the kindest thoughts suggested by the season

Ever Yrs most truly J H N

TO ISAAC WILLIAMS

Oriel Dec 13/38

My dear W

I think your Papers most exceedingly good—and wish to have them for the Tracts as soon as ever you will give them.[2]

Have you sufficiently brought out (perhaps you have, as I cannot be supposed to have mastered them) this remarkable fact—that the re modellers of the Prayer Book *intended* to *Lutheranize* our devotions, I mean to bring in confessions of sin, unworthiness, anti-selfrighteousness, justification by faith only etc. and that these very portions which *they* intended as opposing merit, *do*, as you show, throw the Church in to a lower and sadder state of devotion, or subserve a *different* object.

Ever Yrs affly J H N.

FRIDAY 14 DECEMBER 1838   letters from Mr Norris and Mr Markland   visited Bliss's son   f d   wrote to Mr Norris and Mr Markland

SATURDAY 15 DECEMBER   visited Mrs Ivory.   Bloxam and Ryder dined with me, and R. and J.M. in my (i.e. A.F.'s) rooms   Berkeley returned

SUNDAY 16 DECEMBER   letters from Goldsmid and Trower   preached Number 524[3]   wrote to Trower and anonymous at Post Office

[1] See letter of 3 Nov. to Prevost and that of 7 Nov. from Prevost, placed after.
[2] *Tract* 86, 'Indications of a superintending Providence in the Preservation of the Prayer Book and in the Changes which it has undergone'.
[3] *P.S.* V, 16, 'Sincerity and Hypocrisy'.

TO AN UNKNOWN CORRESPONDENT

Oriel College. Dec 16. 18

Sir,

I consider what you say to be very true—The passages in the Newspaper, to which you direct my attention, are very lamentable; at the same time they are not more so than a great number of things in the world. I suppose we shall find far more things in opposition to the truth than for it in this world; and our first conviction, if we would be comfortable, must be this—We must be surprized at nothing; and much less must we be surprised at strong assertions. There are strong assertions on all sides—if we attend to them we shall be driven to and fro, as if by the winds. We must aim at pleasing Almighty God, and follow what we think He will approve, and then let the opinions of men take their course. In all ages the triumph of evil and falsehood has been a perplexity to those who have wished to follow the truth—we see this in Scripture. At first men fret under it, but after a time they get resigned to it.

These general observations apply to the whole of your letter—I sincerely hope that you will soon be rid of the annoyance which the view of things at present occasions you. And could I say or do anything which might tend to rid you I would.

I am, Sir, Yours faithfully John H Newman.

MONDAY 17 DECEMBER 1838 visited Bliss's son dined in Common Room [Charles] Carey first time, having today taken his degree. Ottley came in evening

TO H. A. WOODGATE

O. C. Dec 17/38

My dear Woodgate,

Your second Lecture, I suspect, is the least striking of the whole batch. This arises from your snuffing[1] so often. The fundamental argument is capital. If you can mend this fault, do. You should vow abstinence from the words, 'argument' 'objection,' 'first,' 'second,' 'deictic,' etc. Ars est celare artem.

It has struck me, there are so many things in your Lectures like my 'Romanism', you *must* read it—and if you agree with me in thinking so, you must say in your Preface, 'Since these Lectures were written, I have read Mr N's book etc and am gratified by having so many of my poor guesses confirmed by the demonstrations of that distinguished individual.'

Ever Yrs affly John H Newman

[1] 'i.e. "snuffing your candle", viz saying what you *have* done or what you *shall* do etc instead of going straight on'. Pencilled note of Newman's, writing long afterwards.

TUESDAY 18 DECEMBER 1838 letters from J. Marriott and Brewer   visited Mrs Ivory for last time   married R. Grey to Sarah Pope   Ottley to breakfast in Common Room Ward with R.[,] Pattison with J M.   College meeting   Nevill dined with R. —Pattison with J M.—Lee with Daman   Mr de Vere,[1] (Mr Todd's friend) in Oxford—he took tea in Common Room

WEDNESDAY 19 DECEMBER   ember day   letter from Keble   Rogers went   walked with Pusey   f.b.   f.d   wrote to J. Marriott

THURSDAY 20 DECEMBER   Vigil of St Thom.   Mr de Vere, J M. and Pattison to breakfast   f d   walked with J M   went to St Peter's to service

TO JOHN KEBLE

Oriel. In Vigilia S. Thom. [20 December] 1838

My dear Keble

I write in a hurry, and shall forget some things I ought to say.—I send the first sheet of the Remains—it must come back here, as I have not verified the quotations from Hoadly and Clarke—Ought not the Title of the Essay to be 'Rationalism *in the interpretation of Scripture*?' for this seems to be *the* subject. I send J Mozley's letter with the queries—which, please, let me have back with the proof. As to whether 'Vol. 3' there seem two reasons for its being '*Series* 2,' (a bad word, what was it in Knox's) 'vol 1'—first, because people do not like to buy a *third* volume without the rest—next because the type is *rather* different;—but I have no strong opinion.

Mr Medley has written to ask why his name is not down among the Translators of the Fathers—*we* do not know—can you tell us what our relations with him are.[2]

By the bye, I would *not* notice H R F's [Froude] 'want of learning—' he always *professed* ignorance. Mr Bunsen has told Arnold that he abused Niebhur and then confessed he had not read him—now, it so happens, he had got it up carefully and lectured Rogers before this—If indeed the *Remains* showed ignorance etc, we must speak,—but else, considering people have a notion (and a true one) he was well read, it seems like putting an idea into their heads.

Please tell Wilson that there is a vast deal about the lesser orders in Thomassin—who does not consider them Apostolical but primitive.[3]

I send a letter of Brewer's—as it relates to a person you know, we want your opinion whether it is safe to agree with him—As to the said Brewer, we must not impute all his mode of speaking to the person he writes for.

As to Prevost, *of course* I *did* judge by what had gone before—but Rogers, who went by the letter itself, did not like its tone[4]

Ever Yrs affly John H Newman

[1] See Wilfrid Ward, *Aubrey de Vere: A Memoir*, London 1904, pp. 29–34.
[2] John Medley collaborated with H. K. Cornish in the translation of St John Chrysostom's Homilies on I Corinthians.
[3] L. Thomassin, *Vetus et Nova Ecclesiae Disciplina*, Lyons 1706, I, 319–40.
[4] Keble wrote on 19 Dec.: 'Many thanks for trusting me with these letters. I am afraid you will think me very prejudiced: but I still think it a great wonder that any one who knew

FRIDAY 21 DECEMBER 1838   St Thos   ember day   sent Keble first proof of H R F's ⟨R H F's⟩ Remains (new series)   Service in Chancel   read Number 272   f d walked with Acland   went to St Peter's to Service   wrote to C Marriott at Rome

SATURDAY 22 DECEMBER   ember day   ½ f b   f d   visited Bliss's son   to St Peter's to service

SUNDAY 23 DECEMBER   4th Advent   letters from Rogers and Henderson   J.M. assisting me in early Communion   did duty morning and afternoon   preached Number 230   Pattison, Berkeley, Mr Gawthorn (whose Si quis I put up) and Ashworth B.C. [Bible Clerk] to dinner.   wrote to Todd, Keble (through Baxter) R W.[,] Rogers and Le bas (through Rivington)

TO JOHN KEBLE

Oriel College ⌜Dec 23. 1838⌝

My dear Keble

I send two fresh Chapters of the Essay on Rationalism—which seem to come between the 3rd and 4th as you have seen them. The former is only in the rough draught—and being written familiarly therefore, perhaps requires modifying in a word or two—tuum est judicium—the other I suppose is perfect. They seem to me the two most impressive ones of the whole—but I dare say not to another.

⌜I am quite ready that all Tracts should undergo the revision of two persons whom your brother chooses—though I don't understand *whom* you mean—[[Isaac]] Williams of course is one—is Prevost the other? Nothing you said from London annoyed me in the least. You have a way of saying things which does not annoy⌝[1]

Ever Yrs affly John H Newman

P.S. I should like the inclosed back soon.

Prevost (to say nothing of other parties at least equally concerned) should have taken at that letter *by itself*; but you were sore from other causes which you mentioned to me. However I trust that now all is set right, and that nothing will occur at all to separate people who on every account—and among the rest for H F's sake—ought to go on together.'

[1] Keble wrote in an undated letter:
'I am not exactly easy in my conscience about that hurried note which I wrote you from London—it seems to me as if I had said something about "where there is a will there is a way" which might hurt you and which I certainly had no particular reason for saying and hardly know what I meant by it. I wish you would consider it unsaid, if you happened to notice it.

Do you think a plan might be adopted of getting the *Tracts* regularly revised by Tom's favourite Duumvirate, leaving people to their own discretion in other publications. There seems an obvious reason for this—viz. that more than one are supposed to be concerned in the Tracts, and to be responsible for them. I do not however myself press it, for there is hardly any thing if any thing at all in the Tracts, that I know of from the responsibility of which I should shrink: but if it satisfied Tom and took off the burthen in some degree from you, those would be two good effects as far as they go: you know better than I whether the delay and trouble occasioned would more than balance these.'

TO R. I. WILBERFORCE

Oriel Dec 23/38

My dear Wilberforce

I have taken a liberty with one or two words of your Article[1], since you saw it—which I had not time to tell you and yet ought to do so. The chief is leaving out the words Pontius Pilate and Judas—which some persons might think rather too light. I suppose you could not give me for the July number some Article such as a Review of Lord Chatham's correspondence which is in course of publication?[2] There is no news here except that Baden Powell is writing a book against the Oxford Tracts,[3] and your friend Mr Cox is the new Rector of Carfax.[4] You may have seen by the papers that Dr Bishop is dead. Copleston has taken Woolcombe's living in Gloucestershire, and is on his year of grace. Mrs Pusey is neither better nor worse than she was 2 months since

Yours ever most sincerely John H Newman

MONDAY 24 DECEMBER 1838 Christmas Eve baptized London's child f b f d went to St Peter's Acland called in evening

TUESDAY 25 DECEMBER Christmas Day did duty morning and afternoon J.M. assisting at Communion preached Number 125[5] dined at Trinity with Copeland —as did J M.[,] Pattison and Berkeley. Cartwright and Smith there

WEDNESDAY 26 DECEMBER St Stephen's letters from Sewell and Cornish did duty in Chancel read Number 62 4th of course of the 23rd Psalm Bloxam, Berkeley etc to dinner others with J M

THURSDAY 27 DECEMBER St John's Eve letters from Moberley Le Bas and R. Hornby did duty in Chancel read Number 233 Eden went dined with Bloxam —where was his sister—also Smith, Faber, Whorwood, J M. etc wrote to J.

FRIDAY 28 DECEMBER Innocents letter from Woodgate Service in Chancel read Number 279 dined by myself in Common Room wrote to Cornish, Woodgate, Hornby, Rogers, Henderson, and proof to Roworth

TO CHARLES CORNISH

Oriel. in festo Ss. Inn. [28 December] 1838

My dear Cornish

Parker has already heard from Devonshire on the subject of the Subscribers—and of course *any one* who has put down his name is entitled to the books at the reduced prices. He has but to state the fact—

[1] 'Prussian Schools', *Brit. Crit.*, 25, 1839 (Jan.), 76–95.
[2] W. S. Taylor and J. H. Pringle(eds.), *Correspondence of William Pitt, Earl of Chatham...*, four volumes, London 1838–40. The article did not appear.
[3] *Tradition Unveiled; or, an Exposition of the Pretensions and Tendency of Authoritative Teaching in the Church*, London 1839. The work was noticed in George Moberly's article, 'Catholic Tradition', *Brit. Crit.*, 25, 1839 (April), 450–79.
[4] William Hayward Cox, Vice-Principal of St Mary Hall.
[5] *P.S.* VIII, 17, 'Religious Joy'.

I have no news for you, except that Faber has returned from Cambridge, and does not give so satisfactory an account as one could wish. These fellows take up every thing as a matter of literature—and their opinions come and go like Spring fashions. At present they are all followers of [F.D.] Maurice, and Mr Whithead (I do not say he is one of them) hearing your Morris[1] preach in St Mary's for me carried down to Cambridge a report of him as if he had been his great Homophone. They are all for what is Catholic, and their definition of Catholicism in any subject matter is an abstraction taking in the widest extent of opinion.

Thank you for your thought about the Paris MS.[2] I forget what the direction was I gave you—this is the best I can now find—

'What is the *number* of the MS in the Royal Library, how is it to be *described*, which is referred to in note y on Fabricius Bibl. Græc. ed. Hamb. vol 8. p 685?'—Harrison *copied* the MS out for me according to this reference —so I know it will *find* it.

Yours most sincerely with kindest thoughts of the Season

John H Newman.

TO THOMAS HENDERSON

Oriel College. In fest Ss. Inn. [28 December] 1838

My dear Henderson,

First let me congratulate you, as I do most sincerely, on the advancement of your little friend Coffin.[3] I was truly glad—his very face is enough to make one like him, if one knew nothing more. It seems he was kind enough to call on me to show his new sleeves, but did not find me in.

And now as to your question. You have not heard correctly what my objection is to the Testimonial,[4] but no wonder, as I have told no one, except one or two persons in and out of Oxford who have asked me. I, as well as others, have tried as much as possible to act for myself, and let others do the like. It is no point of doctrine that is in dispute, but of opinion about historical facts. I am quite willing every one should think his own way. Accordingly Keble wrote to Pusey urging him not to be influenced by what *he* should do—and though I was at Hursley with Keble at the time, yet he did not tell me his reasons for declining to subscribe, though of course one cannot help picking them up more or less. In the same way I was quite pressing with Pusey, at a time when he felt half disposed to subscribe, to do so freely, whatever I might do. Sewell at first was on the Committee and remained some time—but at last it would not do—stomach or conscience

---

[1] J. B. Morris of Exeter College.
[2] See Volume IV, 294.
[3] R. A. Coffin of Christ Church, recently elected Student.
[4] The proposed Martyr's Memorial. See letter of 23 Oct. from Pusey about the origin of the scheme.

could not stand it, and he bolted. The report is that the Bishop too has withdrawn his name, having been favorably disposed at first.

If I must say it in a few words, my reason for not subscribing is, that I cannot trust, I have no sort of confidence in, Cranmer etc, and I will not commit myself to them. Practically speaking, to subscribe is to make them the representative of the English Church—This is the reason they are brought forward; in order to be watchwords against the Romanists. It is not then merely expressing horror and pity at their cruel death—but it is to acknowledge them theologically. This, I am sure, will be the practical effect of it. I will not tie, what may prove a millstone, round my neck. The publication of Froude's Remains was an act of duty to *him*—but else I should not have gone out of my way to attack them—but now when through happy fortune I am emancipated, when I walk in the light of day and the free air, and no longer need invent all sort of fictions and artifices to make out Cranmer or others Catholic, now when I can protest against King Edward's 2nd Book which he brought forward, and leave the defence of his political as well as theological history to those who choose to answer attacks on it, it would be sheer absurdity to bury myself again in the world of shadows, and give myself in the eyes of our adversaries, Romanists and Dissenters, that appearance of unfairness and disingenuousness which they have ever imparted to the English controversialist. No—I can say, do your worst on Cranmer, you do not touch the English Church.—I am perfectly aware indeed that what I gain *controversially*, I lose *at home*. I alienate and disgust brother Churchmen, while I strengthen myself against opponents. And this in consequence is what such men as Hook seem to be saying to those who think with me. 'You dolts—you can do any thing if you fight under Cranmer's colours— you can prove him Catholic, you can teach Catholicism through him—You can prove the Reformation to be a Catholic movement. Yet you double dolts, you play into the hands of your enemies, you stupidly *allow* what they urge, that you *are* against the leading Reformers—and when you might play so fair a game, you [they?] are then against you with an argument especially popular.' Now what do I say to this? Why (continuing the argument on the line of expedience, on which we are moving,) I say that Cranmer will not stand *examination*—that they are worst friends to him who put him up to be criticized—that they are best friends who keep silence. Were I then to bring his name forward, I am thereby by that very act preparing for my own refutation. Men are for him now—they will be less and less so. The more he is talked of, the less he will be borne. It is an unpopular thing to seem to take part against him now—but men will come over to us. The English Church will get ashamed of conduct like his; and therefore, though unpopular at the moment, it is long sighted policy, even in the way of policy, to keep free of him. The controversial gain then is permanent, the unpopularity at home transitory;—but I have no room to go on.

I believe the objection of not liking to speak in that way of a memorial against Romanism was Sewell's; with this meaning. 'It is not right for one branch of the Church to raise monuments to the sins or errors of another.' This was pretty much our Provost's ground also as I am told.

I feel exceedingly obliged by your kind way of accepting my Sermons

Yours most truly John H Newman

TO FREDERIC ROGERS

Oriel: In festo SS. Innoc., 1838.

Faber has returned from Cambridge with doleful accounts, as he gives them, though I have not confidence in his representation. However, I doubt not he has done good by going. He says that two parties are formed, Hookites, which *in fact* includes us, and a sort of Latitudinarians, who *consider* they maintain 'Oxford views'; and they quote the Preface to the 'Remains' to show that they are not members of the 'Establishment,' *that is*, the local Church (which they say is heretical, etc.), but the 'Catholic Church,' an idea or shadow. Merivale has been preaching, and is to publish four sermons which *seem* to make subjective religion all in all[1]—indeed, they seem Maurician, the said Maurice being at present the great doctor at Cambridge. What a set they are! They cannot make religion a reality; nothing more than a literature. Heath (I think) holds by my 'Romanism' and 'Justification,' not by my Sermons; which means, I suppose, not by Catholic views about *Church* and *Sacraments*. An external *bond* is what they want, and what they shrink from. Are they not like Greeks, and we like Romans? 'Graiis ingenium,' etc. 'Tu, Romane, memento . . . parcere subjectis et debellare superbos.'[2]

TO H. A. WOODGATE

Oriel. In fest. Ss. Innoc. 1838

My dear Woodgate,

I think there are objections to not-repeating the words. Pusey wrote a letter to the B. Magazine about November 1836 in which they are well stated.[3] I doubt whether it much shortens time. The rail fills all *at once*, and does not *keep* filling. At Dodsworth's certainly it seemed to me to be no saving, or no great. It annoys some people very much not to have the words addressed to them personally. I think it would myself. It is a privilege, just

[1] Charles Merivale, *The Church of England a faithful Witness of Christ; not destroying the Law but fulfilling it. Four Sermons preached before the University of Cambridge, in November 1838*, Cambridge 1839.
[2] Horace, Ars Poetica, 323–4; Virgil, *Aeneid* VI, 852–4.
[3] *Brit. Mag.*, 10, 1836 (Nov.), 531–8, signed 'Canonicus'. Pusey found it 'painful' that the practice was becoming common at Holy Communion of saying the words 'once only to those assembled round the altar, and then giving the elements severally, in silence, to each individual.'

as in Baptism—and is a part of the Church's maternal kindness. But you will see what Pusey says—

I am ready to look at any thing Combe will send me. Is Mr Spenser in your neighbourhood? he has stung the Standard so cruelly, that the Editor, who one day called *us* 'pious and amiable' the next calls us 'coxcombs' etc etc   With kindest wishes of the season to you and your wife

Ever Yrs affly John H Newman

P.S. I almost think Shuttleworth's book is engaged in the B. C. but do not quite know yet.[1]

SATURDAY 29 DECEMBER 1838   letters from Bowden, Le Bas and Miss Holdsworth dined with J M and Pattison as also Bloxam, young Ashworth, Berkeley
SUNDAY 30 DECEMBER   after Christmas   did duty morning and afternoon Provost assisting me in Sacrament   preached Number 430[2]   young Ashworth, Berkeley etc to dinner in Common Room?

TO JOHN KEBLE

Oriel ⌐Dec 30/38¬

My dear Keble

I send a sort of concluding Chapter of the Essay,[3] which is rescued from a very rough copy—i.e. it is a design written *before* what you have seen, though in order it comes after. I fear you will say I have scribbled it—but I have been much hurried, and my hand gets tired. Also I send the last thing he did ⟨(against Arnold etc)⟩.[4] There are several interpolations of mine in brackets which must be left out—but I have not yet set them right. I should not have thought the Essay would have borne more than the headings of the *chapters*—would each *page* afford a heading? Hooker is a very miscellaneous writer, and there is a reason for it in his case.

I will leave out the sentence about a 'good Sermon.'

⌐I have no objection to Williams and Wilson.¬[5] I will see about the Benedictine.[6]

[1] P. N. Shuttleworth's *Not Tradition but Revelation*, London 1838, was one of several works reviewed in George Moberly's 'Catholic Tradition', *Brit. Crit.*, 25, 1839 (April), 450–79.
[2] *P.S.* VIII, 11, 'Doing Glory to God in Pursuits of the World'.
[3] Froude's 'Essay on Rationalism, as shown in the Interpretation of Scripture', *Remains* III, 1–164.
[4] Froude's 'Remarks upon the Principles to be observed in interpreting Scripture', *Remains* III, 357–83, was a critique of Thomas Arnold's introduction to his third volume of *Sermons*.
[5] I. Williams and R. F. Wilson had been suggested as possible revisors of the *Tracts*.
[6] The Benedictine edition of St John Chrysostom, *Opera Omnia*, thirteen volumes, Paris 1718–38. Keble needed to borrow some volumes for his work on the preface to the Library of the Fathers translation of the Homilies on I Corinthians.

Thanks—I think I shall not be able to leave this place this Christmas. Kindest thoughts of the Season to all at Hursley.

Ever Yrs Affly John H. Newman

TO J. R. BLOXAM

Saturday

My dear Bloxam

I am going to bring a friend with me to dinner, Wood. What hour do you dine?

Ever Yrs J H N

Saturday

My dear B

Williams wishes to see Sewell's letter. Give it to the bearer

Ever Yrs J H N

Oriel Thursday

My dear Bloxam

If you can, come and breakfast with me tomorrow morning to meet a man who wants instruction about organs

Ever Yrs John H Newman

Oriel Tuesday

My dear Bloxam

I rely on your dining with me tomorrow (Wednesday) at $\frac{1}{2}$ past 5 instead of today

Ever Yrs J H N

Appendix

Tracts for the Times 1837–8

Tract 1837

78   2 Feb.   *Catena Patrum*, No. 3. Testimony of Writers of the Later English Church to the Duty of maintaining, *Quod semper, quod ubique, quod ab omnibus traditum est*, 118 pp. [Usually ascribed to H. E. Manning and C. Marriott though Newman may have had the chief responsibility for it]

79   25 Mar.   *On Purgatory* (Against Romanism, No. 3), 61 pp. [Newman]

80   undated   *On Reserve in Communicating Religious Knowledge*, Parts 1–3, 82 pp. [I. Williams]

81   1 Nov.   *Catena Patrum*, No. 4. Testimony of Writers of the Later English Church to the Doctrine of the Eucharistic Sacrifice, with an Historical Account of the Changes made in the Liturgy as to the Expression of that Doctrine, 415 pp. [E. B. Pusey with the assistance of B. Harrison]

82   1 Nov.   *Letter to a Magazine on the Subject of Dr Pusey's Tract on Baptism*, 42 pp. [Newman]

1838

83   29 June   *Advent Sermons on Antichrist*, 54 pp. [Newman]

84   24 Aug.   *Whether a Clergyman of the Church of England be now bound to have Morning and Evening Prayers daily in his Parish Church*, 45 pp. [T. Keble and G. Prevost]

85   21 Sept.   *Lectures on the Scripture Proof of the Doctrines of the Church*, Part I, 115 pp. [Newman]

List of Letters by Correspondents

Abbreviations used in addition to those listed at the beginning of the Volume:

A	Original Autograph.
Bodleian	Bodleian Library, Oxford.
C	Copy, other than those made by Newman.
D	Draft by Newman.
Georgetown	Georgetown University, Washington, D.C.
H	Holograph copy by Newman.
Keble	Keble College, Oxford.
Oriel	Oriel College, Oxford.
Pr	Printed.
Pusey	Pusey House, Oxford.

The abbreviation which describes the source is always the first one after the date of each letter. This is followed immediately by the indication of its present location or owner. When there is no such indication, it means that the source letter is preserved at the Birmingham Oratory. It has not been thought necessary to reproduce the catalogue indications of the Archives at the Oratory, because each of Newman's letters there is separately indexed, and can be traced at once. Next, when it is available, comes the address to which the letter was sent. Any additional holograph copies (with their dates, when known) or drafts are then listed below the source.

Correspondent	Year	Date	Source	Location, Owner, Address
Acland, Thomas Dyke	1837	3 Aug	Pr	A.H.D.Acland, *Memoir and Letters of Sir Thomas Dyke Acland*, London 1902, 82
	1838	17 June	Pr	Op. cit., 106
Anderson, Charles Henry John	1837	23 Feb	A	Lincolnshire Archives *Ad.* Charles Anderson Esqr/Lea/Gainsborough/ Lincolnshire *readdressed* Scawby/ Brigg
Bagot, Richard, Bishop of Oxford	1838	19 Aug	D	
		21 Aug	A	Pusey
			D	
		29 Oct	D	
Bloxam, John Rouse	1837	26 Aug	A	*Ad.* The Revd J R Bloxam/ Magdalen College
	1838	9 June	C	
		[31 Dec]	C	four notes
Boone, James Shergold	1837	7 July	A	Pusey
Bowden, John Edward	1838	17 Jan	A	London Oratory
Bowden, John William	1837	13 Jan	C	
			H	1862
		16 Jan	C	
			H	1862
		26 Feb	C	
			H	1862
		16 Mar	C	
			H	1862
		12 April	C	
			H	1862
		25 April	C	
			H	1862
		6 June	C	
			H	1862
		7 July	C	
			H	1862
		12 July	C	
			H	1862
		25 Aug	C	
			H	1862
		6 Oct	C	
			H	1862
		22 Nov	C	
			H	1862
		12 Dec	C	
			H	1862
	1838	17 Jan	C	
			H	1862
		19 Mar	C	
			H	1862
		15 April	C	
			H	1862
		22 May	C	
			H	1862
		17 Aug	C	
			H	1862
		4 Sept	C	
			H	1862
		21 Sept	C	
			H	1862
		2 Oct	A	*Ad.* [by J.B.Mozley] M. Johnson Esq/J.W.Bowden Esq/Stamps and Taxes/Somerset House/London
		6 Nov	C	
		21 Nov	C	

Correspondent	Year	Date	Source	Location, Owner, Address
Bowden, Mrs John William	1837	23 July	C	
Christie, John Frederic	1837	29 Jan	A	*Ad.* The Revd J F Christie/Badgeworth/Cheltenham
		2 June	A	
		14 June	A	
	1838	5 Aug	A	*Ad.* The Revd J.F.Christie/Badgeworth/Cheltenham
Church, Richard William	1838	17 Aug	A	Pusey
			H	1865
		24 Aug	A	Pusey
			H	1865
		31 Aug	A	Pusey
			H	1865
		21 Sept	A	Pusey
			H	1865
Churton, Edward	1837	14 Mar	A	Pusey
		14 July	A	Pusey *Ad.*[in another hand] Rev. Edward Churton/Crayke/Easingwold/Yorkshire
		3 Sept	A	Pusey *Ad.* The Revd E Churton/Craike/Easingwold/Yorkshire
		6 Oct	A	Pusey *Ad.* The Revd E.Churton/Crayke/Easingwold/Yorkshire
		21 Nov	A	Pusey *Ad.* the same
		4 Dec	A	Pusey *Ad.* the same
	1838	30 Jan	A	Pusey *Ad.* the same
		3 Oct	A	Pusey *Ad.* The Revd Edward Churton/Crayke/Easingwold/Yorkshire
		2 Nov	A	Pusey
		12 Dec	A	Pusey *Ad.* The Revd E. Churton/Crayke/Easingwold/Yorkshire
Clerke, Charles Carr	1838	16 Aug	C	Pusey
			D	
Cornish, Charles	1838	28 Dec	A	Pusey *Ad.* The Revd Charles Cornish/18 Bedford Circus/Exeter
Dowding, William	1837	31 Dec	A	Chichester Theological College *Ad.*—Dowding Esqr/Merton College
Faber, Frederick William	1838	4 July	A	London Oratory *Ad.* The Revd F. W. Faber/University
		25 Sept	A	London Oratory *Ad.* The Revd F. W. Faber,/Stockton on Tees/Durham
Faber, George Stanley	1838	11 April	A	*Ad.* The Revd G. S. Faber/289 Regent Street/London
			D	
		16 May	A	Bodleian *Ad.* The Revd G. S. Faber/at Robert Welbank's Esqr/Tandridge Priory/Godstone
			D	
Fawcett, Joshua	1838	30 May	A	*Ad.* The Revd J. Fawcett/Low Moon[Moor]/Bradford/Yorkshire
Giberne, Maria Rosina	1837	13 Jan	A	*Ad.* Miss M R Giberne/F. Danvers Esqr/Lancaster Place/Wellington Street/Strand/London
			H	1862
		29 Jan	A	Miss M. R. Giberne/—Danvers Esqr/Lancaster Place/Waterloo Bridge/London
			H	1862
		14 Feb	A	*Ad.* Miss M R Giberne/Chesnut Walk/Walthamstow/London
			H	1862

Correspondent	Year	Date	Source	Location, Owner, Address
		7 Mar	A	*Ad.* Miss M. R. Giberne/Chesnut Walk/Walthamstow
			H	1862
		3 May	A	*Ad.* Miss M. R. Giberne/Chesnut Walk/Walthamstow/London *re-addressed* Revd — Hoskins/St George's Place/Canterbury
			H	1862
		24 July	A	*Ad.* Miss M. R. Giberne/M Giberne's Esqr/Chesnut Walk/Walthamstow
			H	1862
		3 Dec	A	*Ad.* Miss M. R. Giberne
			H	1862
	1838	12 April	A	*Ad.* Miss M. R. Giberne/Chesnut Walk/Walthamstow/London *readdressed* at the Rev. — Hoskins/ St George's Place/Canterbury
			H	1862
Golightly, Charles Portales	1837	9 Feb	A	Lambeth Palace Library *Ad.* The Revd C P Golightly
		[9 Feb]	A	Lambeth Palace Library
Henderson, Thomas	1838	8 April	A	Pusey *Ad.* Revd T. Henderson/ Messing Vicarage/Kelvedon [franked by C. Wood]
		2 Aug	A	Pusey
		28 Dec	A	Pusey *Ad.* The Revd T. Henderson/ Messing/Kelvedon/Essex
Holdsworth, Miss	1838	6 Feb	C	
		27 April	Pr	G. H. Harper, *Cardinal Newman and William Froude, F.R.S. A Correspondence*, Baltimore 1933, p. 34
Hook, Walter Farquhar	1838	[1 Mar]	Pr	W.R.W. Stephens, *Life and Letters of Walter Farquar Hook*, London 1880, p. 275
Hope, James Robert	1838	1 Oct	A	*Ad.* J R. Hope Esqr/Merton College
Hornby, James J.	1838	10 April	A	Yale University
			D	
Jacobson, William	1837	7 Aug	A	*Ad.* The Revd W. Jacobson/ Magdalen Hall
Keble, John	1837	12 Feb	A	*Ad.* The Revd John Keble
			H	1885
		23 Feb	A	
			H	1885
		2 Mar	A	*Ad.* The Revd John Keble/ Hursley/Winchester
			H	1885
		31 Mar	A	*Ad.* The Revd John Keble
			H	1885
		14 April	A	
			H	1885
		30 June	A	*Ad.* Revd John Keble
			H	1885
		16 July	A	
		27 Aug(I)	A	*Ad.* [franked] 1837/Oxford August twenty seven/Revd J. Keble/Hursley/Winchester/T. D. Acland Jr.
			H	1885
		27 Aug(II)	A	*Ad.* the same
			H	1885
		17 Sept	A	*Ad.* The Revd John Keble/Hursley/ Winton

Correspondent	Year	Date	Source	Location, Owner, Address
			H	1885
		30 Sept	A	Miss Irene Wilberforce
		26 Oct	A	
			H	1885
		[31] Oct	A	
		3 Nov	A	*Ad.* The Revd John Keble
			H	1885
		20 Nov	A	*Ad.* The Revd John Keble
		[20 Nov]	A	
		[20 Nov]	A	
	1838	20 Jan	A	*Ad.* Revd J. Keble
			H	1885
		24 Jan	A	*Ad.* Revd John Keble/Hursley/ Winchester
			H	1885
		4 Feb	A	*Ad.* The Revd John Keble
		26 Feb	A	
			H	1885
		28 Feb	A	*Ad.* The Revd John Keble
			H	1885
		29 Mar	A	*Ad.* The Revd John Keble/ Hursley/Winton
		7 May	A	*Ad.* The Revd J Keble/Hursley/ Winchester
			H	1885
		[9 Aug]	A	
		14 Aug(I)	A	*Ad.* The Revd John Keble/Hursley/ Winchester
			H	1885
		14 Aug(II)	A	*Ad.* The Revd John Keble
			H	1885
		22 Aug	A	*Ad.* The Revd John Keble/Hursley/ Winchester
			H	1885
		[22 Aug]	A	
		28 Aug	A	*Ad.* The Revd John Keble
			H	1885
		5 Sept	A	*Ad.* The Revd John Keble/Hursley
		13 Sept	A	*Ad.* The Revd John Keble
		30 Sept	A	*Ad.* The Revd John Keble/Hursley/ Winchester
		17 Oct	A	*Ad.* the same
		6 Nov(I)	A	*Ad.* Revd John Keble
		6 Nov(II)	A	
		7 Nov	A	*Ad.* The Revd John Keble/Hursley/ Winchester
		17 Nov	A	
		21 Nov	A	
		28 Nov	A	
		29 Nov	A	
		5 Dec	A	*Ad.* [in another hand] The Revd John Keble/Hursley
		[13 Dec]	A	*Ad.* Revd John Keble/Hursley
		13 Dec	A	*Ad.* The Revd John Keble/Hursley
		20 Dec	A	
		23 Dec	A	
		30 Dec	A	
Lathbury, Thomas	1838	7 Feb	D	
Lifford, Lord	1837	12 Sept	D	
Manning, Henry Edward	1837	24 Feb	A	Cardinal Manning Archives *Ad.* The Revd H Manning/Lavington/ Petworth/Sussex
		12 April	A	Cardinal Manning Archives
		14 July	C	

Correspondent	Year	Date	Source	Location, Owner, Address
		23 July	C	
	1838	12 Jan	A	Cardinal Manning Archives *Ad.* Revd H Manning
		28 Jan	A	Cardinal Manning Archives
		6 Mar	A	Cardinal Manning Archives *Ad.* The Revd H Manning/Lavington/ Petworth/Sussex
		4 April	A	Cardinal Manning Archives
		6 June	A	Cardinal Manning Archives
		9 Aug	A	Cardinal Manning Archives *Ad.* The Revd H. Manning
		29 Aug	A	Cardinal Manning Archives
		18 Oct	A	Cardinal Manning Archives *Ad.* Revd H. Manning/Lavington/Pet- worth/Sussex
		24 Oct	Pr	E. S. Purcell, *Life of Cardinal Manning*, London 1895, I, 137
Mozley, James Bowling	1837	17 Oct	A	
	1838	10 June	C	
		2 Aug	A	*Ad.* The Revd James Mozley/Chol- derton/Amesbury/Wilts
		10 Aug	A	*Ad.* the same
		30 Aug	A	*Ad.* the same
		7 Sept	A	*Ad.* the same
Mozley, John	1838	23 Jan	A	
			H	1873
		7 May	A	
Mozley, Mrs John	1837	5 Jan	A	*Ad.* favoured by T. Stevens Esqr/ Mrs John Mozley/Friargate
			H	1873
		19 Jan	A	
			H	1873
		8 Feb	A	*Ad.* Mrs John Mozley/ Friar gate/ Derby
		21 Feb	A	*Ad.* [Mrs John Moz]ley/ [Friarg] ate/[Der]by
		29 Mar	A	
			H	1873
		25 April	H	1873
		19 May	A	*Ad.* Mrs J Mozley/Friargate/Derby
		4 June	A	
			H	1873
		17 June	Pr	G. Tillotson, *Newman Prose and Poetry*, London 1957, 794.
		19 Aug	A	*Ad.* Mrs John Mozley/Friargate/ Derby
			H	1873
		11 Sept	A	*Ad.* [franked] 1837/Oxford Sep- tember eleven/Mrs J. Mozley/ Friar Gate/Derby/T. D. Acland Jr
		6 Oct	A	*Ad.* Mrs John Mozley/at Rev T. Mozley's/Cholderton/Amesbury
		29 Dec	A	*Ad.* Mrs John Mozley/Friar Gate/ Derby
	1838	29 Jan	A	*Ad.* Mrs John Mozley
			H	1873
		4 Mar	A	
		6 April	A	*Ad.* Mrs John Mozley/Friargate/ Derby
		5 June	A	*Ad.* [franked] Oxford June five 1838/Mrs J. Mozley/Friar Gate/ Derby/R Williams
			H	1873

Correspondent	Year	Date	Source	Location, Owner, Address
		4 July	A	*Ad.* Mrs John Mozley/Friargate/ Derby
		31 Aug	A	*Ad.* the same
			H	1873
		22 Oct	A	*Ad.* Mrs John Mozley/Derby
Mozley, Thomas	1837	25 May	A	
		27 July	A	*Ad.* The Revd T. Mozley/Cholderton Rectory/Amesbury/Wilts
Mozley, Mrs Thomas	1837	2 Jan	H	1873
	1838	9 Jan	H	1873
		28 Mar	H	1873
		2 Nov	A	*Ad.* [in another hand] Revd Thos. Mozley/Cholderton/Amesbury/ Wilts/Mrs T. Mozley
Parker, John Henry	1837	25 Dec	A	*Ad.* J H Parker Esqr/Broad Street
Perceval, Arthur Philip	1837	3 Aug	C	Pusey
	1838	22 Aug	C	Pusey
Pope, Simeon Lloyd	1837	25 April	A	Duke of Norfolk
		18 Dec	A	Duke of Norfolk *Ad.* The Revd S L Pope/Whittlesey/Peterborough (two)
Prevost, George	1838	3 Nov	D	
		13 Dec	D	
Pusey, Edward Bouverie	1837	10 Jan	C	*Ad.* The Revd Dr Pusey/Fairford
		25 Jan	A	
		[12 April]	C	
		16 July	A	Pusey *Ad.* The Revd Dr Pusey/ Sark/favored by Revd J Ashworth.
		24 Oct	A	Pusey
		19 Dec	A	Pusey
	1838	5 Feb	A	Pusey *Ad.* The Revd E B Pusey D D/Ch Ch
		24 April	A	Pusey
		20 May	A	Pusey *Ad.* The Revd Dr Pusey
		30 July	A	Pusey
		13 Aug	A	Pusey *Ad.* The Revd Dr Pusey
		21 Aug	A	Pusey *Ad.* The Revd Dr Pusey/ Weighmouth
		26 Aug	A	Pusey
Pusey, Mrs E.B.	1837	11 Mar	A	Pusey
	1838	13 April	A	Pusey *Ad.* Mrs Pusey/Ch Ch
		21 Oct	A	Pusey *Ad.* Mrs Pusey
Pusey, William Bouverie	1837	16 Dec	A	Pusey *Ad.* W. B. Pusey Esqr/ Dr Pusey's/Ch Ch
Rickards, Samuel	1837	30 May	A	*Ad.* The Revd S. Rickards/ Stowlangtoft/Ixworth/Suffolk
Rogers, Frederic	1837	7 Jan	Pr	*Moz.* II, 220–2
			C	Pusey
		1 June	Pr	*Moz.* II, 231–2
			C	Pusey
		19 June	C	Pusey
		5 July	Pr	*Moz.* II, 237–40
			C	Pusey
		20 July	C	Pusey
		31 Aug	Pr	*Moz.* II, 242–3
			C	Pusey
		25 Sept	Pr	*Moz.* II, 243–4
		6 Oct	C	Pusey
		29 Nov	Pr	*Moz.* II, 246–7
			C	Pusey
	1838	4 Jan	C	Pusey
		7 Jan	C	Pusey
		25 Feb	C	Pusey
		25 July	C	Pusey
		3 Oct	C	Pusey

Correspondent	Year	Date	Source	Location, Owner, Address
		28 Dec	Pr	*Moz.* II, 274–5
Rose, Hugh James	1837	3 Jan	A	*Ad.* The Revd/The Principal/King's College/London
	1838	7 Feb	A	*Ad.* The Revd/The Principal/King's College/Somerset Place/London *readdressed* Revd Francis Garden/The Knowle/Torquay/Devonshire *readdressed* Revd Francis Garden/Bocking/Braintree/Essex
		28 June	A	*Ad.* The Editor of the British Magazine
		8 July	A	*Ad.* The Revd/The Principal/King's College/London
Routh, Martin Joseph	1837	6 Jan	A	
			D	
Routh, Mrs M. J.	1837	6 Jan	D	
Russell, John Fuller	1837	15 Mar	C	
	1838	3 Jan	A	Oriel *Ad.* John F. Russell Esqr/at Messrs Baily and Co/83 Cornhill/London/post pd
Ryder, George Dudley	1838	14 Feb	A	*Ad.* The Revd G. D. Ryder/Easton/Winchester
		30 Nov	A	*Ad.* [franked] Revd G D Ryder/Easton/Winchester/G.[. . . .]
Ryder, Thomas Dudley	1837	[31 Dec]	A	Harrowby MSS.
Sewell, William	1838	14 July	A	Bodleian *Ad.* The Revd W. Sewell/Hermitage/Newport/Isle of Wight
Stone, Mr	1838	26 Feb	H	
Sumner, Charles Richard, bishop of Winchester	1838	30 Nov	Pr	G. H. Sumner, *Life of Charles Richard Sumner*, London 1876, 260
			D	
Sumner, John Bird, Bishop of Chester	1838	30 Nov	D	
Todd, James Henthorne	1837	19 Mar	A	Trinity College, Dublin *Ad.* The Revd J H Todd/Trinity College/Dublin
Townsend, George	1837	17 Sept	D	
		22 Sept(I)	D	not sent
		22 Sept(II)	D	
		13 Oct	A	Pierpont Morgan Collection *Ad.* [in Pusey's hand] Rev. G. Townsend/etc etc/Durham
			D	
Trail, William	1838	20 July	D	
Unknown Correspondents	1837	10 Feb	D	
		24 Feb	D	
		30 Nov	A	Stark Library, University of Texas
	1838	16 Dec	A	
Watson, Joshua	1837	1 Sept	A	Keble
			H	Pusey
		20 Oct	A	Keble
		3 Nov	A	Keble
Wigram, Joseph Cotton	1838	1 June	D	Pusey
Wilberforce, Henry	1837	3 Jan	A	Georgetown *Ad.* The Revd H Wilberforce/Brans Gore/Ringwood/Hants
		29 Jan	A	Georgetown *Ad.* The Revd H W Wilberforce/Brans Gore/Ringwood/Hants *readdressed* The Revd H Wilberforce/Moers Library/Cowes/Isle of Wight
			H	1876

Correspondent	Year	Date	Source	Location, Owner ,Address
		18 Feb	A	Georgetown *Ad.* The Revd H W Wilberforce/Cowes/Isle of Wight
		27 Feb	A	Georgetown
			H	1876
		14 Mar	A	Georgetown
			H	1876
		25 Mar	A	Georgetown *Ad.* [in another hand] The Rev. H. Wilberforce/Brans-gore/Ringwood
			H	1876
		12 April	A	Georgetown *Ad.* The Revd H. W. Wilberforce/Brans Gore/Ring-wood/Hants
		9 May	A	Georgetown
		16 May	A	Georgetown *Ad.* The Revd H W Wilberforce/Brans Gore/Ring-wood/Hants
		31 May	A	Georgetown *Ad.* the same
			H	1876
		2 Aug	A	Georgetown *Ad.* The Revd H W Wilberforce/Brans Gore/Ring-wood/Hants *readdressed* Lavington/ Petworth
			H	1876
		10 Sept	A	Georgetown *Ad.* [franked] 1837/ Oxford September 11/Revd H. Wilberforce/Bransgore/(Hants) Ringwood/T.D. Acland Jr.
			H	1876
		13 Nov	A	Georgetown *Ad.* The Revd H W Wilberforce/Bransgore/Ringwood/ Hants *readdressed* Lavington/ Petworth
			H	1876
		15 Dec	A	Georgetown *Ad.* the same
	1838	7 Jan	A	Georgetown
			H	1876
		15 Mar	A	Ushaw College, Durham *Ad.* The Revd H W Wilberforce/Bransgore/ Ringwood/Hants
			H	1876
		7 May	A	Georgetown *Ad.* Revd Henry Wilberforce/Bransgore/Ringwood/ Hants
		19 May	A	Georgetown
		23 May	A	Georgetown *Ad.* The Revd H W Wilberforce,/Brans Gore/Ring-wood/Hants/post pd
		31 May	A	Georgetown *Ad.* The Revd H W Wilberforce/Brans Gore/Ring-wood/Hants
		5 July	A	Georgetown *Ad.* The Revd H W Wilberforce
		11 July	A	Georgetown *Ad.* [franked] London July eleven 1838/Revd H W. Wilberforce/Bransgore C. Wood
		14 July	A	Georgetown *Ad.* The Revd H. Wilberforce/Brans Gore/Ring-wood/Hants
		19 July	A	Georgetown *Ad.* The Revd H W Wilberforce/Brans Gore/Ring-wood/Hants
		19 Aug	A	Ushaw College, Durham
			H	1876

379

Correspondent	Year	Date	Source	Location, Owner, Address
Wilberforce, Robert Isaac	1837	25 April	A	Miss Irene Wilberforce
		6 Oct	A	Miss Irene Wilberforce
	1838	9 June	A	Miss Irene Wilberforce *Ad.* Revd R. Wilberforce/East Farleigh/Maidstone/Kent
		18 July	A	Miss Irene Wilberforce
		25 Sept	A	Miss Irene Wilberforce
		17 Oct	A	Miss Irene Wilberforce
		23 Dec	A	Miss Irene Wilberforce *Ad.* The Revd R. I. Wilberforce/East Farleigh/Maidstone/Kent
Wilberforce, Samuel	1837	2 Jan	A	*Ad.* The Revd S. Wilberforce/33 Grosvenor Square
		12 May	A	Emmanuel College, Cambridge
		15 Aug	A	Emmanuel College, Cambridge
	1838	18 July	Pr	A. R. Ashwell, *The Life of Samuel Wilberforce*, second edition, London 1883, I, 125
Williams, Isaac	1837	23 Sept	A	I. Williams *Ad.* The Revd I. Williams/at The Revd Sir George Prevost's/Norman Hill/Dursley
		7 Oct	A	I. Williams *Ad.* The Revd I Williams/Trinity College/Oxford
	1838	3 Jan	A	I. Williams *Ad.* The Revd I Williams/The Revd Sir G. Prevost's/Stinchcombe/Dursley *re-addressed* The Venble Archdeacon Froude/Dartington/Totness/Devon
		10 April	A	I. Williams
		26 July	A	I. Williams *Ad.* The Revd I. Williams/Stinchcombe/Dursley/Gloucestershire
		13 Dec	A	*Ad.* The Revd I. Williams/Trinity College
Wilson, Robert Francis	1838	4 Feb	H	1878
		11 Oct	A	Newman Preparatory School, Boston *Ad.* The Revd R. F. Wilson/Hursley/Winchester
Wood, Samuel Francis	1837	2 June	C	
		18 Aug	A	*Ad.* [. . .] Wood Esqr.
	1838	2 Mar	D	
		19 Mar	A	
		23 Mar	A	
		23 Aug	A	*Ad.* S. F. Wood Esqr
Woodgate, Henry Arthur	1837	17 Mar	A	
	1838	23 Feb	A	*Ad.* The Revd H A Woodgate/Tunbridge Wells/Kent
		28 Feb	A	*Ad.* the same
		[1 April]	A	*Ad.* The Revd H A Woodgate/St John's
		23 May	A	
		13 Aug	A	*Ad.* The Revd H. A. Woodgate/Bell Broughton/near Birmingham *readdressed* Tunbridge Wells/Kent
			H	Bodleian
		25 Sept	A	*Ad.* The Revd H. A. Woodgate/Tunbridge Wells/Kent
		22 Nov	A	*Ad.* Revd H A Woodgate/Bellbroughton/Stourbridge
		17 Dec	A	*Ad.* The Revd/H. A. Woodgate
		28 Dec	A	*Ad.* Revd H. A. Woodgate/Bellbroughton/Stourbridge
			H	Bodleian

LIST OF LETTERS BY CORRESPONDENTS

Correspondent	*Year*	*Date*	*Source*	*Location, Owner, Address*
Wordsworth, Christopher	1837	29 Mar	A	Lambeth Palace Library

MEMORANDA AND PUBLIC DOCUMENTS

	Placed at	*Source*	*Subject*
1838	14 Feb	A	The Irish Establishment
	14 Aug	Pr	BISHOP OF OXFORD'S CHARGE

LETTERS TO NEWMAN AND OTHERS

		From	*Placed at*
1837	22 Feb	H. E. Manning	24 Feb
	12 Sept	J. Keble	17 Sept
	21 Sept	G. Townsend	22 Sept
	26 Sept	E. B. Pusey to R. Bagot	22 Sept
	28 Oct	H. E. Manning	30 Oct
	2 Nov	H. E. Manning	4 Nov
	18 Nov	J. F. Russell to a friend	20 Nov
	22 Nov	H. E. Manning	22 Nov
	2 Mar	H. E. Manning	6 Mar
1838	9 April	G. S. Faber	11 April
	12 April	G. S. Faber	11 April
	1 May	G. S. Faber	16 May
	13 July	S. Wilberforce	18 July
	15 Aug	J. Keble	14 Aug
	20 Aug	R. Bagot	21 Aug
	23 Aug	J. Keble	22 Aug
	23 Oct	E. B. Pusey	22 Oct
	2 Nov	G. Prevost	3 Nov
	6 Nov	S. F. Wood	6 Nov
	7 Nov	G. Prevost	3 Nov
	7 Nov	J. Keble	6 Nov
	20 Nov	S. F. Wood	21 Nov
	26 Nov	J. Keble	21 Nov
[1886]	5 Mar	F. Rogers to A. Mozley	12 Dec
	8 Dec	J. Keble	13 Dec

Index of Persons and Places

References are given to *The Dictionary of National Biography*, *The Dictionary of American Biography*, or to the Frederick Boase, *Modern English Biography*. Some of the information is derived from correspondence and other material in the archives of the Birmingham Oratory, and from various private sources. With this volume, Newman's career and the Oxford Movement begin to enter a new phase, and so new biographies have been provided. Reference will be made back to the index of this volume in those of the four remaining volumes. All Colleges referred to are of Oxford, except where otherwise specified.

Abbott, Jacob (1803–79), American Congregationalist minister, author of many works, including *The Corner-Stone*, 1834, which was accused of Arian leanings. It was criticised by Newman in *Tract* 73, and Abbott modified some of the questionable passages in later editions. He had a friendly meeting with Newman in 1843, see *Moz.* II, 372. (*DAB*), 132–3, 134, 226.

Acland, Thomas Dyke (1809–98), entered Christ Church in 1827, and was a Fellow of All Souls from 1831–7. He was friendly with Newman from undergraduate days and often heard him preach. He gradually took up Tractarian views, and, together with his friends S. F. Wood and Robert Williams, was at the centre of a group of London Tractarians. However, later in life he took up Broad Church opinions. He was Conservative M.P. for West Somerset from 1837–47. (*DNB* Supplement), 15, 17, 19, 21, 24, 27–8, 49–50, 52, 70, 88–9, 91, 93–4, 100, 107, 109, 112, 120, 124, 126, 157, 170, 178, 189, 194, 195, 205, 235, 236, 239, 252–4, 257–8, 266, 298, 306, 308–9, 330, 361–2.

Anderdon, William Henry (1816–90), a nephew of Manning, studied at King's College, London, at around the age of fifteen. He entered Balliol College in 1835, and held a scholarship at University College from 1837–43. Influenced by Newman, he visited him at Littlemore in 1843, and continued to correspond with him about his religious difficulties until 1845. He was appointed Vicar of Knighton, Leics., in 1846, where he undertook vigorous apostolic work. He became a Catholic in 1850, and was on the staff of the Catholic University in Dublin under Newman. He joined the Society of Jesus in 1872, 21, 39–40, 52, 54, 69, 212, 241,

249, 257, 282, 294; Mr Anderdon (senior), 69, 255.

Anderson, Charles Henry John (1804–91), entered Oriel in 1823, B.A. 1826, and was influenced by the Oxford Movement. From his College days he was a close friend of Samuel Wilberforce. He became Sheriff of Lincolnshire in 1851, and was responsible for the restoration of many churches in the county. He contributed many papers to the Royal Archaeological Institute and similar bodies, and was the author of *Ancient Models, or Hints on Church Building*, 1841. (*Boase* IV, 25, 31–2, 244, 252.

Arnold, Thomas (1795–1842), the Headmaster of Rugby School. He entered Corpus Christi College in 1811, where he became a friend of John Keble, and was elected Fellow of Oriel in 1815. He took up his post at Rugby in 1827. His liberal views on ecclesiastical matter were naturally directly opposed to those of Newman and the Tractarians. However, Newman always retained a great personal respect for him. He was Regius Professor of Modern History from 1841–2. See *Moz.* II, 440–2, for an account of their meeting in 1842. (*DNB*), 8, 82, 128, 135, 216, 303, 360, 366.

Ashworth, Arthur Howard, entered Oriel in 1838, where he was a Bible Scholar, B.A. 1842. He was appointed to a minor canonry of York Minster in 1853. He died in 1874, 202–3, 361, 366.

Ashworth, John, entered Christ Church in 1832, aged 21, B.A. from Brasenose in 1836. He was one of the divinity students who lodged at Pusey's house, and he became a translator for the Library of the Fathers. He became Rector of Didcot in 1851, 99.

Bowden—*cont.*
100–1, 146, 189, 236, 252, 264–5, 269, 314, 324.

Bowles, Dr Joseph, Rector of Noke, Oxon., died in 1879, 110.

Bowles, Henry Albany, entered St John's College in 1837, aged 18, B.A. 1841. He was Rector of Merrow, Surrey from 1851–84, 241, 245.

Bowyer, George (1811–83), briefly a cadet at Woolwich Military College, was admitted as a student of the Middle Temple in 1836, and was called to the Bar in 1839. Oxford created him an honorary M.A. in 1839 for his *Brit. Crit.* article on the Ecclesiastical Discipline Bill. In 1841 he published *The English Constitution*, the first of his popular series of legal commentaries. He was made a D.C.L. at Oxford in 1844, and appointed reader in law at the Middle Temple in 1850. He became a Catholic in 1850, and later adopted Ultramontane views. He was adviser to Wiseman during the No-Popery agitation. He was M.P. for Dundalk from 1852–68, and for Wexford from 1873–80. (*DNB*), 239.

Bragge, Mr, 115.

Bramston, John (1802–89), entered Oriel in 1820 and met Newman two years later when the latter was a nervous probationer Fellow, (see Volume XIX, 318–19). He was a Fellow of Exeter College from 1825–30, and took orders in 1828. He held various livings in Essex, being Vicar of Great Baddow from 1830–40. He was appointed Dean of Winchester in 1872, retiring from the post in 1883. (*Boase* IV), 17.

Brewer, John Sherren (1810–79), though his father was a Baptist, he joined the Church of England, and entered Queen's College in 1827, gaining a first in 1832. He gained a reputation at Oxford for the extraordinary range of his reading. He was influenced by the Tractarians and always retained a high regard for Newman. He was appointed Lecturer in Classical Literature at King's College, London, in 1839, and Professor of English Language and Literature and Lecturer in Modern History in 1855, succeeding his friend F. D. Maurice, whom he later assisted at the Working Men's College in Great Ormond Street. He was Rector of Toppesford, Essex, from 1876, until his death. He did a good deal of journalistic work and wrote extensively on historical and religious topics. His major work was his edition of the *Letters and Papers of the Reign of Henry VIII* for the Record Office. (*DNB*), 239, 360.

Bridges, Alexander Henry, entered Oriel in 1830, aged 18, B.A. 1835. He became a curate at Beddington, Surrey. He was granted an honorary canonry of Winchester in 1873, 5, 11.

Bridges, Brook Charles, was born in 1815. He entered Oriel in 1833, B.A. 1837, 39, 52, 225, 318, 324, 342.

Bridges, Thomas Edward, entered University College in 1798, aged 15. B.A. from Corpus Christi College in 1802, where he was a Fellow, and, in 1823, was elected President, a post which he held until his death in 1843, 211.

Bridgford, Mr, 333, 334.

Broadhurst, parishioner, 348.

Browell, William Robert (1805 or 6–67), entered Pembroke College in 1824, B.A. 1828, was a Fellow and Tutor of the College, and Public Examiner in 1834. He was Rector of Beaumont-cum-Mose, Essex, from 1839 until his death. (*Boase* I), 42, 51, 173, 342, 348.

Browne, J., LL.B., Minister of Holy Trinity, Cheltenham, since 1827, and an ardent opponent of the Tractarians, 146, 150.

Browne, John Henry (1779–1858), an undergraduate and Fellow of St John's College, Cambridge, was Rector of Cotgrave, near Nottingham from 1811 until his death. He was appointed Archdeacon of Ely in 1816. He was an Evangelical and a critic of the Tractarians, 146, 150.

Browne, Thomas Murray, Vicar of Standish, Gloucs., and Chaplain to the Bishop of Gloucester and Bristol, 83, 190, 333, 334.

Bruce, James, later 8th Earl of Elgin, 51.

Buck, parishioner at Littlemore, 117.

Bull, John (1789 or 90–1858), was a King's Scholar at Westminster, went up to Christ Church, where he was a Student and Censor, in 1808, gaining a double first in 1812. He was Public Examiner in 1817–18, and a Proctor in 1820. He was a Canon of Christ Church from 1830 until his death, and Treasurer from 1832–57. He was a notorious pluralist. (*Boase* I), 122.

Bull, Henry, brother of John, B.A. from Christ Church in 1819, 10.

Buller, Anthony (1809–81), entered Oriel in 1827, B.A. 1831. He was Rector of Tavy St Mary, Devon, from 1833–76. His family were local Devon friends of the Froudes, and he officiated at Hurrell Froude's funeral, 59, 161, 187.

Bunsen, Christian Charles Josias, Baron von, (1791–1860), diplomat and scholar. He was Prussian Ambassador to Rome from 1823–38. He took a keen interest in ecclesiastical matters and was reckoned to be the prime mover in the Jerusalem Bishopric scheme, see *Moz.* II, 352–66, 360.

Bunsen, Henry George, son of the preceding, entered Oriel in 1836, aged 18, B.A. 1840, and was Vicar of Lilleshall, Salop, from 1847–69. He died in 1885, 77, 239, 330, 354.

Burder, George (1814–81), entered Magda-

Mozley—*cont.*

Newman's most regular correspondent out of the family. She certainly did not condone Newman's conversion, but they continued to write regularly. They remained on friendly terms, though she kept a little distance from him until she was sure that her children were fully grown up and not likely to be influenced by him, after which they resumed normal contact, 6, 10, 15, 21–3, 30, 31, 39, 42, 49, 52, 59, 61, 63, 64, 70, 72, 78, 81, 84, 114, 120, 126, 145, 148, 149, 153, 156, 157, 160, 180, 181, 186, 191, 192, 208–9, 224, 240, 253, 259, 260, 262, 268, 303, 311, 316, 324, 327–8, 331, 362.

Mozley, Thomas (1806–93), entered Oriel in 1825, and was one of Newman's pupils, B.A. 1828. He was a Fellow of the College from 1829–37. In 1836 he married Newman's eldest sister Harriett, and left Oxford to become Vicar of Cholderton, Wilts. He was an ardent Tractarian, and succeeded Newman as editor of *Brit. Crit.* in 1841. He made the tone of the journal more extreme and it ceased publication in 1843. In the same year he visited Normandy and was on the verge of becoming a Roman Catholic, but was held back, partly by Newman's advice to wait for two years. He became a leader writer for the *Times* in 1844, and settled in London. He became Vicar of Plymtree, Devon, in 1868, and retired in 1880. When he retired he produced his Oxford *Reminiscences*, the inaccuracy of which greatly annoyed Newman. (*DNB*), 3, 17, 19, 24, 38, 72, 77, 78, 82–3, 86–8, 104, 148–9, 157, 159–61, 191, 241, 268, 277–8, 311, 319, 322, 332, 354.

Mozley, Mrs Thomas (1803–52), Harriett Newman, Newman's eldest sister, married Tom Mozley in 1836, five months after the marriage of Jemima to his brother. She grew more and more out of sympathy with Newman's religious position during the years of the Oxford Movement. She blamed Newman for the near conversion of her husband to Roman Catholicism in 1843, and from that time broke off relations, 3, 17, 21, 22, 28, 31, 45, 62, 65, 72, 78, 83, 105, 109, 114, 120, 126, 149, 153, 180, 186, 190, 192, 205, 208, 221, 224, 236, 237, 240, 246, 268, 271, 311, 318, 319, 322, 333, 335, 342, 354.

Musgrave, Thomas (1788–1860), succeeded Edward Grey as Bishop of Hereford in 1837, and was translated to the Archbishopric of York in 1847. (*DNB*), 108.

Neale, Mr and Mrs, 133.

Neate, Charles (1806–79), entered Lincoln College in 1824, was a scholar from 1826–8, and a Fellow of Oriel from 1828 until his death. He was called to the bar at Lincoln's Inn in 1832, but he ruined his chance at the bar by an intemperate assault on a senior barrister. He was Professor of Political Economy from 1857–62. He was M.P. for Oxford from 1863–8. (*Boase* II), 115, 152, 236.

Nelson, John, B.A. from St. John's College in 1822, 349.

Neville for Nevile, either Charles, who entered Trinity College in 1835, aged 18, was a scholar from 1836–41, and became curate at Thorney, Notts., in 1839; or his brother Henry, who entered the college in 1836, aged 18, and was Rector of Wickenby, Lincs., from 1863 until his death in 1878, 78, 224, 249, 272, 360.

Neville for Nevile, Mr and Mrs, parents of Charles and Henry who were at Trinity College at this time, 78.

Nevins, Mr, 327.

Newman, Charles Robert (1802–84), second son of the Newman family, quarrelled with the family at the time of his father's death, and gave up Christianity. His elder brother obtained a place in the Bank of England for him in 1825, but he resigned in 1832. He then drifted for some years into various temporary posts. From 1842–5 he was at Bonn University, but he did not bother to take a degree. All through these years, and afterwards, he depended upon his family for support. About 1853 he retired to Tenby, and took a room in Alma Cottage, Marsh Road, where his landlady, Mrs Griffiths, looked after him with persistent kindness. Newman made a final visit to him in September 1882. When he died Newman paid for his tomb, and chose the inscription:

Domine, misericordia tua in seculum,
Opera manuum tuarum ne despicias.

6, 7, 16, 21, 22–4, 29–31, 37, 39, 57, 69, 71, 88, 100, 104, 105, 107–9, 115, 138, 149, 186, 190, 209, 213, 218, 223, 239, 315.

Newman, Elizabeth Good (1765–1852), Newman's paternal aunt, to whom he owed part of his early religious instruction and love of the Bible, and to whom he was devoted. He often had to pay her debts, finally in 1828 £700, which he and Francis paid between them, (*A.W.* p. 213). After Jemima Newman married and went to live at Derby, Aunt Elizabeth joined her. She was very distressed at Newman's conversion, but was softened by his letters and visits afterwards, 6, 15, 16, 22, 24, 30, 31, 49, 50, 84, 86, 105, 108, 115, 181, 193, 209, 225, 260, 311.

Newman, Francis William (1805–97), entered Worcester College in 1822, where he was largely supported by his elder brother. At this time he held similar Evangelical religious views to those of his brother. He took a double first in 1826, and was elected Fellow of Balliol. He resigned his Fellowship in 1830 on the grounds of his nonconformist religious

fication were very influential, and are singled out by Newman as representative 'of the pure Lutheran school' (*Jfc.*, p. vii). He was appointed Bishop of Ossory, Ferns, and Leighlin in 1842, and he attacked the Tractarians in episcopal charges and other publications. (*DNB*), 97.

O'Connell, Daniel (1775–1847), leader of the Irish Catholics in Parliament, M.P. for various Irish seats between Emancipation in 1829 and his death, at this time was sitting for Dublin. He was the leading spokesman for the repeal of the Union. (*DNB*), 115, 276, 277.

Ogilvie, Charles Atmore (1793–1873), entered Balliol College in 1811, B.A. 1815. He was a Fellow of the College from 1816–34, and a tutor from 1819–30, and played a great part in the improvement of Balliol's academic standing. 'About 1829 he was looked on as a leader of the high-church party in Oxford, but he gave little active support to the Oxford Movement'. He spent some time as Chaplain to Archbishop Howley, and was appointed Regius Professor of Pastoral Theology in 1842. (*DNB*), 301, 303, 306, 311.

Ogle, James Adey (1792–1857), was at Eton, and entered Trinity College in 1810, and took a first in mathematics in 1813. He studied medicine, took up practice, and was appointed Aldrich Professor of Medicine in 1824, Clinical Professor in 1830, and Regius Professor in 1851. He was Newman's private tutor as an undergraduate and they remained good friends (see *Apo.*, p. 236). He had four sons and five daughters, of whom one married Manuel Johnson, and another J. B. Mozley. (*DNB*), 15, 60, 68–70, 181, 319, 322.

Oldham, John Roberts, entered Oriel in 1827, aged 19, B.A. 1830. He became Vicar of St Paul's Huddersfield in 1834, and was Vicar of Ottershaw, Surrey from 1865 until his death in 1882, 63, 70.

Orger, William, 70, 74.

Orr, Alexander, entered Oriel in 1832, aged 17, B.A. 1836. He was Vicar of Lamby Connor, Co. Antrim from 1847–60, 74.

Ostrehan, Joseph Duncan (1799–1870), was at Worcester College from 1818–22. In the latter year he married Anne Withy, a second cousin of Newman's. He was Vicar of Creech St Michael, Somerset, from 1851 until his death, 50.

Otter, William (1768–1840), was Principal of King's College, London, from 1830–6, when he was appointed Bishop of Chichester. As Bishop he was responsible for the foundation of the Diocesan College, and for the revival of weekly eucharist at the Cathedral. (*DNB*), 156, 209, 294.

Ottley, John Bridges, originally Hooker, he took the additional surname of Ottley in

1820. He entered Oriel in 1815, aged 18, B.A. 1819, and was a Fellow of the College from 1822–5. He became Vicar of Farnborough, Warks., in 1838, and was Vicar of Thorpe Acre, Leics., from 1845 until his death in 1879, 11, 124, 187, 258, 359.

Oxnam, Nutcombe, entered Oriel in 1828, aged 17, and gained a scholarship at Trinity College in the following year. He was a Fellow of Exeter College from 1832–4, and then Vicar of Modbury, Devon, until his death in 1859, 17, 69.

Paine, parishioner, 272.

Painter, 173.

Palgrave, Sir Francis (1788–1861), was of Jewish parentage, and worked at a London solicitors for some years. In 1823 he became a Christian, married, and changed his surname from Cohen. He edited and published many volumes of medieval public records, and in 1838 he was appointed Deputy Keeper of Her Majesty's Records. He published several volumes of medieval English history. (*DNB*), 109, 113, 237, 275, 281, 310, 331.

Palmer, William (1803–85), was at Trinity College, Dublin, B.A. 1824. He was incorporated at Magdalen Hall in 1828, and transferred to Worcester College in 1831. He published his *Origines Liturgicae* in 1832, and this brought him into contact with Keble and Froude. He was deeply involved in the opening stages of the Oxford Movement, but grew alarmed at what he felt was an incautious approach and did not cooperate closely for long. He was an erudite theologian, and was well acquainted with Roman Catholic controversy. His famous *Treatise on the Church of Christ* of 1838 expounded the 'branch theory' of the Church. He was sympathetic to Newman at the time of the *Tract* 90 crisis. However, he launched an attack on the extreme Tractarians in his *Narrative of Events connected with the Tracts for the Times*, 1843. (*DNB*), 52, 64, 99, 156, 176, 209, 217, 221, 244, 262, 270, 272, 298, 302–4, 306, 310, 311, 318, 337, 343, 344, 352.

Palmer, William (1811–79), entered Magdalen as a Demy in 1826, gained a first in Classics in 1832, and was elected Fellow in the following year. In 1833 he went as a Classics tutor to Durham and there took up Tractarian views under Rose's influence. In 1836 he returned to Magdalen and was ordained deacon. He was interested in the Eastern Church, and in 1840 he paid his first visit to Russia. On his second visit to Russia, in 1842, he failed to gain recognition for the Church of England or permission to communicate in the Church of Russia. He was unsettled by Newman's conversion, and in 1849 he travelled to Greece in the hope of